AUTHENTICATING THE ACTIVITIES OF JESUS

AUTHENTICATING THE ACTIVITIES OF JESUS

EDITED BY

BRUCE CHILTON AND CRAIG A. EVANS

BRILL ACADEMIC PUBLISHERS, INC.
BOSTON • LEIDEN
2002

Library of Congress Cataloging-in-Publication Data

Authenticating the activities of Jesus / edited by Bruce Chilton and Craig A. Evans
   p. cm.
   Companion to: Authenticating the words of Jesus.
   Originally published: [L]eiden ; Boston : Brill, 1999, in series: New Testament tools and studies.
   Includes bibliographical references and index.
   ISBN 0–391–04164–9
   1. Jesus Christ—Biography—History and criticism. 2. Jesus Christ—Historicity. 3. Bible. N.T. Gospels—Criticism, interpretation, etc. I. Chilton, Bruce. II. Evans, Craig A.

   BT301.9 .A87 2002
   232.9'08—dc21

                                           2002023240

ISBN 0–391–04164–9

PRINTED IN THE UNITED STATES OF AMERICA

IN MEMORY OF BEN F. MEYER

CONTENTS

PART ONE
METHODS AND ASSUMPTIONS

PART TWO
AUTHENTICATING THE ACTIVITIES OF JESUS

PREFACE

The present volume is a companion to *Authenticating the Words of Jesus* and is intended to review the appropriate criteria and necessary steps in assessing the Jesus tradition, particularly the activities of Jesus. The title *Authenticating the Activities of Jesus* should not be taken to mean that the contributors have as their aim some sort of apologetical goal, whose purpose is to prove that Jesus did everything attributed to him in the Gospels. Rather, the purpose is to clarify what procedures should be undertaken to distinguish tradition and meaning that stem from Jesus from that which stems from later tradents and evangelists. The opening essays by the editors in the *Words* volume should clarify the exegetical and historical goals of both volumes.

The essays by James D. G. Dunn, E. Earle Ellis, William R. Farmer, N. Thomas Wright, Ben F. Meyer, and Martin Hengel appeared in earlier forms in William R. Farmer (ed.), *Crisis in Christology: Essays in Quest of Resolution* (Livonia: Dove, 1995). They have been edited and updated for inclusion in the present volume. The editors express their thanks to Professor Farmer and to the publisher.

The editors are grateful to Dr. Orton for his suggestion and to Dr. Theo Joppe for guiding the completed manuscripts through the press. The editors also wish to thank the series editors, Professors Bruce Metzger and Bart Ehrman, as well as the many contributors, whose labors have made the volumes possible, and Mr. Chris Young for his assistance in the preparation of the indexes.

Bruce Chilton   October, 1998
Bard College
Annandale-on-Hudson, New York

Craig A. Evans
Trinity Western University
Langley, British Columbia

ABBREVIATIONS

AB	Anchor Bible (Commentary)
ABD	D. N. Freedman (ed.), *The Anchor Bible Dictionary* (6 vols., New York: Doubleday, 1992)
ABRL	Anchor Bible Reference Library
ACNT	Augsburg Commentary on the New Testament
AGJU	Arbeiten zur Geschichte des antiken Judentums und des Urchristentums
ANF	A. Roberts and J. Donaldson (eds.), *The Ante-Nicene Fathers* (10 vols., Edinburgh: T. & T. Clark, 1898; repr. Grand Rapids: Eerdmans, 1989)
ANRW	W. Haase and E. Temporini (eds.), *Aufstieg und Niedergang der römischen Welt* (Berlin: de Gruyter, 1979-)
ANTJ	Arbeiten zum Neuen Testament und Judentum
ArBib	The Aramaic Bible
ASOR	American Schools of Oriental Research
ATANT	Abhandlungen zur Theologie des Alten und Neuen Testaments
ATR	*Anglican Theological Review*
BA	*Biblical Archaeologist*
BAGD	W. Bauer, *A Greek-English Lexicon of the New Testament and Other Early Christian Literature* (2nd ed., revised by W. F. Arndt, F. W. Gingrich, and F. W. Danker; Chicago: University of Chicago Press, 1979)
BAR	*Biblical Archaeology Review*
BASOR	*Bulletin of the American Schools of Oriental Research*
BBB	Bonner biblische Beiträge
BDF	B. Blass, A. Debrunner, and R. W. Funk, *A Greek Grammar of the New Testament and Other Early Christian Literature* (Chicago: University of Chicago Press, 1961)
BETL	Bibliotheca ephemeridum theologicarum lovaniensium
BFCT	Beiträge zur Förderung christlicher Theologie
Bib	*Biblica*
BibInt	*Biblical Interpretation*
BibLeb	*Bibel und Leben*
BibOr	Biblica et orientalia
BibRev	*Bible Review*
BibSem	The Biblical Seminar
BIS	Biblical Interpretation Series
BJRL	*Bulletin of the John Rylands University Library of Manchester*
BK	*Bibel und Kirche*
BLG	Biblical Languages: Greek

BNTC	Black's New Testament Commentary
BTB	*Biblical Theology Bulletin*
BU	Biblische Untersuchungen
BWANT	Beiträge zur Wissenschaft vom Alten und Neuen Testament
BZ	*Biblische Zeitschrift*
BZNW	Beihefte zur *Zeitschrift für die neutestamentliche Wissenschaft*
CBQ	*Catholic Biblical Quarterly*
CBQMS	Catholical Biblical Quarterly Monograph Series
CGTC	Cambridge Greek Testament Commentaries
CH	Calwer Hefte
ConBNT	Coniectanea biblica, New Testament
CRINT	Compendia rerum iudaicarum ad novum testamentum
DJD	Discoveries in the Judaean Desert
DJG	J. B. Green, S. McKnight, and I. H. Marshall (eds.), *Dictionary of Jesus and the Gospels* (Downers Grove: InterVarsity, 1992)
DRev	*Downside Review*
DSD	*Dead Sea Discoveries*
EFN	Estudios de Filología Neotestamentaria
EHS	Europäische Hochschulschriften
EKKNT	Evangelisch-katholischer Kommentar zum Neuen Testament
EvQ	*Evangelical Quarterly*
ExpTim	*Expository Times*
FB	Forschung zur Bibel
FBBS	Facet Books, Biblical Series
FRLANT	Forschungen zur Religion und Literatur des Alten und Neuen Testaments
GGA	*Göttingische Gelehrte Anzeigen*
GNS	Good News Studies
Greg	*Gregorianum*
GTA	Göttinger theologische Arbeiter
GTB	Gütersloher Taschenbücher
HBT	*Horizons in Biblical Theology*
HNT	Handbuch zum Neuen Testament
HR	*History of Religions*
HSM	Harvard Semitic Monographs
HTKNT	Herders theologischer Kommentar zum Neuen Testament
HTR	*Harvard Theological Review*
ICC	International Critical Commentary
IEJ	*Israel Exploration Journal*
IKZ	*Internationale katholische Zeitschrift*
IRT	Issues in Religion and Theology
ITQ	*Irish Theological Quarterly*
JAAR	*Journal of the American Academy of Religion*
JAOS	Journal of the American Oriental Society
JBL	*Journal of Biblical Literature*
JE	*Jüdische Enzyklopädie*
JETS	*Journal of the Evangelical Theological Society*
JR	*Journal of Religion*

JSJ	*Journal for the Study of Judaism in the Persian, Hellenistic and Roman Period*
JSJSup	*Journal for the Study of Judaism in the Persian, Hellenistic and Roman Period*, Supplements
JSNT	*Journal for the Study of the New Testament*
JSNTSup	*Journal for the Study of the New Testament*, Supplement Series
JSOTSup	*Journal for the Study of the Old Testament*, Supplement Series
JSPSup	*Journal for the Study of the Pseudepigrapha*, Supplement Series
JTS	*Journal of Theological Studies*
LCL	Loeb Classical Library
LD	Lectio divina
LSJ	Liddell, Scott, Jones, *Greek-English Lexicon*
MeyerK	H. A. W. Meyer (ed.), Kritisch-exegetischer Kommentar über das Neue Testament
NA	E. Nestle and K. Aland (eds.), *Novum Testamentum Graece*
NCB	New Century Bible
NICNT	New International Commentary: New Testament
NIGTC	New International Greek Testament Commentary
NovT	*Novum Testamentum*
NovTSup	Novum Tetamentum, Supplements
NTAbh	Neutestamentliche Abhandlungen
NTOA	Novum Testamentum et Orbis Antiquus
NTS	*New Testament Studies*
NTTS	New Testament Tools and Studies
PG	J. Migne (ed.), *Patrologia graeca*
PGM	K. Preisendanz (ed.), *Papyri graecae magicae*
PTMS	Princeton Theological Monograph Series
RAC	*Reallexikon für Antike und Christentum*
RB	*Revue biblique*
REJ	*Revue des études juives*
RGG	*Religion in Geschichte und Gegenwart*
RHPR	*Revue d'histoire et de philosophie religieuses*
RSR	*Recherches de science religieuse*
RTP	*Revue de théologie et de philosophie*
SAC	Studies in Antiquity & Christianity
SANT	Studien zum Alten und Neuen Testament
SBB	Stuttgarter biblische Beiträge
SBEC	Studies in the Bible and Early Christianity
SBG	Studies in Biblical Greek
SBLDS	Society of Biblical Literature Dissertation Series
SBLMS	Society of Biblical Literature Monograph Series
SBLRBS	Society of Biblical Literature Resources for Biblical Study
SBLSBS	Society of Biblical Literature Sources for Biblical Study
SBLSP	Society of Biblical Literature Seminar Papers
SBS	Stuttgarter Bibelstudien
SBT	Studies in Biblical Theology
ScEccl	*Sciences ecclésiastiques*
SJLA	Studies in Judaism in Late Antiquity

SJT	*Scottish Journal of Theology*
SNT	Studien zum Neuen Testament
SNTSMS	Society for New Testament Studies Monograph Series
SNTU	*Studien zum Neuen Testament und seiner Umwelt* (journal)
SNTU	Studien zum Neuen Testament und seiner Umwelt (monograph series)
SNTW	Studies of the New Testament and its World
SR	*Studies in Religion/Sciences religieuses*
SSEJC	Studies in Scripture in Early Judaism and Christianity
StNeot	Studia Neotestamentica
Str-B	[H. Strack and] P. Billerbeck, *Kommentar zum Neuen Testament aus Talmud und Midrasch* (5 vols., Munich: Beck, 1922-61)
SUNT	Studien zur Umwelt des Neuen Testaments
SVTP	Studia in veteris testamenti pseudepigrapha
TBei	*Theologische Beiträge*
TBl	*Theologische Blätter*
TDNT	G. Kittel and G. Friedrich (eds.), *Theological Dictionary of the New Testament* (1964-74)
TF	Theologische Forschung (monograph series)
TLZ	*Theologische Literaturzeitung*
TRu	*Theologische Rundschau*
TS	*Theological Studies*
TSAJ	Texte und Studien zum antiken Judentum
TU	Texte und Untersuchungen
TynBul	*Tyndale Bulletin*
TZ	*Theologische Zeitschrift*
UBSGNT	United Bible Societies *Greek New Testament*
USQR	*Union Seminary Quarterly Review*
WBC	Word Biblical Commentary
WUNT	Wissenschaftliche Untersuchungen zum Neuen Testament
ZNW	*Zeitschrift für die neutestamentliche Wissenschaft*
ZTK	*Zeitschrift für Theologie und Kirche*

CONTRIBUTORS

Jostein Ådna
Misjonshøgskolen
Stavanger
Norway

Dale C. Allison, Jr.
Pittsburgh Theological Seminary
Pittsburgh, Pennsylvania
USA

Richard J. Bauckham
St. Mary's College
St. Andrews, Fife
Scotland
UK

Bruce Chilton
Bard College
Annandale-on-Hudson, New York
USA

James D. G. Dunn
University of Durham
Durham, England
UK

E. Earle Ellis
Southwestern Baptist Seminary
Fort Worth, Texas
USA

Craig A. Evans
Trinity Western University
Langley, British Columbia
Canada
Roehampton Institute London
London, England
UK

William R. Farmer
University of Dallas
Dallas, Texas
USA

Martin Hengel
University of Tübingen
Federal Republic of Germany

William Klassen
École Biblique et Archéologique
Française
Jerusalem
Israel

Bruce J. Malina
Creighton University
Omaha, Nebraska
USA

Joel Marcus
University of Edinburgh
Edinburgh, Scotland
UK

Byron R. McCane
Converse College
Spartanburg, South Carolina
USA

Ben F. Meyer
McMaster University
Hamilton, Ontario
Canada

J. Ramsey Michaels
Southwest Missouri State University
Springfield, Missouri
USA

Matthew Brook O'Donnell
Roehampton Institute London
London, England
UK

Stanley E. Porter
Roehampton Institute London
London, England
UK

N. Thomas Wright
Lichfield Cathedral
Staffordshire, England
UK

Dieter Zeller
University of Mainz
Federal Republic of Germany

PART ONE

METHODS AND ASSUMPTIONS

AUTHENTICATING THE ACTIVITIES OF JESUS

Craig A. Evans

It is largely to E. P. Sanders's credit that scholars in recent years have come to appreciate the importance of the actions and activities of Jesus. In his influential book, *Jesus and Judaism*, Sanders identified eight facts or activities, about which we may be relatively confident. They are as follows:

1. Jesus was baptized by John the Baptist.
2. Jesus was a Galilean who preached and healed.
3. Jesus called disciples and spoke of there being twelve.
4. Jesus confined his activity to Israel.
5. Jesus engaged in a controversy about the Temple.
6. Jesus was crucified outside Jerusalem by the Roman authorities.
7. After his death Jesus' followers continued as an identifiable movement.
8. At least some Jews persecuted at least parts of the new movement (Gal 1:13, 22; Phil 3:6), and it appears that this persecution endured at least to a time near the end of Paul's career (2 Cor 11:24; Gal 5:11; 6:12; cf. Matt 23:34; 10:17).[1]

In his later, less technical work, *The Historical Figure of Jesus*,[2] Sanders enumerates several other highly probable facts:

1. Jesus was born c. 4 BCE, at the approximate time of the death of Herod the Great.
2. Jesus grew up in Nazareth of Galilee.
3. Although Jesus taught in small villages and towns, he seems to have avoided cities.
4. Jesus ate a final meal with his disciples.
5. Jesus was arrested and interrogated by Jewish authorities, apparently by orders of the High Priest.
6. Although they abandoned Jesus after his arrest, the disciples later "saw" him after his death. This led the disciples to the belief that Jesus would return and found the kingdom.[3]

---

[1]   E. P. Sanders, *Jesus and Judaism* (London: SCM Press; Philadelphia: Fortress, 1985) 11.

[2]   E. P. Sanders, *The Historical Figure of Jesus* (London and New York: Penguin, 1993).

[3]   For a helpful tabulation that compares the "almost indisputable facts" given

I am in essential agreement with Sanders, both with regard to this list and with regard to his emphasis on events and activities. Of course, Sanders has been criticized for giving priority to *facts*, as opposed to the *sayings* of Jesus, which is where most studies traditionally have begun.[4] I am not, however, impressed by this criticism; I believe that it is prudent historical procedure to attempt the construction of the basic framework, even sequence of events (as limited as that may be), in the light of which Jesus' teachings and practices should be studied.

I side with Sanders here for two reasons: (1) The original, specific context of the sayings of Jesus, with rare exceptions, is lost. Consequently, even if we are relatively certain of the authenticity of a significant core of sayings, we are seldom certain of the original setting in which they were uttered and, therefore, of what precisely they originally meant. As I see it, interpretation of the sayings is more vulnerable to the whims of modern subjectivity than are events and "facts." Obviously the "facts" have to be interpreted also, and subjectivity remains a problem, but their context is more certain. In my judgment, what we can recover is a more or less *general* context, not the *specific* contexts of *specific* sayings. (2) Non-Christian sources support certain important facts and so provide significant information for comparative study. As I have argued elsewhere, we have no reliable sources of Jesus' sayings outside of the New Testament.[5] Even if some of these sources were to be accepted as containing historically trustworthy tradition, they give us no useful information as to the setting and context of the sayings.[6] From this I

---

by Sanders in his two books, see M. A. Powell, *Jesus as a Figure in History* (Louisville: Westminster John Knox Press, 1998) 117.

    4   See Sanders, *Jesus and Judaism*, 10-22.

    5   C. A. Evans, *Jesus and His Contemporaries: Comparative Studies* (AGJU 25; Leiden: Brill, 1995) 26-45; idem, "Jesus in non-Christian Sources," in B. D. Chilton and C. A. Evans (eds.), *Studying the Historical Jesus: Evaluations of the State of Current Research* (NTTS 19; Leiden: Brill, 1994) 443-78; idem, with J. H. Charlesworth, "Jesus in the Agrapha and Apocryphal Gospels," in Chilton and Evans (eds.), *Studying the Historical Jesus*, 479-533.

    6   The same conclusion has been reached by J. P. Meier, *A Marginal Jew: Rethinking the Historical Jesus.* Volume One: *The Roots of the Problem and the Person* (ABRL 3; New York: Doubleday, 1991) 56-166. The *Gospel of Thomas*, a favorite extra-canonical source among many scholars, especially those associated with the Jesus Seminar, presents the sayings of Jesus completely free of context.

conclude that the historical framework, made up of several fairly certain facts, must first be clarified and then used as a primary criterion for determining what sayings and episodes ought to be considered the stronger candidates of authentic tradition and how they should be interpreted.

In a recent work N. T. Wright has added a few facts to the list that in my judgment are also probable:

1. Jesus spoke Aramaic, Hebrew, and probably some Greek.
2. Jesus summoned people to repent (*pace* Sanders).
3. Jesus made use of parables to announce the kingdom of God.
4. Jesus effected remarkable cures, including exorcisms, as demonstrations of the truth of his proclamation of the kingdom.
5. Jesus shared in table fellowship with a socially and religiously diverse group, including those whom many Torah-observant Jews would regard as "sinners."[7]

To Sanders's and Wright's several facts one can add a few more complementary details. I think that it is highly probable that Jesus was viewed by the public as a prophet, that the Romans crucified him as "king of the Jews," and that following Easter his followers regarded him as Israel's Messiah. We shall find that many of the sayings of Jesus cohere with these historical elements, often times either explaining them or being explained by them. I think it is also appropriate to retain as *highly* probable Jesus' reference to "twelve." (Sanders expresses less confidence about this tradition in his later book.)[8]

It will be useful to review a number of the proposed facts outlined by Sanders and Wright, supplementing them with the three points recommended above. What emerges is a coherent historical context and framework, in the light of which the sayings of Jesus should be interpreted. Not every one of these elements will be accepted by

---

[7]   N. T. Wright, *Jesus and the Victory of God* (Christian Origins and the Question of God 2; London: SPCK; Minneapolis: Fortress, 1996). Again, it is helpful to see the tabulation provided by Powell, *Jesus*, 154-55.

[8]   See now the very capable defense of the pre-Easter origin of the Twelve in J. P. Meier, "The Circle of the Twelve: Did It Exist during Jesus' Public Ministry?" *JBL* 116 (1997) 635-72. Meier (p. 671 n. 83) exposes the logical weaknesses and implausibility in W. Schmithals's (*The Office of the Apostle in the Early Church* [Nashville: Abingdon, 1969] 69-70) proposal that the tradition of the Twelve is a post-Easter development that quickly faded, yet nonetheless left numerous traces in the Gospels but had no impact on early Christian theology.

scholars. Jürgen Becker, for example, doubts the historicity of the Temple controversy. His important book will be treated below. For his part, Sanders does not think Jesus called for repentance and so he will disagree with part of my supplement to the second fact. The restoration of Israel, implied by the appointment of the Twelve, is not accepted by some of the Jesus Seminar. Readers will discern other points with which they and others disagree. In my opinion, however, the following "facts" can be well supported individually, even in isolation, and taken together form a solid, coherent framework that makes sense and in part finds important parallels in Jewish history of late antiquity.

1. Jesus was baptized by John the Baptist. With little fanfare the Markan evangelist states that Jesus "was baptized by John in the Jordan" (Mark 1:9). But Mark's presentation of this event, especially in the way it is juxtaposed to the narrative of John's activities, is subtle and effective. In effect John becomes the forerunner of Jesus, the forerunner who announces the fulfillment of Isaiah 40, the great passage of Israel's anticipated restoration, as well as the fulfillment of John's prediction of the coming of a "mightier one" who "will baptize [the people] with the Holy Spirit" (Mark 1:8).

The evangelist's skillful and obviously tendentious use of the tradition does not, however, militate against the authenticity of the material itself. In view of the obvious difficulties the story of Jesus' baptism gave the early church, it is highly improbable that the story was invented. Attempts to deal with these difficulties are plainly evident in the Gospels: Matthew qualifies the story by explaining why it is that Jesus would need to undergo a "baptism of repentance for the forgiveness of sins" (Mark 1:4). Matthew does not retain this sentence exactly,[9] but mention of repentance is prominent in his version of the narrative nonetheless (cf. Matt 3:2, 8 [from Q], 11). Jesus wishes to undergo it "to fulfill all righteousness" (Matt 3:15), though exactly how it does that is not made clear. That Jesus really does not need to submit to baptism is emphasized by John's initial refusal to baptize Jesus (Matt 3:14). By having *John* ask to be baptized *by Jesus* seeks to overcome the implication that being baptized by John means that John is the master and Jesus is the

---

9   Indeed his near omission of Mark 1:4 was probably due to a desire to head off the question of why Jesus would go to be baptized by a man who offered a "baptism of repentance."

student. Luke's revision of the story leaves the reader with the impression that John himself did not actually baptize Jesus, for the former had already been imprisoned (Luke 3:19-21). John's Gospel says nothing about Jesus being baptized. Rather, the fourth Gospel tells us that Jesus baptized more disciples than did John (John 3:22; 4:1-2), that some of John's disciples joined Jesus' following (1:37), and that John himself recognized Jesus as "the lamb of God who takes away the sin of the world" (John 1:29).

The potential embarrassment of the baptism of Jesus is further mitigated in various ways. Mark says heaven opened, the Spirit descended on Jesus, and the heavenly voice recognized Jesus as the beloved son, with whom God is well pleased (Mark 1:11). Matthew seconds this account, adding that the descending Spirit perched on Jesus (Matt 3:16). Luke notes that it was the "Holy" Spirit that descended on Jesus and that it did so "in bodily form" (Luke 3:22), perhaps to underscore the reality and substance of Jesus' empowerment through the Spirit. The baptism account is richly embellished in the extracanonical Gospels. The *Gospel of the Ebionites* §4 and the *Gospel of the Hebrews* §2 respectively expand on the numinous elements, while the *Gospel of the Nazarenes* §2, following Matthew's lead, has Jesus expressly reject the need for his baptism. The fourth Gospel, which narrates no baptism, instead has the Baptist proclaim Jesus' superiority and John's preparatory role (John 3:25-30).

The development of the tradition strongly recommends the authenticity of the baptism of Jesus by John. The effort to explain away embarrassing elements, either through correction, augmentation, or omission, makes it clear that there was every reason not to manufacture such a story.[10]

If we agree that Jesus was baptized by John, what does it mean? I think that it implies at the very least that Jesus was in essential agreement with the Baptist's agenda, an agenda that seems to have the restoration of Israel as its goal (through repentance and preparation for an eschatological moment). In Jesus' approximate time we know of at least one other revivalist movement associated with the Jordan River. Here we have in mind Theudas who summoned the crowds to take up their possessions and join him at the famous river (cf. Josephus, *Ant.* 20.5.1 §97-98). In what was probably calculated as a

---

[10] On the authenticity of the baptism of Jesus, as well as discussion of the criterion of embarrassment, see Meier, *A Marginal Jew*, 168-71.

reenactment of Joshua's crossing of the Jordan, Theudas enjoined his following to take up their possessions and join him at this historic spot. At his command, the prophet promised, God would part the waters allowing him and his following to pass through unhindered. It is probable that Theudas believed that such a sign would be but the first step in a new conquest of the Promised Land.

Besides the fact of John's presence at the Jordan River, which by itself could point to Joshua, we have the intriguing utterance that "God is able from these stones to raise up children to Abraham" (Matt 3:9 = Luke 3:8). To what "stones" did John refer? Do we not again have an echo of Joshua tradition? According to Joshua 4 twelve stones representing the twelve tribes of Israel were set up at the Jordan as a memorial to God's covenant with his people. The link in Josh 4:7 between stones (הָאֲבָנִים) and sons (בָּנִים) is especially apposite ("these stones will be for a memorial for the sons of Israel forever"), given evidence of wordplays involving these two sound-alike words.[11] The twelve stones/twelve tribes significance of the "stones" in John's speech gains support from the other probable fact in Jesus' ministry, namely, his appointment of twelve apostles (Mark 3:14; 6:7; Matt 19:28 = Luke 22:30; cf. 1 Cor 15:5). The possible, if not probable correlation between John's preaching and the "stones" to which he makes reference, on the one hand, and the proclamation of Jesus and his speaking, if not appointment, of twelve emissaries, on the other, suggests one more important point of continuity between John and Jesus and at the same time strengthens the probability that Jesus understood his mission in terms of the restoration of Israel. Our suspicion receives important corroboration in the saying about the twelve who will sit on twelve thrones judging the twelve tribes of Israel (Matt 19:30 = Luke 22:28-30). Not only does this saying offer

---

[11]   Josephus (*J.W.* 5.6.3 §272) says that when a Roman siege stone (ἡ πέτρα) approached the ramparts, watchmen would warn that the "son" was coming (ὁ υἱὸς ἔρχεται). This odd epithet, which makes no sense in Greek, in all probability is based on Aramaic or Hebrew, as has been proposed. The possibility that John's words may also allude to Isa 51:1-2 (as recommended by D. C. Allison and W. D. Davies, *A Critical and Exegetical Commentary on the Gospel according to Saint Matthew. Volume I: Introduction and Commentary on Matthew I-VII* [ICC; Edinburgh: T. & T. Clark, 1988] 308) does not need to militate against the Joshua allusion. For the view adopted here, see O. J. F. Seitz, "'What Do These Stones Mean'?" *JBL* 79 (1960) 247-54. Seitz also draws our attention to Josh 5:7 ("their sons, whom he raised up").

important support to such an interpretation, the saying is itself clarified by the probable linkage with John's words and activities at the Jordan River.

2. *Jesus was a Galilean who proclaimed the kingdom of God.* His proclamation of it as the "good news," as "fulfilled," and as "at hand" is consistent with his recognition as a prophet.[12] It is also consistent with the theme of Isaiah 61 ("the Lord has anointed me to proclaim good news"), to which Jesus alludes in tradition which surely is authentic (cf. Matt 11:4-5 = Luke 7:22).[13] Influence of the theology of Second Isaiah is witnessed throughout Jesus' ministry[14]: the provision of food (Mark 6:35-44; 8:1-10; cf. Isa 25:6), healing (Mark 1:29-31, 32-34, 40-45; 2:1-12; 3:1-6; cf. Isa 35:5-6; 61:1-2), and even raising the dead (Mark 5:35-43; Luke 7:11-17; cf. Isa 26:19). Although how much of this tradition derives from the actual activities of Jesus is debated, the contribution of Isaiah can hardly be gainsaid. (On Jesus as healer and exorcist, see below.) An orientation toward Second Isaiah strongly suggests that Jesus understood his

---

[12]   Two passages in particular strongly suggest this: (1) Mark 6:4, where Jesus' self-reference, "A prophet is not without honor except at home," can hardly have been the creation of the early church; and (2) the passage in which the soldiers mockingly ask Jesus to "prophesy" and so identify those who strike him (Mark 14:65; cf. Matt 26:68, where the request for identification is made explicit). The doleful lament in Q, "Jerusalem, Jerusalem, which stones the prophets and kills those sent to you . . ." (Matt 23:37 = Luke 13:34), also implies that Jesus understood himself as a prophet. A few other passages lend additional support (cf. Matt 10:41; Mark 6:15; 8:27-28). Some references to Jesus as a prophet have been added by Matthew (21:11, 46) and Luke (7:16, 39).

[13]   Occurrences of "good news" or "gospel" (בשׂר) are found in the second half of Isaiah. There are five passages in all (Isa 40:1-11; 41:21-29; 52:7-12; 60:1-7; 61:1-11). The summary in Mark 1:15 betrays significant points of dictional coherence with the Aramaic paraphrase of some of these passages from Isaiah. In *Tg.* Isa 40:9 we read *"The kingdom of your God is revealed!"* instead of "Here is your God!" Again, in *Tg.* Isa 52:7 we read *"The kingdom of your God is revealed"* instead of "Your God reigns." The italicized words indicate the places where the Aramaic departs from the Hebrew. The Aramaic diction approximates the gist of Jesus' proclamation: "The time is fulfilled, the kingdom of God is at hand; repent, and believe in the good news." What draws the Aramaic tradition even closer to Jesus' proclamation is that the verses cited above are understood to relate the essence of the message that the prophet is to proclaim.

[14]   For a recent assessment of the influence of Second Isaiah in Jesus' proclamation, see O. Betz, "Jesus' Gospel of the Kingdom," in P. Stuhlmacher (ed.), *The Gospel and the Gospels* (Grand Rapids: Eerdmans, 1991) 53-74.

message and mission in terms of national restoration.

Jesus' proclamation of the kingdom not only presupposed John's earlier call to repentance, it continued it (Matt 12:41 = Luke 11:32; Mark 6:12; Luke 13:3-5; 16:30).[15] Consistent with his role as eschatological prophet Jesus called for repentance and rebuked those who criticized his ready acceptance of those who joined his movement (Matt 11:19 = Luke 7:34). Repentance, moreover, was in some circles understood to be a prerequisite for the deliverance of Israel. It is only in the post-Easter setting that repentance is qualified by the demand for faith in Jesus (cf. Acts 2:38-39; 3:17-21).

3. Jesus called disciples and spoke of there being twelve. Jesus is called "rabbi," his most common designation.[16] His activities of teaching and disciple-making are consistent with what we know of Jewish religious teachers of this period. His allusive, *ad hoc* appeal to Scripture reflects interpretive tendencies that may be traced to the synagogue (as attested in prayers and in the Aramaic paraphrases). His eschatological and charismatic understanding of Scripture is paralleled in important ways at Qumran. As a teacher, or rabbi, Jesus disputed with other teachers about what constituted purity, an important factor in Israel's covenant with God and, from an eschatological perspective, the nation's restoration. Even his actions in the Temple precincts is consistent with his recognition as a rabbi and followed the examples of other rabbis before him (see seventh point below).

The appointment of the twelve, taken with the proclamation of the kingdom of God, virtually makes certain Jesus' hopes for the restoration of Israel. That the twelve signified the twelve tribes of Israel

---

15   Sanders (*Jesus and Judaism*, 226-27) maintains that Jesus regarded the call for national repentance satisfied by John's proclamation and baptism and that Jesus therefore only concerned himself with summoning people, including the wicked, to join him in fellowship in anticipation of the kingdom of God. For criticism of this view, see B. D. Chilton, "Jesus and the Repentance of E. P. Sanders," *TynBul* 39 (1988) 1-18. On the wider question of Jesus' view of repentance and its relation to questions of purity, see Chilton, "E. P. Sanders and the Question of Jesus and Purity," in Chilton and C. A. Evans, *Jesus in Context: Temple, Purity, and Restoration* (AGJU 39; Leiden: Brill, 1997) 221-30.

16   Jesus is called ῥαββί in Mark 9:5; 11:21; 14:45; ῥαββουνί in Mark 10:51. The Greek equivalent διδάσκαλος is found in Mark 4:38; 5:35; 9:17, 38; 10:17, 20, 35; 12:14, 19, 32; 13:1. Some of the usages of κύριος and ἐπιστάτα are probably also Greek equivalents of "rabbi."

can hardly be doubted and that such symbolism pointed to the whole of Israel is highly probable and is consistent with later rabbinic discussion of the regathering of the twelve tribes in the age to come.

4. Jesus confined his activity to Israel. This adds further support to Jesus' mission of restoration of Israel. If only a philosopher, and a cynic one at that, why not more ministry in the cosmopolitan cities within and without Israel? Why no mention of activity in neighboring Tiberias and Sepphoris? The formulation in Matthew 10 may reflect a great deal of editorial work of the evangelist, but surely the command to "go nowhere among the Gentiles, but only go to the lost sheep of the House of Israel" (Matt 10:5-6; cf. 15:24),[17] could not have been generated in the church, even the Matthean church. For one, the saying stands in obvious tension with the Great Commission, whereby the apostles are to make disciples of the nations, but it also stands in tension with the immediate context of the Missionary Discourse. For later in the discourse the disciples are given instructions about what to say and not to fear when brought before the Gentiles (cf. Matt 10:18). The instructions to go only to Israel very likely originated in Jesus, which through contextualization in the Missionary Discourse and in the Great Commission is qualified in an important sense.

The over-all impression one gains is that Jesus was indeed a teacher and prophet to his own people. His teachings may have contained implications for Gentiles and he may have encountered a few Gentiles (such as the Syro-Phoenician woman), but his ministry appears to have been confined for the most part to Israel itself. This limitation is consistent with the view, recommended above, that Jesus' ministry had as its goal Israel's redemption.

5. Jesus was widely regarded as a remarkable healer and exorcist. Any fair reading of the Gospels and other ancient sources (including Josephus)[18] inexorably leads to the conclusion that Jesus was well

---

[17]   The Matthean complexion of these verses is undeniable, yet it is not easy to explain them as Matthean inventions (esp. when the tension with Matt 28:16-20 is taken into account). The assumption that Luke omitted this material from Q is quite reasonable (cf. Luke 9:1-6). For reasons against a redactional origin of Matt 10:5-6, see D. C. Allison, Jr. and W. D. Davies, *A Critical and Exegetical Commentary on the Gospel according to Saint Matthew.* Volume II: *Commentary on Matthew VIII–XVIII* (ICC; Edinburgh: T. & T. Clark, 1991) 168-69.

[18]   In the part of the so-called *Testimonium Flavianum* most scholars regard as authentic, Josephus describes Jesus as a "doer of amazing deeds [παραδόξων ἔργων

known in his time as a healer and exorcist. Historians need not be distracted by scientific and philosophical questions that inquire into the exact nature of these events. It is sufficient for historians to conclude that Jesus engaged in activities that led his contemporaries to view him as a healer and exorcist. Many scholars in recent years have adopted this view.[19]

Scholarship has now moved past its preoccupation with demythologization.[20] The miracle stories are now treated seriously and are widely accepted by Jesus scholars as deriving from Jesus' ministry. Major studies on the historical Jesus discuss the miracles, whether in general terms or in reference to specific miracles, with little or no discussion of myth or the philosophical issues at one time thought to be necessary for any assessment of the miracle traditions in the Gospels.[21] Several specialized studies have appeared in recent years, which conclude that Jesus did things that were viewed as "miracles."[22]

ποιητής]" (*Ant.* 18.3.3 §63). This language is not negative; it is neutral.

[19]   See J. Jeremias, *New Testament Theology* (New York: Scribner's, 1971) 91; B. F. Meyer, *The Aims of Jesus* (London: SCM Press, 1979) 155; Sanders, *Jesus and Judaism*, 166; J. D. Crossan, *The Historical Jesus: The Life of a Jewish Mediterranean Peasant* (San Francisco: HarperCollins, 1991) 318-19; G. Twelftree, *Jesus the Exorcist: A Contribution to the Study of the Historical Jesus* (WUNT 2.54; Tübingen: Mohr [Siebeck], 1993) 98-113. Even the Jesus Seminar, as reported in R. W. Funk (ed.), *The Acts of Jesus: What Did Jesus Really Do? The Search for the Authentic Deeds of Jesus* (San Francisco: HarperCollins, 1998), have accepted many of the miracles (e.g. Mark 1:30-31, Simon's mother-in-law; Mark 1:40-42, the cleansing of the leper; Mark 2:3-5, 12, the paralytic; Mark 5:25-29, the woman with the hemorrhage; Luke 8:1-2, exorcism; Mark 10:46-52, blind Bartimaeus).

[20]   On the declining influence of myth as significant factor in Jesus research, see C. A. Evans, "Life-of-Jesus Research and the Eclipse of Mythology," *TS* 54 (1993) 3-36.

[21]   Many of the most significant studies in Jesus in recent years take the miracles seriously into account, e.g. G. Vermes, *Jesus the Jew: A Historian's Reading of the Gospels* (London: Collins; Philadelphia: Fortress, 1973) 58-82; M. Smith, *Jesus the Magician* (San Francisco: Harper & Row, 1978) 8-20; Meyer, *The Aims of Jesus*, 154-58; A. E. Harvey, *Jesus and the Constraints of History* (London: Duckworth, 1982) 105-18; Sanders, *Jesus and Judaism*, 157-73; M. J. Borg, *Jesus: A New Vision* (San Francisco: Harper & Row, 1987) 57-75; B. Witherington, *The Christology of Jesus* (Minneapolis: Fortress, 1990) 145-77.

[22]   R. H. Fuller, *Interpreting the Miracles* (Philadelphia: Westminster, 1963); German ed., *Die Wunder Jesu in Exegese und Verkündigung* (Düsseldorf: Patmos, 1967). Fuller concludes that "the tradition that Jesus did perform exorcisms and

The principal evidence for this conclusion has been ably summarized by Barry Blackburn. As he puts it,[23]

the miracle-working activity of Jesus—at least exorcisms and healings—easily passes the criterion of multiple attestation.[24] Such miracles are attested in Q, Mark, material unique to Matthew and to Luke, and the Gospel of John (healings only), including the "signs source."[25] Jesus'

---

healings (which may also have been exorcisms originally) is very strong" (p. 39). Fuller's positive assessment anticipated the critical affirmations that have been heard in more recent years. G. Theissen, *Urchristliche Wundergeschichten: Ein Beitrag zur formgeschichtlichen Erforschung der synoptischen Evangelien* (Gütersloh: Mohn, 1974); ET: *The Miracle Stories of the Early Christian Tradition* (Philadelphia: Fortress, 1983) 277: "There is no doubt that Jesus worked miracles, healed the sick and cast out demons"; P. J. Achtemeier, "Miracles and the Historical Jesus: A Study of Mark 9:14-29," *CBQ* 37 (1975) 471-91; O. Betz and W. Grimm, *Wesen und Wirklichkeit der Wunder Jesu* (ANTJ 2; Frankfurt am Main and Bern: Lang, 1977); Smith, *Jesus the Magician*, 101: "In most miracle stories no explanation at all is given; Jesus simply speaks or acts and the miracle is done by his personal power. This trait probably reflects historical fact"; D. Zeller, "Wunder und Bekenntnis: zum Sitz im Leben urchristlicher Wundergeschichten," *BZ* 25 (1981) 204-22; G. Maier, "Zur neutestamentlichen Wunderexegese im 19. und 20. Jahrhundert," in D. Wenham and C. L. Blomberg (eds.), *The Miracles of Jesus* (Gospel Perspectives 6; Sheffield: JSOT Press, 1986) 49-87, 79: "Historische Forschung kann heute mit guten Gründen sagen, dass Jesus damals Wunder getan hat"; Sanders, *Jesus and Judaism*, 157: "There is agreement on the basic facts: Jesus performed miracles, drew crowds and promised the kingdom to sinners"; H. Hendrickx, *The Miracle Stories of the Synoptic Gospels* (London: Chapman; San Francisco: Harper & Row, 1987) 22: "Yes, we can be sure that *Jesus performed real signs which were interpreted by his contemporaries as experiences of an extraordinary power*" (his emphasis); Witherington, *Christology*, 155: "That Jesus performed deeds that were perceived as miracles by both him and his audience is difficult to doubt."

[23] The quoted paragraphs, including the footnotes, are taken from B. L. Blackburn, "The Miracles of Jesus," in Chilton and Evans (eds.), *Studying the Historical Jesus*, 356-57.

[24] Argued *inter alios* by Fuller, *Interpreting the Miracles*, 25; N. Perrin, *Rediscovering the Teaching of Jesus* (New York: Harper & Row, 1976) 65; D. E. Aune, "Magic in Early Christianity," *ANRW* 2.23.2 (1980) 1525; Witherington, *Christology*, 155-56, 201.

[25] Q: Matt 4:3 = Luke 4:3; Matt 8:5-10, 13b = Luke 7:1-10; Matt 11:4-5 = Luke 7:22; Matt 10:8 = Luke 10:9; Matt 11:20-24 = Luke 10:13-15; Matt 9:32-34 = 12:22-29 = Luke 11:14-15, 17-22; *unique Matthean material:* 7:22; 9:27-31; 17:24-27; 21:14; *unique Lukan material:* 4:18, 23-27; 5:1-11; 7:11-17; 8:2; 9:54; 10:17-20; 13:10-17; 13:32; 14:1-6; 17:11-21; 22:51; 23:8, 37, 39; 24:19. The fragments

wonderworking is also attested in various forms of oral tradition isolated by form criticism:[26] (1) controversy, scholastic, and biographical apothegms,[27] (2) dominical sayings, including logia (wisdom sayings), prophetic sayings, church rules, and "I" sayings,[28] (3) miracle stories, (4) legends,[29] and (5) the passion narrative.[30]

(Moreover), Jesus' exorcistic and healing activity is mentioned or implied by a few dominical logia with strong claims to authenticity. Following the charge that Jesus exorcised as a sorcerer, both Mark and Q contain two dominical parables, the former of which, the "divided kingdom" parable (Mark 3:24-26; Matt 12:25-26; Luke 11:17-18), almost certainly originated as a defense against the charge of demonically empowered healings and/or exorcisms. Only so could the language about Satan being divided against himself be meaningfully interpreted. Independently attested by Mark and Q and addressing a charge patently not created by the church, its claim to be an authentic dominical saying is good. Its talk of the βασιλεία τοῦ σατανοῦ certainly comports well with Jesus' principal theme, the kingdom of God.[31]

One of the most revealing episodes, to which Blackburn also draws

---

of the four pericopae that constitute the remains of the Egerton Gospel contain a variant of the Healing of the Leper (Mark 1:40-45 par) and an extra-canonical miracle whose exact nature is uncertain due to lacunae. The critical question is whether this gospel is independent of the Synoptics (*pro* Crossan, *The Historical Jesus*, 428; *contra* J. A. Fitzmyer, *The Gospel According to Luke* [2 vols., AB 28, 28A; Garden City: Doubleday, 1981-85] 1.573).

[26] For convenience I employ the categories and nomenclature proposed by R. Bultmann in his *The History of the Synoptic Tradition* (Oxford: Blackwell, 1972); German orig. *Die Geschichte der synoptischen Tradition* (FRLANT 12; Göttingen: Vandenhoeck & Ruprecht, 1921; 2nd ed., 1931). For a much more recent application of form-critical method which exploits the categories of ancient Greek rhetoric, see K. Berger, *Formgeschichte des Neuen Testaments* (Heidelberg: Quelle und Meyer, 1984).

[27] *Controversy*: Mark 3:1-6 par; Luke 14:1-6; 13:10-17; Mark 3:22-30; 2:1-12 par; *scholastic*: Matt 11:2-19 par; Mark 9:38-40 par; 11:20-25 par; *biographical*: Luke 17:11-19; Matt 17:24-27; Luke 13:31-33. Bultmann also regards Mark 7:24-31 par and Matt 8:5-13 par as apothegms (cf. *History of the Synoptic Tradition*, 38-39).

[28] *Logia*: Mark 3:24-26 par; *prophetic sayings*: Matt 11:21-24 par; 11:5-6 par; 7:22-23 par; *church rules*: Mark 6:8-11 = Matt 10:5-16 = Luke 10:2-12; *"I" sayings*: Matt 12:27-28 par.

[29] Matthew 4:1-11 par appears to presuppose Jesus' reputation as a miracle worker.

[30] Mark 15:31 par.

[31] Advocates of the authenticity of this parable include Meyer, *The Aims of Jesus*, 156; and Crossan, *Historical Jesus*, xix, 318-19.

our attention, is the account in which Jesus is accused of being in league with Satan (Mark 3:22-27):

22 And the scribes who came down from Jerusalem said, "He is possessed by Be-elzebul, and by the prince of demons he casts out the demons." 23 And he called them to him, and said to them in parables, "How can Satan cast out Satan? 24 If a kingdom is divided against itself, that kingdom cannot stand. 25 And if a house is divided against itself, that house will not be able to stand. 26 And if Satan has risen up against himself and is divided, he cannot stand, but is coming to an end. 27 But no one can enter a strong man's house and plunder his goods, unless he first binds the strong man; then indeed he may plunder his house.

What is interesting is the statement that "Satan . . . is coming to an end" (Mark 3:26). An exact Latin equivalent of Mark's ἔχει τέλος ("comes to an end") is found in the *Testament of Moses*: "Then his [i.e. God's] kingdom will appear in his entire creation. And then the devil will come to an end [*finem habebit*], and sadness will be carried away together with him" (10:1).[32] The association of the appearance of God's kingdom and the demise of the devil is the presupposition of the eschatology of both Jesus and the author of the *Testament of Moses*, a pseudepigraphon which in its final form appeared in the first third of the first century CE.[33] What is especially interesting is that what is viewed in the *Testament of Moses* as part of the End, at which time Satan will finally be undone, in Jesus it is viewed as having already been accomplished in his ministry.[34] What is anticipated in the *Testament* is believed to be in the process of fulfillment in Jesus' ministry. We find the same difference in temporal perspective in the comparison of Jesus' proclamation of the kingdom of God and the paraphrasing in the Isaiah Targum. What in the Aramaic tradition is anticipated, in Jesus' proclamation it is fulfilled (see n. 14 above).

Jesus' widespread ministry of exorcism, which included healings

---

32 The Vulgate renders the pertinent part of Mark 3:26 *finem habet*.

33 For text and translation, see J. Tromp, *The Assumption of Moses: A Critical Edition with Commentary* (SVTP 10; Leiden: Brill, 1993) 18-19. On the early first-century date of this writing, see Tromp, 116-17, and J. Priest, "Testament of Moses," in J. H. Charlesworth (ed.), *The Old Testament Pseudepigrapha* (2 vols., ABRL 13-14; New York: Doubleday, 1983-85) 920-21.

34 The point is rightly made by M. de Jonge, *God's Final Envoy: Early Christology and Jesus' Own View of His Mission* (Studying the Historical Jesus; Grand Rapids and Cambridge: Eerdmans, 1998) 53.

that in some ways were thought to involve the countering of Satanic influence, creates a strong presumption that Jesus' aim was the restoration of Israel through the renewing and reviving power of God's presence. The kingdom of Satan has begun to give way to the greater power of the kingdom of God.

6. *Jesus associated with diverse elements of Jewish Palestinian society.* More than two dozen times in the Synoptic Gospels we hear of "sinners," often in reference to Jesus' association with them. In many of these passages "tax (or toll) collectors" are mentioned as well. The authenticity of this tradition can scarcely be doubted, for it appears in all layers of the Synoptic tradition and no convincing reason can be given for assigning its origin to the early Church.

One of the most interesting instances involves a dominical saying in Q, where in contrast to the ascetic John the Baptist Jesus says of himself: "the Son of man came eating and drinking, and they say, 'Behold, a glutton and a drunkard, a friend of tax collectors and sinners!'" (Matt 11:19 = Luke 7:34).[35] Here we have a saying that can hardly have been produced by the early Christian community. This saying offers important corroboration to the Gospels' general portrait of Jesus as frequently in the company of sinners. But the epithet itself, "a glutton and a drunkard," is ominous, as Howard Kee comments:

> The verbal links of this phrase with Deut 21:20 have been noted and discussed[36] but not adequately explored. The fact that the phrase in Q (φάγος καὶ οἰνοπότης) differs sharply from the LXX (συμβολοκοπῶν οἰνοφλυγεῖ) can be used to argue for the authenticity of the saying, since a direct quotation from the LXX, even its wording, would be a likely sign of a later addition to the Q tradition. What has been largely overlooked is the context in which the phrase occurs in Deuteronomy (21:18-21) and the implications which this carries with it for the use of the phrase in the Jesus

---

35 On this saying's authenticity, setting, and meaning, see H. C. Kee, "Jesus: a Glutton and Drunkard," in B. Chilton and C. A. Evans (eds.), *Authenticating the Words of Jesus* (NTTS 28.1; Leiden: Brill, 1998) 311-32.

36 Kee cites J. Jeremias, *The Parables of Jesus* (New York: Scribner's, 1963) 160, and then comments that Fitzmyer (*Luke*, 1.681) dismisses the proposal of a connection, since the Greek of Q differs from the LXX of Deuteronomy. One might also see G. R. Beasley-Murray, *Jesus and the Kingdom of God* (Grand Rapids: Eerdmans, 1986) 235, 391-92 n. 64. Beasley-Murray takes essentially the same position that Kee has adopted. One should also consult the Aramaic tradition, where the language of Deut 21:20 parallels the epithet "glutton and drunkard" more closely (cf. *Tg. Neof.* Deut 21:20: "he is a glutton for meat and a drunkard of wine").

tradition. The passage in Deuteronomy outlines the procedure for dealing with a "stubborn and rebellious son," who refuses to obey his parents. More is at stake than relations within the family, however. He constitutes a threat to the welfare of the community as a whole, as is evident in the court of appeal to which the case is to be referred and the agents through whom the legally prescribed punishment is to be carried out. The problem is not to be resolved by the parents alone. Instead, the charge against the rebel is to be brought to the town council: to the elders gathered at the town gate. The execution of the rebel is to be by stoning, and is to be carried out by all the adult males of the community.[37]

Kee's insights reveal the extent to which Jesus' comment anticipates his fate in Jerusalem. The saying may also shed important light on Jesus' understanding of the kingdom in relation to his mission. From the accusation that he was "a glutton and a drunkard" we should probably infer that Jesus had begun to celebrate the coming of the kingdom of God. It is only when faced the probability of death, that Jesus vows not to "drink again of the fruit of the vine until that day when [he] drink[s] it new in the kingdom of God" (Mark 14:25).

The charge that Jesus was a glutton and drunkard, a friend of tax collectors and sinners also draws attention to the redemptive aims in his ministry. This point is well illustrated in the popular Parable of the Prodigal Son (Luke 15:11-32).[38] The prodigal is said to have "squandered his property in loose living" (v. 13) and is later accused by his older brother of having cavorted "with harlots" (v. 30). But despite his sins, having repented he is to be received with joy (vv. 24, 32). The natural inference from what is said of the prodigal and what is said of Jesus is that the latter's association with sinners was part of the restoration of Israel. Jesus sought to reclaim "sinners" and enjoined the righteous to receive them. The kingdom of God, then, entailed a call to repentance and a ready acceptance of the penitent into full participation, even celebration, in the new community.

7. Jesus engaged in a controversy about the Temple. This controversy centered on criticism of the ruling priests.[39] This is consistent

---

[37]   Kee, "Jesus: a Glutton and Drunkard," 329.

[38]   Even the Jesus Seminar accepts this parable as probably authentic; cf. R. W. Funk and R. W. Hoover (eds.), *The Five Gospels: The Search for the Authentic Words of Jesus* (Sonoma: Polebridge Press; New York: Macmillan, 1993) 356-57.

[39]   In no sense did Jesus criticize the practice of sacrifice or the "externals" of Judaism. This kind of interpretation derives from Christian apologetic and polemic, not from exegesis and history. The principal pericopes that underscore controversy

with Jesus' being a rabbi, for on occasion rabbis did this sort of thing.[40] It is consistent with his role as prophet, for the later prophet Jesus son of Ananias did something similar.[41] It is also consistent with Jesus' concern for the fate of Israel, for if Temple polity is defective, Israel's restoration will be postponed.

The appeal to Isa 56:7 is highly significant and should not be dismissed as a Christian invention, either to deflect charges that Jesus was attacking the Temple or to find some scriptural warrant to justify his actions. The saying, "my house shall be a house of prayer for the nations" (Mark 11:17), cannot easily be explained as deriving from the early Church.[42] Why would early Christians wish to claim the Temple as the house of prayer for the nations? Would not such a view stand in tension with the Church? The assumption of Christian

---

between Jesus and the ruling priests are Mark 11:15-18, 27-33; 12:1-12, 38-40, 41-44; 14:53-52, 53-65; 15:1, 11, 31-32.

40   Pharisees incite the crowd to pelt Alexander Jannaeus before he could offer sacrifice (Josephus, *Ant.* 13.13.5 §372-373); rabbis encourage youths to damage an eagle Herod had mounted over a Temple gate (Josephus, *J.W.* 1.33.2–4 §648-655); and Rabbi Simeon ben Gamaliel protests the overcharge for doves (*m. Ker.* 1:7). On these incidents and their potential relevance for understanding the actions of Jesus in the Temple precincts, see B. D. Chilton, *The Temple of Jesus: His Sacrificial Program within a Cultural History of Sacrifice* (University Park: Penn State Press, 1992) 100-111.

41   Jesus son of Ananias cried out words apparently based on Jer 7:34, was cuffed by some of the inhabitants of Jerusalem, was treated sympathetically by others, and finally was hauled in before the Roman governor. After interrogation, which included the infamous Roman scourging, the hapless Jesus was released, the governor having decided he was nothing more than a harmless lunatic (cf. Josephus, *J.W.* 6.5.3 §300-309).

42   Consistent with their assumption that "Citations of scripture are usually a sign of the interpretive voice of the evangelist or the early Christian community," the Jesus Seminar thinks Mark 11:17 does not derive from Jesus; cf. Funk and Hoover (eds.), *The Five Gospels*, 97-98. In his recent work, J. Becker (*Jesus von Nazaret* [de Gruyter Lehrbuch; Berlin and New York: de Gruyter, 1996] 408; ET: *Jesus of Nazareth* [Berlin and New York: de Gruyter, 1998] 332) also opines that the allusions to Isaiah and Jeremiah are the work of the evangelist. He concludes this for two reasons: (1) The Old Testament quotations are recalled to explain the scene; and (2) the quotations are septuagintal. On the contrary, the quotations hardly offer an explanation that would serve Christian interests or clarify Christian ideas, while affiliation with the LXX proves nothing, given the complexities of Hebrew, Greek, and Aramaic biblical texts in the pre-70 period (as attested by the Dead Sea Scrolls). Besides, the LXX in this case is a literal translation of the (proto-) MT.

origin becomes even more problematic, if Mark's Gospel was not published until after the destruction of the Temple in 70. It is better to understand the saying as originating with Jesus, for it is consistent with his restorative theology, as the fuller context of the prophetic oracle suggests. Isaiah 56:1-8 constitutes an oracle that looks forward to the day when all the peoples of the world will come to Jerusalem. Jesus' appeal to this oracle, which forms the scriptural presupposition for his complaint against Temple polity, is consistent with his proclamation of the appearance of the kingdom. The kingdom is at hand, Temple polity should reflect it.[43]

The general historicity of the Temple controversy is corroborated in an important way in Josephus. According to him, Pilate condemned Jesus to death "upon hearing him accused by the first men among us [τῶν πρώτων ἀνδρῶν παρ' ἡμῖν]" (*Ant.* 18.3.3 §64). Who are these "first men among us"? The most probable candidates are Jerusalem's ruling priests and associates. First-century usage supports this suggestion. The author of Luke-Acts refers to Israel's leaders as the "first of the people": "And he was teaching daily in the Temple. The chief priests and the scribes and the principal men of the people [οἱ πρῶτοι τοῦ λαοῦ] were seeking to destroy him" (Luke 19:47). Luke links these "first" ones with "the ruling priests and the scribes." Two additional examples in Acts should be cited: "And the chief priests and the principal men of the Jews [οἱ πρῶτοι τῶν Ἰουδαίων] informed him (i.e. Governor Festus) against Paul" (Acts 25:2); "After three days (Paul) called together the principal men of the Jews [τοὺς ὄντας τῶν Ἰουδαίων πρώτους]" (Acts 28:17). Examples from Josephus are instructive: "There came to (Ezra) certain men who accused some of the common people as well as Levites and priests of having violated the constitution and broken the laws of the country . . . No sooner did he hear this than he rent his clothes for grief . . . because the first men among the people [τοὺς πρώτους τοῦ λαοῦ] were guilty of this charge" (*Ant.* 11.5.3 §140-141). Here, the "first men" are synonymous with the Levites and priests. In a text closer to the one that concerns us, Josephus describes Vitellius'

---

43   For the details of this line of interpretation, see C. A. Evans, "From 'House of Prayer' to 'Cave of Robbers': Jesus' Prophetic Criticism of the Temple Establishment," in C. A. Evans and S. Talmon (eds.), *The Quest for Context and Meaning: Studies in Biblical Intertextuality in Honor of James A. Sanders* (BIS 28; Leiden: Brill, 1997) 417-42.

movement against Aretas: "Since he had started to lead his army through the land of Judea, the Jews of the highest standing [ἄνδρες οἱ πρῶτοι] went to meet him and entreated him not to march through their land. For, they said, it was contrary to their tradition to allow images . . . to be brought upon their soil" (*Ant.* 18.5.3 §121). These "first men" who are concerned that Roman icons not be allowed to pass through Judea were in all probability religious leaders. Vitellius accommodated their wishes. Accordingly, the "first men" of the *Testimonium Flavianum* should be understood as ruling priests and their associates. If this is correct, then we have in Josephus an important point of agreement with the New Testament Gospels, which tell us that the ruling priests had Jesus arrested and handed over to Pilate.

8. *Jesus ate a final meal with his disciples.* In this meal Jesus spoke of not drinking wine "until that day" when he drinks it new in the kingdom of God, a passage mentioned above. We now consider it in its own right. Mark 14:22-25 reads:

> 22 And as they were eating, he took bread, and blessed, and broke it, and gave it to them, and said, "Take; this is my body." 23 And he took a cup, and when he had given thanks he gave it to them, and they all drank of it. 24 And he said to them, "This is my blood of the covenant, which is poured out for many. 25 Truly, I say to you, I shall not drink again of the fruit of the vine until that day when I drink it new in the kingdom of God."

Jesus' anticipation that he will not drink wine again until he drinks it in the kingdom of God clearly attests an expectation of Israel's restoration. The authenticity of the statement is virtually guaranteed by the extreme improbability that the Markan evangelist or tradents that preceded him, decades after Jesus' death, would create a saying whose fulfillment seemed problematic. The Pauline version, which is some twenty years earlier than the Markan version, does not retain this part of the tradition. Its absence may have been the result of deliberate omission. The material should be judged as largely authentic. However, the Jesus Seminar does not agree, for "most Fellows were convinced that the supper tradition has been so overlaid with Christianizing elements and interpretation that it is impossible to recover anything of an original event, much less any of the original words spoken by Jesus."[44] This judgment is too skeptical, for the words are

---

44   Funk and Hoover (eds.), *The Five Gospels*, 118. Jesus' words in Mark 14:22b, 24b-25 are rated as "gray," which expresses grave reservations.

attested in Paul, though admittedly in a somewhat different form. According to 1 Cor 11:23-25:

> For I received from the Lord what I also delivered to you, that the Lord Jesus on the night when he was betrayed took bread, 24 and when he had given thanks, he broke it, and said, "This is my body which is for you. Do this in remembrance of me." 25 In the same way also the cup, after supper, saying, "This cup is the new covenant in my blood. Do this, as often as you drink it, in remembrance of me."

Paul's form of the tradition underscores the memorial aspect of the words of institution, a feature totally absent from the Markan version. This is important to note. The memorializing of the words of the Last Supper shifts the emphasis away from Jesus' anticipation of the imminent fullness of the kingdom, which his reference to drinking wine surely implies. Mark's form is primitive, the Pauline form— attested in Luke 22:19—is secondary.

Jesus' expectation to drink wine "anew" (καινόν) in the kingdom anticipates not only the restoration of Israel, a "kingdom of God" in which the reign of God is felt throughout the nation and the world,[45] but it also anticipates an active administrative role for himself and his disciples. The Q saying about the twelve sitting on thrones judging the twelve tribes of Israel, as well as the Markan saying about the disciples not administering Israel the way the Gentiles and mighty men of the world lord it over others, is part of this kingdom hope. Both of these sayings require some attention.

The Q Saying about the Twelve Judging the Twelve Tribes reads:

> Truly, I say to you, in the new world, when the Son of man shall sit on his glorious throne, you who have followed me will also sit on twelve thrones, judging the twelve tribes of Israel. (Matt 19:28)

> 28 You are those who have continued with me in my trials; 29 and I assign to you, as my Father assigned to me, a kingdom, 30 that you may eat and drink at my table in my kingdom, and sit on thrones judging the twelve tribes of Israel. (Luke 22:28-30)

The Markan saying about Serving One Another reads:

> 42 You know that those who are supposed to rule over the Gentiles lord it over them, and their great men exercise authority over them. 43 But it shall not be so among you; but whoever would be great among you must be your

---

[45] For more on this matter, see B. Chilton, "Regnum Dei Deus Est," *SJT* 31 (1978) 261-70; idem, "The Kingdom of God in Recent Discussion," in Chilton and Evans (eds.), *Studying the Historical Jesus*, 255-80.

servant, 44 and whoever would be first among you must be slave of all. 45 For the Son of man also came not to be served but to serve, and to give his life as a ransom for many. (Mark 10:42-45)

I have argued elsewhere that these materials may have been linked in Jesus' teaching, part of it perhaps in a form something like this:

The sons of Zebedee said to him, "Grant us to sit, one at your right hand and one at your left, in your glory." But Jesus said to them, "You do not know what you are asking. To sit at my right hand or at my left is not mine to grant, but it is for those for whom it has been prepared. Truly I say to you, when I sit on my glorious throne, you who have followed [or continued with] me will also sit on twelve thrones, judging the twelve tribes of Israel."[46]

The hope for the full manifestation of the kingdom of God, which brings with it Israel's restoration, entails a shaking up of the political and economic structures of Israel. Old administrators must go (as seen in the Parable of the Wicked Vineyard Tenants), serious social and religious wrongs must be set right (as seen in the warning about the scribes who plunder widows, as seen in the widow's last mite), and new administrators, "who do the will of God" (Mark 3:35), must assume positions of leadership (as seen in the Markan and Q sayings).

In his final meal with his disciples, which left an indelible imprint on the collective memory of his earliest followers, Jesus spoke of the coming of the kingdom and of "blood of the covenant." However that last phrase was originally intended,[47] it is very probably part of Jesus' hope for Israel's restoration. Dom Crossan is right to say that the

---

[46]   C. A. Evans, "The Twelve Thrones of Israel: Scripture and Politics in Luke 22:24-30," in Chilton and Evans, *Jesus in Context*, 473 n. 46. For arguments in support of the authenticity of these materials, see pp. 470-73 and notes.

[47]   On its meaning as an alternative to the shedding of animal blood in the Temple precincts, see Chilton, *The Temple of Jesus*, 152-54; idem, "The Purity of the Kingdom as Conveyed in Jesus' Meals," in E. H. Lovering, Jr. (ed.), *Society of Biblical Literature 1992 Seminar Papers* (SBLSP 31; Atlanta: Scholars Press, 1992) 473-88, esp. 487-88. Chilton's interpretation has been accepted by B. Lang, "The Roots of the Eucharist in Jesus' Praxis," in Lovering, Jr. (ed.), *Society of Biblical Literature 1992 Seminar Papers*, 467-72. Whether we accept the traditional interpretation that Jesus saw the cup and bread as in some way signifying his anticipated death, or we accept Chilton's proposal that the elements were meant as substitutes to the body and blood of the animal of sacrifice (i.e. better to eat bread and drink wine in purity than to slaughter an animal inappropriately acquired and offered), we are still left with the impression that Jesus envisioned, indeed had called for national renewal and with it a higher form of purity.

"Last Supper" came to be remembered as such because it was in fact the last supper shared by Jesus and his disciples,[48] but this does not take away from the probable fact that Jesus spoke of covenant and the kingdom of God.

Although the final meal became theologized, institutionalized, and taken up in the liturgy of the early Church, the fact that it stood out in the Church's memory and that statements about a covenant and a vow not to drink wine until it could be drunk in the kingdom of God were partly remembered attest to its importance and provide us with a context, in the light of which other sayings (and activities) may be better interpreted.

9. *Jesus was crucified as "king of the Jews" outside Jerusalem by the Roman authorities.* The execution of Jesus by the Romans as ὁ βασιλεὺς τῶν Ἰουδαίων (Mark 15:26 parr.) is one of the single most important data we have. In Latin the inscription probably read something like *IESUS NAZARENUS REX IUDAEORUM*, while the Hebrew may have read מלך היהודים.[49] David Catchpole doubts the historicity of the *titulus*, suspecting that it has been drawn from the earlier material in Mark 15.[50] But Mark wishes to portray Jesus as the "Christ," the "son of God," not as the "king of the Jews." The Roman Senate, and later emperor Augustus, recognized Herod the Great as "king of the Jews," or "king of Judea" (Josephus, *Ant.* 14.1.3 §9: Ἡρώδῃ . . . βασιλεῖ τῶν Ἰουδίων; 14.11.4 §280: βασιλέα τῆς Ἰουδαίας; 15.11.4 §409: ὁ τῶν Ἰουδαίων βασιλεὺς Ἡρώδης; cf. *J.W.* 1.14.4 §282-285; *Ant.* 14.14.4 §282-285). Only Romans call Jesus "king of the Jews."[51] In contrast, the mocking priests call Jesus "king of Israel" (vv. 31-32). Christians, however, regarded Jesus as

---

48   J. D. Crossan, *The Historical Jesus: The Life of a Mediterranean Jewish Peasant* (San Francisco: HarperCollins, 1991) 361.

49   The trilingual tradition of the *titulus* rests only on John 19:20.

50   D. R. Catchpole, "The 'Triumphal' Entry," in E. Bammel and C. F. D. Moule (eds.), *Jesus and the Politics of His Day* (Cambridge: Cambridge University Press, 1984) 319-34, esp. 328. W. Bousset (*Kyrios Christos* [Göttingen: Vandenhoeck & Ruprecht, 1913] 56) viewed the *titulus* as unhistorical, an "erbauliche Betrachtung der gläubigen Jesusgemeinde." But in what sense could the *titulus*, which for early Christians inadequately described Jesus, serve as an "edifying meditation"?

51   See also *Ant.* 15.10.5 §373, where an Essene greets the young Herod as βασιλέα Ἰουδαίων. Although the Essene is Jewish, the prophetic greeting conveys the Roman epithet, not a religious, Jewish one.

the Messiah, the son of God, and never call him "king of the Jews." In view of these considerations I have to agree with the majority of scholars who accept the *titulus* and its wording as historical and genuine.[52]

The *titulus* accordingly gives us a great deal of insight into the nature of Jesus' activities and how his contemporaries apparently viewed him. If Jesus was in fact executed as a royal claimant, then we probably should regard the entry, in which Jesus is mounted on the animal (evidently as a conscious enactment of Zech 9:9), as also historical. For it would have been a symbolic act such as this that would have contributed to the growing belief that Jesus was in some sense a king. Jesus' execution as "king of the Jews," moreover, may suggest that the woman's anointing of Jesus in Mark 14:3-9 was a messianic anointing, only later understood in the light of Easter as a preparation for burial. Other traditions, such as the cry of blind son of Timaeus, in which he addresses Jesus as "Son of David" (Mark 10:47-48), also receive a measure of corroboration.

The crucifixion of Jesus as "king of the Jews," therefore, seriously weakens attempts to interpret Jesus in non-messianic ways. The Jesus Seminar's portrait of Jesus more in terms of a Cynic philosopher stumbles on the nature of Jesus' death. At most a pest, neither Jewish nor Roman authorities would have paid much attention to him. A good beating, perhaps imprisonment, would have been more than sufficient. Execution, however—and an execution by crucifixion at that—calls for a much better explanation of the nature of Jesus' words and activities. When we notice that the substance of his message centered on the "kingdom of God," we may justifiably suspect that his execution of the "king of the Jews" was related and that this correlation surely points to a messianic agenda of some sort.

10. After his death Jesus' followers continued as an identifiable

---

[52]   G. Schneider, "The Political Charge," in Bammel and Moule (eds.), *Jesus and the Politics of His Day*, 403-14. On p. 403 Schneider comments that the *titulus* is "historically unimpeachable." Other supporters for the historicity of the *titulus* include J. Wellhausen, *Das Evangelium Marci* (Berlin: G. Reimer, 1909) 130-31; P. Winter, *On the Trial of Jesus* (Studia Judaica: Forschungen zur Wissenschaft des Judentums 1; Berlin: de Gruyter, 1961) 108; E. Dinkler, *Signum Crucis* (Tübingen: Mohr [Siebeck], 1967) 306; E. Bammel, "The *titulus*," in Bammel and Moule (eds.), *Jesus and the Politics of His Day*, 353-64. On p. 363 Bammel concludes that the "wording of the *titulus* as it is reported in the Gospels is in all likelihood authentic."

movement and were called "Christians" because of their belief that Jesus was the Christ, the Messiah of Israel. The widespread understanding of Jesus as Israel's Messiah, and therefore God's "Son" (in keeping with Psalm 2 and 2 Samuel 7—all part of the Davidic royal tradition), strongly recommends a messianic element that reaches back to the period of Jesus' ministry. If nothing messianic was present in Jesus' ministry, if only primarily implicit, this widespread messianic understanding of Jesus is hard to explain. After all, there appears to have been no competing interpretations of Jesus among his followers, that is, some messianic and others non-messianic.

The force of this point seems lost on many who claim that the recognition of Jesus as Messiah originated only in the post-Easter setting. Had there been no messianic element in Jesus' teaching or activity, at least nothing discernible to his following, then it is very hard to understand where post-Easter Messianism came from. The resurrection alone cannot account for this widespread belief, for there is no pre-Christian messianic tradition that viewed resurrection as in some way evidence of a person's messianic identity. The early Church, it should be remembered, usually found the proclamation of Jesus' resurrection an insufficient apologetic in Jewish settings. Alone, the resurrection of Jesus could not compensate for the enormity of the problem of his rejection by the ruling priests, his ostensible defeat at the hands of the Roman authorities, and his shameful execution. The Messiah was to "remain forever" (John 12:34).

Although due allowance must be made for its obvious apologetic slant, the question with which Justin Martyr credits Trypho the Jew very likely approximates the misgivings many Jews would have entertained when hearing Christian claims:

> Then Trypho remarked, "Be assured that all our nation awaits the Messiah; and we admit that all the Scriptures which you have quoted refer to him. Moreover, I also admit that the name of Jesus by which the son of Nun was called, has inclined me very strongly to adopt this view. But we are in doubt about whether the Messiah should be so shamefully crucified. For whoever is crucified is said in the Law to be accursed, so that I am very skeptical on this point. It is quite clear, to be sure, that the Scriptures announce that the Messiah had to suffer; but we wish to learn if you can prove it to us whether by suffering he was cursed." (*Dialogue with Typho* 89.1)

> "Lead us on, then," [Trypho] said, "by the Scriptures, that we may also be persuaded by you; for we know that he should suffer and be led as a sheep.

> But prove to us whether he must also be crucified and die such disgraceful
> and dishonorable death, cursed by the Law. For we cannot bring ourselves
> even to consider this." (*Dialogue with Typho* 90.1)

Trypho is quite accommodating in his concession that "the Scriptures
announce that the Messiah had to suffer," but remains skeptical due
to the shameful and dishonorable nature of Jesus' suffering, ending
in a form of death that brings to mind Deut 21:23 and the idea of one
who dies in such a manner is "cursed of God."

Of course, Jewish critics were not alone in mocking the Christian
proclamation that the crucified Galilean was none other than Israel's
King and God's Messiah. According to Origen, Celsus regarded the
notion as absurd, that someone betrayed, abandoned, captured, and
executed could be regarded as God and Savior. The whole notion is
preposterous (cf. Origen, *Contra Celsum* 2.9, 35, 68; 6.10, 34, 36).[53]
To make any headway at all, especially in a Jewish context, a
Christian apologetic would have to explain the circumstances of the
passion and would have to show how the passion was in keeping with
scriptural expectation.[54] Proclamation of the resurrection would in
itself constitute an insufficient apologetic.

From these considerations it seems prudent to conclude that the
origin of the messianic understanding of Jesus is pre-Passion, not
post-Easter. The resurrection of Jesus served to revive messianic
categories; it did not create them.

Postscript

At this point we might briefly compare the recent work of the
Jesus Seminar with the probable facts outlined above. The Seminar
has affirmed the following:

1. Jesus was an itinerant teacher in Galilee.
2. Jesus practiced prayer in seclusion.
3. Jesus preached in the synagogues of Galilee.

---

[53]See M. Hengel, *Crucifixion in the Ancient World and the Folly of the
Message of the Cross* (Philadelphia: Fortress, 1977) 1-10; idem, "Christological
Titles in Early Christianity," in J. H. Charlesworth, ed., *The Messiah: Developments in Earliest Judaism and Christianity* (Minneapolis: Fortress, 1992) 425-48,
esp. 425-30.

[54]   I have argued in *Word and Glory: On the Exegetical and Theological Background of John's Prologue* (JSNTSup 89; Sheffield: JSOT Press, 1993) 172-84
that this is precisely what the fourth evangelist has attempted to do, in his use of
scriptural testimonies.

4. Jesus proclaimed the kingdom of God.
5. Jesus cured some sick people.
6. Jesus drove out what were thought to be demons.
7. Jesus enjoyed a certain amount of popularity in Galilee and surrounding regions.[55] (pp. 61, 66-67, 171)

Other incidents recorded in the New Testament Gospels regarded by the Seminar as probable include Jesus' baptism by John, his association with "sinners," for which he was criticized, his use of parables, plucking and eating grain on the Sabbath, scribal criticism for allowing his disciples to eat with unwashed hands, his being accused of being demon empowered, his negative reception in his hometown, his driving out vendors in the Temple precincts, desertion by his disciples, his being handed over to Pilate, who flogged him and had him crucified. The Seminar believes that the hearing before the Jewish Council and the trial before Pilate are propaganda, not historical. Indeed, with the regard to the latter, the Seminar states: "It is not just the content of the trial but the fact of a trial that lacks historical foundation."[56] Accordingly, the Seminar does think Jesus was brought before the High Priest.[57]

What is therefore absent in the Seminar's findings is the question that Caiaphas the High Priest put to Jesus: "Are you the Messiah, the son of the Blessed?" as well as the detail that Jesus was crucified as "king of the Jews" (Mark 14:61; 15:2, 9, 12, 18, 26).[58] The evidence for the historicity of both of these elements is strong, especially for the latter, which in turn lends important support to the former. These two details also receive important support, as already noted, from the facts that before his death Jesus proclaimed the kingdom of God, and after his death his disciples proclaimed him to be the Messiah, the king of Israel. Logic strongly suggests that a messianic element was present in Jesus' teaching and activities, if only implicitly, and that this best accounts for this development.

What is absent in the Seminar's work is a convincing explanation of what led to Jesus' death. Key elements in the Temple controversy are discounted, as well as Jesus' appearance before the High Priest.

---

[55]   Funk (ed.), *The Acts of Jesus*, 61, 66-67, 171. See the convenient summary of five points on p. 171 ("These observations are almost certainly historical.")

[56]   Funk (ed.), *The Acts of Jesus*, 152.

[57]   See Funk (ed.), *The Acts of Jesus*, 146, where Mark 14:53 is rated "pink."

[58]   See Funk (ed.), *The Acts of Jesus*, 146-48. Most of this material is rated "black."

The Seminar's portrait of Jesus as a teacher (but not messianic claimant) is insufficient to account for what happened to Jesus and the ideas his following entertained in the aftermath. One remembers Sanders's appreciation of one important aspect of the work of the late Morton Smith.[59] Sanders describes it as "a serious effort to explain historically some of the principal puzzles about Jesus, specifically why he attracted attention, why he was executed, and why he was subsequently deified . . . regarding Jesus as essentially a teacher does not answer these and related questions."[60]

The point is a good one. Much about Jesus' teaching and activities can be inferred from the results. Why was he executed? Why did his followers regard him as Israel's Messiah, despite what by all accounts should have been viewed as his disqualification?[61] The weighty relevance of these questions does not seem to have been adequately appreciated by the Jesus Seminar.

The "probable" facts that have been surveyed above form a coherent picture and provide a plausible framework into which the sayings of Jesus may be placed. What emerges is a man whose public life began in association with and apparent support of the baptizing ministry of John. We immediately suspect an agenda of national restoration. Consistent with this suspicion is Jesus' subsequent proclamation of the kingdom of God, a proclamation that appears to be an Aramaic interpretation of Second Isaiah's "good news." This observation adds further support to the idea of national restoration, for Second Isaiah proclaims the coming new exodus. Again, consistent with this theme Jesus calls disciples and speaks of "twelve." The twelve surely represent the twelve tribes of Israel. Jesus' focus on Israel is supported when we observe that he confined his activity to Israel. His healings and especially his exorcisms were understood by

---

59   M. Smith, *Jesus the Magician* (San Francisco: Harper & Row, 1978).

60   Sanders, *Jesus and Judaism*, 7.

61   See also R. Morgan, "*Non Angli sed Angeli*: Some Anglican Reactions to German Gospel Criticism," in S. Sykes and D. Holmes (eds.), *New Studies in Theology* I (London: Duckworth, 1980) 1-30; idem, "Günther Bornkamm in England," in D. Lührmann and G. Strecker (eds.), *Kirche: Festschrift für Günther Bornkamm zum 75. Geburtstag* (Tübingen: Mohr [Siebeck], 1980) 491-506. Morgan rightly calls attention to the significance of the results of Jesus' ministry and death. From the results we may infer some general things about what Jesus did. The approach taken by A. E. Harvey's *Jesus and the Constraints of History: The Bampton Lectures, 1980* (London: Duckworth, 1982) is similar.

Jesus as evidence of the powerful presence of the kingdom of God and the beginning of the demise of Satan. His exorcisms, in some sense a "rescue operation," is consistent with his ministry of reclamation, as seen in association with "sinners" and other Jewish people who were marginalized.

When Jesus takes his program to Jerusalem he encounters serious opposition from the ruling priests. Jesus demonstrates in the Temple precincts, evidently as part of a criticism leveled against Temple polity. This action provokes further antagonism, which in turn leads to threats about the loss of the ruling priests' hegemony. In his final meal with his disciples, which may have been a Passover meal (which again would be consistent with Second Isaiah's promise of a new exodus), Jesus vows that he will not drink wine again until he drinks it "new" in the kingdom of God. His subsequent arrest and crucifixion as "king of the Jews" confirm the messianic and national element in his ministry. This belief is further confirmed when his disciples, upon hearing about and in many cases personally experiencing the resurrected Jesus, with confidence proclaim their master as Israel's Messiah.

Critical research of the life and teaching of Jesus should take into account this framework, or provide compelling reasons for why Jesus should be interpreted outside of it. The essays that make up the balance of the present volume are devoted to these issues and operate from assumptions that are for the most part illustrative of the general overview taken here. We hope to bring to the fore the more convincing parts of the Third Quest, while criticizing dubious assumptions and implausible conclusions. We proceed on the assumption that authenticating the activities of Jesus is just as important as authenticating his words.

CAN THE THIRD QUEST HOPE TO SUCCEED?

James D. G. Dunn

I

In his influential and significant study, *A New Quest of the Historical Jesus*, James M. Robinson entitled his second chapter "The Impossibility and Illegitimacy of the Original Quest."[1] It was *impossible* because "the Gospels are primary sources for the history of the early Church, and only secondarily sources for the history of Jesus"; "the twentieth century presupposes the kerygmatic nature of the Gospels, and feels really confident in asserting the historicity of its details only where their origin cannot be explained in terms of the life of the Church." It was *illegitimate* because such historical inquiry runs counter to faith: "whereas the kerygma calls for existential commitment to the meaning of Jesus, the original quest was an attempt to avoid the risk of faith by supplying objectively verified proof for its 'faith.'"[2]

These two words, "impossible," "illegitimate," sum up the failure of the 19th century quest, or at least the reasons for that failure when Rudolf Bultmann colossus-like still bestrode the narrow world of New Testament scholarship. To the two key questions, the answer was a resounding negative. *Can* the 20th century scholar hope to penetrate back into the historical reality of Jesus in the early 30s of the common era? "No! Not with any confidence; there are too many layers of post-Easter reflection and tradition intervening," came the reply. Does the 20th century believer *need* to penetrate back to the historical Jesus? Equally came the reply, "No! On the contrary, faith which seeks to undergird itself by history destroys itself." The same two questions cannot be ignored, otherwise they will return to haunt any renewed interest in the life of Jesus. The same two words, "impossible," "illegitimate," remain in place to bedevil any attempt to revive the quest and to close off the way back to Jesus with the

---

[1]   J. M. Robinson, *A New Quest of the Historical Jesus* (SBT 25; London: SCM Press, 1959) 26-47.

[2]   Robinson, *New Quest*, 35, 37-38, 44.

sign, "No Through Road."

It is true, of course, that the so-called "New Quest" provided what most probably regard as an effective answer to the "illegitimacy" charge. Faith may properly look to history for *information* as distinct from *legitimation*. Since the Gospels are themselves kerygma, the kerygma validates interest in the "What" of Jesus' life as well as the "That." To make faith depend on the mathematical point of Jesus' crucifixion[3] is to encourage and invite faith in a docetic or mythical Christ.[4] And the argument could be reinforced by observing the importance of the incarnation in Christian theology. An incarnational theology places incalculable weight on the thirty or so years of Jesus' life, and particularly on the first three years of the 30s.[5] The claim is that in Jesus' life, in that ministry, God revealed himself more fully and definitively than ever before or since. The revelatory significance of that life makes it inconceivable that Christian theology should disregard that life or regard it as inconsequential if nothing is to be known of that life. On the contrary, knowledge of that life, or at least of Jesus' ministry, in which the significance of his life comes to focus, is essential if the revelation of the incarnation is to have any content beyond the mere "That."

At the same time as the road-block of "illegitimacy" has been largely dismantled,[6] however, the road-block of "impossibility" seems to have been strengthened rather than weakened. It was put back in place by the failure of the second or "new quest." That became bogged down in unending debate over particular texts and in

---

3   The words of S. Kierkegaard have often been referred to: "If the contemporary generation (of Jesus) had left nothing behind them but these words: 'We have believed that in such and such a year the God appeared among us in the humble form of a servant, that he lived and taught in our community, and finally died,' it would be more than enough" (*Philosophical Fragments* [²1962] 130).

4   This was the principal argument in the famous essay of E. Käsemann, "Das Problem des historischen Jesus," *ZTK* 51 (1954) 125-53; ET: "The Problem of the Historical Jesus," in *Essays on New Testament Themes* (SBT 41; London: SCM Press; Philadelphia: Fortress, 1964) 15-47.

5   On the normal dating for Jesus' ministry.

6   But note the protest of L. T. Johnson, *The Real Jesus* (San Francisco: HarperCollins, 1996) 81-166, in which he echoes the earlier protest of M. Kähler, *Der sogenannte historische Jesus und der geschichtliche, biblische Christus* (Leipzig: A. Deichert, 1892; 2nd ed., 1896; repr., 1956); ET: *The So-Called Historical Jesus and the Historic Biblical Christ* (Philadelphia: Fortress, 1964).

unresolved disputes regarding criteria for recognizing authentic words of Jesus.[7] And the road-block was massively reinforced by the growing sense of crisis regarding the historical method itself.[8] The less objective meaning there was to be found in a text, the less control there could be on the meanings read from such texts, the more intangible became the historical Jesus, the more frustrating became any quest. No wonder so many have turned their attention to redaction criticism, to reconstructing the social contexts of the Gospels, or to a narrative criticism which concerns itself with the world of the text rather than the historical reality of its characters. The fact that the second quest has enjoyed a recent flowering in the portrayal of a Jesus draped in Cynic clothes, based on dubious presuppositions regarding the spread of Cynic philosophy in Jesus' early environment, questionable analysis and dating of sources, and specious arguments which equate analogy with genealogy,[9] simply underlines the severity of the crisis.

In the face of such intractable problems of principle and method, what hope can any further quest have? Can a third quest hope to succeed? Somewhat surprisingly, an affirmative answer, even a strongly affirmative answer can be given. The rest of this paper will be devoted to fleshing out this confidence and to arguing that the "impossibility" barricade can be circumvented, even if not wholly removed.

II

What distinguishes the so-called "third quest of the historical Jesus" is the conviction that any attempt to build up a historical picture of Jesus of Nazareth must begin from the fact that he was a first century Jew operating in a first century milieu. We can confidently assume that Jesus was brought up as a religious Jew. There is no dispute that his ministry was carried out within the land

---

[7] See e.g. D. G. A. Calvert, "An Examination of the Criteria for Distinguishing the Authentic Words of Jesus," *NTS* 18 (1971-72) 209-19; J. P. Meier, *A Marginal Jew*, vol. 1 (ABRL; New York: Doubleday, 1991) 167-95.

[8] See e.g. J. Bowden, *Jesus: The Unanswered Questions* (London: SCM Press, 1988).

[9] See particularly the critique of B. L. Mack, J. D. Crossan, and F. G. Downing by N. T. Wright, *Jesus and the Victory of God* (London: SPCK; Philadelphia: Fortress, 1996) 28-82.

of Israel. His execution on the charge of being a messianic pretender ("king of the Jews") is generally reckoned to be part of the bedrock data in the Gospel tradition. What more natural, what more inevitable than to pursue a quest of the historical Jesus the Jew?[10]

Such a statement seems very obvious, but it is one which generations of scholarship seem to have resisted. As the rationalist preacher, the ideal man, the teacher of liberal ethics, so beloved in the first quest, the historical Jesus was not only to be liberated from the distorting layers of subsequent dogma, but he could also be presented as the one who liberated the quintessential spirit of religion from the outmoded garb of Jewish cult and myth. The existential Jesus of Bultmann could make the quantum leap into the present moment of encounter without any dependence on his historical background. And the principal criterion used in the second quest, the criterion of dissimilarity, tried to make a virtue out of what second questers perceived as a necessity by reconstructing their picture of Jesus out of what distinguished Jesus from his historical context and set him over against his Jewish milieu. The older quests, we may say, multiplied their difficulties by setting out to find a Jesus who was somewhat like an isolated island in the south Pacific, when all the time he was more like a headland on the great land mass of ancient Israel and second Temple Judaism.

A contributory factor of no little significance here is the still mounting reaction, not least in New Testament scholarship, as indeed in Christian scholarship generally, against the denigration of Judaism which has been such a deeply rooted and long-standing feature of Christian theology. The repentance and penitence required by the Holocaust, though in some circumstances in danger of being overplayed, have still to be fully worked through at this point. The mindset which figures Judaism as the religion of law to be set over against Christianity as the gospel, with the chief task being to show how Jesus belongs with the latter rather than the former, still seems to operate at a deep subconscious level. And the portrayal of the Pharisees as archetypal legalists and bigots is still popular. Oddly enough, despite several potent earlier contributions on Jesus the Jew,[11] it was E. P. Sanders's work on *Paul* which caused the penny to

---

10   The case is well made by Wright, *Jesus*, 83-124.

11   We may mention particularly J. Jeremias, *New Testament Theology, Vol. 1: The Proclamation of Jesus* (London: SCM Press, 1971), notable for its apprecia-

drop finally in New Testament scholarship.[12] If traditional New Testament scholarship had misrepresented the Judaism with which *Paul* had to do, how much more was it necessary for *Jesus'* relationship to his ancestral Judaism to be reassessed. In that sense, Sanders' *Jesus and Judaism* (1985)[13] has to be reckoned as the real beginning of the third quest.

The prospects for the third quest have also been considerably eased by the fresh insights into the character of second Temple Judaism which have come to us during the last fifty years. Here the discovery of the Dead Sea Scrolls has pride of place. More than anything else they have broken open the idea of a monolithic, monochrome Judaism, particularly as set over against the distinctiveness of newly emerging Christianity. It has now become possible to envisage Jesus, as also "the sect of the Nazarenes," within the diversity of late second Temple Judaism in a way which was hardly thinkable before. This breakthrough has been accompanied and reinforced by other important developments—particularly the breakdown of the previously quite sharp distinction between Judaism and Hellenism,[14] the recognition that the portrayals of rabbinic Judaism in Mishnah and Talmud could not simply be projected backwards into the first century,[15] and the renewed interest in the rich range of apocryphal and pseudepigraphical Jewish literature as further testimony to the diversity of second Temple Judaism.[16] In short, it is no exaggeration to say that scholarship is in a stronger position than ever before to sketch in a clearer and sharper picture of Judaism in the land of Israel at the time of Jesus.

---

tion of Jesus as an Aramaic speaker; G. Vermes, *Jesus the Jew* (London: Collins, 1973), an old-fashioned presentation, but of subtle influence; B. F. Meyer, *The Aims of Jesus* (London: SCM Press, 1979), whose articulation of hermeneutical issues has been given too little consideration; J. K. Riches, *Jesus and the Transformation of Judaism* (London: Darton, Longman & Todd, 1980), which didn't quite come off; A. E. Harvey, *Jesus and the Constraints of History* (London: Duckworth, 1982), whose title indicates an important perspective only partially achieved; and B. Chilton, *A Galilean Rabbi and His Bible* (London: SPCK, 1984), overly dependent on a particular thesis.

[12] E. P. Sanders, *Paul and Palestinian Judaism* (London: SCM Press, 1977).

[13] E. P. Sanders, *Jesus and Judaism* (London: SCM Press, 1985).

[14] M. Hengel, *Judaism and Hellenism* (2 vols., London: SCM Press, 1974).

[15] The many works of J. Neusner have been particularly important here.

[16] See e.g. J. H. Charlesworth (ed.), *The Old Testament Pseudepigrapha* (2 vols., London: Darton, Longman & Todd; New York: Doubleday, 1983-85).

Not least of importance is the fact that the New Testament documents themselves can and should be counted as part of the evidence for the character and diversity of first century Jewish literature. Paul is the only Pharisee from whom we have first hand documentation from before 70 CE. And if the letters of Paul have to be counted as Jewish literature in an important sense, then how much more the Gospels. Even if one or more of the Gospels has to be attributed to a Gentile author, the traditions which they contain (we need only reckon with the Synoptic Gospels at this point) can hardly fail to be classified as "Jewish."

In short, whatever the motivation behind earlier quests of the historical Jesus, everything invites and urges the attempt to see Jesus within the context of first century Judaism and to ask both what light the Gospel traditions shed on that Judaism and what light that Judaism sheds on the Jesus tradition.

III

If protest needs to be lodged against the attempt, implicit or explicit, to begin by distancing Jesus from his ancestral religion, protest needs equally to be lodged against the equivalent attempt to distance Jesus from the churches which grew up from his work. This latter dichotomy has also been a spin-off from earlier phases of the quest. The original quest began precisely as a reaction against the ecclesiastical Christ, the Christ of dogma: back to the historical Jesus, the real Jesus, was the primary motivation. In this phase it could be argued that only by thus distancing Jesus from subsequent Christology would it be possible to rediscover him. But in the reaction against the first quest the distinction between historical Jesus and Christ of faith was retained and given fresh emphasis by kerygmatic theology. And in the second quest the criterion of double dissimilarity set the distinctiveness of Jesus over against church as well as Judaism.[17] Again, the motivation was understandable: the search was the old one for an invulnerable base on which to build a strong historical portrayal. But in seeking to avoid the Christianized Jesus as well as the Jewish Jesus, the method inevitably promoted the idiosyncratic Jesus, who could hardly be more than an enigma to Jew

---

[17]   The clearest exposition was by N. Perrin, *Rediscovering the Teaching of Jesus* (London: SCM Press; New York: Harper & Row, 1967) 39-43.

and Christian alike.[18]

But if the starting assumption of a fair degree of continuity between Jesus and his native religion has a priori persuasiveness, then it can hardly make less sense to assume a fair degree of continuity between Jesus and what followed. Here the issue is not so much that of portraying a Jesus who is "big" enough to explain the extraordinary growth of the Jesus movement after his death.[19] It is rather the continuity implicit in the self-identity of the first Christian churches. Here, after all, were small house groups who designated themselves by reference to Jesus the Christ, or Christ Jesus. Sociology teaches us that such groups would almost certainly require founding traditions to explain to themselves as well as to others why they had formed distinct social groupings, why they were "Christians." It is unlikely that a bare kerygmatic formula like 1 Cor 15:1-8 would provide sufficient material for self-identification. Even the initiatory myths of the mystery cults told a more elaborate story. And stories of such diverse figures as Jeremiah and Diogenes were preserved by their disciples as part of the legitimation for their own commitment. Of course, counter examples can be named: we know very little of Qumran's Teacher of Righteousness. On the other hand, the Teacher of Righteousness never gave his name to the movement he initiated, whereas the first Christians could only explain themselves by reference to him whom they called "(the) Christ."

This a priori logic is supported by the evidence that the passing on of tradition was part of church founding from the first. Paul was careful to refer back to such foundation traditions on several occasions (e.g. 1 Cor 11:2; 15:1-3; Phil 4:9; Col 2:6-7; 1 Thess 4:1; 2 Thess 2:15; 3:6). It is true that the lack of *explicit* reference to Jesus tradition within the Pauline letters appears to point in the opposite direction. But, as I have argued elsewhere, there are a fair number of *allusions* to Jesus' teaching and behaviour in Paul's letters, and, more to the point, allusions are just what we would expect when

---

[18]   For early critique, see M. D. Hooker, "Christology and Methodology," *NTS* 17 (1970-71) 480-87.

[19]   Sanders put the point well by referring to the second half of "Klausner's test": a good hypothesis regarding Jesus will explain why the movement initiated by him eventually broke with Judaism (*Jesus*, 18). Wright reiterates the point in his own terms: e.g. "Jesus must be understood as a comprehensible and yet, so to speak, crucifiable first-century Jew, whatever the theological or hermeneutical consequences" (*Jesus*, 86).

there was a large body of shared tradition to which allusion could be made without further identification.[20] In other words, the letters were not themselves the medium of initial instruction regarding founding traditions, but were able to draw on and refer back to these traditions as to something well enough known as part of their shared heritage. If further confirmation is needed, it is provided by the prominence of teachers within the earliest Christian churches (Acts 13:1; Rom 12:7; 1 Cor 12:28; Eph 4:11). Teachers, indeed, seem to have been the first regularly paid ministry within Christianity (Gal 6:6). Why teachers? Why else than to serve as the congregation's repository of oral tradition? What else would Christian teachers teach? A Christian interpretation of the scriptures, no doubt. But also, we can surely safely assume, the traditions which distinguished house churches from house synagogues or other religious, trade or burial societies.

There is a further argument here which needs to be given some weight, even though it has rarely been deployed.[21] Since the rise of form criticism it has been a regular assumption that sayings first uttered in the name of Jesus by early Christian prophets were incorporated into the Jesus tradition.[22] And that this happened in at least some measure seems probable.[23] But if prophetic utterance is invoked at this point then we also have to consider the long established recognition that inspiration could give rise to *false* prophecy. The need to test prophecy and to have tests for prophecy was recognized more or less from the beginning of Israel's reliance on prophecy.[24] And as soon as we begin to read of prophets

---

20   See my "Jesus Tradition in Paul," in B. Chilton and C. A. Evans (eds.), *Studying the Historical Jesus: Evaluations of the State of Current Research* (NTTS 19; Leiden: Brill, 1994) 155-78, esp. 176-78.

21   In what follows I draw on my "Prophetic 'I'-Sayings and the Jesus Tradition: the importance of testing prophetic utterances within early Christianity," *NTS* 24 (1977-78) 175-98.

22   The most thorough study is that of M. E. Boring, *Sayings of the Risen Jesus: Christian Prophecy in the Synoptic Tradition* (SNTSMS 46; Cambridge: Cambridge University Press, 1982).

23   A popular and highly plausible example is Matt 18:20 (see e.g. Boring, *Sayings of the Risen Jesus*, 214).

24   E.g. Deut 13:1-5; 1 Kgs 22:1-38; Isa 28:7; Jer 28:9. The ancient proverb, "Is Saul also among the prophets?" (1 Sam 10:12; 19:24), reflects an early recognition of the ambiguity of the prophetic experience.

operating in the earliest churches we find the same concern reflected. Already in what may be the earliest writing in the New Testament Paul counsels: "Do not despise prophecy, but test everything, hold to the good and avoid every form of evil" (1 Thess 5:20-22). And the concern runs through the New Testament into the second century churches (*Did.* 11:7-8; 12:1; Hermas, *Mand.* 11:7, 11, 16): "Believe not every spirit, but test the spirits . . ." (1 John 4:1).

Once this point has been grasped, it gives rise to an important corollary of relevance for present discussion. The corollary is that wherever prophecy was active in the earliest churches it is likely to have been accompanied by what we might call a hermeneutic of suspicion. The prophetic utterance would not automatically have been assumed to be inspired by the Spirit of Jesus or the words to be words of (the exalted) Christ. The awareness that such utterances must be tested seems to have been continuous through Israel's prophetic experience and into Christianity's prophetic experience.

The next step in the logic is the decisive one. What test would be applied to such utterances? One of the consistent answers is in effect the test of already recognized and established tradition. It was denial of or departure from foundational tradition which most clearly attested a false prophecy, which should therefore *not* be given any credence (Deut 13:2-3; 1 Cor 12:3; 1 John 4:2-3).

When this insight is brought to the issue of prophetic utterances becoming incorporated into the Jesus tradition the result is quite far-reaching. For it means, first, that *any prophecy claiming to be from the exalted Christ would be tested by what was already known to be the sort of thing Jesus had said.* This again implies the existence in most churches of such a canon (the word is not inappropriate) of foundational Jesus tradition. But it also implies, second, that only prophetic utterances which *cohered* with that assured foundational material were likely to have been accepted as sayings of Jesus. Which means, thirdly, that any *distinctive* saying or motif within the Jesus tradition is likely to have come from the original teaching of Jesus, since otherwise, if it originated as a prophetic utterance, it is unlikely to have been accepted as a saying of Jesus by the church in which it was first uttered. In other words, we have here emerging an interesting and potentially important fresh criterion for recognizing original Jesus tradition—a reverse criterion of coherence: the *less* closely a saying or motif coheres with the rest of the Jesus tradition, the *more* likely is it that the saying or motif goes back to Jesus himself.

In short, there is quite substantial circumstantial evidence both that the first churches would have and actually did cherish and refer to Jesus tradition, provided for them as foundational tradition by their founding apostle(s), and that they would have been alert to the danger of diluting or contaminating that vital foundational tradition by incorporation into it of material incoherent with it.

IV

All this a priori reasoning and circumstantial evidence is given immeasurably greater credibility by the most important fact of all: that *we have immediately to hand clear evidence of the sort of tradition these earliest churches possessed and of how they regarded and handled that tradition.* I refer, of course, to the Synoptic Gospels themselves.

Here, in the first place, we must take with due seriousness the starting point of form criticism—that is, the recognition that behind the written Gospels earlier forms of the tradition can be clearly enough discerned, and the assumption that these earlier forms indicate the way in which this tradition was preserved and used in the first churches. Despite this, some discussions of Synoptic pericopes at times almost seem to assume that when a copy of Mark or Matthew or Luke was first received by any church, that was the first time the church had heard the Jesus tradition contained therein. How ludicrous! In fact, it is almost self-evident that the Synoptists proceeded by gathering and ordering Jesus tradition which had already been in circulation, that is, *had already been well enough known to various churches, for at least some years if not decades.* Where else did they find the tradition? Stored up, unused, in an old box at the back of some teacher's house? Stored up, unrehearsed, in the failing memory of an old apostle? Hardly! On the contrary, it is much more likely that when the Synoptics were first received by various churches, these churches *already* possessed (in oral or written form) their own versions of much of the material. They would be able to compare the evangelist's version of much of the tradition with their own version.

This, surely, must be part at least of the explanation of the variations between Gospels. To treat such variations solely in terms of redaction of written sources betrays a gross failure of historical reconstruction. The corollary, of course, is that the task of tracing the history of particular forms becomes immeasurably more difficult, since it is no longer a case of tracing a simple linear development. But if such complexity and uncertainty is closer to historical reality, then any resort to more simplified hypotheses is a flight into false security whose outcome deserves little trust.

Secondly, *we have evidence of the way the Jesus tradition was actually handled in the process of transmission.* For within the Synoptics themselves we can discern the effects of at least two if not three retellings of various traditions.[25] I refer, of course, to the universally recognized fact of literary interdependence between the Synoptic Gospels. In terms of the principal consensus, we can see how Matthew and Luke used tradition derived from or shared with Mark, how, less confidently, Matthew and Luke used Q material, and how, much more speculatively, any of these three or four writings made use of earlier forms and blocks of material. The firmest data are the first mentioned—how Matthew and Luke used tradition derived from or shared with Mark—and this is where we should obviously start. To start elsewhere is likely to lead quickly into a quagmire of speculative hypotheses, such as two or more recensions of Q,[26] and to provide little or no secure ground on which to build.

When, however, we look at the clearest example of tradition-history (Mark as a source for Matthew and Luke) an important conclusion soon emerges.[27] That is the clear evidence of a deep and genuine respect for the story being told or the saying recorded. Again and again, even when material is reordered or a story told differently, we can be confident that the same event or the same saying is in view. And even when dialogue or sayings have been modified (to avoid possible misunderstanding),[28] there is evidence of a concern to hold as closely as possible to the earlier form, that is, evidence of a respect for the earlier form of the tradition. This is not to discount the equally clear evidence of editing—the reworking of material, the modification and elaboration of earlier forms, and so on. But over all, the strong thrust of the evidence is of a consistency

---

[25]   I do not say two or three layers of tradition, since I believe the image of multiple layers is misleading; see later in this section.

[26]   See again Wright's critique (*Jesus*, 41-4).

[27]   I draw on my semi-popular *The Evidence for Jesus* (London: SCM Press; Philadelphia: Westminster, 1985) 1-29.

[28]   For good examples, cf. Mark 6:5-6 with Matt 13:58 and Mark 10:17-18 with Matt 19:16-17.

and coherence between the earlier material and the evangelist's redaction of it, not of an editing which changes character and introduces abrupt discontinuities. Of course, a detailed substantiation of this argument would cover many pages. But if there is anything in the above summary, it provides a far sounder basis for tracing the pre-Gospel history of the material than speculative hypotheses about the redaction by any of the Synoptists of imaginatively reconstructed sources no longer extant.

Thirdly, in taking seriously the fact that most of the pre-history of the Synoptic tradition was in oral form, we should note how much of the material and process visible to us conforms to the character of oral tradition. So far as we can tell, the communication of oral tradition was typically characterized by traditional themes focused in a number of fixed points, and elaborated in the re-telling with motifs and formulae characteristic of the particular re-teller. What did this mean in practice?[29] The best example comes in fact in Acts, in the three tellings of Paul's conversion (Acts 9, 22, 26). The episode in view is clearly the same in each case, with the commission of Saul as missionary to the Gentiles a common theme. Each telling focuses in the brief encounter between Jesus and Saul which is word for word across all three tellings.[30] And yet the details and development of the narrative are very different. What is worth noting is that the differences between the three tellings are very similar to the differences between parallel pericopes in two or three different Gospels. And yet the three retellings in Acts appear *in the same document*. In other words, such differences are to be reckoned not only in terms of literary redaction of written sources; we must also reckon in terms of retellings of the same story even by the same narrator but adapted to different circumstances. Within the Synoptics themselves the best example is probably the healing of the centurion's boy (Matt 8:5-13 = Luke 7:1-10), with the same feature of a word for word core, but differently developed in the different retellings of the two Evangelists.[31]

---

29   For the character of oral tradition in the ancient world see particularly H. Wansbrough (ed.), *Jesus and the Oral Gospel Tradition* (JSNTSup 64; Sheffield: JSOT Press, 1991); K. E. Bailey, "Informal Controlled Oral Tradition and the Synoptic Gospels," *Asia Journal of Theology* 5 (1991) 34-54.

30   "Saul, Saul, why do you persecute me? . . . Who are you, Lord? . . . I am Jesus, whom you are persecuting; . . . Rise . . ." (Acts 9:5-6; 22:7-10; 26:14-16).

31   See further my *Evidence*, 14-16.

An important corollary follows from this. It is that the usual model of analysing the pre-written Gospel history of the Synoptic tradition is probably wrong. That model assumes layers of tradition, layers of redaction upon redaction, separating the final Gospel form from any putative original deriving from Jesus' own ministry. In consequence the trail leading back to an original Jesus word often becomes so tortuous that the quester is unable to pursue it beyond two or three layers at the most and must give up having penetrated no further back than, say, the 40s. But why should we assume that the process of transmission was a sequence of successive editings of individual forms? On the model of oral transmission we should rather assume a substantial store of remembered episodes and teaching from Jesus' ministry, remembered by the congregations' teachers as a prime part of their responsibility, with retellings usually focused in particular sayings fairly fixed in content, but otherwise variously elaborated. In other words, the model is not so much that of an archaeological tell, with success depending on ability to dig down through many strata. A better model is that of forms somewhat like space satellites circling round the remembered Jesus, with the forms of the 60s and 70s not necessarily further from Jesus than those of the 40s and 50s.[32] In short, in an oral culture, where the outline, theme and fixed points of a cherished tradition were probably soon established and remained relatively constant, the later pre-written retellings were probably little or no further from the original than the first retellings.

Finally, we need also to reckon with a point now fairly widely acknowledged. It is that Bultmann's denial that the Gospels were biographies was almost certainly misplaced. What he really meant is that they were not *modern* biographies and therefore did not facilitate a modern biographer's interest in "the life and personality of Jesus."[33] But it is now clear that the Gospels are very similar in

---

[32] The image is not all that good, but it can be elaborated to depict John's Gospel as on a higher orbit, or to include the possibility of forms drifting out of the gravity of the remembered Jesus, or being caught by a countervailing gravity. The earlier image of a trajectory could be fitted to this also: e.g. Q material on a trajectory leading to a *Gospel of Thomas* no longer held within the original gravity field.

[33] I echo here the famous comment of Bultmann (*Jesus and the Word* [London: Collins Fontana, 1958] 14): "I do indeed think that we can know almost nothing concerning the life and personality of Jesus, since the early Christian

type to *ancient* biographies: that is, their interest is not the modern one of tracing how an individual's character developed over time; rather their concern is with the portrayal of a historical character by means of recounting episodes and sayings which document that character.[34] Of course, a Gospel is not simply a biography; it is propaganda; it is kerygma. But then neither were ancient biographies wholly dispassionate and objective. In other words, the overlap between Gospel and ancient biography remains substantial and significant. In short, the genre itself tells us at once that there was a considerable historical interest in the formulating, retelling and collecting into Gospel format of the material which now comprises the Synoptic Gospels.

In summary of this section of the argument, then, we may simply say that a priori deductions, circumstantial evidence, the character of the Synoptic tradition and the clearest indications regarding its transmission, and the very character of the Gospels themselves all reinforce each other and point firmly to the conclusion that a careful scrutiny of the Synoptic tradition is likely to lead us back at many points to Jesus as he was remembered from the first.

V

Bearing all this in mind, how then should we proceed? When we put together the lessons to be learned from the failure of the previous quests and the potential for the third quest, two important points seem to emerge, one of principle, the other of procedure.

First the point of principle. The Synoptic tradition provides evidence not so much for what Jesus did or said in itself, but for what Jesus was *remembered* as doing or saying by his first disciples, or as we might say, for the impact of what he did and said on his first disciples. What we actually have in the Synoptic tradition are the memories of the first disciples—not Jesus himself, but the remembered Jesus. The idea that we can get back to an objective historical reality, which we can wholly separate and disentangle from the disciples' memories, and which we can then use as a check and

---

sources show no interest in either, are moreover fragmentary and often legendary."

[34]   See further D. E. Aune, *The New Testament in its Literary Environment* (Philadelphia: Westminster, 1987) 46-76; R. A. Burridge, *What are the Gospels? A Comparison with Graeco-Roman Biography* (SNTSMS 70; Cambridge: Cambridge University Press, 1992).

control over the way the tradition was developed during the oral and earliest written transmission, is simply unrealistic. This observation would have been more obvious had more attention been given to the narrative tradition, as distinct from the sayings tradition, over the past 150 years. For narratives about Jesus never began with Jesus; at best they began with eyewitnesses. From the first we are confronted not so much with Jesus, but with how he was perceived. And the same is actually true of the sayings tradition: at best what we have are the teachings of Jesus as they impacted on the individuals who stored them in their memories and began the process of oral transmission.

The point can be given heavy theological (and methodological) weight, as it was by Martin Kähler and most recently by Luke Johnson.[35] That is to say, the point can be stated in terms of the unrecoverability of the historical Jesus because the biblical Christ and the perspective of Christian faith infuses the whole, every last form, narrative or saying. But that too is an inadequate formulation. For the point being made here is not the same as saying that the portrayal of Jesus is entirely post-Easter in creation and the product of developed faith. The point is rather that the original impulse behind these records were *sayings of Jesus as heard and received*, and *actions of Jesus as witnessed and retained in the memory* (both parts of each phrase being important). We have to add in both cases, *and as reflected on thereafter*, of course. But what we have in these traditions is not just the end-product of that reflection. It is rather the faith creating word/event, as itself a force shaping faith and as retained and rehearsed by the faith thus created and being created. In other words, the Jesus tradition gives immediate access not to a dispassionately recorded word or deed, nor only to the end product (the faith of the 50s, 60s, 70s, or 80s), but also to the process between the two, to the tradition which began with the initial impact of word or deed and which continued to influence intermediate retellers of the tradition until crystallized in Mark's or Matthew's or Luke's account. In short, we must take seriously the depth of the tradition as well as its final form.[36]

---

[35] See above n. 6.

[36] The argument here is similar to that between J. A. Sanders and B. S. Childs on "canonical criticism," in which I side with Sanders; see e.g. my "Levels of Canonical Authority," *HBT* 4 (1982) 13-60, esp. 15 and n.14.

At the same time we might observe that to make this point is simply to recognize the nature of the evidence which any biographer has to weigh who has no access to any writings of the biography's subject. That is to say, a portrayal of Jesus as seen through the eyes and heard through the ears of his first disciples is neither an illegitimate nor an impossible task, and such a portrayal, carefully drawn in terms of the evidence available, should not be dismissed or disparaged as inadmissible. After all, it is precisely the impact which Jesus made and which resulted in the emergence of Christianity which we want to recover. Of course it would be wonderful and intriguing if we could portray Jesus as seen by Pilate or Herod, by Caiaphas or the house of Shammai. But we simply do not have sufficient evidence for that, and even if we had, what would it tell us about the character and impact of a ministry which transformed fishermen and toll collectors into apostles? In terms of pivotal individuals on whom the history of the world has turned, it is the latter in whom we are most interested. And the Synoptic tradition and the Gospels are precisely what we need for the task.

Second the point of procedure. We need to attend first to the broad picture, otherwise we are liable to become quickly bogged down and lost in a mire of details over individual disputed sayings. The criteria for recognizing "authentic" tradition are usually thought about in reference only to individual sayings. But there is a prior criterion which emerges more or less directly out of the considerations marshaled above, and to which appeal should be made before turning to particular detail. The criterion is this: any feature which is *characteristic of and relatively distinctive within the Jesus tradition* is most likely to go back to Jesus, that is, to reflect the original impact of Jesus on several at least of his first disciples. The logic is straightforward: if a feature is characteristic and relatively distinctive within the Jesus tradition, then the most obvious explanation of its presence in the Jesus tradition is that it reflects the characteristic and relatively distinctive impact which Jesus made on his first followers.

When we apply this prior criterion to the Jesus tradition a remarkably full portrayal quickly begins to emerge: a Galilean who emerged from the circle of John the Baptist and who ministered for a lengthy period, most of his ministry, in the small towns and villages of Galilee; a preacher whose main emphasis was the royal rule of God; a healer who was famous for his exorcisms in particular; a teacher who characteristically taught in aphorisms and parables, who successfully summoned many to follow him, and who had a close circle of twelve; a prophet who somehow challenged the Temple authorities and who was crucified in Jerusalem on the charge of being a messianic pretender.[37] We could elaborate in the same vein. For example, when we encounter a thoroughly consistent and distinctive feature—a tradition which depicts Jesus regularly using the phrase "son of man" and virtually no other use of the phrase—it simply beggars scholarship to deny that this feature stemmed from a remembered speech usage of Jesus himself. To argue otherwise is the *reductio ad absurdum* of rational debate.[38] Similarly, but more controversially, it would seem to me to be highly implausible to deny to that first layer of remembered Jesus a consistent feature in the Jesus tradition, such as talk of the royal rule of God coming to full eschatological expression in the near future.[39]

Of course, the above claims need to be demonstrated in more detail. But if such a broad picture can be sketched in with some confidence, then we are in a much better position to evaluate key particulars. The question again and again will be *not* so much, "Is this detail or that detail historically reliable?," but "Does this particular build into a coherent and consistent picture of the person who made the impact of the broader picture?" "What was the impact of this person which resulted in this episode or saying being originally formulated?" Of course much of the detail will be hazy and disputed; debates over the biographies of the great and the good have found it ever so. But the broad picture of Jesus can still be sound, even if much of the detail remains vague. And the tradition will provide at least a number of specific features which illuminate the quality of personal encounter which caused them first to be recorded.

In short, there is a historical (or perhaps better, historic) Jesus who is the legitimate and possible goal of the third quest. Not a quasi-objective Jesus, Cynic or otherwise, who may or may not be significant for Christian faith. But the Jesus who historically

---

[37] Cf. Sanders's list of "almost indisputable facts"; cf. Sanders, *Jesus*, 11; idem, *The Historical Figure of Jesus* (London: Penguin, 1993) 10-11.

[38] Nevertheless the argument has often been made; see those cited in my *Christology in the Making* (London: SCM Press, 1980; 2nd ed., 1989) 300 n.99.

[39] Nevertheless such denial is characteristic of the findings of the Jesus Seminar.

speaking *was* significant for the first flowering of Christian faith. That quest, I believe, has good hope of success.

THE SYNOPTIC GOSPELS AND HISTORY

E. Earle Ellis

The four New Testament Gospels are virtually the only source for our knowledge of the acts and teachings of the earthly Jesus.[1] They are received by the Christian church as the work of inspired writers, apostles and prophets, who were guided by the Spirit of God to give a true portrayal and interpretation of his life and work, and they are also historical documents whose origin and formation can be investigated and in some measure discovered. Written some time after Jesus' death and resurrection, they have been subjected to careful and prolonged study to determine their background and the degree to which they accurately reflect his pre-resurrection ministry. The historical investigation of the Gospels has taken mainly four routes: (1) the attempt to identify underlying documents (known as "source criticism"), (2) the attempt to identify individual literary units and analyze their formation and character (known as "form criticism"), (3) the attempt to trace changes in these units during their transmission prior to their use by the evangelists (known as "tradition criticism"), and, finally, (4) the attempt to identify changes that each evangelist himself made in composing his Gospel (known as "redaction" or "composition criticism"). Each of these avenues of research is perfectly legitimate but, as in other areas of historical reconstruction, the results arrived at are heavily influenced if not determined by the world-view with which the historian approaches the texts and by his other historical and methodological assumptions.[2]

---

[1] There is a brief reference to his ministry by the first-century Jewish historian, Josephus (*Ant.* 18.3.3 §63-64), and a few additional sayings of the earthly Jesus recorded elsewhere in the New Testament (e.g. Acts 20:35) and in other sources; cf. J. Jeremias, *Unknown Sayings of Jesus* (London: SPCK, 1958).

[2] I address these questions in more detail in E. E. Ellis, "Gospel Criticism: A Perspective on the State of the Art," in P. Stuhlmacher (ed.), *The Gospel and the Gospels* (Grand Rapids: Eerdmans, 1991) 26-52; idem, "The Historical Jesus and the Gospels," in J. Ådna et al. (eds.), *Evangelium–Schriftauslegung–Kirche* (P. Stuhlmacher Festschrift; Göttingen: Vandenhoeck & Ruprecht, 1997) 94-106; idem, "New Directions in the History of Early Christianity," in T. W. Hillard et al.

I

An assumption that may be addressed at the outset is the view, still held in some quarters, that history writing is an objective science in which the historian is a neutral observer and evaluator of probabilities. This view has been effectively discredited by such writers as Carl Becker, H. S. Commager, and, for biblical history, Alan Richardson,[3] and its fallacies illustrated again in the work of John Kenyon on critical historians in Britain.[4]

As Bernard Lonergan[5] and others have reminded us, the term "history" may be employed in two senses, that which is written and that which is written about. It is history in the former sense that is presented to us both by the Evangelists and by modern historians of early Christianity. Such history is by its very nature interpretive and modern historians, including of course the present writer, are no less subjectively involved in their reconstructions than the Evangelists were in theirs. As one who very early had to contrast the history of the War between the States received at my grandmother's knee and in Jefferson Davis's *The Rise and Fall of the Confederate Government*[6] with that presented, for example, by Charles A. Beard in the public school text-books of my high school years. I later read the diverse accounts of the ministry of Christ and historicity of the Gospels by, say, F. W. Farrar, C. H. Dodd and B. Gerhardsson[7] on

---

(eds.), *Ancient History in a Modern University* (E. A. Judge Festschrift; 2 vols., Grand Rapids: Eerdmans, 1998) 2.71-92.

3   C. Becker, "Detachment and the Writing of History," *Atlantic Monthly* 106 (Oct. 1910) 524-36; repr. in idem, *Essays* (Westport: Greenwood, 1972) 3-28; H. S. Commager, *The Study of History* (Columbus: C. E. Merrill, 1966) 43-60; A. Richardson, *History Sacred and Profane* (London: SCM Press; Philadelphia: Westminster, 1964) 83-183.

4   J. P. Kenyon, *The History Men* (London: Weidenfeld and Nicolson, 1983; Pittsburgh: University of Pittsburgh Press, 1984).

5   B. Lonergan, *Method in Theology* (London: Darton, Longman & Todd; New York: Herder and Herder, 1972) 175.

6   J. Davis, *The Rise and Fall of the Confederate Government* (2 vols., New York: D. Appleton, 1881; repr. New York: T. Yoseloff, 1958).

7   F. W. Farrar, *The Life of Christ* (London and New York: 1874; repr. 1912); C. H. Dodd, *The Founder of Christianity* (London: Collier-Macmillan; New York: Macmillan, 1971); idem, "The Framework of the Gospel Narrative," in Dodd, *New Testament Studies* (Manchester: Manchester University Press, 1953) 1-11; B. Gerhardsson, *Memory and Manuscript* (Lund: Gleerup, 1961; repr. Grand Rapids: Eerdmans, 1998).

the one hand and D. F. Strauss and R. Bultmann on the other with a distinct sense of *déjà vu*.[8]

The subjectivity inevitably involved in the reconstruction of the past does not, of course, diminish the importance of a proper method or excuse us from criticizing historical reconstructions that are demonstrably defective in this or other respects. A currently widespread view of the origins of the Gospels with its skeptical attitude toward their historicity seems to me to warrant such criticism, specifically, (1) in its misrepresentation of its own confessional presuppositions as a scientific or critical stance, (2) in its misuse of historical method and (3) in its mistaken historical and literary assumptions.

1. The historical study of the Gospels has been marked for the past two centuries by a cleavage in world-views, characterized on the one side by deism and on the other by Christian theism or, in the categories of H. Thielicke by Cartesian and non-Cartesian assumptions.[9] In the mid-twentieth century it was dominated in many circles by a Cartesian, that is, rationalistic approach for which R. Bultmann was probably the most influential representative. Regarding history and the natural world as a closed continuum of cause and effect "in which historical happenings cannot be rent by the interference of supernatural transcendent powers,"[10] Bultmann dismissed, and indeed on a priori grounds had to dismiss, large portions of the Gospels as later mythological creations. On the same grounds he had to limit the "authentic" sayings of Jesus to those he regarded as originating in Jesus' earthly ministry since no exalted Lord could, in fact, speak to

---

[8]   D. F. Strauss, *Das Leben Jesu kritisch bearbeitet* (2 Vols., Tübingen: C. F. Osiander, 1835-36; repr. in 1984; 3rd ed., 1838-39; 4th ed., 1840); ET: *The Life of Jesus, critically examined* (3 vols., London: Chapman, 1846; Philadelphia: Fortress, 1972; Lives of Jesus Series; London: SCM Press, 1973); R. Bultmann, *Jesus* (Berlin: Deutsche Bibliothek, 1926); ET: *Jesus and the Word* (New York: Scribner's, 1934; repr. 1958).

[9]   H. Thielicke, *The Evangelical Faith* (3 vols., Grand Rapids: Eerdmans, 1974-81) 1.30-173.

[10]   R. Bultmann, *Existence and Faith* (New York: Harper & Row, 1960) 292 (German text: *TZ* 13 [1957] 411-12); cf. idem, "Neues Testament und Mythologie," Part II of Bultmann, *Offenbarung und Heilsgeschehen* (BEvT 7; Munich: Kaiser, 1941); repr. in H.-W. Bartsch (ed.), *Kerygma und Mythos: Ein theologisches Gespräch* (TF 1; Hamburg-Bergstedt: Reich und Heidrich, 1948; 4th ed., 1960) 18; ET: "New Testament and Mythology," *Kerygma and Myth: A Theological Debate* (London: SPCK, 1953; 2nd ed., 1964) 7.

and through the Gospel traditioners and Evangelists. These attitudes and conclusions which Bultmann and other rationalist historians represented as "scientific" and "critical" were in fact only the expression and predetermined result of their world-view, that is, their philosophical and thus ultimately confessional commitments.

2. Other questions of method are not unrelated to these philosophical assumptions, for example, the assignment of the "burden of proof" in determining whether a particular episode in the Gospels originated in the pre-resurrection mission of Jesus and the criteria by which its pre-resurrection origin could be established. The proposed criteria were (1) an episode's attestation in more than one Gospel, (2) its lack of so-called "developed," that is, post-resurrection tendencies, (3) its dissimilarity from the idiom or ideas found in contemporary Judaism or early Christianity and (4) its coherence with other Gospel material thought to be authentic. Some of the criteria raise certain probabilities and some simply beg the question, but none of them produce any "assured results."[11] As the critiques of M. D. Hooker and E. L. Mascall have pointed out, the conclusions drawn from them were "very largely the result of (the scholar's) own presuppositions and prejudices."[12] Moreover, the criteria received an importance beyond their due from the assumption, adopted by E. Käsemann and others, that the Gospel accounts should be regarded as post-resurrection creations unless proven otherwise.[13] Does this view of the burden of proof accord with good historical method?

According to E. Bernheim's classic text on historical method the

---

[11]   Cf. Ellis, "Gospel Criticism," 30-31.

[12]   M. D. Hooker, "On Using the Wrong Tool," *Theology* 75 (1972) 581; cf. idem, "Christology and Methodology," *NTS* 17 (1970-71) 480-87; E. L. Mascall, *Theology and the Gospel of Christ* (London: SPCK, 1977) 87-97.

[13]   E. Käsemann, "Das Problem des historischen Jesus," *ZTK* 51 (1954) 125-53; repr. in Käsemann, *Exegetische Versuche und Besinnungen* (vol. 1; Göttingen: Vandenhoeck & Ruprecht, 1960) 187-214, here 205; ET: "The Problem of the Historical Jesus," in Käsemann, *Essays on New Testament Themes* (SBT 41; London: SCM Press, 1964) 15-47, here 37. He was followed by the Anglo-American writers N. Perrin, *Rediscovering the Teaching of Jesus* (London: SCM Press; New York: Harper & Row, 1967) 39, and J. M. Robinson, *A New Quest of the Historical Jesus* (SBT 25; London: SCM Press, 1959; repr. Missoula: Scholars, 1979) 38. The latter is critiqued by R. P. Martin, "The New Quest of the Historical Jesus," in C. F. H. Henry (ed.), *Jesus of Nazareth: Savior and Lord* (Grand Rapids: Eerdmans, 1966) 25-45.

historian has the two-fold task of testing the genuineness and demonstrating the nongenuineness of his sources.[14] Applied to the Gospels this means, as W. G. Kümmel has rightly seen[15] that the historian must demonstrate that any part of the Gospel materials is created in the post-resurrection church since the Gospels present their accounts in the context of the pre-resurrection mission of Jesus. In a word good historical method requires that a Gospel passage be received as an account of Jesus' earthly ministry unless it is shown that it cannot have originated there.

II

Under the influence of R. Bultmann and M. Dibelius[16] the classical form criticism raised many doubts about the historicity of the Synoptic Gospels, but it was shaped by a number of literary and historical assumptions which themselves are increasingly seen to have a doubtful historical basis. It assumed, first of all, that the Gospel traditions were transmitted for decades exclusively in oral form and began to be fixed in writing only when the early Christian anticipation of a soon end of the world faded. This theory foundered with the discovery in 1947 of the library of the Qumran sect, a group contemporaneous with the ministry of Jesus and the early church which combined intense expectation of the End with prolific writing. Qumran shows that such expectations did not inhibit writing but actually were a spur to it.[17] Also, the widespread literacy in first-

---

14 E. Bernheim, *Lehrbuch der historischen Methode* (Leipzig: Duncker & Humblot, 1903; repr. New York: B. Franklin, 1960) 332; C. Langlois and C. Seignobos (*Introduction to the Study of History* [New York: Barnes and Noble, 1966; orig., 1898] 157) are more skeptical.

15 W. G. Kümmel, *Dreissig Jahre Jesusforschung (1950-80)* (BBB 60; ed. H. Merklein; Bonn: Hanstein, 1985) 28-29; cf. *TRu* 31 (1965-66) 42-43.

16 R. Bultmann, *Die Geschichte der synoptischen Tradition* (FRLANT 12; Göttingen: Vandenhoeck & Ruprecht, 1921; 2nd ed., 1931; 3rd ed., 1958); ET: *The History of the Synoptic Tradition* (Oxford: Basil Blackwell; New York: Harper & Row, 1963); idem, *Die Erforschung der synoptischen Evangelien* (2nd ed., Giessen: Töpelmann, 1930) ET: R. Bultmann and K. Kundsin, *Form Criticism: Two Essays on New Testament Research* (New York: Harper & Row, 1962) 11-76; M. Dibelius, *Die Formgeschichte des Evangeliums* (Tübingen: Mohr [Siebeck], 1919; 2nd ed., 1933); ET: *From Tradition to Gospel* (New York: Scribner's, 1934; repr. Cambridge and London: James Clarke, 1971).

17 Cf. E. E. Ellis, "New Directions in Form Criticism," in Ellis, *Prophecy and*

century Palestinian Judaism,[18] together with the different language backgrounds of Jesus' followers—some Greek, some Aramaic, some bilingual—would have facilitated the rapid written formulations and transmission of at least some of Jesus' teaching.[19] Finally, the factor that occasioned writing in early Christianity, the separation of the believers from the teaching leadership, was already present in the ministry of Jesus who had groups of adherents in the towns of Galilee, Judea and probably on the Phoenician coast, the Decapolis and Perea. There are good grounds, then, for supposing not only that the traditioning of Jesus' acts and teachings began during his earthly ministry, as H. Schürmann has argued,[20] but also that some of them were given written formulation at that time.

Secondly, the early form criticism tied the theory of oral transmission to the conjecture that Gospel traditions were mediated like folk traditions, being freely altered and even created ad hoc by various and sundry wandering charismatic jackleg preachers. This view, however, was rooted more in the eighteenth century romanticism of J. G. Herder[21] than in an understanding of the handling of religious tradition in first-century Judaism. As O. Cullmann, B. Gerhardsson, H. Riesenfeld and R. Riesner have demonstrated,[22] the

---

Hermeneutic in Early Christianity (Tübingen: Mohr [Siebeck]; Grand Rapids: Eerdmans, 1978) 237-53; idem, "Gospel Criticism," 39-43.

18   Cf. Josephus, *Against Apion* 2.25 §204: The Law "orders that (children) should be taught to read . . ."; cf. idem, *Ant.* 12.4.9 §209; Philo, *Embassy to Gaius* 115, 210. Further, see R. Riesner, *Jesus als Lehrer* (WUNT 2.7; Tübingen: Mohr [Siebeck], 1981; 4th ed., 1998) 112-15.

19   Jesus had hearers and doubtless some converts from Syria (Matt 4:25), the Decapolis (Matt 4:25; Mark 3:8; 5:20; 7:31), Tyre and Sidon (Mark 3:8; 7:24, 31; Matt 15:21).

20   H. Schürmann, "Die vorösterlichen Anfänge der Logientradition," in Schürmann, *Traditionsgeschichtliche Untersuchungen zu den synoptischen Evangelien* (Kommentare und Beiträge zum Alten und Neuen Testament; Düsseldorf: Patmos, 1968) 39-65; idem, *Jesus* (Paderborn: Bonifatius, 1993) 380-97.

21   J. G. Herder, *Vom Erlöser der Menschen* (Riga: Hartknoch, 1796); idem, *Von Sohn Gottes* (Riga: Hartknoch, 1797); repr. in idem, *Sämtliche Werke* (ed. B. Suphan, 33 vols., Hildesheim: Olms, 1994; orig. 1877-1913) 19.197, 213-14, 417-18, cited in W. G. Kümmel, *The New Testament: The History of its Problems* (Nashville: Abingdon, 1972) 79-83.

22   O. Cullmann, "The Tradition," in Cullmann, *The Early Church* (London: SCM Press; Philadelphia: Westminster, 1956) 55-99; B. Gerhardsson *The Origins of the Gospel Traditions* (Philadelphia: Fortress, 1979); H. Riesenfeld *The Gospel*

Judaism of the period treated such traditions very carefully, and the New Testament writers in numerous passages applied to apostolic traditions the same technical terminology found elsewhere in Judaism for "delivering," "receiving," "learning," "holding," "keeping," and "guarding," the traditioned "teaching."[23] In this way they both identified their traditions as "holy word" and showed their concern for a careful and ordered transmission of it. The word and work of Jesus were an important albeit distinct part of these apostolic traditions.

Luke (1:2-4) used one of the same technical terms, speaking of eyewitnesses who "delivered to us" the things contained in his Gospel and about which his patron Theophilus had been instructed. Similarly, the amanuenses or co-worker-secretaries who composed the Gospel of John speak of the Evangelist, the beloved disciple, "who is witnessing concerning these things and who wrote these things," as an eyewitness and a member of the inner circle of Jesus' disciples.[24] In the same connection it is not insignificant that those to whom Jesus entrusted his teachings are not called "preachers" but "pupils" and "apostles," semi-technical terms for those who represent and mediate the teachings and instructions of their mentor or principal.[25]

A third fundamental axiom of classical form criticism is also historically doubtful, that is, that the geographical and chronological framework of the Gospels was wholly the creation of the traditioners and Evangelists. The Gospels are not chronologues, of course, and the Evangelists feel free, as did the Roman historian Suetonius, to organize their presentation on thematic or other lines. However, if

---

Tradition (Philadelphia: Fortress, 1970) 1-29; Riesner, *Jesus als Lehrer.*

[23] Rom 6:17; 16:17; 1 Cor 11:2, 23; 15:3; Phil 4:9; Col 2:6-7; 2 Thess 2:15; 3:6; 2 Tim 3:14; Titus 1:9; 2 John 9-10; Jude 3: Rev 2:13, 24. Cf. *ʾAbot* 1:1; Philo, *The Worse Attacks the Better* 65-68; W. Bacher, *Die exegetische Terminologie der jüdischen Traditionsliteratur* (2 vols. in 1; Darmstadt: Wissenschaftliche Buchgesellschaft, 1965) 1.94ff.; 2.234-35 *et passim.*

[24] John 19:35; 21:24-25; cf. 13:23; 18:15-16; 19:26-27; 20:1-10; 21:7, 21-23. Cf. J. A. T. Robinson, *Redating the New Testament* (Philadelphia: Westminster, 1976) 298-311. *Pace* S. S. Smalley, *John: Evangelist and Interpreter* (Exeter: Paternoster; Nashville: Nelson, [3]1984) 80ff. and R. E. Brown, *The Gospel According to John* (2 vols., AB 28, 28A; Garden City: Doubleday, 1970) 1.ci-cii, who distinguish the Evangelist from the Beloved Disciple.

[25] On parallels with other rabbis and their disciples and other Jewish usage cf. Mark 2:18 = Luke 5:33; K. H. Rengstorf, "ἀπόστολος," *TDNT* 1 (1964) 413-43; "μαθητής," *TDNT* 4 (1967) 431-55.

C. H. Dodd's schematic framework of Jesus' ministry is not fully acceptable,[26] K. L. Schmidt's views are much less satisfactory.[27] Among other things Schmidt drew too sharp a dichotomy between editorial and traditional elements in the Gospels and did not recognize that the Evangelists' editorial arrangements, such as the journey to Jerusalem in Luke (9:51–19:44), are often simply a reworking of received traditions.

If the early form criticism built upon a poor foundation, is there a better explanation of the origin and formation of our Gospels?

III

An acceptable reconstruction of the formation of the Gospels must take into account both first-century Jewish attitudes toward the transmission of religious traditions and the charismatic, prophetic character of the ministry of Jesus and of the primitive church. With respect to the former B. Gerhardsson's conception of a controlled transmission of Gospel traditions marked a clear advance beyond the earlier form criticism, but his rabbinic analogy was unable to account for the kind of alteration and elaboration of Gospel traditions that one observes even when comparing one Gospel with another. Indeed, the traditioners and Evangelists seem to handle Jesus' word with the same kind of freedom that they use with another type of "holy word," the Old Testament scriptures. Their conduct in this respect is best explained by a prophetic consciousness.

Jesus viewed himself[28] and was perceived by others[29] to be the bearer of the prophetic Spirit, and he promised the same Spirit to his followers.[30] Already in his earthly ministry the apostles were sent on their missions of teaching, healing and exorcisms in the role of prophets whether, as J. Jeremias has argued, the Spirit was already

---

26   C. H. Dodd, "The Framework of the Gospel Narrative," in Dodd, *New Testament Studies*, 1-11.

27   K. L. Schmidt, *Der Rahmen der Geschichte Jesu: Literarkritische Untersuchungen zur ältesten Jesusüberlieferung* (Berlin: Trowitzsch, 1919; repr. Darmstadt: Wissenschaftliche Buchgesellschaft, 1964).

28   Matt 13:57 = Mark 6:4 = Luke 4:18, 24; 13:33-34; John 4:44; cf. Matt 12:28 = Luke 11:20.

29   Mark 6:15; 8:28; cf. 8:11; 14:65 = Matt 26:67-68 = Luke 22:63-64; 24:19.

30   Matt 10:19-20 = Mark 13:11 = Luke 21:15; 12:12; John 7:38-39; 14:17-18, 26; 16:7; cf. Matt 3:11 = Mark 1:8 = Luke 3:16.

conferred on them[31] or, perhaps not very different, whether the Spirit of Jesus was active in their use of his name. It is clear in any case that the Gospel traditioners included themselves among those who according to Matt 5:12, 13:11, Luke 21:15 and other passages fulfilled a prophetic role both in their preaching and persecution and also in their writing as "wise men and scribes," that is, scripture teachers.[32] This prophetic consciousness best explains their boldness and confidence both in their christological contemporization of Old Testament texts and in their similar treatment of the holy word of Jesus.

There are few if any historical or literary grounds to suppose that the Gospel traditions created events in Jesus' life or, indeed, that they mixed to any great degree oracles from the exalted Jesus into the Gospel traditions. If a proper historical critical method is followed, proper presuppositions observed and the practices of first-century Palestinian Judaism considered, the Gospels of the New Testament will be found to be a reliable presentation and faithful portrait of the teachings and acts of the pre-resurrection mission of Jesus.

---

[31]   J. Jeremias, *New Testament Theology* (New York: Scribner's, 1971) 79. Cf. Matt 10:1; Mark 6:7, 30; Luke 9:1-2; 10:9, 17.

[32]   Matt 13:52; 23:34; cf. Luke 11:49-51. Cf. Wis 7:27; Philo, *On the Giants* 5, 22; idem *On the Unchangeableness of God* 1, 3: prophet = wise man.

REFLECTIONS UPON "THE HISTORICAL PERIMETERS FOR UNDERSTANDING THE AIMS OF JESUS"*

William R. Farmer

As carefully crafted as the title for this essay may be, it remains ambiguous. By the "aims of Jesus" do we mean Ben Meyer's stunning book by that title?[1] If so, we would be obliged to undertake a social historical analysis of Gospel criticism in Germany during the nineteenth century and position Meyer's book within the context of the history of ideas from Reimarus to the present. That is a task worth undertaking, but it is not my present task. Rather, by the "aims of Jesus" I refer not to Meyer's book itself, but the subject of that book, namely the guiding purposes of Jesus, which to understand helps us make the most sense out of as much as possible of all the relevant data bearing on the question of Christian origins.

I think it is fair to say that before Meyer wrote his book, this subject was generally regarded in higher circles of theological scholarship as off limits. One of the basic assumptions of mid-twentieth century critical reflection has been that the self-consciousness of Jesus is beyond recovery. To attempt to penetrate behind the earliest strata of the Synoptic tradition as formulated in the primitive Palestinian Christian communities has been to defy the gods of reason and correct academic behavior.

We have yet to take the full measure of Ben Meyer's achievements in his book *The Aims of Jesus*, but for this observer, it already appears that the whole question of what we can know, and/or what we should attempt to understand about Jesus, has been recast in a very constructive way by Meyer's soundly grounded and comprehensive study. The very formulation: "the aims of Jesus," serves to make it clear that what is under investigation is not his personality which may be beyond recovery, nor his private life, which in any

---

* This essay is a shorter version of a paper presented for discussion at a symposium honoring Professor Ben F. Meyer held at McMaster University, December 1989.

[1] B. F. Meyer, *The Aims of Jesus* (London: SCM Press, 1979).

case belongs to the gossip columns rather than the annals of responsible theological scholarship. What is under investigation is the public career of Jesus. What did he do and say that can make sense out what emerged from what he did and said? Of course Jesus did not speak and act within a vacuum, and every historical reconstruction must make sense in terms of what we can know about the circumstances of the time—social, historical, political et al. Jesus did do something He did say something. And what he did and said stands in some consequential relationship to what happened to his people and what happened to him. And what happened to his people and what happened to Jesus as a consequence of what he did and said stands in some consequential relationship to the Church which from the earliest period has served as the custodian of his oracles, and the perpetuator of his purposes.

We turn now to our topic: "The Historical Perimeters for Understanding the Aims of Jesus."

These historical perimeters include what may be called basic presuppositions, which while they may not be established are regarded by most critics as not only plausible but intrinsically probable.

We may begin with further reference to the common-sense assumptions of continuity between Jesus and the community which bears and cherishes his memory. Jesus did do something with his life and did teach or preach something. Is it not reasonable to conclude that this something provided the Church an initial impetus, that is, that authentic Christian life and faith, at one or more decisive points, is commensurate with the original intention of Jesus and the effect he had upon the life and faith of his disciples? Is it not reasonable to think that, however much our understanding of existence may have broadened, deepened, or changed, nothing has happened which sets aside, nullifies or contravenes the significance of original event.

In addition to this general pre-understanding there are several rather specific presuppositions or material assumptions that are important to this study.

The first is the *historical existence* of Jesus. The fact that some intelligent persons sincerely doubt whether Jesus ever-existed as an historical personage, and that theologians have felt constrained to allow for this doubt, reminds us that in the intellectual history of the West this is still an item of unfinished business.

The second is the sanity of Jesus. Jesus' sanity is hardly capable of competent definition or diagnosis. But the fact that it has been challenged deserves to be noted. There is no reason in principle why historical studies of Jesus presupposing that he was suffering from one or another mental illness should not be attempted. However, such studies as have been made seem incomplete and their results uncertain.

The third is the *integrity* of Jesus. The point at issue here is primarily this: did Jesus intend to deceive his followers or did he allow them to be deceived? Sensitive pastors are aware of the fact that there are members of their flocks whose faith in their integrity sometimes disposes them to be uncritically naive with regard to the problems pastors experience in maintaining at all times personal integrity in their ministries. Therefore, when the integrity on the part of Jesus is assumed by an historian, this assumption must not be made naively, but should be regarded as a presupposition, for it tends to limit the range of human experience by which the historian judges probabilities and improbabilities in his reconstruction of the past, by leaving out of consideration possibilities which might otherwise be entertained if the suggestion that Jesus may not have been a person of integrity were really taken seriously. To say that Jesus was a person of integrity does not rule out the possibility that he sometimes may have been conscious of failing to adhere to or wholeheartedly affirm what he preached. Such questions are virtually impossible to settle because of the difficulties with which any investigation into the self-consciousness of Jesus is fraught. The materials we have for understanding Jesus do not afford us as much of this kind of knowledge about him as we could wish. The basic question is: did Jesus mean what he said; did he intend others to take his words seriously and did he himself take seriously the understanding of existence to which he gave expression in his teaching? It is an affirmative answer to this question which is presupposed in this essay. The degree to which anyone hesitates to agree that Jesus was in this sense a person of integrity should lead her/him to a corresponding degree of skepticism regarding the possibility of ever knowing with any degree of probability what aims of Jesus actually were, since any conclusions that may be drawn on this matter presuppose such integrity on Jesus' part.

In the fourth place it is presupposed that within the primitive Church there were those who *remembered* Jesus. That Jesus was remembered in the Church by those who had known him is intrinsically probable from virtually every point of view, but since it has never been demonstrated it needs to be listed as something assumed in any investigation of the "aims of Jesus." In the fifth place it is assumed that all the gospels were written relatively late, i.e. probably a full generation after the events described. The evidence on which such dating is based is admittedly tenuous.

The sixth matter that is presupposed or assumed is closely related to the fourth and fifth. It is that *within the tradition preserved in the gospels, the memory of Jesus is preserved.* The alternative that, in the period between the time when Jesus was remembered in the primitive Church and the time the gospels were written, the memory of Jesus was completely or effectively lost is a real one. An although few would support this alternative, the fact that the contrary is assumed deserves noting.

Finally, we frequently presuppose that it is possible *to distinguish between what was remembered about Jesus and what has been added.* This analysis can be accomplished with the aid of contemporary knowledge of the relevant ancient languages; environmental research into the life situation of Jesus and of the first-century Church; literary and historical criticism (including source, form-critical and redactional analysis); and a reasonably perceptive understanding of human existence, informed by the humanities and social science disciplines. It is not presupposed that *all* the genuine remembrances can be identified, but that *in a significant number and variety of passages* in the gospels it is possible to distinguish between what has been remembered and what has been added. In this connection it can be said that it is to the enduring credit of Professor Joachim Jeremias that he was able to take the form-critical methods of his more skeptical German colleagues and by a careful and judicious application of the principles of form-critical inquiry, demonstrate to the satisfaction of most critics that one could separate the later redactional additions coming from the exegetical tradition of the early church from the earlier parables of Jesus. This triumph of Jeremias, more than his famous "Abba" triumph, accounts for the basic shift that has come over the so-called quest for the historical Jesus. It broke the back of radical skepticism and more than any other single development in German New Testament scholarship to the twentieth century, has served to open up the real possibility of an hermeneutic that can reconcile the demands of the academy with the vital interest of the church.

We turn now to a second category of historical perimeters for understanding the Aims of Jesus. These are facts or conclusions that need not be presupposed. They can all be demonstrated explicitly or inferred from circumstantial evidence.

PRELIMINARY METHODOLOGICAL CONSIDERATIONS

The chief methodological problem in writing about the aims of Jesus is chronology. Since the turn of century, critical theology has been aware of the historical uncertainty of the gospel chronologies. This has led to a virtual moratorium on writing "lives of Jesus" according to the nineteenth-century mode. The classic twentieth-century reconstruction by Bultmann in his *Jesus and the Word* is largely restricted to the reconstruction of Jesus' message. Bornkamm's *Jesus of Nazareth* is an improvement on Bultmann, primarily by taking into account the intervening parable research of Dodd (*The Parables of the Kingdom*) and Jeremias (*The Parables of Jesus*).[2]

A peculiar merit of the approach here to be presented is that it goes beyond the simple reconstruction of Jesus' message. Without uncritical dependence upon the gospel chronologies, it attempts to explicate Jesus' teachings within the context of an intrinsic development in his public career. To this extent it serves in a modest way to demonstrate the possibility of a "story of Jesus" acceptable to historians, a story which is not essentially different from the story of Jesus familiar to us from the Gospels.

The gospel tradition originated with Jesus and those who worked with him and experienced his saving influence. It developed in the earliest Christian communities where Jesus was remembered and worshipped as the crucified and resurrected Lord. The traditions' canonical function in the church calls for theological and historical reflection upon the way it developed into the forms given to it in the Gospels and upon the relationship of these Gospels to one another and to Scripture as a whole.

---

2   G. Bornkamm, *Jesus von Nazareth* (Urban-Bücher 19; Stuttgart: Kohlhammer, 1956; 11th ed., 1977); ET: *Jesus of Nazareth* (New York: Harper & Row, 1960; repr. Minneapolis: Fortress, 1995); C. H. Dodd, *The Parables of the Kingdom* (London: Nisbet, 1935; 2nd ed., New York: Scribner's, 1961); J. Jeremias, *Die Gleichnisse Jesu* (Zürich: Zwingli, 1947; 10th ed., Göttingen: Vandenhoeck & Ruprecht, 1984); ET: *The Parables of Jesus* (London: SCM Press, 1963; 3rd ed., New York: Scribner's, 1972).

The Gospels embody tradition concerning Jesus. Between Jesus and the Gospels stands the traditioning process, by which the Gospel stories and sayings of Jesus were handed on. These traditions were oral and written and included sayings both of Jesus and of early Christian prophets speaking in the name of Jesus. They also included accounts of eyewitnesses concerning the actions and character of Jesus and later modifications of this tradition made to meet the changing needs of different Christian communities.

This traditioning process has never ceased. It flourished up to and through the period when the Gospels were written and achieved manifold expression during the second and third centuries. It was normed with the adoption of the fourfold Gospel canon, which in turn has enhanced the traditioning process through its influence upon the visual, arts, music, literature, and preaching.

The canonical Gospels afford us our best access to the earliest traditions concerning Jesus. From a form-critical study of the Gospels, it is clear that the Jesus tradition was already richly developed by the time the Gospels were written. A study of this developed tradition is rewarding because it helps clarify the character of Jesus and improves our understanding of the evangelists' purpose in writing the Gospels.

The Gospels represent Jesus as he was remembered and worshipped in certain Christian communities a generation after the beginning of the church. This is clear from the traditions concerning Jesus that the evangelists used, which include not only traditions that originated with Jesus himself and his first associates, but also many which reflect the needs of later Christian communities.

Christianity as a religious movement began with Jesus and his disciples in Palestine, a meeting place for diverse cultural influences. This does not mean, however, that no viable distinctions can be made between the environment of Jesus and that of the evangelists. The environment of Jesus of Nazareth was spatially Palestinian and temporally pre-Pauline. Therefore, whatever he did and said, however distinctive it may have been, would have been accommodated to those who shared this environment. Presumably tradition concerning Jesus' words and actions, which achieved stable form at a very early date, would tend to reflect this environment both conceptually and pictorially.

On the other hand, the environment of the evangelists was extra-Palestinian and post-Pauline. We can assume that what the evangelists wrote was accommodated accordingly. The other New Testament writings make clear that the social and theological forces set in motion by Jesus and his disciples broke out of the original Palestinian environment at an early period. The Acts of the Apostles views this transition in retrospect. More importantly, however, the transition is seen firsthand in the letters of Paul. Thus, Paul's writings are an important control in distinguishing between the environment of Jesus and that of the evangelists.

In his letters it is clear that Paul considered carrying the gospel to the Gentiles his special vocation. This vocation committed him to lengthy journeys among people far removed from Palestine. Therefore Paul himself reflects the transitional situation, not simply because he was a Jew engaged in a mission to gentiles, but also because he knew Jerusalem and met there with those who were apostles before him. He was concerned that these leaders understand that such changes in missionary policy as he had introduced in his efforts to expedite the spread of the gospel did not affect its saving truth. In fact, Paul was prepared to question the integrity of these apostles when they conducted themselves in a manner he perceived as prejudicial to the truth of this gospel.

Basically, then, what is seen in Paul's letters is one way in which it was possible to adapt the gospel so that it was viable for predominantly gentile churches in Asia Minor and points west.

The works of the Jewish historian Josephus serve not only as background material to the letters of Paul and the rest of the New Testament writings, but also provide a basis for observing the contrast between the environments of Jesus and the evangelists. Like Paul, Josephus was basically of the pharisaic persuasion. Unlike Paul and most other New Testament writers, however, Josephus reflects first-century Judaism unchanged by Christian belief. Similarly, the manuscripts from the caves of the Judean desert, Jewish writings from the intertestamental period, and some Mishnaic and other rabbinic materials all afford access to first-century Palestinian Judaism unaffected by Christian belief. These Jewish writings together with the works of Josephus provide a reliable control in determining the nature of the religious, social, economic, and political environment of Jesus. In other words, in the effort to delineate the environment of Jesus, the modern historian is not confined to the limited and selective circle of New Testament writings.

When a tradition concerning Jesus or a saying attributed to him comes alive against the background of his environment as it is known through a study of the topography, geography, and climate of Palestine and the history of Palestinian Judaism prior to AD 70, then an element in the tradition is isolated or identified which may be early. If this tradition would be unintelligible outside Palestine or unfamiliar in gentile-oriented circles, then the probabilities increase that such a saying or story belongs to an early stage in the development of the tradition. Material in the Gospels which presupposes the death and resurrection of Jesus and reflects a situation where he is remembered and worshipped as a transcendent being represents tradition which may have originated in some post-Easter Christian community. Such tradition could have developed either early or late, either in Jewish or gentile circles. Paul's letters preserve evidence that mythopoeic tendencies were at work at a very early date in some Christian communities, producing powerful christological statements about Jesus.

There are four major turning points in the development of the tradition leading from Jesus to the Gospels: (1) Jesus' baptism by John followed by the arrest, imprisonment, and death of the Baptist; (2) Jesus' challenge of religious authorities climaxing in his cleansing of the Temple followed by a final institutionalizing meal with his disciples, his arrest, trial, death, and resurrection and the emergence of a post-Easter messianic community; (3) sectarian conflict and division within the Jewish-Christian messianic community over the manner by which Gentiles were to be admitted to full membership; and (4) the inspiring rediscovery and renewal of ecumenical unity in the aftermath of the martyrdom of chief apostles Peter and Paul in Rome and the outbreak of the catastrophic Roman-Jewish military conflict. From this outline it may be seen that the crucial matter is not where a tradition belongs in some temporal progression marked off by decisive periods in a developmental sequence.

The public career of Jesus falls between the first and second of these decisive periods and took place in Palestine. The Gospels were written during or following the fourth and are extra-Palestinian in provenance. Paul's letters provide us with an indispensable control for understanding how the Jesus tradition developed between the second and fourth turning points by illuminating the third. Paul himself was intimately acquainted with both the Jewish-Palestinian environment of Jesus and with the extra-Palestinian, gentile-oriented environment of the evangelists, and his life and work provide an indispensable historiographical bridge between the two.

Because of both the historical uncertainty concerning the gospel chronologies and the mythopoeic character of much of Jesus' "life and ministry," it is best to focus our attention on sayings of Jesus which originated during the period of his earthly ministry if we wish to reflect on the aims of the actual Jesus.

Within the corpus of the tradition which originated during the period of Jesus' earthly ministry, the parables afford the best key for understanding his career and character. However, the following points concerning the parables merit consideration: (1) the parables are not to be interpreted allegorically (Jülicher); 2) in his parables Jesus proclaims that the eschatological kingdom of God has already broken into reality (Dodd); (3) form criticism enables the critic to identify the parables of Jesus as belonging to the genre of rabbinic parables, while as a whole presenting theologically distinctive content (Jeremias); and (4) form criticism enables the critic to distinguish the original form of Jesus' parables from the additions that were made by the early church (Jeremias). Once these matters concerning the parables become clear, it is possible to recapture the most adequate image of Jesus' career and character.

To do this it is also necessary to meet minimal chronological requirements. One need only recognize that Jesus' public ministry began with his baptism at the hands of John, whose identity is established by the historian Josephus; that Jesus' ministry ended in crucifixion in response to the fateful decisions of the procurator Pontius Pilate and the high priest Caiaphas, whose identities are also established by Josephus; and that between the beginning and end of Jesus' ministry a two-fold and compound crisis occurred. Central to this crisis was opposition to Jesus by the religious authorities, who felt challenged by his practice of eating with tax collectors and sinners. Recognizing this fact makes it possible to perceive a credible relationship between Jesus' ministry and his death and to develop an intrinsic chronology for his earthly career.

This can be accomplished by arranging the sayings of Jesus and particularly his parables in relationship to this twofold and compound crisis. For example, a parable in which Jesus rebukes the self-righteousness of those who resent God's mercy toward repentant sinners would have been prompted by his decision to defend his action of eating with tax collectors and sinners against the criticism of the Pharisees. This is a decision, however, that could not have come until after a decision by the Pharisees to criticize such conduct, which decision could not have been made before some tax collectors and sinners had decided to accept Jesus' invitation to table fellowship. This decision in turn could not have taken place until after Jesus' decision to invite repentant tax collectors and sinners into the intimacy of his table fellowship. And this decision of Jesus could not have taken place until some of these persons had decided to respond to his gracious call to repentance, which could not have come until after Jesus' decision to leave the sparsely settled regions of the wilderness of Judea where he had been with John and to carry his gracious call to repentance into the more densely populated urban areas of Israel.

With this necessary sequence of decisive moments in Jesus' public career, it is possible to reconstruct in outline form the essential development of his message. The ability to do this rests on the premise that the parables and other sayings of Jesus were not conceived all at once, but like the letters of Paul, were composed in response to particular situations. The essential outlines of this development are as follows:

1. Jesus followed John the Baptist, proclaiming the imminent coming of the kingdom of God.

2. His initial message issued in:

(a) A gracious call to repentance

(b) A positive response from "tax collectors and sinners."

(c) The acceptance of sinners into table fellowship, which created a new community that existed in anticipation of the coming kingdom.

3. Jesus' ministry was beset by two separate crises; and a third occurred which was compounded by interaction between the other two.

(a) An internal crisis developed among Jesus' followers because of uncertainty concerning the coming of the kingdom.

(b) An external crisis developed because of the Pharisees' resistance to Jesus' message and his table fellowship with sinners. Jesus rebuked the Pharisees and declared that it was better to be a repentant sinner than a self-righteous keeper of the law. The attitude of the Pharisees toward Jesus became increasingly hostile, and they plotted his death. Even in the face of death, Jesus reaffirmed the truth of his message.

(c) The external conflict with the Pharisees compounded the internal uncertainty among the faithful, raising the question: should we really allow sinners in our fellowship? Jesus assured his disciples that God would separate the just from the unjust. God alone, not some ritual, would decide who is justified and who is not.

On the basis of this analysis of Jesus' ministry and message, the image of Jesus is that of one who in the face of God's imminent destruction of the wicked issued God's gracious call to repentance, and with compassion and joy received sinners into his fellowship. Moreover, it is the image of one who defended this action in the fact of criticism and rebuked the self-righteous attitude of those authorities who resented God's mercy toward repentant sinners. The significance of this image of Jesus' lifestyle is both theological and existential. There is in the parables of Jesus a theology of grace, a theology which is ethically and morally concerned with the little ones—those who are disadvantaged and victimized by the social and religious structures of their existence. This is a theology out of which comes a call to repentance and a promise of God's salvation to all who respond. In short, Jesus' parables demonstrate beyond reasonable doubt that the one who communicated these parables and their message provides the primal historical and theological context within which to reflect on the meaning of the cross and the resurrection.

When the parables of Jesus preserved in the Gospel of Matthew are analyzed theologically and compared to the parables of Jesus preserved in the Gospel of Luke, in every case the theology of the parables in Matthew can be matched by the theology of one or more of the parables in Luke. Moreover, the theology of Jesus' parables is essentially the same as the theology of Paul. Since we learn from Paul himself that he preached the faith of the church he once persecuted, it follows that Paul preached a pre-Pauline faith. The historian has no alternative but to conclude that the theology common to Paul and to the two streams of parable tradition preserved separately in Matthew and Luke goes back to Jesus. To imagine that these three streams of tradition converge in some unidentified pre-Pauline theologian would be to create an unnecessary set of historical and theological problems.

It is important to clarify one further point. There is solid textual basis for making a fundamental theological distinction between Jesus and John the Baptist. Liberation theologies can be strengthened if they are careful not to blur this distinction and if they do not wrongly conclude that the polarizing effect of John's preaching should be attributed also to Jesus and identified as the cause for Jesus' execution at the hands of the political establishment.

Such a conclusion would be a vast oversimplification of a complex question and would leave important evidence unexplained—evidence both from the parables in Luke and Matthew and from Paul's account of his pre-Christian persecution of the church. This evidence indicates that the religious authorities, who were drawn from the righteous elements within the established world of Jewish piety, were opposed to Jesus' message and conduct. The woes of Jesus (which, to be sure, were added to in the bitterest of terms during the persecution of the church in which Paul the Pharisee took part) and his cleansing of the Temple polarized his relationship with the religious authorities and sealed his fate. Jesus' fate was not in the first instance sealed by direct confrontation with Pilate and his political authority or with Roman military forces stationed in the capital. Thus, while the words of the psalmist "zeal for thy house has consumed me" (Ps 69:9) have been cited in Scripture in connection with Jesus' cleansing of the Temple (John 2:17), Jesus was categorically more than a zealot or political activist.

There is no one category (like carpenter, king, teacher, or exorcist) that can do justice to the unique career of Jesus. The best way in which to approach an understanding of Jesus as an historical figure is to focus on his role as religious reformer (like Bernard of Clairvaux or Romero of Salvador). He certainly taught his disciples to love their enemies. any reconstruction that stumbles on that fact will not stand up to criticism. The reconstruction offered here clarifies the relationship between religion and politics in Jesus' environment and focuses attention on what is truly liberating in Christianity.

The theology which comes to expression in the words and actions of Jesus is a theology which works against every form of oppression and exploitation and binds together all persons who love God and thirst after righteousness. It is a theology which calls for resourcement and renewal in the life of the church and for political involvement in the struggle for justice in society—for self-sacrifice and a readiness for martyrdom as exemplified in the lives of Mahatma Gandhi, Martin Luther King, Jr., and Archbishop Oscar Romero. Jesus' prophetic power to unmask hypocrisy and self-righteousness is absolutely central to this theology and very distinctive of it.

Where certain parables of Jesus are interpreted within the context of initial developments in his ministry and specifically within the context of his gracious call for repentance, they enable the historian to make informed suggestions about the intention of Jesus as he responded to the exigencies and difficulties he encountered. How was one to understand the delay in the coming of the kingdom which John had pronounced to be at hand, especially after John's arrest and execution? And if one were to undertake to continue proclaiming the coming of the kingdom, how should he or she perceive this ministry? Was it to be understood as the work of God to be carried out during an extension of the period of grace in the face of the coming judgment? If so, was it not reasonable to expect that in due season, failing the fruits of repentance, this period of grace would come to a sudden and just end (Luke 13:6-9)? As for those who would mistakenly hold back because of their fear that the cost of repentance might be too great, was it not important for their sake to emphasize the joy of the kingdom (Matt 13:44-45)? Should not those who were delinquent in setting their houses in order be reminded of the inevitability of judgment (Matt 21:33-41; Luke 20:9-16), the appropriateness of radical action in the face of certain change (Luke 16:1-8b), the folly of not trusting God (Matt 25:14-30; Luke 19:11-27), and the suddenness and unexpectedness of God's judgment (Matt 24:45-51; Luke 12:42-46; 13:1-5)?

Certainly parables which dramatically illustrate the folly of postponing repentance (Matt 22:1-10; 25:1-13; Luke 13:6-9) and which teach the wisdom of living in ready expectation of God's gracious judgment (Luke 12:35-38) most likely would have originated in situations where such expectations would be enlivened and heightened—in the period of Jesus' active ministry after his baptism into the movement of John and his decision to continue proclaiming the imminence of the kingdom following John's arrest and death.

Even within this period it is possible to postulate development. Presumably Jesus would have understood the lesson the authorities intended by John's execution: "A disciple is not above his teacher: (Matt 10:24). Jesus' decision to carry on would have been realistic only if he understood that he did so at great risk. Although John had been beheaded, a more unusual form of execution was crucifixion. For Jesus to say "Take up (your) cross and follow me" (Matt 16:24) was his way of making clear that he had placed himself outside the discipline and protection of the established world of Jewish piety, and was calling upon others to do the same. This established world of Jewish piety derived its earthly jurisdiction from Rome. Thus, in coming into conflict with the religious authorities, Jesus was risking the ultimate wrath of Roman power. To speak in this way was a determined response to a policy of oppression which had been calculated to discourage dangerous rhetoric associated with messianic activity. But Jesus was not intimidated by what the authorities did to John. He continued to preach. "No one can serve two masters . . . You cannot serve God and mammon . . . Repent, and engage in the service of God . . . for the kingdom of heaven is at hand" (Matt 6:24; 3:2).

When Jesus said, "Take up (your) cross and follow me" (Matt 16:24) or "Leave the dead to bury their own dead" (Matt 8:22), he took upon himself the full measure of God's absolute demand which was entailed in messianic leadership. With such startling statements Jesus challenged others to free themselves from a paralyzing fear of human authorities both those who sat in Moses' seat and those who represented the emperor. In the former saying, Jesus unobtrusively clarified the all-important question of whether he was naively calling others into a course of action where the sacrifices being risked might be greater than he himself was prepared to bear.

"What will it profit a man, if he gains the whole world and forfeits his life?" (Matt 16:26). "Whoever would save his life will lose it" (Matt 16:25). Such brave and bold words staved off the disintegrating effects of temptation to abandon hope for the kingdom's coming, once news of John's arrest and imprisonment was followed by confirmation of his death. Even so, such sayings do not seem to carry one to the heart of Jesus' message. They simply show that Jesus gave expression to qualities that help account for his emergence as a leader in Israel, greater than John.

If we are to trust the earliest and most reliable tradition, Jesus saw himself in prophetic continuity with John in commitment to the call for national repentance in the face of the imminent coming of the kingdom (Matt 11:7b-19). But Jesus saw himself in radical discontinuity with John regarding the basis for admission into the kingdom (Matt 21:28-32). John's strictures against the moral laxities of the people were uncompromising and the ostensible cause for his death was his denunciation of immorality in high places. With Jesus it was otherwise. The misdeeds of the wealthy and powerful did not seem to preoccupy him, though he was not unmindful of the plight of the rich (Matt 19:23-24; Luke 16:19-31). Jesus came to save sinners, not to condemn them. As children of their Father in heaven, they in turn were counseled to love their enemies even as God loved his (Matt 5:43-48). They were admonished not to put forgiveness on any calculated basis, but to forgive freely, boldly, unconditionally, and from the heart—not seven times, but seventy times even (Matt 18:21-35).

The fellowship of such a community of forgiven and forgiving sinners was poignant and joyful. "There will be more joy in heaven over one sinner who repents than over ninety-nine righteous persons who need no repentance" (Luke 15:7). Therefore, Jesus ate with sinners and celebrated their repentance (Luke 15:1-10). Such radical doctrine and practice was difficult to justify by legal precedent from Jewish scriptures. So revolutionary an attitude on the part of Jesus could only irritate authorities whose social importance rested upon their mastery of the exegetical intricacies of a life-encompassing legal system.

In this respect, the relationship of Jesus to the Pharisees calls for some clarification. Their opposition to his practice of admitting tax collectors and sinners into intimacy of table fellowship was rooted in two distinguishable legal concerns. First, there were the explicit food laws, called kashrut, which forbade eating pork, a kid seethed in its mother's milk, meat with the blood still in it, and the like. These laws had governed the diet of Jews for centuries and served to keep them from eating with gentiles or other Jews who lived and ate like gentiles. Second, there was the purity code which, when applied to the laity, separated Jew from Jew socially. Such social separation was going on in the time of Jesus when some groups of Jews were applying the priestly purity code to the laity. The Jews who did this, called *ḥaberim* in rabbinic sources, were eventually followed by the rabbis, who attempted to extend the provisions of the purity code to all Israelites.

Since gentiles were present in the Holy Land, righteous Jews were affected in different ways as far as eating was concerned. They sometimes found it helpful to band together to see that the *kashrut* laws were fully observed (and the purity code, too, when that was of concern to them). A common table where proper precautions regarding these laws were observed was in order among righteous Jews who, when away from home, could not depend upon this service being rendered by members of their respective families.

The admission of unrighteous Jews (those lax in their observance of the *kashrut* laws) into the table fellowship of those who were righteous was permitted at the discretion of the leaders of the group. Such admissions were defended on the grounds of *ḥesed* (covenantal love) and justified as a means of recruiting new members for the fellowship or for the renewal movement, as the case might be.

The Pharisees as righteous Jews, that is, as observants of the Law of Moses, including the *kashrut* laws, had no particular grounds for objecting to this practical way of facilitating the observance of the law within the wider community. To the extent that the Pharisees were looked to by the authorities, that is, the Roman-backed high priestly oligarchy, as the party best able to police the land in terms of observing the law, or to the extent that they were recognized by the people (and so perceived themselves) to be authorized by God to police the land, the Pharisees were nervous about any situation where the righteousness of those observing the law was being dangerously imputed to the unrighteous. (This is precisely what Jesus' acceptance of sinners at table fellowship implied.) Such nervousness could best be allayed by requiring a probationary period during which anyone seeking admission to an eating group could give evidence of a sincere intent to become truly and enduringly observant.

A scandalous feature of Jesus' admitting unrighteous Jews into the intimacy of his table fellowship was the absence of any fixed probationary period. The most liberal of the *haberim* required one month (*t. Dem.* 2.10-12) and the Essenes required two or three years.

Compared to the more established religious groups, then, Jesus' fellowship appeared dangerously subversive of that law upon whose strict observance the Pharisees placed such great importance. In any case, simple prudence dictated that the Pharisees take the precautionary step of warning righteous Jews who were most likely to heed their warning. (Because of political restraints placed upon them that curtailed that zeal for the law, there was generally little the Pharisees could do against tax collectors and others who lived like gentiles, except to excommunicate them from their table fellowship.)

The Pharisees were certainly not the only righteous Jews in Palestine. The Qumran community constituted a haven for those who wanted to be right with God according to the Law of Moses. Doubtless there were other such righteous communities. But the special status of the Pharisees in the eyes of the people and their role in the power structure of the established world of Jewish piety, attested by Josephus, justify regarding some of the New Testament evidence about them as valid.

First, Paul was a Pharisee, and he was granted police power by Jewish authorities. He was not granted those powers because he was a Pharisee, but since he was a Pharisee he had credentials that stood him in good stead in carrying out his police duties. The local people present at the arrests Paul made, whose cooperation with the arresting authorities was important, knew that Paul was a Pharisee. Therefore they assented to his authority as derived from God, not from Rome. Second, Jesus recognized the Pharisees as righteous and alluded to them when his teaching required the example of a righteous person (for example, the parable of the tax collector and the Pharisee in the Temple). Third, Jesus perceived a difference between the righteousness practiced by the Pharisees and the obedience he taught his disciples to render to God. Fourth, Jesus at times came into conflict with the Pharisees, for example, over Sabbath observance and over his practice of admitting sinners into the intimacy of his table fellowship. This latter opposition possible arose only in those cases where the sinners were guilty of notorious transgression, as with tax collectors. Finally, Jesus recognized that the Pharisees possessed authority to rule on the interpretation of the Law of Moses. Taken as a legal guild, however, their example discredited their ultimate authority as reliable exponents of God's requirements of his sons and daughters.

Whether Jesus is responsible for the woes against the Pharisees is an historical question affected by the source paradigm that is applied. According to the two-document hypothesis, Matthew 23 can be understood as an expanded Matthean construction representing development of tradition from Q, some of which was also known to Mark. On form-critical grounds, however, even assuming the two-document hypothesis, there is much against this view. The tradition preserved in Matthew 23 reflects the influence of oral tradition, Jewish and Palestinian in provenance. Regarding Matthew as the earliest of the extant Gospels removes all doubt about the Jewish-Christian and Palestinian origin of most if not all of the tradition in Matthew 23.

It is possible on form-critical grounds to reconstruct the more original form of the woes and to separate the tradition that has been added. Paul's own testimony of his attack upon the church fits the historical requirement of a kind of violent persecution which, when inflicted by some Pharisees upon some Christians, would explain these bitter additions. The woes themselves, however, may well be authentic to Jesus. They certainly are profoundly consonant with the best-attested sayings of Jesus.

Thus, it is clear that one can give a credible account of the importance of the Pharisees for understanding the New Testament, especially the importance of their opposition to Jesus' table fellowship with tax collectors and sinners, without settling the question as to the extent the purity code was being applied to all Israelites in the time of Jesus. Depending upon the extent that the purity code was applied and whether the Pharisees had any interest at all in gaining wide acceptance of it among the laity, Jesus' table fellowship with tax collectors and sinners could have been of added concern to the Pharisees. A concern would have been there in any case, based simply on the *kashrut* laws. It would not have been only the Pharisees' concern, but one shared by all righteous Jews, to one degree or another.

It was normative that righteous Jews not eat with sinners. As one who came in the way of righteousness, John had not eaten with sinners. But Jesus did. This marks a profound theological difference between John and Jesus (Matt 11:16-19).

The objection of scribes and Pharisees to Jesus' practice of eating with tax collectors and sinners led to a major crisis for Jesus. Succumbing to pressure to abandon this practice would possibly have brought Jesus favor; instead, he struck at an important root of the problem—the self-righteousness of a scrupulous religious establishment.

Jesus represented the legal authorities' emphasis on minutiae of the law and their neglect of justice, mercy, and faith as the counsel of "blind guides" (Matt 23:23-24). This, however, may be a caricature. In any case, Jesus himself came from a religious background so akin to Pharisaism as to command the respect of the Pharisees. Their anxiety over what he was doing may have been rooted in the perception that one of their own kind was endangering the interests of "the righteous." Jesus openly said that he did not come to call the righteous (Matt 9:9-13). Although he himself was known as a righteous man, in eating with sinners Jesus was breaking down the barriers by which many righteous Jews maintained an inner group strength. This group strength was necessary to withstand external pressures to compromise religious scruples in the interests of achieving an improved economy and a more cosmopolitan society.

Jesus' table fellowship with tax collectors and sinners may not have been in the first instance the nucleus of a new community. Nevertheless, it was based upon the recognition that God is the Father of all. Indeed, if a man has a hundred sheep and one goes astray, will he not leave the ninety-nine to search for the one that is lost? And having found it, will he not put it on his shoulder and bring it back rejoicing and call to his friends, "Rejoice with me, for I have found my sheep which was lost" (Luke 15:3-6; cf. Matt 18:10-14)? How much more will our heavenly Father rejoice over the return of a lost son (Luke 15:11-24)? Therefore, how appropriate that we celebrate the repentance of those lost sons of Abraham who, once dead in trespasses, are now alive through God's merciful judgment (Luke 15:25-32; 19:1,10).

By such forceful imagery as this, Jesus defended his practice of table fellowship with tax collectors and sinners. Parables like the one about the lost son and his elder brother (Luke 15:11-32) or the laborers in the vineyard (Matt 20:1-16) were first created in response to this crisis in Jesus' ministry. They were used to defend the gospel of God's unmerited and unconditional acceptance of the repentant sinner. Similarly, the parable about the great banquet (Matt 22:1-10; Luke 14:16-24) served to remind the righteous that they had no ground for complaint over the eschatological acceptance of sinners since they themselves had turned their backs on the kingdom (cf. Matt 23:13).

These parables in themselves were probably not intended to alienate the scribes and Pharisees, but to forestall their inquisitorial activity among the disciples. Nor is a parable like that of the Pharisee and the tax collector in the Temple (Luke 18:9-14) designed to hurt rather than to heal. The Pharisee in the parable does not represent all Pharisees and certainly not the ideal Pharisee. But to make his point that goodness can become demonic and destructive when it leads good men to isolate themselves from others, Jesus chose a man from one of the most virtuous circles of Jewish society. If such a man, no matter how moral, places his trust in his own righteousness and despises others, he goes from the house of God to his own house in a wrong relationship to God. However, a sinner who places his or her trust in the mercy of God goes home in a right relationship to God.

The love God has for the sinner shows no lack of love for the righteous. "All that is mine is yours," says the father to his elder son, but "it was fitting to make merry and be glad, for this your brother was dead, and is alive; he was lost, and is found" (Luke 15:31-32). This noble and heartfelt sentiment did not go completely unheeded, but lodged itself within the collective unconscious of the Pharisaic community, there to work its way inexorably against every tendency toward hard-heartedness, within the ranks of the righteous.

Subsequently, the elder brother, a strict Pharisee, while persecuting the church, was won over by the powerful reality of God's love. He became a staunch defender of what some regarded as an illicit table fellowship, but which he himself saw being at the heart of the gospel for which Jesus had died (Gal 2:11-21).

In spite of the cogency of Jesus' defense of the gospel of God's mercy toward repentant sinners, opposition from the religious establishment stiffened. In this period of opposition from religious authorities responsible for upholding the law in the towns and cities outside Jerusalem, Jesus formulated his woes against the "scribes and Pharisees." These utterances are uncompromising. By this time the issue had become clear; Israel was at the crossroads. The people could either follow those whom Jesus characterized as "blind guides," who hypocritically held in their hands the keys of the kingdom but who neither entered themselves nor allowed others to enter (Matt 23:13), or they could follow Jesus. Irony turned to bitter sarcasm in the judgment: "Woe to you, scribes and Pharisees, hypocrites! For you build the tombs of prophets and adorn the monuments of the righteous, say, 'If we had lived in the days of our fathers we would not have taken part with them in shedding the blood of the prophets'" (Matt 23:29-30). You hypocrites, Jesus said, because in so speaking you condemn yourselves as among those who murder prophets. For as you dissociate yourselves from those who have done evil and vainly imagine that had you been in their place you would not have committed the sins they committed, you show yourselves to be the very kind of self-righteous persons who will condone the killing of those God sends us as his messengers.

Uncompromising words like these sealed the fate of Jesus. By their use he unmasked what many in positions of privilege and power could not bear to have unmasked. Jesus penetrated the facade of goodness behind which persons hid their lust for power. He represented them to be like "whitewashed tombs, which outwardly appear beautiful, but within . . . are full of dead men's bones" (Matt 23:27).

After invective like this, the legal authorities were beside themselves to find some charge on which to get rid of Jesus. The compliance of high priestly circles and the rest of the Jerusalem oligarchy was assured once Jesus made it clear that he called for changes not only in men's hearts, but in the institutions of Zion—specifically within the central institution, the Temple itself (Matt 21:12-13).

With the Pharisees, the high priests, and the elders of the people in concert, the Roman authorities, had they insisted on due process, would have risked a tear in the delicately woven fabric of political collaboration. This collaboration enabled Rome to maintain viable control over a key sector in the defensive perimeter of its frontier with the Parthians, who were an ever-present threat to the stability of the eastern provinces. Ostensibly, in the interest of maintaining Jewish law and Roman order, Jesus was executed. This was done in spite of the fact that Jesus programmatically insisted that he came "not to destroy the law, but to fulfill it" (Matt 5:17). Moreover, Jesus taught his disciples that unless their righteousness exceeded that of the scribes and Pharisees, they would never enter the Kingdom of Heaven (Matt 5:20). Yet it can hardly be doubted that in fulfilling the "law and the prophets," Jesus ran afoul of the scribes and Pharisees. This occurred not only when he ate with tax collectors and sinners, but also in regard to other matters as, for example, the Sabbath observance (Matt 12:1-8; Luke 14:5). Jesus certainly challenged Jewish legal authority and, as for Roman order, it was to be replaced by the Kingdom of Heaven. So the die had been cast well in advance. While Jesus died a righteous man by the standards of the Kingdom of Heaven, he did not go to the cross innocent of breaking the law as it was represented by the mores of the local populace. Nor was he innocent of disturbing the peace as it was preserved in and through imperial order. He was crucified in the end by the Romans as a political criminal. We can imagine the mixed feelings of anguish and relief on the part of responsible Jewish authorities. Yet we are not in a position to know with any degree of certainty the motives of the principals who were involved in his death.

This outline of essential developments between the death of John and the death of Jesus illustrates how tradition originating with Jesus, which is preserved in the Gospels, can be set within the context of his life situation. The tradition can be seen to come alive against the historical background of the Jews in Palestine when Herod Agrippa was Tetrarch of Galilee and Perea, when John the Baptist had been preaching a baptism of repentance in the Jordan valley, and when Pontius Pilate was procurator of Judea.

In retrospect, on the basis of what can be supported by historical inquiry, is it possible to say something about the character of Jesus and about his public ministry? Jesus' character is the mark he left or "engraved" upon his disciples, including the tax collectors and sinners he admitted into the intimacy of his table fellowship. This fellowship heard Jesus gladly and remembered his words and actions. Members of this fellowship took responsibility for formulating and handing on to the earliest churches such authentic sayings of Jesus as in fact have been preserved in the Gospels.

To the degree that the understanding of life expressed in these authentic sayings was actually represented by Jesus in his own life situation, that is, through his words and actions—to this degree it is possible to speak about the character of Jesus. Confining the inquiry to that nucleus of sayings which beyond a reasonable doubt can be accepted as authentic sayings of Jesus, it is possible to conclude that in rebuking self-righteousness and chiding those who resented God's mercy toward sinners, Jesus disclosed something about the kind of person he was. He can be seen as a public figure in relationship to other figures. His contemporaries could understand his human concern for others, and many were moved by it. They saw not only his friendship for tax collectors and sinners, but more. They saw a concern for community.

Pretentiousness and self-righteousness on the part of individuals or groups is one of the most serious corrupting influences affecting the health and integrity of communal existence. Individual and collective self-righteousness on the part of authorities, when unchallenged is like a hard cement by which outmoded and unjust ecclesiastical, economic, political, and social structures are kept defensible in the face of justified opposition from advocates of social or religious reforms. Privileged individuals or castes are secure only so long as it is possible for society to perceive their positions of privilege as clothed with the garments of righteousness. To pull aside these garments and to expose hypocrisy and abuse is a revolutionary act of a most radical nature.

Jesus exposed hypocrisy and abuse. For him to rebuke the prideful self-righteousness of religious authorities was to strike at an important source of contra-redemptive influence in his own life situation and to encourage the continuation of the individual and covenantal renewal that was taking place in response to his preaching. Those whom Jesus had helped to perceive themselves as sinners dependent upon the unmerited grace of God were glad to know that he not only received sinners, but defended this action when it was criticized. And insofar as it was possible, they were moved to go and do likewise.

There was in this compassionate but disconcerting stance of Jesus a dynamic source of redemptive power which worked against the attempt of the established world of Jewish piety to structure human existence on the exclusive ground of the mosaic covenant. Such a source of power provided the basis for a distinctive style of life wherein Jesus and his disciples worked joyfully for a reconciling mode of human existence open to God's grace and to a future conditioned by (1) sin and the expectation of God's imminent destruction of sinners; (2) the unbounded sovereign love of God; and (3) a faith which led them to submit to the judgment of God and to trust themselves utterly to the mercy that was intrinsic to and inherent in God's love. This is a style of life grounded in God's sovereign love which results in a new creation (Paul), and being born again (John). Jesus likened this new style of life to "becoming like a child."

This personal structuring and restructuring of their historical existence, this shaping of the realities of their human environment, and the compassion and joy associated with this creative stance sustained and gave theological depth and direction to their fellowship. Clearly there is more to Jesus than this. But this understanding of his public career and character carries the investigator to the very heart of what can be shown as both essential and enduring in Jesus.

FIVE GOSPELS BUT NO GOSPEL
JESUS AND THE SEMINAR

N. Thomas Wright

LOOKING FOR JESUS

People have been looking for Jesus for a long time, but never quite like this. The "Quest of the Historical Jesus" has been proceeding, in fits and starts, for two hundred years. Its story has often been told;[1] in recent years there has been a flurry, not to say a flood, of writing about Jesus, and debates of all sorts, about every aspect of the evidence, and every conceivable reconstruction of Jesus' life, teaching, work, and death, have been running to and fro.[2] Most of

---

[1]   N. T. Wright, "Quest for the Historical Jesus," *ABD* 3.796-802.

[2]   We may note, for instance W. R. *Farmer, Maccabees, Zealots, and Josephus: An Enquiry into Jewish Nationalism in the Greco-Roman Period* (New York: Columbia University Press, 1956); G. B. Caird, *Jesus and the Jewish Nation* (London: Athlone Press, 1965); G. Vermes, *Jesus the Jew: A Historian's Reading of the Gospels* (London: Collins; Philadelphia: Fortress, 1973); idem, *Jesus and the World of Judaism* (London: SCM, 1983; Philadelphia: Fortress, 1984); idem, *The Religion of Jesus the Jew* (London: SCM; Minneapolis: Fortress, 1993); B. F. Meyer, *The Aims of Jesus* (London: SCM, 1979); idem, *Christus Faber: The Master-Builder and the House of God* (PTMS 29; Allison Park: Pickwick, 1992); idem, "Jesus Christ," in D. N. Freedman et al. (eds.), *The Anchor Bible Dictionary* (6 vols., New York: Doubleday, 1992) 3.773-96; A. E. Harvey, *Jesus and the Constraints of History: The Bampton Lectures, 1980* (London: Duckworth, 1982); M. J. Borg, *Conflict, Holiness, and Politics in the Teachings of Jesus* (SBEC 5; New York and Toronto: Mellen, 1984); idem, *Jesus: A New Vision* (San Francisco: Harper & Row, 1987); E. P. Sanders, *Jesus and Judaism* (London: SCM; Philadelphia: Fortress, 1985); idem, *The Historical Figure of Jesus* (London and New York: Penguin, 1993); G. Theissen, *Der Schatten des Galiläers. Historische Jesus-forschung in erzählender Form* (Munich: Kaiser, 1986); ET: *The Shadow of the Galilean: The Quest of the Historical Jesus in Narrative Form* (Philadelphia: Fortress, 1987); R. A. Horsley, *Jesus and the Spiral of Violence: Popular Jewish Resistance in Roman Palestine* (San Francisco: Harper & Row, 1987); S. Freyne, *Galilee, Jesus and the Gospels: Literary Approaches and Historical Investigations* (Philadelphia: Fortress, 1988); J. H. Charlesworth, *Jesus within Judaism* (ABRL; New York: Doubleday, 1988); B. Witherington, *The Christology of Jesus* (Minneapolis: Fortress, 1990); J. P. Meier, *A Marginal Jew: Rethinking*

this writing has been produced by individual scholars, working independently. But in the last few years a new corporate venture has emerged, attempting by a process of discussion and voting to arrive at an answer to the question: "What did Jesus really say?" This group has called itself "The Jesus Seminar," and among its many recent publications one stands out as a kind of flagship: *The Five Gospels*, published late in 1993 by Macmillan (though emanating from the Seminar's own publishing house, Polebridge Press). This is the subject of the present chapter.

No doubt there are at least as many opinions about the "The Jesus Seminar" as the Seminar itself holds about Jesus. Passions, in fact, already run high on the subject, and may run higher yet before the storm abates. Some of the Seminar's members treat any questioning of its work like a slap in the face—though not with the turning of the other cheek, as one might have thought considering that that saying received the rare accolade of a red vote (meaning authentic; see below).[3] In other quarters, one only has to mention the Seminar to provoke a wry smile, or even guffaws of laughter. At a packed and high-profile meeting of the Society of Biblical Literature's "Pauline Theology" seminar in 1991, the person in the chair—one of the most senior and respected of North American biblical scholars—rejected a call for a vote on the subject that had been under discussion by simply saying, "This ain't the Jesus Seminar." This was greeted with laughter and applause in about equal measure.

So what is the Jesus Seminar up to, and what should be think about it? It has now completed many years of detailed and painstaking work, and, though it may well all deserve discussing, there is no

---

the Historical Jesus. Volume One: *The Roots of the Problem and the Person* (ABRL 3; New York: Doubleday, 1991); idem, *A Marginal Jew: Rethinking the Historical Jesus.* Volume Two: *Mentor, Message, and Miracles* (ABRL 9; New York: Doubleday, 1994); J. D. Crossan, *The Historical Jesus: The Life of a Mediterranean Jewish Peasant* (San Francisco: HarperCollins, 1991); B. Chilton, *The Temple of Jesus: His Sacrificial Program within a Cultural History of Sacrifice* (University Park: Penn State Press, 1992); idem and C. A. Evans, *Jesus in Context: Temple, Purity, and Restoration* (AGJU 39; Leiden: Brill, 1997); C. A. Evans, *Jesus and His Contemporaries: Comparative Studies* (AGJU 25; Leiden: Brill, 1995).

3   Matt 5:39; cf. R. W. Funk and R. W. Hoover (eds.), *The Five Gospels: The Search for the Authentic Words of Jesus* (Sonoma: Polebridge; New York: Macmillan, 1993) 143-45.

space here to go into its many products, with all their presuppositions, methods, decisions, and results.[4] I have, in any case, written
about all that elsewhere.[5] I want in this essay to concentrate on *The
Five Gospels*, the book towards which all else was preliminary.

The "Five Gospels" in question are (in case there was any doubt)
Mark, Matthew, Luke, John, and *Thomas*. The inclusion of the last
of these will still raise one or two eyebrows, through it is by now
well known that the Seminar takes kindly to *Thomas*, not least
because of its apparent similarity with (some reconstructions of) the
hypothetical source "Q"—and, as we shall see, the portrait of Jesus
which it appears to support. More striking is the technique with
which the Seminar's results are displayed. The old "red letter testaments" picked out all the words of Jesus in red; this one accords that
status to the favored few among the sayings, those which the Seminar
voted as highly likely to emanate from Jesus himself. The rest of
Jesus' sayings are set in pink, gray, and black, on a rough sliding
scale of the probability and improbability of their coming from
Jesus; I shall discuss the precise nuances of the colors presently. Each
saying, story, or group of sayings/stories is then commented on, and
the reasons for the voting are explained, sometimes briefly, sometimes up to a few pages. The text is broken up from time to time by
"cameo essays" on key topics (the kingdom of God, the son of man,
and so forth). The text is attractively laid out, with diagrams and
occasional pictures. Everything is presented about as clearly as it
could be; nobody, from high school student upwards, could fail to
see what was being said. All in all, it is a substantial product, and
whatever one thinks of the actual results, it clearly represents a great
deal of hard labor.

A New Translation

Six features of the book call for general comment right from the
start. First, it uses what the Seminar has called "The Scholars Version" [sic]—its own translation of the four canonical Gospels and

---

4   See, for instance, R. W. Funk, B. B. Scott, and J. R. Butts (eds.), *The
Parables of Jesus: Red Letter Edition. A Report of the Jesus Seminar* (Sonoma:
Polebridge, 1988); R. J. Miller, *The Complete Gospels: Annotated Scholars Version* (Sonoma: Polebridge, 1992); and the Seminar's journal, *Forum: Foundations
and Facets*.

5   N. T. Wright, *Jesus and the Victory of God* (Christian Origins and the
Question of God 2; London: SPCK; Minneapolis: Fortress, 1996) 28-82.

Thomas. This is an attempt to represent, in colloquial American English, the original flavor of the Greek. Now it is our turn to be slapped in the face:

> Although Jesus was indignant, he stretched out his hand, touched him, and says to him, "Okay—you're clean!"[6]

> The king came in to see the guests for himself and noticed this man not properly attired. And he says to him, "Look, pal, how'd you get in here without dressing for the occasion?"[7]

> When Jesus noticed their trust, he said, "Mister, your sins have been forgiven you."[8]

I have no objection to colloquial translations—though one might have thought this would be the People's Version, not the Scholars'. What I do find somewhat objectionable is the dismissive tone of the introduction, which explains that other versions are "faintly Victorian" and set a context of "polite religious discourse suitable for a Puritan parlor."[9] The New Revised Standard Version comes in for particular criticism; one suspects that its main fault in the eyes of the SV translators is that it is a lineal descendant, on one side of the family at any rate, of the old King James Version, which, as we shall see, represents all that Seminar abominates by way of American religion. The authors make great play of the fact that, unlike most Bible translations, this one both includes the non-canonical Thomas and is not authorized by any ecclesiastical or religious bodies. Instead, pompously, "The Scholars Version is authorized by scholars."[10]

Present and Absent Friends

But, second, which scholars? Seventy-four names are listed in the back of the book, and there have been other members, quite influential in earlier stages of the debate, who are not explicitly mentioned here.[11] Some of them are household names in the world of New

---

6   Mark 1:41; Funk and Hoover (eds.), *The Five Gospels*, 43. There is a hint here that the transaction between Jesus and the leper was not a healing, but simply Jesus' declaration that he should no longer be treated as an outcast.

7   Matt 22:12; Funk and Hoover (eds.), *The Five Gospels*, 234.

8   Luke 5:20; Funk and Hoover (eds.), *The Five Gospels*, 283.

9   Funk and Hoover (eds.), *The Five Gospels*, xiii-xviii, here at xiv.

10   Funk and Hoover (eds.), *The Five Gospels*, xviii.

11   For example, Burton Mack, author of *A Myth of Innocence: Mark and Christian Origins* (Minneapolis: Fortress, 1988) and other works which have had a profound impact on the work of the Jesus Seminar. Over 200 members are reported

Testament studies: Robert Funk himself, the driving force behind the entire enterprise, whose earlier work on the Greek grammar of the New Testament is universally recognized as authoritative; Dominic Crossan, whose combination of enormous erudition, subtlety of thought, and felicitous writing style have rightly ensured him widespread respect; James Robinson, whose work on the Nag Hammadi texts has placed the entire discipline in his debt; Marcus Borg, Bruce Chilton, and Walter Wink, all of whom have made distinguished and distinctive contributions to the study of Jesus in his context (and to much else besides); Ron Cameron, whose forthright and provocative writings on *Thomas* and related topics are rightly famous; John Kloppenborg, one of the leading specialists on the hypothetical source "Q." In any list of contemporary North American biblical scholars, all these would find a place of honor.

But one could compile a very long list of North American New Testament scholars, including several who have written importantly about Jesus, who are not among those present, and whose work has had no visible impact on the Seminar at all. The most obvious is Ed Sanders, whose work, massive in its learning, and almost unique in its influence over the present state of scholarship worldwide, seems to have been ignored by the Seminar—except for one tiny particular, and that precisely where Sanders is at his weakest.[12] Another figure whose work has been totally ignored is Ben F. Meyer, who has more understanding of how ancient texts work in his little finger than many of the Jesus Seminar seem to have in their entire word-processors, and whose writing on Jesus is utterly rigorous, utterly scholarly, and utterly different in its results from anything in the volume we are considering.[13] So, too, one looks in vain for members of the teaching faculties of many of the leading North American colleges and universities. There is nobody currently teaching at

---

to have belonged at one stage or another; Funk and Hoover (eds.), *The Five Gospels*, 34.

[12] Cf. Sanders, *Jesus and Judaism*, remarkably absent from the bibliography of *The Five Gospels*; cf. too Sanders, *The Historical Figure of Jesus*. E. P. Sanders and M. Davies, *Studying the Synoptic Gospels* (London: SCM; Philadelphia: Trinity Press International, 1989), is listed in the bibliography of *The Five Gospels* as "an excellent guide," though anyone taking it seriously would be forced to reject a good deal of the Jesus Seminar's methods and results. See below.

[13] Cf. esp. Meyer, *The Aims of Jesus*; idem, *Christus Faber*; idem, "Jesus Christ."

Harvard, Yale, Princeton, Duke, McGill, or Stanford. Toronto is well represented; so is Claremont (not least by its graduates); several Fellows of the Seminar have doctorates from Harvard. But where is the rest of the guild—those who, for instance, flock to the "Historical Jesus" sessions of the annual meeting of the Society of Biblical Literature? They are conspicuous by their absence.

No doubt some within the Seminar would suggest that this comment is academic snobbery, but they cannot have it both ways. The Jesus Seminar is in something of a cleft stick at this point. On the one hand, the members are determined to present to the general public the findings which "scholars" have come up with. Away with secrecy, and hole-in-a-corner scholarship, they say: it is time for scholars to come out of their closets, to boldly say what no one has said before. They must, therefore, present themselves as the pundits, the ones in the know, the ones the public can trust as the reputable, even the authorized, spokespersons for the serious tradition of biblical scholarship.[14] But, on the other hand, they lash out at the "elitism" of their critics within the broader academic world[15]—while saying on the next page that attacks on members of the Seminar have tended to come from "those who lack academic credentials." Sauce for the goose and sauce for the gander: either academic credentials matter, in which case the Seminar should listen to those who possess them in abundance and are deeply critical of their work, or they don't matter, in which case the Seminar should stop priding itself on its own, over against the common herd. The attitude to critics expressed in this book reminds me of John 7:49: in the Scholars Version, it reads: "As for this rabble, they are ignorant of the Law! Damn them!" It becomes apparent that the work we have here does

---

[14]   For example, see Funk and Hoover (eds.), *The Five Gospels*, 34-35, whose triumphalism is as breathtaking as it is unwarranted: "Critical scholars practice their craft by submitting their work to the judgment of peers. Untested work is not highly regarded. The scholarship represented by the Fellows of the Jesus Seminar is the kind that has come to prevail in all the great universities of the world." Only in the most general terms is the last sentence true; the present essay is a response to the invitation of the previous sentences.

[15]   For examples, see Funk and Hoover (eds.), *The Five Gospels*, 1: the present book is "a dramatic exit from windowless studies"; 34: "we have been intimidated by promotion and tenure committees . . . It is time for us to quit the library and speak up . . ."; the Seminar's methods have been attacked by "many elitist academic critics who deplored [its] public face."

not represnt "scholars," as simply as that; it represents some scholars, and that mostly (with some interesting exceptions) from a very narrow band among serious contemporary readers of the Gospels worldwide.[16]

These comments about the make-up of the Seminar highlight a point which must be clearly made before we go one step further. Though this book claims, on every page, to speak for all the Fellows of the Seminar, it becomes increasingly apparent that it comes from the Seminar's Chair, Robert W. Funk (R. W. Hoover is named as co-author, though there is no indication of which author drafted which parts). Dissentient voices are, of course, recorded in the reporting of voting patterns. But it would be a mistake to saddle all, perhaps even most, of the Fellows with the point of view, and the arguments, that we find on page after page. Only occasionally is this really acknowledged. In the bibliography, for instance, one of Marcus Borg's books is listed, with the comment "It goes almost without saying that he didn't vote with the majority on every issue."[17] One suspects that that is something of an understatement. In the present essay, therefore, I am discussing the work of Funk and Hoover, not necessarily that of other Fellows; we may note, though, that the whole layout and intent of the book predisposes the reader—not least the non-academic reader, who is clearly in view—to assume that the verdicts reached are those of "scholars" in a much broader sense.

A Driving Agenda

There is, thirdly, a further agenda involved at this point, which is, one may suspect, the major force which motivates the project in general and several (though by no means all) of its members. They are fundamentally antifundamentalist. Listen to these wonderfully objective, value-free, scholarly comments, taken from the book's introduction:

> Once the discrepancy between the Jesus of history and the Christ of faith emerged from under the smothering cloud of the historic creeds, it was only a matter of time before scholars sought to disengage [the two] . . . It is ironic that Roman Catholic scholars are emerging from the dark ages of

---

16   There is, for instance, a good deal of important work on Jesus emanating from Latin America; but one would not guess it from reading the Seminar's publications.

17   Funk and Hoover (eds.), *The Five Gospels*, 540, referring to Borg, *Jesus: A New Vision*.

theological tyranny just as many Protestant scholars are reentering it as a consequence of the the dictatorial tactics of the Southern Baptist Convention and other fundamentalisms.[18]

With the council of Nicea in 325, the orthodox party solidified its hold on the Christian tradition and other wings of the Christian movment [sic] were choked off.[19]

There are only two positions allowed, it seems. One must either be some kind of close-minded fundamentalist, adhering to some approximation of the historic creeds of the Christian church; one notes that this lumps together Athanasius, Aquinas, Barth, Pannenberg, and Moltmann along with the TV evangelists who are among the real targets of the polemic. Or one must be non-judgmentally open to the free-for-all hurly-burly of Gnosis, Cynicism, esoteric wisdom, folklore and so on represnted by various groups in the first three centuries—and to the baby-and-bathwater methodological skepticism adopted by the Seminar.[20] The strange thing is that there are several members of the Seminar itself who represent neither point of view; has the author of this introduction forgotten who some of his colleagues are? Unfortunately, as we shall see, this either-or has so dominated the landscape that a great many decisions of the Seminar simply reflect a shallow polarization which has precious little to do with the first century and, one suspects, a great deal to do with the twentieth, not least in North America. One suspects that several members of the Seminar do not actually *know* very many ordinary, non-fundamentalist, orthodox Christians. Would it be going too far to venture the supposition that more than one leading member of the Jesus Seminar is doing his (or her) best to exorcize the memory of a strict fundamentalist background? Unfortunately, the attempt to escape from one's own past is not a good basis for the attempt to reconstruct someone else's.

This question has another aspect to it which must be noted carefully. It is now endemic in North American Biblical Studies that very few practitioners have studied philosophy or theology at any depth.

---

18   Funk and Hoover (eds.), *The Five Gospels*, 7-8.

19   Funk and Hoover (eds.), *The Five Gospels*, 35.

20   It is interesting to compare the Seminar's work with the comment on the Gospels made by a leading secular historian, J. M. Roberts: "[the Gospels] need not be rejected; more more inadequate evidence about far more intractable subjects has often to be employed" (*History of the Word* [2nd ed., Oxford: Helicon, 1992] 210).

Such study, indeed, is sometimes regarded with suspicion, as though it might prejudice the pure, objective, neutral reading of the text. Leave aside for the moment the impossibility of such objectivity (see below). The real problem is that if one is to discuss what are essentially theological and philosophical issues, in terms both of the method required for serious study of Jesus and of the content and implications of Jesus' proclamation, one really requires more sophistication than the Seminar, in this book at least, can offer. This will become apparent as we proceed.

Which Gospels?

The fourth introductory point concerns the treament of the different "Gospels." As I said, it is now commonplace to treat the book known as the *Gospel of Thomas* alongside the canonical Gospels. If we are studying the entire Gospel tradition, this is clearly mandatory. The Seminar is to be congratulated for pushing this fact into the public eye (and for the marvellous work of producing texts of a large number of relevant documents which had not been easily available hitherto). But, when all is said and done, huge questions remain about the relevance of *Thomas* for the study of Jesus. By no means all students of it agree with the majority of the Seminar in placing it early and independent of the canonical Gospels.[21] If members of the public are interested in knowing what "scholars" think, they ought to be told fair and square that diagrams in which a hypothetical first edition of *Thomas* is placed in 50s of the first century are thoroughly tendentious, and belong out on a limb of current scholarship.[22]

In particular, we should not accept without question the assumption that *Thomas*, and for that matter fragments like the Egerton papyrus, are (or belong to) gospels. It all depends on what you mean. *Thomas* does not call itself a "gospel." Nor, for that matter, do Matthew, Luke, and John; and the opening note in Mark ("The beginning of the gospel of Jesus Christ") may well refer, not to the book which then follows, but to the events which it purports to record. The

---

[21] In favor: S. J. Patterson, *The Gospel of Thomas and Jesus* (Sonoma: Polebridge, 1993), noted in the bibliography as being influential in the Seminar. Against: C. M. Tuckett, *Nag Hammadi and the Gospel Tradition: Synoptic Tradition in the Nag Hammadi Library* (Studies of the New Testament and its World; Edinburgh: T. & T. Clark, 1986); idem, "Thomas and the Synoptics," *NovT* 30 (1988) 132-57.

[22] See Funk and Hoover (eds.), *The Five Gospels*, 18, 128.

meaning of the word "gospel" in the first two centuries of the Christian era is, in fact, quite controversial;[23] sufficient to note here that to call *Thomas*, and for that matter "Q," "gospels" is to make quite a far-reaching decision. It is to say that these works are to be regarded as *proclamations* about Jesus, of the same sort as the four better-known "gospels," despite the fact that they do not narrate the story of Jesus, do not (for the most part) proclaim him as Messiah, do not tell of his death and resurrection—do not, in fact, do the very things which seem, from the Pauline evidence, to be what the earliest Christians regarded as "gospel." Bringing Paul into the picture at this point is of course itself controversial, but not nearly so much as making Thomas contemporary with him.[24]

I suggest that nothing would be lost, and a good deal of clarity regained, if, instead of referring to *Thomas*, and indeed "Q," as "gospels," and thereby supposing that they record the theology of an entire group within very early Christianity, we see them as what they are (supposing for the moment that "Q" ever existed): collections of sayings. Calling them "gospels" obscures the obvious difference of genre between them and the four ordinarily so called. In an attempt to gain a hearing for different supposed presentations of Jesus, the

---

[23]   For example, see H. Koester, *Ancient Christian Gospels: Their History and Development* (London and Philadelphia: Trinity Press International, 1990), on which see N. T. Wright, *The New Testament and the People of God* (Christian Origins and the Question of God 1; London: SPCK; Minneapolis: Fortress, 1992) 371-443; and, for some comments on Paul's meaning of the term, N. T. Wright, "Gospel and Theology in Galatians," in L. A. Jervis and P. Richardson (eds.), *Gospel in Paul: Studies on Corinthians, Galatians and Romans for Richard N. Longenecker* (JSNTSup 108; Sheffield: Sheffield Academic Press, 1994) 222-39.

[24]   The suggestion (Funk and Hoover [eds.], *The Five Gospels*, 500-501) that the Gnosticism in *Thomas* is very like what we find in John and Paul would be laughable if it did not reveal culpable ignorance of the entire drift of Pauline studies in the last forty years. The brief sketch of how *Thomas* got its name (p. 20) reveals an astonishing naivety, speaking of the apostle being "revered in the Syrian church as an apostle," and giving as evidence for this Matt 10:3; Mark 3:18; Luke 6:15; Acts 1:13; John 11:16; 20:24; 21:2. The attribution to Thomas, we are told, "tells us nothing about the author," but "may indicate where this gospel was written." In which of the above texts do we find evidence for Thomas in Syria? If the writers applied the same skepticism to claims about Thomas as they do, on the same page, to claims about the other four (the evidence of Papias, for instance), it would quickly become clear how little evidence there is for an early date, or a Syrian provenance, for the Thomas collection.

current fashion distorts precisely that sort of literary analysis that "scholars" ought to favor.

In fact, although *The Five Gospels* prints all of John as well as the others, it is clear that John is regarded a priori as having little or nothing to do with Jesus himself. This, indeed, is one of the Seminar's vaunted "seven pillars of scholarly wisdom."[25] But here we see quite sharply, what we shall observe in more detail presently: the Seminar's method has not been to examine each saying all by itself and decide about it, but to start with a fairly clear picture of Jesus and early Christianity, and simply run through the material imposing this picture on the texts.

All Cats Are Gray in the Dark

A note, next, on the color-coding of the sayings. This is clearly meant to convey a definite and precise meaning. The "ordinary reader," browsing through *The Five Gospels*, picks up quite quickly that red or pink is a quite rare accolade, that black is common, and that gray, close enough (it seems) to black, also dominates at several points. The book's cover reflects something of this balance, with a small red box on a large black background, and in the small red box the words "WHAT DID JESUS REALLY SAY?" It seems fairly clear that red denotes what Jesus said, black what he did not, and that pink and gray are softer variants on these two.

Not so simple, however. The voting system was quite complex.[26] There are two cumbersome sets of "meanings" for the four colors, and an intricate system of numberings for the votes, which were then averaged out. This means that in any given case, especially in relation to pink and gray, the color on the page does not represent what "scholars," even the small selection of scholarly opinion represented in the Seminar, actually think. A pink vote almost certainly means that, on the one hand, a sizeable minority believed Jesus actually said these words, while a substantial minority were convinced, or nearly convinced, that he did not. Most, in fact, did not vote pink; yet that is what appears on the page. (I am reminded of the notorious funda-

---

25   Funk and Hoover (eds.), *The Five Gospels*, 3. The sayings of Jesus in John are voted almost uniformly black, with 4:43 a solitary pink ("a prophet gets no respect on his own turf"), 12:24-25 and 13:20 a lonely pair of grays ("unless the kernel of wheat falls to the earth and dies . . ." and "if they welcome the person I send, they welcome me . . .").

26   Described in Funk and Hoover (eds.), *The Five Gospels*, 34-37.

mentalist attempts to harmonize how many times the rooster crowed when Peter denied Jesus. One of the only ways of doing it is to say that the rooster crowed, not three, but nine times. Thus a supposed doctrine of scriptural inerrancy is "preserved"—at the enormous cost of saying that what actually happened *is what none of the texts record*.) Thus, the Jesus Seminar could print a text in pink or gray, *even though the great majority of the Seminar voted red or black.* The colors, especially the two middle ones, cannot be taken as more than an averaging out of widely divergent opinion. It is perfectly possible that the color on the page, if gray or pink, is one for which nobody voted at all.

In particular, the gray sayings conceal a very interesting phenomenon. Spies on the Seminar report that in some cases the gray verdict could be seen as a victory—for those who, against the grain of the Seminar, think Jesus might well have said the words concerned. Take Luke 19:42-44 for an example. This stern warning about the coming destruction of Jerusalem fits with an "apocalyptic" strand of teaching which, in almost all other cases, the Fellows of the Seminar voted black by a substantial margin. But on this occasion a paper was given arguing that the words could indeed have been spoken by Jesus. Enough Fellows were persuaded by this to pull the vote up to gray— a quite remarkable victory for those who voted red or pink. Seen from within the Seminar, where a good number start with the assumption that virtually no sayings go back to Jesus himself, gray can thus mean "well, maybe there is a possibility after all . . ." Seen from outside, of course—in other words, from the perspective of those for whom the Seminar's products, particularly this book, are designed—it conveys a very different message, namely "probably not."

Another example of this occurs in the summary account of the vote on Matt 18:3 ("If you don't do an about-face and become like children, you will never enter Heaven's domain"). The following is typical of literally dozens of passages:

> The opinion was evenly divided. Some red and a large number of pink votes, in favor of authenticity, were offset by substantial gray and black votes. The result was a compromise gray designation for this version and all its parallels.[27]

Or again, in dealing with the Parable of the Two Sons, and the

---

27   Funk and Hoover (eds.), *The Five Gospels*, 213.

subsequent saying (Matt 21:28-31a and 21:31b):

> Fifty-eight percent of the Fellows voted red or pink for the parable, 53
> percent for the saying in v. 31b. A substantial number of gray and black
> votes pulled the weighted average into the gray category.[28]

Without using a pocket calculator, I confess I cannot understand
how, if a majority in each case thought the saying authentic or probably authentic, the "weighted average" turned out to be "probably
inauthentic." A voting system that produces a result like this ought to
be scrapped. The average reader, seeing the passage printed as gray,
will conclude that "scholars" think it is probably inauthentic; whereas, even with the small company of the Seminar, the majority would
clearly disagree.[29]

In evaluating the color scheme, therefore, it is important not to
think that consensus has been reached. The Seminar's voting methods
and results remind one somewhat of Italian politics: with propor-
tional representation, everybody's votes count to some extent, but the
result is serious instability. Gray and pink sayings are like the smile
on a politician's face when a deal has been struck between minority
parties; the informed observer knows that the coalition is a patch-up
job, which will not stand the test of time. The reader, particularly
the reader outside the scholarly guild, should beware. This volume is
only a snapshot of what some scholars think within one particular
context and after a certain set of debates. But even the snapshot is out
of focus, and the colors have been affected by the process of development. This may be fine if what one wants is an impressionistic idea
of the state of play. But the Seminar promises, and claims to offer,
much more than that. It claims to tell the unvarnished truth. And
therein lies the sixth and final point for comment at this stage.

Jumping on the Bandwagon after the Wheels Came Off

Perhaps the deepest flaw in terms of apparent method is that this
book appeals constantly, as does all the literature of the Jesus Seminar, to the possibility that by the application of supposedly scientific
or "scholarly" criteria one will arrive at a definite answer to the
question as to what Jesus actually said. This jumps out of the very

---

[28]   Funk and Hoover (eds.), *The Five Gospels*, 232.

[29]   See also Funk and Hoover (eds.), *The Five Gospels*, 250, on Matt 24:32-
33: 54% voted either red or pink, but a 35% black vote resulted in a gray compromise (for which, apparently, only the remaining 11% had voted).

cover of the book: the subtitle ("The Search for the Authentic Words of Jesus") has the word "authentic" underlined, and the sub-subtitle, "What did Jesus Really Say?" is clearly intended to emphasize the "really." The whole enterprise seems to offer the possibility of objectivity certainty, of methods which will produce results as watertight as $2 + 2 = 4$.

The puzzle about this is that it buys heavily into exactly the sort of positivism that is now routinely abandoned by the great majority of scholars working in the fields of history and texts—including by several members of the Jesus Seminar themselves. The idea that by historical investigation one might arrive at a position of unbiased objective certainty, of absolute unconditioned knowledge, about anything, has been shot to pieces by critiques from a variety of points of view. All knowledge is conditioned by the context and agenda of the knower; all reconstructions are somebody's reconstructions, and each "somebody" sees the world through their own eyes and not their neighbor's. This is so widely acknowledged that one would have thought it unnecessary to state, let alone to stress. The positivistic bandwagon got stuck in the mud some time ago, and a succession of critics, looking back to Marx, Nietzsche and Frend but now loosely gathered under the umbrella of postmodernism, has cheerfully pulled its wheels off altogether. This, of course, has not filtered through to the popular media, who still want to know whether something "actually happened" or not. The Jesus Seminar, in its desire to go public with the results of scholarship, has apparently been lured into giving the public what it wants, rather than what scholarship can in fact provide. As the previous discussion about voting and color-coding makes clear, the one thing this book cannot offer is an answer to the question on its front cover. All it can do is to report, in a manner that will often mislead the ordinary reader, what some scholars think Jesus may have said.

At this point some members of the Seminar will want to protest. They know very well that positivism is a dead-end street. They fully appreciate that most of the color-codings, especially the pink and gray, are compromise solutions hiding a good deal of debate and uncertainty. Unfortunately, such subtleties were totally lost on whoever wrote the blurb on the back of the book, which encourages the average reader, for whom the book is designed, to assume that the colors in the book provide certain, objective, copper-bottomed, positivistic answers:

> Did Jesus really give the Sermon on the Mount? Is the Lord's Prayer composed of his authentic words? *THE FIVE GOSPELS* answers these questions in a bold, dynamic work that will startle the world of traditional biblical interpretation . . . In pursuit of the historical Jesus, [the scholars] used their collective expertise to determine the authenticity of the more than 1,500 sayings attributed to him. Their remarkable findings appear in this book . . .

> Only those sayings that appear in red type are considered by the Seminar to be close to what Jesus actually said . . . *According to the Seminar, no more than 20 percent of the sayings attributed to Jesus were uttered by him* . . .[30]

Underneath the rhetoric about making the results of scholarship generally available, therefore, we find a new form of an old divide between the scholars and the simple folk. The introduction to this book castigates those scholars who "knew" of the problems about finding the historical Jesus (not to mention the Christ of the church's faith), but who kept these "findings" from the public, who wanted to have their fragile faith confirmed. The Seminar claims to have bridged this divide. But then the Seminar, whose members clearly know that their own work is culture-conditioned, and that the color-coding system repeatedly hides compromise and serious disagreement, keeps these facts from its own public, which wants to have *its fragile faith in positivism* supported and confirmed. At this meta-level, encouraging the reading public to think that the old Enlightenment bandwagon is still rolling along, when in fact the wheels came off it some time ago, is just as irresponsible as the preacher who hides from the congregation the fact that there are serious questions to be faced about the origin and nature of early Christianity.

This is not to say, of course, that all "results" of Jesus-scholarship are tenuous and uncertain. There is such a thing as genuine historical knowledge, and it does allow us to make definite claims about Jesus. But it is not to be attained by the route of positivism, still less by the dubious method of vote-taking within a small circle of scholars. It is to be attained by the route of critical realism—a historical method which proceeds, not by atomistic discussion of isolated elements, but by the serious process of hypothesis and verification, during which the perspective of the historian is itself taken into account. I have written about this elsewhere.[31] A good many scholars are pursuing

---

30   The emphasis is in the original.
31   Wright, *The New Testament and the People of God*, 81-120.

this path to a lesser or greater extent. The Jesus Seminar has chosen not to do so.

TOWARDS A NEW PORTRAIT

The introduction to the book contains a lengthy section (pp. 16-34) setting out the "rules of written evidence" and "the rules of oral evidence" which the Seminar formulated and adopted for use in its work. There are thirty-six of these "rules." But again and again throughout the book, the "rules" boil down to three guiding principles which are wheeled out almost ad nauseam as the justification for accepting, or more usually for rejecting, a particular saying or set of sayings.

These three actual guiding principles may be formulated as follows. First, the Seminar in fact presupposes a particular portrait of Jesus. Second, the Seminar adopts a particular, and highly misleading, position about eschatology and apocalyptic, particularly about the kingdom of God; this too was presupposed. Third, the Seminar assumes a particular picture of the early church, especially its interest in and transmission of material about Jesus. In each case there is every reason to reject the principle in question. We must look at each in turn.

Jesus the Distinctive Sage

As we just saw, the explicit intention of the Seminar was to examine all the sayings and vote on them one by one, allowing a portrait of Jesus to emerge slowly and bit by bit. Thus, for instance, the editors can speak of Matt 7:16b, which was voted pink, as being placed "into the red/pink database *for determining who Jesus was*" (p. 157, emphasis added). But what has in fact happened is exactly the reverse. For the majority of Fellows at least, what comes first is an assumption about who Jesus really was, which is then used as the yardstick for measuring, and often ruling out, a good many sayings.

This assumption focusses on the portrait of Jesus as a "traveling sage and wonder-worker" (p. 128). Sayings can be assessed according to whether they fit with this.[32] The Fellows, or at least their spokespersons in this volume, somehow know that Jesus is a "reticent sage who does not initiate debate or offer to cast out demons, and

---

[32]   For example, see Funk and Hoover (eds.), *The Five Gospels*, 326, on "daily bread" in the Matthean and Lukan versions of the Lord's Prayer.

who does not speak of himself in the first person" (p. 265). On this basis they feel able to make judgments about sayings which, since they make Jesus do some of these things, cannot be his. As a reticent sage, Jesus "did not formally enlist followers" (p. 284); he used secular proverbs, having "perhaps acquired his knowledge of common lore from itinerant philosophers who visited Galilee while he was growing up" (p. 287). He does not, however, quote the Hebrew scriptures very often (pp. 376, 380), so that when we find such quotations attributed to him, they almost certainly come from the early church, which, unlike Jesus, was very concerned to understand his work in the light of the scriptures.

As a reticent sage, Jesus did not, of course, predict his own death (pp. 94, 208, and very frequently); still less did he refer to himself in any way as Messiah or Son of God (pp. 75, 312, and regularly). Among the reasons given for this latter assumption is the remarkable argument:

> Jesus taught that the last will be first and the first will be last. He admonished his followers to be servants of everyone. He urged humility as the cardinal virtue by both word and example. Given these terms, it is difficult to imagine Jesus making claims for himself . . . unless, of course, he thought that nothing he said applied to himself.[33]

What the writers seem to ignore is precisely that Jesus taught these things. By what right? Even at the level of teaching, Jesus' words carry an implicit self-reference. When we put even a small amount of his teaching into its first-century Jewish context (see below), it was inevitable that questions should be asked about who he thought he was; and virtually inevitable that he would reflect on such a question himself. Instead of this context, however, the Seminar's spokespersons offer one that may perhaps be thought just a little anachronistic:

> Like the cowboy hero of the American West exemplified by Gary Cooper, the sage of the ancient Near East was laconic, slow to speech, a person of few words. The sage does not provoke encounters . . . As a rule, the sage is self-effacing, modest, unostentatious.[34]

Jesus, then, was not aware that he had a specific mission to carry out (p. 70). He did not organize "formal missions" (p. 311). He was not "given to institution building" (p. 213). The older liberalism was right after all: Jesus' teaching was about being nice to people, not

---

33   Funk and Hoover (eds.), *The Five Gospels*, 33.
34   Funk and Hoover (eds.), *The Five Gospels*, 32.

about warning them of punishment in store for the wicked (pp. 170, 181, 289-90, 320, and frequently).[35]

In particular, when Jesus did speak it was almost always in pithy, subversive, disturbing aphorisms. (This, of course, was the presupposition for the Seminar's whole enterprise, of breaking up the text into isolated sayings and voting separately on them.) Thus, in rejecting Luke 22:36-37, the editors comment: "there is nothing in the words attributed to Jesus that cuts against the social grain, that would surprise or shock his friends, or that reflects exaggeration, humor, or paradox . . . [thus] nothing in this passage commends itself as authentically from Jesus" (p. 391). Proverbs that "are not particularly vivid or provocative" or which "do not surprise or shock" "belong to the stock of common lore and so are not of Jesus' invention" (p. 157). It is admitted that Jesus could have used such proverbs, but again and again they attract a gray or black vote.[36]

The Seminar claims, then, that a portrait of Jesus "begins to emerge" from their work at certain points (p. 340). Not so. The portrait was in the mind all along. It is, for the most part, a shallow and one-dimensional portrait, developed through anachronistic parallels (the laconic cowboy) and ignoring the actual first-century context. Its attractive and indeed sometimes compelling features, of Jesus as the subversive sage, challenging the status quo with teasing epigrams and parables, has been achieved at the huge cost of

---

35   The Seminar nevertheless held, we are told, that the judgmental sayings in Matt 11:21-14 (for example) were uttered by a Christian prophet "speaking in the spirit and the name of Jesus" (Funk and Hoover [eds.], *The Five Gospels*, 181; cf. 320). We are to assume, it seems, that the prophet in question misunderstood that spirit, and misused that name, quite drastically. "Jesus . . . would not have told Capernaum to go to Hell after instructing his disciples to love their enemies" (p. 320). This touching naivety is rightly questioned at 214: "prophetic anger does not entirely contradict the injunction to love one's enemies. It is possible for the two to be combined in one person."

36   There seems to be an added confusion at this point. According to all the Seminar's literature, the voting was supposed to be on the question of whether Jesus said things, not on where he was the first to say them. But frequently the votes seem to have reflected the latter point instead: e.g. Funk and Hoover (eds.), *The Five Gospels*, 106, 168, 176, 240, 298-99, 337 and elsewhere. This produces a strange heads-I-win/tails-you-lose situation. The secular, non-Jewish sages who (according to the Seminar) may have influenced Jesus in his early days provide us, we are told, with the model for how he spoke. But if a saying looks as though it came from such common stock, it still does not attract a pink or red vote.

screening out a whole range of material which several of the leading Jesus-scholars around the world, in major, serious, and contemporary works of historical reconstruction, would regard as absolutely central. By far the most important of these is the material often designated "apocalyptic"; and, within that, Jesus' announcement of the kingdom of God—or, as the Seminar often puts it, "heaven's imperial rule." The rejection of this material is the largest and most central presupposition that the Seminar brings to its entire work, and it deserves a separate section.

The Resolutely Non-Apocalyptic Jesus

The most thoroughgoing way in which the Seminar applies the criterion of dissimilarity, according to which Jesus stands out from his surrounding context, is in relation to apocalyptic. Here this reader at least had a strange sense of *déjà vu*. Nearly three decades ago Klaus Koch wrote a book describing, among other things, what he called "the agonised attempt to save Jesus from apocalyptic."[37] Albert Schweitzer, at the turn of the century, had described Jesus as an apocalyptic visionary; many theologians after Schweitzer found this too much to stomach, and neatly extracted Jesus from his surrounding Jewish, and apocalyptic, context. This was normally done for apologetic motives: if Jesus predicted the end of the world, he was wrong, and this has serious implications for Christology.

The Jesus Seminar, of course, harbors no such motive. Instead, it has a different one, no less all-pervading: Jesus must not in any way appear to give sanction to contemporary apocalyptic preaching, such as that on offer in the fundamentalist movements against which the Seminar is reacting so strongly. Jesus must not, therefore, have supposed that the end of the world was at hand, or that God was about to judge people, or that the Son of Man (whom the Seminar persists in misleadingly calling the Son of Adam) would shortly "come on the clouds." All these things form the scriptural basis for much stock-in-trade fundamentalist preaching; the Seminar therefore wishes to rule them out of court.[38] The older flight from apocalyptic was designed

---

[37] K. Koch, *The Rediscovery of Apocalyptic: A Polemical Work on a Neglected Area of Biblical Studies and its Damaging Effects on Theology and Philosophy* (SBT 2.22; London: SCM, 1972 [German original, 1970]).

[38] Any who think this analysis over-suspicious should spend half a day reading through the Seminar's journal *Forum: Foundations and Facets*, and the work of Burton Mack in particular, which was heavily influential on the Seminar's decisions

to save orthodox Christianity; the newer one is designed to subvert it.

But, though the motive is different, the effect is the same. Although John the Baptist is described as "the precursor and mentor of Jesus" (p. 128), Jesus' own ministry and message were utterly distinct. John pronounced apocalyptic-style warnings of impending judgment; Jesus did not. Likewise, the very early church (though not the Seminar's hypothetical early Q, and not *Thomas*) reinterpreted Jesus' sayings in an apocalyptic style which distorted Jesus' own intention. Thus Matt 10:7, in which Jesus tells the disciples to announce that "Heaven's imperial rule is closing in," is an "apocalyptically oriented summary," which "was not, however, the point of view of Jesus" (p. 168). So, too, the warnings of judgment on cities that rejected the disciples are "alien to Jesus, although not to the early disciples, who may have reverted to John the Baptist's apocalyptic message and threat of judgment, or they may simply have been influenced by apocalyptic ideas that were everywhere in the air" (p. 169).

Stated as baldly as this, the agenda is exposed for what it is: a further agonized attempt to rescue Jesus from contamination with the dreaded "apocalyptic." By what means does the Seminar know, *a priori*, that Jesus so firmly rejected something which was "everywhere in the air," which was absolutely central to the work of John, who is acknowledged as Jesus' "precursor and mentor," and which was fundamental, in some shape or form, to all forms of early Christianity known to us—except, of course, to the *Thomas* collection? (We had better leave the doubly hypothetical "Early Q" out of account, since the only reason for inventing a non-apocalyptic "Early Q," when so many "apocalyptic" sayings are in the Matthew/Luke parallels upon which the Q hypothesis rests, is the very assumption we are examining, that Jesus and one strand of his followers did not make use of this world of thought.) If almost everyone else thought and spoke like that, how do they know that Jesus did not?[39] The

---

at this point; cf. B. L. Mack, "The Kingdom Sayings in Mark," *Forum* 3 (1987) 3-47; idem, *A Myth of Innocence.*

[39]   See also Funk and Hoover (eds.), *The Five Gospels,* 112, where the comment (on Mark 13:14-20) that "almost anyone could have formulated these warnings" is followed at once by the report of near-unanimity among the Fellows that "Jesus was not the author of any of these sayings." In place of the distinctive Jesus of some traditional Christology, who stood out from everyone else because of his divinity, we have the distinctive Jesus of the Seminar, who was certainly

answer is that they do not. This "conclusion" was, in their phrase, "in the air" from the inception of the Seminar. It was a starting point, not a result. It may even, we may suspect, have been one of the reasons why the Seminar came into existence in the first place.

But this view of apocalyptic, and of Jesus' participation in it, can be controverted again and again by serious study of the first-century phenomenon which goes by that name. I have argued in detail elsewhere, in line with a fair amount of contemporary scholarship, that "apocalyptic" is best understood as a complex metaphor-system through which many Jews of the period expressed their aspirations, not for other-worldly bliss, nor for a "big bang" which would end the space-time world, but for social, political, and above all theological liberation.[40] This enables us to affirm that Schweitzer and others were absolutely right to see Jesus as part of apocalyptic Judaism, while denying Schweitzer's unhistorical notion (shared, of course, by fundamentalists) that apocalyptic language was designed to be taken literally. The Seminar is fighting a shadow.

In particular, the language of the Kingdom of God has been studied in great detail by scholars with far more awareness of the first-century Jewish context than is evident in the present book.[41] There is no sign that this scholarship has been even noted, let alone taken seriously, by the Seminar. Instead, there is a persistent and muddled repetition of outdated and/or naive points of view:

> Mark 13 is an apocalypse (an apocalypse tells of events that are to take place at the end of history. In Mark's version, the end of history will occur when the son of Adam appears on the clouds and gathers God's chosen people from the ends of the earth). This and related themes make Mark 13 sound much like the Book of Revelation . . .

> A notable feature of early Christian instruction is that teaching about last

---

incapable of saying things that almost anyone else at the time might have said. This is almost a secular version of the Docetic heresy.

40   Wright, *The New Testament and the People of God*, 280-338.

41   For details, see e.g. (among a great many) B. Chilton (ed.), *The Kingdom of God in the Teaching of Jesus* (IRT 5; London: SPCK; Philadelphia: Fortress, 1984); idem, *God in Strength: Jesus' Announcement of the Kingdom* (SNTU 1; Freistadt: Plöchl, 1979; repr. BibSem 8; Sheffield: JSOT Press, 1987); G. R. Beasley-Murray, *Jesus and the Kingdom of God* (Grand Rapids: Eerdmans, 1986); R. S. Barbour (ed.), *The Kingdom of God and Human Society: Essays by Members of the Scripture, Theology and Society Group* (Edinburgh: T. & T. Clark, 1993); and the discussions in the other works about Jesus referred to above in n. 2.

things (termed *eschatology*) occurs at the conclusion of the catechism or manual of instruction. Paul tended to put such matters toward the close of his letters, for example, in 1 Thess 5:1-13 and 1 Corinthians 15. In the second-century Christian manual known as the Didache, instruction in eschatology also comes last, in chapter 16.

Mark thus appropriatedly makes Jesus' discourse on last things his final public discourse . . .[42]

An apocalypse is a form of literature in which a human agent is guided on an otherworldly tour by means of visions. On that tour, the agent learns about a supernatural world unknown to ordinary folk, and the secrets of the future are also revealed . . .

The so-called little apocalypse assembled by Mark in chapter 13, and copied by Matthew and Luke, is not actually an apocalypse in form. But it has the same function . . .[43]

The comment about Paul shows, as clearly as anything else, the shallow and largely spurious level of analysis employed here. Paul is just as capable of talking about (what we call) "the last things" at other points in his letters (e.g. 2 Corinthians 5). And the whole statement —it is hardly an argument—is designed to minimize the role of "apocalyptic" in the Gospel accounts, isolating Mark 13 and its parallels from the rest of the text, in a way which, as the last comment quoted tacitly admits, does great violence both to that chapter and to the rest of the synoptic tradition.[44]

It is with discussion of the Kingdom of God (or whatever it is to be called; "Heaven's Imperial Rule" does have the virtue of jolting or confronting a contemporary reader in a way that "Kingdom of God" has largely ceased to do) that the problem is focussed most clearly. The "cameo essay" on the subject (pp. 136-37) is extremely revealing; and what it reveals is a string of misunderstandings, prejudices, and false antitheses.

The essay sets out four categories. First, there is the preaching of John the Baptist. Second, there are sayings of Jesus which speak of God's rule as future. Third, there are sayings of Jesus which speak of God's rule as present. Fourth, there is a passage from Paul. Already there are problems. (a) The passage quoted from John the Baptist (Matt 3:7, 10) does not mention the Kingdom of God, and in any

---

42   Funk and Hoover (eds.), *The Five Gospels*, 107

43   Funk and Hoover (eds.), *The Five Gospels*, 246.

44   See Wright, *The New Testament and the People of God*, 394-95.

case would be regarded by many as a later formulation, not necessarily giving us access to John himself. (b) The main passage quoted as an example of sayings of Jesus about God's future rule is Mark 13:24-27 and 30, which again does not mention the Kingdom of God, but speaks instead of the son of man coming on the clouds. (c) One of the passages quoted as illustrating sayings of Jesus about God's rule as present in Luke 11:2, which is the petition from the Lord's Prayer, here translated as "Impose your imperial rule." If this indicates that the kingdom is already present, why is one commanded to pray for it as though it were not yet here? (d) The single passage quoted from Paul is 1 Thess 4:15-17, which says nothing about the Kingdom of God, but speaks of the dead rising, the Lord descending, and the living Christians being caught up in the air. There are, of course, passages in Paul which speak explicitly about the Kingdom of God, and in some that kingdom is a present reality (e.g. Rom 14:17). The only reason I can imagine for quoting 1 Thessalonians 4 in this context is that the author of the essay is assuming an equation between "future Kingdom of God" and "end-time apocalyptic events," and taking passages about the latter, which fundamentalists have interpreted in a particular way (e.g. the "rapture") as expressions of this "apocalyptic" view of the kingdom. But each stage in this line of thought is quite unwarranted. Indeed, the author of the essay more or less agrees with the fundamentalist interpretation of the key texts, in order then to dismiss them as indices of Jesus' mind.

The discussion which follows the citation of these texts poses an utterly spurious either-or:

> Does this phrase [Kingdom of God] refer to God's direct intervention in the future, something connected with the end of the world and the last judgment, or did Jesus employ the phrase to indicate something already present and of more elusive nature?

> The first of these options is usually termed apocalyptic, a view fully expressed in the book of Revelation, which is an apocalypse.[45]

Here we have it: "apocalyptic" is, more or less, "that which fundamentalists believe about the end of the world." The author seems to imply that the fundamentalists have actually read some of the texts correctly. So much the worse for the texts; clearly the Seminar is going to take a different view, which will involve ditching those wicked "apocalyptic" ideas and setting up its own alternative. But if

---

45 Funk and Hoover (eds.), *The Five Gospels*, 37.

this loaded argument functions like a shopkeeper putting extra weights onto the scales, what follows is the equivalent of leaning on them with both elbows:

> Did Jesus share this [apocalyptic] view, or was his vision more subtle, less bombastic and threatening?
>
> The Fellows . . . are inclined to the second option: Jesus conceived of God's rule as all around him but difficult to discern . . . But Jesus' uncommon views were obfuscated by the more pedestrian conceptions of John, on the one hand, and by the equally pedestrian views of the early Christian community, on the other.[46]

As we saw before, Jesus seems to have been radically different from his "predecessor and mentor," and was radically misunderstood by almost all his followers from the very beginning. In particular, despite the other passages (e.g. p. 7) in which the authors regard Paul as the great Hellenizer, or gnosticizer, of the gospel, they wheel him out this time as another representative of Jewish-style apocalyptic:

> The views of John the Baptist and Paul are apocalyptically oriented. The early church aside from Paul shares Paul's view. The only question is whether the set of texts that represent God's rule as present were obfuscated by the pessimistic apocalyptic notions of Jesus' immediate predecessors, contemporaries, and successors.[47]

"Apocalyptic," then, is unsubtle, bombastic, threatening, obfuscatory, pedestrian, and pessimistic—and shared by everybody from John the Baptist through to the early church, apart from Jesus himself. This picture is then fitted into the broader old-liberal agenda, as follows: future-kingdom sayings are about judgment and condemnation, while Jesus instead offered forgiveness, mercy, and inclusiveness.[48] The evidenced adduced to support this astonishing piece of rhetoric—and this remarkably old-fashioned, almost pre-Schweitzer, view of Jesus —is the existence of texts about the Kingdom as a present reality, such as Luke 17:20-21, 11:20, and *Thomas* §113. In addition, the parables are supposed to represent the kingdom as a present, rather than a future, reality. The Jesus Seminar therefore voted "present-kingdom" sayings pink,[49] and "future-kingdom" sayings black. It was

---

46   Funk and Hoover (eds.), *The Five Gospels*, 137.

47   Funk and Hoover (eds.), *The Five Gospels*, 137.

48   Funk and Hoover (eds.), *The Five Gospels*, 157

49   For example, *Thomas* §113: the explicit reason given for the vote is that this saying provides "a counterweight to the view that Jesus espoused popular apocalypticism" (Funk and Hoover [eds.], *The Five Gospels*, 531). Here, no doubt, is

as easy as that.

I have to say that if I had been served up this "cameo essay" by a first-year undergraduate, I would quickly have deduced that the student, while very ingenious, was unfamiliar both with some of the basic secondary discussions of the topic,[50] and, more damaging still, with the meaning of the primary texts in their first-century context. The determination to rule fundamentalism off the map altogether has so dominated the discussion (if not the Seminar itself, at least in this apparently authoritative interpretation of its work) that texts of great subtlety and variety have been forced into a tight and utterly spurious either/or and played off against one another. It would be one thing to find a student doing this. When two senior academics do it, after having gone on record as saying that "critical scholars practice their craft by submitting their work to the judgment of peers," while "non-critical scholars are those who put dogmatic considerations first and insist that the factual evidence confirm theological premises,"[51] the uncomfortable suspicion is aroused that it is the latter description, not the former, that fits the work we have in our hands. Sadly, this suspicion can only be confirmed by the bombastic, threatening and utterly pedestrian nature of the discussion itself.

There is, of course, a good deal more to be said about the Kingdom of God in the teaching of Jesus. There is need for much discussion and careful reconstruction. This, however, cannot be the place for it. We conclude that, when it comes to the central theme of the teaching of Jesus, the Seminar, at least as reported in this volume (and with dissentient voices drowned out by the voting averages and by those who voted black for everything on principle), allowed itself to make

---

one of the real reasons for the Seminar's long-running love-affair with *Thomas*: the collecton offers apparent historical grounds for dumping apocalyptic.

[50] For example, G. E. Ladd, *Jesus and the Kingdom: The Eschatology of Biblical Realism* (London: SPCK, 1966); Chilton (ed.), *The Kingdom of God*; idem, *God in Strength*; Beasley-Murray, *Jesus and the Kingdom*; Barbour (ed.), *The Kingdom of God*; and the many recent discussion of the parables, e.g. M. Boucher, *The Mysterious Parable: A Literary Study* (CBQMS 6; Washington: Catholic Biblical Association, 1977); K. E. Bailey, *Poet and Peasant/Through Peasant Eyes* (Grand Rapids: Eerdmans, 1983); J. Drury, *The Parables in the Gospels: History and Allegory* (London: SPCK, 1985). The major earlier discussions, involving such magisterial figures as Dodd and Jeremias, might as well not have happened.

[51] Funk and Hoover (eds.), *The Five Gospels*, 34.

its key decisions on the basis of an ill-informed and ill-advised disjunction between two ill-defined types of kingdom-sayings. The entire history of debate this century on the subject of Jesus and eschatology goes by the board. It is one thing to disagree with the line of thought running, broadly, from Schweitzer to Sanders. It is something else to ignore it altogether. Eschatology and apocalyptic, and "Kingdom of God" within that, has here been misunderstood, misanalyzed, and wrongly marginalized.

Two tail-pieces to this discussion: first, the effect of the Seminar's portrait of Jesus at this point is to minimalize his Jewishness. The authors claim, of course, that Jesus was "not the first Christian" (p. 24); that is, he does not belong to the Christian movement, but (presumably) to Judaism. But only minimally—if the Seminar's analysis of "Kingdom of God" were to be accepted. Quite unintentionally, of course, the Seminar has reproduced one of the most dubious features of the older liberal picture of Jesus. Judaism only appears as the dark backcloth against which the jewel of Jesus' message—not now as a *Christian* message, but as a subversive, present-kingdom, almost proto-gnostic, possibly-Cynic, laconic-cowboy message—shines the more brightly. We do not actually know anything about wandering pagan philosophers whom Jesus might have met in the days of his youth. There is no evidence for them. But they are brought in of necessity; otherwise one might have to admit that Jesus' language about the Kindom of God was thoroughly Jewish, and belonged within the Jewish setting and aspirations of his day.

At the same time, the authors are clearly anxious not to play Jesus off against "Jews." They are very much aware that some allegorical readings of Jesus' teaching have produced tragic consequences for Jewish-Christian relations (p. 234). They are so coy about using the word "Jew" that they insist on saying "Judean" instead—even, amusingly, when the Jews in question are mostly Galileans, not Judeans at all (e.g. p. 168). But they seem unaware that, within our own century, the attempt to paint Judaism as dark, pessimistic, bombastic, pedestrian religion, expecting a great and cataclysmic final judgment, and to paint Jesus as having countered this by offering (the supposedly unJewish message of) mercy and love and forgiveness, has itself generated tragic consequences.

Second, there are all sorts of signs that the authors, representing some but surely not all of the Seminar, simply do not understand how first-century Judaism, in all its plurality, works. The discussion of "hallowed be your name" in Matt 6:9 implies that there is a paradox in Jesus using the form "Abba" and then asking "that the name be regarded as sacred" (p. 149). There may, no doubt, be a paradox there, but not at that simplistic level. The point of asking that the divine name be hallowed is, as has very often been pointed out, that the name is hallowed when the people of God are vindicated, rescued from their enemies. This discussion is sadly typical of many points where quite basic perspectives on central texts seem to be ignored altogether. Thus, for instance, we read that Luke 23:31 ("if they do this when the wood is green, what will they do when it is dry?") is enigmatic, which is undoubtedly true. But then, when the authors say "no one knows what it means, although it, too, must have something to do with the fall of Jerusalem" (pp. 395-96), one wonders if they bothered to check any of the major commentaries.

In particular, the authors offer (p. 242) a brief discussion of first-century Pharisaism, in order to substantiate the Seminar's decision to cast black votes for most of the sayings in Matthew 23. They repeat uncritically the line which Sanders took from Morton Smith, though there was never much evidence for it and always plenty against it: the Pharisees were based in Judea, not Galilee, so Jesus may not have come into contact with them or even known much about them (pp. 242, 244).[52] This is backed up in a way which neither Sanders nor Smith suggests: "The teachings of the rabbis in Jesus' day were all circulated by word of mouth; it was not until the third century C.E. that rabbinic traditions took written form in the Mishnah." This last statement is of course true, but totally irrelevant, implying as it does that word-of-mouth circulation would be a casual, inefficient, uncertain thing, so that, lacking written texts, Jesus would not have known much about Pharisaic teaching. As we shall see presently, however, in a substantially oral culture, oral teaching will have circulated far more widely, and far more effectively, than written texts.

The authors further suggest that the Pharisees became the dominant party after the fall of Jerusalem, and that "at the council of Jamnia,

---

52 See Sanders, *Jesus and Judaism*; M. Smith, "Palestinian Judaism in the First Century," in H. Fischel (ed.), *Essays in Greco-Roman and Related Talmudic Literature* (New York: Ktav, 1977) 183-97. Sanders (*The Historical Figure*) has toned this right down, perhaps as a result of his further researches reflected in his *Judaism: Practice and Belief, 63 BCE–66 CE* (London: SCM; Philadelphia: Trinity Press International, 1992). For discussion, see Wright, *The New Testament and the People of God*, 181-203; on this point, see esp. 195-96.

in 90 C.E., the Pharisees laid the foundations for the survival of Judaism in its modern form—rabbinic Judaism." Meanwhile, even in the last quarter of the first century, the "emerging church, in its Palestinian and Syrian locales, was still largely a sectarian movement within Judaism."

All this comprises so many half-truths and inaccuracies that one is tempted to wonder whether it is worth reading further in a book supposedly about the first century.[53] It is highly likely that the Pharisees were already very influential, quite possibly the most influential group, within the pluriform Judaism of the pre-70 period. The group that became dominant after 70 was one variety of Pharisees, namely the Hillelites, over against another variety, the Shammaites. But even this was not achieved overnight; it was only with the collapse of the second revolt, in 135, that the shift of influence was complete. In addition, our knowledge of the council of Jamnia is very nebulous; its date and achievements are very uncertain. The later rabbinic traditions about it are, most likely, far more heavily overlaid with subsequent reinterpretations than almost anything we find in the Gospels. To use it as a fixed point for establishing early Christian material is like a hiker taking a compass bearing on a sheep. Finally, we do not actually know very much at all about the church in Palestine and Syria in the last quarter of the century. What we do know is that a sharp division between the church, precisely in Palestine and Syria, and Pharisaic Judaism of the more zealous (i.e. Shammaite) variety had already taken place *in the first five years after Jesus' death*. We know this because of Saul of Tarsus, alias the apostle Paul, who, for neither the first nor the last time, puts a spoke in the wheel of the Jesus Seminar's speculative reconstructions of early Christianity.

Lest all these criticisms be misunderstood, I should stress: there is nothing wrong with trying to popularize the results of scholarship. Quick overviews of complex issues are necessary in such work. But popularization sometimes reveals crucial weaknesses which a more highflown and abstract language would have masked. So it is in this case. Serious contemporary research on first-century Judaisms by no means rules out the possibility, which must then be decided (and interpreted) on quite other grounds, that Jesus did come into sharp

---

53   On all of the following, see Wright, *The New Testament and the People of God*, 145-338.

confrontation with the Pharisees. What the discussion tells us is that the Seminar, or at least its spokespersons in this book, are not to be trusted to know their way around the details of the first century, which they are supposed to be describing.[54]

Oral Culture, Storytelling, and Isolated Sayings

The third driving principle behind a great many of the Seminar's decisions can be stated quite baldly.[55] It is assumed that only isolated sayings of Jesus circulated in the earliest post-Easter period. Unless a saying can be conceived as having enough intrinsic interest and, as it were, staying power to survive being passed on by word of mouth, all by itself and without any context, we can assume that it cannot be original to Jesus. Words of Jesus which fail this test, and which occur within more extended narratives, are simply part of the storyteller's art, or of the evangelist's theology.[56] This is, at its heart, an assumption about the nature of early Christianity.

Examples of this principle in operation could be picked from almost anywhere in the book's 500 and more pages. Here are some taken at random:

> The words ascribed to Jesus in this story [rebuking winds and wave; Mark 4:35-41] would not have circulated independently during the oral period; they reflect what the storyteller imagined Jesus would have said on such an occasion.[57]

> The stories Mark has collected in chapter five of his gospel contain words

---

[54] Compare Funk and Hoover (eds.), *The Five Gospels*, 362-63, where we are blithely told that "people in the ancient world" (which people? all people? Jews?) "though that the sky was held up by mountains that serve as pillars at the edge of the world." No doubt some people thought that. To offer it as an interpretative grid for a text in the Gospels (Luke 17:6, which is in any case about trees, not mountains) is rather like trying to interpret a Mozart opera by means of nuclear physics.

[55] See Funk and Hoover (eds.), *The Five Gospels*, 25-29, discussed below.

[56] Even at the level of reporting what is in the text, the Seminar's spokespersons here leave much to be desired. In Funk and Hoover (eds.), *The Five Gospels*, 210, commenting on Matthew's Transfiguration narrative (17:1-9), they declare that, by contrast with Matthew, "in Mark's version, Jesus says nothing at all," and say that in this respect Luke has followed Mark. However, in Mark 9:9 we find a saying of Jesus, parallel to that in Matt 17:9, but simply in indirect speech: "He instructed them not to describe what they had seen to anyone, until the son of Adam rise from the dead." Funk, as a grammarian, would surely acknowledge that *oratio obliqua* is still *oratio*.

[57] Funk and Hoover (eds.), *The Five Gospels*, 60

ascribed to Jesus that are suitable only for the occasion. They are not particularly memorable, are not aphorisms or parables, and would not have
circulated independently during the oral period. They cannot, therefore, be
traced back to Jesus.[58]

The words ascribed to Jesus [during the healing of the blind man in Mark
8:22-26] are the invention of the evangelist. Because they are incidental dialogue and not memorable pronouncements, they would not have been
remembered as exact words of Jesus.[59]

Jesus' public discourse is remembered to have consisted primarily of aphorisms, parables, or a challenge followed by a verbal retort. Matt 4:17 does
not fall into any of these categories.[60]

The remarks quoted from Jesus [in Matt 8:5-13] are intelligible only as part
of the narrative and could not have circulated as a separate saying apart from
this narrative context. They were accordingly voted black.[61]

The words attributed to Jesus in the story of the feeding of the crowd all
belong to the narrative texture of the story. They cannot be classified as
aphorisms or parables and so could not have circulated independently
during the oral period, 30–50 C.E. As a consequence, they cannot be traced
back to Jesus, but must have been created by the storyteller.[62]

The basis for these judgments is found in the extended discussion
or oral memory and tradition in the introduction (pp. 25-29). It is
impossible, without quoting the entire section and discussing it line
by line, to show the extent of the misunderstandings it reveals.
Though the authors regularly refer to oral cultures, the only actual
examples they give come from a very non-oral culture, that of their
own modern Western world.[63] Referring to what Thucydides says

---

[58]   Funk and Hoover (eds.), *The Five Gospels*, 62.

[59]   Funk and Hoover (eds.), *The Five Gospels*, 75.

[60]   Funk and Hoover (eds.), *The Five Gospels*, 134. Procrustes would have
been proud of this one.

[61]   Funk and Hoover (eds.), *The Five Gospels*, 160.

[62]   Funk and Hoover (eds.), *The Five Gospels*, 205, compare with 199-200.

[63]   "We" rephrase jokes and witticisms, such as those of Oscar Wilde (Funk
and Hoover [eds.], *The Five Gospels*, 27); "we know" that oral memory "retains
little else" other than sayings and anecdotes that are short, provocative, and memorable (p. 28); "recent experiments with memory" have reached various conclusions
about the capacity of memory, emphasizing that, though people remember the gist
of what was said, they do not recall the exact phrases. All of these examples are
100% irrelevant when we are considering a genuinely oral culture, such as still
exists in certain parts of the world, not least among peasant communities in the
Middle East. On the whole topic, see K. E. Bailey, "Informal Controlled Oral Tra-

about making up speeches to suit the occasion (p. 27) is not to the point; the speeches in question tend to be longer by far than any of Jesus' reported discourses, even the Sermon on the Mount and the Johannine "farewell discourses." In any case, Thucydides was a man of learning and letters, and to that extent less representative of a genuinely oral culture.

The theory that sayings, aphorisms, memorable oneliners, and sometimes parables are the things that survive, whereas *stories* about Jesus, with his words embedded within them, do not, is clearly promulgated with one eye on the results. "It is highly probable," we are told—this, recall, at the introductory level, before we have examined a single saying!—that the earliest layer of the Gospel tradition was made up almost entirely of single aphorisms and parables that circulated by word of mouth, without narrative context—precisely as that tradition is recorded in "Q" and *Thomas*.[64]

With the evidence thus well and truly cooked in advance, it is not surprising that the portrait of Jesus-the-quizzical-sage "emerges" from the subsequent discussion. It could not help doing so. The theory about what sort of material survives in oral tradition, I suggest, was designed to produce exactly this result.

Against this whole line of thought we must set the serious study of genuinely oral traditions that has gone on in various quarters recently.[65] Communities that live in an oral culture tend to be *storytelling* communities. They sit around in long evenings telling and listening to stories—the same stories, over and over again. Such stories, especially when they are involved with memorable happenings that have determined in some way the existence and life of the particular group in question, acquire a fairly fixed form, down to precise phraseology (in narrative as well as in recorded speech), extremely early in their life—often within a day or so of the original incident taking place. They retain that form, and phraseology, as long as they are told. Each village and community has its recognized

---

dition and the Synoptic Gospels," *Asia Journal of Theology* 5 (1991) 34-54.

64 Funk and Hoover (eds.), *The Five Gospels*, 28.

65 For example, see H. Wansbrough (ed.), *Jesus and the Oral Gospel Tradition* (JSNTSup 64; Sheffield: JSOT Press, 1991), referring to a large amount of earlier work; Bailey, "Informal Controlled Oral Tradition," 34-54. The following discussion depends on these and similar studies, and builds on Wright, *The New Testament and the People of God*, 418-43; and idem, *Jesus and the Victory of God*, 133-37.

storytellers, the accredited bearers of its traditions; but the whole community knows the stories by heart, and if the teller varies them even slightly they will let him know in no uncertain terms. This matters quite a lot in cultures where, to this day, the desire to avoid "shame" is a powerful motivation.

Such cultures do also repeat, and hence transmit, proverbs and pithy sayings. Indeed, they tend to know far more proverbs than the orally starved modern Western world. But the circulation of such individual sayings is only the tip of the iceberg; the rest is narrative, narrative with embedded dialogue, heard, repeated again and again within minutes, hours and days of the original incident, and fixed in memories the like of which few in the modern Western world can imagine. The storyteller in such a culture has no license to invent or adapt at will. The less important the story, the more adaptation may be possible; but the more important the story, the more the entire community, in a process that is informal but very effective, will keep a close watch on the precise form and wording with which the story is told.

And the stories about Jesus were nothing if not important. Even the Jesus Seminar admits that Jesus was an itinerant wonder-worker. Very well. Supposing a woman in a village is suddenly healed after a lengthy illness. Even today, even in a non-oral culture, the story of such an event would quickly spread among friends, neighbors and relatives, acquiring a fixed form within the first two or three retellings and retaining it, other things being equal, thereafter. In a culture where storytelling was and is an art-form, a memorable event such as this, especially if it were also seen as a sign that Israel's God was now at last at work to do what he had always promised, would be told at once in specific ways, told so as to be not just a celebration of a healing but also a celebration of the Kingdom of God. Events and stories of this order are community-forming, and the stories which form communities do not get freely or loosely adapted. One does not disturb the foundations of the house in which one is living.

What about detached aphorisms, then? Clearly, a memorable saying is a memorable saying, and could circulate independently. But what about sayings which sometimes have a context and sometimes not? I suggest that the following hypothesis is far more likely than that proposed by the Seminar.[66] It was only later, when the communities had been scattered through external circumstances (such as sundry persecutions, and the disastrous Jewish War of 66–70), that individual memorable sayings, which might very well have enjoyed a flourishing earlier life *within various narrative settings*, would become detached from those settings and become *chreiai*, isolated pithy sayings with minimal narrative context, such as we find (of course) in *Thomas*, and also to some extent in Luke. It is heavily ironic that the reason often given for supposing Luke's version of "Q" to be earlier than Matthew's is that Luke's versions of "Q" sayings are more chreia-like, while Matthew's are more embedded in Jewish, and often in narrative, contexts. Unless one had been fairly well brainwashed by the idea that Jesus-traditions consisted originally of non-Jewish, detached sayings, and only in the second generation acquired a Jewish setting, complete with scriptural overtones and so forth, the most natural historical hypothesis here would have been this: that Jesus' earliest hearers, being Jews, eager for their God to act in their present circumstances, would have told stories about Jesus in a thoroughly Jewish way, with scriptural echoes both deliberate and accidental. Then, later on, the church which was leaving the tight storytelling communities, and going out into the wider Hellenistic world, would find it easier to detach sayings from their original narrative context and present them, like the sayings of wise teachers in the Greco-Roman world, as isolated nuggets of wisdom.

The Jesus Seminar's view of oral tradition is thus based, not on the most likely historical hypothesis, but on the same view of the distinctive Jesus that we have seen to dominate their whole picture. Jesus would not have quoted Scripture;[67] he did not share, or address, the

---

66 Sometimes the absence of narrative context in the *Thomas* collection is remarked on (e.g. Funk and Hoover [eds.], *The Five Gospels*, 122) as though this were of great significance—which it clearly is not, since *Thomas* never has any such contexts. Waving *Thomas* around (e.g. p. 102), as though its detached sayings somehow prove that the saying first circulated independently and only subsequently acquired its synoptic context, constitutes an empty celebration of a circular argument.

67 For example, Funk and Hoover (eds.), *The Five Gospels*, 174, where the reference to Micah in Matt 10:34-36 is given as a reason for inauthenticity. Compare p. 201, where we are told that "scholars believe that most, perhaps all, quotations from scripture attributed to Jesus are secondary accretions." This is quite breathtaking, both in its ignoring of serious and well-known scholarly traditions in

aspirations of his contemporary Jews; he did not even follow the line taken by his "precursor and mentor." Nothing much memorable ever happened to him, or if it did we do not know about it. He was not involved in incidents which made a deep impression on the onlookers, causing them to go at once and tell what they had seen over and over again, with the anecdote quickly fixing itself into a pattern, and the words of Jesus, including incidental words, becoming part of that regularly repeated story. He never spoke about himself (the more one thinks about this suggestion, the more absurd it becomes); his conversation consisted only of subversive, teasing aphorisms. He must, in short, have been a very peculiar human being (as one Fellow of the Seminar pointed out to me, a Jesus who always and only uttered pithy aphorisms would start to look like some of the less credible cinematic Jesuses). Such a person would in fact be quite maddening. More importantly, as a historian I find it incredible that such a Jesus could have been a significant historical figure. It is not at all clear why people would have followed him, died for him, loved him, invented rich and powerful stories about him, and (within an almost incredibly short time, and within a context of continuing Jewish monotheism) worshipped him.[68]

Perhaps the greatest weakness of the whole construct lies just here. In order to sustain their home-made view of Jesus, the authors of this book, and presumably a fair number at least of Fellows of the Jesus Seminar, have had to invent, as well, an entire picture of the early church out of not much more than thin air. Sometimes they have borrowed other people's inventions, but they, too, are based on little or nothing. Paul, as we have seen, is the one major fixed point in early Christianity; we know that he was active, travelling, preaching and writing in the 40s and 50s, but we do not know anything at all, with the same certainty, about almost anyone else. We do not know that "Q" even existed; notoriously, there is a growing body of opinion that it did not (though one would never guess this from reading *The Five Gospels*), even as there is a growing body of opinion,

---

which Jesus is seen as a major expositor of Scripture, and in the extraordinary nonJewishness of the portrait which emerges.

[68]   On the worship of Jesus and Jewish monotheism, see N. T. Wright, *The Climax of the Covenant: Christ and the Law in Pauline Theology* (Edinburgh: T. & T. Clark; Minneapolis: Fortress, 1991) 18-136; Wright, *The New Testament and the People of God*, 457.

represented strongly within the Jesus Seminar, that expounds ever more complex theories about its origin, development, historical setting, and theologies.[69] Of course, once scholars are allowed to invent whole communities at will, anything is possible. Any jigsaw puzzle can be solved if we are allowed to create new pieces for it at a whim. But we should not imagine that historical scholarship built on this principle is of any great value.

CONCLUSION

Let me be quite clear, in bringing the discussion to a close, on several points at which misunderstanding of what I have said might perhaps arise.

First, I have no quarrel with the enterprise of publishing as much of the early Jesus-material as possible, from both the canonical and non-canonical sources, and bringing every scrap of possibly relevant evidence into full play. Indeed, I am deeply grateful for the immense labor and effort that members of the Seminar have expended to enable all of us involved in the search for Jesus to study these texts more easily. But, as with recent controversies about the Dead Sea Scrolls, the Seminar should be wary of suggesting that those who find the canonical material to be more reliable than the non-canonical are part of a conspiracy of silence, inspired by thoroughly non-historical motives, that is, by the desire for some form of closed-minded traditional Christianity. Frankly, *both* the desire to "prove" orthodoxy *and* the desire to "disprove" it ought to be anathema to the serious historian. The first of these is, of course, the way to what is normally called fundamentalism; the second, taken by at least some (and they are clearly influential) in the Jesus Seminar, is no less closed-minded, and in fact fundamentalist, in practice. Hatred of orthodoxy is just as unhistorical a starting point as love of it.

Second, I have no quarrel with popularizaton. I totally agree with Robert Funk that the results of scholarship are far too important, on this of all questions, to be confined to the classroom and library. I will go further. The Jesus Seminar, in this and in several other of its publications, has done as good a job of popularization as any scholarly group or individual I have ever seen. Its charts, diagrams, tables, layout, and so forth are exemplary. I am not, in short, in any way a

---

[69] The problematical nature of this aspect of "Q studies" is treated by C. A. Evans in his chap. on assumptions and methodology (in *Authenticating the Words*).

scholarly snob, who wants to keep the discussion within a charmed circle. My problems lie elsewhere. The thing which is thus being often brilliantly communiciated, especially in *The Five Gospels*, is not the assured result of scholarship. It is a compromise of pseudo-democratic scholarship, based on principles we have seen good reason to question, employing methods that many reputable scholars would avoid, ignoring a great deal of very serious (and by no means necessarily conservative) contemporary scholarship, making erroneous and anachronistic assumptions about the early church and its cultural context, and apparently driven by a strong, and strongly distorting, contemporary agenda. There was no point in popularizing all this. One should only popularize scholarship when it has passed the text this book itself suggests: submitting work to the judgment of peers (p. 34). For what it is worth, my judgment is that *The Five Gospels* does not pass the test. Any non-scholar reading this book is likely to be seriously misled, not only about Jesus, but about the state of serious scholarship. This is culpably irresponsible.

Third, I repeat what I said early on: I have no quarrel with the scholarship of many members of the Seminar. Some I am privileged to count as friends, and I trust that what I have said here will not put that friendship in jeopardy. From within the Seminar, as we saw, several of the discussions, not least some of the votes that ended up gray, must appear as highly significant, points of potential advance in understanding. Several Fellows have done sterling work in persuading others within the Seminar to adopt, or at least to allow for, views other than their original ones; pulling votes up from black to gray may indicate, for many, an opening of an otherwise closed mind. From within certain circles in the North American academy, this is quite a significant achievement. From outside the Seminar, however, the present volume cannot but appear as a disaster, for which the individual Fellows cannot and must not be held responsible, since they did not write it. The two authors of this book are men whose work in other fields I admire and have used a good deal: Funk's Greek grammar is always close at hand, and Hoover's work on a key Greek term used once by Paul is foundational, I am persuaded, for the correct understanding of a much controverted and hugely important passage.[70] But they, as the named authors, must unfortunately

---

70   R. W. Funk, *A Greek Grammar of the New Testament and Other Early Christian Literature* (5th ed., Chicago and London: University of Chicago Press,

bear responsibility for this, the flagship work of the Jesus Seminar. It does them no credit. Indeed, it obscures any good work that the Seminar itself may have done.

Fourth, and perhaps most importantly of all: I agree completely with the Seminar that the search for Jesus in his historical context is possible, vital, and urgent. I am as convinced as they are that if the church ignores such a search it is living in a fool's paradise. What is more, my own study of Jesus leads me to think that "conservative" and "orthodox" Christianity, in the twentieth century at least, has often, indeed quite regularly, missed the point of Jesus' sayings and deeds almost entirely. But the way to address this problem is not, and cannot be, the way taken by the Jesus Seminar. One cannot tackle serious historical problems by taking them to bits and voting on the bits one by one. The only way forward must be the way of genuine historiography; and one may search *The Five Gospels* from cover to cover in vain for such a thing. There are a good many people engaged in serious historical study of Jesus at the moment, but the Seminar in its corporate identity (as opposed to some of its individual members) cannot be reckoned among their number.

Fifth, in conclusion, I question whether the Jesus proposed by *The Five Gospels* constitutes, or offers, good news, i.e. "gospel," at all. The main thing this Jesus has to offer, it sometimes appears, is the news that the fundamentalists are wrong. Some of us believed that anyway, on quite other grounds. Aside from that, Jesus becomes a quizzical teacher of wisdom, to be ranged alongside other quizzical teachers of wisdom, from many traditions. No reason emerges as to why we should take this teacher any more or less seriously than any other. It is not clear why even a sustained attempt to follow his maxims, his isolated aphorisms, should offer hope in a world threatened by ecological disasters, nuclear holocausts, resurgent tribalisms— and, for those insulated from such things in certain parts of the Western world, the moral and spiritual bankruptcy of materialism. The whole point of calling Gospels "Gospels" was, I suggest that they did contain reason for hope, good news to a world that badly needed it.

The Five Gospels, in other words, systematically deconstructs its own title. If this book gives us the truth about Jesus, about the early church, and about the writing of the five books here studied, there is

---

1973); R. W. Hoover, "The *harpagmos* Enigma: A Philological Solution," *HTR* 64 (1971) 95-119; see Wright, *The Climax of the Covenant*, 56-98.

no gospel, no good news. There is only good advice, and we have no reason for thinking that it will have any effect. Many members of the Jesus Seminar would disagree strongly with this conclusion, but this book does not give us any means of seeing why. In any case, those who persist in seeing the Seminar's portrait of Jesus as somehow good news are bound to say, as the book does on almost every page, that Matthew, Mark, Luke, and John got it all wrong, producing their own variations on the pedestrian, bombastic, apocalyptic, and essentially fundamentalist worldview. If the Seminar insists on retaining the word "Gospels" in the title, then, it is the word "five" that is deconstructed: all one is left with is *Thomas* and, of course, the doubly hypothetical "Early Q."

From a historical point of view it might of course be true that there is no good news to be had. Christianity as a whole might simply have been whistling in the dark for two thousand years. Subversive aphorisms may be the only comfort, the only hope, we have. But this question must be addressed precisely *from a historical point of view*. And, when all is said and done, *The Five Gospels* is of no help whatever in that task. There is such a thing as the serious contemporary search for Jesus in his historical context. This particular book makes no contribution to it.

THE IMPLICATIONS OF TEXTUAL VARIANTS FOR AUTHENTICATING THE ACTIVITIES OF JESUS

Stanley E. Porter and Matthew Brook O'Donnell

1. INTRODUCTION

In our paper in the previous volume of this two-volume work on authenticating the words and actions of Jesus, we argued that systematic research into variation among the manuscripts of the New Testament containing the words of Jesus was noticeably absent among recent work on the Historical Jesus. We carried out a detailed study of the textual variants in the words of Jesus in the Synoptic Gospels as recorded by the Nestle–Aland[27] and suggested the need for a reconsideration of both the criteria used for authenticating the words of Jesus and those operational in textual criticism. Of particular concern was the seeming lack of attention in Historical Jesus studies to the precise wording of the words of Jesus as they are found in the Greek text of the New Testament. This disregard is largely due to the Aramaic Hypothesis, which, though showing signs of decline, has had a central influence upon the manner in which Historical Jesus research has been carried out. As a result of this, we suggested that it was in fact not so much the words of Jesus but rather the *concepts* of Jesus that were being studied. From that standpoint, the lack of attention to the textual variants is understandable—syntactical, morphological and even lexical variation is less significant if the question is "Could Jesus have said something along these lines?" instead of "Did Jesus say this or not?"

In this paper, we do not propose to carry out a detailed classification of the variants regarding the actions of Jesus, as we did in the first study of the words of Jesus. One reason for this is the difficulty in extracting just the actions of Jesus from the text of the Synoptic Gospels. The question of how much of a clause or verse should be considered as part of an action of Jesus is assessed in the first section. Here we develop categories for classification of the actions of Jesus, introducing distinctions regarding processes that may prove helpful in subsequent research. Then, in the next several sections, we focus specifically on the processes attributed to Jesus in Mark's Gospel, which are realized by the verbal forms in the Greek text. We use the same classifications for variants that we used in the previous paper, although we will cite examples selectively. These categories of variants include addition/insertion, subtraction/omission, lexical differentiation/replacement, morphological alteration (e.g. tense-form/ aspect, mood, voice, case, number), and syntax, usually pertaining to word order. These sections examine the textual variants in several pericopes from Mark (and their Synoptic parallels) in the light of their potential significance for Historical Jesus research (we also include an appendix with further instances for examination).

2. EXTRACTING THE ACTIONS OF JESUS

1. What Counts as an Action of Jesus?

In investigating the words of Jesus, it was a relatively simple task, with the aid of a standard red-letter edition of the New Testament, to extract the words attributed to Jesus from the Synoptic Gospels. Repeating this procedure for the actions of Jesus, on the other hand, is not such a self-evident task. Consider, for instance, the first verses in Mark where any actions of the character, Jesus, are found (Mark 1:9-10):

9 καὶ ἐγένετο ἐν ἐκείναις ταῖς ἡμέραις ἦλθεν Ἰησοῦς ἀπὸ Ναζαρὲτ τῆς Γαλιλαίας καὶ ἐβαπτίσθη εἰς τὸν Ἰορδάνην ὑπὸ Ἰωάννου. 10 καὶ εὐθὺς ἀναβαίνων ἐκ τοῦ ὕδατος εἶδεν σχιζομένους τοὺς οὐρανοὺς καὶ τὸ πνεῦμα ὡς περιτεράν καταβαῖνον * εἰς αὐτόν.

The underlined words are those that have variant readings in the Nestle–Aland[27], and the asterisk indicates that certain manuscripts add words at this point—in this case, καὶ μένον is found in ℵ (W) 33. How much of these two verses should be classified as belonging to the actions of Jesus? If we were to consider solely the processes (verbal forms) of which Jesus was the subject or actor then η and ει are the only words that should be included in a corpus of the actions of Jesus. In addition, the grammaticalized actor, Ἰησοῦς, should also be included in these words. For our present purpose, none of these words exhibit textual variants. But what about the prepositional phrase ἀπὸ Ναζαρέτ ("from Nazareth")? It modifies the verb η, which we have classified as an action of Jesus, and thus serves as an adjunct in that clause.[1] It is related to the action of Jesus, providing a locative origin for the process. There are two variants for the word Ναζαρέτ (attested in ℵ B L Γ Δ 28 33 565 600 892 1241 2427 2542 1844 *l*2211), one reading Ναζαράτ (A P) and the other Ναζαρέθ (D K W Θ *f*[1, 13] *l*4224), which was formerly read in the Nestle–Aland[26]. Further, what about the action of John upon Jesus? "Jesus was baptized (ἐβαπτίσθη) in the Jordan *by John*" (v. 9). Should this be counted as an action of Jesus? In one sense, it certainly relates to something that Jesus was involved in—he was baptized. Similarly, the Spirit is said to have descended *upon Jesus* (εἰς αὐτόν). The text reading εἰς αὐτόν is supported by B L (W) *f*[1, 13] 33 2427 Majority text. In line with the parallels in Matt 3:16 and Luke 3:22, there is a variant ἐπ' αὐτόν supported by important manuscripts (ℵ A L W Θ *f*[1] 33 Majority text). If this clause is included in the actions of Jesus, then the significant textual variant καὶ μένον ("and remained") should be taken into consideration. Finally, what about the clause καὶ ἐγένετο ἐν ἐκείναις ταῖς ἡμέραις ("And it happened in those days") —does that constitute a part of the actions of Jesus? It is less connected with the actions of Jesus ("he came . . . he saw") than the information that Nazareth was the place from which he did the action and that John was the person who baptized him. However, it may still be considered as an element in the actions of Jesus, and thus the variants for the words καὶ ἐγένετο need to be considered.

2. Types and Levels of Action

These observations have led us to propose different types of actions or levels of activity for classifying the actions of Jesus. These are summarized in the chart below. Direct actions (Level 1) are those in which Jesus is the grammatical subject, and actor or agent of a process. These are usually instances where a finite active voice verb form is found, though appropriate genitive absolutes and infinitives,

---

[1]   On the elements in a Greek clause, see S. E. Porter, *Idioms of the Greek New Testament* (BLG 2; Sheffield: Sheffield Academic Press, 2nd edn, 1994) 286-97. The three major components of a clause are *subject* (S) *predicate* (P) and *complement* (C). The complement includes everything in the clause that is not either the main verb and its modifiers (predicate) or grammatical subject and its modifiers (subject), and is sometimes divided into further units, including that of *adjunct* (A). The complement includes direct and/or indirect objects and prepositional phrases (the latter often treated as adjuncts). These categories are used in the chart below.

with reference to Jesus in the genitive or accusative case respectively, would also qualify for inclusion here. In the above example, the words ἦλθεν Ἰησοῦς . . . εἶδεν σχιζομένους τοὺς οὐρανούς are classified as direct actions. At the next level (Level 2) are indirect actions of Jesus. These include passive constructions where Jesus is the grammatical subject, but the recipient of an action performed by either a stated or an unstated agent. For example, "Jesus was baptized by John" (Mark 1:9). It also includes examples where Jesus is the recipient (grammatical object) of the action of another individual or group, such as "John baptized Jesus in the Jordan." Level 3 consists of concomitant actions, that is, elements of a clause in which Jesus as the grammatical subject (as either actor [Level 1] or acted upon [Level 2]) is not directly involved, by that complement, but that occur alongside or in support of the major actions. Level 3 elements are usually types of clause complements, such as the prepositional phrase ἀπὸ Ναζαρέτ. Finally, discursive actions (Level 4) are the furthest away from the direct action of the clause and communicate temporal, locative or other discourse information in which the other levels of action occur. For instance, καὶ ἐγένετο ἐν ἐκείναις ταῖς ἡμέραις is classified as a discursive action.

Level	Type of Action	Clause Component(s)
1	Direct	Subject
		Predicate (active)
2	Indirect	(Grammatical) Subject
		Predicate (passive)
		Complement (agent), or
		Complement (recipient)
3	Concomitant	Complement
4	Discursive	Deixis (indicating when, where, etc.)

We have found these four levels of activity, on which the direct, indirect, concomitant and discursive actions of Jesus take place, to be a useful classificatory device for investigating the textual variants in the actions of Jesus. The next four sections consider specific examples at each level of action. These example have been selected on more or less an *ad hoc* basis from Mark's Gospel, but they all have some direct relevance for issues related to Historical Jesus research. However, they also serve to illustrate the necessity for an analytical framework through which to consider the actions of any characters within the Gospel narratives, in this case Jesus.

3. THE DIRECT ACTIONS OF JESUS (LEVEL 1)

Since this essay is part of this larger project on authenticating the actions of Jesus, within the limited space available we will devote our greatest amount of attention to the direct actions of Jesus (Level 1). We treat here three significant examples, from two categories of textual variant.

Lexical alteration/differentiation in the actions of Jesus, particularly the direct actions of Jesus, is the most likely place for conceptual variation to take place. The reason for this is that these types of variant show places where a different verb has been used to describe an action of Jesus. The semantic classifications found in the Louw–Nida lexicon[2] provide a useful tool for charting lexical differences as variants change semantic domains or sub-domains. Such a shift in domains or sub-domains, indicating a shift in sense of the verb, and hence distinction in the action, has obvious implications for studying the nature of the actions of Jesus, and, with it, raises questions regarding authenticating these actions. As we outlined in our previous study, and has been confirmed in this study as well, it unfortunately appears to be the case that most work on the words and actions of Jesus pays little attention to the specific wording of the Greek text, that is, what Jesus actually said or did according to the account, but is more interested in the concepts that lie behind them, that is, whether Jesus said or did something somewhat like what is reported. The primary reason for this neglect of the Greek words of Jesus appears to be the view that they may merely represent an Aramaic original. It is less easy to account for the lack of concern regarding the actions of Jesus.

Mark 2:23 (69).[3] This example of lexical alteration/differentiation in the direct actions of Jesus is representative of a number of variant readings in the Synoptic Gospels' reporting of the actions of Jesus. These are cases where a root lexical item has variants with different

---

[2]   J. P. Louw and E. A. Nida, *A Greek–English Lexicon Based upon Semantic Domains* (2 vols., New York: United Bible Societies, 1988).

[3]   As in the previous article, we refer to the Synoptic pericope numbers in A. Huck, *Synopsis of the First Three Gospels* (rev. H. Lietzmann and F. L. Cross; Oxford: Blackwell, 9th edn, 1949), by reference number in parenthesis.

prepositional prefixes. At Mark 2:23, Nestle–Aland[27] reads καὶ ἐγένετο αὐτὸν ἐν τοῖς σάββασιν παραπορεύεσθαι διὰ τῶν σπορί-μων ("And it happened on the Sabbath for him to *pass through* the grainfields"). The infinitive παραπορεύεσθαι is found in 𝔓[88] ℵ Θ 700 892 *l*2211. The variant reading διαπορεύεσθαι ("to pass through") is found in B (C) D 2427 and πορεύεσθαι ("to go") in W, *f*[13]. Luke's parallel has the infinitive διαπορεύεσθαι (Luke 6:1) and Matthew's has the finite un-prefixed form ἐπορεύθη (Matt 12:1). The textual evidence is strongly Alexandrian for παραπορεύεσθαι with 𝔓[88] and ℵ, but more balanced with both Alexandrian (B) and Western (D) testimony for διαπορεύεσθαι. On the basis of accounting for the origins of the variants, Taylor asserts that

> The change to διαπορεύεσθαι can readily be explained as the substitution of a more exact expression and an assimilation to Lk. vi. I, whereas there is no reason why διαπορεύεσθαι should be replaced by παραπορεύεσθαι.[4]

Thus, the text-critical canon of dissimilarity favours παραπορεύ-εσθαι as the original Markan reading. In addition, assuming Markan priority, Taylor suggests that Matthew and Luke's readings are "clearly meant as improvements,"[5] but then cites Moulton's suggestion that Mark's καὶ ἐγένετο with the infinitive[6] "is perhaps a primitive assimilation to Lk 6[1]."[7] It is not clear how Taylor reconciles these two positions. Either Matthew and Luke are "improving" on Mark, or the text of Mark is an early assimilation to Luke, but it is difficult to see how both can be the case. Moulton makes his comment in the context of his discussion of supposed Hebraisms in Luke, particularly the forty or more occurrences of καὶ ἐγένετο.[8]

---

4   V. Taylor, *The Gospel According to St. Mark: The Greek Text with Introduction, Notes and Indexes* (London: Macmillan, 1959) 215.

5   Taylor, *Gospel According to St. Mark*, 215.

6   καὶ ἐγένετο occurs four times in Mark: 2:23; 4:4; 9:3; 9:26. Mark 2:23 is the only instance in the Gospel where there is a catenative construction (see Porter, *Idioms of the Greek New Testament*, 197-98), which occurs three times in the Gospel of Luke: 6:1; 6:6; 16:22.

7   J. H. Moulton, *A Grammar of New Testament Greek*. I. *Prolegomena* (Edinburgh: T. & T. Clark, 3rd edn, 1908) 17. In a footnote, Moulton suggests "Παραπορεύεσθαι (ℵ A L D *al*) may be a relic of Mk's original text." Presumably this indicates that Moulton was using a text that had the διαπορεύεσθαι reading.

8   Moulton is particularly responding to Dalman's list of "Semitisms in the Synoptic Gospels" (G. Dalman, *The Words of Jesus: Considered in the Light of*

In terms of the semantics of each of the three verbs, they are obviously closely related, and concern linear movement. The Louw–Nida lexicon places all three words in domain 15, "Linear Movement"[9] (παραπορεύομαι [15.28], διαπορεύομαι [15.21, 22] and πορεύομαι [15.10, 18, 34]), although within different sub-domains. Taking the "a" sense for each word, the three different sub-domains are: πορεύομαι "Move, Come/Go," διαπορεύομαι "Travel, Journey" and παραπορεύομαι "Pass, Cross Over, Go Through, Go Around." The basic sense of all three of these verbs is the same, it must be noted, but each has a different extended sense. The sub-domains of the Louw–Nida lexicon are generally ordered from less to greater specificity in meaning,[10] an ordering reflected in these three verbs, with πορεύομαι being the least and παραπορεύομαι the most specific. Thus, whereas all three Gospels are in agreement that Jesus was involved in linear movement regarding grainfields, the variations in word choice in the Synoptic accounts, mirrored in Mark's textual variants, raise the question of what specific action Jesus was performing. Gundry thinks that the author of Mark's Gospel has deliberately separated the action of Jesus (παραπορεύομαι) from that of his disciples (οἱ μαθηταὶ αὐτοῦ ἤρξαντο ὁδὸν ποιεῖν τίλλοντες τοὺς στάχυς "His disciples began to make a path plucking heads grain"). He suggests that the purpose of this separation

> Is to make a clean separation between Jesus' going along *without* plucking ears of grain and the disciples' making their way *while* plucking ears of grain; for the Pharisees will not raise a question about Jesus' conduct, but only about the conduct of his disciples, and he will defend their conduct, not his own.[11]

It is plausible to think that, assuming Markan priority, the writer of Mark's Gospel is reflecting a specific view of the actions of Jesus, as reflected in the form of verb selected. Jesus is depicted as passing

Post-Biblical Jewish Writings and the Aramaic Language [trans. D. M. Kay; Edinburgh: T. & T. Clark, 1909] 17-36). For a more recent discussion of Mark 2:23 as an alleged Semitism, see E. C. Maloney, *Semitic Interference in Marcan Syntax* (SBLDS 51; Chico: Scholars Press, 1981) 85-86.

9   Louw and Nida, *Greek–English Lexicon*, 1.181-211. Domain 15 is a large and complex domain, with 33 sub-domains.

10   E. A. Nida and J. P. Louw, *Lexical Semantics of the Greek New Testament* (SBLRBS 25; Atlanta: Scholars Press, 1992) 110-11.

11   R. H. Gundry, *Mark: A Commentary for His Apology for the Cross* (Grand Rapids: Eerdmans, 1993) 140 (his emphasis).

through the field, not plucking the grain, while his disciples are specifically described as plucking the grain. The use of the verb παραπορεύεσθαι, with the prefixed preposition παρά, followed by the prepositional phrase with διά, seems at least compatible with this sense, if not require it.[12] This distinction in the action is confirmed by other features of Mark's account in relation to Matthew and Luke. For example, Mark is the only writer to specify a separate set of movements for the disciples (ἤρξαντο ὁδὸν ποιεῖν), with the other two Gospels seeming to include the disciples in the action of Jesus. Matthew states that "Jesus went (ἐπορεύθη) through the grainfields and his disciples were hungry and began to pluck heads of grain" (Matt 12:1), seemingly including the disciples in the action of the verb ἐπορεύθη. Luke's version is closer to Mark's, with καὶ ἐγένετο with the infinitive construction, and states that "his disciples were plucking and eating heads of grain, rubbing them with their hands" (Luke 6:1). The focus is placed upon their action of plucking and eating the grain, and not their moving through the field. It seems to be assumed in the Lukan account that the disciples are included in Jesus' travelling through the field (διαπορεύεσθαι διὰ σπορίμων). There are also implications of the textual variants in Mark for Synoptic relations. As Taylor notes (see above), the Markan reading with παραπορεύεσθαι can account best for the other variants in a way that the other variants cannot. Further, the distinction in the actions seems to have been lost by the other (later) Synoptic writers. Perhaps neither appreciated the distinction being made between what Jesus and his disciples did as they passed through the fields, even though this distinction in Mark is confirmed by the reaction of the Pharisees to the disciples' but not Jesus' actions. Luke retains the sense of passing through, but Matthew loses any sense but that of the action of movement, and both have the Pharisees enquiring regarding Jesus and the disciples' behaviour.

The conclusions to be drawn from the previous discussion, especially regarding authenticating the actions of Jesus, will rest partly on the solution to the Synoptic problem that one adopts. But leaving that issue aside for the moment, this example illustrates the importance of analyzing the textual variants of the actions of Jesus,

---

12   On the semantics of the prepositions παρά and διά, see Porter, *Idioms of the Greek New Testament*, 166-68, 148-51, where the glosses "alongside, parallel to or beside" and "through" are suggested for παρά and διά respectively.

especially in comparison of the Synoptic accounts. In this instance, the variants in Mark point to an early (if not authentic) description of a specific action of Jesus, over against those of his disciples. One is also able to account for the reactions to Jesus' actions (in this instance, the lack of reaction to his actions) and the nature of the other Synoptic accounts. It should be in terms of these specific actions of Jesus that any test of authenticity is made.

There are also numerous examples of morphological alteration in the direct actions of Jesus. Frequently finite verbs are replaced by infinite constructions, such as an adverbial participle phrase, a genitive absolute clause, or a form of the infinitive. Two examples are illustrative of the relation of this kind of variant to the actions of Jesus.

Mark 3:33 (89). Jesus' mother and brothers have come to the house in which Jesus is staying, and they send a messenger inside to inform him of their presence.[13] Nestle–Aland[27] gives the reading καὶ ἀποκριθεὶς αὐτοῖς λέγει ("And answering them he said"), found in ℵ B (C) L Δ 892 2427. The mood of the two verbal forms is switched in the reading in A D (Θ) Majority text, which is καὶ ἀπεκρίθη αὐτοῖς λέγων ("And he answered them saying"). Both of these readings are comprised of a single clause. There are, however, two additional variant readings that instead use two finite verb forms. The first has relatively weak manuscript evidence (*f*[1, (13)] 28 700 2542), ἀπεκρίθη αὐτοῖς καὶ λέγει ("He answered and he said"). Notice that the tense-forms of the verbs do not vary in these three readings, ἀποκρίνομαι being in the aorist tense-form and λέγω in the present. The fourth variant listed in the apparatus of Nestle–Aland[27] for this clause is ὃς δὲ ἀπεκρίθη καὶ εἶπεν αὐτοῖς ("And he answered and he said to them"), found in W (33). Here there is a complex of variation: addition of the relative pronoun, making anaphoric reference to Jesus, and the use of two clauses, with the third-person personal pronoun (αὐτοῖς) moving to the second clause after ει, which has altered in both mood and tense-form.

In this instance, the external evidence seems strongly to support the choice of the Nestle–Aland[27] committee. However, it is

---

[13] For another analysis that appreciates the textual variants, one of few that we have discovered, see G. D. Kilpatrick, "Jesus, his Family and his Disciples," *JSNT* 15 (1982) 3-19; repr. in C. A. Evans and S. E. Porter (eds.), *The Historical Jesus: A Sheffield Reader* (BibSem 33; Sheffield: Sheffield Academic Press, 1995) 13-28.

noteworthy that little attention is given to variation in this and other similar constructions in either commentaries or specific Historical Jesus research. Gundry highlights the use of the present-tense form with λέγω because it "stresses the rhetorical question that follows (v 33),"[14] but makes no mention of the variant (λέγων), which would remove the "historic present" upon which he bases his argument, and thus presumably alter his point regarding stress on the question. Likewise, Taylor makes no mention of variant readings, suggesting that "the construction ἀποκριθεὶς εἶπεν (or λέγει) is very common in the Synoptic Gospels."[15] A variation in tense-form (aorist or present) does not seem to be of concern to Taylor here, as he posits that the construction "reflects the influence of the LXX," as well as the use of Aramaic.[16] On the one hand, the morphological variation listed above probably appears to be of little consequence when it comes to authenticating the actions of Jesus, particularly if one accepts the widely asserted view that the use of two semantically related verb forms in an adverbial participle–finite verb construction reflects a Semitic idiom, and is a result of Aramaic and/or Septuagintal influence.[17] On the other hand, given that commentators draw attention to the frequency with which this "idiom" occurs in the Synoptic Gospels,[18] it perhaps warrants closer attention.

In our previous paper dealing with the textual variants in the words of Jesus, we suggested that one of the problems in both Historical Jesus research and textual criticism was a failure to pay attention to the larger picture, that is, to examine patterns both within the text and within the different textual traditions. An understanding of the tendencies of an author or scribe in such choices as tense-form and word-order guards against the problems of making text-critical decisions on a case by case, atomistic basis.

---

14   Gundry, *Mark*, 178.

15   Taylor, *Gospel According to St. Mark*, 246. He notes that this construction occurs 15 times in Mark, 45 in Matthew, 38 in Luke but not once in John. On this construction, see S. E. Porter, *Verbal Aspect in the Greek of the New Testament. with Reference to Tense and Mood* (SBG 1; New York: Peter Lang, 1989) 120-26.

16   Taylor, *Gospel According to St. Mark*, 246. Guelich cites Taylor and notes that Mark 3:33 is "the first Markan use of this Semitism common in the LXX" (R. A. Guelich, *Mark 1–8:26* [WBC 34A; Dallas: Word, 1989] 168).

17   For discussion, see Porter, *Verbal Aspect*, 137-38, with bibliography cited.

18   But not John, who, according to Taylor, prefers the paratactic construction ἀπεκρίθη καὶ ει (*Gospel According to St. Mark*, 246).

Obviously such an examination cannot reveal any hard and fast rule for these features. There are many factors that influence tense-form choice and the position of a subject group, for instance, within a clause. The following table shows the occurrences of ἀποκρίνομαι followed by λέγω in the Gospel of Mark. Of the 18 examples[19] found in Nestle-Aland[27], only two are paratactic constructions, with two finite verb-forms in separate clauses (Mark 7:28 and 12:34). This fact could be taken as internal evidence against the paratactic variant readings for Mark 3:33, in addition to the weak external evidence.[20] Of the 16 (or 17) remaining instances with a single complex clause (hypotactic construction), there is only one where λέγω occurs as an adverbial participle modifying the verb ἀποκρίνομαι—Mark 15:9, ὁ δὲ Πιλᾶτος ἀπεκρίθη αὐτοῖς λέγων ("And Pilate answered them saying"). All the other instances are either an adverbial participle form of ἀποκρίνομαι, modifying λέγω, or a substantival use of the participle (ὁ ἀποκριθείς) as the subject of λέγω. This raises the question of whether this pattern should be taken as internal evidence against the reading in A D (Θ) Majority text, καὶ ἀπεκρίθη αὐτοῖς λέγων ("And he answered them saying").

3:33	καὶ ἀποκριθεὶς αὐτοῖς λέγει	A–P
6:37	ὁ δὲ ἀποκριθεὶς ει [αὐτοῖς][21]	S–P–C
7:28	ἡ δὲ ἀπεκρίθη καὶ λέγει αὐτῷ	S–P and P–C
8:29	ἀποκριθεὶς ὁ Πέτρος λέγει αὐτῷ	A–S–P–C
9:5	ἀποκριθεὶς ὁ Πέτρος λέγει τῷ Ἰησοῦ	A–S–P–C
9:19	ὁ δὲ ἀποκριθεὶς αὐτοῖς λέγει	S–P
10:3	ὁ δὲ ἀποκριθεὶς ει αὐτοῖς	S–P–C
10:24	ὁ δὲ Ἰησοῦς πάλιν ἀποκριθεὶς λέγει αὐτοῖς	S–A–P–C
10:51	καὶ ἀποκριθεὶς αὐτῷ ὁ Ἰησοῦς εἶπεν	A–S–P
11:14	καὶ ἀποκριθεὶς ει αὐτῇ	A–P–C
11:22	καὶ ἀποκριθεὶς ὁ Ἰησοῦς λέγει αὐτοῖς	A–S–P–C
11:33	καὶ ἀποκριθέντες [τῷ Ἰησοῦ λέγουσιν][22]	A–P

---

19   Although listed in the table, the second example from Mark 11:33 does not have ἀποκριθείς in the printed text.

20   ἀπεκρίθη αὐτοῖς καὶ λέγει (f¹, (13) 28 700 2542) and ὁ ς δὲ ἀπεκρίθη καὶ ει αὐτοῖς (W [33]).

21   αὐτοῖς is omitted by A L f¹ 33 892 2427.

22   The order of verb and indirect object is transposed in A D f¹ Majority text. The Nestle–Aland[27] reading, τῷ Ἰησοῦ λέγουσιν, is attested by 𝔓45vid ℵ B C L N W Δ Θ Ψ f¹³ 28 33 579 892 2427 2542.

11:33	καὶ [ἀποκριθεὶς]²³ ὁ Ἰησοῦς λέγει αὐτοῖς	[A]–S–P–C
12:34	ἀπεκρίθη εἶπεν αὐτῷ	P and P–C
12:35	καὶ ἀποκριθεὶς ὁ Ἰησοῦς ἔλεγεν	A–S–P
14:48	καὶ ἀποκριθεὶς ὁ Ἰησοῦς ει αὐτοῖς	A–S–P–C
15:2	ὁ δὲ ἀποκριθεὶς αὐτῷ λέγει	S–P
15:9	ὁ δὲ Πιλᾶτος ἀπεκρίθη αὐτοῖς λέγων	S–P–C
15:12	ὁ δὲ Πιλᾶτος πάλιν ἀποκριθεὶς ἔλεγεν αὐτοῖς	S–A–P–C

As noted above, in the case of Mark 3:33 the external evidence seems strongly in favour of the Nestle–Aland²⁷ reading. However, the suggested method for examining patterns within an author to aid in the decision regarding a particular variant appears to merit consideration. The third column of the table indicates word-group order for the ἀποκρίνομαι–λέγω construction in Mark. Again, the recognition of a particular pattern might be suggestive in one direction when examining syntactical word-order variants.

The parallels to the Markan pericope contain the same construction: Matt 12:48, ὁ δὲ ἀποκριθεὶς εἶπεν τῷ λέγοντι αὐτῷ²⁴ ("And the one answering said to the one speaking to him") and Luke 8:21, ὁ δὲ ἀποκριθεὶς εἶπεν πρὸς αὐτούς²⁵ ("And the one answering said to them"), with no significant variation.

Mark 6:6 (108). A second example of morphological variation in the direct actions of Jesus concerns an alteration in tense-form. Following a hostile reception in Jesus' home town (τὴν πατρίδα αὐτοῦ) and his inability to perform many miracles there, Mark reports that Jesus "was amazed on account of their faithlessness" (ἐθαύμαζεν διὰ τὴν ἀπιστίαν αὐτῶν). The imperfect indicative (ἐθαύμαζεν) read in the text of Nestle–Aland²⁷ is found in A C D L W Θ f¹, ¹³ 33 Majority text. Previous editions, specifically Nestle–Aland²⁵, read an aorist indicative (ἐθαύμασεν) supported by ℵ B 565 2427. Taylor has the aorist form in his text, noting the imperfect variant in his apparatus, but making no comment.²⁶ Gundry suggests that "the imperfect tense of ἐθαύμαζεν appears to make his

---

23   Nestle–Aland²⁷ does not include ἀποκριθεὶς in this verse, following ℵ B C L N Γ Δ Ψ 33 579 892 2427. It is found in A D K f¹, ¹³ (28) 1241.

24   There are a number of variant readings for τῷ λέγοντι αὐτῷ (ℵ B D 33 892 1424): C L Θ f¹, ¹³ Majority text read τῷ ει αὐτῷ, Z omits αὐτῷ and W omits the whole phrase.

25   𝔓⁷⁵ has αὐτόν for αὐτούς.

26   Taylor, *Gospel According to St. Mark*, 301.

marvelling concurrent with the towns people's astonishment."[27] Meier points out that there are few references to Jesus being "surprised" in the Gospel traditions and that "throughout all Four Gospels—with the notable exception of Matt 8:10 par. and Mark 6:6—references to Jesus' being astonished are simply absent."[28]

The imperfect tense-form, like the present tense-form, grammaticalizes imperfective aspect, but, in opposition to the present indicative, it also grammaticalizes remoteness.[29] The aorist tense-form grammaticalizes perfective aspect, and neither the imperfect nor the aorist indicative grammaticalizes absolute temporal reference. So the question concerning variants in this verse is one of aspectual distinction. Aspectual choice is a result of the "author/speaker's reasoned subjective choice of conception of a process,"[30] separate from the objective reality which is being described. The implications of these grammatical points for Historical Jesus research are that, even if a choice between two readings, which differ in tense-form, can be made on the basis of strong textual evidence, we are not necessarily taking a step towards authenticating an action of Jesus by arguing for selection of a particular aspect or tense form. Aspect is an inherently textually-based feature,[31] not one grounded in a particular objective, external world. Therefore, one can only speak with certainty about the choice of aspect made by the author, and not necessarily about the objective nature of the process it is describing. This fact heightens the need for greater attention to be paid to the larger

---

27   Gundry, *Mark*, 293. He makes no reference to the variant reading with the aorist indicative. But he does make an attempt to examine Mark's use of tense-forms within this section, noting that the towns people's astonishment (ἐξεπλήσ-σοντο [3:2]), their taking offense at Jesus (ἐσκανδαλίζοντο [3:3]) and his inability to perform miracles (οὐκ ἐδύνατο [3:5]) are also conveyed by imperfect tense-forms.

28   J. P. Meier, *A Marginal Jew: Rethinking the Historical Jesus. II. Mentor, Message, and Miracles* (ABRL; New York: Doubleday, 1994) 725; cf. 771 n. 206. He makes no reference to the variant reading in Mark 6:6. Note that in the Matthean parallel to Mark 6:1-7 there is no reference to Jesus' amazement. The other occurrence of θαυμάζω with Jesus as the subject that Meier makes reference to uses an aorist indicative (ἐθαύμασεν) in both Matt 8:10 and Luke 7:9.

29   See Porter, *Verbal Aspect*, 198-211, esp. 207-208. For a less technical description, see Porter, *Idioms of the Greek New Testament*, 20-45, esp. 33-35.

30   Porter, *Verbal Aspect*, 1.

31   The term *text* here is being used in the broadest sense as referring to the result of language use, either spoken or written.

context of individual variants, particularly patterns within a particular author,[32] when making decisions in cases of morphological alteration.

4. THE INDIRECT ACTIONS OF JESUS (LEVEL 2)

In section two, we described indirect actions of Jesus as including passive constructions where Jesus is the grammatical subject, but the recipient of an action performed by either a stated or an unstated agent (Level 2). However, aside from the example from Mark 1:9, "he was baptized into the Jordan by John" (ἐβαπτίσθη εἰς τὸν Ἰορδάνην ὑπὸ Ἰωάννου), presented in that section, there are few examples of passive constructions with Jesus as the grammatical subject in Mark's Gospel, to say nothing of instances with textual variants. It is thus necessary to concentrate upon examples in this category of action where Jesus is the recipient (grammatical object) of the action of another individual or group of individuals.

Mark 14:65 (241). Two variant readings in this verse serve to illustrate cases of addition/insertion and omission/deletion in various manuscripts regarding the indirect actions of Jesus. The Nestle–Aland[27] reads: καὶ ἤρξαντό τινες ἐμπτύειν αὐτῷ καὶ περικαλύπτειν αὐτοῦ τὸ πρόσωπον ("And certain ones began to spit on him and to cover his face"). There are two variants attached to this part of the sentence (which contains two further infinitive clauses). The first, found in (D) Θ 565 700, inserts the phrase αὐτοῦ τῷ προσώπῳ ("on his face") for αὐτῷ. This is similar to Matt 26:67, τότε ἐνέπτυσαν εἰς τὸ πρόσωπον αὐτοῦ ("Then they spat on his face").[33] The apparatus of Nestle–Aland[27] does not indicate the basis of the reading in their printed text, although the UBSGNT[4], which has added this variant to its apparatus since the previous edition, indicates that it is

---

[32]   This is particularly the case with aspectual choice, but also other linguistic features in the Greek language. One of the most useful ways to visualize aspectual usage in narrative is in terms of planes of discourse. The model describes the way in which the different tense-forms play different roles in presenting background (perfective aspect >> aorist tense-form), foreground (imperfective aspect >> present and imperfect tense-forms) and frontground (stative aspect >> perfect and pluperfect tense-forms) information. See Porter, *Verbal Aspect*, 92-93; *idem*, *Idioms of the Greek New Testament*, 23.

[33]   Assuming Markan priority, Matthew has altered Mark's complex clause with four infinitival clauses to three finite clauses, omitting reference to blindfolding (περικαλύπτω) and inserting ἐρράπισαν ("they hit *him*").

found in אַ A B C L W Δ $f^{1, 13}$ 28 33 157 and other minuscules.[34] The second variant is that Bezae (D) omits the reference to Jesus being blindfolded (καὶ περικαλύπτειν αὐτοῦ τὸ πρόσωπον), which is again in line with Matthew's version. Luke, however, retains reference to this action (Luke 22:64). Taylor, in his comments on Mark 14:65, suggests that the verse's "interpretation is complicated by textual problems."[35] He notes that Matthew and Luke include the question τίς ἐστιν ὁ παίσας σε; ("Who is the one striking you?") among the words of those beating Jesus. This question is found in some Markan manuscripts as well (N W X [Δ] Θ f^{13} 33 565 579 700 892 1424 2542).[36] Taylor suggests that this reading "is probably an assimilation to the text of Lk or Mt,"[37] but then points out that "if it is omitted, the reference to blindfolding becomes superfluous."[38] The Greek text upon which his commentary is purportedly based, "a modified form of the text of Westcott and Hort,"[39] however, has the same text as that of the Nestle–Aland[27].[40] That the phrase, καὶ περικαλύπτειν αὐτοῦ τὸ πρόσωπον, is an addition is, according to Taylor, supported by Luke having περικαλύψαντες, as well as the question τίς ἐστιν ὁ παίσας σε; In support of his position, he cites Streeter, who devotes considerable attention to the Synoptic parallels for this pericope, viewing the various manuscripts of Matthew and

---

[34]   In the second edition of his textual commentary, Metzger asserts that the witnesses that have replaced αὐτῷ with αὐτοῦ τῷ προσώπῳ were "no doubt influenced by the parallel account in Mt 26.67" (*A Textual Commentary on the Greek New Testament* [London: United Bible Societies, 1st edn, 1971; Stuttgart: Deutsche Bibelgesellschaft, 2nd edn, 1994] 96-97). The variant is given an "A" rating in the UBSGNT[4]. Given the lack of discussion of the variant in the commentary, and the posited certainty of this rating, it is more than a little puzzling that the variant has been introduced into the new edition.

[35]   Taylor, *Gospel According to St. Mark*, 571.

[36]   The shorter reading (προφήτευσον) without the question is given a "C" rating in the UBSGNT[3] and upgraded to a "B" in the UBSGNT[4]. Metzger's commentary is, however, unchanged. He states that the longer reading "appears to be an assimilation to the text of Matthew (26.68) or Luke (22.64)" (*Textual Commentary*, 1st edn, 155; 2nd edn, 97).

[37]   Taylor, *Gospel According to St. Mark*, 571.

[38]   Taylor, *Gospel According to St. Mark*, 571.

[39]   Taylor, *Gospel According to St. Mark*, vi.

[40]   See B. F. Westcott and F. J. A. Hort, *The New Testament in the Original Greek* (vol. 1; Cambridge: Macmillan, 1881) *ad loc.*

Mark as exhibiting particularly complex assimilation.[41] Based on the observation that virtually all the manuscripts of Matthew have the question "Who struck you?" but not the reference to blindfolding, and that the blindfolding is omitted by D and others in Mark, Streeter questions whether Matthew would have omitted the blindfolding if he had seen it in his source. This is reinforced by the fact that the question, "Who struck you?" seems to depend upon the inability of Jesus to see who had done it.[42] This observation leads Streeter to posit that:

> The original text of Matthew and of Mark omitted *both* the veiling and the words "Who is it, etc." These two stand or fall together. In Luke they are both original; and from Luke the first has got into the Alexandrian (but not into the earliest Antiochene and Western) text of Mark; the second has got into all the texts of Matthew.[43]

If this analysis of the origin of the text is accepted, the implications of this position for authenticating the indirect actions of Jesus are obvious, particularly if Markan priority is assumed. Luke's reference to blindfolding and the accompanying question are, if he is the one who originated them, historically questionable and most likely redactionally motivated, and not original to an earlier source.

In contrast, however, Gundry thinks that the text of Mark 14:65 is original to him, and that he has not included the question, "Who struck you?" because he is more interested in the actions of those beating Jesus, "because those actions fulfil the passion predictions."[44] He notes that Matt 26:67-68 has reference to Jesus' face but not to it being covered, while Luke has no mention of Jesus' face but includes the covering. For Gundry, this fact "favors that the original text of

---

41   Streeter questions whether the passage might not be one that "has specially invited assimilation, and this to such an extent that it has taken place independently along three different lines of transmission" (B. H. Streeter, *The Four Gospels: A Study of Origins* [London: Macmillan, 1936] 326). The question τίς ἐστιν ὁ παίσας σε; in Mark "is influentially supported in each of three main streams of textual tradition."

42   Referring to the blindfolding, Streeter suggests that Matthew "would have been unlikely to omit such a striking point, if it had occurred in his source, more especially as the whole point of the taunt '*Prophesy* who it is that struck thee' depends upon the fact that He was prevented by the veil from *seeing* who did it" (Streeter, *Four Gospels*, 326).

43   Streeter, *Four Gospels*, 326-27.

44   Gundry, *Mark*, 887.

Mark 14:65 mentioned both."[45] In reference to the omission of the clause concerning the covering of Jesus' face in D, Gundry suggests a number of possibilities:

> Apparently Mark's omitting to tell the purpose for which Jesus' face was covered led to scribal omission of that element. Or Matthew's omission of the covering may have led to scribal omission in Mark of the face as well as of the covering. Or both of these factors may have been at work.[46]

In contrast to Streeter, Gundry suggests that Matthew omits the blindfolding because he is making an allusion to Isa 50:6, which does not mention blindfolding.

Whether one accepts Taylor's or Gundry's analyses, or some other estimation, one is left with the realization that how one evaluates the textual variants in this passage in Mark has direct bearing on what one thinks regarding the indirect actions of Jesus. In other words, one's decision on the original wording of the text determines whether one is able to plausibly argue that Jesus' being spat upon and his being blindfolded were actual indirect actions performed on Jesus and recorded in the earliest Gospel sources.

5. THE CONCOMITANT ACTIONS OF JESUS (LEVEL 3)

Concomitant actions (Level 3) are those that accompany those of Jesus. Whereas they are less important in terms of Historical Jesus research into what Jesus may or may not have himself actually done, they are important for the context in which Jesus acted, and there are examples with variants that merit discussion.

Mark 10:49 (193). This example of morphological alteration in the concomitant actions of Jesus is interesting from a number of standpoints, not least in simply establishing what is or is not an action or a word of Jesus. First, the textual witnesses that support the two major readings are relatively close in terms of quality. The Nestle–Aland[27] text has the reading καὶ στὰς ὁ Ἰησοῦς εἶπεν· φωνήσατε αὐτόν ("And standing Jesus said, 'Call him!'"), which is attested by ℵ B C L Δ Ψ 579 892 1241 1424 2427. The variant found in the apparatus of the Nestle–Aland[27] has the witnesses A D W Θ ƒ[1), 13] Majority text, and reads καὶ στὰς ὁ Ἰησοῦς εἶπεν αὐτὸν φωνηθῆναι ("And standing Jesus said for him to be called"). The difference here

---

45   Gundry, *Mark*, 918.
46   Gundry, *Mark*, 918.

is between reported direct and indirect speech of Jesus. The parallels in Matt 20:32 and Luke 18:40 contain a description of Jesus calling the blind men (in Matthew) or of his ordering the man to be brought to him (in Luke).[47] If the reading selected by Nestle–Aland[27] is accepted, then the words φωνήσατε αὐτόν should be included among the words of Jesus and evaluated as such. But if, instead, the variant reading is adopted, then the passive aorist infinitive with the accusative αὐτόν acting as grammatical subject should be read, and the passage interpreted as an action of Jesus.[48] One of the reasons that Nestle–Aland[27] selected its reading for Mark 10:49 (direct speech) may have been that selecting the alternate reading would bring the Markan text more in line with Matthew and Luke. Their observing the text-critical canon of dissimilarity may thus have led to the acceptance of φωνήσατε αὐτόν. However, in a different verse in Mark (Mark 1:39 [16]), where there are two readings with similar external witnesses as 10:49,[49] Elliott argues that:

> If the criterion of author's style takes precedence over the rule of dissimilarity as I believe it should, then ἦν at Mark 1:39 should be printed as original—not ἦλθεν.[50]

As Elliott rightly points out, there are a number of factors to weigh in determining what text should be read. These include what he refers to as elements of the "author's style," as well as other, larger features of the text, such as the flow of thought within and between pericopes.

The kind of indirect speech found in the variant of Mark 10:49 is relatively rare in the Gospels,[51] where the verb that would have been

---

47   Taylor notes how in Mark and Luke "the direct speech is omitted and the facts briefly summarized," suggesting that both Gospels are toning down Mark's "vivid picture" (*Gospel According to St. Mark*, 448-49).

48   On indirect discourse in the New Testament, see Porter, *Idioms of the Greek New Testament*, 268-75, esp. 270-71 on the use of the infinitive to report indirect speech.

49   Nestle–Aland[27] has καὶ ἦλθεν κηρύσσων ("And he came preaching"), attested by ℵ B L Q 892 2427, but A C D W *f*[1, 13] 33 Majority text read καὶ ἦν κηρύσσων ("And he was preaching"), in line with the parallel in Luke 4:44.

50   J. K. Elliott, "The Relevance of Textual Criticism to the Synoptic Problem," in *Essays and Studies in New Testament Textual* Criticism (EFN 3; Cordoba: Ediciones El Almendro, 1992) 154.

51   See Matt 16:12; 20:23; Mark 5:43; 8:7; 12:18; Luke 19:15; 20:7; 23:2; 24:23.

used in direct speech is placed in the infinitive mood.[52] There are two other examples of this kind in Mark: (1) 5:43, καὶ εἶπεν δοθῆναι αὐτῇ φαγεῖν ("And he said *for something* to be given to her to eat") and (2) 8:7, εἶπεν καὶ ταῦτα παρατιθέναι ("He said also these things to place"). Tentative reconstructions of each saying could conceivably use an imperative form: δότε αὐτὴν φαγεῖν ("Give her *something* to eat") and παρατίθετε ταῦτα ("Place these things").

The direct-speech form of this construction, reporting the words of Jesus in Mark, is much more common (we have noted nearly 40 occurrences in a quick count). On this basis, internal criteria would seem to support the Nestle–Aland[27] reading. However, it is necessary to consider how the two readings fit within the pericope (Mark 10:46-52). The characters found in the paragraph are Jesus, Bartimaeus (the blind man), the disciples and a great crowd (ὄχλου ἱκανοῦ). The disciples and the crowd are clearly minor characters, and neither is mentioned by means of grammaticalized reference (an explicit word group) or through anaphoric reference (the use of a pronoun to point back to a previous grammaticalization of the referent) after their introduction in v. 46. The one exception is the ambiguous "many" (πολλοί) in v. 48, who order the blind man to be silent. Jesus and Bartimaeus, on the other hand, are frequent referents within the paragraph.[53] This observation has a bearing on the textual variants under consideration. The text as it reads in Nestle–Aland[27] has a second-person plural imperative form (φωνήσατε). The reading in A D W Θ f[(1), 13] Majority text (αὐτὸν φωνηθῆναι) places what was said in a dependent clause, and thus in a much less prominent position. In general, indirect speech can be considered as less prominent than direct speech. If the reading with the imperative is accepted, then a minor character group is given prominence (the referent of the second-person plural is not clear; is it the disciples, the crowd, or both?). On the other hand, if the infinitive construction is accepted, then "they" remain as minor characters within the discourse. On the basis of this consideration of the discourse features of the pericope and in the light of the evenness

---

52   Porter, *Idioms of the Greek New Testament*, 270.

53   Bartimaeus: Grammaticalized reference [3 times] vv. 46, 50, 51; Anaphoric reference [6 times] vv. 48 (2 times), 50, 51 (2 times), 52. Jesus: Grammaticalized reference [9 times] vv. 47 (4 times), 48, 49, 50, 51, 52; Anaphoric reference [4 times] vv. 46 (2 times), 51, 52.

of the external evidence, we suggest that the reading in the apparatus of Nestle–Aland[27] with the infinitive and indirect speech should be accepted. This places these words among the concomitant actions of Jesus (as the complement of the verb ϵι), instead of being among the words of Jesus (φωνήσατε αὐτόν).

6. THE DISCURSIVE ACTIONS OF JESUS (LEVEL 4)

The discursive actions of Jesus provide necessary support for the structure of a pericope, establishing such factors as the time or location of a set of events (Level 4). These are often referred to as deictic indicators, and, according to our analysis of the four types of actions presented above, would include the well-known καὶ ἐγένετο construction. There are other discursive patterns with variants worth considering as well.

Mark 9:2 (124). An example of addition/insertion in the discursive actions of Jesus is found in Mark's account of the transfiguration. Jesus reportedly takes three of his disciples, Peter, James and John, up a high mountain and "he was transformed before them" (καὶ μετεμορφώθη ἔμπροσθεν αὐτῶν). The apparatus of the Nestle–Aland[27] indicates that 𝔓45 W Θ ƒ13 (565) insert a temporal infinitive clause, ἐν τῷ προσεύχεσθαι αὐτούς ("while they were praying"), just before the verb μετεμορφώθη, which it modifies. Similarly, Θ 28 have ἐν τῷ προσεύχεσθαι αὐτόν ("while he was praying"). This latter reading is similar to Luke's καὶ ἐγένετο ἐν τῷ προσεύχεσθαι αὐτόν ("And it happened while he was praying") in Luke 9:29.[54] Matthew's version (17:2) has the same reading as Mark 9:2 in the Nestle–Aland[27] (καὶ μετεμορφώθη ἔμπροσθεν αὐτῶν).[55] The question arises concerning exactly what the disciples and/or Jesus were doing at the time when he was changed before them. Luke introduces the disciples in 9:28 as accompanying Jesus when *he* went up the mountain in order to pray (ἀνέβη εἰς τὸ ὄρος προσεύξασθαι). They are not mentioned again until v. 32, where they are described as being sound asleep (η βεβαρημένοι ὕπνῳ), and then gradually awakening and seeing the glorified Jesus (διαγρηγορήσαντες δὲ εἶδον

---

54   There is a morphological variation, προσεύξασθαι for προσεύχεσθαι, in 𝔓45 א* Ψ. Luke's account does not use the verb μεταμορφόω.

55   There is a variant reading in D that inserts μεταμορφωθεὶς ὁ Ἰησοῦς for μετεμορφώθη, but no readings that add a temporal clause as in Luke 9:29 or the variant in Mark 9:2.

τὴν δόξαν αὐτοῦ). Luke's portrayal of the disciples then reveals their impiety and sloth—Jesus is praying (v. 29), but they are sleeping and do not see his transformation, until the figures that appear with Jesus are about to leave (v. 33). Matthew's and Mark's accounts, on the other hand, indicate that Jesus was "changed before them" (Matt 17:2; Mark 9:2). This is a more neutral picture of the disciples. If the variant, "while they were praying," is accepted, then it presents a much more positive, pious view of the disciples.

Taylor dismisses the reading in Mark 9:2 as simply an assimilation to Luke 9:28, which is "Luke's interpretative addition" to Mark's reference to solitude (κατ' ἰδίαν μόνους).[56] Meier suggests that Mark may have made an addition to the traditional transfiguration story by placing "his favorite trio of disciples, Peter, James, and John" at this "secret epiphany."[57] He also discusses the embarrassment for the early Church caused by Jesus' saying in Mark 9:1 just before the transfiguration account, "Truly I say to you that there are certain ones standing here who will surely not taste death until they might see the Kingdom of God come in a state of power." He states:

> Mark most likely intended his readers to see the prophecy fulfilled, at least partially, in the transfiguration story. Peter, James, and John fit perfectly the designation of "some of those standing here" . . . Mark can solve the problem of the non-fulfillment of 9:1 by placing it just before the transfiguration, which is made into its (at least partial) fulfillment.[58]

If this is the case, then Mark would apparently want to portray the disciples in a positive light, given that they are the fulfillment of the prophecy. Interestingly, this does not seem to be a concern of Luke, whose account of the transfiguration also follows the prophecy concerning the kingdom (Luke 9:27). Is this perhaps because Luke has modified the saying by removing ἔρχομαι? He simply has "they will certainly not taste death ἔως ἂν ἴδωσιν τὴν βασιλείαν τοῦ θεοῦ ('until they might see the kingdom of God')." By removing reference to the "coming of the kingdom of God," the saying becomes less of an embarrassment for Luke, who does not need to portray the disciples in a more positive and pious light.

---

56 Taylor, *Gospel According to St. Mark*, 389.
57 Meier, *Marginal Jew*, 2.778.
58 Meier, *Marginal Jew*, 2.342. On the criterion of embarrassment, see J. P. Meier, *A Marginal Jew: Rethinking the Historical Jesus*. I. *The Roots of the Problem and the Person* (ABRL; New York: Doubleday, 1991) 168-71.

The implications of this set of variants for authenticating the discursive actions of Jesus appear to be several. One could well argue that the development of this set of variants points to Luke's action actually representing the earliest account of the actions, if not the original occurrence, in which the disciples are inattentive and asleep. Mark's and Matthew's accounts omit reference to the disciples sleeping, perhaps for two reasons. As noted above, one might well be best explained in relation to the criterion of embarrassment, in which their slothfulness is seen to be out of keeping with later Church attempts to display the disciples in a more positive light. The other reason might be because of the need to present the transfiguration account as a (partial) fulfillment of the prophecy concerning the coming of the kingdom. In any event, the textual variants, especially in the Markan account, help to raise important questions regarding this Synoptic account.

7. CONCLUSION

As in our previous paper on textual variants in the words of Jesus, study of the textual variants in the actions of Jesus pushes the Historical Jesus scholar to pay particular attention to the exact wording of the Greek text as a means of helping to evaluate the authenticity of the specific actions of Jesus. If one is content to speak in relatively vague and imprecise ways about the kinds of things that Jesus may or may not have done, study of the textual variants in the Synoptic Gospel accounts may have less apparent immediacy. Without assessing the textual variants, one may be able to conclude that Jesus did, or did not, do something such as travel to Jerusalem. This has some merit, but can only function to the extent of the criteria developed for such a purpose. Our investigation has uncovered that there is a surprising lack of even definition of what it means to speak of an action of Jesus. As a result, to aid those who are interested in a more specific analysis and assessment, in conjunction with the major types of textual variants, we have differentiated four major types of actions and their relations to the actions of Jesus as a primary figure in the Gospel accounts. By using this four-fold differentiation of verbal processes, we have been able to discuss in more specific terms actions where Jesus is the agent or instigator, actions where Jesus is the recipient, actions that occur concomitantly with the actions of Jesus, and actions of a discursive type, which set the temporal and locative sphere for other actions. These criteria, we believe, could form the basis for future discussion of the actions of Jesus, apart from treatment of textual variants. We have also noted that many of the variants regarding the actions of Jesus involve Synoptic parallels, and hence raise further questions regarding text-critical criteria for evaluating such variants. In our study, we have refrained from concluding for each of the examples above whether the action depicted is or is not authentic, but have instead tried to develop criteria in relation to textual variants that need to be taken into account in future Historical Jesus research.

APPENDIX

1. Examples of Textual Variants in the Direct Activities of Jesus

(a) Addition/Insertion

Vs. (Huck No.)	Reading	Witnesses
6:31 (112)	καὶ λέγει αὐτοῖς "And he said to them"	None listed in NestleAland[27]
	καὶ λέγει αὐτοῖς ὁ Ἰησοῦς "And Jesus said to them"	D Θ f[13] 28 565 700 2542
14:22 (236)	καὶ ἐσθιόντων αὐτῶν λαβῶν ἄρτον "And while they were eating, taking bread"	ℵ[1] B D W f[13] 565 2427
	καὶ ἐσθιόντων αὐτῶν λαβῶν ὁ Ἰησοῦς τὸν ἄρτον "And while they were eating, taking the bread Jesus"	Σ
	καὶ ἐσθιόντων αὐτῶν λαβῶν ὁ Ἰησοῦς ἄρτον "And while they were eating, taking the bread Jesus"	ℵ[*,2] A C L Θ Ψ f[1] Mj

(b) Subtraction/Omission

Vs. (Huck No.)	Reading	Witnesses
2:19 (54)	καὶ ειαὐτοῖς ὁ Ἰησοῦς "And Jesus said to them"	None listed in NestleAland[27]
	καὶ ειαὐτοῖς "And he said to them"	D W 28 1424

(c) Lexical Differentiation/Replacement

Vs. (Huck No.)	Reading	Witnesses
8:22 (121)	ἐξήνεγκεν αὐτὸν ἔξω τῆς κώμης "And they carried him out of the village"	ℵ B C L Δ Θ 33 579 892 2427
	ἐξήγαγεν αὐτὸν ἔξω τῆς κώμης "And they led him out of the village"	A D W f[1, 13] 2427 Mj

(d) Morphological Alteration

Vs. (Huck No.)	Reading	Witnesses
6:48 (113)	καὶ ἰδὼν αὐτούς "And seeing them"	ℵ B D L W Δ Θ 579 892 1241 1424 2427
	καὶ εἶδεν αὐτούς "And he saw them"	𝔓[45] A f[1, 13] 33 Mj

(e) Syntactical Word Order

Vs. (Huck No.)	Reading	Witnesses
6:2 (108)	ἤρξατο διδάσκειν ἐν τῇ συναγωγῇ "He began to teach in the synagogue"	ℵ B C D L Δ (Θ) 33 579 892
	ἤρξατο ἐν τῇ συναγωγῇ διδάσκειν "He began in the synagogue to teach"	𝔓[45vid] A W 0126 f[1, 13] Mj
6:5 (108)	καὶ οὐκ ἐδύνατο ἐκεῖ ποιῆσαι οὐδεμίαν δύναμιν "And he was not able there to do nothing miraculous"	ℵ B C L Δ Θ f[1] 892 2427 2542
	καὶ οὐκ ἐδύνατο ἐκεῖ οὐδεμίαν δύναμιν ποιῆσαι "And he was not able there nothing miraculous to do"	A f[13] 33 Mj
	καὶ οὐκ ἐδύνατο ἐκεῖ οὐδεμίαν ποιῆσαι δύναμιν "And he was not able there nothing to do miraculous"	D 565 700

2. Examples of Textual Variants in the Indirect Activities of Jesus

(a) Addition/Insertion

Vs. (Huck No.)	Reading	Witnesses
14:53 (241)	καὶ συνέρχονται "And they came together"	ℵ D L W Δ Θ f¹³ 565 700 892 2542
	καὶ συνέρχονται αὐτῷ "And they came together to him"	A B Ψ 2427 Mj
	καὶ συνέρχονται πρὸς αὐτὸν "And they came together towards him"	C
	καὶ συνέρχονται αὐτοῦ "And they came together with him"	1

(b) Subtraction/Omission

Vs. (Huck No.)	Reading	Witnesses
15:20 (247)	καὶ ἐξάγουσιν αὐτὸν ἵνα σταυρώσωσιν αὐτόν "And they led him out in order that they might crucify him"	None listed in NestleAland²⁷
	καὶ ἐξάγουσιν αὐτὸν ἵνα σταυρώσωσιν "And they led him out in order that they might crucify"	ℵ D f¹ 28 700 1424 l844

(c) Lexical Differentiation/Replacement

Vs. (Huck No.)	Reading	Witnesses
15:1 (242)	δήσαντες τὸν Ἰησοῦν ἀπήνεγκαν καὶ παρέδωκαν Πιλάτῳ "Binding Jesus they carried him away and handed him over to Pilate"	None listed in NestleAland[27]
	δήσαντες τὸν Ἰησοῦν ἀπήγαγον καὶ παρέδωκαν Πιλάτῳ "Binding Jesus they led him away and handed him over to Pilate"	C D W Θ f[1] 565 700 892 1424 2542
15:24 (249)	καὶ ἐσταύρωσαν αὐτόν "And they crucified him"	None listed in NestleAland[27]
	καὶ ἐφύλασσον αὐτόν "And they were guarding him"	D

3. Examples of Textual Variants in the Concomitant Actions of Jesus

(a) Addition/Insertion

Vs. (Huck No.)	Reading	Witnesses
7:17 (115)	εἰσῆλθεν εἰς οι "And he went into a house"	None listed in NestleAland[27]
	εἰσῆλθεν εἰς τὸν οι "And he went into the house"	ℵ (D 565) Δ
8:1 (118)	προσκαλεσάμενος τοὺς μαθητάς "Calling the disciples"	ℵ D L N 0131 f¹ 28 892 *l*2211
	προσκαλεσάμενος τοὺς μαθητὰς αὐτοῦ "Calling his disciples"	A B W Θ f¹³ 33 2427 Mj
	προσκαλεσάμενος τοὺς μαθητὰς πάλιν "Calling the disciples again"	Δ
15:17 (247)	καὶ ἐνδιδύσκουσιν αὐτὸν πορφύραν "And they dressed him in a purple garment"	None listed in NestleAland[27]
	καὶ ἐνδιδύσκουσιν αὐτὸν χλαμύδα κοκκίνην καὶ πορφύραν "And they dressed him in a scarlet cloak and purple garment"	Θ f¹³ 565 700 2542 *l*844

(b) Subtraction/Omission

Vs. (Huck No.)	Reading	Witnesses
6:41 (112)	καὶ λαβὼν τοὺς πέντε ἄρτους καὶ τοὺς δύο ἰχθύας "And taking the five loaves and the two fish"	None listed in NestleAland[27]
	καὶ λαβὼν τοὺς ἄρτους καὶ τοὺς ἰχθύας "And taking the loaves and the fish"	𝔓45
6:48 (113)	ἔρχεται πρὸς αὐτοὺς περιπατῶν ἐπὶ τῆς θαλάσσης "He came towards them walking on the sea"	None listed in NestleAland[27]
	ἔρχεται περιπατῶν ἐπὶ τῆς θαλάσσης "He came walking on the sea"	D W Θ 565

9:25 (126)	ἐπετίμησεν τῷ πνεύματι τῷ ἀκαθάρτῳ "He ordered the unclean spirit"	None listed in NestleAland[27]
	ἐπετίμησεν τῷ πνεύματι "He ordered the spirit"	$\mathfrak{P}^{45}$ W f[1]

(c) Lexical Differentiation/Replacement

Vs. (Huck No.)	Reading	Witnesses
12:41 (212)	καὶ καθίσας κατέναντι τοῦ γαζοφυλακίου "And sitting opposite the temple offering box"	None listed in NestleAland[27]
	καὶ καθίσας ἀπέναντι τοῦ γαζοφυλακίου "And sitting before the temple offering box"	B Ψ 33 579 1424 2427

(d) Syntactical Word Order

Vs. (Huck No.)	Reading	Witnesses
4:1 (90)	ὥστε αὐτὸν εἰς πλοῖον ἐμβάντα καθῆσθαι ἐν τῇ θαλάσσῃ "so that he in a boat stepped to sit on the sea"	ℵ B* C L Θ 33 565 892 1241 1424 2427
	ὥστε αὐτὸν εἰς τὸ πλοῖον ἐμβάντα καθῆσθαι ἐν τῇ θαλάσσῃ "so that he in the boat stepped to sit on the sea"	B² D W Δ
	ὥστε αὐτὸν ἐμβάντα εἰς τὸ πλοῖον καθῆσθαι ἐν τῇ θαλάσσῃ "so that he stepped in the boat to sit on the sea"	A f[(13)] Mj
	ὥστε αὐτὸν ἐμβάντα εἰς πλοῖον καθῆσθαι ἐν τῇ θαλάσσῃ "so that he stepped in a boat to sit on the sea"	K f[1] 2542

4. Examples of Textual Variants in the Discursive Activities of Jesus

(a) Addition/Insertion

Vs. (Huck No.)	Reading	Witnesses
6:47 (113)	καὶ ὀψίας γενομένης ητὸ πλοῖν ἐν μέσῳτῆς θαλάσσης "And as evening was coming, and the boat was in the middle of the sea"	None listed in NestleAland[27]
	καὶ ὀψίας γενομένης ηπάλαι τὸ πλοῖν ἐν μέσῳτῆς θαλάσσης "And as evening was coming, and the boat was already in the middle of the sea"	𝔓[45], D, f1, 28, 2542

(b) Subtraction/Omission

Vs. (Huck No.)	Reading	Witnesses
6:48 (113)	περὶ τετάρτην φυλακὴν τῆς νυκτὸς "Around the fourth watch of the night"	None listed in NestleAland[27]
	περὶ τετάρτην φυλακὴν "Around the fourth watch"	𝔓[45]
10:46 (193)	καὶ ἔρχονται εἰς Ἰεριχώ "And they came into Jerico"	None listed in NestleAland[27]
	(omitted)	B*

(c) Lexical Differentiation/Replacement

Vs. (Huck No.)	Reading	Witnesses
8:22 (121)	καὶ ἔρχονται εἰς Βηθσαϊδάν "And they came into Bethsaida"	None listed in NestleAland[27]
	καὶ ἔρχονται εἰς Βηθανινάν "And they came into Bethany"	D 1424
10:46 (193)	καὶ ἐκπορευομένου αὐτοῦ ἀπὸ Ἰερχὼ καὶ τῶν μαθητῶν αὐτοῦ "And he was going out from Jericho and his disciples"	None listed in NestleAland[27]
	καὶ ἐκπορευομένου αὐτοῦ ἐκείθεν μετὰ τῶν μαθητῶν αὐτοῦ "And he was going out from there with his disciples"	D (Θ 700)
15:25 (249)	ηδὲ ὥρα τρίτη "And it was the third hour"	None listed in NestleAland[27]
	ηδὲ ὥρα ἕκτη "And it was the sixth hour"	Θ

(d) Syntactical Word Order

Vs. (Huck No.)	Reading	Witnesses
11:13 (199)	ὁ γὰρ καιρὸς οὐκ ησύκων "For the season was not of figs"	ℵ B C* L Δ Ψ 892 2427
	οὐ γὰρ ηκαιρὸς σύκων "For it was not a season of figs"	A C² (D W) Θ 0188 f(1), 13 33 Mj

PART TWO

AUTHENTICATING THE ACTIVITIES OF JESUS

APPOINTED DEED, APPOINTED DOER
JESUS AND THE SCRIPTURES[*]

Ben F. Meyer

Of the many indices to Jesus' consciousness of his mission to Israel, three kinds are especially revealing: his identification of himself and his disciples as eschatological antitypes of Israel, her kings and prophets; his allusion to divinely appointed eschatological "measures" (of time, of evil, of revelation) being fulfilled to the brim: and his pointing, as to signs of the times, to the enactment, in his own activities, of God's promise of salvation for the end-time. We begin our effort of reflection with the observation that these three facets of the consciousness of Jesus exhibit a point of convergence: a full awareness of being charged with the climactic and final mission to Israel as promised and previewed in the Scriptures.

Second, we shall *independently* (i.e. without dependence on the foregoing) establish this same conclusion by a cumulative and convergent argument drawing on five data in the Gospel narratives, the historicity of which has won almost universal agreement. These are: Jesus' proclamation that the reign of God was at hand; the fact that Jesus spoke and acted "with authority"; that he was widely known as and was a wonder worker; that he "cleansed"—or mounted a demonstration at—the Jerusalem Temple; and that he died crucified, condemned by the Romans as "the king of the Jews." From these as yet disparate and unelucidated data I propose to argue to the main currents of the Gospels' Christology. All the themes belonging to these main currents, according to the argument, derived from Jesus and reflected his grasp of the Scriptures as bearing on his own mission.

The form of the argument is as follows: the above-mentioned data, of which the historicity is all but universally accepted, establish Jesus' consciousness of being charged with God's "climactic and definitive" mission to Israel in view of the imminent consummation

[*] The present study appeared in an earlier form in W. R. Farmer (ed.), *Crisis in Christology: Essays in Quest of Resolution* (Livonia: Dove, 1995) 311-32.

of history, or the reign of God. *But to speak of a "climactic and definitive mission" in the context of imminent consummation of history is to imply the imminent consummation of fulfillment of the whole of eschatological promise and prophecy.* It follows that we ought positively to expect to find on Jesus' part not only an eschatological consciousness, but on marked by *the awareness of present fulfillment*, a phenomenon without parallel in ancient Israel.[1]

Crucial to the argument is the ascertainment that, like his contemporaries, Jesus understood the great soteriological themes of the Scriptures as prophetic, that is, as awaiting fulfillment from the moment at which the end-time would break out. This is why we should positively expect the bearer of God's climactic and definitive mission *to focus on and to coordinate these themes.*

The sheer sweep and power of the argument—from the consciousness of an eschatological mission, through the necessity of all the Scriptures to come to fulfillment, to the main currents of the messianology or Christology of the Gospels—invite us to press it for its validity, i.e. to test the sufficiency of its premises and the cogency of its logic. Do the Gospels in fact exhibit the requisite data? Do they confirm that Jesus, like others who looked for the eschatological consummation, read the Scriptures as prophecy awaiting its moment of convergent fulfillment? Is there any plausible escape from the argument?

Finally, this argument evokes an antecedent expectation that the profusion, the positive explosion, of christological speech following

---

[1]   On whether the realized element in the eschatology of Jesus and of earliest Christianity has any true parallel in ancient Judaism, see D. C. Allison, Jr., *The End of the Ages Has Come: An Interpretation of the Passion and Resurrection of Jesus* (Philadelphia: Fortress, 1985; repr. Studies of the New Testament and Its World; Edinburgh: T. & T. Clark, 1987) 91-92. Here Allison significantly nuances the account of "realized eschatology in D. E. Aune, *The Cultic Setting of Realized Eschatology in Early Christianity* (NovTSup 28; Leiden: Brill, 1967). But despite his clarity on the main issues, Allison himself has been led to suppose that *T. Job* 39:9–40:6 might offer a true parallel to the realized eschatology of the resurrection of Jesus. In presenting the "resurrection" of Job's children, however the writer of the testament never steps out of the narrative world of Job into that shared by write and reader. This does not hold for New Testament texts on the resurrection of Jesus, as 1 Cor 15:3-8 unequivocally shows by its accent on available living witnesses to whom the risen Christ had appeared. Moreover, this difference grounds another: the impact attributed to Jesus' resurrection vs. the total lack of impact of the "resurrection" of Job's children.

on "the Easter experience of the disciples" will have been rooted in Jesus' own self-understanding. We shall accordingly conclude by entertaining the question of whether this expectation is confirmed.

THREE SORTS OF INDICES
TO JESUS' CONSCIOUSNESS OF HIS MISSION

Three words—the Temple riddle (Mark 14:58 = Matt 26:61 = John 2:19; cf. Mark 15:29 = Matt 27:40; Acts 6:14), the response to Antipas (Luke 13:32), and the Jonah saying in response to the demand for a sign (Matt 12:39 = Luke 11:29; cf. Mark 8:12; Matt 16:4)—share a set of sharply profiled traits that reflect the Jesus of history: first, a context of clash with authoritative or elite forces in Israel; second, the "three-days" motif, which evokes (in consciously enigmatic fashion) the divine governance of the life and fate of Jesus;[2] third, a consequent and unmistakable note of perfect confidence. Jesus clearly regarded the looming crisis (or eschatological ordeal) in the light of its subjection to God's royal sovereignty.

Two of these sayings present "types" of salvation: the sanctuary (Greek: ναός; Hebrew: הֵיכָל; Aramaic: הֵיכְלָא) of the Temple is presented as a type of the messianic community of salvation, transfigured in the reign of God.[3] Jonah, saved from the sea-monster, is presented as a type of one raised from the dead, returning (at the great consummation, the say of "the [son of] Man") to confound those who pressed Jesus for a "sign." There would be no sign but that one![4] Both sayings thus belong to the series of words presenting Jesus and his disciples as eschatological antitypes of familiar biblical figures: Moses (Matt 5:17, 21-48; cf. John 6:14; 7:40), David (Mark 12:35-37 = Matt 22:41-46 = Luke 20:41-44; Mark 2:25-26 = Matt 12:3-4 = Luke 6:3-4), Solomon (Matt 12:42 = Luke 11:31), Elisha (Mark 6:35-44 = Matt 14:15-21 = Luke 9:12-17), Isaiah (Mark 4:12 = Matt 13:13; Luke 8:10), the Servant of the Lord (Mark 10:45 = Matt 20:28; Mark 14:24 = Matt 26:28; Luke 22:20; John 6:51), the

---

2   J. Jeremias, "Die Drei-Tage-Worte der Evangelien," in G. Jeremias, H.-W. Kuhn, and H. Stegemann (eds.), *Tradition und Glaube* (K. G. Kuhn Festschrift; Göttingen: Vandenhoeck & Ruprecht, 1971) 221-29, here 227.

3   Jeremias, "Die Drei-Tage-Worte"; B. F. Meyer, "The 'Inside' of the Jesus Event," in Meyer, *Critical Realism and the New Testament* (Allison Park: Pickwick, 1989) 157-72.

4   J. Jeremias, "Ιωνᾶς," *TDNT* 3 (1965) 406-10.

one like a [son of] man and the tribes and prophets of Israel (Mark 3:13-14 = Matt 10:1-2 = Luke 6:13; Matt 5:12 = Luke 6:23). The typological interpretation of the early Church was not an independent development; it was grounded historically in Jesus' own use of typology. The two typological texts adduced here (the riddle of the new sanctuary and the sign of Jonah) are, in particular, words of Jesus;[5] nor is the eschatological character of the antitypes open to reasonable doubt.

Second, we meet the motif of divinely appointed measure of all things and its specific application to the Eschaton in the Markan form of the public proclamation: πεπλήρωται ὁ καιρός ("the time is fulfilled" or "filled full"). Though the verb is used variously of time, the probable image here is a great vase that with the years has been slowly filled until at last it is full to the brim.[6] As Paul Joüon pointed out long ago,[7] the parallelism of πεπλήρωται and ἤγγικεν suggests that the latter means "has arrived" (substratum: קָרֵב). The whole is aligned closely with the "today" and "fulfilled" motifs in Luke 6:21 ("Today this Scripture has been fulfilled [πεπλήρωται] in your hearing").

Elsewhere Jesus applied the same filling-up-to-the-appointed-measure motif to "evil" and to "revelation." "This evil generation" (of unbelievers and killers of God's envoys) will find itself overwhelmed by the rapidly approaching ordeal/tribulation, when God will exact from it the blood-debt for all the murders recorded in the Scriptures from first to last (i.e. from Cain's fratricide in Genesis 4 to the stoning of Zechariah in 2 Chr 24:20-25; cf. Matt 23:34-36 =

---

5   Respecting Jesus' use of typology, a detailed special study is still lacking; meantime, see R. T. France, *Jesus and the Old Testament* (London: Tyndale, 1971) 38-82; L. Goppelt, *Typos—The Typological Interpretation of the Old Testament in the New* (Grand Rapids: Eerdmans, 1982) 61-106; C. A. Evans, "Typology," *DJG* (1992) 862-66.

6   F. Zorell, *Lexicon Graecum Novi Testamenti* (Paris: Lethielleux, 1931) 1079 (on πλήρωμα); see also 1076 (on πληρόω). For Mark 1:15 it follows that καιρός here is not punctiliar but equivalent to χρόνος. Among recent treatments, see J. Marcus, "'The Time Has Been Fulfilled!' (Mark 1.15)," in J. Marcus and M. L. Soards (eds.), *Apocalyptic and the New Testament: Essays in Honor of J. Louis Martyn* (JSNTSup 24; Sheffield: JSOT Press, 1989) 49-68. On the theme of eschatological measure, see R. Stuhlmann, *Das eschatologische Mass im Neuen Testament* (Göttingen: Vandenhoeck & Ruprecht, 1983).

7   P. Joüon, "Notes philologiques sur les Évangiles," *RSR* 17 (1927) 537-40, here 538.

Luke 11:49-51). Fill up, then, the measure of your fathers! (Matt 23:32), spoken to persons already set on the death of Jesus (Matt 21:45-46), is a bitterly ironic summons to bring to completion with this prospective crime the last wave of evil allotted to history.

By contrast, the final measure of revelation allotted to Israel is bestowed, now at last, through the agency of Jesus. "Do not think that I have come to annul the Law [or the prophets]; I have come, not to annul but to complete" (Matt 5:17).[8] This motif of the eschatological completion of God's revelation is carried through in the following antitheses (cf. Matt 5:21-22, 27-28, 33-34, 38-39, 43-44) as well as in the accounts of Jesus' teaching in general, e.g. in the move, from Moses' provisional legislation on divorce (Deuteronomy 24) to the eschatological restoration of the idea of paradise (Gen 2:24), enacted anew from the already inaugurated restoration of Israel (Matt 19:3-9 = Mark 10:2-10). In short, Jesus here presents himself as the prophet like Moses, bringing to Israel the final measure of revealed truth.

Third and last, when John in prison sent the question to Jesus, "Are you he who is to come [Ps 118:26], or shall we look for another?" Jesus allowed his actions to speak for him; in the urgent staccato of two-beat rhythm, he answered: Go and tell John what you hear and see:

> blind men see,
> cripples walk,
> lepers are cleansed,
> deaf persons hear,
> dead persons are raised,
> and good news is broken to the poor!
> (Matt 11:5 = Luke 7:22-23)

Jesus is saying that his own public activity in Israel must be read as the superabundant fulfillment of eschatological promises (Isa 35:5-6; 29:18-19; 61:1).[9] He had come as the messianic consolation of Israel (Isa 40:1; Tg. Isa 33:20). Like the answer to the High Priest in the Sanhedrin hearing (Matt 26:64; cf. Luke 22:70), Jesus response is averse to claims (in manner), while entirely affirmative (in substance).

---

[8]   J. Jeremias, *New Testament Theology: I. The Proclamation of Jesus* (New York: Scribner's, 1971) 82-85.

[9]   "Superabundant," especially inasmuch as the Isaianic texts on which Jesus drew do not include reference to raising the dead.

It seems to me that these three phenomena—self-identification as eschatological antitype, the claim that in him and his mission the divine measures assigned to the Eschaton were being brought to completion, and, finally, the specific invitation to interpret his public activity as the fulfillment of eschatological promise and prophecy—are inexplicable except as attesting a unique consciousness: that of mediating God's last, climactic visitation of his people. (We are looking back from two millennia later; this should not distract us into supposing that the Jesus of the public ministry envisioned a long history still to come.)[10] The historicity of the texts is solidly probable and their central meaning appears to be perfectly clear. Let him who has ears hear. But since the music of these texts apparently falls outside the auditory range of many professional listeners, I shall propose a distinct and independent consideration of texts equally intelligible and still more widely acknowledged to be historical, namely, the five data listed in the introduction to this essay.

DID JESUS ANNOUNCE THE IMMINENT END OF HISTORY?

We take it that scholarship has copiously established the historicity of the proclamation of Jesus. The one relevant issue that has not found universal agreement bears on its eschatological character. When Jesus spoke of the imminence of the reign of God (Greek: βασιλεία τοῦ θεοῦ; Aramaic: מַלְכוּתָא דִּי־אֱלָהָא), was this meant to signify the imminence of the end of history? Starting a hundred years ago with Johannes Weiss, this question has periodically appeared to have been settled in the affirmative—only to be upset by some new effort of revisionist scholarship.

In 1935 C. H. Dodd offered a brilliant reconstruction of Jesus' scenario of the future, which included an affirmation of the imminent end of history.[11] But Dodd followed his reconstruction with a historico-hermeneutical account of what it finally meant. The account, under the name "realized eschatology," left nothing still to be expected in the future, whether by Jesus or by the believer today. (In this Dodd was followed by T. F. Glasson[12] and J. A. T.

---

10   B. F. Meyer, *The Aims of Jesus* (London: SCM Press, 1979) 202-208.

11   C. H. Dodd, *The Parables of the Kingdom* (London: Nisbet, 1935) 34-110.

12   T. F. Glasson, *The Second Advent: The Origin of the New Testament Doctrine* (London: Epworth, 1945; 3rd ed., 1963). See also idem, "Schweitzer's Influence: Blessing or Bane?" in B. D. Chilton (ed.), *The Kingdom of God in the*

Robinson,[13] who worked out this view with such consistency that its latent defects became patent.)

Meantime, in an article little noticed (it appeared during the Second World War in a journal that ceased publication before the war was over), Joachim Jeremias offered a positive appreciation of Dodd's historical reconstruction, adding a number of corrections and refinements, and dropping Dodd's unhelpful attempt to free Jesus from the liability of a mythical view of the future.[14]

In the post-War period, existentialist kerygma theology also had its say. Ernst Käsemann attempted, like Dodd, to save Jesus from the luggage of apocalyptic expectations, but forgoing Dodd's laborious indirection. Without flinching at the necessary literary and historical surgery on the Gospels, Käsemann directly attributed to the historical Jesus an exclusively realized eschatology.[15]

Yet another rescue attempt was mounted by George B. Caird.[16] Caird did not contest that Jesus spoke the language of apocalyptic eschatology. The issue was whether he meant this language literally or metaphorically. According to Caird, Jesus expected a metaphorical end of the world. On the literal plane this corresponded to the end of the current era in human history. (Disciples of Caird today include Marcus Borg and N. Thomas Wright.)[17]

Several of these efforts to interpret the proclamation of Jesus came under critical review in 1985 by Dale C. Allison, Jr., in a

---

Teaching of Jesus (IRT 5; London: SPCK; Philadelphia: Fortress, 1984) 107-20.

13   J. A. T. Robinson, *Jesus and His Coming* (2nd ed., Philadelphia: Westminster, 1979).

14   J. Jeremias, "Eine neue Schau der Zukunftsaussagen Jesu," *TBl* 20 (1941) 216-22.

15   E. Käsemann, "Sätze heiligen Rechtes im Neuen Testament," "Die Anfänge christlicher Theologie," and "Zum Thema der urchristlichen Apokalyptik," in Käsemann, *Exegetische Versuche und Besinnungen* (2 vols., Göttingen: Vandenhoeck & Ruprecht, 1965) 2.69-131; ET: "Sentences of Holy Law in the New Testament," "The Beginnings of Christian Theology," and "On the Subject of Primitive Christian Apocalyptic," in Käsemann, *New Testament Questions of Today* (Philadelphia: Fortress, 1969) 66-137.

16   G. B. Caird, *Jesus and the Jewish Nation* (London: Athlone, 1965); idem, *The Language and Imagery of the Bible* (Philadelphia: Westminster, 1980).

17   M. J. Borg, *Conflict, Holiness and Politics in the Teaching of Jesus* (SBEC 5; New York and Toronto: Mellen, 1984); idem, *Jesus: A New Vision* (San Francisco: Harper & Row, 1987); N. T. Wright, *The New Testament and the People of God* (Minneapolis: Fortress, 1992) 332-34.

monograph based on an earlier doctoral dissertation.[18] Allison
conclusively showed that many of them (those especially of Glasson,
Robinson, and Caird) were unsalvageable. His account (though he
was apparently unaware of this) was largely a reprise of Joachim
Jeremias's 1941 reconstruction of Jesus' scenario for the end-time.
Indeed, Jeremias's brief presentation was in certain details more
exact,[19] though Allison's monograph provided a fullness of
treatment—in the framing of the question, the survey of the Gospel
sources, and the repertory of relevant intertestamental and other
Jewish literature—that far surpassed the reach of Jeremias's short
review-article.

Having recently taken up anew the question of Jesus' future
scenario,[20] I shall not review the entire question here. Let it suffice
to say that Johannes Weiss was right at least about Jesus' expectation
of the imminent end of the world. Just prior to Jesus, the Baptist
proclaimed the imminence of the last judgment. Just after Jesus, Paul
repeatedly indicated his hope and expectation of the imminent
parousia of the Lord. In the interim between the Baptist and Paul,
Jesus affirmed that the last judgment, for which the men of Nineveh
and the Queen of the South were to be raised from the dead, was on
the brink.[21]

What Weiss and Schweitzer missed, and what Dodd caught, was
the present realization in Jesus' own time of at least part of Israel's
heritage of eschatological promise and prophecy. To this should be
added the nascent Christian community's unambiguous affirmation of

[18]   See n. 1 above.

[19]   In his numerous historical-Jesus studies Jeremias repeatedly affirmed that
Jesus understood his coming suffering to inaugurate the eschatological ordeal. The
metaphor Jeremias used in *Neutestamentliche Theologie: I. Die Verkündigung Jesu*
(Göttingen: Vandenhoeck & Ruprecht, 1971) 231, was that his suffering would
constitute *der Auftakt* (the first syllable, first beat, opening phrase, prelude) of the
eschatological ordeal. The choice of the term "prelude" in the English translation,
however, led Allison (*The End of the Ages*, 118) (a) to suppose that in Jeremias's
reconstruction Jesus took his own suffering to precede, but not to belong to, the
ordeal; and (b) to find fault with Jeremias's failure to prove the view thus mistakenly attributed to him. (For his own part, Allison [*The End of the Ages*, 117-28] took
the tribulation to be already underway during Jesus' ministry.) See how some of
the most relevant texts (e.g. Matt 26:18; Luke 12:49; 13:33; John 12:19; 16:16) are
read in Jeremias, "Drei-Tage-Worte" and *New Testament Theology*, 127-41.

[20]   B. F. Meyer, "Jesus' Scenario of the Future," *DRev* 109 (1991) 1-15.

[21]   See, e.g., Allison, *The End of the Ages*, 111 n. 40.

the era of fulfillment as having *already arrived*. Both in Jesus himself and in the Easter community of his followers there were two facets of the eschatological consciousness: first, a consciousness of eschatological promise/prophecy "already fulfilled"; second, the complementary consciousness of promise/prophecy "still to be fulfilled." Together these facets of eschatological consciousness commend, as the most useful terminological rubric both for the views of Jesus and for those of the post-Easter Church, "eschatology inaugurated and in process of realization."

FOUR MORE DATA ACKNOWLEDGED TO BE CERTAINLY HISTORICAL

No one doubts the historicity of Jesus' proclamation of the reign of God. Similarly, the historicity of the following is secure: (1) Jesus impressed his contemporaries of one who spoke and acted "as having authority" (Greek: ὡς ἐξουσίαν ἔχων; Aramaic: כְּשַׁלִּיט; cf. Mark 1:22 = Matt 7:29 = Luke 4:22; Mark 1:27 = Luke 4:26). What sort of authority? Not, emphatically, the authority of the professional trained theologian (Mark 11:28 = Matt 21:23 = Luke 20:2); rather that of a charismatic wielding supernatural power over demons, a power that he could and did sovereignly transmit to his disciples (Mark 3:15 = Matt 10:1; Mark 6:7 = Luke 9:1). More, Jesus acted as one bearing the authority to remit sins (Mark 2:10 = Matt 9:5 = Luke 5:24)—in short, like the plenipotentiary of a new economy of salvation.[22]

(2) Once, when some Pharisees delivered a threat against Jesus' life, allegedly from Antipas, Jesus coolly responded with a memorable word on his invulnerability until the moment of God's choosing, when he would indeed be subject to the onslaught of Satan:

> Behold, I drive out demons
> and perform cures
> today and tomorrow,
> and on the third day I complete my course.
> (Luke 13:32)

Since the three-days motif connotes God's sovereignly appointed plan, the sense of the text is: "(Tell that fox that) I cannot be touched until the divinely appointed time." Quite incidentally, however, the

---

[22]   A point made cogently by N. T. Wright in an unpublished paper presented at a McMaster University seminar (14 December 1989) on hermeneutics and the historical Jesus.

saying defines the public career of Jesus under the rubric of exorcisms and cures, thus significantly adding to the sum of testimonies
to Jesus' career as a wonder worker.

Central to these testimonies is a series of sayings: (a) the double
mašal on Beelzebul and the advent of the reign of God (Matt 12:27-
28 = Luke 11:18-20); (b) the *mašal* on dynasties and households
divided against themselves (Mark 3:24-26 = Matt 12:25-26 = Luke
11:17-18); (c) the *mašal* on the binding of the strong man (Mark
3:27 = Matt 12:29 = Luke 11:21); (d) the inference that, if (in the
context established by Jesus' proclamation) it was by God's power
that he drove out demons, *the reign of God had already* (virtually)[23]
come (Matt 12:28 = Luke 11:20). This last motif epitomizes at least
one of the many facets of Jesus' wonder working.

(3) The historic drama of the cleansing of the Temple, as I have
recently argued elsewhere,[24] has been underplayed both by the
Gospels themselves and by recent historical-Jesus research. The
historicity of the event is not in doubt.[25] The meaning of the event is
clearly many-faceted.[26] In the present context, however, the critical
point is that in all its aspects the cleansing is peculiarly charged with
an implicit claim to plenary authority over the destiny, the definitive
restoration, of Israel. A secondary matter is the provenance, in the
public life of Jesus, of the riddle on the new sanctuary. It seems to
me to belong, with mid-range probability, to the follow-up on the
cleansing of the Temple. This follow-up was hardly the question of

---

[23]   The scholastics, building on the Aristotelian distinction of potency and act,
differentiated within "act" between what was formally and what was virtually
actual—a distinction often appropriate to the advance presence of God's reign.

[24]   B. F. Meyer, "The Expiation Motif in the Eucharistic Words: A Key to the
History of Jesus?" *Greg* 69 (1988) 461-87, here 481-84.

[25]   Contrary to R. J. Miller, "The (A)historicity of Jesus' Temple Demonstration: A Test Case in Methodology," in E. H. Lovering, Jr. (ed.), *Society of Biblical
Literature 1991 Seminar Papers* (SBLSP 30; Atlanta: Scholars, 1991) 235-52.

[26]   Among these facets was one that, recently and independently, J. Neusner
("Money-Changers in the Temple: The Mishnah's Explanation," *NTS* 35 [1989]
287-90) and I ("Expiation Motif," 482-84) inferred from the negative stance toward
the cult implicit in Jesus' demonstration at the Temple, namely, that the counterpart
of the Temple cleansing must be the last supper. See now B. Chilton, *A Feast of
Meanings: Eucharistic Theologies from Jesus through Johannine Circles* (NovTSup
72; Leiden: Brill, 1994); idem, "Ideological Diets in a Feast of Meanings," in B.
Chilton and C. A. Evans, *Jesus in Context: Temple, Purity, and Restoration*
(AGJU 39; Leiden: Brill, 1997) 59-89.

ἐξουσία/רְשׁוּת (Mark 11:27-33 = Matt 21:23-27 = Luke 20:1-8); it must rather have been the demand for a sign, as John presents it (John 2:18-19). But whatever the precise source of this word, it is clear that in Jesus' riddling answer (some like: "Destroy this sanctuary and after three days I will build it"; cf. John 2:19 and Mark 14:58), the "authority" was that of the son of David/son of God (2 Sam 7:12; 1 Chr 17:12-13; Ps 2:7; 110:3; 4QFlor 11) commissioned to build God's house (2 Sam 7:13-14; 1 Chr 17:12-13; Hag 1:1-2; 2:20-23; Zech 6:12-13). Inasmuch as "God's house" in texts such as these was open to signifying God's eschatologically restored people (ἐκκλησία/עֵדָה/קָהָל), and since this is precisely the sense of the new sanctuary in Jesus' word, the cleansing itself as well as this word (which, in the present hypothesis, immediately followed on the cleansing) showed that Jesus understood the restoration of Israel to belong to his mission—indeed, as its central task.[27]

(4) In the light of the above ascertainments, the *titulus* on the cross, "the king of the Jews" (ὁ βασιλεὺς τῶν Ἰουδαίων), makes excellent historical sense. In the passion story the key religious question (as shown by Mark 14:61 = Matt 26:63; cf. Luke 22:67) had been whether Jesus would acknowledge his claim, up till now exclusively implicit in the public forum, to be the appointed agent (the Messiah) of the appointed eschatological act (the restoration of Israel). When the Sanhedrists presented this question to Pilate, they gave it a political twist. The *titulus*, doubtless a product of Pilate's own malicious irony, is a solid index to the crime of which Jesus was accused: pretension to royal dominion. The *titulus*, besides being well attested (Mark 15:26 = Matt 27:37 = Luke 23:39 = John 19:19), interlocks easily with the other data on the Sanhedrin's effort to bring about the suppression of Jesus.

Our purpose is not to deal on its own merits with each of the five data adduced here; it is rather to point to the fact that, taken collectively, they converge on Jesus' consciousness of being the bearer of a divinely appointed, climactic and definitive, mission to Israel. Once again, consider these data cumulatively: (a) He proclaims the imminence of the divine saving act celebrated in the prophets as the

---

27   Hence the thesis (in Meyer, "The 'Inside' of the Jesus Event," 169) that "to predicate 'Messiah' of Jesus in the sense he himself intended is to grasp the 'inside' of the Jesus event as the single task of re-creating Israel—and the nations by assimilation to Israel—in fulfillment of the Scriptures."

eschatological restoration of God's people. (b) But he does not just announce it. His public performance, including teaching and wonder working, strikes his contemporaries as maximally authoritative, the authority deriving directly from God. (c) When threatened by Antipas—just as when questioned by the Baptist—his response points to his career as wonder worker: it accords with the divine plan and proceeds under its protection (Luke 13:32) and it fulfills the promises of the Scriptures (Matt 11:5 = Luke 7:22-23). (d) When "reign of God" is taken in the sense that Jesus intended, namely, as God's definitive act of salvation,[28] its correlates include new covenant, new sanctuary, new cult.[29] The thrust of the symbolic action at the Temple accordingly appears to intend the end of the old (Mosaic) dispensation and to intimate some new, implicitly messianic, dispensation. (e) The last wisp of remaining ambiguity is dissipated by the *titulus* on the cross. The conclusion that we find imposed on us (again, not from these five data taken singly but from the five taken cumulatively and collectively) is that Jesus did indeed think of himself as called to a climactic and definitive mission to Israel.

THE SCRIPTURES MUST BE FULFILLED

Many years ago John Downing, in an article on Jesus and martyrdom,[30] offered an apparently irrefutable observation: Jesus, by his proclamation of the imminent coming of the reign of God, implicitly defined himself as God's last voice, the last prophetic envoy to Israel. "He was the last prophet," argued Downing, "for men's reactions to him and to his preaching determined their eschatological destiny (Luke xii.8 and par.)."[31] Or, in the expression of Amos Wilder, Jesus' role was "that of mediator of God's final

---

28   The case was made by G. Dalman (*The Words of Jesus* [Edinburgh: T. & T. Clark, 1902] 96-101), who differentiated this from other senses of the phrase in ancient Judaism.

29   See J. Behm, "διαθήκη," *TDNT* 2 (1964) 124-34, esp. 128, 132-33; Jeremias, *Die Abendmahlsworte Jesu* (Göttingen: Vandenhoeck & Ruprecht, 1960) 217-18: the (new) covenant is "Korrelatbegriff zu βασιλεία τοῦ οὐρανοῦ"; ET: *The Eucharistic Words of Jesus* (London: SCM Press, 1966) 226. But what holds for new covenant holds for new sanctuary and new cult. On the new Temple/sanctuary, see E. P. Sanders, *Jesus and Judaism* (London: SCM Press, 1985) 77-90.

30   J. Downing, "Jesus and Martyrdom," *JTS* 14 (1963) 279-93.

31   Downing, "Jesus and Martyrdom," 286-87.

controversy with his people."[32]

Keeping in mind this motif of "last envoy, last prophet" (which Jesus himself made thematic and emphatic by his warnings to the crowds that time was running out, that the great judgment was on the brink), we should perhaps bring it into relation with the biblical conception of God's word and of his fidelity to his word.

YHWH could be counted on. Thus, when Joshua's work was done, the narrator of his story writes:

> So YHWH gave unto Israel all the land
> that he swore to give unto their fathers,
> and they possessed it and inhabited it;
> and YHWH gave them rest round about
> according to all that he swore unto their fathers;
> and there stood not one of their enemies against them;
> YHWH delivered all their enemies into their hand.
> There failed not aught of all the good things
> that YHWH had spoken unto the house of Israel.
> All came to pass.
> (Josh 21:42-43; English: 21:42-45)

The key word is "all." YHWH gave Israel all the land he had promised, and he gave them rest according to all he had sworn. Of all their enemies not one withstood them; YHWH delivered them all into their hands. Of all the good things that he had said, not one failed. In a word, בָּא הַכֹּל: all came to pass.

This passage is not only repeated again and again in fragmentary fashion in the texts that follow in the book of Joshua; it also epitomizes the biblical theme of YHWH's צְדָקָה/righteousness and his אֱמוּנָה/fidelity, motifs endlessly recurrent in the Scriptures. We are moreover in the presence of a massive index to the way in which Israel would come to understand promise and prophecy for the end-time. The whole of it, all without exception, would come to pass. That specifically included the salvation of the nations by assimilation to eschatologically restored Israel.

The background to new developments in the reading of the Scriptures might be sketched in a few strokes. The traumatic events of the sixth century—the loss of king and aristocracy in 597, the far more violent and severe losses in the capture of Jerusalem and

---

[32]   A. N. Wilder, "Eschatology and the Speech-Modes of the Gospel," in E. Dinkler (ed.), *Zeit und Geschichte: Dankesgabe an Rudolf Bultmann zum 80. Geburtstag* (Tübingen: Mohr [Siebeck], 1964) 19-30, here 29.

destruction of the Temple in 587, another deportation in 582; return followed by disillusionment; rifts and factions in the Judean restoration—are diversely reflected in the new foundations laid by prophecy (Trito-Isaiah and Deutero-Zechariah) and by the reforms of Ezra and Nehemiah. The true restoration of Israel became a leading theme and an ongoing, contentious issue. The transcendent terms into which Trito-Isaiah and Deutero-Zechariah transposed the restoration theme opened the era of proto-apocalyptic, remotely preparing the scene for new forms of faith-literature.

The Macedonian conquest of the East similarly instigated new developments in the way indentured Israel envisaged the salvation of the nation. The probably influx from the eastern Diaspora of mantic wise men (not the representatives of proverbial wisdom such as we find in Ben Sira) may well explain the origins and salient features of the book of Daniel.[33]

In Qumran we find a systematic way of reading the Scriptures, one facet of which is the specification of "the (prophetic) meaning" (*pešer*), which focuses on the community, its origins, status, and destiny. The biblical books partly retain their original sense, but by the time of Jesus they (the prophets in particular) were read as pointing toward definitive fulfillment at the outbreak of the end-time. Qumran furnishes the fullest data on this;[34] but we find it also in intertestamental literature,[35] in the Targums,[36] and in John the Baptist (e.g. John 1:23 on Isa 40:3; cf. Mark 1:3 = Matt 3:4 = Luke 3:4).

---

[33] J. J. Collins, *The Apocalyptic Vision of the Book of Daniel* (HSM 16; Missoula: Scholars Press, 1977) 56-57.

[34] Though there are numerous good general expositions (e.g. O. Betz, *Offenbarung und Schriftforschung in der Qumransekte* [WUNT 6; Tübingen: Mohr (Siebeck), 1960]; M. P. Horgan, *Pesharim: Qumran Interpretation of Biblical Books* [CBQMS 8; Washington: Catholic Biblical Association, 1979]), to understand concretely the Essenes' style of interpreting, special studies of individual tests (e.g. W. H. Brownlee, *The Midrash Pesher of Habakkuk* [SBLMS 24; Missoula: Scholars Press, 1979]) are indispensable.

[35] See J. Barton, *Oracles of God* (Oxford: Oxford University Press, 1986); C. Rowland, "The Inter-Testamental Literature," in J. Rogerson, C. Rowland, and B. Lindards (eds.), *The History of Christian Theology: II. The Use of the Bible* (Grand Rapids: Eerdmans, 1988) 153-225.

[36] In the present context, see esp. B. Chilton, *A Galilean Rabbi and His Bible: Jesus' Use of the Interpreted Scripture of His Time* (GNS 8; Wilmington: Glazier, 1984); and idem, *The Isaiah Targum* (ArBib 11; Wilmington: Glazier, 1987).

Paul, looking back, would say, "Whatever promises God has made, their Yes is in him" (2 Cor 1:2). Similarly, Jesus himself, repudiating the charge of annulling the Scriptures, claimed rather to bring them to completion and fulfillment (Matt 5:17 = Luke 16:17; Matt 11:5 = Luke 7:22).

In the introduction to this essay we sketched an argument according to which a consciousness like that of Jesus, i.e. of one charged with a climactic and definitive mission to God's people, should lead us to expect to find in him a phenomenon otherwise unexampled in ancient Israel: the conviction that God's promises for the end-time *were already being fulfilled.*[37] Now we may be more specific. We should expect to find that, as time passed and the fulfillment of the whole-to-be-fulfilled was inaugurated and underway, Jesus should somehow indicate (a) that some of this whole-to-be-fulfilled had now, already, found fulfillment; (b) that some of it was now finding fulfillment (i.e. during his public career); (c) that some of it was about to find fulfillment; and (d) that, since the prominent, perhaps dominant, end-time scenario (e.g. Dan 12:1-2) posits a distinction between the great affliction and its cessation (e.g. with the resurrection of the dead), all the rest, i.e. whatever of prophecy remains still outstanding (including the very resolution of the ordeal) would find fulfillment when the mission of Jesus would be crowned by the advent of God's "reign."

In point of fact, we find among the data of the Gospel story the full confirmation of this multiple expectation. (a) After Antipas' execution of the Baptist, we learn that in Jesus' view God had already fulfilled the Elijah promise/prophecy (Mal 3:23-24; English: 4:5-6; Sir 48:10) in the mission of John. (b) Earlier, by way of answer to the Baptist's query, Jesus pointed to his own career of wonder working and proclaiming as bringing prophetic oracles of salvation to fulfillment here and now. (c) Again, he instructed the inner circle of his disciples that he was destined by prophetic necessity to be repudiated and killed (in accord with the role of the Servant of the

---

37   Chilton (*God in Strength: Jesus' Announcement of the Kingdom* [SNTU 1; Freistadt: Plöchl, 1979; repr. BibSem 8; Sheffield: JSOT Press, 1987]; idem, *A Galilean Rabbi*, 148-98) has observed that Jesus proclaims as fulfilled what is anticipated in the Aramaic paraphrase of Isaiah (to which the later Isaiah Targum gives witness). The Aramaic's "the kingdom of your God is revealed" (cf. *Tg.* Isa 52:7: אתגליאת מלכותא דאלהיך) in the language of Jesus becomes "the kingdom of God has come" (Mark 1:15: ἤγγικεν ἡ βασιλεία τοῦ θεοῦ).

Lord who, to be sure, was equally destined to be vindicated and glorified; see Mark 9:1 and its many parallels);[38] moreover, the disciples were to share in this suffering, which would signal the outbreak of the eschatological ordeal. (d) Finally, once the tribulation or ordeal had run its fierce but brief course, he would complete his work as the Davidic master-builder of the new sanctuary (i.e. of the people of the new covenant) (Mark 14:58 = Matt 26:61 = John 2:19; cf. Acts 6:14), a saying that, once more, inescapably implied the total reversal of his personal fate. This would be the moment at which the gentile world would be judged and saved (Matt 8:11 = Luke 13:29).[39]

These data of fulfillment—not exhaustive, but merely representative of the full picture offered by the Gospels—are telling. They meet our expectation that, given the kind of consciousness of mission that we can with assurance affirm of Jesus, and given the ancient Judaic view of the Scriptures as having the aspect of prophecy to be fulfilled in the Eschaton, we should expect to find in him the conviction that *in this last, climactic mission to Israel, and therefore in the bearer of this last, climactic mission, the Scriptures—all the Scriptures without remainder—had, of divine or prophetic necessity, to come to fulfillment.*

JESUS: PROXIMATE SOURCE OF THE MESSIANOLOGY OF THE GOSPELS

If the Scriptures had prophetically spoken, as Jesus was fully persuaded that they had, of God's decisive saving act, namely, the restoration of Israel, of the *mebasser* or herald who was to announce it (Isa 52:7), of the prophet like Moses who was to reveal its demands (Deut 18:15, 18), of the Davidic Messiah anointed to accomplish it (2 Sam 7:13-16; cf. 4QFlor), of the Servant who would extend it to the ends of the earth (Isa 49:6), of the one like a (son of) man whose triumph would seal it (Dan 7:9-27), it follows that we are

---

38   See Jeremias, *New Testament Theology*, 281-86, on Mark 9:31 and its many parallels.

39   See the still valuable B. Sundkler, "Jesus et les païens," *RHPR* 16 (1936) 462-99; J. Jeremias, *Jesu Verheissung für die Völker* (Stuttgart: Kohlhammer, 1956); ET: *Jesus' Promise to the Nations* (SBT 24; London: SCM Press, 1958); J. Dupont, "'Beaucoup viendront du levant et du couchant . . .' (Matthieu 8,11-12; Luc 13,28-29)," *ScEccl* 9 (1967) 153-67.

faced immediately with prophecies and promises which, precisely at that last moment, called inescapably for fulfillment.

How might we form an idea of what, in the Scriptures, Jesus took to be soteriologically significant, to call for fulfillment? The clues must be sought in the Gospel texts. After an initial period of public activity as the ally of the Baptist until the latter's arrest (John 3:22-26),[40] Jesus inaugurated his own independent public career in Galilee (Mark 1:14 = Matt 4:12 = Luke 4:14) with the public proclamation, made especially in synagogues but also out-of-doors: "The reign of God is at hand/has arrived!" (Greek: ἤγγικεν ἡ βασιλεία τοῦ θεοῦ/ Aramaic: מַלְכוּתָא דִּי־אֱלָהָא קְרֵבַת). To many who heard it, these words surely recalled the *Qaddiš* prayer (יִמְלוֹךְ מַלְכוּתיה: "may he allow his reign to reign . . .") recited weekly in the Synagogue and just as surely evoked the news of salvation epitomized in the cry מָלַךְ אֱלֹהָיִךְ, "your God reigns!" (Isa 52:7). This accordingly suggests that Jesus spoke in the voice of the Isaianic מְבַשֵּׂר/εὐαγγελιζ-όμενος—a figure interpreted at Qumran in "messianic" terms: "one anointed with the Spirit" (11QMelch 2:18).[41] In Isaiah, then, Jesus found both his career as proclaimer of salvation and the essential burden of his proclamation.

Though, as it happens, we have no confirmatory textual index, it is highly probable that, like his contemporaries, Jesus took the promise of a prophet like Moses (Deut 15:15, 18) to await its fulfillment in the end-time—and concretely to find this fulfillment in his own act of bringing to completion the last measure, the fullness, of revealed truth (Matt 5:17).

It is quite out of the question that Jesus should not have been aware of the many strands of biblical tradition promising a new David or son of David appointed to mediate God's act of restoring his people. Let it suffice to refer to the riddle of the new sanctuary (Mark 14:58 = Matt 26:61 = John 2:19) with its biblical antecedents on the one appointed to build God's house (2 Sam 7:12-13; cf. 1 Chr 12:13-14; Hag 2:20-23; Zech 6:12-13). There are, of course, many other texts that show Jesus' hold on motifs of royal messianism (e.g. the

---

40   On Jesus as "baptizer," see Meyer, *Aims of Jesus*, 122-24.

41   J. A. Fitzmyer, "Further Light on Melchizedek from Qumran Cave 11," *JBL* 86 (1967) 25-41; repr. in Fitzmyer, *Essays on the Semitic Background of the New Testament* (London: Geoffrey Chapman, 1971; repr. SBLSBS 5; Missoula: Scholars Press, 1974) 245-67.

Caesarea Philippi scene;[42] the royal entry into Jerusalem;[43] repeated use of shepherd imagery).[44]

So far as the Isaianic Servant passages are concerned, we find at least two pieces of evidence for Jesus' awareness especially of the last, great passage as soteriologically significant prophecy. These two crucial texts are Mark 10:45 = Matt 20:28 (the ransom word, which specifies the beneficiaries of the ransom as "many" [cf. Isa 52:14-15; 53:11-12], and for which Peter Stuhlmacher has provided both a striking exegesis and a persuasive argument in favor of historicity),[45] and Mark 14:24 = Matt 26:28 (the word over the cup, which brings together two motifs of Isaiah 53: the "pouring out" of the Servant's life [Isa 53:12] and, again, the "many").

The two most significant indices to Jesus' keen awareness of the great apocalyptic scene of Daniel 7 are, first, his references to the thrones for the court of judgment (Dan 7:9-10) in Matt 19:28 = Luke 22:29 and, second, the "little flock" saying in Luke 12:32, where the motif of transferring to the disciples a share in royal dominion is derived from Dan 7:27.[46] We might add that the Lukan form of Jesus' words in the Sanhedrin scene (Luke 22:69), which takes nothing from Daniel 7 except the term Son of man, is probably prior to the parallels in Mark and Matthew and probably authentic.[47]

Our conclusion is that Jesus, in the consciousness of election to a climactic and definitive mission to Israel, sought and found in the

---

[42]   Meyer, *Aims of Jesus*, 185-97.

[43]   Meyer, *Aims of Jesus*, 168-70, 199.

[44]   On messianic shepherd imagery, see Ezek 34:23-24; 37:24; Zech 13:7-9; cf. 12:10; 13:1-6. On shepherd imagery in the Gospels, see G. Dalman, "Arbeit und Sitte in Palästina vi," *BFCT* 2.41 (1939) 249-50, 253-55.

[45]   P. Stuhlmacher, "Existenzstellvertretung für die Vielen: Mk 10,45 (Mt 20,28)," in R. Albertz et al. (eds), *Werden und Wirken des Alten Testaments* (C. Westermann Festschrift; Göttingen: Vandenhoeck & Ruprecht, 1980) 412-27; repr. in Stuhlmacher, *Versöhnung, Gesetz und Gerechtigkeit. Aufsätze zur biblischen Theologie* (Göttingen: Vandenhoeck & Ruprecht, 1981) 27-42; ET: "Vicariously Giving His Life for Many, Mark 10:45 (Matt. 20:28)," in Stuhlmacher, *Reconciliation, Law, and Righteousness* (Philadelphia: Fortress, 1986) 16-29.

[46]   O. Betz, *Jesus und das Danielbuch: II. Die Menschensohnworte Jesu und die Zukunftserwartung des Paulus (Daniel 7,13-14)* (ANTJ 6.2; Frankfurt am Main: Lang, 1985). On the two texts adduced, see Jeremias, *New Testament Theology*, 205 n. 4, 265.

[47]   B. F. Meyer, "How Jesus Charged Language with Meaning: A Study in Rhetoric," *SR* 19 (1990) 273-85, here 285, with n. 32.

Scriptures the specifications of God's eschatological deed and the specifications of his own role as the chosen instrumental doer of that deed. By ineluctable logic these Scriptures could not, in Jesus' view, fail to find fulfillment in the drama of his own mission and in its swiftly approaching climax—the ordeal and its resolution. All the Scriptures must find fulfillment, whether in the now of his mission or in the rapidly approaching ordeal and final triumph. If the Baptist had fulfilled the Elijah role, Jesus with his disciples was to fulfill the roles of servant of the Lord and Davidic builder of the house of God. Moreover, though Jesus never simply relaxed that altereity which typified his words on the Son of man,[48] picturing him, for example, as witnessing for or against people in accord with how they had stood vis-à-vis Jesus (Mark 8:38; Matt 10:33 = Luke 12:9), it is ultimately inescapable that he understood himself as destined to perform the triumphant role of the Son of man. It is an attractive hypothesis that, adopting a deliberately ambiguous use of "Son of man" (Greek: υἱὸς ἀνθρώπου/Aramaic: בַּר אֱנָשׁ), he applied it both to humanity in general and to himself (in his prediction of the passion, in Mark 9:31 parr.).[49] If Luke 22:69 is an authentic word, we are given a hint of Jesus' focus on Psalm 110; this in turn grounds the hypothesis that he provided at least a hint (e.g. Mark 12:35-37 = Matt 22:41-46 = Luke 20:41-44) that he himself, now the lowly son of David, but soon to be transcendently enthroned— therefore David's "lord"—at the right hand of God.[50] This, of course, correlates and converges with the role of the Son of man on the "Day when the Son of man will be revealed" (Luke 17:30; cf. vv. 24, 31). Nevertheless, for the disciples only the Easter experience would definitively break down the altereity that somehow differentiated between Jesus and "the (Son of) man." (In the light of that breakdown, it is amazing that the original form of the sayings, which exhibit it, should have been so well preserved in the tradition.)

The procedure of the above argument, one that puts a premium on the value of heuristic anticipations, has been consciously and inevitably schematic. First, we acknowledge evidence for Jesus' firm

---

[48]   Jeremias, *New Testament Theology*, 265-66, and, still more relevantly and incisively, 275-76.

[49]   See above n. 38.

[50]   On the sense of the pericope on David's son and David's lord, see Jeremias, *New Testament Theology*, 259, 276.

personal conviction of election. He was a man with a mission; the mission bore on and belonged to the climactic and definitive saving act of God. Jesus accordingly found himself called to function as God's (intimately instrumental) agent with respect to what the Scriptures defined as the final restoration of Israel, comprehending (by assimilation to Israel) the salvation of the nations. Second, to this we added the observation that Jesus could not have failed to expect that the sum total of scriptural promise and prophecy was bound by divine necessity to come to fulfillment in connection with his own mission. Third, we consequently found ourselves in the position of being able to articulate a set of significant anticipations: that the accounts of Jesus should yield evidence (a) of eschatology inaugurated and in process of realization; (b) of eschatology in accord with the schema of crisis to be followed by resolution (Dan 12:1-2; cf. Isaiah 53) and hence of some elements of fulfillment postponed until the moment of resolution; (c) on Jesus' part, of some reflection on and correlation of such soteriological themes (interpreted as prophecy) as the herald of salvation, the awaited prophet, the royal Messiah, the Servant of the Lord, and the one like a man in Daniel 7; (d) on the disciples' part, of the probably fragmentary, only partly thematic, and gradually developing knowledge or realization of the eschatological roles of Jesus. Fourth, we found that these anticipations were solidly met by the data of the Gospels. Fifth, we concluded that Jesus himself had been the principal source of the earliest post-Easter messianology/Christology.

We should add that in this reconstruction Jesus is seen as intent on listening to the Scriptures for the orientation of his life and mission. We do not, however, find in him one constantly and restlessly engaged in adjustments, revisions, changes of heart and mind. The paucity of messianic self-revelation accorded on the part of Jesus neither with simple ignorance nor with any supposed sense of personal ordinariness, but with an economy of revelation that withheld the secret of his person and destiny out of realism and wisdom respecting his listeners. Hence the special importance that accrues to the esoteric traditions in the Gospels. It should be added that the disciples were neither swift nor deft in construing the intentions and paradoxical self-disclosures of Jesus. The conditions of the possibility of accurate comprehension were not given except with the so-called Easter experience. But what this experience generated in the disciples was not the celebration of new, previously unknown messianic and soteriological themes. *All* had been repeatedly adumbrated, if not made thematic, by Jesus.

CONCLUSION

We have offered the reader an experiment, a mode of investigation (moving from heuristic anticipations to the interpretation of the data) hitherto little used in biblical criticism,[51] though it has been successfully brought to bear on other fields.[52] Its principal advantage is that the orientation of the investigation, made explicit from the start, derives less from the undiscussed preferences of the investigator (which in some measure are always present, albeit most variously in how, from scholar to scholar, they relate to the purity of the desire to know) but from a grasp of procedures spontaneously operative in ancient Judaism. The orientation in question here derives from the manner in which Jesus and his contemporaries typically read the Scriptures.

We moved (a) from the evidence of Jesus' conviction of personal election to a mission bearing on God's climactic saving act (b) through the Scriptures, read as prophecy reserved for eschatological fulfillment, (c) to the anticipation, *and its satisfaction*, of a many-sided, scripturally prophesied role and destiny. To the chosen one the Scriptures revealed in advance the saving mission and its bearer— deed and doer alike in all their variety.

Among the limits of this procedure two are noteworthy: its schematic character and its essential incompleteness vis-à-vis the reality of Jesus and his mission. (Where do we find in the Scriptures so much as a hint of Jesus' initiatives toward notorious sinners? Where do they foretell his heavy accent on forgiveness and the rejection of resentment and vengeance?) Its two main strengths are also noteworthy: the orienting principle of the inquiry is a set of verifiable observations about antiquity which markedly diminish that ever widening gap between ourselves and the suppositions operative in ancient Judaism but not among us. Of these we tend to be

---

[51]   An exception (though perhaps not an altogether successful one) is the collaboration of W. Thüsing and K. Rahner, *A New Christology* (New York: Seabury, 1980).

[52]   An example is the argument from human problem to heuristic specification of the divine solution in B. Lonergan, *Insight* (New York: Longmans, Green, 1958) 687-730.

oblivious or amnesiac, or at least we systematically minimize them. The result is to find that data—unambiguous in context—tend, without that context, to grow dim and almost to vanish before our eyes in a cloud of ambiguity.

Those who suppose that scholarship consists in a leisurely cultivation of ambiguity and in recoil from "closure," including the closure intrinsic to framing arguments and drawing conclusions, are likely to repudiate the procedure either with cool disdain or the vehemence of offended theology.[53] Those, on the other hand, who think that historical inquiry should devise new ways of heading for historical conclusions may well find some merit in the procedure.

---

[53]   The recoil from the closure proper to judgments of credibility and to beliefs pervades Northrop Frye's transactions with the Bible in *The Great Code* (London and New York: Harcourt Brace Jovanovich, 1982). If ideology is the rationalization of alienation, this is ideological, transparently alienated as it is from belief, which Frye conceives single- and narrow-mindedly as headed for religious war. See my essay, "A Tricky Business: Ascribing New Meaning to Old Texts," *Greg* 71 (1990) 745-61.

THE ITINERANT JESUS AND HIS HOME TOWN

J. Ramsey Michaels

The only saying of Jesus in the entire Gospel of John judged likely to be authentic by the Jesus Seminar is found in John 4:44 (προφήτης ἐν τῇ ἰδίᾳ πατρίδι τιμὴν οὐκ ἔχει), translated by the Seminar as "A prophet gets no respect on his own turf."[1] The more common rendering is "A prophet has no honor in his own country" (RSV, NIV). The Seminar opted to print all the varied forms of this saying (John 4:44; Matt 13:57; Mark 6:4; Luke 4:24; and *Gospel of Thomas* §31) in pink, indicating substantial authenticity. Normally, the Jesus Seminar does not accept sayings judged to be proverbial, or mere expressions of conventional wisdom,[2] but in this instance the editors concluded, "In spite of its seemingly proverbial character, a majority of the fellows were of the opinion that the simple proverb was plausible in the context of Jesus' activity and the rejection of him in his own village; his rejection is not something the evangelists would have invented. Accordingly, the saying merits a pink designation."[3]

John 4:44

John 4:44 comes within a parenthetical comment by the Gospel writer, and therefore has no actual narrative context of its own. At

---

[1]   R. W. Funk and R. W. Hoover (eds.), *The Five Gospels: The Search for the Authentic Words of Jesus* (New York: Macmillan, 1993) 412. The only Johannine sayings printed in gray (indicating some kind of indirect relationship to authentic words of Jesus) are John 12:24, 25 and 13:20.

[2]   See, for example, Epictetus, *Discourses* 3.16.11: "It is for this reason that the philosophers advise us to leave even our own countries [καὶ τῶν πατρίδων], because old habits distract us and do not allow a beginning to be made of another custom, and we cannot bear to have men meet us and say, 'Look, So-and-so is philosophizing, although he is this sort of a person or that'" (Loeb edition, 2.107-109); Dio Chrysostom, *Discourses* 47.6: "It was the opinion of all the philosophers that life in their own native land [ἐν τῇ πατρίδι] was hard" (Loeb edition, 4.251). The classic parallel to the saying of Jesus is Philostratus, *Epistle* 44: "Other men regard me as the equal of the gods, and some of them even as a god, but until now my own country [ἡ πατρίς] alone ignores me" (Loeb edition, 2.437).

[3]   Funk and Hoover (eds.), *The Five Gospels*, 491.

the point when Jesus left Sychar in Samaria to go to Galilee, the writer recalls that Jesus once said this (αὐτὸς γὰρ Ἰησοῦς ἐμαρτύρησεν), but does not tell us when or under what circumstances. Moreover, it is cited as indirect rather than direct discourse, a summary rather than an exact quotation. In the synoptic Gospels, by contrast, the narrative context is quite specific. In Luke a very similar saying, "No prophet is acceptable in his home town" (οὐδεὶς προφήτης δεκτός ἐστιν ἐν τῇ πατρίδι αὐτοῦ, Luke 4:24) is linked explicitly to "Nazara [i.e. Nazareth], where he was brought up" (4:16).[4] Matthew and Mark have a longer, negative form of the same pronouncement, "A prophet is not without honor except in his home town"(Οὐκ ἔστιν προφήτης ἄτιμος εἰ μὴ ἐν τῇ πατρίδι), with Matthew adding the words, "and in his own house" (καὶ ἐν τῇ οἰκίᾳ αὐτου, Matt 13:57), and Mark adding, "and among his relatives and in his own house" (καὶ ἐν τοῖς συγγενεῦσιν αὐτοῦ καὶ ἐν τῇ οἰκίᾳ αὐτοῦ, Mark 6:4). Explicit references in Matthew and Mark to Jesus' mother Mary, to his brothers James, Joseph (or Joses), Judas, and Simon, and to his sisters (Matt 13:55-56; Mark 6:3), underscore the point that Jesus found no honor as a prophet even in his immediate family.[5] In Matthew and Mark, as in Luke, the setting is Jesus' actual home town, or πατρίς (Matt 13:54; Mark 6:1), and it is likely, though not absolutely certain, that these two Gospels also identified the home town as Nazareth. Mark mentions Nazareth by name only once, when "Jesus came from Nazareth of Galilee and was baptized in the Jordan by John" (1:9), but refers four times to Jesus as a "Nazarene" (1:24; 10:47; 14:67; 16:6). According to Matthew, Joseph "settled down" (κατῴκησεν) with his family in Nazareth (2:23), but Jesus later left Nazareth and "settled down" (κατῴκησεν) in Capernaum (4:13). Yet Matthew too has Jesus later identified by the crowds in Jerusalem as "the prophet Jesus who is from Nazareth of Galilee" (21:11).

In John the saying has no apparent connection with Jesus' actual home town or family, even though Jesus is clearly a native of Nazareth as in the other Gospels. His first disciples call him "Jesus

---

4   Jesus imagines that the townspeople of Nazareth will say, "whatever things we have heard done in Capernaum, do *here in your home town*" (ὧδε ἐν τῇ πατρίδι σου, Luke 4:23; cf. also Luke 1:26; 2:4, 39, 51).

5   See also Matt 12:46-50 = Mark 3:31-35; Matt 19:29 = Mark 10:29-30.

from Nazareth, son of Joseph" (1:45),[6] and Nathanael asks, "Can
anything good come out of Nazareth?" (1:46). But Jesus never comes
to Nazareth in the Gospel of John. The question of his antecedents
comes up not in Nazareth, but Capernaum.[7] Interpreters, therefore,
have rather consistently translated ἐν τῇ ἰδίᾳ πατρίδι in John 4:44
not "in his home town," but "in his own country," whether understood as Galilee or Judea..[8] They have further assumed that the key
to understanding the text is the precise identification of the πατρίς.
Is the country Galilee, Judea, or some other region? If Galilee,[9] how
does the saying provide a reason for going there? Was Jesus
deliberately looking for a place where he would have "no honor"? If
so, his hopes seem to have been disappointed, for the narrator
immediately mentions that when he arrived "the Galileans welcomed
him" (v. 45).[10] The saying is more naturally understood as explaining
why Jesus would avoid a place or leave it than why he would seek it
out. Yet if he meant Judea,[11] why is the saying quoted at 4:44 instead

---

6   For "son of Joseph," cf. Luke 4:22 (also Matt 13:55, "the son of the
carpenter").

7   Within a dialog said to take place while Jesus was "teaching in synagogue at
Capernaum" (6:59), a group identified as "the Jews" (οἱ Ἰουδαῖοι) asks, "Is this
not Jesus the son of Joseph, whose father and mother we know?" (6:42).

8   This is the case with most English versions, which tend to translate πατρίς
as "home town" in the synoptics, but "country" in John 4:44. Rudolf Bultmann is
quite emphatic on the point: "Πατρίς v. 44 of course means 'fatherland' and not
'home-town'" (The Gospel of John: A Commentary [Philadelphia: Westminster,
1971] 204).

9   This is the majority view. See, e.g. R. E. Brown, The Gospel according to
John I–XII (AB 29; Garden City: Doubleday, 1966) 187; R. Schnackenburg, The
Gospel according to John (New York: Crossroad, 1982) 1.462; D. A. Carson, The
Gospel According to St. John (Grand Rapids: Eerdmans, 1991) 235-36; E.
Haenchen, John 1: A Commentary on the Gospel of John Chapters 1–6
(Hermeneia; Philadelphia: Fortress, 1984) 234. These authors appeal simply to the
fact that Jesus in the Gospel of John is a Galilean (1:45; 6:42; 7:41, 52).

10   John Wesley solved the problem with the comment, "He went into Galilee
—that is, into the Country of Galilee; but not to Nazareth. It was at that town only
that he had no Honour. Therefore he went to other towns" (Explanatory Notes
upon the New Testament [London: William Bowyer, 1755] 234).

11   This view that John means Judea (or Jerusalem) is as old as Origen,
Commentary on John 13.372 (translated by Ronald E. Heine, in Fathers of the
Church 89 [Washington: Catholic University of America, 1993] 148). Among
moderns, see B. F. Westcott, The Gospel according to John (Grand Rapids:
Eerdmans, 1950) 77-78.

of at 4:3, when he first left Judea for Galilee? And even then, the reason for his departure was not that he found no honor in Judea, but that he found so much honor it was an embarrassment to him (cf. 3:26; 4:1-3). Nor, despite the immediate context, can the πατρίς be Samaria. Even though his enemies will later denounce him as a Samaritan (8:48), the clear presumption throughout Jesus' encounter with the Samaritan woman is that she is a Samaritan and he a Jew (4:9, 19, 22).

The difficulties besetting every specific identification of the πατρίς raise the intriguing possibility that the interpretation of John 4:44 may not depend on such an identification at all. Rudolf Bultmann drops an unintentional clue to this effect in his commentary on the passage. In listing various interpretations, he mentions in passing those of Alfred Loisy and Emmanuel Hirsch:

> Loisy thinks that Samaria, because it was part of Palestine, was also Jesus' πατρίς; since he had found no honour there, he must now leave on the principle stated in v. 44! Similarly, Hirsch (who takes v. 44 as a gloss, as do others): Jesus leaves Samaria so quickly lest it become a πατρίς for him.[12]

Bultmann's "similarly" conceals a significant difference between the two interpretations. While Loisy identifies the πατρίς with Samaria, Hirsch makes no specific identification at all. The relevant passage in Hirsch's work bears this out:[13]

> Der Sinn dieses Zusatzes kann dann bloss sein, die Kürze des Verweilens bei den Samaritern zu begründen. Jesus blieb nicht solange, dass die Samariterstadt seine πατρίς wurde, weil ein Prophet nichts gilt da, wo er eine Heimat hat oder zu haben versucht. Das Wort sieht das Wandern und nicht lange bleiben also dem Propheten gemäss an.[14]

Hirsch's interpretation is by no means dependent on his judgment that v. 44 is a redactor's gloss. His appeal is simply to the notion that Jesus was regarded at some stage of the tradition as an itinerant

---

12 Bultmann, *John*, 205.

13 Caution is obviously necessary in dealing with German theologians from the Nazi era (such as Hirsch, or even Bultmann) on the subject of Jesus' Jewish roots. Yet we are dealing here with a kind of two-edged sword: whatever Jesus' πατρίς may have been, it was a place where he had "no honor." It is best, therefore, to take Hirsch's proposal at face value and judge it on its merits, aside from political issues.

14 E. Hirsch, *Studien zum vierten Evangelium* (Tübingen: Mohr [Siebeck], 1936) 55.

prophet. Such a prophet who stays in a town more than two days wears out his welcome. In effect he makes the town his πατρίς, and has no honor there. Instead of serving to explain why Jesus was rejected in his actual home town, it becomes in John the explanation of why he kept moving instead of settling down in one place. On this interpretation, πατρίς is a town or village in John 4:44, just as in the synoptics, not a whole region such as Judea or Galilee. But it is *any* village, not a particular one. The question in the immediate context is how long Jesus will remain in the Samaritan village of Sychar (4:5), but under other circumstances it might have been Bethany or Cana or Capernaum. The point is simply to reinforce the notion that Jesus' ministry was an itinerant one.

Read in this light, John 4:44 recalls the principle laid down in the second-century in the *Didache*: "Let every apostle who comes to you be received as the Lord, but he shall stay only one day or if necessary a second as well; but if he stays three days, he is a false prophet" (*Did.* 11:4-5). These instructions belong to what the writer calls the "behavior of the Lord" (τοὺς τρόπους κυρίου, lit. "the ways of the Lord," *Did.* 11:8), a phrase suggesting a tradition about Jesus' own practice during his ministry. It is natural to ask whether or not this was consistently Jesus' practice in the Gospel of John. Many commentators have pointed out a six-day sequence in John 1:19–2:11, and one could make a case that Jesus spent four days in "Bethany beyond Jordan" (1:28), the sequence being punctuated by the repeated phrase, "the next day" in 1:29, 35, and 43. But Jesus did not appear on the scene until the second day (v. 29), and on the fourth "decided to leave for Galilee" (v. 43). When he arrived at the Cana wedding, it was said to be "the third day" (2:1), not the sixth, and after the wedding Jesus moved on with his disciples and relatives to Capernaum, where he remained "not many days" (2:12). Later he remained at the same "Bethany beyond Jordan" for an undetermined period of time (10:40), and when he learned that his friend Lazarus was sick he "remained two days in the place where he was" (11:6). Similarly, we are told that he stayed "two days" with the Samaritans at Sychar (4:40), and after the two days left for Galilee (4:43). The feast of Tabernacles in Jerusalem was a seven-day feast, but Jesus did not arrive at the Temple until "it was already the middle of the feast" (7:14).

It appears that time designations in this Gospel, *when they are precise*, do tend to agree with the tradition about itinerant prophets found in the *Didache*. Other time intervals are left indeterminate, perhaps deliberately,[15] but nothing in the Gospel flatly violates that tradition—*until* Jesus comes to Jerusalem! He arrives in Bethany (*not* "beyond Jordan," but near Jerusalem) "six days before Passover" (12:1), and proceeds from there, after his anointing by Mary, into Jerusalem (12:12-19), where he remains until his death and resurrection. For this reason, those interpreters who have argued that in the final analysis Jesus' πατρίς is specifically the city of Jerusalem have a point worthy of consideration.[16] Jerusalem is preeminently the place where Jesus has "no honor," or rather where the honor he does have proves false. The form of the parenthetical aside in John 4:44 is noticeably similar to that of another such comment made by the narrator in connection with Jesus' first visit to Jerusalem (2:24-25). This can be shown as follows:

> *John 2:24-25*: But Jesus himself [αὐτὸς δὲ 'Ιησοῦς] did not entrust himself to them because he knew all things, and because he had no need for anyone to testify about human beings [περὶ τοῦ ἀνθρώπου], for he himself knew [αὐτὸς γὰρ ἐγίνωσκεν] what was in humans [ἐν τῷ ἀνθρώπῳ].

> *John 4:44*: For Jesus himself testified[17] [αὐτὸς γὰρ 'Ιησοῦς ἐμαρτύρησεν] that a prophet has no honor in his home town.

The almost formulaic similarity suggests that the same narrator (probably the Gospel writer) is at work in both places. The narrator reminds us in the first instance that Jesus did not trust the people of Jerusalem, or in fact human beings generally,[18] and in the second that Jesus had actually said something to that effect. The implication of Jesus' remark is that he chose for himself an itinerant ministry, with no "home town" in this world. This, the narrator tells is, is why

---

15   Not only 2:12; 7:14; and 10:40, but 3:22, when Jesus "remained" with his disciples somewhere in Judea and baptized, and 11:54, when he "remained" with them at a place called Ephraim for an unspecified length of time.

16   See, e.g. E. C. Hoskyns, *The Fourth Gospel* (London: Faber and Faber, 1947) 260-61; and J. Willemse, "La Patrie de Jésus selon Saint Jean," *NTS* 11 (1964-65) 349-64.

17   Or "had testified." Notice that ἐμαρτύρησεν in 4:44 is aorist, in contrast to the imperfects ἐπίστευεν ("entrusted") in 2:24 and ἐγίνωσκεν ("knew") in 2:25. This rendering would imply that the narrator understood Jesus' comment about the prophet without honor to have preceded his departure from Samaria in chap. 4.

18   Cf. 5:41-42, where Jesus reinforces the point of 2:24-25 in his own words: "I do not receive glory from human beings [παρὰ ἀνθρώπων], and what's more I know you [ἀλλὰ ἔγνωκα ὑμᾶς], that you do not have the love of God in you."

he left Sychar in Samaria after only two days—despite the Samaritans' faith (vv. 41-42)—and moved on to Cana in Galilee (4:43-46).

The larger Johannine setting of the principle that "A prophet has no honor in his home town" (προφήτης ἐν τῇ ἰδίᾳ πατρίδι τιμὴν οὐκ ἔχει) is of course the notice that Jesus "came to his own [εἰς τὰ ἴδια],[19] and his own people [οἱ ἴδιοι] did not receive him" (1:11). Implicitly, the accent is at first on Jesus' rejection *by* his πατρίς— and by the world[20]—but because Jesus knows the end from the beginning (2:24-25) this theme quickly gives way to Jesus' rejection *of* his πατρίς in favor of an itinerant ministry. "His own" are no longer the people of the world, but "his own who are in the world" (τοὺς ἰδίους τοὺς ἐν τῷ κόσμῳ, 13:1), that is, his disciples.[21] Moreover, God is "his own Father" (πατέρα ἴδιον, 5:18), and Jesus seeks not "his own glory" (τὴν δόξαν τὴν ἰδίαν), but that of his Father (7:18; cf. 8:50, 54). Jesus "honors" his Father (τιμῶ, 8:49), and his Father, in turn, has committed "all judgment" into his hands, "so that all might honor [τιμῶσι] the Son just as they honor the Father. Whoever does not honor [ὁ μὴ τιμῶν] the Son does not honor the Father who sent him" (5:23). Jesus in the Gospel of John is not a poor beggar looking for "honor" in the world and finding none, but a Stranger who knows where he comes from and where he is going (8:14). In a way he is the model for the well-known ancient portrait of believing Christians as those who "dwell in their own fatherlands [πατρίδας . . . ἰδίας], but as if sojourners in them; they share all things as citizens, and suffer all things as strangers. Every foreign country is their fatherland [πᾶσα ξένη πατρίς], and every fatherland is a foreign country [πᾶσα πατρὶς ξένη]."[22]

Luke 4:24 and Gospel of Thomas §31

The tension in John's Gospel between the rejection of Jesus by his πατρίς (1:11) and his own conscious rejection of *any* πατρίς in this

---

19   According to the RSV, "his own home" (see 16:32, where Jesus tells his disciples that they will be scattered "each to his own home," and 19:27, where the beloved disciple takes Jesus' mother "to his own home").

20   See 1:10: "He was in the world, and the world was made through him, and yet the world did not know him."

21   Cf. "his own sheep" (τὰ ἴδια πρόβατα, 10:3, and vv. 4, 12. Also 15:19: "If you were of the world, the world would love its own [τὸ ἴδιον], but because you are not of the world, but I have chosen you out of the world, the world hates you."

22   *Epistle to Diognetus 5.5* (Loeb edition of *Apostolic Fathers* 2.359-61).

world (4:44) finds a parallel, perhaps unexpectedly, in the Gospel of
Luke. After reading from Isaiah 61:1-2 in the synagogue at
Nazareth, and concluding that "Today this scripture is fulfilled in
your ears" (Luke 4:17-21), Jesus challenges the citizens of the town
by almost literally putting words in their mouth: "Doubtless you will
quote to me this proverb: 'Doctor, heal yourself! Whatever we have
heard done in Capernaum, do also here in your home town'" (v 23).
Then Jesus gives his answer: "Truly, I say to you that no prophet is
acceptable in his home town" (v 24).[23] Here it is a question of a
prophet being "acceptable" (δέκτος), rather than of finding "honor"
(τιμή) in his home town. But "acceptable" to whom? Perhaps because
of the parallel passages in the other Gospels, commentators have
customarily taken it as acceptable *to* the home town, or the people
who live there. The usage of δέκτος, however, in the New Testament
and ancient literature generally does not bear this out, as Bauer's
lexicon tacitly admits: "only here of human recognition, elsewhere
always of recognition by God."[24] It is clearly a matter of
"recognition by God" in the immediately-preceding Scripture quotation, where Jesus announces his intention "to proclaim the acceptable
[δέκτον] year of the Lord" (4:19), and the burden of proof is on
those who would read it merely as human recognition in 4:24.

That the Lukan form of the saying about the prophet is not Luke's
creation is evident from the *Gospel of Thomas* §31: "Jesus said: No
prophet is acceptable in his village; no doctor heals those who know
him"[25] (or, in the Greek of POxy 1.6: λέγει Ἰ(ησοῦ)ς· οὐκ ἔστιν
δεκτὸς προφήτης ἐν τῇ π(ατ)ρίδι αὐτ[ο]ῦ, οὐδὲ ἰατρὸς ποιεῖ
θεραπείας εἰς τοὺς γεινώσκοντας αὐτό[ν]).[26] This form of the

23   This translation reads οὐδείς as an adjective modifying "prophet." Another
possible translation takes οὐδείς as a pronoun: "No one is acceptable as a prophet
in his home town" (see BAGD 591-92).

24   BAGD 174. Cf. also J. Nolland, *Luke 1–9:20* (WBC 35A; Dallas: Word,
1989) 200.

25   Most scholars now agree that the *Thomas* sayings are generally independent
of the canonical Gospels. Although a case could be made here for dependence on
Luke, it would imply rather cumbersome editorial work on Luke by the compilers
of the sayings material. More likely, the two pronouncements about the doctor and
the prophet were linked in a pre-Lukan sayings collection now partially represented
in the Oxyrhynchus Papyri and the *Gospel of Thomas*.

26   For the text, see K. Aland, *Synopsis Quattuor Evengeliorum* (Stuttgart:
Deutsche Bibelgesellschaft, 1995) 50; and E. Klostermann (ed.), *Apocrypha II*

pronouncement is in two parts, one about a prophet and one about a doctor. The latter sounds like an appropriate reply to the words of Luke 4:23a, "Doctor, heal yourself!"[27] The accompanying demand, "Whatever we have heard done in Capernaum, do also here in your home town" (v. 23b) made it clear that "Heal yourself" really meant "Heal those who are closest to you (i.e. heal us)." In Luke 4:24 Jesus changes the image from doctor to prophet, while in Thomas both images—we can hardly call them metaphors, for Jesus is *literally* both healer and prophet—are at work simultaneously. The understanding of δέκτος appears to be the same in these texts as in Luke. Just as "No doctor heals those who know him" sounds more like a stated policy of doctors than of patients, so "No prophet is acceptable in his home town" should be read not as a complaint but as the stated policy of an itinerant prophet. If prophecy is an itinerant calling, then no prophet *acceptable to God* (that is, no true prophet) stays home.

In Luke 4, this principle is borne out by the example of two prophets who were also healers: Elijah, who was sent not to the "many widows in Israel," but to "a widow at Zarephath in Sidon" (vv. 25-26), and Elisha, who cleansed Naaman the Syrian instead of the "many lepers in Israel" (v. 27). Both went to foreigners on their own initiative, not because they were first rejected in their "home town" or "native country." Jesus too has his own agenda, not one determined by the response of this place or that. Though he is in fact rejected in Luke (and almost killed) by the citizens of Nazareth (vv. 28-30), his is the action, theirs the reaction. He moves on to Capernaum, as an itinerant prophet should,[28] and after casting out a demon in the

---

Evangelien (Berlin: de Gruyter, 1929) 19.

[27] A different but equally appropriate reply to such a demand can be found in another context in the canonical Gospel tradition: "Not those who are well have need of a doctor, but those who are sick" (Matt 9:12 = Mark 2:17 = Luke 5:31).

[28] The tension in Luke between the notion that Jesus visited Capernaum first and then Nazareth (based on the words Jesus attributes to the townspeople of Nazareth, 4:23), and the notion that he went first to Nazareth and then to Capernaum (based on Luke's actual narrative sequence) is well known. It is usually attributed to Luke's tacit acknowledgment of the Markan narrative, in which Jesus reaches Capernaum already in chap. 1 and Nazareth not until chap. 6. As Luke's narrative stands, the summary reference in 4:14-15 to a teaching ministry in the synagogues of Galilee allows for an earlier visit to Capernaum without mentioning it explicitly.

synagogue and performing other exorcisms and healings (4:31-42) bids farewell to that town too: "I must proclaim the gospel of the kingdom of God to the other towns also, because for this I was sent" (v. 43). With this, he continues "making proclamation in the synagogues of Judea" (v. 44). The scope of Jesus' ministry is the whole of Jewish Palestine, [29] but as Luke's Gospel unfolds it becomes apparent that his goal is Jerusalem. "As the days drew near for him to be taken up," Luke tells us, "he set his face to go [τοῦ πορεύεσθαι] to Jerusalem" (9:51, and note the repetition of πορεύεσθαι, "go," in vv. 52-53, 56, 57). Later, when some Pharisees urge him to "Get out and go on from here [πορεύου ἐντεῦθεν], for Herod wants to kill you" (13:31), he replies, "Go and tell that fox, 'Look, I drive out demons and accomplish healings today and tomorrow [σήμερον καὶ αὔριον], and on the third day I am finished' [τῇ τρίτῃ τελειοῦμαι]" (v. 32). Then he continues, sounding redundant: "Nevertheless [πλήν], I must [δεῖ με] go on my way today and tomorrow and the next day [σήμερον καὶ αὔριον καὶ τῇ ἐχομένῃ πορεύεσθαι], for it is not possible that a prophet should be killed outside of Jerusalem" (v. 33). This saying in turn occasions the lament, "Jerusalem, Jerusalem, she who kills the prophets and stones those who are sent to her! How often I wanted to gather your children in the way a hen gathers her brood under her wings, and you would not! See, your house is left to you. And I tell you , you will not see me until the time when you say 'Blessed is he who comes in the name of the Lord'" (vv 34-35; cf. Matt 23:37-39).

Jesus' response to the Pharisees' warning reinforces his role as itinerant prophet, but only if vv. 32 and 33 are read together. To a casual modern reader, v. 33 may appear to be merely a repetition of v. 32, but it is not. Verse 32 by itself is simply Jesus' way of telling the Pharisees, "I'll go when I'm good and ready." He has his own agenda of exorcism and healing, and will not have his hand forced by Herod's threats. The exchange recalls a similar warning from his own disciples in John 11:8, expressing surprise that he would return

---

29   This is indicated by the striking "Judea" (corrected in some manuscripts to "Galilee") in v. 44. "Judea" is probably meant not in contrast to Galilee (the focus of 4:14-15), but as a wider designation for all of Palestine (see Nolland, *Luke*, 216, who cites Luke 1:5; 6:17; 7:17; 23:5; and the book of Acts generally). Luke 4:44, therefore, signals an expansion or widening of Jesus' horizons as an itinerant prophet, even though much that follows still takes place in Galilee.

to Judea: "Rabbi, just now the Judeans were trying to stone you, and you are going there again?" "Are there not twelve hours of daylight?" he replied. "If anyone walks in the daytime, he does not stumble, because he sees the light of this world. But if anyone walks at night, he stumbles, because the light is not with him" (John 11:9-10). The point of both replies is that Jesus is not in danger until his "hour," or appointed time of death, has come. Until then, he is invulnerable (see John 7:30; 8:20; and cf. 8:59; 10:39; and Luke 4:30). Jesus will not go on his way simply because the Pharisees tell him he is in danger. Yet, as v. 33 reminds us, *he goes nonetheless*. The conjunction πλήν ("and yet," or "nonetheless") should be given its full force. Jesus does precisely what the Pharisees urge him to do (v 33), but only after making it very clear that he is doing it on his own initiative and not theirs (v. 32). They tell him to "go" (πορεύου, v. 31), and in reply he defiantly tells them in turn, "Go [πορευθέντες] and tell that fox, 'Look, I drive out demons and accomplish healings today and tomorrow, and on the third day I am finished'" (v. 32). But then he announces his own intention to "go" [πορεύεσθαι] after all—not at their request but out of divine necessity: "I must [δεῖ με] go on my way today and tomorrow and the next day, for it is not possible that a prophet should be killed outside of Jerusalem" (v. 33). He does what he is urged to do, but not *because* of the urging. As an itinerant prophet, he moves according to God's plan, and no one else's.[30]

Conclusions: Did Luke and John Get It Right?

The evidence of John 4:44 and Luke 4:24 suggests that both Gospels use the saying about a prophet not being "acceptable" or not having "honor" in his home town to dramatize Jesus' calling as an

---

[30]   The incident recalls two others in John's Gospel where Jesus is asked (implicitly or explicitly) to do something, seems at first to refuse, but then, after establishing his independence of all human agendas, accedes to the request. The first was his mother's comment at the Cana wedding that "They have no wine" (John 2:3), to which Jesus first replied, "What has that to do with me? My hour has not yet come?" (v 4), but to which he then responded with his first miracle (vv. 5-11). The second was his brothers' advice in Galilee before the Feast of Tabernacles to "Leave here and go to Judea, so that your disciples too may see the works you are doing . . . . as long as you are doing these things, show yourself to the world" (John 7:3-4). Again Jesus first refused (vv. 6-9), but then went after all, "not publicly but in secret" (v. 10).

itinerant prophet. They do so independently, however, and in very different ways. In this respect, they stand apart from Mark and Matthew, who read the saying simply as Jesus' reaction to hostility in his home town and immediate family on one occasion. Luke retains Mark's connection to the literal home town and makes it even more explicitly Nazareth, but also makes the traditional proverb programmatic for the whole of Jesus' ministry. The *Gospel of Thomas* provides evidence, first, that the Lukan form of the saying circulated more widely than Luke and is probably older than Luke, and second, that it is not necessarily linked to Nazareth. John's Gospel confirms this by inserting a slightly different form of the proverb into its account of Jesus' departure from the village of Sychar in Samaria after a two-day visit. Luke, in its own very different setting, preserves a recollection that the itinerant nature of Jesus' ministry was as much a problem for the people of an unnamed Samaritan village as for the people of Nazareth. Just after Jesus "set his face to go [πορεύεσθαι] to Jerusalem" (Luke 9:51), he "sent messengers [presumably his disciples] before his face, and they went [πορευθέντες] and entered a village of the Samaritans, so as to prepare for him" (v. 52).[31] But Luke quickly adds, "they did not receive him, because his face was headed [πορευόμενον] for Jerusalem" (v. 53). After Jesus' rebuked his disciples for wanting to call down fire from heaven on these Samaritans, "they went on [ἐπορεύθησαν] to another village" (v. 56)—but whether in Samaria, Judea, or Galilee we are not told!

The independent testimony of Luke (with the support of the *Thomas* tradition) and of John's Gospel is that Jesus did not merely quote a familiar proverb about prophets being unwelcome at home, but that he transformed it into a guiding principle for his ministry. The proverb's significance for him was by no means limited to a specific incident in Nazareth. Though widely known as "the Nazarene" (either ὁ Ναζαρηνός[32] or ὁ Ναζωραῖος[33]), Jesus never

---

31 Cf. 10:1: "After this, the Lord appointed seventy [two] others, and sent them two by two before his face, to every town and place where he was going to come."

32 Mark 1:24; 10:47; 14:67; 16:6 ; Luke 4:34; 24:19.

33 Matthew 2:23; 26:71; Luke 18:37; John 18:5, 7; 19:19; Acts 2:22; 3:6; 4:10; 6:14; 22:8; 26:9. Jesus's followers, accordingly, were known by their enemies as a "sect of the Nazarenes" (i.e. τῶν Ναζωραίων αἱρέσεως, Acts 24:5). Ναζωραῖος, with its play on both "Nazareth" and "nazirite" (in the sense of one who, like Samson, took vows of holiness), may well have been first used ironically by Jesus'

applied that term to himself during his ministry, and only once assented to its use by others.[34] Rather, he was an itinerant prophet who called no town or village his home.

This is not, of course, a startling conclusion. The saying, "Foxes have holes, and the birds of the sky have nests, but the Son of man has nowhere to lay his head" (Matt 8:20 = Luke 9:58) is well known and widely accepted as authentic.[35] But the saying about the prophet in Luke and John testifies to greater intentionality on Jesus' part. It is not a matter of "Poor Jesus, he had no home," but of a conscious purpose in his life to keep moving from village to village through Galilee, Samaria, and Judea toward the city where all true prophets come to grief (Luke 13:33). Echoes of that intention are, as we have seen, present even in John, who has Jesus coming to Jerusalem not once but four times (in chaps. 2, 5, 7, and 12). In short, the Jesus Seminar was right: John 4:44 should be printed in pink. I am tempted to be playful, and say "That's a start. Now let's look again at the other 878 verses in John," but I will resist that. The point is rather that the Jesus Seminar seems to have come to the right decision for the wrong reason—not that "the simple proverb was plausible in the context of Jesus' activity and the rejection of him in his own village,"[36] but that Jesus himself transformed a simple proverb into something quite different, the marching orders of his own prophetic mission.

This is where the issue is joined. Was it Jesus himself, or was the transformation of the proverb the work of the early church? Certainly Luke knows of prophets who were not itinerant as Jesus was, but who seem to have been "stationed," at least for a time, in particular congregations. Their roles included being emissaries auth-

---

enemies, and only later taken up (as in the book of Acts) by his own followers.

34   In John 18:4, Jesus asked the soldiers who had come to arrest him, "Who are you looking for?" They replied, "Jesus the Nazarene," and he said, "I am he" (ἐγώ εἰμι, v. 5; cf. vv. 7-8). The term "Nazarene" (Ναζωραῖος here) is their term, not his, and the distinctive Johannine significance of ἐγώ εἰμι is well-known (see John 8:24, 28, 59; 13:19). The *risen* Jesus, however, in the second of Paul's accounts of his Damascus road experience, does tell Paul, "I am Jesus the Nazarene (again Ναζωραῖος), whom you are persecuting" (Acts 22:8). In each instance, Jesus (whether earthly or risen) seems to be represented as accommodating his speech to the vocabulary and the expectations of his (unbelieving) hearers.

35   See Funk and Hoover, *The Five Gospels*, 160-61, 316-17.

36   Funk and Hoover, *The Five Gospels*, 491 (see above, n. 3).

orized to deliver messages from Jerusalem to sister congregations—
Agabus and others to Antioch (Acts 11:27), Agabus to Caesarea
(21:10), and Silas and Judas Barsabbas to Antioch (Acts 15:22,
32)[37]—and appointing missionaries from their number to proclaim
the Christian gospel where it had not yet gone—that is, the several
"prophets and teachers" at Antioch through whom the Holy Spirit
spoke explicitly about Paul and Barnabas (Acts 13:1). But Luke
knows of no itinerant Christian prophets in quite the sense implied
by Luke 4:24 ("acceptable" to God precisely because they did not
stay in one place), or even in the sense of John 4:44 (because they
refused to stay anywhere longer than two days). Luke and John are
willing to attribute such a lifestyle to Jesus, but unwilling to make it
exemplary for all (perhaps not for any) Christian prophets or
missionaries. Even though Jesus tells his disciples in John's Gospel,
"As the Father has sent me, so I send you" (John 20:21; cf. 17:18),
and warns them of hatred and rejection in the world (John 15:18-
16:3), there is no evidence that the Johannine community was in any
way an itinerant or transient community. On the contrary, what little
evidence the so-called Johannine writings do provide points rather
toward a suspicion of itinerant teachers. "If anyone comes to you,"
the Elder writes, "and does not bring this teaching, do not receive
him into your house or say 'Welcome,' for whoever says 'Welcome'
to such a person shares in his evil deeds" (2 John 10-11).[38]

As we have seen, only the *Didache* seems to reflect the practice of
Jesus implied by John 4:44 and Luke 4:24. Even here, the person
who comes and is to be "received as the Lord" is an 'apostle'

---

37   These, David Aune notes, are "the only NT examples of trips taken by
prophets for the specific purpose of exercising their prophetic gifts" (*Prophecy in
Early Christianity and the Ancient Mediterranean World* [Grand Rapids: Eerdmans,
1983] 212).

38   Most of the other evidence from 1, 2, and 3 John is ambiguous. 1 John
2:19, for example, could refer to "those who went out from us" as itinerant
missionaries who proved to be false, but more likely refers to schism within a
Johannine congregation. Similarly, the "false prophets who have gone out into the
world" (1 John 4:1) could be itinerant false prophets, but are just as likely false
prophets pure and simple (the same is true in 2 John 7). On the positive side, the
"brothers" to whom the Elder refers in 3 John, to whom Gaius showed hospitality
(vv. 5-8) while Diotrephes did not (v. 10), could be itinerant prophets or teachers,
but could just as easily be emissaries from the Elder's congregation similar to the
emissaries from Jerusalem we meet in the book of Acts.

(ἀπόστολος, *Did.* 11:4, probably in the sense of missionary), not a prophet. Such a person is to "stay only one day or if necessary a second as well; but if he stays three days, he is a false prophet" (11:5). Later, the authors of the *Didache* state that "every true prophet [πᾶς δὲ προφήτης ἀληθινός] who who wants to settle among you is 'worthy of his food.' Likewise a true teacher is himself worthy, like the workman, of his food. Therefore, you shall take the firstfruit of the winepress and of the threshing floor, and of oxen and sheep, and give them as firstfruit to the prophets, for they are your high priests. But if you have no prophet, give to the poor" (13:1-4). David Aune argues that the *Didache* is distinguishing between "apostles," who are only allowed to stay two days, and "prophets," who are allowed, even encouraged to settle down in the community.[39] Yet the heading to the whole section is, "Now concerning the apostles and prophets" (11:3), with no clear distinction between the two groups. When an "apostle" violates the rules by staying more than two days, we are told, "he is a false prophet" (ψευδοπροφήτης, 11:5), and the text then adds that "when the apostle goes forth, let him take nothing but bread until he turn in for the night; and if he asks for money, he is a false prophet" (ψευδοπροφήτης, 11:6). The authors conclude that "not everyone who speaks in a spirit is a prophet, unless he has the behavior [literally 'the ways'] of the Lord. From their behavior, then, the false prophet and the prophet shall be known" (11:8).

The terminology suggests that "apostle" and "prophet' are being used almost interchangeably.[40] "Apostle," or missionary, appears to be the larger category, of which "prophets" (itinerant prophets in particular) are a subset. The principle articulated in *Didache* 11 is repeated in chap. 12: "If he who comes is itinerant [παροδιός], help him as much as you can, but he shall not remain with you more than two days, or three if need be" (12:2). But then the authors add, "But

---

[39]   Aune, *Prophecy in Early Christianity*, 213: "Unlike other Christians who visit the community, prophets are not limited to a maximum length of time for their stay."

[40]   Aune disagrees: "The term 'false prophet' as used here does not imply that the apostles depicted in the Didache functioned as prophets; rather, the term 'false prophet' is used here as a general term for a charlatan" (*Prophecy in Early Christianity*, 412 n. 210; cf. 409 n. 148). But the fact that within four verses "apostle" and "prophet" are contrasted in such similar ways to "false prophet" suggests the contrary.

if he wants to settle among you, being a craftsman, let him work and eat. If he has no craft, provide for him according to your understanding, so that no one will live in idleness with you as a Christian. If he refuses, he is making traffic of Christ. Beware of such" (12:3-5). When they go on to state that "every true prophet who wants to settle among you is "worthy of his food" (13:1), they are not really saying anything new. Whether one is specifically a prophet, or a traveler in a more general sense, the rule about staying only two days is not a hard and fast one. If one has a serious desire to give up itinerancy, settle down in the community, and become a contributing member, every effort is made to honor that desire.

In short, the evidence of the *Didache* is that while Jesus' saying about prophets seems to have been *adapted* to the Christian communities in view there, it did not originate in such communities. Nor is it likely that the communities supposedly represented in the so-called "Q" material common to Matthew and Luke are responsible for transforming a familiar proverb into a justification of the itinerant lifestyle. Although a number of sayings commonly assigned to "Q" do call hearers to such a lifestyle (Matt 8:18-22 = Luke 9:57-62, for example), this kind of material is no more characteristic of "Q" than of other Gospel traditions. In Mark, for example, Jesus sends out his disciples and tells them, "Whenever you enter a house, stay there until you go out, and whatever place does not receive you or listen to you, go out from there and shake off the dust that is under your feet, as a witness to them" (Mark 6:10-11; cf. Matt 10:11-14; Luke 9:4-5, 10:5-12). Jesus' disciples are itinerant during his ministry, but their wanderings are not aimless: "When they persecute you in this city," he concludes in Matthew, "flee to the next, for truly I say to you, you will not complete the cities of Israel until the Son of man has come" (Matt 10:23). Jesus' own marching orders are theirs as well, and their goal no less than his, is Jerusalem (cf. Matt 23:34, with vv. 35-39).

The post-resurrection churches were different. So far as we know, they were not sustained by itinerant prophets, and their goal was not Jerusalem. Yet they preserved and handed down Gospel traditions about itinerancy even when these did not coincide with how they actually functioned as communities. They seem to have maintained a continuity of interpretation but not of practice. As for the specific saying about prophets in their home town, it is not found in "Q" (unless the *Thomas* tradition can somehow be traced to "Q"), but does occur independently in Mark (followed by Matthew), in Luke and the *Gospel of Thomas*, and in John. It passes with flying colors the criterion of multiple attestation. In this essay I have tried to show how Luke and John, each in its own way, assimilated the saying to their distinctive presentations of Jesus and his mission, while remaining generally true to Jesus' own intention.

BEHIND THE TEMPTATIONS OF JESUS
Q 4:1-13 AND MARK 1:12-13

Dale C. Allison, Jr.

Matt 4:1-11 and Luke 4:1-13 tell a story in which Jesus is thrice tempted by the devil. The two accounts are so close that a common origin within Q is, for those of us who accept the existence of that source, assured. There is also a temptation narrative in Mark 1:12-13. This, by comparison, is much shorter and in other respects different. Here we fail to read about multiplying stones into bread, or about obtaining the kingdoms of the world, or about leaping off the pinnacle of the temple. How are the two accounts related?

One possibility is that the cryptic Mark 1:12-13 is an abbreviation of the story more faithfully preserved in Q.[1] A second is that Q offers us an expansion of the story that Mark retained intact.[2] Given how hard it is to see how one might have reduced Q 4:1-13 to the very different Mark 1:12-13 or expanded the latter to create the former, the most likely alternative is a third, namely, that both of our stories are independent and so grew out of something not quite like either one.[3] It is the purpose of this essay to explore this last possibility and then to consider the implications for study of the historical Jesus.

---

[1] So e.g. J. Lambrecht, "Mark 1.1-15: Markan Redaction of Q?," *NTS* 38 (1992) 376-78 (defending the thesis that Mark knew and used Q). Compare A. B. Lord, "The Gospels as Oral Traditional Literature," in W. O. Walker, Jr. (ed.), *The Relationships among the Gospels: An Interdisciplinary Dialogue* (San Antonio: Trinity University Press, 1978) 63. For objections see J. B. Gibson, *The Temptations of Jesus in Early Christianity* (JSNTSup 112; Sheffield: Sheffield Academic Press, 1995) 38-40.

[2] See R. E. Brown, *New Testament Essays* (Garden City: Doubleday, 1968) 263-64. W. Wilkens ("Die Versuchung Jesu nach Matthäus," *NTS* 28 [1982] 479-89) argues that Matthew created his temptation story from Markan materials and that Luke then followed Matthew.

[3] So also J. Dupont, *Les tentations de Jésus au désert* (StNeot 4; Bruges: Desclée de Brouwer, 1968) 80-97. These pages include a review of scholarly opinions.

THE ACCOUNTS IN MARK AND Q

Mark 1:12-13 tells us that, after his baptism, Jesus was driven out
(the verb is ἐκβάλλει) by the Spirit into the wilderness, where he
spent forty days. During that time he was tempted by the devil. We
are also told that Jesus was with "wild animals"[4] and that angels
waited upon him. These last two observations, so rapidly recounted,
were not, it appears, added to satisfy either a novelistic impulse or
the historian's eye for detail.[5] They were rather inserted for a
theological end; and, although I cannot argue the point here, the key
to Mark's cryptic narrative most likely lies in Jewish traditions
about the first man, Adam.[6] In paradise Adam lived in peace with the
animals[7] and was guarded by and/or honored by angels.[8] There too

---

4   R. Bauckham ("Jesus and the Wild Animals (Mark 1:13): A Christological
Image for an Ecological Age," in J. B. Green and M. Turner [eds.], *Jesus of
Nazareth: Lord and Christ* [Grand Rapids: Eerdmans, 1994] 8-10) shows that there
is a connotation of danger.

5   See Gibson, *Temptations*, 65.

6   So too A Feuillet, "L'épisode de la tentation d'après l'Evangile selon saint
Marc (1,12-13)," *EstBib* 19 (1960) 49-73; J. Gnilka, *Das Evangelium nach Markus*
(2 vols., EKKNT 2.1-2; Zürich: Benziger; Neukirchen-Vluyn: Neukirchener
Verlag, 1978-79) 1.58; U. Mell, "Jesu Taufe durch Johannes (Markus 1,9-15)—
zur narrativen Christologie vom neuen Adam," *BZ* 40 (1996) 161-78; R. Pesch,
"Anfang des Evangeliums Jesu Christi: Eine Studie zum Prolog des Markus-
evangeliums (Mark 1,1-15)," in G. Bornkamm and K. Rahner (eds.), *Die Zeit
Jesu: Festschrift für Heinrich Schlier* (Freiburg: Herder, 1970) 130-33; and P.
Pokorný, "The Temptation Stories and their Intention," *NTS* 20 (1974) 115-27.
Contrast Gibson, *Temptations*, 66-67. Patristic texts also interpret Jesus' tempta-
tion as the undoing of Adam's sin: Justin, *Dial.* 103; Irenaeus, *Adv. haer.* 5.21.2;
Athanasius, *Frag. in Matt* (in PG 27.1368A); etc. Perhaps Luke prefaced his temp-
tation account with a genealogy that concludes with Adam (Luke 3:38) because the
evangelist viewed Jesus' victory over temptation as a reversal of Adam's failure.
Compare J. Jeremias, "Ἀδάμ," *TDNT* 1 (1964) 141; C. A. Evans, "Jesus and the
Spirit: On the Origin and Ministry of the Second Son of God," in C. A. Evans and
J. A. Sanders, *Luke and Scripture: Essays on the Function of Authoritative
Tradition in Luke-Acts* (Minneapolis: Fortress, 1993) 26-45, esp. 36-38.

7   Gen 2:18-20 (here Adam names the animals). See further *Jub.* 3:1-3, 28;
Adam and Eve 8:1-3; 37:1-3; *Apoc. Mos.* 15:3; 16:2 ("the beasts . . . associate with
you" [Adam]); 24:4; 29:14, 16; *2 En.* 58:2-6. The motif already appears in the *Epic
of Gilgamesh*: Utnapishtim lived in a place where "the bird of death did not utter the
cry of death, the lion did not devour, the wolf did not tear the lamb . . . ." Recall
also Plato's comments on the age of Cronos (*Polit.* 271E). According to *b. Sanh.*
59b, humans were vegetarians before the fall, and many have rightly interpreted

he was fed by angels[9] or (according to another tradition) ate the food of angels, manna.[10] But after succumbing to the temptation of the serpent he was cast out (the verb is ἐξέβαλεν in Gen 3:24 LXX). This sequence of events is turned upside down in Mark. Jesus is first cast out. Then he is tempted. Then he gains companionship with the animals[11] and the service of angels (which probably includes

---

Gen 1:29-30 to mean, in accord with much ancient thought, that human beings and animals were originally vegetarians (contrast Gen 9:3). Thus Isa 11:7 and 65:25 (the lion will eat straw) mark a return to paradise. In Jewish legend Adam actually has intercourse with the various beasts before Eve is given to him.

8   *Adam and Eve* 13:3-15:3 (the angels worship Adam); 21:1-3 (the angels assist Eve even after the fall); 22:1-2 (Michael teaches Adam how to farm); 33:1-3 (two angels guard Adam and Eve); *Apoc. Mos.* 29:1-6, 14 (angels intercede for Adam after the fall); *Apoc. Sed.* 5:2 (the angels worship Adam).

9   *ʾAbot R. Nat.* A §1: "Adam was reclining in the Garden of Eden and the ministering angels stood before him, roasting meat for him and cooling wine for him."

10   *Adam and Eve* 4:2: "And Adam said to Eve, 'The Lord apportioned this for animals and beasts to eat, but for us there used to be the food of angels.'"

11   See the apocryphal accounts in *Gos. Ps.-Matt.* 19 and 35 (ANF 8.376, 381). For the eschatological taming of animals, see Isa 11:6-9; 65:25; Hos 2:18; Philo, *De praem.* 85-90; Luke 10:19; *2 Bar.* 73:6; *Sib. Or.* 3:788-95; Papias in Irenaeus, *Adv. haer.* 5.33.3-4. Late rabbinic texts in Str-B 4/2.964-65. For full discussion, see Bauckham, "Wild Animals," 3-21, and E. Fascher, "Jesus und die Tierre," *TLZ* 90 (1965) 561-70. There are also Roman parallels—see Horace's *16th Epode* and Virgil's *Fourth Ecloge*—as well as parallels from the history of religions in general. For Islamic parallels, see A. Jeffery, "The Descent of Jesus in Muhammadan Eschatology," in S. E. Johnson (ed.), *The Joy of Study* (New York: Macmillan, 1951) 111-12. Although Bauckham mutes Mark's Adam christology at the expense of a David christology, he does effectively dispose of the proposals that the wild animals are simply part of the wilderness setting or allies of Satan (an idea common with the church Fathers).

The theme of taming the wild beasts (note already Job 5:22-23) also appears in early Christian stories about monks and ascetics, where it is sometimes understood as a return to paradise; see e.g. Sulpicius Severus, *Dial.* 1.13 (this concerns an unnamed monk who, although he lives in the desert, has a garden with much water and a tame lion), and PG 65.380D-381A (*Apophthegmata Patrum*, Abba Paul, where Paul of the Thebaid, who can handle snakes, says, "If someone has obtained purity, everything is in submission to him, as it was to Adam, when he was in paradise before he transgressed the commandment"). For discussion see P. Nagel, *Die Motivierung der Askese in der alten Kirche und der Ursprung des Mönchtums* (TU 95; Berlin: Akademie-Verlag, 1966) 55-62.

being fed by them, as in 1 Kgs 19:5-8):[12]

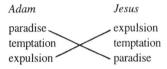

Another way to depict the contrast between the two stories is in terms of results:

Adam succumbs to temptation

• no longer are the beasts "with" Adam
• no longer do the angels serve Adam
• no longer does Adam have the food of angels

Jesus overcomes temptation

• the beasts are with Jesus
• the angels serve Jesus
• Jesus has the food of angels

If *T. Levi* 18:10 prophesies that the Messiah will open the gates of Eden and remove the sword that has guarded it since Adam and Eve fell, then in Mark 1:12-13, Jesus, by his victory over Satan, sees paradise restored around him.[13] Such a reading is all the more likely given that, in the immediately preceding pericope, the descent of the Holy Spirit as a dove over the waters is intended to recall the creation account of Gen 1:1-2.[14] Moreover, Christian baptism was, from a very early time, associated with recovery of the Adamic image,[15] so the association of Jesus' baptism with paradisiacal themes would be natural.

---

12   Compare *'Abot R. Nat.* A §1 (as quoted in n. 9). Mark's clause is, "and the angels served (διηκόνουν) him." BAGD, s.v., gives the first meaning of verb as "wait on someone at table," and this is the sense it has just a few verses later, in Mark 1:31, where Peter's mother-in-law "serves" Jesus and the disciples. See further E. Best, *The Temptation and the Passion: The Markan Soteriology* (SNTSMS 2; Cambridge: University Press, 1965) 9-10.

13   Whether Mark's "forty days" is part of his Adam typology is unclear. *Jub.* 3:9 relates that Adam was placed in Eden forty days after he was created, and in *Adam and Eve* 6:1, 3, Adam does penance for forty days. Is this a coincidence, or was this period of time firmly associated with the Adam legends?

14   See my article, "The Baptism of Jesus and a New Dead Sea Scroll," *BAR* 18 (1992) 489-95.

15   A. Meeks, "The Image of the Androgyne: Some Uses of a Symbol in Earliest Christianity," *HR* 13 (1974) 165-208.

If the Jesus of Mark 1:12-13 undoes the work of Adam, then one is inevitably reminded of Paul's christology, in which Adam's disobedience and its attendant effects are contrasted with Jesus' obedience and its attendant effects (Rom 5:12-21; 1 Cor 15:21-23, 45-49). Indeed, one wonders, given the other intriguing connections between Mark and Paul,[16] whether Mark 1:12-13 was composed under Paul's influence.

Q holds something very different. Here Jesus is implicitly compared and contrasted not with Adam but with Israel in the wilderness. Q 4:3 quotes LXX Deut 8:3 ("And he afflicted you, and he made you famished, and he fed you with manna, which your fathers knew not, in order to teach you that man shall not live by bread alone, but that man shall live by everything that proceeds from the mouth of God"). Q 4:12 quotes LXX Deut 6:16 ("You shall not tempt the Lord your God, as you tempted him in the temptation [at Massah]"). And Q 4:7 quotes LXX Deut 6:13 ("You shall fear the Lord your God, and him only shall you serve"). Q offers us a haggadic tale in which, as Tertullian, *De bapt.* 20, already recognized, Jesus repeats Israel's history in the desert:

> *The temptations of Israel and Jesus*
>
> forty years/days in wilderness (Exod 16:35; Q 4:2)
> temptation by hunger (Exod 16:2-8; Q 4:2-3)
> temptation to put God to the test (Exod 17:1-3; Q 4:9-12)
> temptation to idolatry (Exodus 32; Q 4:5-8)[17]

Who first formulated Q's temptation narrative? According to common opinion, Q opened with five sections which, from T. W. Manson on, have often been reckoned a larger literary unit:[18]

> the Proclamation of John the Baptist, Q 3:7-9, 16-17
> the Temptations of Jesus, Q 4:1-13
> the Sermon on the Plain, Q 6:20-49
> the Centurion's Servant, Q 7:1-10
> John and Jesus, Q 7:18-35

---

16 K. Romaniuk, "Le Problème des Paulinismes dans l'Évangile de Marc," *NTS* 23 (1977) 266-74.

17 See further B. Gerhardsson, *The Testing of God's Son (Matt 4:1-11 & Par.)* (ConBNT 2.1; Lund: Gleerup, 1966). Note also the popular yet instructive work of A. Farrer, *The Triple Victory: Christ's Temptation according to St. Matthew* (Cambridge: Cowley, 1990).

18 T. W. Manson, *The Sayings of Jesus* (London: SCM Press, 1949) 5.

We seem to have here a large chiasmus. The opening and closing units concern John the Baptist and have much in common, as can be seen at a glance:

Q 3:7-9 + 16-17	Q 7:18-35
John speaks about Jesus	Jesus speaks about John
John foresees an	Jesus claims to be
eschatological figure	the eschatological figure
who is coming (3:16).	who is coming (7:19-23)
John speaks to the "crowds"	Jesus speaks to the "crowds"
and addresses them as "you"	and addresses them as "you"
(3:7)	(7:24)
John speaks of God	Jesus speaks of wisdom
raising up	being justified by
"children" to Abraham (3:8)	her "children" (7:35)

Q 7:18-35 was deliberately designed to recall 3:7-9 + 16-17.

Q 4:1-13 and 7:1-10 likewise belong together.[19] They offer the only extended narratives in Q[20] and its only real dialogues. Everywhere else we meet only sayings, although occasionally these do have a narrative setting. So the two sections correspond formally. Their contents, furthermore, are also similar. In both a figure of authority asks Jesus to make use of his supernatural powers. While in 4:1-13 Satan wants him to multiply bread and throw himself off the temple, in 7:1-10 the centurion wants him to heal his son or servant. The difference is that whereas the requests of the former are illegitimate, the request of the latter is not.

What then of the center of Q 3-7, namely, the sermon on the plain, Q 6:20-49? While this has been outlined in several ways, it seems plain enough that the beginning and end correspond. The sermon opens with blessings: "Blessed are you poor, etc." (6:20-23). It ends with a warning, with the parable about the person who hears and does not do and so is likened to a house which the storm destroys (6:47-49). "Thus," in the words of C. M. Tuckett, "the whole sermon may be seen as dominated by a grand *inclusio*, setting the whole under the rubric of eschatological promises and warning . . . ."[21]

---

19 Cf. E. Sevenich-Bax, *Israels Konfrontation mit den letzten Boten der Weisheit: Form, Funktion und Interdependenz der Weisheitselemente in der Logienquelle* (Altenberge: Oros, 1993) 265-67.

20 The only other narrative is the very brief and hardly comparable 11:14.

21 C. M. Tuckett, "The Son of Man in Q," in M. C. De Boer (ed.), *From Jesus to John: Essays on Jesus and New Testament Christology in Honour of*

One is, accordingly, encouraged to think that Q's first five units were arranged in a large chiasmus in which each correlation was a pair of opposites:[22]

> A John speaks to the crowds about the coming one
>   B A figure of authority asks for a miracle that Jesus refuses
>   C Blessings
>   Main body of sermon
>   C' Warnings
>   B' A figure in authority asks for a miracle Jesus that grants
> A' The coming one speaks to the crowds about John

If this is the right analysis, one must ask to what extent 4:1-13, the Q temptation story, was redacted in order to make it balance 7:1-10, the healing of the centurian's son/servant.[23] We know from the close parallel to the latter in John 4:46-54 that the story of the healing of the centurion's son or servant must have come to Q pretty much as it is.[24] But we have no such assurance with regard to Q's temptation narrative. Maybe a desire to supply a counterpart to 7:1-10 was one of the factors that turned a pre-Q temptation story into an extended narrative with a dialogue having as its subject Jesus' ability to do miracles.

BEHIND MARK AND Q

However that may be, if one sets Mark's account beside the reconstructed text of Q,[25] the following motifs are shared:

• The Spirit as initiator of the experience

Marinus de Jonge (JSNTSup 84; Sheffield: Academic Press, 1993) 206.

[22] For more details and for the use of chiasmus elsewhere in Q, see the first chapter of my book, *The Jesus Tradition in Q* (Valley Forge: Trinity Press International, 1997).

[23] On other grounds Pokorný ("Intention," 125-26) suggests a redactional origin for Q 4:1-13; and A. Lindemann ("Die Versuchungsgeschichte Jesu nach der Logienquelle und das Vaterunser," in D.-A. Koch, G. Sellin, and A. Lindemann [eds.], *Jesu Rede von Gott und ihre Nachgeschichte im frühen Christentum: Beiträge zur Verkündigung Jesu und zum Kerygma der Kirche* [Gütersloh: Mohn, 1989] 91-100) argues further that the Q temptation story may be a partial exposition of Q's Lord's Prayer.

[24] For John 4:46-54 as an independent version of the story in Q, see U. Wegner, *Der Hauptmann von Kafarnaum* (WUNT 2.14; Tübingen: Mohr [Siebeck], 1985) 18-74.

[25] Throughout this essay I shall use the text of the International Q Project.

* Location in the wilderness
* Temptation by devil (so Mark) or Satan (so Q)
* Forty days
* Fasting and/or food from angels[26]
* Angels as servants

One guesses that somewhere behind Mark and Q was an Ur-text that contained at least what our present narratives have in common. Although this hypothetical Ur-text cannot be reconstructed, it is worth speculating on one point. Only two figures in the Hebrew Bible fast for forty days—Moses on Sinai (Exod 24:18) and Elijah on his way to Horeb (1 Kgs 19:8). Many, when commenting on Jesus' temptations, have been reminded either of one or of both of these experiences.[27] The fasts of Moses and Elijah also took place in the wilderness, which further brings the synoptic stories into line with them. But the presence of angels as servants makes us think of Elijah's experience as opposed to that of Moses. For nothing similar is found in the Pentateuch.[28] In 1 Kings 19, by contrast, Elijah is twice given food by an angel (vv. 6-8)—a striking fact if "the angels served" is taken to refer to the angels feeding Jesus.

All this raises the tantalizing possibility that an early version of the temptation narrative presented Jesus not as the new Israel or the last Adam but as an eschatological prophet like Elijah. In line with this hypothesis, several portions of the Jesus tradition preserve episodes in which Jesus is like Elijah.[29] Furthermore, because Christians came

---

26   In Mark the service of the angels implies Jesus' fasting; see n. 12. Moreover, since it is the angels who feed Jesus, and since manna was spoken of as "the bread of angels" (Ps 75:28; 2 Esdr 1:19; Wis 16:20), Mark's text may envisage Jesus being fed manna. This is so striking because manna is what Israel ate in the wilderness, and Q's text has in its background Israel's hunger during the exodus.

27   E.g. Irenaeus, *Adv. haer.* 5.21.2; Eusebius, *Dem. ev.* 3.2; Chrysostom, *Hom. on Matt.* 13:2; Augustine, *Serm.* 252.11; *Ep.* 55.28; Calvin, *Inst.* 4.12.20; Bauckham, "Wild Animals," 8. See further K.-P. Köppen, *Die Auslegung der Versuchungsgeschichte unter besonderer Berücksichtigung der Alten Kirche* (BGBE 4; Tübingen: Mohr [Siebeck], 1961) 15-23.

28   Later Jewish tradition does, however, put angels on Sinai with Moses (compare Gal 3:19), and the Samaritan text, *Memar Marqah* 4:6, has Moses eating the bread of angels.

29   See e.g. Mark 1:16-20 (this is modelled upon 1 Kgs 19:19-21, where Elijah calls Elisha); 6:15 and 8:28 (some people say Jesus is Elijah); Luke 4:25-26 (Jesus compares his own situation to that of Elijah); 7:11-17 (the resurrection of the widow's son at Nain recalls Elijah's miracle in 1 Kgs 17:17-24); 9:61-62 (compare

to identify John the Baptist as the messenger of Mal 4:5-6, such parallelism tended to disintegrate as time moved on.[30] Is this what happened with the temptation story? Did an Elijah typology become an Israel typology in one part of the tradition and an Adam typology in another?

Some support for this conjecture may be drawn from Matthew's redactional activity. When the First Evangelist redacted Q 4:1-13 he glossed its Israel typology with his own Moses typology.[31] Further, it did not require much reworking to achieve this—just a few additions here and there.[32] This matters because the story of Elijah in 1 Kings 19 is itself a collection of intertextual echoes: it is modelled on traditions about Moses on Sinai.[33] So if an early version of the temptation narrative of Jesus—what I have called the Ur-text—drew upon 1 Kings 19 and depicted Jesus as being like Elijah, it only makes sense that a descendant of that Ur-text could easily have been turned into a Moses typology—for the elements that recalled the story of Elijah and Horeb could equally have recalled Moses and Sinai.

THE TEMPTATIONS AND JESUS OF NAZARETH

But what, if anything, does all this have to do with Jesus of Nazareth? According to E. P. Sanders, "It is reasonable to think that Jesus really did fast and pray before beginning his active ministry and that he was subject to temptation. The safest conclusion is that the synoptic gospels, especially Matthew and Luke, are 'mythological' elaborations based on fact."[34] Is Sanders right, or is his

---

1 Kgs 19:19-21). For pertinent texts from John, see J. L. Martyn, "We have found Elijah," in R. Hamerton-Kelly and R. Scroggs (eds.), *Jews, Greeks and Christians: Religious Cultures in Late Antiquity* (SJLA 21; Leiden: Brill, 1976) 180-219.

[30]   See Martyn, "We have found Elijah"; and P. Katz, "Jesus als Vorläufer des Christus: Mögliche Hinweise in den Evangelien auf Elia als den 'Typos' Jesu," *TZ* 52 (1996) 225-35. The latter finds an Elijah typology in Mark's temptation narrative.

[31]   D. C. Allison, Jr., *The New Moses: A Matthean Typology* (Minneapolis: Fortress, 1993) 165-72.

[32]   See Allison, *The New Moses*.

[33]   See Allison, Jr., *The New Moses*, 39-45. The parallels, so many of which are obvious, are already catalogued in *Pesiq. R.* 4.2.

[34]   E. P. Sanders, *The Historical Figure of Jesus* (London: Penguin, 1993) 117.

evaluation overly sanguine?[35]

The accounts of Jesus' baptism prove that an event widely regarded as historical can be embellished by mythological motifs. Perhaps it is the same with the temptation accounts. Certainly religious people have sometimes gone into seclusion and interpreted their experiences in solitude as combat with evil spirits. One need think only of Anthony of Egypt and other early Christian monastics.[36] And yet we can hardly be encouraged by what we have found so far—a Q text with an Israel typology, a Markan text with an Adam christology, and a hypothetical Ur-text in which Jesus was perhaps an eschatological prophet like Elijah. In each case we seemingly have to do with post-Easter christologies, not literal reports of an historical experience, nor even with symbolic accounts of such an experience.[37] T. W. Manson's contention that our story goes back to Jesus himself, that it was a "parabolic narrative form for the instruction of his disciples,"[38] hardly appears to agree with the evidence.

There is a further difficulty in our way. Although commentators on the synoptics often neglect to mention it, fictitious narratives

---

[35] For a plausible attempt to explain the temptation traditions without any reference to an event in the life of Jesus, see D. F. Strauss, *The Life of Jesus Critically Examined* (Philadelphia: Fortress, 1972) 259-63.

[36] It is also interesting that, according to M. Dods (in J. Hastings [ed.], *A Dictionary of Christ and the Gospels* [2 vols., Edinburgh: T. & T. Clark, 1908] s.v., "Temptation (in the Wilderness)") there is an old Persian custom of retiring to a desert place, fasting for forty days, and fearlessly facing the jinns that take the forms of lion, tiger, and dragon—all for the purpose of gaining power over demons. Dods' authority for this is a paper by E. Bevan in *Transactions of the Society of Historical Theology* 1901-1902, which I have not seen.

[37] But see the interpretation of J. Jeremias, *New Testament Theology* (New York: Scribner's, 1971) 68-75. Some of the church fathers were persuaded that the story in Matthew and Luke records visionary events. See V. Kesich, "The Antiocheans and the Temptation Story," in F. L. Cross (ed.), *Studia Patristica 7* (TU 92; Berlin: Akadamie-Verlag, 1966) 496-502. Origen (*De prin.* 4.3.1) already observed that there is no earthly place from which all the kingdoms of the world can be seen at once.

[38] T. W. Manson, *The Servant-Messiah: A Study of the Public Ministry of Jesus* (Cambridge: University Press, 1953) 55. Compare the recent judgment of R. H. Stein, *Jesus the Messiah: A Survey of the Life of Christ* (Downers Grove: Inter-Varsity, 1996) 103: we have here a "piece of spiritual autobiography." So too earlier Dupont, *Tentations*, 97-100.

about heroes and religious founders tend to exhibit certain recurring patterns, and among them is the trial that takes place shortly after entering manhood and/or near the beginning of an adult vocation.[39] Buddhist sources, for instance, relate that Gautama, immediately before his enlightenment, entered into a battle with Mara, the evil one or tempter, and that after Buddha's enlightenment Mara sought to keep him from returning to the world.[40] Zoroastrian legend recounts that, shortly after its founder's conversion, a demon encountered Zoroaster in the wilderness and besought him to give up the true faith.[41] Gregory Thaumaturgus is supposed to have trounced the devils in a pagan temple very early in his spectacular career.[42] Manifestly we have here to do with a common motif in world-wide folklore and the history of religions which presumably has its explanation in religious psychology.[43] But who would want to defend the historicity of the stories just referred to, or posit a factual nucleus behind Oedipus' confrontation with the Sphinx, or Perseus' contest with a dragon, or Abraham's encounter with Azazel on Horeb?[44] Why should it be any different with the synoptic narratives?

Nonetheless, awareness of the parallels does not by itself or once and for all allow us to dismiss Sanders' proposal. For a couple of sayings in the Jesus tradition, sayings often reckoned authentic, might refer to a particular, triumphant encounter of Jesus with the devil.

The first saying is Mark 3:27: "But no one can enter a strong man's house and plunder his property without first tying up the strong man; then indeed he may plunder his house." Some commentators

---

[39]   See L. Raglan, *The Hero: A Study in Tradition, Myth, and Drama* (London: Watts, 1949) 177-99.

[40]   E. Conze, *Buddhism: Its Essence and Development* (New York: Harper & Row, 1959) 35. Some sources also have Buddha fasting for forty days.

[41]   *Vendidad* 19:8.

[42]   The story is told in Gregory of Nyssa's *Panegyric on Gregory Thaumaturgus* (in PG 46.893-958).

[43]   See Raglan, *Hero*. Relevant too is O. Rank, *The Myth of the Birth of the Hero: A Psychological Interpretation of Mythology* (New York: Brunner, 1952).

[44]   See *Apocalypse of Abraham* 13–14. This is a development of Genesis 15, where God makes a covenant with Abraham. Here too we have a forty-day fast (*Apoc. Abr.* 13:2) and the assistance of an angel (13:2). Note also the tale in *b. Sanh.* 89b, so reminiscent of Q 4:1-13, in which Satan and Abraham enter into debate by citing Scriptures against each other.

have considered this an allusion to the episode recorded in Matt 4:1-11 par. According to C. J. Cadoux, "It is difficult to see what else this victory [referred to in Mark 3:27] could have been but his successful resistance to the Temptation that beset him in the wilderness shortly after his baptism."[45] This might be correct.

Regrettably, however, one knows no way of demonstrating this. The truth is that Mark 3:27 may not even refer to a definite experience. Jesus might, for all we know, have uttered Mark 3:27 while reflecting upon his ministry in its entirety. That is, he may no more have been alluding to a particular event than when he said he had come not to bring peace to the earth but a sword (Q 12:51-53). Even if one were to suspect otherwise, our text remains a parable devoid of concrete detail. Certainly there is no need to connect it with the Adam typology in Mark or the Israel typology in Q. In other words, Mark 3:27 does not confirm that the canonical temptation accounts preserve historical memories, dimmed or otherwise.

The second saying is Luke 10:18, where Jesus declares that he saw Satan fall like lightning from heaven.[46] This logion, which probably assumes the identity of stars with angels,[47] once no doubt circulated apart from its present context, and it too may originally have been a figurative way of referring to a personal victory Jesus had while wrestling with Satan in the wilderness. Cadoux at least thought that this verse might hark back to Jesus' temptation in the wilderness.[48]

One problem with this proposal is that Luke 10:18 does not clearly attribute Satan's fall to Jesus' own actions: Jesus sees something but he does not claim to have been its cause. Moreover, Joel Marcus has recently made the intriguing argument, which is worth considering, that the original *Sitz im Leben* of Luke 10:18 was not Jesus'

---

45   C. J. Cadoux, *The Historic Mission of Jesus* (New York: Harper & Brothers, 1941) 66. So too H. B. Swete, *Commentary on Mark* (London: Macmillan, 1913) 67; J. Jeremias, *New Testament Theology* (New York: Scribner's, 1971) 72-73; J. W. Miller, *Jesus at Thirty: A Psychological and Historical Portrait* (Minneapolis: Fortress, 1997) 57; and N. T. Wright, *Jesus and the Victory of God* (Minneapolis: Fortress, 1996) 457-49. Best (*The Temptation and the Passion*, 7-15) argues that Mark 3:27, on the level of Markan redaction, refers back to 1:12-13.

46   On this, see esp. U. B. Müller, "Vision und Botschaft: Erwägungen zur prophetischen Struktur der Verkündigung Jesus," *ZTK* 74 (1977) 416-48.

47   Particularly interesting for comparison is *T. Sol.* 20:16-17, where falling stars are identified with demons.

48   Cadoux, *Historic Mission*, 66.

temptation in the wilderness but his baptism in the Jordan.[49] This might very well be the right guess. Maybe in the Jordan Jesus had a vision which persuaded him that Satan had been deposed, that the time of eschatological salvation had arrived.

But it is equally possible that Luke 10:18 was not initially a declaration of victory but a call to arms. When Satan or demons fall from heaven in *1 Enoch* 86; *Adam and Eve* 16:1-3; Revelation 12; and *T. Sol.* 20:16-17,[50] they do not tumble to utter defeat. Rather do they come down from heaven to do battle with human beings or to harm them in some way. Hence, if one sets aside as secondary the Lukan context in which it is now found, one can envisage Luke 10:18 as being, on Jesus' lips an announcement that the last times have come: Satan has fallen from the skies and is now amongst us to do eschatological battle.[51] The meaning would then be close to *Sib. Or.* 8:190-92, where the falling of the stars and the arrival of a great comet betoken not the end of the evil but the beginning of "impending toil, war, and slaughter."[52]

Yet this interpretation of Luke 10:18 remains as hypothetical as the others. It cannot be confirmed or disconfirmed. All we can conclude is that the possibility of interpretations other than that of Cadoux means that Luke 10:18 can hardly be called upon as firm support for a historical episode behind Q 4:1-13 or Mark 1:12-13.

Having come to this skeptical result it might seem that we can go no further. Yet more is to be said. For even if we are inclined to deny that Jesus, near the beginning of his ministry, went into the wilderness and there underwent a time of testing, this need not mean that the temptation texts tell us nothing at all about him. Nils Dahl once observed that uncertainty about the historicity of an individual word or episode is not crippling for life of Jesus research, for "the fact that the word or occurrence found a place within the tradition

---

J. Marcus, "Jesus' Baptismal Vision," *NTS* 41 (1995) 512-21.

[50]   Compare also 4 Ezra 5:5: "and the stars shall fall" may mean that evil powers will descend and add to the chaos of the latter days.

[51]   Such a proposal could be harmonized with Marcus' suggestion that Luke 10:18 was uttered in connection with Jesus' baptism.

[52]   Compare also the passage from the *Bundahishn* quoted in R. C. Zaehner, *The Teachings of the Magi: A Compendium of Zoroastrian Beliefs* (New York: Macmillan, 1956) 148 ("And Gōchihr, the serpent in the heavenly sphere, will fall from the summit of the Moon to the earth, and the earth will suffer pain like unto the pain a sheep feels when a wolf rends out its wool").

about Jesus indicates that it agreed with the total picture as it existed within the circle of the disciples."[53] William Walker expressed the same thought this way: "If the early Church did, in fact, create traditions about Jesus (and it surely did), it would no doubt have attempted, at least for the most part, to create such traditions as would fit 'reasonably well' into the general picture of Jesus which it had received through the prior traditions."[54] This proposition seems sensible enough, and it follows that even stories that do not reproduce historical events may tell us indirectly about Jesus because they incorporate features which his followers knew to be congruent with what he was all about. I now wish to argue that this was the case with the temptation narratives in Mark and Q.

(1) Q 4:1-13 explicitly, and Mark 1:12-13 implicitly, inform us that Jesus was victorious over Satan. Now whether or not Jesus once went into the wilderness and there bested temptation, the tradition about him is full of texts in which he vanquishes evil. One thinks first of all of the stories of exorcism. Even though we may have difficulty evaluating the historicity of particular episodes, in the aggregate they must give us a good idea of the sorts of things Jesus did.[55] We have every reason to believe that Jesus was not just an exorcist but a highly successful one.[56] There are further authentic sayings in which Jesus assumes that he has gotten the better of Satan, sayings such as Q 11:20 ("But if I by the finger of God cast out demons, then the kingdom of God has come to you") and 21-22 = Mark 3:27 (the parable of the strong man). So the traditions stemming from Jesus leave one with the same impression that one gets from the temptation stories: when Jesus confronted Satan and evil spirits, he overcame them.[57]

(2) In Q's temptation narrative the devil asks Jesus to turn bread into stones and to cast himself down from the pinnacle of the Temple

---

53   N. A. Dahl, *The Crucified Messiah and Other Essays* (Minneapolis: Augsburg, 1974) 67.

54   W. O. Walker, "The Quest for the Historical Jesus: A Discussion of Methodology," *ATR* 51 (1969) 50.

55   B. Kollmann, *Jesus und die Christen als Wundertäter: Studien zu Magie, Medizin und Schamanismus in Antike und Christentum* (FRLANT 170; Göttingen: Vandenhoeck & Ruprecht, 1996) 174-215.

56   Note Q 11:14; Mark 1:12-13, 21-28, 34, 39; 5:1-20; 6:7, 13; 7:24-20; 9:14-29.

57   See further Dupont, *Tentations*, 119-26.

in the expectation that angels will lift him up. The text assumes that Jesus has the power to perform miracles. This too, it goes without saying, accords with the rest of the tradition and with the historical facts behind it. Jesus was perceived to be a miracle worker, and he must have shared this estimate of himself.[58] Again one may appeal to Q 11:20, which links Jesus' successful ministry of exorcism with the advent of God's eschatological kingdom. So once more the impression gained from Q 4:1-13—in this case, that Jesus was a miracle worker—coheres with our knowledge of the historical Jesus.

(3) If Q 4:1-13 assumes that Jesus could do miracles, it also tells us that he did not do so indiscriminately. When the devil asks him to do give proof of his ability, he refuses. This circumstance harmonizes with what we find elsewhere in the synoptics.[59] In Q 11:29-30, in a saying widely attributed to Jesus, he says that his generation seeks a sign and then adds that it will see nothing other than the sign of Jonah. While the statement is partly enigmatic—what exactly is the sign of Jonah?—its implications appear to be the same as those of Mark 8:11-13: when the Pharisees tempted Jesus to prove himself by some great miracle, he denied their request (compare Q 12:54-56; Luke 11:16; 17:20). So Jesus' unwillingness to perform for Satan in Q 4:1-13 is matched by his refusal to perform miraculous signs for more mundane opponents.

(4) Mark 1:12 says that the Spirit drove Jesus into the wilderness. Q 4:1, although it cannot be exactly reconstructed, must have said something similar. The point to be made here is that Jesus himself probably associated his work with the eschatological gift of the Spirit. It is true that explicit references to the Spirit are few and far between in the words attributed to Jesus, and also true that perhaps not a single one of these goes back to him.[60] The evidence is, however, sufficient for the inference that he associated his activities with the prophecies of Deutero-Isaiah and indeed thought of himself as the

---

[58]   Pertinent texts include Q 7:1-10, 19-22; 10:9; 11:14-20; Mark 1:21-28, 29-31, 32-34, 40-45; 2:1-12; 3:1-6, 22; 5:1-20, 21-43; 6:30-44, 47-52; 7:24-30, 31-37; 8:22-26; 9:14-29; 10:46-52; Matt 9:27-31; 14:28-33; 26:53; Luke 13:32; 14:1-6; John 2:1-11; 5:2-9; 9:1-12; 11:28-44. Note that in Mark 3:22 Jesus' enemies do not deny that he does miracles; they question only the source of his power.

[59]   Compare Dupont, *Tentations*, 113-15.

[60]   C. K. Barrett, *The Holy Spirit and the Gospel Tradition* (London: SPCK, 1947).

anointed herald of Isaiah 61.[61] That herald declares: "The Spirit of the Lord is upon me, because the Lord has anointed me; he has sent me to bring good news to the oppressed, to bind up the broken hearted, to proclaim liberty to the captives, and release to the prisoners . . . to comfort all who mourn." If Jesus did indeed think of himself as the anointed prophet of Isaiah 61, then the temptation narratives do not lead us astray when they associate Jesus' ministry with the Spirit.

(5) In Q 4:1-13 Jesus quotes Scripture more than once. Some scholars would find this out of character. For them almost all of the scriptural citations and allusions in the Jesus tradition come from the church. Others of us, however, believe there is good cause for thinking that Jesus was much concerned with the prophetic tradition and with the interpretation of Torah.[62] If this is the correct point of view, then Q's picture of Jesus using the Pentateuch and Psalms to interpret his experience would be faithful to his memory: Jesus was a pious man who quoted from the Jewish Bible.

(6) Q 4:1-13 depicts Jesus as a man of great faith in God. Jesus says that it is written, "Worship the Lord your God, and serve only him" (Q 4:8, citing Deut 6:13). He also declares that God is not to be tested (4:12). And when he is hungry he refuses to obey the devil by turning stones into loaves: Jesus continues, despite his need, to wait upon God (4:3-4). What we see in all this is a person whose life is fully entrusted to the divinity. This utter dependence upon God is also what we see throughout the dominical sayings. Jesus goes not just without amenities but without necessities—without home, without family, without work, without money—and trusts that his heavenly Father will take care of him. He teaches prayer for daily bread and declares that the God who feeds the birds will gives good things to those he loves even more.[63]

(7) In Q 4:5-7 Satan offers Jesus all the kingdoms of the world and

---

[61] J. D. G. Dunn, *Jesus and the Spirit: A Study of the Religious and Charismatic Experience of Jesus and the First Christians as Reflected in the New Testament* (London: SCM Press, 1975) 41-67; and A. E. Harvey, *Jesus and the Constraints of History* (Philadelphia: Westminster, 1982) 140-53.

[62] For a thorough overview, see B. D. Chilton and C. A. Evans, "Jesus and Israel's Scriptures," in B. D. Chilton and C. A. Evans (eds.), *Studying the Historical Jesus: Evaluations of the State of Current Research* (NTTS 19; Leiden: Brill, 1994) 281-335.

[63] E.g. Q 11:3, 9-13; 12:24.

their splendor. Jesus refuses. This coheres with the likely circumstance that Jesus, who was crucified as a messianic pretender, expected
to become king in Jerusalem but waited upon God to make him so.[64]
John 6:15 is probably accurate when it recounts that Jesus withdrew
when the crowds "were about to come and take him by force to make
him king." So when he turns down the devil's offer in Q 4:5-7, his
refusal is analogous to a refusal he probably made during his public
ministry.

(8) Finally, both Mark and Q tell us that Jesus spent time alone in
the desert. Q says he also fasted during that time, and the idea is
probably implicit in Mark. Many would no doubt affirm that this
does not accord with what we know about Jesus. Modern scholars,
typically on the basis of Mark 2:18-20[65] and Q 7:31-35,[66] routinely
assert, in the words of John Dominic Crossan, that whereas "John
lived an apocalyptic asceticism . . . Jesus did just the opposite."[67] But
the "eating and drinking" of Q 7:31-35[68] takes up the polemical
language of Jesus' adversaries[69] and so can hardly be reckoned an
objective description of his activities.[70] As for Mark 2:18-20,[71] it is
not a blanket denial of the legitimacy of all fasting, for the Torah
itself prescribes fasting for the day of atonement.[72] The passage
entails only that Jesus, unlike some others, did not set aside fixed
days every week for fasting. Thus "it is going too far to conclude

---

64   This is a controversial proposition which I cannot argue in this context.

65   "As long as the bridegroom is with them they cannot fast." Compare
GThom. §104.

66   Here the Son of man, in contrast to John, has come "eating and drinking."

67   J. D. Crossan, *The Historical Jesus: The Life of a Mediterranean Jewish
Peasant* (San Francisco: HarperCollins, 1991) 260.

68   For its unity and authenticity, see U. Luz, *Das Evangelium nach Matthäus,
2. Teilband Matt 8-17* (EKKNT 1.2; Neukirchen: Neukirchener, 1990) 184.

69   On its stereotypical character, and indeed scriptural background in Deut
21:20, see D. Daube, *Appeasement or Resistance and Other Essays on New
Testament Judaism* (Berkeley: University of California, 1987) 23-26.

70   Those who make so much of Q 7:31-35 always neglect to remind us that
Jesus himself, in Q 17:26-30, uses "eating and drinking" with a pejorative sense:
"Just as it was in the [proverbially wicked] days of Noah, so too it will be in the
days of the Son of man. They were eating and drinking, etc." (cf. also Q 12:45).

71   Most believe this unit rests upon something Jesus said; cf. Crossan,
Historical Jesus, 259-60.

72   Lev 16:29-31; 23:32; Num 29:7-11; cf. Philo, *Spec. leg.* 2:195; *m. Yom.*
8:1.

from the practice of the disciples in Mark 2:18 that non-fasting was for Jesus a form of life."[73] The truth is that some aspects of Jesus' behavior and proclamation merit the adjective, "ascetic."[74] He and those around him practiced a rigorous self-denial for religious ends.[75] They chose to forsake money and live in poverty.[76] They elected to leave their villages and wander about without sandals.[77] They abandoned families and business.[78] And some of them, to whom Jesus addressed words of warning about the dangers of the sexual impulse,[79] evidently adopted celibacy, as did Jesus himself.[80] So, despite his celebration of the presence of the kingdom, he obviously lived something other than a life of indulgence. Rather, if he preached judgment and called people to repentance,[81] he embodied repentance in his own person (as when he submitted to John's baptism "for the remission of sins," Mark 1:4). We should accordingly be open-minded when the tradition, including the

---

[73]   J. Behm, "νῆστις," *TDNT* 4 (1967) 932 n. 59.

[74]   I explore this topic in my recent book, *Jesus of Nazareth: Millenarian Prophet* (Minneapolis: Fortress, 1998).

[75]   See e.g. Q 14:11, 27; 17:33; Mark 8:34; 9:43-48; GThom. §55.

[76]   Cf. P. Nagel, *Die Motivierung der Askese in der alten Kirche und der Ursprung des Mönchtums* (TU 95; Berlin: Akademie, 1966) 6-7. Relevant texts include Q 10:4, 7-8; 12:22-31; Mark 10:17-27. Luke 8:1-3 may be correct in remembering that certain women provided for Jesus and his disciples out of their resources.

[77]   Mark 1:16-20; Q 9:57-58; 10:4; etc.

[78]   Mark 1:16-20; 2:14; 10:28-31; Q 9:59-60; 12:51-53; 14:26.

[79]   See esp. Matt 5:27-28 and Mark 9:43-48. For the authenticity of these complexes, see J. Gnilka, *Das Matthäusevangelium I. Teil* (HTKNT 1.2; Freiburg: Herder, 1988) 163-64. On the original application of the latter to sexual sins, see W. Deming, "Mark 9.42-10.12, Matthew 5.27-32, and *b. Nid.* 13b: A First Century Discussion of Male Sexuality," *NTS* 36 (1990) 130-41; and K. Niederwimmer, *Askese und Mysterium: Über Ehe, Ehescheidung und Eheverzicht in den Anfängen des christlichen Glaubens* (FRLANT 113; Göttingen: Vandenhoeck & Ruprecht, 1975) 29-33. On Mark 12:18-27, which envisages the possibility of human nature without the sexual impulse, see W. D. Davies and D. C. Allison, Jr., *A Critical and Exegetical Commentary on the Gospel according to Saint Matthew* (3 vols., ICC; Edinburgh: T. & T. Clark, 1988, 1991, 1997) 3.221-34.

[80]   Matt 19:12 is best explained as Jesus' own retort to those who mocked his single state; see J. Blinzler, "Εἰσὶν εὐνοῦχοι," *ZNW* 48 (1957) 254-70. And that he uses the plural, "eunuchs," may tell us that his words included some of his followers.

[81]   J. Becker, *Jesus von Nazaret* (Berlin: Walter de Gruyter, 1966) 58-99.

temptation narratives, sometimes associates Jesus with "desert asceticism."[82] The canonical temptation narratives, when they depict Jesus fasting by himself in the desert, may accurately remember the sort of thing Jesus sometimes did.

CONCLUDING REFLECTIONS

It remains possible, despite all necessary skepticism, that Q 4:1-13 and Mark 1:12-13 retain something of Jesus' own interpretation of a foundational religious experience. But even if one thinks otherwise it would be simplistic to label our complex unhistorical. Fiction can bring us facts. Today's readers learn much history from historical novels. In like manner some of the traditions about Jesus which are, in the strict sense, not historical, surely give us a faithful impression of the sort of person he was or the sort of thing that he typically did. This, as I have argued, appears to be the case with the temptation narratives. Apart from Q 4:1-13 and Mark 1:12-13, we know that Jesus waged a successful campaign against Satan, that he was a miracle worker who did not perform for opponents on demand, that he was a man of the Spirit who trusted in God and lived in the Scriptures, that he waited upon God to make him king in Jerusalem, and that, despite his experience of the presence of the kingdom, he practiced rigorous self-denial and discipline. Thus even if nothing resembling Q 4:1-13 or Mark 1:12-13 ever took place, and even if Sanders's very minimal reconstruction of an historical kernel is too optimistic, the sources do not, from one point of view, mislead us in any serious way. For we still come away with a fair sense of several things that characterized Jesus. That is, Q 4:1-13 and Mark 1:12-13, although they seem to be haggadic fiction, remain indirect carriers of information about the historical Jesus.

---

[82] G. Anderson (*Sage, Saint and Sophist: Holy Men and their Associates in the Early Roman Empire* [London: Routledge, 1994] 44) uses this phrase of Jesus. Texts that place Jesus in the wilderness and/or depict him seeking solitude include Q 4:1; Mark 1:35, 45; 6:31-44; 8:1-10; and John 3:22. On the historical value of this last notice, see the fascinating article of J. Murphy-O'Connor, "John the Baptist and Jesus: History and Hypotheses," *NTS* 36 (1990) 359-74.

AN EXORCISM OF HISTORY: MARK 1:21-28

Bruce Chilton

INTRODUCTION: FINDING HISTORY AGAIN IN EXEGESIS

Some recent fashions would have us approach the Gospels in a synthetic manner, as literary entities which have insights and fresh perspectives to offer.[1] To a considerable extent, the fashion is a timely corrective of purely analytic approaches, which may give rise to the false impression that the Gospels are merely layers of tradition and redaction. Particularly, a more integrative approach to the Scripture may help to correct some forms of the odd notions that only the earliest layer of a text can possibly be "historical," and that only traditions which are historical in that sense can possibly be authoritative. Literary criticism permits of the necessary distinction between historicity and authority, because its premise is that texts communicate, quite aside from the question of whether they communicate as history. But while there is a distinction to be made, it should not be pressed to the point of a divorce. Authority *is* more than a matter of what actually happened in the past; after all, the past is often unrecoverable, and may prove to be quite unlike the present when it is recovered. But it would be an odd sort of faith in Jesus, a historical figure, which took no notice of what he actually said and did to the extent that can be made known. Again, literary meaning[2] is

---

[1]   See J. D. Kingsbury, *The Christology of Mark's Gospel* (Philadelphia: Fortress, 1983); R. A. Culpepper, *The Anatomy of the Fourth Gospel: A Study in Literary Design* (Philadelphia: Fortress, 1983). For an attempt to reconcile redaction criticism and the newer, literary movement, see R. M. Fowler, *Loaves and Fishes: The Function of the Feeding Stories in the Gospel of Mark* (SBLDS 54; Chico: Scholars, 1981), and the reviews in *JTS* 34 (1983) 593-96 and *JBL* 103 (1984) 290-92. That Fowler tries to reconcile the approaches is surely to be welcomed at a time when even some experienced scholars appear to believe that the historical dimension can be ignored within literary criticism. See Chilton, "Biblical Authority, Canonical Criticism, and Generative Exegesis," in C. A. Evans and S. Talmon (eds.), *The Quest for Context and Meaning. Studies in Biblical Intertextuality in Honor of James A. Sanders* (BIS 28; Leiden: Brill, 1997) 343-55.

[2]   See W. Ray, *Literary Meaning: From Phenomenology to Deconstruction*

more than a matter of historical content, but one's evaluation of a
document in literary terms, and the consequent judgment of the
grounds of its authority, will depend to some extent on its historical
accuracy. In the present paper, I should like to represent a redaction-
critical and tradition-critical approach which is chastened, but not
converted, by recent discussion. The attempt will be made to relate a
redaction-critical with a literary-critical orientation; the question of
how such a hearing influences the perceived authority of a text lies
outside the present purpose.[3]

The present approach is "chastened," in the sense that a simplistic
picture of Mark, as a mechanical compilation of earlier units which
are easily distinguished from "the Evangelist's" theology, will be
eschewed. If it is reasonable to speak of "Mark" at all, the name
should refer to the document as a whole and the process of
generating meanings which lead to the document, not to the purely
hypothetical idea of a final redactor. And any suggestion to the effect
that meaning is inherent in redaction alone, or that history is only to
be discovered in traditional material, should be avoided as simple
prejudice. But the present approach is also "not converted," in the
sense that, however fiction should be evaluated,[4] the Gospels are
palpably not the compositions of single authors.[5] The documents as
we hear them (and we *should* hear them as we read them, if we wish
to comport ourselves with the purposes for which they were

(Oxford: Blackwell, 1984), as a readable introduction to more recent theories of
meaning.

3   And is in any case taken up in my article, cited in the first note.

4   Fiction has, for understandable reasons, been the especial interest of literary
critics, some of whom would define historical writing as a species of story (J. Barr,
"Story and History in Biblical Theology," *JR* 56 [1977] 1-17). That is a matter for
further discussion, but quite beside the purpose of the present paper. The present
point resides purely in the observation that the Gospels are not the compositions of
single authors. To attempt to skirt that reality by using jargon of an "implied author"
(see Culpepper, *Anatomy*) simply shows that the paraphernalia of modern literary
theory should not be applied unreflectively to the study of the Gospels.

5   See Chilton, "An evangelical and critical approach to the sayings of Jesus,"
Themelios 3 (1978) 78-85. The programme of the earlier article was solely
developed in respect of the tradition of Jesus' sayings. The present contribution is
designed to cope with narrative material. See *A Galilean Rabbi and His Bible:
Jesus' Use of the Interpreted Scripture of His Time* (GNS 7; Wilmington: Glazier,
1984) 71-78 (also published by SPCK in London, with the subtitle *Jesus' own
interpretation of Isaiah*).

produced) probably derive from many witnesses, ranging from oral tradents to professional scribes (see Luke 1:1-4). To this extent, distinctions within each Gospel are a part of its literary character; to attempt to homogenize such distinctions in the quest for the significance of "the text as it now stands" may do violence to that character.[6] In the present inquiry, the term "redaction" is used to speak of those features of Mark 1:21-28 which serve to anchor the story in well-established themes within the Gospel; "tradition" is used to speak of more unusual features, which do not serve the interests of larger themes, but rather seem to belong to the material which was incorporated into the redactional whole.

These definitions introduce qualifications into current usage, but they appear to be necessary. Normally, redaction is ascribed to "the Evangelist," who is understood to have been responsible for the theological meaning of a given Gospel, while his tradition, frequently styled as "a kernel" of some sort, is held to approximate to a historical datum. What is unfortunate about such a picture is that it misleads. The process of framing an entire Gospel may have required the work of more than one "redactor," the purpose of redaction may or may not have been primarily "theological" (whatever one may mean by that term), and the last person in the process need not have been the one most determinative of the overall result. The material incorporated during the course of redaction, in turn, may be more of theological than of historical interest. Because we have only texts before us, without reliable external evidence of the persons and motives behind them, attention should initially be

---

6   The phrase is that of J. Barr, "Hearing the Bible as Literature," *BJRL* 56 (1973) 10-33, 25, and he uses it in discussing the contribution of Meir Weiss in his sympathetic survey of attempts to appreciate the Bible from a literary point of view. In his conclusion, he seems to me at least to approach the very difficulty here at issue (p. 34): "The literature is its own meaning; we cannot expect to identify a set of external realities of which it is the linguistic sign, and nobody approaches other literatures in such a way." The "external realities" Barr here has in mind are theological exegeses of the Bible, but he tentatively applies the attitude of the dictum to Jesus' birth and resurrection (p. 16). The last clause in the quotation is in any case an exaggeration; the approach which Barr rather dogmatically excludes is, for good or ill, common among classicists. The statement on the whole is, as a generalization, only applicable to modern fiction, and then only because the post-Enlightenment tendency has been to expunge the historical element from what is called literature, and to de-emphasize the literary element in what is called history.

directed to the shape of those texts. The consideration of a passage will then begin with seeing how it relates to the Gospel in which it is found. The passage may be found to cohere with the tendencies of redaction, and/or to manifest its own particular tendencies.

THE EXEGESIS OF REDACTION

The redactional emphases of the first exorcism story in Mark seem evident. It is presented as the first event in a long day of healing at Capernaum (vv. 21-34, inclusive), and the introductory words (καὶ εἰσπορεύονται εἰς Καφαρναούμ) are typically Markan in respect of diction (see 5:40) and syntax (see 8:22; 11:15, 27).[7] The day of what we might call authoritative healing at Capernaum[8] is paradigmatic; Jesus is to preach elsewhere, just as he does here (v. 38). But what justification have we for speaking of "authoritative healing," and for linking that to preaching? The justification lies in the redactional framework which presents the stories about healing in general, and the exorcism story in particular. The entry into Capernaum is but preliminary to Jesus' entry into the synagogue in order to teach (v. 21b-c). The reference to the Sabbath may seem superfluous, until it is remembered that within Mark the Sabbath is often the time of controversy (see 2:23, 24, 27, 28; 3:2), much as the synagogue often is the place of controversy (see 3:1; 12:38, 39; 13:9). The time and place are occasions of amazement, just as they later will be when Jesus teaches in his home country (6:2). "Sabbath," "synagogue," "teach" and "amazed" are all shared by 1:22 and 6:2. Although the emphases of the two passages are quite different, it is plain from

---

7   Overall, this evaluation was followed by "the Jesus Seminar," in a discussion based to some extent on my unpublished dissertation, *Khristos Epiphanes. A redaction critical study of Mark 1:21-28* (New York: The General Theological Seminary, 1974). See R. W. Funk (ed.), *The Acts of Jesus: The Search for the Authentic Deeds of Jesus* (San Francisco: HarperCollins, 1998) 57-59. Stylistically, the appearance of the clause is infelicitous, in that the use of the two impersonal forms, εἰσπορεύονται (v. 21) and ἐξεπλήσσοντο (v. 22), involves a change in subjects from the disciples to the congregation in the synagogue.

8   See R. Pesch, "Ein Tag vollmächtigen Wirkens Jesu in Kapharnaum (Mk 1, 21-34.35-39)," *BibLeb* 9 (1968) 114-28, 177-95, 261-77; J. Gnilka, *Das Evangelium nach Markus* (EKKNT 2.1; Zürich: Benziger; Neukirchen-Vluyn: Neukirchener, 1978) 76. But the observation was alreay made by E. Lohmeyer, *Das Evangelium des Markus* (MeyK 2; Göttingen: Vandenhoeck & Ruprecht, 1951) 34.

Markan usage that the verbal form ἐξεπλήσσοντο in the earlier story by no means suggests the response of the congregation was unequivocally positive.[9] Those in the synagogue are astounded, and they correctly perceive Jesus' "authority" as different from that of the scribes; they (implicitly) will tell the tale of what happened in the synagogue (v. 28). But there is room for misunderstanding, as subsequent Markan narrative will demonstrate. For now, however, what is established is the authority of Jesus' teaching. That is the redactional category under which the exorcism is introduced. It is, in this sense, an instance of healing with authority (see v. 27), an instance of the ministry which is to be conducted outside Capernaum (v. 38).

It has frequently been observed that "teaching" in Mark is used to characterize Jesus' ministry in such a way that the emphasis falls more on the one who teaches than on the content of his teaching.[10] That would appear to be the case in 11:18 (which is reminiscent of 1:22), since the paramount issue for the high priests and scribes (again, see 1:22) is how to destroy Jesus himself.[11] Verbal usages of διδάσκω would appear to confirm the personal emphasis which Jesus' teaching involves within Mark (see 2:13; 6:6, 34; 14:49, none of which specify the content of Jesus' teaching).[12] The point seems to be rather that Jesus taught habitually (see 10:1, ὡς εἰώθει) and that he became known in his teaching. One must conclude from 1:15 that Jesus' message is understood to concern the kingdom of God, but v. 22b-c would appear to focus more on the manner of Jesus' teaching (ὡς ἐξουσίαν ἔχων καὶ οὐχ ὡς οἱ γραμματεῖς) than on its matter. The comparison with the scribes invites attention, since scribes feature prominently in the opposition to Jesus (see 2:6; 3:22; 11:18;

---

[9]   In 7:37 and 11:18, the verb indicates a positive response. But 10:26 is ambiguous in this regard.

[10]   See A. M. Ambrozic, *The Hidden Kingdom: A Redaction-Critical Study of the References to the Kingdom of God in Mark's Gospel* (CBQMS 2; Washington: Catholic Biblical Association, 1972) 84-85. For a fuller discussion of the phenomenon, see R. T. France, "Mark and the Teaching of Jesus," in R. T. France and D. Wenham (eds.), *Studies of History and Tradition in the Four Gospels* (Gospel Perspectives 1; Sheffield: JSOT Press, 1980) 101-36.

[11]   Ἀπόλλυμι is also the language of contention in 1:24, albeit in a different connection (see below).

[12]   Mark 12:35-37 is something of an exception, in that an instance of teaching is given.

12:35, 38).[13] Commentators will, no doubt, insist on trying to discover in what precise way Jesus differed from the scribes.[14] If they succeed, it will not be because of any information which Mark here provides: the focus of v. 22 is the uniqueness of Jesus, not the ground of the comparison with scribes. In contrast with them, Jesus' authority becomes plain; the particulars of the contrast are not at issue.

To some extent, this authority is none other than the power to exorcise demons (see v. 27d; 3:15; 6:7).[15] But far more to the point, ἐξουσία is—directly or indirectly—the basis on which he acts (11:28-29, 33). Verse 27 makes this point evident within the terms of reference of the present story. To general amazement (see the wording of 9:10, 15), Jesus' teaching is recognized as new, that is non-scribal (v. 22), because he commands unclean spirits and is obeyed. The recognition of "teaching" provokes the question: "what is this?" It is a primitive sort of question, even less appropriate than the disciples' befuddled "who then is this?" at 4:41. But these are as yet early days in the literary context of the Gospel. For the moment, the scribes constitute a contrasting group, not an opposition; the teaching does not yet occasion scandal. The Sabbath is still kept[16]; the synagogue is—for the only time on this, the first reported day of Jesus' ministry with disciples—the place where Jesus' *exousia* is disclosed without occasioning overt resistance (see 3:1-6; 6:1-6).[17] If the recognition of Jesus is partial, and couched in terms redolent of

---

13   But see 12:28, 34; scribes are not merely enemies in Mark. See M. J. Cook, *Mark's Treatment of the Jewish Leaders* (NovTSup 51; Leiden: Brill, 1978).

14   See E. Haenchen, *Der Weg Jesu: Eine Erklärung des Markus-Evangeliums und der kanonischen Parallelen* (Berlin: de Gruyter, 1966) 86, 87, for an instant identification of the scribes with the later rabbis.

15   See J. Starr, "The Meaning of 'Authority' in Mark 1, 22," *HTR* 23 (1930) 302-305; and R. Reitzenstein, *Die hellenistischen Mysterienreligionen* (Leipzig: Teubner, 1927) 363. See also the translation of J. E. Steely, *Hellenistic Mystery-Religions: Their Basic Ideas and Significance* (Pittsburgh: Pickwick, 1978).

16   It is of note in this connection that v. 32 has the populace wait for sundown, the end of the Sabbath, before bringing the diseased to Jesus.

17   Even at this early stage, however, the synagogue is called "their synagogue" (v. 23). In that the pronoun refers back to the (merely implicit) subject of ἐξεπλήσσοντο in v. 22, it may be taken to mean "Jewish synagogue," as in v. 39. The attitude towards Judaism is similar to what is found at 7:3-4. See Chilton, "A Generative Exegesis of Mark 7:1-23," *The Journal of Higher Criticism* 3.1 (1996) 18-37.

future conflict, at least for a moment, starting from a single day in Capernaum, his fame can go forth unimpeded (v. 28), just as he himself can (v. 39).

Within its redactional frame (vv. 21-22, 27-28), the exorcism therefore raises the question of Jesus' authority in an acute way, and on two levels. At the level of the people in the story, whose identity is never specified, the question concerns both the teaching and the exorcism: taken together, they are altogether new and strangely efficacious in the Markan presentation. Incipient conflict in no way diminishes Jesus' authority; comparison with scribal teaching makes it all the more apparent. There is a partial disclosure of Jesus' identity, even to his contemporaries. At the level of the reader or—more properly, given the expectations with which the document was composed—the hearer of the Gospel, the disclosure is more complete. He or she knows whom this story concerns (1:1), and how its principal has been designated by God (1:11). The general outline of Jesus' ministry as recounted in the Gospel is probably already known to the hearer, so that there is some poignancy in the not yet hardened reaction of the congregation in the synagogue: the watershed presented by the crucifixion has not yet been passed. Between those in the synagogue in Capernaum and those in Mark's congregation there is not yet a world of difference. The former are amazed (v. 22), but disciples can be, as well (10:26); the former—all of them (ἅπαντες)—are astounded (v. 27), but an even more emphatic derivative of the same verb (θαμβέομαι) is used of Jesus in Gethsemane (14:33) and of the women at the tomb (16:5). Before a divine epiphany, of whatever sort, composure ceases to be a virtue; the attitude of those in the synagogue is quite appropriate, given the new teaching and healing[18] authority which confronts them. Within the Markan style of presentation, Jesus is disclosed as wielding a divine but confusing authority, both to his contemporaries and to Mark's hearers. The latter enjoy a position of privilege as compared to the former, but it is the relative privilege of knowledge, not an inalienable possession. Those who hear the Gospel know more of the story, and yet—in the end—awe such as is shown in the synagogue is

---

[18]   That the exorcism is seen within the context of healing, whatever its distinctive elements, is suggested by its association with vv. 29-34a. See D.-A. Koch, *Die Bedeutung der Wundererzählungen für die Christologie des Markusevangeliums* (Berlin: de Gruyter, 1975).

the only appropriate response, provisional though it may be.[19] The Gospel represents the disturbing "new teaching with authority" (v. 27, construed in a manner different from that of the Revised Standard Version) which challenges ordinary expectations of how God operates.

The Markan presentation therefore invites us, in our privileged position as hearers (even as hearers who happen to be reading), to participate in the response of Jesus' contemporaries, and thereby to learn and develop our own attitude. But there is also a third level at which the Markan presentation seeks to disclose the authority of Jesus. Within the body of the exorcism story (vv. 23-26), one or two striking features, which are coherent with the tendencies of Markan redaction, are evident. The first oddity is the immediate usage by the demon[20] in v. 24a-b of the first person plural, "what have we to do with you . . . have you come to destroy us?" In v. 24c, however, the demon says, "*I* know who you are" (οἶδά σε τίς εἶ), and is addressed by Jesus in the singular of the second person aorist imperative in v. 25b (φιμώθητι καὶ ἔξελθε ἐξ αὐτοῦ). The plurality of the demons might have been an original feature of this story, as in that of the Gerasene demoniac (Mark 5:1-20), but the narrative as we have it (vv. 23, 26) as well as some of the direct discourse of the demon (v. 24c) and of Jesus (v. 25b), tells somewhat against this possibility. The plural usage seems rather more to belong to the Markan scheme, according to which demons or unclean spirits are regularly referred to in the plural when they are spoken of in relation to Jesus (see 1:34, 39; 3:11-12). The usage, of course, interrupts the narrative flow of the passage, which requires only a single demon; but within Mark as a whole, symmetry with 5:1-20, and some allusion to the

---

[19] Given that the amazement/astonishment of Jesus' contemporaries can lead to scandal, there is perhaps a certain suggestion that awe is no guarantee that one has understood correctly. It is a necessary, but in itself insufficient, response.

[20] At first, it is not apparent whether it is the unclean spirit or the demoniac that is speaking, although the masculine participle makes it appear the voice is the man's (see R. G. Bratcher and E. A. Nida, *A Translator's Handbook of the Gospel of Mark* [Leiden: Brill, 1961] 49). But v. 25 makes it clear that Jesus thinks he is addressing the demon in the story. The ambiguity should not be pressed for significance, however. Possession involved the control of the boy by an alien spirit, at least in the understanding of those who told stories such as this. See F. Annen, "Die Dämonenaustreibungen Jesu in den synoptischen Evangelien," *Theologische Berichte* 5 (1976) 107-46, esp. 108.

special knowledge of demons in general, is achieved. The present story is the most specific instance of what the later, summary passages intimate: the knowledge of the demons (1:34) that Jesus is God's son (3:11). To those who know the pattern of the Gospel, a special disclosure of Jesus' authority is here offered. They will know that the demon's (or demons') identification of Jesus as the "holy one of God" (v. 24d) is insightful, but partial. The demons in Mark serve to keep Jesus' divine identity in the forefront of hearers' minds. But even as compared to the demons' knowledge, theirs is more complete.

In another sense, however, the demons' fearful knowledge of Jesus points to an authority even beyond the hearers' present experience. The unclean spirit of 1:24 speaks as a representative of a force, or group of forces, which fears for its very existence: "have you come to destroy us?" (ἦλθες ἀπολέσαι ἡμᾶς;). Generally, it is odd to speak of an exorcist destroying a demon; the verbs "binding" (δέω) or "tormenting" (βασανίζω, see Mark 5:7) would have been more conventional.[21] The demons here seem to tremble before an eschatological destruction[22] (see the use of the verb ἀπόλλυμι at 12:9), not simply a displacement from the person they occupy. While the Markan reference to the temptation of Jesus by Satan (1:13) is so spare as to make any guesses as to its precise outcome largely speculative, the narrative line of 1:21-28, 34, 39; 3:11, 12, 20-27; 5:1-20 presupposes that the rule of the demons has been broken, and that a new era dawns. In that new era, the Markan hearer is a stranger. He knows more of it than Jesus' contemporaries in the synagogue, but the new and the unexpected still have the upper hand. Because the disclosure of Jesus' authority in the story is of an eschatological nature, the hearer realizes that even his or her

---

[21] See O. Bauernfeind, *Die Worte der Dämonen im Markusevangelium* (Stuttgart: Kohlhammer, 1927) 24-25; and Chilton, *Khristos Epiphanes*.

[22] See V. Taylor, *The Gospel according to St. Mark* (London: Macmillan, 1952) 174, where 1 *Enoch* 69:27; Luke 10:18; Rev. 20:10 are cited by way of comparison; and Annen, "Dämonenaustreibungen," 126, citing the *Testaments of Simeon* 6:6 and *Levi* 18:12. A case has been made against seeing Satan as strictly associated with demons in general by M. Limbeck, "Jesus und die Dämonen," *BK* 30 (1975) 7-11. But see R. Yates, "Jesus and the Demonic in the Synoptic Gospels," *ITQ* 44 (1977) 39-57; J. D. G. Dunn and G. Twelftree, "Demon-Possession and Exorcism in the New Testament," *Churchman 94* (1980) 210-25, esp. 217-218; Annen, "Dämonenaustreibungen," 180-82.

knowledge of Jesus as God's son is but an intimation of what is as unknown as it is irresistible. Even for the hearer, it is a new teaching which needs to be learned afresh at each moment, as the future comes closer.

Three dimensions of disclosure are therefore realized in the Markan emphasis on Jesus' authority. At the level of past, historical experience, Jesus' contemporaries express an amazement, which may border on scandal, at a new, efficacious "teaching." At the level of present, literary experience, the hearer is invited to know more than Jesus' contemporaries, to look more to the teacher than to his message. And at the level of future, eschatologically anticipated experience, the broken power of the demons intimates a new reality which otherwise is only a matter of hope. The attentive hearer (to whom Mark seems especially addressed [see 13:14]) need not, of course, be consciously aware of the three dimensions of disclosure as he/she hears. But any hearing of the text which excluded one or more of them would be incomplete. To hear the text purely historically, or purely literarily, or purely eschatologically, would be one-sided, and unacceptable as an account of what is said. The three dimensions are all involved in appreciating the Markan redaction at the moment one hears.

Particular attention might nonetheless be given to the historical level of the Markan discourse. The literary disclosure of Jesus' authority in the text can be appreciated by placing the story in context; similarly, the eschatological level of address is appreciable as soon as it is placed within the framework of primitive Christian expectation. But the text as it stands seems to make a categorical statement about the past; in that claim, it places itself at the bar of history. If the text is an historical nonsense, its claim to disclose Jesus' authority is purely theoretical, at least as far as hearers with a sense of the past are concerned. But if the text is historically tenable in the hearer's mind, he or she might then see even in the literary and eschatological dimensions of the story an assertion about the real world. In any sort of hearing, of course, the hearer permits his or her own world to be influenced by the world of the text. That is why hearing of a serious sort is fundamentally an act of disciplined imagination. In Mark 1:21-28, however, the world of the text claims to be more than imaginary; Jesus' authority is presented, not only as a literary motif and an eschatological hope, but as instanced in an event. Whether one sees that presentation as historically true or false will therefore influence one's hearing of the text. That is to say, the issue of historicity is not only a function of an *a priori* historical interest in Jesus; it is also part and parcel of considered literary awareness and of a critical analysis of the religious system the Gospel is evoked by and seeks to evoke.

In general terms, there is a good degree of coincidence between this story in its Markan presentation and the kerygma of the New Testament. The eschatological significance of Jesus' exorcisms is claimed in a saying attributed to Jesus himself, and widely accepted as authentic (Matt 12:28 = Luke 11:20).[23] More particularly, some of Jesus' parables, including the one about the strong man, make the claim that his exorcisms signify the end of Satan's régime (Mark 3:23-27 = Matt 12:25-29 = Luke 11:17-22), which—in effect—is what is implicitly claimed in Mark's Gospel by virtue of the ordering of 1:21-28 shortly after the temptation story. Even on the supposition that these sayings are authentic, of course, one could not infer immediately that this particular Markan exorcism story is historical. It is possible that the Markan presentation accords with a theological claim which is itself not based on any fact, or—at any rate—which is not based on the understanding that the present story is factual. But at least we should grant that Mark 1:21-28 accords with an early (perhaps, the earliest) understanding of Jesus' exorcisms, as eschatologically redolent. Similarly, the literary emphasis of Mark on the demons' knowledge and disclosure of Jesus' identity is not merely an inventive motif,[24] but an element in early Christian theology (see Acts 19:13-17; and Jas 2:19 [noted again below]). Within the generally acceptable understanding that Jesus was known among his followers as a successful exorcist whose success was a seal of who he was and an eschatological portent, the Markan story of the exorcism in the synagogue seems at home. It is difficult to imagine how Jesus could have gained the reputation he did unless such stories were circulated, and harder still to understand why Mark begins with the particular story it does unless the story was at least credible. In other words, we should recognize from the outset

---

23   See Chilton, *Pure Kingdom: Jesus' Vision of God* (Studying the Historical Jesus 1; Eerdmans: Grand Rapids and London: SPCK, 1996) 67-70.

24   See H. Räisänen, *Das "Messiasgeheimnis" im Markusevangelium: Ein redaktionskritischer Versuch* (Helsinki: Suomalainen Tiedeakatemia, 1976) 91-93; and M.-J. Lagrange, *L'Evangile selon Marc* (Paris: Gabalda, 1947) 23.

that, whatever we might make of the story, in its own time it was considered tenable.[25]

INITIAL EXEGESIS OF TRADITION

The observation of certain features of the text encourages the view that it is far from a composition designed merely to illustrate Markan themes. The story manifests oddities which do not appear to be redactional, but rather suggest it had its own individual character before it was taken up into Mark's Gospel. The first and most striking oddity is found in the opening statement of the demon (v. 24). Except for the first person plural usage, the initial Τί ἡμῖν καὶ σοί fits well within the convention of exorcism stories: the demon attempts to deflect his antagonist with an abrupt put off: "We have nothing for you."[26] But the demon in the story goes further. He

---

[25]   It is interesting that Robert Funk rather proudly notes that, in coming to this evaluation, the Jesus Seminar comes out looking more conservative than a contemporary Catholic exegete; see *The Acts of Jesus*, 57-59, 77-79. He might have mentioned that only considerable discussion brought us to that point, and to the acknowledgment that Jesus cleansed the man with outbreak in Mark 1:40-45 (pp. 61-63). Those two evaluations are tightly linked, since in both cleansings and exorcisms within the Gospels purity is a prominent concern.

[26]   See Bauernfeind, *Worte*, 7. As Räisänen (*Das "Messiasgeheimnis" im Markusevangelium*, 92 n. 9) observes, Bauernfeind based many of his generalizations on the assumption that texts of a magical nature are immediately relevant to the question of Jesus' exorcisms. To an extent, however, the *religionsgeschichtliche* approach he employed justified such a procedure, although the approach has since been discredited (see C. Colpe, *Die religionsgeschichtliche Schule: Darstellung und Kritik ihres Bildes vom gnostischen Erlösermythus* [Göttingen: Vandenhoeck & Ruprecht, 1961]; H. C. Kee, *Miracle in the Early Christian World: A Study in Sociohistorical Method* [New Haven: Yale University Press, 1983]). In any case, Bauernfeind's findings can be checked against more obviously relevant texts. A list of useful analogies to exorcism stories in the Gospels might include Tobit 6–8, 1QapGen 20:12-32 (cf. J. A. Fitzmyer, *The Genesis Apocryphon of Qumran Cave 1* [BibOr 18A; Rome: Biblical Institute Press, 1971]), *Ant.* 8.2.5 §46-48 (cf. H. St. J. Thackeray and R. Marcus, *Josephus V* [LCL 281; London: Heinemann; Cambridge: Harvard University Press, 1934]), and *Life of Apollonius* 3.38; 4.20 (from a later period; cf. F. C. Conybeare, *Philostratus: The Life of Apollonius of Tyana* [LCL 16-17; London: Heinemann, 1912]). Reference might also be made to K. Preisendanz, *Papyri Graecae Magicae* (Leipzig: Teubner, 1928), and the revision undertaken by A. Henrichs, *Die griechischen Zauberpapyri* (Stuttgart: Teubner, 1973-74), which offers actual instances of the language of exorcism and incantation, but the dates of the documents are too late to permit of a direct comparison

names the exorcist quite precisely as Ἰησοῦ [ὁ] Ναζαρηνέ, a designation which only appears in Mark in direct or indirect discourse.[27]
Demons were commonly thought to possess supernatural insight in
antiquity, but this one is portrayed as naming Jesus in quite a formal
sense: "I know who you are, the holy one of God." In the literature
which mentions exorcism, the technique of naming (sometimes with
multiple designations) generally appears as the means by which the
exorcist gains control over the demon.[28] That convention is here

---

with the Gospels. (See also the remarks of Kee, *Miracle*, 214-15.) The question of
chronology must also be borne in mind when one uses G. A. Deissmann's *Light
from the Ancient East* (London: Hodder & Stoughton, 1910). It is also worth
noting that there are not many stories of exorcisms in the literature of early Judaism.
But the evidence does not suggest that such stories differed entirely from those of
Hellenistic literature. Moreover, this is an area in which the chronology of sources
may have little to do with the practices they relate. C. Bonner, for example,
demonstrates that elements in the narrative of Josephus resemble a contemporary
story ("The Violence of Departing Demons," *HTR* 37 [1944] 334-36). See also
Bauernfeind, *Worte*, 13 n. 3, which gives a sure indication that the practitioners of
Religionsgeschichte were not as naive in respect of chronology as is sometimes
alleged; and J. M. Hull, *Hellenistic Magic and the Synoptic Tradition* (SBT 28;
London: SCM Press, 1974).

   27   See H. H. Schaeder, "Ναζαρηνός, Ναζαραῖος," *TDNT* 4 (1967) 874-79.
The understanding of the term in this material is discussed below.

   28   See Annen, "Dämonenaustreibungen," 121, citing the work of Limbeck; but
their supposition that this feature is theologically motivated does not bear examination. Bauernfeind (*Worte*, 3-18) presents the classic form of the observation. His
position is attacked by A. Fridrichsen, "Jesu Kampf gegen die unreinen Geisten,"
in A. Suhl (ed.), *Der Wunderbegriff im Neuen Testament* (Darmstadt: Wissenschaftliche Buchgesellschaft, 1980) 248-65, 251-52. Fridrichsen's argument that
the demon's words amount to a confession is, however, only tenable within the
Markan context, not within the context of the tradition. The oddity of the demon's
speech is mentioned by C. Bonner ("The Technique of Exorcism," *HTR* 36 [1943]
39-49, 44), who in turn ascribes the observation to Loisy. For usage of ἅγιος, see
Testament of Solomon as cited by Bonner. Haenchen (*Weg*, 88) rejects the idea,
raised by Lohmeyer, that the naming represents an attempt to control one's
adversary, by saying, "Jesus ist doch für den Dämon kein 'Rumpelstilzchen'!"
Were this observation couched in the form of an argument, one might respond to it.
See R. Pesch, *Der Besessene von Gerasa: Entstehung und Überlieferung einer
Wundergeschichte* (Stuttgart: Katholisches Bibelwerk, 1972) 26 (see 32-33), who
characterizes Mark 5:7 as a parody of an exorcistic formula. Such words should be
distinguished from those in which demons might recognize the power of exorcists
(see Pesch, *Der Besessene von Gerasa*, 34; Annen, "Dämonenaustreibung," 120-
21 for examples).

reversed: the demon, in effect, attempts to exorcise Jesus, much as at 5:7 (see Luke 8:28). No doubt, the demon acts with the mere intention of warding Jesus off; the fact remains that it utilizes exorcistic means to do so. Jesus' counter-measure in v. 25[29] proves effective, but the demon departs only with violence, "convulsing" the man and screaming (v. 26). Comparison might be made with 9:26, where the same verb (σπαράσσω) is used to describe such a violent seizure that onlookers believe the victim is dead when it is over. It is true that exorcism stories sometimes include physical "evidence" of a demon's departure; the most famous example is probably that of Eleazar in Josephus, who commanded a demon to knock over a container of water as it departed.[30] But the present story is odd in the violence it stresses. (Because the mention of violence occurs just when one might expect a clear statement of the success of the exorcism, to speak of a stress on violence appears appropriate.) Both the attempt of the demon to gain control over Jesus, and its final, furious attempt to injure the demoniac are also, of course, hardly consistent with the Markan emphasis on the magisterial authority of Jesus' exorcism.

Although these features of the story amount to a coherent version (and help to confirm that it is traditional in substance), they are not easily explained as theologically motivated elements. Such christological point as there might be in having a demon in a synagogue call Jesus "the holy one of God" is dissipated, first of all by the strong resistance of the demon to Jesus, but also by the vagueness of the designation.[31] It has been suggested from time to time that stories about the exorcisms of Jesus might have circulated among those who were interested more in the style of the exorcisms than in the person of the exorcist.[32] But the relative absence of technical detail and practical

---

29   See Dunn and Twelftree, "Demon-Possession," 212; T. A. Burkill, *Mysterious Revelation: An Examination of the Philosophy of St. Mark's Gospel* (Ithaca: Cornell University, 1963) 73.

30   See *Ant.* 8.2.5 §46-48.

31   See Lagrange, *Marc*, 22-23. Although this description might be held to be disappointingly general, it seems more adequate than the attempt to see the phrase in a specifically messianic (so H. B. Swete, *The Gospel according to St. Mark* [London: Macmillan, 1913] 19), high priestly (so Lohmeyer, *Markus*, 37), or charismatic (so Haenchen, *Weg*, 87 n. 5) light.

32   See E. Trocmé, *La formation de l'Evangile selon Marc* (Paris: Presses Universitaires, 1963) 42-43. Pesch (*Der Besessene von Gerasa*, 48-49) speaks of quite a different cycle in respect of the story of the Gerasene demoniac. But he

advice (in the style, say, of the Magical Papyri) would seem to tell against speculation of this kind, at least in the case of the present passage. More to the point, the peculiar features of the story are no better accounted for on the supposition it belonged to an exorcism cycle than they are on the supposition it was transmitted by disciples of Jesus. The question of who the pre-Markan tradents of the story were is best left open for the moment, which implies there is something of a mystery as to why it was told. The theological usefulness of the story to the disciples, once it originated, is evident; but the story cannot be explained as a mere reflection of their theology.

In the absence of certainty, or even information, about the story-tellers and their motives, the odd elements of the story are difficult to evaluate. They might conceivably represent theological or typical features of which we are ignorant, but in which the story-tellers (be they disciples, folk exorcists, or whatever) and their audiences delighted. But the presently available evidence concerning conventions of exorcism stories in general lends no support to such an understanding. Moreover, the story is somewhat out of step with what we know of disciples' claims about Jesus' exorcisms in particular. As we have already observed, the Markan redaction presents the point of the story as the manifestation of Jesus' authority, not the struggle of one exorcistic oath against another. The Matthean redaction handles the difficulty in a more dramatic way, by referring to it, if at all, only in respect of Jesus' teaching, and in very summary form (7:28-29). Although the Lukan parallel of the story (4:31-37) has reference to the demon's adjuration of Jesus (4:34),[33] the description of the violence done by the demon is weaker than in Mark. Instead of σπαράσσω, ῥίπτω is used to speak of the demon's action, and the reassurance is added that it did no damage (4:35). In the end, it would appear unwise to try to explain the peculiar features of the story with reference to convention of theological tendency.

INITIAL EXEGESIS OF HISTORY

The understanding that an exorcism of the sort described was

---

clearly distinguishes 1:21-28 from this complex, and argues that the earlier exorcism story is to some extent the paradigm of the later (pp. 41-42).

[33] See also 8:29 as compared to Mark 5:7, and Pesch, *Der Besessene von Gerasa*, 52-53. But compare Luke 8:28 with Mark 5:7, and see Pesch, 61.

believed by the story-tellers to have happened would, on the other hand, adequately account for its presence in the Gospels, and for the relative importance ascribed to it within the Markan redaction. Above all, it would explain the existence of the odd features of the story: Jesus was believed on one occasion to be resisted in a synagogue by a demon who addressed him as both "Nazarene" and "the holy one of God" as part of a vain attempt to exorcise the exorcist and/or kill the demoniac. As the story was told, the ultimate victory of Jesus was stressed more and more, until it came to be seen as a manifestation of his authority. At the end of the day, the aspect of struggle which the story reveals only links in with the Markan outline insofar as it is in proximity to the temptation story. The attempt of the demons to stop Jesus by naming him is submerged in the motif of the demons' knowledge of Jesus' identity (see 1:34d). In other words, a tradition history of the story is not difficult to construe on the supposition that it was told originally to speak of an actual event; just those features which suggest it is in *that* sense historical are difficult to account for as secondary elaborations.

Pre-modern hearers of Mark would have required no tradition critical consideration to be convinced that the story-tellers intended to speak of an occurrence, and that they accomplished their intention. Even for them, however, an element of unexpected struggle and violence was present, an element which is softened in Luke and expunged in Matthew. Markan hearers were invited to perceive Jesus' authority in all its dimensions, historical, literary, and eschatological, as disclosed in continuing combat with the agents of Satan. For them, Jesus had joined combat and begun the long battle for victory, but the fight had still to be waged in his name (see 9:38-40).

Modern hearers of Mark are put in a different position, not by the text, but by their own understanding of the world. For us, the meaning of Jesus' authority within Mark is still conveyed by the text, and we can appreciate the significance which might be attached to this sort of authority. But among educated Westerners, to think of demons at all, much less of demons uttering exorcistic formulae and convulsing their victims, has long been considered more appropriate within the realm of fantasy, rather than of fact. (The commonly voiced objection that there are certain instances of demoniacal thinking and experience in our culture does not refute the general observation that such instances are not consonant with our usual apprehension.) A critical hearing of the evidence will not necessarily resolve our dilemma, because it is not within the province of exegetes or historians to rule on matters of natural science. To say, for example, that the story is true and our view of the world too narrow, is a perfectly respectable philosophical reflection, but it can hardly be commended on strictly textual or historical grounds. Similarly, to say that demons do not exist and stories which suppose they do are misleading, has the attractive ring of rational consistency about it, but it would seem to reduce history to *a priori* notions of what is possible.

Within the discipline of historical exegesis, the text is neither an absolute, nor an inconvenience to be overcome: the task of the hearer as exegete is to understand what the text he or she is hearing offers. In the present case, what is offered is a picture of Jesus' authority based on the report of an exorcism which, in the minds of those who told the story, actually occurred. The claim of actuality, so far as criticism can determine, lies at the very origin of the story; without it, we can understand neither why the story was told, nor why it was incorporated as it now is within Mark. In this sense, the speech of the demon and Jesus' eventual exorcism of it are historical events. History in this case contradicts received notions of ordinary reality. One might easily construct an alternative diagnosis of the demoniac, along the lines, say, of a dissociative reaction.[34] But constructions of that sort would only impose an alien point of view on the text, and are more exercises in natural philosophy than in exegesis. The story raises in our minds the phenomenological question whether demons exist, without settling it; what would have been experienced by a modern observer in ancient Capernaum remains a mystery. If we cannot accept the terms of reference with which the story works, it will not help us to its meaning if we invent new terms of reference for it. Even the attempt to impose the demonic conventions of the story on the modern hearer is an exercise in inventing terms of reference, since demons are not a normal part of our world view.

---

[34] See N. Cameron, *Personality Development and Psychopathology: A Dynamic Approach* (Boston: Houghton Mifflin, 1963) 338-72, who deals with the rather rare occurrence of multiple personality within this category (pp. 358-60). It should be observed that schizophrenia is described quite differently, as regression expressed by the production of delusions and/or hallucinations (p. 584). See also *The Psychiatric Clinics of North America* 7 (1984). On the generally problematic nature of attempts at retrospective diagnosis, see R. Hengel and M. Hengel, "Die Heilungen Jesu und medizinisches Denken," in *Wunderbegriff*, 338-73.

The story does not preach the existence of demons; it merely takes them for granted.

Above all, exercises in the alternative reconstruction of the event described do not explain why the text emerged as it has; they relinquish the study of the text in favor of a general study of the phenomenology of exorcism. In the present case, to say that all alleged instances of possession are really a species of psychological disturbance[35] might make some hearers more comfortable with the story, but it would not account for its impact on those who heard and told it, or for the precise words attributed to the demon. Rather, the historicity of the text, quite aside from the ontological question of the existence of demons, should be accepted on exegetical grounds as one facet of its effectiveness as a literary whole. History is essentially the study of human events, and of the factors which occasioned and influenced those events.[36] By an act of sympathy, historians attempt to understand the recorded impact of events on people; how people perceived events is therefore part of the historical record. The exorcism reported in Mark 1:21-28 should be accepted as one factor in the recognition of Jesus' identity by his followers.[37] Usually, such conditioning factors—such as economic climate, and popular expectations of the time—can be recognized as possible realities in the present, as well as the past. Historians normally speak of the

---

[35]   Before psychological explanations of such events are accepted, however, it must be appreciated that the entire notion of mental disease has come under attack, both on practical grounds (see W. E. Broen, *Schizophrenia: Research and Theory* [New York: Academic, 1968]; T. R. Sarbin and J. C. Mancuso, *Schizophrenia: Medical Diagnosis or Moral Verdict?* [Oxford: Pergamon, 1980]) and moral grounds (see J. Coulter, *Approaches to Insanity: A Philosophical and Sociological Study* [London: Robertson, 1973]; T. Szasz, *The Myth of Psychotherapy: Mental Healing as Religion, Rhetoric, and Repression* [Oxford: Oxford University, 1979]).

[36]   See B. J. F. Lonergan, *Method in Theology* (New York: Herder & Herder, 1972) 178-96, 220-24.

[37]   Annen ("Dämonenaustreibung," 115-17) puts his finger on a difficulty which has been created for (and by) critical scholarship. Critics are willing to say Jesus exorcized in general, but not which stories are historical (see Dunn and Twelftree, "Demon-Possession"). But general statements cannot possibly do justice to the particularity of texts, in this case, the struggle of the demon and its naming of Jesus. The force of any story lies precisely in its unusual elements; their appreciation as historical, mythical, theoretical, fantastic, or whatever, is part of the hearer's task.

conditioning factors of the past in the comforting knowledge that they would easily be recognized in the present. But there are occasions, and this is one of them, when the historical conditions of the past have no obvious analogies in the present; whether that is because human perceptions have changed over time, or because the actuality perceived has itself altered, no one can say with certainty. An event may be said to be historical without being repeatable in the present. On such occasions, historical inquiry must itself be exorcised of the pretension to speak of what is true for all time, and rest content with a reasoned, exegetical account of how what is written came to be, and how that influences our appreciation of the received form of the text. The historical question centers fundamentally on what people perceived, and how they acted on their perception; the question of how ancient experience relates to modern experience is a distinct, interpretative matter.[38]

EXEGESIS OF TRADITION: A SECOND LOOK

The struggle to come to terms with Jesus' exorcisms is evident not only in contemporary discussion, but in the text of Mark. Nowhere is that plainer than in the story of the Gerasene demoniac (Mark 5:1-20), which in some particulars bears a striking resemblance to the story of the exorcism in the synagogue. Jesus is placed on the eastern side of the sea of Galilee, in explicitly gentile territory. The already emphatic impurity of the locale is, at it were, squared by the approach of a maniac who inhabits the cemetery of the Gerasenes. The unclean spirit within him calls himself "legion," an evident reference to the recent occupation by the Romans (under Pompey) and the use of the region of the Decapolis for administrative purposes.[39] Now we understand how impure the place is, and why it is appropriate to think of it—as the reference to the tombs suggests —in terms of death itself. Finally, however, impurity squared becomes impurity cubed, with the request of the demons to entire a herd of about two thousand pigs. The narrative puts Jesus in confrontation with uncleanness, if not to the "nth" degree, then cubed.

Jesus' characteristic activity within Galilee put him into contact

---

[38]   See A. Suhl, "Die Wunder Jesu: Ereignis und Überlieferung," in *Wunderbegriff*, 464-509.

[39]   See J. J. Rousseau and R. Arav, *Jesus and His World. An Archaeological and Cultural Dictionary* (Minneapolis: Fortress, 1995) 85-87, 97-99.

with those whom many teachers would have considered of doubtful purity, or as simply impure. The failure to pay tithe, for example, was held by Pharisees to render one unfit for fellowship (in Mishnah, see the tractate *Demai*). A well-known saying of Jesus, widely held to be authentic, attests Jesus' own awareness that this habit of table-fellowship with dubious examples of Israel was notorious (see Matt 11:19 = Luke 7:34, from "Q").[40] But the story of the Gerasene maniac pushes the issue of uncleanness well beyond debatable questions: here is a man who lives in a cemetery in gentile territory occupied by the Romans, whose unclean spirit calls itself "legion" ("troops") and likes the company of swine.

The maniac may be understood to be an Israelite or not. His proximity to the pigs is no disqualification; Jesus' own parable of the wayward son conceives of pig-keeping as the supreme symbol that a Jew has hit rock bottom (see Luke 15:11-32). The reference to Jesus as "the son of God Most High," however, probably suggests that the maniac is a gentile, since "God Most High" is a title of the God of Israel which is classically used by non-Israelites (see Melchizedek in Gen 14:19; Balaam in Num 24:16; the Philippian slave girl in Acts 16:17).

Whether the maniac is identified as a Jew or not, the outcome of his encounter is plainly indicated. The pigs are drowned, the demons are confined to the deep, and Jesus is cordially invited to depart from the area. His purity is such that he can indeed encounter what is triply impure, the gentile domain of Roman mortuary demons and swine, but the result is a disaster for uncleanness itself. Jesus can abide what is impure, but what is impure cannot survive before him.

Within its own particular terms of reference, the story of the legion of demons might be compared to the story of Nadab and Abihu, the sons of Aaron, in the Hebrew Bible (Lev 10:1-3). When they offered an unauthorized, unwanted form of sacrifice by fire, they were themselves consumed with fire. As fire is the answer to fire in Leviticus, drowned pigs are the answer to impure spirits in the Synoptic Gospels. In both cases, the underlying dynamic of the narratives is that the pure and the impure are incompatible, and that it is the pure which destroys the impure when they meet, by driving uncleanness to self-immolation.

The narrative of the demonic legion and the Gerasene swine is an

---

40   See *Pure Kingdom*, 80, 83, 112, 142.

explicit marker of the limits of Jesus' characteristic activity. Seàn Freyne has observed that Jesus is not placed by the Gospels in any of the urban centers which modern archaeologists have excavated.[41] We can say much more about Sepphoris and Tiberias, for example, than was once the case, but we find Jesus there no more than in Tyre or Sidon. Fishing towns such as Bethsaida and Capernaum, agricultural settlements such as Nazareth and Chorazin, rather provided his focus of activity. Even in Jerusalem, we find him staying out in the village of Bethany. The story of the legion may to some extent permit us to say why Jesus avoided the centers of Roman civilization in his area.

The very conception of the story projects Jesus' practice of purity as inclusive, willing to engage both the man from the tombs and the request of the legion to enter the swine, and to do so on for him unusual territory. But his apparent willingness to accede to their desire is a disaster for them and for the economy of the region. Implicitly, insofar as the demons take the name of legion, Roman hegemony itself is threatened. From the perspective of this story, Jesus did not avoid Caesarea and Sepphoris and Tyre and Sidon because he feared the contact of impurity; rather, his avoidance was a matter of containing the power of his own purity. The whole irony of the encounter is that Jesus' trip east, in the direction of Roman influence, banishes the demons, kills the pigs, upsets the prosperity which the Romans and their legions have brought.[42]

As purity delineated the Israel which the Pharisees attained to and which the Essenes insisted upon, so purity was at the center of Jesus' program.[43] According to his ideal, the purity of the kingdom could

---

[41] See "The Geography, Politics, and Economics of Galilee and the Quest for the Historical Jesus," in B. D. Chilton and C. A. Evans (eds.), *Studying the Historical Jesus. Evaluations of the State of Current Research* (NTTS 19; Leiden: Brill, 1994), 75-121, esp. 120-21.

[42] This irony was extensively discussed within the meeting of the Jesus Seminar which found that an historical event generated the story. Robert Funk was visibly annoyed with the finding at the time, and now writes, "The Fellows of the Jesus Seminar concluded that some vague historical event might lie behind the story" (*The Acts of Jesus*, 78). The Seminar might well have gone further in assertions of historicity had there been greater participation by those who are interested in history, but in any case the discussion was much more pointed, and the results sometimes more accommodating of a positively historical concern, than Funk indicates.

[43] See Chilton, *The Temple of Jesus: His Sacrificial Program Within a Cultural History of Sacrifice* (University Park: Penn State University Press, 1992).

be celebrated in meals of fellowship within Israel. The generic purity of Israel was assumed, without the addition of Pharisaic or Essene rules of tithing and preparation. But within Jesus' practice, precisely which "Israel" was assumed to be pure? Jesus' own activity draws us a map of Israel as communities in which Jewish settlements, supported by fishing and/or agriculture, supported themselves and were productive for other Jews. Those communities might be in the territory of Herod Antipas, such as Nazareth and Capernaum and Chorazin, or in the territory of Herod Philip, such as Bethsaida. Political boundaries as such do not seem to have been considered an issue.

What was an issue, the story of the legion informs us, was the capacity and willingness to join the circle of Israel by means of the practice of purity. Absent those conditions, contact with Jesus' purity might be disastrous. Once purity in Jesus' teaching and practice is understood to be a positive value, the condition of Israel which is consistent with the kingdom of God, then the story of the legion becomes sensible. Apart from the context of purity, the story seems an arbitrary display of power; within that context, the story articulates the implicit limitation of Jesus' ministry to non-urban Israel.

Within non-urban Israel, fellowship might be joined by offering of one's own produce, on the assumption that the products of Israel were suitably pure. At the same time, forgiveness is clearly a feature of Jesus' movement, in which a regular prayer to be forgiven was characteristic (see Matt 6:12 = Luke 11:4). But to that which is outside Jesus' Israel, to the world of unclean spirits, of swine and cemeteries, of that all the legion represent, Jesus' purity is a threatening practice. There, generic cleanness may not be assumed and forgiveness is neither asked nor offered; it is a world which is simply incompatible with Jesus' vision. The end of the story, in the request that Jesus depart, is the limiting boundary of what constitutes Israel. As in the Mishnah, so for Jesus, Israel is marked off from non-Israel by the practice of purity. In Jesus' case, the purity at issue is more generic than in Mishnah, a matter of producing more than a matter of tithing, and yet the fundamental, defining role of purity remains constant.

But how is it that the implicit limitation to agricultural Israel within Jesus' program became so emphatic and clearly delineated in this story? That overt focus on purity within the story of the

Gerasene maniac is the likely contribution of James and his circle. The importance of James as a central authority within a primitive stage of Christianity is evident from a reading of Acts and Galatians.[44] A passage within the Gospels will be the focus of attention here, in order to elucidate James' influence within the oral and literary formation of the texts. To lay the groundwork for a consideration of James' concern for the Temple (a pivotal topic within any discussion of purity), we begin with the description of James provided by Hegesippus, a Christian writer from the second century.

Hegesippus—as cited by Eusebius (see *Hist. Eccl.* 2.23.1-18)— characterizes James, Jesus' brother, as the person who exercised immediate control of the church in Jerusalem. Although Peter had initially gathered a group of Jesus' followers in Jerusalem, his interests and activities further afield left the way open for James to become the natural head of the community there. That change, and political changes in Jerusalem itself, made the Temple the effective center of the local community of Jesus' followers. James practiced a careful and idiosyncratic purity in the interests of worship in the Temple. He abstained from wine and animal flesh, did not cut his hair or beard, and forsook oil and bathing. According to Hegesippus, those special practices gave him access even to the sanctuary. Josephus reports he was killed in the Temple c. 62 at the instigation of the High Priest Ananus during the interregnum of the Roman governors Festus and Albinus (*Ant.* 20.9.1 §197-203). Hegesippus gives a more circumstantial, less politically informed, account of the martyrdom.

In addition to the sort of close association with the Temple which could and did result in conflict with the authorities there, the circle of James is expressly claimed in Acts to have exerted authority as far away as Antioch, by means of emissaries who spoke Greek (Acts 15:13-35). The particulars of the dispute (with both Pauline and Petrine understandings of purity) will not detain us here, because they have been discussed at some length (see note 44). What is of immediate import is that James alone determines the outcome of apostolic policy. James in Acts agrees that Gentiles who turn to God are not be encumbered with needless regulations (15:19), and yet he

---

[44]   See J. Neusner and B. D. Chilton, *Revelation: The Torah and the Bible* (Christianity and Judaism: The Formative Categories 1; Valley Forge: Trinity Press International, 1995) 118-23.

insists they be instructed by letter to abstain "from the pollutions of idols, and from fornication, and from what is strangled, and from blood" (v. 20).

The grounds given for the Jacobean policy are that the law of Moses is commonly acknowledged (Acts 15:21); the implication is that to disregard such elemental considerations of purity as James specifies would be to dishonor Moses. Judas Barsabbas and Silas are then dispatched with Paul and Barnabas to deliver the letter in Antioch along with their personal testimony (vv. 22-29), and are said particularly to continue their instruction as prophets (v. 32-33). They refer to the regulations of purity as necessities (v. 28), and no amount of Lukan gloss can conceal that what they insist upon is a serious challenge of Paul's position (compare 1 Corinthians 8).

James' devotion to the Temple is also reflected in Acts 21. When Paul arrives in Jerusalem, James and the presbyters with him express concern at the rumor that Paul is telling Jews who live among the gentiles not to circumcise. Their advice is for Paul to demonstrate his piety by purifying himself, paying the expenses of four men under a vow, and entering the Temple with them (Acts 21:17-26). The result is a disastrous misunderstanding. Paul is accused of introducing "Greeks" into the Temple, a riot ensues, and Paul himself is arrested (21:27-36). James is not mentioned again in Acts, but Hegesippus' description shows his devotion to the Temple did not wane.

Within the Gospels, certain passages reflect the exceptional devotion of James' circle to the Temple. The best example is Mark 7:6-13 (and, with an inverted structure, Matt 15:3-9); although the topic of the chapter overall is purity, the issue addressed in the passage itself is the sanctity of the Temple in particular (Mark 7:6-13). The issue is spelled out in terms of a dispute concerning *qorban*, the Aramaic term for a cultic gift (Mark 7:11).

The dispute reflects Jesus' own stance, that what is owed to one's parents cannot be sheltered by declaring it dedicated to the Temple. The crucial point of such a gambit of sheltering is that one might continue to use the property after its dedication to the Temple, while what was given to a person would be transferred forthwith.[45] The basic complaint about the practice, especially as stated in the simple

---

45   See Z. W. Falk, "Notes and Observations on Talmudic Vows," *HTR* 59 (1966) 309-312.

epigram of Mark 7:11-12, derives from Jesus. The complaint is characteristic of him; quite aside from his occupation of the Temple, he criticized commercial arrangements there (see Matt 17:24-27[46]; Mark 12:41-44; Luke 21:1-4).

The dominical epigram has here been enveloped in a much more elaborate argument, crafted within the circle of James. Mark 7:6-13 is a syllogism, developed by means of scriptural terms of reference. Isaiah's complaint (29:13) frames the entire argument: the people claim to honor God, but their heart is as far from him as their vain worship, rooted in human commandments (Mark 7:6b-7). That statement is related in Mark 7:10-12 to the tradition of *qorban*, taken as an invalidation of the Mosaic prescription to honor parents. The simple and unavoidable conclusion is that the tradition violates the command of God (Mark 7:8-9, 13).

The argument as it stands insists upon the integrity of the Temple and the strict regulation of conduct there; it attacks opponents for too little concern for the Temple, not too much. At the same time, the passage presents Jesus as maintaining a literal loyalty to the Scriptures which the Pharisees did not. (The actual form of citation, however, is derived from the Greek translation of the Hebrew Bible, the Septuagint. That is a sign of the Hellenistic phase of the cycle of tradition which James inspired.) Those aspects of the presentation of Jesus' saying are typical of the circle of James.

Regular worship in the Temple only became a characteristic feature of Jesus' movement after the crucifixion and resurrection. Before then, Jesus' conflict with the cultic authorities over the most basic issues of how offerings should be brought to the Temple resulted in deadly opposition to him. But one of the most surprising developments of the period after that time is that a group of Jesus' followers continued to reside in Jerusalem, and that worship in the Temple was one of their primary purposes there. The removal of Caiaphas from the high priesthood in the year 36/37 CE (see *Ant.* 18.4.3 §90-95), and the consequent reversal of his reforms (to which

---

[46]   See Chilton, "A Coin of Three Realms: Matthew 17.24-27," in D. J. A. Clines, S. E. Fowl, S. E. Porter (eds.), *The Bible in Three Dimensions. Essays in Celebration of Forty Years of Biblical Studies in the University of Sheffield* (JSOTSup 87; Sheffield: JSOT, 1990) 269-82; repr. in B. D. Chilton and C. A. Evans, *Jesus in Context: Temple, Purity, and Restoration* (AGJU 39; Leiden: Brill, 1997) 339-51.

Jesus himself had objected), fed the conviction of Jesus' followers that he who had been crucified had also been vindicated.

Acts pictures Peter as the first leader of a tightly knit group, which broke bread at home and held property in common (see Acts 1:12-26; 2:46; 3:1-26; 4:1-37; 5:1-11). But Peter is also represented as active much further afield. A shift in leadership of the community in Jerusalem, from Peter to James, became necessary, and Acts clearly attests it (see Act 12:17). Acts 12:17 also reflects an important (and overlooked) aspect of the shift in power from Peter to James. Peter has been imprisoned at the command of Herod Agrippa, and is delivered by means of an angel. Greeted by companions in the house he goes to, he orders them to tell James of his release, and departs to an unspecified place. Peter had aroused priestly opposition in a way James did not (see Acts 4:1-31; 5:12-42), and the priests were able to use their influence with Herod. In contrast, James managed to adapt Jesus' message to a greater devotion to the Temple than most Jews demonstrated. Just that devotion is reflected in the scriptural syllogism regarding *qorban*, as well as in Hegesippus' description of James.

The syllogism in regard to *qorban* also assumes that devotion to Jesus' teaching is consistent with a greater than ordinary loyalty to the Temple. Hegesippus' account of the death of James conveys the same assumption, in its reference to the attempt by a member of a priestly family to save James from death in the last moments of his life. Indeed, the entire scene of his martyrdom unfolds in the context of the Temple at the time of Passover, and reflects the particular devotion of James' circle both to that feast and to the conduct of sacrificial worship in the Temple.[47]

Typically, the circle of James applied the Scriptures directly to the situation of Jesus' followers, on the assumption of their regulative authority. James cited the reference of Amos to the restoration of the house of David (in Amos 9:11-12). As James develops the meaning of Amos in Acts 15:16-21, the gentiles are to recognize the triumph of David, and that implies that they are to remain gentiles. They are not a part of Israel, although they are to keep basic rules of purity in order to honor the law of Israel.

James' focus was on Jesus' role as the ultimate arbiter within the

---

[47]   See B. D. Chilton, *A Feast of Meanings: Eucharistic Theologies from Jesus through Johannine Circles* (NovTSup 72; Leiden: Brill, 1994) 93-108.

Davidic line, and there was never any question in his mind but that the Temple was the natural place to worship God and acknowledge Jesus. Embracing the Temple as central meant for James, as it meant for everyone associated with worship there, maintaining the purity which it was understood that God required in his house, and keeping it better than many of those associated with the priesthood. That is the point of the Scriptural syllogism regarding *qorban*. According to James, Jesus' purity involved excluding gentiles, even those who acknowledged some rudiments of purity out of loyalty to the Mosaic law, from the interior courts of the Temple. There, only Israel was to be involved in sacrifice, and followers of Jesus were to accept particular responsibility for such sacrifice (so Acts 21:17-36). The line of demarcation between Israel and non-Israel was no invention within the circle of James, but a natural result of seeing Jesus as the triumphant scion of the house of David.

Peter's imprisonment by Herod Agrippa can be dated rather precisely to the year 44 CE.[48] By that time, then, James had emerged as a prominent authority, the natural leader of the group in Jerusalem. Earlier, in reference to his visit to Jerusalem in 35 CE, Paul refers to meeting Peter and James, but he alludes to receiving instruction only from Peter (see Gal 1:18-19). During the intervening period, c. 40 CE, the circle of James promulgated its own instructional gospel, comparable to Peter's and building upon it. That was the basis of James' authority, which the apostolic council reflected in Acts 15 confirmed. That council is usually dated in the year 49 CE. When Judas Barsabbas and Silas were sent by the council to deliver its judgment (which was originally James' opinion) in Antioch, it authorized James' version of the gospel to be delivered in Greek. When Acts 15:32-33 refers to Judas and Silas as prolonging their visit in Antioch after they had read the letter from the council, we are given a glimpse into to process by which materials originally framed in Aramaic were rendered into Greek. At that moment, the importance of non-Jewish testimony to Jesus within its own environment (rather than within Israel) was emphasized. The sequel to the story of the legion, in which the restored maniac is portrayed as preaching among his own people (Mark 5:18-20), is an example of that development.

---

[48]   See C. K. Barrett, *The Acts of the Apostles* (ICC; Edinburgh: T. & T. Clark, 1994) 592.

At the same time, we are shown how James' classic understanding of Israel was considered authoritative, even for the largely non-Jewish congregation in Antioch. Here, in the place where Jesus' followers were first called "Christians" (so Acts 11:26), it is accepted after a considerable controversy that, although Gentiles may not be required to circumcise, neither may they be considered one with Israel. James' Israel consisted of those who recognized Jesus, the scion of the Davidic line, as the guardian of true, non-commercial purity in the Temple.

The nature of the vow fulfilled within the Temple which James was especially devoted to seems quite clear. It is to be fulfilled when the men shave their heads (so Acts 21:24). We are evidently dealing with a Nazirite vow.[49] As set out in Numbers 6, a Nazirite was to let his hair and beard grow for the time of his vow, abstain completely from grapes, and avoid approaching any dead body. At the close of the period of the vow, he was to shave his head, and offer his hair in proximity to the altar (so Num 6:18). The end of this time of being holy, the LORD's property, is marked by enabling the Nazirite to drink wine again (6:20).

Just these practices of holiness are attributed by Hegesippus (as cited by Eusebius, *Hist. Eccl.* 2.23) to James. The additional notice, that he avoided oil and using an enclosed bath, is consistent with the especial concern for purity among Nazirites. They were to avoid any contact with death (Num 6:6-12), and the avoidance of all uncleanness—which is incompatible with sanctity—follows naturally. The avoidance of oil is also attributed by Josephus to the Essenes (*J.W.* 2.8.3 §123), and the reason seems plain: oil, as a fluid pressed from fruit, was considered to absorb impurity to such an extent that extreme care in its preparation was vital.[50] Absent complete assurance, abstinence was a wise policy. James' vegetarianism also comports with a concern to avoid contact with any kind of corpse. Finally, although Hegesippus' assertion that James could actually enter the sanctuary seems exaggerated, his acceptance of a Nazirite

---

49   See R. Tomes, "Why did Paul Get his Hair Cut? (Acts 18.18; 21.23-24), in C. M. Tuckett (ed.), *Luke's Literary Achievement: Collected Essays* (JSNTSup 116; Sheffield: Sheffield Academic Press, 1995) 188-97. Tomes rightly points out that there is considerable deviation from the prescriptions of Numbers 6 here, but Mishnah (see below) amply attests such flexibility within the practice of the vow.

50   See Josephus, *J.W.* 2.30.4–5 §590-594; *m. Menaḥ.* 8:3-5; and the whole of *Makširin*. The point of departure for the concern is Lev 11:34.

regime, such as Acts 21 explicitly associates him with, would account for such a remembrance of him, in that Nazirites were to be presented in the vicinity of the sanctuary.

As it turned out, James' advice proved disastrous for Paul. Paul's entry into the Temple caused a riot, because it was supposed he was bringing non-Jews in. As a result, he was arrested by a Roman officer, and so began the long legal contention which resulted ultimately in his death (Acts 21:27-28:21). The extent to which James might have anticipated such a result can not be known, but it does seem obvious that his commitment to a Nazirite ideology blinded him to the political dangers which threatened the movement of which he was the nearest thing to the head.

Indeed, our suggestion that James was a Nazirite,[51] and saw his brother's movement as focused on producing more Nazirites, enables us to address an old and as yet unsolved problem of research. Jesus, bearing a common name, is sometimes referred to as "of Nazareth" in the Gospels, and that reflects how he was specified in his own time. There is no doubt but that a geographical reference is involved (see John 1:45-46).[52] But more is going on here. Actually, Jesus is rarely called "of Nazareth" or "from Nazareth," although he was probably known to have come from there. He is usually called "Nazoraean" or "Nazarene." Why the adjective, and why the uncertainty in spelling? The Septuagint shows us that there were many different transliterations of "Nazirite." That reflects uncertainty as to

---

51   See the more global construction of R. H. Eisenman, *James the Brother of Jesus: The Key to Unlocking the Secrets of Early Christianity and the Dead Sea Scrolls* (New York: Viking, 1996). It is sometimes argued that Jesus himself was a Nazirite. So an as yet unpublished paper by Marcus Bockmuehl, given at the meeting of the Studiorum Novi Testamenti Societas in Birmingham in 1997. Of all the arguments adduced, the most attractive is that Yeshua's statement concerning wine and the kingdom involves his accepting Nazirite vows. See P. Lebeau, *Le vin nouveau du Royaume: Etude exégétique et patristique sur la Parole eschatologique de Jésus à la Cène* (Paris: Desclée, 1966); M. Wojciechowski, "Le naziréat et la Passion (Mc 14,25a; 15:23)," *Bib* 65 (1984) 94-96. But the form of Yeshua's statement has not been rightly understood, owing to its Semitic syntax. He is not promising never to drink wine, but only to drink wine in association with his celebration of the kingdom. See Chilton, *A Feast of Meanings*, 169-71.

52   Indeed, there was even a place called Bethlehem of Nazareth, according to the Talmud; see Chilton, *God in Strength: Jesus' Announcement of the Kingdom* (SNTU 1; Freistadt: Plöchl, 1979; repr. BibSem 8; Sheffield: JSOT Press, 1987) 311-13.

how to convey the term in Greek. (That uncertainty is not in the least surprising, since even the Mishnah refers to differing pronunciations [see *Nazir* 1:1].) Some of the variants are in fact very close to what we find used to describe Jesus in the Gospels.

In the Gospel according to Mark, the first usage is in the mouth of the unclean spirit in the synagogue, who says to Jesus (Mark 1:24):

> We have nothing for you, Nazarene Jesus!
> Have you come to destroy us?
> I know who you are—the holy one of God!

In this usage, "Nazarene" in the first line clearly parallels "the holy one of God" in the last line. The demon knows Jesus' true identity, but those in the synagogue where the exorcism occurs do not. And they do not hear the demons, because Jesus silences them (so Mark 1:25). This is part of the well known theme of the "Messianic secret" in Mark.[53]

For James and those who were associated with him, Jesus' true identity was his status as a Nazirite. The demons saw what others did not, and after the resurrection the knowledge of the holy one of God could be openly acknowledged and practiced. That practice could include men, women, and slaves, in accordance with the Mishnah (*Nazir* 9:1). In the Christian movement, the custom was apparently widespread. In Acts 18:18, it is said that even Paul "had his head shorn in Kenkhraea, because he had a vow." Such vows in regard to hair alone were held in Mishnah to equate to a Nazirite vow (*Nazir* 1:1), so that what Paul thought of his vow from his own perspective, many would have seen him as falling in with the program of James, the brother of Jesus. Under the influence of James, they might have said, even Paul was concerned with getting it right.

THE EXEGESIS OF HISTORY: A SECOND LOOK

The formative influence of the circle of James on this story provides it with a clear meaning, which feeds the overarching Markan motif of the messianic secret. The unclean spirits in the synagogue and the demons which enter the swine appreciate Jesus' Nazirite status, which is hidden to his contemporaries. He himself

---

53   See Chilton, "Exorcism and History: Mark 1:21-28," in D. Wenham and C. L. Blomberg (eds.), *The Miracles of Jesus* (Gospel Perspectives 6; Sheffield: JSOT Press, 1986) 253-71.

silences the demons, because Nazirite practice in Jesus' name is to develop after the resurrection within the circle of James. The premature acknowledgment by the unclean spirits is *because* they are unclean, not because they believe and then act on their belief. As the letter of James puts the matter, "Do you believe that God is one? You do well! Even the demons believe—and quake!" (Jas 2:19).

The underlying assumption of the Jacobean exegesis of Jesus' exorcism is that Jesus' practice involves the confrontation with impurity and its replacement with purity. The particular contribution of James' circle is the claim that the source of Jesus' ability was his Nazirite status. But within Jesus' lifetime, his exorcism appear to have been a source of contention. There are rather clear indications that Jesus and his brothers were on strained terms. Within chap. 3 of Mark, for example, we encounter the following scene:

> [31]And his mother and his brothers come and standing outside, they sent a delegation to him, calling him. [32]And a crowd sat around him, and they say to him,
>> "Look, your mother and your brothers and your sisters seek you outside."
> [33]He replied and says,
>> "Who is my mother and my brothers?"
> [34]He looks around at those sitting in a circle about him, and says,
>> "Look: my mother and my brothers. [35]Whoever does the will of God, he is my brother and sister and mother."

Not a picture of family bliss, and evidently an echo of the earlier statement (3:21) that there were those associated with Jesus who tried to prevent him from engaging in exorcism. They said he was "beside himself." Now he says they are not true family.

Jesus was known to have confronted the origins of impurity, "unclean spirits," and to have entered into violent contention with them, even within a synagogue. The violence of that confrontation was disturbing to many of his followers and to his family. After the resurrection, the memory of that struggle was cast in terms of the special sanctity which attached to Jesus, a secret Nazirite, "the holy one of God."

THE BEELZEBUL CONTROVERSY AND THE ESCHATOLOGIES OF JESUS

Joel Marcus

LOGIC AND GRAMMAR

I start with a simple question: what is the rhetorical purpose of the Parable of the Divided Kingdom in Mark 3:23-26 = Q 11:17-18?[1] It seems obvious that the parable is designed to refute the charge that immediately precedes it, namely the slander of Jesus' opponents that he casts out demons by means of Beelzebul, the demons' ruler (Mark 3:22b = Q 11:15b).[2] In the view of these opponents, then, Jesus' exorcisms are a feint by Satan against himself, designed, apparently, to convey the false impression that Jesus is on the divine side in the conflict between the devil and God.[3] But how exactly does the

---

[1]   As is customary, I use the Lukan chapter and verse numbers for Q passages.

[2]   M. Smith (*Jesus the Magician* [New York: Harper & Row, 1978] 32-33) takes "Beelzebul" as the name for Jesus' familiar spirit; Jesus' question, "Can Satan cast out Satan?" suggests only that *others* identified this familiar with Satan. But this is a strange claim to make, when it is Jesus himself who makes the connection between Beelzebul and Satan; his argument would have no force unless the equivalence were accepted by both sides in the dispute. By New Testament times, "Beelzebul," which originally meant "Baal is raised" (see M. Held "The Root ZBL/SBL in Akkadian, Ugaritic and Biblical Hebrew," *JAOS* 88 [1968] 90-96), had probably become an alternate name for Satan, the ruler of the demonic hordes, though the equivalence is not made explicit apart from our passage and parallel New Testament texts; see however *T. Sol.* 3:6; 6:1-2; Origen, *Celsus* 8.25; and cf. Rev 12:9 arm, which has "Beelzebul" for διάβολος (cf. W. D. Davies and D. C. Allison, Jr., *A Critical and Exegetical Commentary on the Gospel According to Saint Matthew* [3 vols., ICC; Edinburgh: T. & T. Clark, 1988-97] 2.195-96). As Davies and Allison show, Satan had several aliases in Second Temple times, such as "Asmodeus" (Tob 3:8), "Belial" (*Jub.* 1:20; QL; 2 Cor 6:15), and "Mastema" (*Jub.* 10:8; 11:5; QL), and "Beelzebul" could certainly have been another one; against H.-J. Klauck (*Allegorie und Allegorese in synoptischen Gleichnistexten* [NTAbh 13; Münster: Aschendorff, 1978] 179), who asserts that the identification was first made in the post-Easter period.

[3]   Klauck (*Allegorie und Allegorese*, 178) speaks of the alleged tactic as a trick of war (*Kriegslist*) for the purpose of blinding the crowd. The Church Fathers

Parable of the Divided Kingdom contribute to refuting this charge?

In response, it needs first to be recognized that Jesus' refutation employs a species of logical argument.[4] Although the passage omits several of the steps in this argument, it is fairly easy to reconstruct most of them on the basis of those that are present, and they are displayed below. But the third step is not so obvious, and it is indicated by a blank line.

1. If Jesus casts out demons by means of Beelzebul/Satan, as his opponents charge, then Satan's kingdom has become divided.

2. A divided Satanic kingdom implies a Satanic kingdom laid waste, and one that cannot stand.

3. x x x x x x x x x x x x x x x x x x x x x x x x x x x x x x x x x x x

4. Therefore Satan's kingdom has not become divided.

5. Jesus, then, does not cast out demons by means of Beelzebul/Satan: Q.E.D.

What is the missing line of the argument? What sort of statement would follow from 1 and 2, and lead to 4 and 5? The only logical answer is an argument that negates the implications alluded to in line 2: that Satan's kingdom has been laid waste and is unable to stand. The controversy, in other words, is a *reductio ad absurdum*: it is patently absurd to think that Satan's kingdom has been laid waste or is about to fall; therefore it cannot be divided in the way that Jesus' opponents allege.[5] The missing link, then, is some such statement as,

---

accused pagan wonder-workers of a similar strategy; see the passage of Eusebius cited in Section II below and cf. Tatian, *Address to the Greeks* 18, and Irenaeus, *Against Heresies* 2.31.2.

4   See V. K. Robbins, "Rhetorical Composition and the Beelzebul Controversy," in B. L. Mack and V. K. Robbins, *Patterns of Persuasion in the Gospels* (Foundations and Facets: Literary Facets; Sonoma: Polebridge, 1989) 161-93.

5   The only other example of *reductio ad absurdum* in the strict sense in the Synoptic tradition is Mark 2:19. But other passages come close by showing the fallaciousness (though not the absurdity) of an alternative position, often through a question or counter-question; see Mark 3:4; 11:30; 12:35-37; Luke 13:15; 14:5 (cf. R. Bultmann, *The History of the Synoptic Tradition* [New York: Harper & Row, 1963] 41-45). Bultmann rightly asserts that *reductio* is frequent in rabbinic arguments; one example he cites is *Num. Rab.* 3.2 (on Num 3:6), in which a Roman matron charges that God is arbitrary because he chooses whom he pleases. "He [R. Jose] brought her a basket of figs and she scrutinised them well, picking the best

"But Satan's kingdom has obviously not been laid waste, and is not about to fall."[6]

It is understandable that this fairly obvious logic has often been avoided in the past: it conflicts with two sayings in the immediate context, Q 11:20 (the logion about casting out demons by the finger of God)[7] and Mark 3:27 = Q 11:21-22 (the Parable of the Strong Man), both of which imply that Satan's kingdom has suffered a devastating divine blow. As Christopher Evans summarizes this discrepancy: "[Luke 11:18] presupposes that the kingdom of Satan is evidently intact and shows no sign of being fatally divided, whereas in vv 20ff. it is supposed that it is on the point of collapse."[8]

Evans's contention that the two passages clash with each other can be verified by a close look at each of them individually. On the one hand, as we have just seen the very form of the argument in the Parable of the Divided Kingdom implies that Satan's kingdom remains strong; this impression cannot be weakened to the assertion that it merely continues to exist. Attention to the Greek here is important: the word for "kingdom" is of course βασιλεία, which in most New Testament instances means royal rule or power rather

---

and eating. Said he to her: 'You, apparently, know how to select, but the Holy One, blessed be He, does not know how to select!'" (Soncino trans.). See also *t. Soṭa* 15.11 (= *b. B. Bat.* 60b), in which R. Joshua converses with ascetics who abstain from meat and wine because the Temple in which these items used to be sacrificed has been destroyed. R. Joshua counters that by the same reasoning they should also abstain from bread, fruit, and water.

[6]   See W. L. Lane, *The Gospel of Mark* (NICNT; Grand Rapids: Eerdmans, 1974) 142-43: "[The Markan Jesus'] argument is cumulative in its force: If what you say is true there exists the impossible circumstance that Satan is destroying his own realm. For it is self-evident that a kingdom divided against itself will fall, while a household divided against itself cannot be established. If your accusation is factual, then Satan has become divided in his allegiance. This should mean that he has become powerless. *Yet this is clearly not so* [emphasis in original]. Satan remains strong, and this fact exposes the fallacy of your charge."

[7]   Luke's "finger of God," as opposed to Matthew's "Spirit of God," is probably original; see J. P. Meier, *A Marginal Jew: Rethinking the Historical Jesus*. Vol. 2: *Mentor, Message, and Miracles* (ABRL 9; New York: Doubleday, 1994) 410-11.

[8]   C. F. Evans, *Saint Luke* (New Testament Commentaries; London: SCM Press; Philadelphia: Trinity Press International, 1990) 491; cf. C. E. B. Cranfield, *The Gospel according to Saint Mark* (CGTC; Cambridge: Cambridge University Press, 1959) 138.

than the place in which that rule is exercised. If, as seems likely, βασιλεία in our passage retains at least some of this dynamic nuance, making it more or less synonymous with kingly strength,[9] then the Parable of the Divided Kingdom implies that Satan's βασιλεία, his royal power, remains unshaken.

On the other hand, the Parable of the Strong Man and the saying about casting out demons by the finger of God imply that Satan's kingdom has been invaded in a violent, devastating way. The Devil's house has been assaulted and plundered, and he himself has been paralyzed, trussed up so securely that he is henceforth unable to prevent Jesus, the Stronger Man, from rescuing the human beings he had previously held in thrall. Therefore a significant aspect of Satan's βασιλεία, namely his sovereignty over the human race, is ended;[10] it has been replaced by the βασιλεία τοῦ θεοῦ, which is manifest in Jesus' exorcisms "by the finger of God."

This interpretation is supported by history-of-religions parallels from early Judaism and Christianity, in which the binding of Satan and/or evil spirits is synonymous with their disempowerment (see in their contexts *1 Enoch* 10:4; *Jub.* 5:6; 10:7-11; *T. Levi* 18:12; *Rev* 20:1-3).[11] Especially significant here are *Jub.* 5:6, where the binding

---

9   See B. D. Chilton, *God in Strength: Jesus' Announcement of the Kingdom* (SNTU 1; Freistadt: Plöchl, 1979; repr. BibSem 8; Sheffield: JSOT Press, 1987), and J. Marcus, *The Mystery of the Kingdom of God* (SBLDS 90; Atlanta: Scholars Press, 1986). Contrary to S. Åalen, "'Reign' and 'House' in the Kingdom of God in the Gospels," *NTS* 8 (1961-62) 215-40, and J. C. O'Neill, "The Kingdom of God," *NovT* 35 (1993) 130-41, the parallelism between βασιλεία and house does not mean that the βασιλεία is primarily conceived as a place; it is rather the collectivity of subjects ruled by the king, just as the "house" or "household" is, in the ancient hierarchical family, the collectivity of family members ruled by the head-of-household, usually the father. (Mark 3:25 is certainly not talking about the division against itself of a house as a physical object!) The idea of royal rule, then, maintains its primacy in New Testament usages of βασιλεία, even when, as here, the meaning shifts slightly to the subjects of that rule.

10   Our passage speaks of two aspects of Satan's βασιλεία: his rule over his own demonic "household," which is foregrounded in Mark 3:23-26 = Q 11:17-18, and his rule over the human world, which is foregrounded in Mark 3:27 = Q 11:20-21. But these two aspects of the Devil's βασιλεία are interconnected—cf. 1 Tim 3:4-5!

11   The binding of evil spirits may be a temporary measure awaiting the final judgment (e.g. *1 Enoch* 10:11-12; Jude 6), but it may also signify perpetual captivity as an eternal punishment (e.g. *1 Enoch* 14:5; cf. *PGM* 4.1245-48, on which see below, n. 86).

of the evil angels is parallel to their being "uprooted from all their dominion," and *Jub.* 10:7-8, where Mastema complains that if all his subordinate spirits are bound, "I will not be able to exercise the authority[12] of my will among the children of men."[13] Thus the binding of Satan and other evil spirits signifies the end of their βασιλεία, and is incompatible with a parable that implies that Satan's βασιλεία is intact. The tension between the two parts of the passage, then, is striking: one part, the Parable of the Divided Kingdom, implies the continuity of Satan's rule, whereas the other part, the Parable of the Strong Man and the saying about casting out demons by the finger of God, implies its overthrow.

In a moment I will try to treat this tension with the seriousness it deserves. First, however, I will examine some ways that scholars have found of mitigating it. These fall into three general categories: (1) interpretations that assert that the details of the Parable of the Divided Kingdom should not be pressed, (2) interpretations that focus on the grammar of the Parable of the Divided Kingdom, and (3) interpretations that focus on the logic of the two parables.

Interpretations that assert that the details of the Parable of the Divided Kingdom should not be pressed. These can be dealt with in short order. Klauck suggests that the details are unimportant, because the only purpose of the parable is to show that Jesus' exorcisms are God's work, not Satan's, i.e. the Q.E.D. in the outline of the argument above.[14] But this suggestion ignores the polemical setting of the discussion. In such a context it is important not only to assert one's conclusion, but also to demonstrate it, and an illogical proposition, or one that contradicts other parts of the argument,

---

12   On the equivalence of "authority" to βασιλεία, see e.g. Dan 7:14 LXX, where ἐξουσία and βασιλεία are parallel to each other.

13   Trans. from J. H. Charlesworth (ed.), *The Old Testament Pseudepigrapha* (2 vols., ABRL 13-14; New York: Doubleday, 1983-85) 2.76; the comparison and contrast with our passage is especially striking because in the context Mastema is called "the prince of spirits" (cf. Greek *Jub.* 17:16, where he is dubbed ὁ ἄρχων τῶν δαιμονίων, just as Beelzebul is in Mark 3:22 = Q 11:15). Cf. also Melito, *Passover* 102, in which Christ says, "I am the one that destroyed death and triumphed over the enemy and trod down Hades and bound the strong one and carried off men to the heights of heaven" (trans. of S. G. Hall cited in H. W. Hollander and M. de Jonge, *The Testaments of the Twelve Patriarchs: A Commentary* [SVTP 8; Leiden: Brill, 1985] 182).

14   Klauck, *Allegorie und Allegorese*, 178-79.

makes for a poor demonstration.[15]

Similarly inadequate is the analysis of scholars such as Böcher and Twelftree, who assert or imply, on the basis of Mark 3:23b ("how can Satan cast out Satan?"), that the argument in the Parable of the Divided Kingdom hinges not on the question of Satan's strength or weakness but on the assumption that the demonic realm is an indivisible whole.[16] This assumption of demonic unity is applicable at most to 3:23, not to 3:24-26, and indeed the latter seems to contradict it, since it implies that Jesus can rout individual demons without necessarily destabilizing Satan's overall rule.

Interpretations that focus on the grammar of the Parable of the Divided Kingdom. These are worthy of more serious consideration, since they actually try to deal with the text. The main way in which they do so is by separating the saying about Satan revolting against himself in Mark 3:26 = Q 11:18 from the metaphors of the divided kingdom and house in Mark 3:24-25 = Q 11:17. Gnilka, for example, observes that in Mark 3:26 the grammatical form of the protasis changes from $\dot{\epsilon}\acute{\alpha}\nu$ + aorist subjunctive to $\epsilon\dot{\iota}$ + aorist indicative. For Gnilka this shift implies that the argument has moved from a premise that Jesus disputes to one that he accepts--namely that Satan has risen up against himself, and that therefore his power is at an end.[17]

The major problem with this interpretation is that, despite the

---

[15]   Against U. Luz, *Das Evangelium nach Matthäus (Mt 8–17)* (EKKNT 1.2; Zürich: Benziger; Neukirchen-Vluyn: Neukirchener Verlag, 1990) 259-60 and n. 61, who claims that the arguments in Matt 12:25-27 are more rhetorical than substantial; he compares *Pes. Rab Kah.* 4:7, where Yoḥanan ben Zakkai, in a controversy with an obstreperous Gentile, uses demonological assumptions that he himself later admits to his disciples are "an argument of straw." But the stakes are much higher in our passage, in which a charge of sorcery is being leveled at Jesus; were it sustained, this charge might carry the death penalty (see Exod 22:18; Lev 20:27; and cf. *m. Sanh.* 7:4, in which possession of a familiar spirit and sorcery are capital offenses). In such a context a sound rebuttal is imperative.

[16]   O. Böcher, *Christus Exorcista: Dämonismus und Taufe im Neuen Testament* (BWANT 96; Stuttgart: Kohlhammer, 1972) 162; and G. H. Twelftree, *Jesus the Exorcist: A Contribution to the Study of the Historical Jesus* (WUNT 2.54; Tübingen: Mohr [Siebeck], 1993; repr. Peabody: Hendrickson, 1993) 106.

[17]   J. Gnilka, *Das Evangelium nach Markus* (2 vols., EKKNT 2.1-2; Zürich: Benziger; Neukirchen-Vluyn: Neukirchener Verlag, 1978) 1.150; cf. S. E. Porter, *Verbal Aspect in the Greek of the New Testament, with Reference to Tense and Mood* (SBG 1; New York and Bern: Peter Lang, 1989) 310.

difference in form of the conditional sentence in 3:26, for which other explanations are available,[18] that verse is so closely parallel to 3:24-25 that it is difficult to see how they can have radically different meanings.[19] In the flow of the argument, all three verses, 3:24, 3:25, and 3:26, seem to serve the same purpose, namely to refute the charge of 3:22 that Jesus casts out demons by means of the ruler of the demons, and thus to justify the negative implication of the rhetorical question in 3:23b: "How can Satan cast out Satan?" Gnilka's explanation makes hash of this thought progression; why should Jesus suddenly accept the premise of 3:26a, that Satan has risen against himself, when he has been arguing against it consistently since 3:23b?

One possible way around this problem is to assert that, in 3:26a, Jesus is not so much wholeheartedly accepting the premise that Satan has rebelled against himself as momentarily granting it for the sake of argument, in order to move on and make his own point. Twelftree, for example, paraphrases 3:26 thus: "Even if he were exorcising by Satan, even if Satan were divided against himself, Jesus' exorcisms would still mark the destruction of Satan and his kingdom."[20] But nothing in the context suggests this "even if" argumentation; one would expect a more disjunctive conjunction, such as ἀλλά or εἰ καί, if such a dramatic shift were being made in the flow of the discourse.[21] Moreover, it would fatally weaken Jesus'

---

18   The form has probably changed from that in 3:24-25 because Jesus is now abandoning general analogies (dominion, house) and directly taking up the particular case presented by the supposition of his adversaries that his exorcisms mean that Satan has gone to war against himself; see M. Zerwick, *Biblical Greek Illustrated from Examples* (Rome: Scripta Pontifici Instituti Biblici, 1963) §306; and cf. BDF §372 (1b). But this does not necessarily mean that Jesus *accepts* his opponents' premise; rather, we are probably dealing with an unreal conditional (see below). Cf. J. M. Winger's analysis of unreal conditional sentences in Paul ("Unreal Conditions in the Letters of Paul," *JBL* 105 [1986] 110-12); one of the common types is the condition that is said to be true by someone else. In this class Paul always uses the indicative and typically proceeds by *reductio ad absurdum*; see Rom 4:2, 14; 1 Cor 15:13, 15, 16, 29, 32; Gal 2:21; 3:18, 21; 5:11, all of which Winger considers to be *reductio ad absurdum* except for Gal 3:18 and 5:11.

19   Gnilka himself (*Markus*, 1.150) seems to acknowledge this difficulty when he says that there is a certain discrepancy (*Unstimmigkeit*) in the argument.

20   Twelftree, *Jesus the Exorcist*, 106.

21   Confusingly, Twelftree combines his "even if" interpretation with a recognition that our passage is a *reductio ad absurdum*. But an "even if" argument and a

argument to grant even momentarily that Satan might have risen up against himself, since this admission would lend plausibility to his opponents' charge that Jesus accomplishes his exorcisms by Satanic agency. An "even if" argument, to be sure, can be combined with a direct argument against a premise, but only if the premise is of secondary importance to the overall discussion. But this is not the case in the present context, where the matter at issue is precisely whether or not Jesus' exorcisms mean that Satan's kingdom is divided against itself.[22]

Interpretations that focus on the logic of the two parables. The interpretations of Gnilka and Twelftree shade over into the third and most important type of attempt to reconcile the Parable of the Divided Kingdom with the Parable of the Strong Man and the saying about casting out demons by the finger of God: exegeses that focus on the logic of the two parables. Some of these suggest that the two sections are addressing concerns different from that of whether or not Satan's kingdom is strong. Several commentators, for example, assert that the point at issue in the two parables is not *whether* Satan's kingship is under threat, but *how* it is being attacked. What is being denied in the Parable of the Divided Kingdom is that Satan's kingdom is *self*-destructing, not that it is being undermined; Jesus goes on in the Parable of the Strong Man (and in the saying about casting out demons by the finger of God in Q) to assert that through his onslaught the Devil's dominion is being reduced by an outside force rather than through internal division.[23]

---

reductio ad absurdum are incompatible; the "even if" argument intends to show that the premise is irrelevant, whereas the *reductio* assumes that it is relevant in the highest degree, but impossible of fulfillment, and that therefore its opposite must be true.

22   Another, rather desperate attempt to weaken the force of Mark 3:26 = Q 11:18 is R. H. Gundry's suggestion that the apodosis here, which speaks of Satan's destruction, is true "even though the supposition in the preceding 'if'-clause is absurd" (*Mark: A Commentary on His Apology for the Cross* [Grand Rapids: Eerdmans, 1993] 173). But it flouts every rule of logic to use a patently absurd premise to justify a true conclusion, and one wonders how such an obtuse rhetorical procedure could be presumed to be effective in a polemical situation.

23   C. K. Barrett (*The Holy Spirit and the Gospel Tradition* [London: SCM Press; New York: Macmillan, 1947] 60), H. Anderson (*The Gospel of Mark* (NCB; Grand Rapids: Eerdmans, 1976)1976:123), and D. H. Juel (*Mark* [ACNT; Minneapolis: Augsburg, 1990] 63) agree on this basic point. Significantly, how-

This is a clever way of putting the Parable of the Divided Kingdom together with the Parable of the Strong Man, and it may well correspond to the canonical writers' understanding of the link between the two sections. But it is difficult to see how it really makes sense of the line of thought in Mark 3:23-26 = Q 11:17-18. For if the force of Jesus' argument were that Satan's kingdom was being exploded rather than imploded, how well would it serve that argument for him to mention that divided kingdoms end up being devastated? Surely invaded kingdoms do too! But Jesus cannot really afford to leave the two putative explanations on an equal footing; his interpretation of his exorcisms, rather, must trump that of his opponents by appealing to outward circumstances that are visible to all and an unambiguous testimony to the superiority, not just the equality, of his interpretation of them. He must demonstrate, that is, that his opponents' contention that he casts out demons by Satan is patently untrue, and this he does by showing that it would lead to a consequence that obviously does not exist, namely the fatal weakening of Satan's empire. The problem with the distinction between internal revolt and external invasion, then, is that it does not lead to an absurdity; but it is precisely a reduction to absurdity that is required for the argument to be effective.[24]

The Parable of the Divided Kingdom in Mark 3:23-26 = Q 11:17-18 as a whole, then, is a *reductio ad absurdum*: if the charge of demonic collusion were true, then Jesus' exorcisms would testify to a division within and consequent collapse of Satan's kingdom; but such a collapse is refuted by the continued and obvious strength of Satan.[25] There is, however, one final line of defense against this

---

ever, they differ on what the combined passage implies about Satan's power; Barrett and Anderson think that it suggests that Satan is still strong, whereas Juel thinks that it implies that Satan has come to an end.

[24]   Barrett (*The Holy Spirit*, 60-61) sets forth the distinction between revolt and invasion as a way of understanding the passage in its present context, but he recognizes that this does not correspond to the original meaning of Mark 3:23-26, which on its own implies that "the empire of Satan still holds out" and is therefore disharmonious with the Parable of the Strong Man.

[25]   W. Schmithals (*Das Evangelium nach Markus* [2 vols., GTB 503-504; Gütersloh: Mohn; Würzburg: Echter Verlag, 1979] 222) recognizes that the argument is a *reductio ad absurdum*, but the conclusion he draws is fallacious: "In view of the untenableness of that absurd reproach, one must conclude from the demon exorcisms that Satan has been shorn of his power." But if Mark 3:24-26 pars.

interpretation. This is the claim that the Parable of the Divided Kingdom does not have in view "objective" reality but reality as it is viewed from the perspective of Satan. In other words, these verses are indeed a *reductio ad absurdum*, but not because the assumption of Satan's self-division is contradicted by the present state of the world, in which Satan's power is manifest. They are rather a *reductio* because Satan would not do anything as irrational as rising up against himself, when he knows that such a strategy would lead only to the downfall of his kingdom. Satan's revolt against himself, then, is being weighed as a subjective possibility rather than as an accomplished fact. So Pesch, for example, says, "It is not the intention of Satan to destroy himself, to cast himself out (v 23b). Therefore the reproach against Jesus is senseless."[26] Davies and Allison, similarly, speak of "a *reductio ad absurdum* which affirms Satan's rational behaviour. Would it make sense for the devil to give a human being power if that power was in turn to ransack the kingdom of demons?"[27] And Robbins concurs, giving the theory a scholarly pedigree by asserting that Mark 3:23-26 = Q 11:17-18 is an "argument from implausibity" (ἐκ τοῦ ἀπιθάνου):[28] "It is unlikely that Satan would be willing to cast out an underling, because he would be divided against himself, and this division would destroy him and his domain."[29] Or, as Barrett succinctly puts it, "The argument is simply, Satan is not casting out Satan, because 'Satan is not such a fool.'"[30]

But there are two problems with this exegesis, which I will call the "Satanic intentionality" interpretation. The first is that there is

---

really are a *reductio ad absurdum*, that argumentative form is premised on the evident power of Satan; it cannot, then, be an argument for his powerlessness. Moreover, Schmithals' way of stating the alternatives is too categorical, since a portrayal of Satan as a spent force is not the only alternative to a depiction of him as a Machiavellian ruler who employs Jesus as a double agent. One might rather surmise, as I will argue below, that Jesus' exorcisms are successful individual raids against Satan's underlings that do not constitute a frontal assault on Satan himself.

26   R. Pesch *Das Markusevangelium* (2 vols., HTKNT 2.1-2; Freiburg: Herder, 1976) 1.214-15.

27   Davies and Allison, *Matthew*, 2.337-38.

28   Robbins consistently translates the Greek phrase as "argument *for* implausibility," but the ἐκ is better translated "from": Jesus is arguing *from* implausibility *for* something else, namely that he is not Satan's agent.

29   Robbins, "Rhetorical Compostition," 165.

30   Barrett, *The Holy Spirit*, 61-62, quoting T. W. Manson.

simply no independent evidence for it; nothing in the passage directly indicates that Jesus is hypothesizing about Satan's thought-processes. The second and more weighty problem has to do with the form of the conditional sentence in Mark 3:26 = Q 11:18: both of these verses have εἰ + aorist indicative in the protasis,[31] which under normal conditions should refer to a past condition.[32] But for the "Satanic intentionality" interpretation, which focuses not on the objective situation but on Satan's presumed cogitations about it, one would expect in the protasis either ἐάν + subjunctive or εἰ + future indicative, since the contemplated self-division of Satan would have to be future from his own point of view: "[Satan knows that] if ever he becomes divided against himself, his kingdom will not be able to stand."[33] As opposed to this, the εἰ + aorist indicative conditional form of 3:26 seems to point toward a real or contrary-to-fact division of Satan's kingdom that is past from the perspective of the person from whose outlook the condition is being formulated;[34] if

---

[31] εἰ ... ἀνέστη .. καὶ ἐμερίσθη in Mark and εἰ ... [δι]εμερίσθη in Q. I realize, of course, that Jesus spoke Aramaic rather than (or at least more than) Greek, but we have to assume that the Greek forms are being mobilized to create a fairly accurate rendering of the nuance of the Aramaic original. Aramaic has an unambiguous way of indicating a contrary-to-fact conditional, the use of the particle אִילּוּ rather than אִם for "if."

[32] Porter, whose interpretation of the Greek tense system is resolutely atemporal, disputes this (*Verbal Aspect*, 297-300). But see below, n. 34.

[33] Even if the main verb here were past ("Satan *knew*"), the form of the conditional sentence would still need to be ἐάν + aorist subjunctive or εἰ + future indicative: "Satan knew that if ever he became divided against himself, his dominion would not have been able to stand." In Greek, as opposed to English, a past main verb does not change the tense of the conditional clause dependent on it.

[34] Porter (*Verbal Aspect*, 298-99) argues, on the basis of the parallel with ἐάν + subjunctive in 3:24-25, that the aorist indicative in Mark 3:26 is atemporal; the only reason that the Markan Jesus switches to the εἰ + aorist indicative form in 3:26 is to move from the hypothetical state of affairs referred to in 3:24-25 to "an assertion about the specific situation of address" in 3:26. But as I have argued above, if this means that Jesus suddenly accepts the premise in 3:26a, it must be explained why he has implicitly rejected it in 3:24-25. Besides, if a movement from hypothetical to actual were the *only* reason for the change in form of the protasis, Mark would probably use the unambiguous εἰ + *present* indicative rather than the ambiguous εἰ + aorist indicative, or in some other way give a clear signal of the change to actuality.

Porter cites John 15:20; Gal 2:17; Matt 10:25b; and Rom 3:3, 7 as other instances in which εἰ + aorist indicative does not refer to the past. In none of these

that person were Satan himself, it would be too late to do anything about it, and the sentence would be senseless. Mark 3:26 = Q 11:18, therefore, is not based on speculations about Satanic reasoning processes.[35]

Rather, in view of the argument so far, it seems safe to conclude that Jesus' point is that the internal division postulated in Mark 3:26a = Q 11:18a cannot have happened, because if it had occurred something else, namely the fatal weakening of Satan's kingdom, would rapidly have transpired—which is patently not the case. The sentence, in other words, is a form of past unreal condition,[36] an interpretation compatible with its form.

The textbook form of the past unreal condition, to be sure, is εἰ + aorist indicative in the protasis, ἄν + aorist indicative in the apodosis. Our verse conforms to this pattern only in the protasis; the apodosis has present indicative without ἄν (Mark) or future indicative without ἄν (Q). As Winger has shown, however, writers

---

cases, however, is a past reference impossible, or even in my opinion unlikely, despite Porter's arguments. With regard to John 15:20, I am puzzled, in view of such passages as 7:7; 8:23, 39-59, by Porter's claim that the hatred of "the world" for Jesus has not yet shown itself in the Johannine narrative. Similarly, εἰ τὸν οἰκοδεσπότην Βεελζεβοὺλ ἐπεκάλεσαν in Matt 10:25 is a glance back at 9:34. In Rom 3:3 Paul is discussing the election of Israel, which is rooted in the Sinai event in the past, to which the previous verse makes an explicit reference with a verb that is cognate to the one at issue in 3:3 (ἐπιστεύθησαν / εἰ ἠπίστησαν). In Rom 3:7 Paul seems to be speaking in the person of Israel of the history of God's dealings with the nation; very similar language is used for the same subject in Rom 5:20. In Gal 2:17 Paul is defending his past conduct in Antioch, when he and Peter were found by strict Jewish Christians to be "sinners" for associating with Gentiles.

It is certainly true that the aorist indicative can occasionally have a present reference, but as Michael Winger has pointed out in private correspondence, "the occasional uses of any tense with non-standard time reference actually *depend* on the normal time reference for their effect." In the present instance neither the Vulgate nor the Peshita supports Porter's non-temporal understanding of the aorist in 3:26a; the Vulgate changes from *si* + present subjunctive in 3:24-25 to *si* + perfect indicative in 3:26, and the Peshita changes from *'en* (= if) + imperfect in 3:24-25 to *'en* + perfect in 3:26.

35   Similarly Gundry, *Mark*, 173: "Jesus is not arguing for the psychological impossibility of thinking that Satan would not use him to cast out the demons because they serve Satan and because Satan is too smart to work against his own cause. The impossibility has to do with Satan's action, not with our thinking" (shouldn't the last two words read "*Satan's* thinking"?).

36   Cf. R. A. Guelich, *Mark 1–8:26* (WBC 34A; Dallas: Word, 1989) 176.

of ancient Greek, including early Christian authors such as Paul, often formulated conditional sentences they regarded as unreal without using secondary tenses or ἄν.[37] A New Testament example of a past unreal condition that is parallel in form to the Markan version (εἰ + aorist indicative in protasis, present indicative in apodosis) is provided by Rom 4:2: εἰ γὰρ Ἀβραὰμ ἐξ ἔργων ἐδικαιώθη, ἔχει καύχημα (cf. 1 Cor 15:14, 17). An example that is parallel in form to the Q version (εἰ + aorist indicative in protasis, future indicative in apodosis) is provided by John 15:20: εἰ τὸν λόγον μου ἐτήρησαν, καὶ τὸν ὑμέτερον τηρήσουσιν. In 1 Cor 12:19 the apodosis of an unreal conditional is in the form of a question, as in Q 11:18. As Winger demonstrates, moreover, Paul's unreal conditions include some "that someone other than Paul apparently claims are fulfilled. Paul at any rate puts these conditions forward only to deny them, usually by *reductio ad absurdum* . . ."[38] Paul can vary the form because he takes the condition to be refuted at face value, so that he does not need to overemphasize the point with the ἄν + secondary tense form.

These remarks, I would suggest, apply to the Beelzebul controversy as well. The proposition that Jesus casts out demons by Beelzebul has been put forward by Jesus' opponents. Jesus responds to this suggestion with a *reductio ad absurdum*, which concludes with a conditional sentence implying that, if the opponents' charge were true, Satan's kingdom would have fallen. This sentence does not need to be in the standard unreal form, indeed its statement in such a form would represent rhetorical overkill, because the proposition of a bound Satan is refuted at face value by the obvious strength of evil in the world.[39] For it is a standard theme in Jewish traditions, especially apocalyptic ones, that the sad state of the world testifies to the sovereignty of Satan over the present age.[40] We may apply to the theory of Satan's strength what someone has said about the idea of

---

[37] Winger, "Unreal Conditions," 1986.

[38] The Pauline passages are cited above, n. 18.

[39] Cf. Luz, *Matthäus*, 259: "The logic is formally convincing if one takes it as self-evident that the kingdom of Satan is intact."

[40] See e.g. 1QS 1:18-19; 2:19; 1QM 14:9; *T. Zeb.* 9:8; *T. Dan* 5:10-11; *Jub.* 10:31; *Apoc. Elijah* 1:3-4; cf. *1 Enoch* 9:1, 6-9; 10:7-8; 16:1-3; 19:1; 1 Cor 2:6; John 12:31; 14:30; 16:11. The Qumran passages are especially close to ours because in them the present world-age is designated "the dominion of Belial" (ממשלת בליעל); cf. *Apoc. Ab.* 23:12-13, which speaks of the dominion of Azazel.

original sin: it is the only Christian doctrine that is empirically verifiable.

HISTORY AND THEOLOGY

The Parable of the Divided Kingdom, then, is a *reductio ad absurdum*, and there is a real and irreduceable difference between its portrayal of a strong Satan, on the one hand, and the depiction of a paralyzed Satan in the Parable of the Strong Man and, by inference, in the saying about casting out demons by the finger of God, on the other. Indeed, the sheer number, variety, and inventiveness of the methods that scholars have used to avoid this conclusion is itself an indirect testimony to its validity.[41]

The tension between the two portions of the passage immediately suggests that neither the Markan nor the Q context is an original unity, a suggestion which many literary observations confirm.[42]

---

[41]   Some good scholars end up tying themselves in knots when they try to unravel the twisted line of thought in our passage. Guelich (*Mark*, 175), for example, writes, "One would assume that the response to Jesus' question ["How can Satan cast out Satan?"] would be negative. From the viewpoint of the narrator and the reader who knows that Jesus is not working in collaboration with Satan, Satan is not casting out Satan. Yet the argument that follows operates *reductio ad absurdum* with this premise to show that Satan has indeed 'met his end' (3:26)." But surely the *reductio ad absurdum* shows exactly the opposite! Juel (*Mark*, 63), similarly, paraphrases Mark 3:23-27 thus: "Their evaluation is absurd. Attributing his power to cast out demons to demonic possession violates common sense . . . For a ruler to take up arms against himself would be the prelude to disaster. Divided households cannot survive. In fact, if Satan's host is at war with itself, people ought to rejoice—for he has come to an end. Jesus offers the only reasonable interpretation of what is occurring--someone has invaded the domain of the strong man (Satan)—and that someone is the 'stronger one' of whom John the Baptist spoke. Satan is being deposed and his domain plundered." The conclusion of this paraphrase says that Satan's dominion has come to an end, but its beginning suggests that it has not.

[42]   As for Mark, not only does the theme change from the strength of Satan to his weakness in 3:27, which is probably an independent logion (see V. Taylor, *The Gospel According to St. Mark* [2nd ed., London: Macmillan; New York: St. Martin's, 1966] 240-41), but it changes again in 3:28-29, where Mark introduces the saying about the sin against the Holy Spirit; only with difficulty can he link this saying with the preceding discussion by means of the parenthetical remark in 3:30. The original independence of 3:28-29 is confirmed by its introductory formula Ἀμὴν λέγω ὑμῖν, which Mark usually uses to insert unattached traditions into a context, and by its apparent absence in Q.

Might then the theological friction between the parts, like the literary awkwardness of the composition, be the result of the church laying its clumsy hands on the Jesus tradition? In other words, is one (or even both) of the tensive elements, the portrait of a powerful Satan and/or the portrait of one who has been bound, to be ascribed to later Christian reflection rather than to Jesus?[43]

This is an alluring but ultimately unsatisfactory solution, because a good case can be made that both of the conflicting traditions go back to the historical Jesus. As for the portrayal of Satan disarmed, both the saying about casting out demons by the finger of God in Q 11:20 and the Parable of the Strong Man in Mark 3:27 = Q 11:21-22 are full of the sort of eschatological dynamism that is characteristic of the teaching of Jesus,[44] and they both link exorcism with a conviction about eschatological advent, a linkage that is almost nonexistent outside of the teaching of Jesus.[45] As Meier points out,

---

The Q passage, also, has grown by accretion; it contains three sayings that are absent in Mark, Q 11:19 (by whom do your sons cast out demons), 11:20 (if I by the finger/Spirit of God), and 11:23 (the one who is not with me is against me). Of these, the first two are in tension with each other; as Bultmann points out, if the connection between Q 11:19 and 11:20 were original, "it would follow that the Jewish exorcists also cast out demons by the Spirit, and that their activity also demonstrated the coming of the Kingdom," which is contrary to the overall context (*History of the Synoptic Tradition*, 14). The saying about casting out demons by the finger/Spirit of God in Q 11:20, moreover, was probably originally independent of the Parable of the Strong Man, which alludes to Jesus' victory over Satan; it is not present in Mark, even though it would fit his theology and the Markan context well.

On all this, cf. Meier, *A Marginal Jew*, 407-411.

43   Cf. A. Fridrichsen, *The Problem of Miracle in Primitive Christianity* (Minneapolis: Augsburg, 1972 [orig. 1925]) 102-10.

44   See Bultmann, *History of the Synoptic Tradition*, 162; Davies and Allison, *Matthew*, 2.339, 342.

45   See G. Theissen, *The Miracle Stories of the Early Christian Tradition* (SNTW; Edinburgh: T. & T. Clark, 1983) 277-80; and Twelftree, *Jesus the Exorcist*, 184-89, 219-20. *1 Enoch* 10:4; 55:4; *T. Moses* 10:1-3; *Pesiq. R.* 36; and *Sipra* §262 (on Lev 26:6) speak of eschatological judgment on, destruction of, or the rendering harmless of Satan, his angels, and/or demons, but none of them speaks of exorcism; on the latter passage, see below, n. 86. Similarly, several passages in the *Testaments of the Twelve Patriarchs* refer in an eschatological context to treading evil spirits under foot (*T. Sim.* 6:6; *T. Levi* 18:12 [which also speaks of Beliar being bound]; *T. Zeb.* 9:8), but none of them talks explicitly about exorcism, although a related passage, *T. Dan* 5:10-11, speaks of "taking the captivity from

moreover,[46] in the saying about casting out demons Jesus speaks distinctively of the *coming* of the kingdom of God and of exorcism by the finger of God. Further, the Parable of the Strong Man makes its point with graphic, even violent imagery that alludes rather than expounding the point explicitly; this is the customary style of Jesus' parabolic method.[47] And it is like other authentic parables of Jesus in which he compares God or himself to lawless characters.[48]

But the Parable of Satan's House and Kingdom, which implies the opposite evaluation of Satan's power, also has a strong claim to authenticity. As Klauck points out, it is indisputable that the historical Jesus was an exorcist,[49] and therefore it is logical that his opponents would have wanted to come up with an unfavorable interpretation of his power over demons; the *Sitz* of the parable, then, has an intrinsic plausibility. As the previous analysis has shown, moreover, the parable represents an ingenious refutation of the charge of demonic complicity, and it is easier to attribute this sort of clever riposte to an *ad hoc* comment of Jesus than it is to ascribe it to the apologetics of the later church.[50] The use of the parabolic form is, again, typical of Jesus, and the image of the collapse of a kingdom and house is the sort of violent, gripping metaphor that he seems to have favored; its arresting quality was exploited centuries later by Abraham Lincoln.

I should briefly take up a couple of challenges to my view. One comes from a scholar who usually deserves a hearing—Bultmann. He

---

Beliar, the souls of the saints." These passages from the *Testaments*, in any case, may be Christian or reflect Christian influence.

46   Meier, *A Marginal Jew*, 413-17.

47   See C. H. Dodd, *The Parables of the Kingdom* (London: Nisbet, 1935; repr. Glasgow: Collins, 1961); J. D. Crossan, *In Parables: The Challenge of the Historical Jesus* (New York: Harper & Row, 1973).

48   See e.g. the Parables of the Unjust Steward (Luke 16:1-8), the Unjust Judge (Luke 18:1-8), and the Thief in the Night (Matt 24:43 = Luke 12:39). Other parables also feature violated norms: see e.g. the harsh treatment of the man lacking a wedding garment in Matt 22:11-13 and the unfairness of the employer in the Parable of the Laborers in the Vineyard (Matt 20:1-16; cf. J. Marcus, "Blanks and Gaps in the Parable of the Sower," *BibInt* 5 [1997] 1-16, here 6 n. 15).

49   Klauck, *Allegorie und Allegorese*, 178. Cf. Twelftree, *Jesus the Exorcist*, 142 nn. 24-25, for a list of exegetes who agree. D. E. Aune ("Magic in Early Christianity," *ANRW* II.23.2 [1980] 1507-57, here 1525-26) has some particularly trenchant arguments.

50   Cf. Fridrichsen, *The Problem of Miracle*, 105-106.

questions the authenticity of the Parable of the Kingdom and House on the ground that "it is in fact hardly thinkable that a mere exorcism of a demon would give rise to an accusation of being in league with the Devil."[51] We are not dealing, however, with a "mere exorcism of a demon" but with a series of exorcisms by one who operates outside of official channels.[52] Such activities in such a context can easily inspire a charge of demonic collusion; the demons' obedience to the exorcist may be seen by hostile critics as an indication that he is on the demons' side, on the principle that "it takes one to know one" (and to manipulate one).[53] For the exorcist inhabits a dangerously liminal space by the mere fact of his commerce with the demons,[54] and this commerce may either lead to his own possession[55] or testify that he is already possessed.[56]

---

[51]   Bultmann, *History of the Synoptic Tradition*, 49 n. 1.

[52]   Cf. B. J. Malina and J. H. Neyrey, *Calling Jesus Names: The Social Value of Labels in Matthew* (Foundations and Facets. Sonoma: Polebridge, 1988) 20-25. There is much that is instructive in Malina and Neyrey's analysis of the Beelzebul controversy in its Matthean context, but is it accurate to term the charge against Jesus a witchcraft accusation (p. 25)? In sociological discussions, including those cited by Malina and Neyrey, a "witch" is someone who causes harm to others by supernatural means; see for example M. Douglas, *Witchcraft Confessions and Accusations* (London: Tavistock, 1970) xxxvi; M. Marwick (ed.), *Witchcraft and Sorcery: Selected Readings* (New York: Penguin, 1970) 11; and K. Thomas, *Religion and the Decline of Magic: Studies in Popular Beliefs in Sixteenth- and Seventeenth-Century England* (Harmondsworth and New York: Penguin, 1971) 517-34, 551-54. But Jesus is not accused of causing harm in this sort of way in Mark 3:22 = Q 11:15; it is admitted that he has done something good, namely exorcism; the accusation is that he has accomplished this good deed by diabolical means.

[53]   As O. Böcher points out (*Dämonenfurcht und Dämonenabwehr: Ein Beitrag zur Vorgeschichte der christlichen Taufe* (BWANT 90; Stuttgart: Kohlhammer, 1970] 161-67; idem, *Christus Exorcista*, 77), the idea of driving out a demon by a demon corresponds to the homoeopathic nature of ancient magic.

[54]   See I. M. Lewis, *Religion in Context: Cults and Charisma* (2nd ed. Cambridge and New York: Cambridge University Press, 1996) 137-38.

[55]   See T. K. Oesterreich, *Possession Demoniacal and Other Among Primitive Races, in Antiquity, the Middle Ages, and Modern Times* (London: Kegan Paul, Trench, Trubner, 1930) 80, 92, 161; N. P. Spanos and J. Gottlieb, "Demonic Possession, Mesmerism, and Hysteria: A Social Psychological Perspective on Their Historical Interrelations," in B. P. Levack (ed.), *Articles on Witchcraft, Magic and Demonology*, vol. 9 (New York and London: Gardland, 1992) 263-82, here 272. A classic example is provided by Fr. Surin, the exorcist of Soeur Jeanne

Eusebius (*On Philostratus* 26) provides an ancient example when he reports the popular opinion ("as they say") that Apollonius of Tyana drove out demons by a demon. The accusation must have been commonplace, for it causes the Church Father either to forget or to ignore that the same charge had been leveled at Jesus.[57]

Instead of ascribing Mark 3:22-26 = Q 11:17-18 to Jesus, Bultmann attributes it to the early church's defense of him against Jewish charges that diabolical powers had been the mainstay of his entire ministry.[58] But it would be strange for the church to defend Jesus in a way that conflicted with the early Christian conviction that his advent was the beginning of the end of Satan's reign (cf. e.g. John 12:31; 16:11; 1 Cor 2:8; Col 2:14-15; Heb 2:14). This implausibility is recognized by M. Smith, who says: "This implicitly anti-eschatological saying [3:22-26] was the nucleus to which the collections of other sayings on the subject [in 3:20-30] were attached; it therefore must be very early, and it contradicts the general eschatological expectations of later gospel material. Why, then, was it preserved? Perhaps because it was genuine."[59]

Smith is happy with the anti-eschatological thrust of Mark 3:23-26 pars., since it fits into his non-eschatological picture of "Jesus the magician." But he adopts two different and somewhat contradictory strategies for putting this "anti-eschatological" saying together with the rest of the passage. At one point he tries to give the passage a

---

of Loudun, as described by A. Huxley, *The Devils of Loudun* (London: Chatto & Windus, 1952) 273-78, 283.

[56] See I. M. Lewis, "A Structural Approach to Witchcraft and Spirit-Possession," in M. Douglas (ed.), *Witchcraft Confessions and Accusations* (London: Tavistock, 1970) 293-309, here 304-305. In early modern Europe, Protestants frequently alleged that Catholic exorcisms worked through the collusion of demons; see S. Clark, *Thinking with Demons: The Idea of Witchcraft in Early Modern Europe* (Oxford: Clarendon Press, 1997) 360, 421. For a sixteenth-century case in which a demon accused his exorcist of being a witch, see Thomas, *Religion and the Decline of Magic*, 575. In contemporary charismatic Christian circles, similarly, the charge is widespread that "occult" (i.e. non-Christian) healers perform their miracles through the power of Satan; see e.g. P. Horrobin, *Healing Through Deliverance: The Biblical Basis* (Chichester: Sovereign World, 1991) 231-35.

[57] Cf. Smith, *Jesus the Magician*, 205.

[58] Bultmann is followed by W. Weiss, *Eine neue Lehre in Vollmacht: Die Streit- und Schulgespräche des Markus-Evangeliums* (BZNW 52; Berlin: de Gruyter, 1989) 171.

[59] Smith, *Jesus the Magician*, 205.

unitary meaning by imposing a non-eschatological sense on Q 11:20 also: "the finger of God" is the power in magic, and "the kingdom of God" is the accessibility of this power.[60] This interpretation, however, is unconvincing in view of the eschatological significance of "kingdom of God" elsewhere in the Synoptic tradition,[61] and Smith has problems with the clearly eschatological thrust of the Parable of the Strong Man, which he paraphrases but does not explicate. At another point he forswears any attempt to give the passage a unitary meaning, arguing instead that "the variety of demonological diagnoses in Mark 3:20-30 suggests that they [all] come from good tradition. Later invention would have said only, 'He has an unclean spirit,' as the evangelist does in his explanatory note at the end (3:30) . . . ."[62] But this correct observation still leaves unexplained how the variety of contradictory demonological diagnoses in 3:20-30 could all have come from Jesus.

We cannot, then, alleviate the tension between the different attitudes toward Satan's strength in our passage simply by dismissing one or the other of the component parts as *unjesuanisch*, or by glossing over the clash between them. A more sensible course, I would suggest, is to hypothesize that Jesus' thinking on the subject of Satan's dominion over the earth underwent a development. Early in his ministry he performed exorcisms without drawing the conclusion that he or anyone else had overthrown Satan; this early stage in Jesus' understanding of his charismatic gift is reflected in Mark 3:23-26 = Q 11:17-18. That Jesus held such an opinion is perfectly plausible, since most of the Jewish exorcists known to us maintained similar views; as we have seen above, the linkage between exorcism and eschatological advent or the defeat of Satan is rarely if ever made in Jewish traditions that antedate the New Testament. This early Jesus was, to be sure, probably in some sense an apocalyptic thinker, as the language about Satan's dominion seems to indicate,[63]

---

60   Smith, *Jesus the Magician*, 130.

61   Cf. Meier, *A Marginal Jew*, 237-508.

62   Smith, *Jesus the Magician*, 32-33. But there is an inconsistency here as well; Smith goes on to say that the variety of demonological analyses corresponds to "the actual situation," thus implying that Mark 3:20-30 as a whole comes from a particular occasion in the ministry of Jesus. But his acknowledgment on p. 205 that 3:22-26 was the nucleus to which "later Gospel material" was attached suggests the opposite.

63   This imagery seems to place Mark 3:26 = Q 11:18 in an apocalyptic context

but that does not necessarily mean that he would have interpreted his exorcisms as signs of eschatological advent. The people whom he exorcised, rather, were individual brands plucked from the Satanic fire of the present evil age; he did not yet see himself as the fireman whose task it was to put the fire out. His practical response to the evil in the world, then, was episodic rather than programmatic, the sort of response that Wilson characterizes as "thaumaturgical":

> The individual's concern is relief from present and specific ills by special dispensations. The demand for supernatural help is personal and local: its operation is magical. Salvation is immediate but has no general application beyond the given case and others like it...The evils feared are all highly specific, and it is from their particular incidence (not from their universal operation) that salvation is sought.[64]

Later, however, Jesus came to see his exorcistic ministry in a different, more exalted way that Wilson would characterize as millenarian. He began to view himself as the effective opponent of Satan, the Stronger One whose exorcisms testified to his role as the spearhead of the inbreaking age of God's dominion; it is this stage in his self-understanding that is reflected in Mark 3:27 = Q 11:20-22.[65]

---

because of the implication that Satan rules the world; cf. the Qumran passages cited above in n. 40. On subjection to evil cosmic powers as a characteristic of one "track" of apocalyptic thought, see M. C. de Boer, "Paul and Jewish Apocalyptic Eschatology," in J. Marcus and M. L. Soards (eds.), *Apocalyptic and the New Testament: Essays in Honor of J. Louis Martyn* (JSNTSup 24; Sheffield: JSOT Press, 1989) 169-90, esp. 174-75. I use "apocalyptic" to denote the form of thought that is found in ancient Jewish and Christian apocalypses, a view of the world that is dominated by cosmic dualism, an orientation toward the supernatural world, and a conviction that the eschaton is either very close or has already arrived; cf. J. Marcus, "Modern and Ancient Jewish Apocalypticism," *JR* 76 (1996) 2 n. 5, for bibliography on the question of definition.

64   B. Wilson, *Magic and the Millennium* (St. Albans: Paladin, 1973) 24-25.

65   The Parable of the Strong Man in Mark 3:27 = Q 11:21-22 and the saying in Q 11:20 about the demonstration of the advent of the kingdom of God in Jesus' exorcisms were probably originally independent of each other (see above, n. 42). But even without the proximity of the Strong Man parable, Q 11:20 implies that Jesus' exorcisms are a victory over Satan, since the arrival of the dominion of God, which is spoken of in one breath with the rout of the demons, implies the defeat of the rival dominion of Satan; cf. *T. Moses* 10:1. Similarly, the Markan and Matthean versions of the Strong Man Parable speak of the Stronger One "binding" the Strong Man, which is language associated with exorcism (e.g. Tobit 3:17; 8:3; *PGM* 4.1245-1248) and with divine judgment on the demons (e.g. *1 Enoch* 10:4, 12;

I have argued elsewhere that Jesus' conviction of eschatological advent and of his own unique role within that advent came to him at the time of his baptism by John, when he saw Satan thrown down from heaven (Luke 10:18) and arrived at the conclusion that the dominion of the Devil was now being replaced by the dominion of God.[66] It would make sense that the same visionary event was the turning point in Jesus' understanding of the significance of his exorcisms.[67]

This sort of changed evaluation is, in a way, logical; if miracles begin to occur on a wide enough scale, it may start to seem to the miracle-worker and/or his followers that these extraordinary events do not merely represent "the activity of God in territory held largely by the devil" but a momentous alteration in the structure of the universe, the beginning of the longed-for defeat of cosmic evil.[68] Such a change in world-view has sociological precedents; Wilson cites several Third World examples of thaumaturgical movements that mutated into millenarian ones, entitling the relevant chapter of

---

13:1) and on Satan (*T. Lev.* 18:12); cf. R. H. Hiers, "'Binding' and 'Loosing': The Matthean Authorizations," *JBL* 104 (1985) 233-50, esp. 235-39. This language was probably originally in Q, though it is absent in Luke 11:22-23 (cf. Fridrichsen, *The Problem of Miracle*, 108; Evans, *Luke*, 492-93). Moreover, ancient Jewish thinkers could view the human body as the dwelling-place of Satan (see e.g. *T. Naph.* 8:6), so a parable about a strong man's *house* might immediately awaken demonological associations. Even without the proximity of Q 11:20, then, the Strong Man Parable implies exorcism (cf. B. Kollmann, *Jesus und die Christen als Wundertäter: Studien zu Magie, Medizin und Schamanismus in Antike und Christentum* [FRLANT 170; Göttingen: Vandenhoeck & Ruprecht, 1996] 190).

[66] J. Marcus, "Jesus' Baptismal Vision," *NTS* 41 (1995) 512-21.

[67] I realize that the Gospels (and Acts 10:37) present Jesus' baptism by John as the starting point of his public activity; they know nothing of an exorcistic ministry (or any other sort) before that point. But this schema may reflect the church's theological conviction that John was Elijah, the messenger who paved the way for Jesus the Messiah (see Mark 1:2-4; 9:11-13, etc.) rather than strict historical chronology. In any case, I am not claiming that a major portion of Jesus' public ministry preceded his baptism, only a preliminary stage that was basically limited to exorcisms. But he still may have had followers who could have remembered his sayings.

[68] The quotation is from F. O'Connor, *Mystery and Manners: Occasional Prose* (eds. S. & R. Fitzgerald; New York: Farrar, Straus & Giroux, 1961) 118. Cf. Clark, *Thinking with Demons*, 405-406, who notes that the premonitions of the last times of the sixteenth-century priest, Pierre Crespet, seem to have been prompted by possession cases.

his book "From Magic to the Millennium—and Back."[69] (The "and back" part will not concern us here, though it is a fair description of certain aspects of the development of Christianity after the first generation or so.) Closer to Jesus religiously if not chronologically, there is a Jewish parallel in the transformation since the beginning of the twentieth century of the *Ḥabad* (Lubavitch) Ḥasidic sect, which had previously been thaumaturgical in Wilson's sense, into a movement that retained and even increased its emphasis on miracles, but now interpreted them as signs of the imminence and eventually the arrival of messianic redemption.[70]

Although in the case of Jesus this change from "magic" to "millennium" was sealed by the visionary event of the baptism, it may have been prepared for by other factors. For example, the opposition that his sensationally successful and popular exorcistic ministry provoked in more mainstream groups such as the scribes[71] could have pushed him in a millenarian direction even before his baptism, and could indeed have been partly responsible for his joining himself with the Baptist movement in the first place. Wilson describes the analogous apocalyptic transformation of the movement started by Simon Kimbangu, a faith healer whose successful ministry in the Belgian Congo of the 1920's aroused official concern and led quickly to his arrest and imprisonment. This persecution "set the seal on the mutation into a revolutionist movement of an originally thaumaturgical revival."[72] Similarly, Jesus' exorcisms could have provoked harrassment from envious and fearful authorities who were concerned about the growing popularity and influence with the people of a charismatic figure who had no link with official circles. The plausibility of this scenario is supported by the unease with which other Galilean faith-healers and miracle-workers (*Ḥasidim*)

---

69   Wilson, *Magic and the Millennium*, 348-83.

70   See A. Ravitzky, *Messianism, Zionism, and Jewish Religious Radicalism* (Chicago Studies in the History of Judaism; Chicago and London: University of Chicago Press, 1996) 193-203.

71   It is probably significant that the manifestations of scribal hostility to Jesus in Mark 2:1-3:6 are immediately preceded by the series of healing miracles described in 1:21-45. This juxtaposition may well reflect a scribal antipathy to displays of free-lance charismatic power both in Mark's own day and in the time of Jesus; cf. below on official discomfort with wonder-workers such as Ḥanina ben Dosa and Ḥoni the Circle-drawer.

72   Wilson, *Magic and the Millennium*, 367-73.

were regarded by religious officials, as documented by Green and Vermes.[73] The more intense opposition provoked by Jesus' more sensational charismatic ministry[74] could have helped radicalize him, pushing him towards the apocalypticism of the Baptist.

Theoretically it could have been the other way around—Jesus could have moved from "millennium" to "magic," from a conviction of Satan's defeat to a more "realistic" acknowledgment of the devil's continuing power in the world. Or he might have held at one and the same time, or at least perhaps on different days of the same week, apparently contradictory ideas about Satan's power or the lack of it, just as some scholars claim that he concurrently maintained seemingly opposite notions about whether or not the eschaton had arrived.[75]

But the verse I put under the microscope in my earlier article, Luke 10:18, seems to point in another direction. For that verse implies a *change* in the status of Satan, a movement from power to disempowerment. Previously—before Jesus' baptism—Satan was enthroned in heaven, "the prince of the power of the air" (Eph 2:2; cf. Job 1:6; *Asc. Isa.* 7:9; Philo, *Giants* 6). Now, however, he has fallen like lightning from this exalted status (cf. *1 Enoch* 16:2-3; 54:4-5; 90:21, 24; Rev 12:7-12),[76] and this fall is linked in the Lukan

---

73   W. C. Green, "Palestinian Holy Men: Charismatic Leadership and Rabbinic Tradition," *ANRW* II.19.2 (1979) 619-47; and G. Vermes, *Jesus the Jew: A Historian's Reading of the Gospels* (Philadelphia: Fortress, 1981) 69-82. See for example the complaint of Šimon ben Šetaḥ against the impudence of Jesus' fellow Galilean miracle-worker Ḥoni the Circle-Drawer in *m. Taʿan.* 3:8. Aune ("Magic in Early Christianity," 1539) rightly notes that in Vermes's analysis, which interprets Jesus exclusively as a Galilean *Ḥasid*, "the apocalyptic framework within which Jesus' activities and teachings took place has unaccountably receded into the background." But Jesus could have been more like the *Ḥasidim* at an early stage in his career.

74   On the far greater concentration of miracle-stories about Jesus than about other contemporary pagan and Jewish wonder workers, see J. M. Hull, *Hellenistic Magic and the Synoptic Tradition* (SBT 2.28; London: SCM Press, 1974) 63; Smith, *Jesus the Magician*, 109; and Twelftree, *Jesus the Exorcist*, 48-49.

75   Cf. W. G. Kümmel, *Promise and Fulfillment: The Eschatological Message of Jesus* (SBT 23; London: SCM Press; Naperville: Allenson, 1957). On the ability of apocalyptic thinkers to hold seemingly contradictory opinions at the same time, see Marcus, "Modern and Ancient Jewish Apocalypticism," 19 n. 82.

76   In Rev 12:7-12, to be sure, Satan's expulsion from heaven has not rendered him completely powerless; he is still strong enough to wreak havoc on "earth and

context with the submission of the demons to Jesus' power.[77] Jesus now sees that his exorcisms, and those of people who cast out demons in his name, have been made possible by the overthrow of Satan.[78] The tension between Mark 3:23-26 = Q 11:17-18 and Mark 3:27 = Q 11:20-22, then, does not reflect a clash between concurrently held opinions but a *progression* in understanding, corresponding to the *event* of Satan's fall from heaven.

CONGRUENT SAYINGS

But doesn't this attempt to reconstruct an early phase in Jesus' eschatological thinking from one puzzling saying rely on too thin an evidential basis to be convincing? Is there any verification of the hypothesis from other parts of the Synoptic tradition? At least two of the sayings in the immediate 'Q context, and perhaps one in a different Markan setting, are coherent with my interpretation of Mark 3:23-26 = Q 11:17-18 and could belong to the same pre-baptismal stage.

The first is the very next verse in Q: "And if I cast out demons by Beelzebul, by whom do your sons cast them out? Therefore they will be your judges" (Q 11:19). This saying continues the *reductio ad absurdum* reasoning of the Parable of the Kingdom and House in Mark 3:23-26 = Q 11:17-18, and the first part of it is parallel to Mark 3:24-26 = Q 11:18 in form (conditional clause with εἰ in

---

sea," and to make war with the saints, and indeed his deposition from heaven seems to have increased his wrath against the inhabitants of the earth. Yet he has been decisively weakened, since vv. 10-11 announce that "the salvation and the power and the kingdom (βασιλεία) of our God have come, for the accuser of our brethren has been thrown down, . . . and they have conquered him by the blood of the Lamb and by the word of their testimony, for they loved not their lives even unto death." For Christians, therefore, Satan's fall means victory, even if it is achieved at the cost of their lives, whereas for non-Christians it seems to mean only exposure to the terrors of the end-time.

77   The Lukan context, though perhaps not original (see Marcus, "Jesus' Baptismal Vision," 514-15), is correct to link Satan's fall with with a decisive weakening of his power. See the related saying in John 12:31, which links Satan's expulsion with "the judgment of this world."

78   It remains an open question how Jesus, after his baptism and vision of Satan's fall, would have interpreted the exorcisms he had performed earlier, before those events—perhaps as signs that Satan's dominion was beginning to crack? But it is uncertain that he was given to such retrospective thinking, or to such consistency.

protasis, rhetorical question in apodosis). It is also coherent with the world-view expressed in Mark 3:23-26 = Q 11:17-18, but it clashes with Jesus' mature thinking. Jesus portrays himself as one of a number of contemporary figures who perform exorcisms; the fact that these exorcisms are taking place drives him to no conclusions about eschatological advent or about his own unique role in it. Indeed, such uniqueness would seem to be excluded by the saying, since any feature ascribed to Jesus' exorcisms would also need to be ascribed to those of other exorcists who do not follow him.[79] Nor do we find here the realized eschatology of the Parable of the Strong Man and the saying about casting out demons by the power of God; although there is an element of end-expectation in the saying, it refers to the future rather than to the present ("therefore they *will be* your judges").

In this saying, then, reaction to the eschatological figure of Jesus is not the critical criterion of a judgment already taking place, as it will be in Jesus' later thought; it is not the case that one must either fall into step behind Jesus on the apocalpytic battlefield, or be revealed as an enemy of the salvific power that is breaking into the world through him, as will be the situation in the saying that occurs a few verses afterwards in Q, "The one who is not with me is against me" (Q 11:23).[80] To be sure, a harsh judgment is implied against those who put a sinister construction on Jesus' exorcisms, but it is no harsher than the verdict rendered on those who censure other exorcists ("therefore they will be your judges"), and nothing is explicitly said about the position of those who simply do not take a

---

[79]   See the citation of Bultmann above, n. 42; cf. A. D. Jacobson, "The Literary Unity of Q," *JBL* 101 (1982) 365-89, here 381. But Jacobson unconvincingly tries to maintain the literary unity of the Q version by asserting that "the coming of the kingdom is the presupposition for all exorcisms," not just for those of Jesus. Mark 3:27 = Q 11:21-22, however, speaks of a strong *man* who has bound Satan, not of strong *men*, and Q 11:20 speaks of *Jesus'* exorcisms ("if I by the finger of God"), not of exorcisms in general (cf. Davies and Allison, *Matthew*, 2.339).

[80]   This more sectarian attitude is similar to that expressed in 1600 by George More, the chief supporter of the Puritan exorcist John Darrell: "If the Church of England have this power to cast out devils, then the Church of Rome is a false church; for there can be but one true church, the principal mark whereof (as they say) is to work miracles, and of them this is the greatest, namely to cast out devils" (cited in Thomas, *Religion and the Decline of Magic*, 577; cf. 587).

stand vis-à-vis Jesus. Indeed, it is possible that the pre-baptismal Jesus' attitude toward such fence-sitters was not that of Q 11:23 but the opposite viewpoint expressed in Mark 9:40, "He who is not against us [exorcists?] is for us." This more open attitude corresponds to the probable social location position of the pre-baptismal Jesus. As a healer and exorcist who was not yet the center of a large movement that could support him financially, he was probably largely dependent for his sustenance on fees or contributions from those whom he had cured.[81] A person in such a position would probably not embrace the sort of "me against the world" attitude that is expressed in Q 11:23.

A parallel, one among many to the ministry of Jesus, may be cited from the career of the Baal Shem Tov or Besht, the founder of modern Hasidism. The Besht began his ministry as one of numerous *baalei shem* (lit. "masters of the Name [of God]"), faith-healers who were active in Polish Jewry in the early eighteenth century. "At a time when trained physicians were rare—indeed, in the small towns and villages were unheard of—the *baalei shem* took the place of doctors in the treatment of physical and emotional ailments . . ." The Besht first turned to this calling out of poverty, earning his living by means of the fees he collected for miraculous cures and for the therapeutic amulets that he provided. Only gradually did he emerge as pre-eminent among the *baalei shem* and become famous for his compassionate teaching as well as his miraculous cures, eventually earning the sobriquet Baal Shem *Tov*, "the *good* baal shem."[82] It is plausible that these basic points were matched in the early career of

---

[81]   On fees charged by ancient exorcists and faith-healers see Philo, *Special Laws* 3.100-101; Lucian, *Alexander the False Prophet* 22-23; *Lover of Lies* 15-16; Origen, *Celsus* 1.68; contrast what is said about Thomas in *Acts of Thomas* 20; cf. Acts 8:18-19 (see S. R. Garrett, *The Demise of the Devil: Magic and the Demonic in Luke's Writings* [Minneapolis: Fortress, 1989] 70, 145 n. 39; Kollmann, *Jesus und die Christen*, 362-78). These sources are all negative toward the venality of the healers, but the taking of fees does not necessarily indicate greed or corruption; even faith-healers need to make a living. The sixteenth- and seventeenth-century English healers discussed by Thomas (*Religion and the Decline of Magic*, 210) normally expected a fee; cf. also below on the Baal Shem Tov.

[82]   S. Dubnow, "The Beginnings: The Baal Shem Tov (Besht) and the Center in Podolia," in G. D. Hundert (ed.), *Essential Papers on Hasidism: Origins to Present* (Essential Papers on Jewish Studies; New York and London: New York University Press, 1994) 25-57, here 31-32.

Jesus. He started out as one of a number of first-century Galilean wonder-workers, earning his living through his healings, and he saw himself as being in a sort of loose alliance with these other charismatics. Only later did he become pre-eminent among these healers and begin to reveal his gifts as a teacher.

One other logion in the Q context may be linked with the pre-baptismal Jesus, and it may provide a hint about a factor that led Jesus eventually to ally himself with John the Baptist's penitential and apocalyptic movement, to become convinced of eschatological advent, and to come to see his exorcisms in a more programmatic way.[83] This is the passage about the return of the unclean spirit in Q 11:24-26. On the surface this is a strange thing for Jesus to say, since he was an exorcist, yet the saying seems to acknowledge that the end result of exorcism is that the supposedly healed person ends up in worse shape than he or she was in before. The evicted demon finds seven friends more powerful than himself, and with their help he reoccupies his previous human host in a much more formidable way than formerly. Most exegetes have either opted for an allegorical interpretation of this saying or have claimed that in it Jesus was speaking about exorcists other than himself.[84]

But why couldn't this be the pre-baptismal Jesus talking about his own exorcisms and their lack of lasting effectiveness? Why couldn't this saying be the *cri de coeur* of an exorcist who, like a battlefield medic, comes to the depressing realization that he mends his patients only to send them back into the thick of the fighting, where they will be mauled still more terribly by the enemy?[85] And may not such sobering reflections have led Jesus to begin thinking more deeply

---

[83]   For another factor which may have driven Jesus to the Baptist's apocalyptic movement, see the discussion of the effect of persecution above.

[84]   See the surveys in Luz, *Matthäus*, 282-84; Davies and Allison, *Matthew*, 2.359-60; and D. C. Allison, *The Jesus Tradition in Q* (Valley Forge: Trinity Press International, 1997) 122-23.

[85]   See Böcher (*Christus Exorcista*, 17) and Hull (*Hellenistic Magic*, 102), who recognize that the passage is simply a summary of ancient demonology; cf. Allison, *The Jesus Tradition*, 120-32. In *Acts of Thomas* 46 a demon threatens that after his exorcist departs he will repossess the woman from whom he has just been cast out; anxiety about re-possession is also reflected in Mark 9:25; Tobit 6:8, 17; Josephus, *Ant.* 8.2.5 §46-47; and Philostratus, *Life of Apollonius* 4.20. In charismatic Christian circles today, such anxiety is still very real; see e.g. J. Wimber, *Power Healing* (London: Hodder & Stoughton, 1986) 243.

about the scope of the opposition to the human wholeness that his healings were meant to impart, and to wonder whether God might not be calling him to attack the problem directly at its source?[86]

CONCLUDING QUESTIONS AND SPECULATIONS

One of the problems with thinking you have a good thesis is knowing how far to push it, and when to stop. In the present case, I believe I have shown that certain parts of the Beelzebul controversy reflect an early stage in Jesus' ministry, in which he had not yet become convinced that Satan had fallen from heaven. Rather, he was still sure, and could treat it as a self-evident fact, that Satan was enthroned in a position of cosmic lordship. Later, however, after his baptism, he became convinced of Satan's deposition from power, and saw his own exorcisms as evidence for the progressing overthrow of the Satanic regime.

Could this theory also help to resolve the tension between realized and futuristic eschatology in the Synoptic tradition generally? Might it be that the futuristic eschatology belongs to the early, pre-baptismal phrase of Jesus' ministry, before he had seen Satan fall, while the realized eschatology belongs to the later, post-baptismal phase? I acknowledged earlier that apocalyptic thinkers are able to hold together seemingly irreconcilable convictions about eschatological advent, and this ability would provide an alternate way of explaining the clash between futuristic and realized eschatology in the tradition. But would it not be a neater solution to suppose that there was a discernable progression in Jesus' thought, from a hope that was only a hope, to a hope that was conceived as being in

---

[86] In both ancient and modern times, demons have usually been treated by rituals of location or relocation (see J. Z. Smith, "Towards Interpreting Demonic Powers in Hellenistic and Roman Antiquity," in *ANRW* II.17.1 [1978] 425-39, esp. 428-29, 438). But the apocalyptic goal of the later Jesus and of the church was the *extermination* of the demons, not just their eviction from particular human subjects; Jesus was viewed not merely as a supernatural policeman who moved the vagrant spirits on, but as their eschatological liquidator. Mark 1:24, for example, describes the demons screaming in fear, "Have you come *to destroy us*?" Cf. *T. Judah* 25:3; Eusebius, *Proof of the Gospel* 6.13; Ignatius, *Eph.* 19:2-3; and *PGM* 4.1245-1248; the latter invokes Jesus in order to bind and destroy a demon. See also the interesting passage in *Sipra* §262 (on Lev 26:6) cited by Barrett (*The Holy Spirit*, 59), in which R. Judah and R. Šimʿon debate whether at the eschaton God will destroy the demons or merely render them harmless.

process of realization?

To pose the question in this way is immediately to hear alarm bells ringing. Neat solutions are often wrong solutions, especially when one is dealing with a figure as complex as Jesus and an area as irrational as eschatology. Yet I do not think that this neatness should necessarily prevent the hypothesis from being investigated; neat solutions are *sometimes* correct. In any case, once we let go of the theological *a priori* that throughout his career Jesus must have consistently preached and taught the same doctrine, that because he was the incarnate Word his thought could not have undergone significant development, the main obstacle is removed to at least considering the possibility that his thinking on the subject of eschatology progressed, and that different parts of the Synoptic tradition reflect different phases in this thought.[87] Several commentators have been willing to consider such a possibility,[88] and there are also those who have argued that Paul's eschatological thought changed.[89]

I realize that there is a certain similarity between this broader hypothesis and the theory of John Kloppenborg (1987) and others that the earliest layer of Q was less apocalyptic than its later stages.[90] This thesis has been subjected to searching critiques by Horsley (1989), Attridge (1992), Tuckett (1992) and Allison (1997),[91] and I

---

[87] It may seem odd that these different attitudes of Jesus toward eschatology are preserved within a single passage, Mark 3:20-30 pars. But it is characteristic of the Synoptic tradition (as it is of the later rabbinic tradition) to collect together in one place different and even contradictory sayings that deal with the same subject; another Synoptic example that deals with eschatology is Luke 17:20-37, which preserves attitudes toward the presence or futurity of the kingdom of God that are in great tension with each other.

[88] See e.g. A. Schweitzer, *The Quest of the Historical Jesus* (New York: Macmillan, 1968 [orig. 1906]); F. Mussner, "Gab es eine 'galiläische Krise'?" in P. Hoffmann (ed.), *Orientierung an Jesus: Zur Theologie der Synoptiker. Für Josef Schmid* (Freiburg: Herder, 1973) 235-52; J. D. Crossan, *The Historical Jesus: The Life of a Mediterranean Jewish Peasant* (San Francisco: HarperCollins, 1991) 237-38; Davies and Allison, *Matthew*, 2.270-71.

[89] E.g. C. H. Dodd, *New Testament Studies* (Manchester: Manchester University Press, 1953) 109-18.

[90] J. S. Kloppenborg, *The Formation of Q: Trajectories in Ancient Wisdom Collections* (SAC; Philadelphia: Fortress, 1987).

[91] R. A. Horsley, "Questions About Redactional Strata and the Social Relations Reflected in Q," in D. J. Lull (ed.), *Society of Biblical Literature 1989*

would like to distinguish my own position from it. I am clear, whereas Kloppenborg is not, that both of the layers of tradition I have distinguished come from the historical Jesus. Further, I have specifically stated that the early Jesus as well as the later one was probably an apocalyptic thinker, whereas for Kloppenborg the earliest layer of Q is much less apocalyptic than sapiential, and others have used this conclusion as the basis for asserting that Jesus himself was a wisdom teacher rather than an apocalypticist.[92]

I must admit, however, that my exact formulation contains a qualifier: the pre-baptismal Jesus was "in some sense" an apocalypticist. This qualification hints that the apocalyptic framework may have been more central to Jesus' later, post-baptismal thinking than it was to his pre-baptismal thought. I make this qualification partly because according to my interpretation of Mark 3:22-26 = Q 11:17-18, the pre-baptismal Jesus thought that something significant, namely his exorcisms, was being accomplished in the present, even though it was not yet the time of apocalyptic fulfillment. In this sense apocalypticism was not yet as crucial to him as it became after his baptism, when he began to see his exorcisms as signs of eschatological advent.

Also, I must acknowledge that my appropriation of Wilson's analysis of progression from thaumaturgical to millenarian movements might suggest that Jesus started out as a "simple" exorcist and wonder-worker, and that he became an apocalyptic one only later, after experiencing persecution from official quarters for the success of his faith healing. One might synthesize these conceptions by postulating a progression from the non-apocalyptic thaumaturgy of the "early early" Jesus to the futuristic apocalyptic eschatology of the early Jesus to the fulfilled apocalyptic eschatology of the post-baptismal Jesus. In fact, this sort of progression would make a certain amount of sense; it corresponds, for example, to the development of the Ḥabad Ḥasidic movement, to which I referred above, from the non-apocalyptic thaumaturgy of its beginnings, to

---

Seminar Papers (SBLSP 28; Atlanta: Scholars Press, 1989) 175-209; H. W. Attridge, "Reflections on Research into Q," *Semeia* 55 (1992) 223-34; C. M. Tuckett, "On the Stratification of Q: A Response," *Semeia* 55 (1992) 213-22; and Allison, *The Jesus Traditions*, 3-8.

[92]   E.g. B. L. Mack, "Q and the Gospel of Mark: Revising Christian Origins," *Semeia* 55 (1992) 15-39.

the "catastrophic," futuristic messianism of the World War II period, to the triumphant, fulfilled messianism of the most recent decades.[93]

Such a progression is an intriguing possibility, but I do not think that it has the same degree of probability as the basic thesis of this essay.[94] The latter is the more limited contention that Jesus' eschatological thought underwent a discernable change on at least one significant subject, namely the status of Satan in the government of the cosmos. If this hypothesis weathers the test of critical scrutiny, perhaps subsequent scholarship will be able to build on it to formulate a more comprehensive theory about the development of Jesus' view of the end and of the world's standing in relation to it.

---

[93]   See Ravitzky, *Messianism, Zionism*, 193-203. Ravitzky thinks that the persecutions of Jews throughout the first half of this century played a decisive role in moving R. Joseph Isaac Schneerson toward an acute messianic hope; they were for him the birth pangs of the Messiah, which would soon be followed by redemption. Ravitzky therefore calls R. Joseph's messianism "catastrophic." R. Joseph's post-war successor, R. Menachem Mendel Schneerson, saw this hope as being fulfilled in his own days and perhaps in his own person; hence his messianism was "triumphant." The contrast between the catastrophic messianism of R. Joseph and the triumphant messianism of R. Menaḥem corresponds to the difference between the apocalypticism of John the Baptist and that of the later Jesus, but it may also correspond to two different stages in the development of Jesus' own apocalypticism—a "catastrophic" phase that flowed out of his early persecutions by the authorities, and a "triumphant" phase that followed his baptism.

[94]   The main evidence for the "early early" non-apocalyptic stage in Jesus' career is the sociological typology mapped out by Wilson, which is supported by Jewish examples such as the Baal Shem Tov and perhaps Vermes's Ḥasidim. But there is no hard evidence in the Jesus tradition itself.

THE ENCOUNTER OF JESUS WITH THE GERASENE DEMONIAC*

Jostein Ådna

The account of Jesus and the Gerasene demoniac in Mark 5:1-20 is the most dramatic and astounding exorcism story in the Gospels. It has a slightly shorter, but basically corresponding parallel in Luke 8:26-39, whereas the Matthean parallel in Matt 8:28-34 is both remarkably much shorter[1] and less dramatic. In this article I will try to investigate whether and, if so, to what degree this narrative presents an authentic historical account of an encounter between Jesus and a demon-possessed man which happened at a particular time and place during his pre-Easter ministry.

LITERARY-CRITICAL AND TRADITIO-CRITICAL ANALYSES OF MARK 5:1-20

Some twenty-five years ago, Franz Annen submitted a doctoral dissertation on Mark 5:1-20 parr. to the Pontifical Biblical Institute in Rome, which he later revised slightly and published under the title *Heil für die Heiden: Zur Bedeutung und Geschichte der Tradition vom bessenenen Gerasener (Mk 5,1-20 parr.)*.[2] As a full-scale monograph on the text(s) which will serve as the primary textual basis for our investigation, Annen's study deserves more attention than it has traditionally received.[3] Particularly in the realm of

---

*   I thank my friend, Prof. James M. Scott, Trinity Western University, for having corrected and polished my English.

[1]   The Markan version comprises 325 words in 20 verses, the Lukan version 293 words in 14 verses, and the Matthean one solely 135 words in seven verses. (These numbers are taken from Annen, *Heil* [cf. n. 2], 22, 30.)

[2]   F. Annen, *Heil für die Heiden: Zur Bedeutung und Geschichte der Tradition vom besessenen Gerasener (Mk 5,1-20 parr.)* (Frankfurter Theologische Studien 20; Frankfurt am Main: Josef Knecht, 1976).

[3]   Even the major monograph during the recent years on Jesus as an exorcist, produced by Graham H. Twelftree (*Jesus the Exorcist: A Contribution to the Study of the Historical Jesus* [WUNT 2.54; Tübingen: Mohr (Siebeck), 1993]), which generally considers and discusses German scholarly contributions, practically

literary criticism, Annen has done very solid work from which we may gladly profit.

The first result of Annen's literary-critical analysis which is of relevance to us is the affirmation of Markan priority; Luke and Matthew have not had any other sources than Mark 5:1-20 at their disposal when formulating the text in Luke 8:26-39 and Matt 8:28-34, respectively.[4] Consequently, for our purpose of reconstructing the oldest possible version of the tradition as the basis for our historical quest, we may concentrate on Mark 5:1-20 and ignore its synoptic parallels.[5]

A Pre-Markan Version of the Story

Despite vigorous statements to the contrary in recent years, it seems likely that Mark redacted the source behind Mark 5:1-20.[6] Of course, the literary-critical evaluation of certain minute details in the text remains disputable and more or less hypothetical. Nevertheless, in my opinion, Annen has succeeded in reconstructing a coherent pre-Markan version of the story which can serve as a sufficiently convincing, general basis for any further traditio-historical

---

ignores Annen's study. In contrast, J. P. Meier (*A Marginal Jew: Rethinking the Historical Jesus, Vol. 2: Mentor, Message, and Miracles* [ABRL; New York: Doubleday, 1994] 650-53, 664-67) values and profits extensively from Annen in his treatment of Mark 5:1-20. In English the title of Annen's monograph might be rendered "Salvation for the Gentiles: The Meaning and History of the Tradition about the Possessed Gerasene."

4   Annen compares the texts of Mark and Luke in *Heil*, 21-29, and of Mark and Matthew on pp. 29-38. This analysis is considerably abbreviated over against the literary critical comparison of the different Gospel versions in his unpublished dissertation from 1973, also entitled *Heil für die Heiden*; cf. there pp. 26-56 for Mark–Luke and pp. 61-76 for Mark–Matthew.

5   For a redaction critical analysis of the Matthean and Lukan versions of the story cf. R. Pesch, *Der Besessene von Gerasa: Entstehung und Überlieferung einer Wundergeschichte* (SBS 56; Stuttgart: Katholisches Bibelwerk, 1972) 50-64; and Annen, *Heil*, 206-209. Generally, the commentaries on the Gospels of Matthew and Luke are to be consulted on the particular aspects of the versions of these two evangelists.

6   An outspoken contestant of any editorial changes by Mark is for example Rudolf Pesch; cf. both his article, "The Markan Version of the Healing of the Gerasene Demoniac," *Ecumenical Review* 23 (1971) 349-76, esp. 351-52, 374; and the parallel, slightly expanded German version, *Der Besessene*, 14-17, 49.

considerations.[7] The reconstructed text reads as follows:[8]

([1-]2*)[9] And at the seaside a man from Gerasa with an unclean spirit came from the tombs to meet Jesus,[10] (3a) he had his dwelling in the tombs;[11] (4)

---

[7] Cf. his analysis of "Tradition und Redaktion bei Mk" in *Heil*, 39-74. After the detailed investigation of single verses and units on pp. 40-69 he sums up his results on p. 70 by printing the Greek text of Mark 5:1-20 with distinctions between the pre-Markan traditional text and the editorial changes, marked by underlinings. (Annen distinguishes thereby, as far as possible, between "redaktionell" = _____, "vielleicht redaktionell" = _ _ _ _, and "redaktionell formuliert, aber inhaltlich traditionell" = _ _ _ _ _.) When more or less taking over Annen's analysis we are to take note of his explicit and methodologically justified reservation with regard to the limits of exact distinctions: "Es ist ohne weiteres möglich, daß hinter den als redaktionell bezeichneten Versen Tradition steht, die aber im Text nicht mehr greifbar wird. Andererseits ist nicht nur möglich, sondern fast sicher, daß Mk auch in den als traditionell bezeichneten Versen der Perikope eingegriffen hat, nur eben nicht in einer Weise, die als charakteristisch für ihn gelten kann" (*Heil*, 70-71). Without explicitly disclosing his evaluation R. H. Gundry (*Mark: A Commentary on His Apology for the Cross* [Grand Rapids: Eerdmans, 1993] 266) makes a seemingly positive mention of Annen's "detailed attempt to separate redaction from tradition."

[8] My rendering of Annen's German text in *Heil*, 71, in which I try to stay as close to the Greek text as possible without militating against basic grammatical rules and idiomatical preferences of today's English. With regard to the status of this text Annen's introductory commentary to his German translation is fully valid also for this English rendering: "Die . . . Übersetzung darf . . . nicht als (übersetzter) Wortlaut der vormk Erzählung verstanden werden. Sie will lediglich . . . klar machen, welche Textteile der uns vorliegenden mk Erzählung als traditionell erkennbar sind" (ibid.).

[9] To simplify the relating of this reconstructed pre-Markan text to the canonical text of Mark I include the counting of verses. An asterisk marks that only a part of the respective vers(es) is traced back to the pre-Markan version of the story.

[10] Cf. the analysis in Annen, *Heil*, 40-44. "Für Mk 5,1 ergibt sich . . . ziemlich klar, daß die Formulierung mk Redaktionsarbeit entstammt, daß aber der Name Gerasa schon in der Tradition mit der Erzählung verbunden war und wohl auch das Meer (θάλασσα) schon vor Mk in der Einleitung erwähnt wurde" (43). "Sowohl V 2a wie 18a sind . . . mit großer Wahrscheinlichkeit ebenfalls redaktionell, genau wie V 1" (43). V. 2b—ὑπήντησεν αὐτῷ ἐκ τῶν μνημείων ἄνθρωπος ἐν πνεύματι ἀκαθάρτῳ—however, represents tradition (cf. 44). As an independent tradition, not yet included into a narrative context, the story surely explicitly mentioned the name of Jesus in the opening statement.

[11] V. 3a, which is also traditional (cf. Annen, *Heil*, 45), is a relative clause (ὃς τὴν κατοίκησιν εἶχεν ἐν τοῖς μνήμασιν), but because of the necessary word order

and he had often been restrained with fetters and chains, and the chains had been torn apart by him and the fetters had been broken, and no one was strong enough to subdue him;[12] (5) and always, night and day,[13] in the tombs and in the mountains he was crying out and bruising himself with stones. (6) And when he saw Jesus from a distance, he ran and did obeisance to him, (7) and shouting at the top of his voice, he spoke: "What have you to do with me, Jesus, son of the most high God? I adjure you by God, do not torment me."[14] (9*) And he asked him, "What is your name?" And he said to him, "Legion is my name."[15] (11) But there on the hillside a large herd of pigs was feeding;[16] (12*) and they begged him saying, "Send us into the pigs."[17] (13) And he gave them permission. And after the

---

in the preceding main clause I render it as a main clause, as well, because the relative pronoun "who" (= ὅς) would wrongly have referred back to Jesus instead of the demoniac. V. 3b is probably editorial (*Heil*, 45-46).

12   Annen (*Heil*, 46) holds the syntactical construction with διά + infinitives to be an editorial feature, but considers the content of the whole v. 4 to be traditional: διὰ τὸ αὐτὸν πολλάκις πέδαις καὶ ἁλύσεσιν δεδέσθαι καὶ διεσπάσθαι ὑπ᾽ αὐτοῦ τὰς ἁλύσεις καὶ τὰς πέδας συντετρῖφθαι, καὶ οὐδεὶς ἴσχυεν αὐτὸν δαμάσαι.

13   Annen (*Heil*, 71) has here, without commenting on it and at variance with his Greek text on p. 70, reversed the word order of νυκτὸς καὶ ἡμέρας to "Tag und Nacht." I see no reason why not to stick to the word order of Mark, because the formulation here probably already at the pre-Markan level, "as elsewhere, reflects a Jewish method of reckoning twenty-four hour days from sunset to sunset (cf. 4:27)" (Gundry, *Mark*, 249).

14   According to Annen (*Heil*, 46-50) vv. 5-7, with the probable exception of the historical present λέγει in v. 7, are completely traditional: (5) καὶ διὰ παντὸς νυκτὸς καὶ ἡμέρας ἐν τοῖς μνήμασιν καὶ ἐν τοῖς ὄρεσιν ἦν κράζων καὶ κατακόπτων ἑαυτὸν λίθοις. (6) καὶ ἰδὼν τὸν Ἰησοῦν ἀπὸ μακρόθεν ἔδραμεν καὶ προσεκύνησεν αὐτῷ (7) καὶ κράξας φωνῇ μεγάλῃ λέγει, Τί ἐμοὶ καὶ σοί, Ἰησοῦ υἱὲ τοῦ θεοῦ τοῦ ὑψίστου; ὁρκίζω σε τὸν θεόν, μή με βασανίσῃς. Verse 8 he considers to be editorial (cf. *Heil*, 50-52).

15   Annen sums up his extensive discussion of v. 9 in *Heil*, 52-54, as follows: "Für V 9 ergibt sich also, daß Mk die Einleitungen zu den direkten Reden gestaltet hat. Die Frage Jesu Τί ὄνομά σοι und die Antwort Λεγιὼν ὄνομά μοι sind vormk. Für die Erklärung ὅτι πολλοί ἐσμεν läßt sich keine sichere Entscheidung treffen" (54). When it comes to v. 10, however, Annen is clear in his judgement in favour of a Markan editorial addition (cf. *Heil*, 54-55).

16   Annen's discussion of v. 11 (ἦν δὲ ἐκεῖ πρὸς τῷ ὄρει ἀγέλη χοίρων μεγάλη βοσκομένη) in *Heil*, 55-56, reaches the conclusion: "Mit Ausnahme des Anfangs ἦν δὲ ἐκεῖ, der redaktioneller Anschluß sein könnte, ist . . . V 11 ziemlich eindeutig vormk" (56).

17   Annen's analysis of v. 12 (*Heil*, 56) leads to the following result: "V 12ab [i.e.: καὶ παρεκάλεσαν αὐτὸν λέγοντες, Πέμψον ἡμᾶς εἰς τοὺς χοίρους] ist also ziemlich sicher vormk. V 12c [i.e. the rest of the verse] dagegen kann sehr wohl

unclean spirits had come out, they went into the pigs, and the herd rushed down the steep bank into the sea—about two thousand in number—, and they were drowned in the sea.[18] (14*) And those tendering them ran off to the town; and people came to see what it was that had happened.[19] (15*) And they saw the demoniac, dressed and in his right mind, (the very man) who had had the legion, and they were afraid.[20] (16*) And those who had seen what had happened to the demoniac, reported to them.[21] (19*) And Jesus spoke to him, "Go forth and tell how much the Lord has done to you and how he has had mercy on you."[22]

---

aus der Redaktion stammen, für die einiges spricht, während nichts eindeutig auf Tradition hinweist" (57).

[18]   According to Annen (*Heil*, 57-58) all elements of v. 13, including the delayed apposition ὡς δισχίλιοι, are traditional: καὶ ἐπέτρεψεν αὐτοῖς. καὶ ἐξελθόντα τὰ πνεύματα τὰ ἀκάθαρτα εἰσῆλθον εἰς τοὺς χοίρους, καὶ ὥρμησεν ἡ ἀγέλη κατὰ τοῦ κρημνοῦ εἰς τὴν θάλασσαν, ὡς δισχίλιοι, καὶ ἐπνίγοντο ἐν τῇ θαλάσσῃ.

[19]   With regard to v. 14 Annen (*Heil*, 58-59) reaches the following conclusion: "Im Ganzen ist also Mk 5,14 wohl vormk. Es gibt aber Gründe, die es möglich erscheinen lassen, daß καὶ ἀπήγγειλαν und καὶ εἰς τοὺς ἀγρούς redaktionelle Zutaten sind" (59). With these probably editorial additions left out the Greek text, on which the above translation of v. 14* rests, reads: καὶ οἱ βόσκοντες αὐτοὺς ἔφυγον εἰς τὴν πόλιν· καὶ ἦλθον ἰδεῖν τί ἐστιν τὸ γεγονός.

[20]   The extensive discussion of v. 15 by Annen (*Heil*, 59-61) concludes in the following evaluation: "Die Formulierung von V 15 ist . . . bis θεωροῦσιν redaktionell; nachher fehlen außer für καθήμενον Spuren mk Eingreifens. Anstelle von θεωροῦσιν muß aber wohl schon vor Mk ein Verb des Sehens, Findens o.ä. gestanden haben, um mit dem Folgenden zu verbinden" (61). For the above rendering of v. 15* I have, following Annen's German text (*Heil*, 71), hypothetically constructed the beginning of the sentence as καί followed by an aorist plural of θεωρεῖν or some other verb with the meaning "to see." The rest of the presupposed Greek text of v. 15* reads: . . . τὸν δαιμονιζόμενον ἱματισμένον καὶ σωφρονοῦντα, τὸν ἐσχηκότα τὸν λεγιῶνα, καὶ ἐφοβήθησαν.

[21]   It is very difficult to reach any certain conclusions with regard to v. 16. Annen (*Heil*, 61-62) leaves out the last four words καὶ περὶ τῶν χοίρων and accepts the rest as tradition: καὶ διηγήσαντο αὐτοῖς οἱ ἰδόντες πῶς ἐγένετο τῷ δαιμονιζομένῳ. Verses 17 and 18 are completely editorial; cf. *Heil*, 43, 63-64.

[22]   Annen's investigation of v. 19 (*Heil*, 64-67) leads to the following result: "V 19ab, also die Einleitung der Worte Jesu, ist redaktionell formuliert. ὕπαγε ist ein traditionelles Motiv, ebenso ὅσα ὁ κύριός σοι πεποίηκεν καὶ ἠλέησέν σε. ἀπαγγέλειν ist hier wohl ebenfalls traditionell; es hat wie der ganze mit ὅσα eingeleitete Nebensatz atl Kolorit. Dagegen ist εἰς τὸν οἶκόν σου πρὸς τοὺς σούς eher redaktionell" (66-67). In the rendering above I have once more followed Annen's own guess in formulating the lost introduction which has been replaced by the Markan linkage between the preceding editorial v. 18 and the traditional elements in v. 19: "Und Jesus sprach zu ihm" (*Heil*, 71). In accordance with the cited

The Structure of the Pre-Markan Version

This hypothetically reconstructed, pre-Markan version of the story can conveniently be divided into the following sixteen elements: (*1*) Introduction, v. (1-)2*; (*2*) description of the demoniac's state, vv. 3a, 4-5; (*3*) his obeisance to Jesus, v. 6; followed by (*4*) the attempt of the demon(iac) to defend itself/himself against the encountered excorsist, v. 7, and by (*5*) Jesus' question as to the name of the demon, v. 9*. Further we have (*6*) the presentation of the herd of pigs, v. 11; (*7*) the demon's (respectively: the demons') plea for lenience, v. 12*; (*8*) Jesus' permission, v. 13a; (*9*) the transfer of the unclean spirits from the man to the pigs, v. 13b; followed by (*10*) the pigs running into the sea and drowning, v.13c. Finally, the story contains further (*11*) the reaction of the swineherds, v. 14a*; (*12*) people coming to observe what has happened, vv. 14b, 15a*; (*13*) description of the changed state of the demoniac, v. 15b*; (*14*) the awe of those observing his changed condition, v. 15c; (*15*) report by the eyewitnesses, v. 16*; and—as the last element—(*16*) Jesus' instruction to the healed man, v. 19*.

Structurally, these elements can be arranged in three scenes:

Introduction:	v. (1-)2*	(*1*)	Presentation of the two main figures and of the place
Scene 1:	vv. 3-9*	(*2-5*)	The encounter between the demoniac and Jesus The disclosure of the name "Legion" (*5*) functions as a bridge to the next scene
Scene 2:	vv. 11-13*	(*6-10*)	The episode with the herd of pigs The flight of the swineherds (*11*) functions as a bridge to the next scene
Scene 3:	vv. 14-19*	(*11-16*)	The result of the exorcism and its effect on people

It is possible to argue for an alternative structural analysis, if one attaches the episode with the pigs (elements *6-10*) directly to the preceding encounter between the demoniac and Jesus as the integral continuation and outcome of the confrontation.[23] Nevertheless, our

evaluation of Annen the rest of v. 19* reads: Ὕπαγε καὶ ἀπάγγειλον αὐτοῖς ὅσα ὁ κύριός σοι πεποίηκεν καὶ ἠλέησέν σε. Finally, in spite of some doubts with regard to details, the whole v. 20 most likely belongs to the Markan redaction (cf. *Heil*, 67-69).

23   Thus, for example Pesch, "Healing," 350-51, and idem, *Der Besessene*, 14, takes the account of the disease in vv. 3-5 (*2*) to the introduction and collects

proposed tripartite structure for the story is justified if the following points are taken into consideration. In every scene a new set of persons or actors is introduced: (1) the demoniac and Jesus, (2) the herd of pigs, (3) different groups of witnesses to the event. Furthermore, every scene concentrates on a particular theme or main motif: In the first scene there is the *presentation* of the miserable man from Gerasa (element *2*, vv. 3a, 4-5), of the identity of Jesus as "son of the most high God" in the cry of the demon(iac) (element *4*, v. 7), and, finally, of the multiform character of the demon expressed by its name "Legion" (element *5*, v. 9*). In the second scene we witness the transfer of the demons described as a dramatic *"flight"* into the herd of pigs (element *9*, v. 13b), causing the pigs themselves to flee away into the sea (element *10*, v. 13c). Opening the third scene is the flight of the swineherds (element *11*, v. 14a*), causing people to come out to the site where the event had taken place and letting them become *witnesses*, awe-struck by Jesus' mighty deed (elements *12 + 14*, vv. 14b, 15a* + 15c). Those who had actually seen what had happened to the demoniac, as well as the healed man himself, become active *witnesses* in the sense that they tell others about the event (elements *15 + 16*, vv. 16* + 19*).[24] Finally, this placing of the episode with the pigs as a single scene inside the unfolding of the story has the obvious advantage of being able to respect its integral position within what appears to be a coherent narrative,[25] and simultaneously to reflect the fact that it is a unit of its own and that the rest of the story is imaginable without this scene.[26]

---

vv. 6-13 under the heading "Jesus' encounter and conversation [German: *Auseinandersetzung*] with the demon."

[24]   This presentation joins fairly closely Annen's analysis of "Ablauf der Erzählung" and "Struktur der Erzählung" in *Heil*, 103-107. However, he includes the flight of the herdsmen in v. 14 into scene two, whereas I have put this bridging element between the second and third scenes into the latter one because their behaviour already belongs to the chain of reactions to the event and helps call forth the further reactions of witnesses.

[25]   Cf. Annen, *Heil*, 106: ". . . die Schweine-Episode (erklärt und begründet) den Gegensatz zwischen dem Zustand des ἄνθρωπος ἐν πνεύματι ἀκαθάρτῳ (V 3-5) und dem Zustand des Mannes, der die Legion gehabt hatte (τὸν ἐσχηκότα τὸν λεγιῶνα V 15) . . . Die drei Szenen sind nicht einfach lose aneinander gereiht, sondern erzählerisch sehr geschickt miteinander *verbunden*, so daß sich im ganzen eine recht einheitliche Erzählung ergibt" (Annen' emphasis).

[26]   For example, Gundry (*Mark*, 248) lets the episode with the pigs in vv. 11-13 appear as a part of its own within his division of the story into altogether six

The Search for Further Earlier Stages of the Story

With the historical question as the guiding principle to our discussion we ask next whether it is possible to trace the tradition of Jesus' encounter with the Gerasene demoniac even further back to one or more levels behind the reconstructed pre-Markan version.

The German scholar Rudolf Pesch undertook in the early seventies an attempt to do precisely this and suggested a fourfold development of the story, in which the fourth stage represents the text in its canonical, Markan form.[27] The major tools which Pesch employs in his traditio-historical reconstruction of the transmission process are a form-critical analysis and an investigation of the themes or motifs contained in the text.[28] According to his form-critical analysis, the long narrative in Mark 5:1-20 contains the typical formal characteristics of exorcism stories; moreover, "it also includes certain features derived from the themes of the ancient stories of miraculous healing" and "some of the typical features of the exorcism ritual."[29] This systematizing of the form-critical elements serves as a warrant for the traditio-historical inferences insofar as Pesch conjectures an original story consisting of the five extant characteristics of exorcism stories, i.e. (1) the "encounter" between the exorcist and the demoniac (vv. 1-2*, 5*), (2) the defensive reaction of the demon (vv. 6*, 7), (3) the *apopompe*[30] (v. 8*), (4)

---

parts (*pace* Pesch, cf. n. 23 above). He inserts the flight of the herdsmen into the "the response of the people in the region (vv 14-17)" (*pace* Annen; cf. n. 24 above).

27 As noted in n. 6 Pesch contests any editorial changes by the evangelist Mark. The canonical text is, therefore, according to him identical with the form given to it when it was incorporated into the catena of miracle stories, which additionally contained the story of the storm on the lake and the story of Jairus' daughter and the woman with the issue of blood, now to be found in Mark 4:35–5:43. The editor including the story of the Gerasene demoniac into this catena only made minor changes, adding the necessary combining references to the journey on the lake (vv. 1-2, 18), the plural ἦλθον in v. 1, taking notice of the presence of the disciples, and perhaps the drowning of the pigs in v. 13. Cf. Pesch, "Healing," 351, 353, 355-56, 374; idem, *Der Besessene*, 17, 19, 22-23, 48.

28 Pesch (*Der Besessene*, 21-40) gives this part of his study the heading "Form- und motivgeschichtliche Analyse," and "History of the Forms and Themes of the Passage," respectively ("Healing," 354-68).

29 Pesch, "Healing," 354-55 (the direct quotations are to be found on each one of these two pages); idem, *Der Besessene*, 21-22.

30 I.e. the exorcist's command expelling the demon.

the exit of the demon (v. 13*), and (5) the amazement of the onlookers (vv. 15* and 20d [καὶ πάντες ἐθαύμαζον] or 17) and the spread of the exorcist's fame (vv. [11,] 14a* + 16*).[31] Particularly because the defensive reaction in Mark 5:7, "described wholly in thematic terms," seems to be dependent on Mark 1:24, i.e. the corresponding element in the story about the demoniac in the synagogue in Caparnaum in Mark 1:21-28,[32] Pesch contemplates the possibility that the whole story is a secondary creation dependent on the story taken up in Mark 1, or "at least that the narrative was not created from direct observation."[33] In his fixing of the form-critical characteristics of an exorcism story—and also of the additional features of miraculous healing and of exorcism ritual—Pesch shows a considerable dependence on Rudolf Bultmann's classical definitions.[34] Even though Pesch undoubtedly succeeds in bringing us much closer to a sympathetic understanding of this strange and astounding narrative than the classical form critics did,[35] he still

---

[31]   These five formal characteristics of exorcism stories are first shortly listed in "Healing," 354, and idem, *Der Besessene*, 21; then follows a more detailed discussion of each of these form critical elements on pp. 355-60, respectively pp. 22-29; and, finally, in the part of his study entitled "History of the Transmission and Editing of the Passage" (pp. 368-76), and "Überlieferungs- und redaktions-geschichtliche Analyse I: Von der Urform zum Markustext" (pp. 41-49), Pesch undertakes the traditio-historical application of the form critical analysis, reconstruc-ting the original exorcism story consisting of these five characteristics (cf. pp. 368-71/41-45). Where Pesch only includes a part of a verse into his reconstructed original version, I have marked that in the references above with an asterisk. For information about the exact conjectures cf. the references to Pesch's two studies.

[32]   Pesch, "Healing," 357-58 (quotation taken from p. 357); idem, *Der Besessene*, 25-26. Whereas our story includes a lot of additional features, Pesch considers Mark 1:21-28 to represent "the classical pattern" of an exorcism story ("Healing," 354; *Der Besessene*, 21).

[33]   Pesch, "Healing," 370-71; idem, *Der Besessene*, 44.

[34]   Cf. his explicit references to the relevant passages in R. Bultmann, *Die Geschichte der synoptischen Tradition* (7th ed., Göttingen: Vandenhoeck & Ruprecht, 1967) 224, 236ff., and 238f., in the three footnotes related to the three forms that Pesch detects in Mark 5:1-20: "Healing," 354-55 nn. 7-9; idem, *Der Besessene*, 21 nn. 23-25.

[35]   Cf. Pesch's own characterisation of the classical form critics: "Critics who see the preservation of this strange story as marking a 'fall' into unorthodox preaching and unorthodox gospel-writing have to now found it simplest to dismiss it as an obvious transference of a popular tale to Jesus. The only remaining problem is whether it was a popular tale about duping or being duped by the devil and

seems to fall into the trap of classical form criticism when claiming as the point of departure for the transmission process an original version in the "pure" form of exorcism stories and when drawing historical conclusions on this basis.

Franz Annen has, in my opinion, chosen a much more well-founded approach when examining the validity of the Bultmannian "Gattung" of exorcism story (in German: *Dämonenaustreibung*).[36] Restricting the comparative material to texts which are older than or contemporary with the pre-Markan version of the story about the Gerasene demoniac, Annen concludes that it is actually justified to classify a "Gattung" of this kind, but it was obviously handled with great freedom and variation.[37] In his judgement, even those features which occur regularly in exorcism stories, and, thus, in this sense can be labelled typical, do not have their origin in the force of formal standardisation, but likely reflect current demonological beliefs and exorcistic practices.[38] Instead of ascribing supplementary or non-typical features in a story to other forms and viewing the extant text as a mixture—a "Mischform" as opposed to a "reine Form"—reflecting a development within the tradition corresponding to more successive stages in a transmission process, Annen pleads for due respect for the individual particularity of each individual story: "Die Aussage einer Dämonenaustreibungserzählung aus ihren topischen Elementen (oder der Gattung) allein erheben zu wollen, ist eine unerlaubte Verallgemeinerung. Jede Erzählung ist für sich zu untersuchen; ihre individuellen Elemente haben dabei eher mehr

---

whether the tale was originally Jewish or pagan" ("Healing," 349-50). In the corresponding passage of the German version (*Der Besessene*, 10) Pesch quotes Bultmann's judgement explicitly: ". . . daß hier ein volkstümlicher Schwank auf Jesus übertragen ist, kann nicht zweifelhaft sein" (Bultmann, *Geschichte*, 225).

36   Annen, *Heil*, 115-27.

37   Annen, *Heil*, 125: "Eine genaue parallele Form zur Gerasener-Erzählung, die alle Elemente der bulmannschen [sic] Gattung aufweisen würde, fehlt also im NT. Doch weisen Mk 1,21-28; Mk 9,14-29 und Apg 16,16-19 eine recht große Ähnlichkeit auf. Man kann also im Falle der ntl Erzählungen tatsächlich von einer literarischen Gattung sprechen, die allerdings sehr frei gehandhabt wird."

38   Annen, *Heil*, 126: ". . . einzelne Elemente der Dämonenaustreibungen," which "immer wieder auftauchen . . ., drängen sich dem Erzähler . . . offensichtlich nicht von einer festen literarischen Gattung her auf, sondern spiegeln wohl eher dämonologische Ansichten und exorzistische Praktiken der Zeit wieder, soweit sie sich nicht einfach von der erzählten Sache her ergeben."

Gewicht als die topischen."[39]

Hence, with regard to the historical question Annen warns against a premature judgement grounded on a form critical analysis.[40] Pesch, too, acknowledges that the original story which he reconstructs "is localized and contains a few vivid concrete details ... The question arises therefore, whether there is not preserved here an authentic local historical tradition."[41] However, this deliberation is immediately followed by the aforementioned statement of probable dependence on Mark 1:21-28,[42] and Pesch leaves his readers in uncertainty regarding his evaluation of the historical question. Instead, he goes on with his reconstruction of the further stages in the transmission of the story, concentrating on the message and the *Sitz im Leben* of each level.[43]

In my opinion, Rudolf Pesch's traditio-historical analysis rests on too many uncertainties and methodologically untenable premises to be convincing.[44] In one instance, however, there is a striking

---

[39]   Annen, *Heil*, 126.

[40]   Annen, *Heil*, 127: ". . . da nicht nur die Dämonologie, sondern auch exorzistische Praktiken die topischen Elemente bestimmten, ist es sehr wohl möglich, daß hinter diesen öfters ein wirkliches Geschehen stand. Außerdem enthält keine Erzählung *nur* topische Elemente. Die Historizität der Erzählungen muß von andern Kriterien her beurteilt werden" (Annen's emphasis).

[41]   Pesch, "Healing," 370; cf. idem, *Der Besessene*, 44.

[42]   Doubled by the earlier and seemingly even stronger statement in "Healing," 368: The original story about the Gerasene demoniac was "rather like and possibly modelled on the story handed down in Mk. 1,21-28" (cf. idem, *Der Besessene*, 41).

[43]   The original version was a "mission-promoting miracle story" (Pesch, "Healing," 374; cf. idem, *Der Besessene*, 48), originating "probably in Hellenistic Jewish Christian circles in Galilee" ("Healing," 368; cf. *Der Besessene*, 41). For further details about this first level in the transmission, cf. pp. 286-87 above and n. 31. At the second stage, on the basis of Isaiah 65 (and Psalm 67), "the Gerasene demoniac is presented as a prototype of the Gentile world," and "the narrative was expanded into a demonstration of Jesus' superiority over pagan disorder" ("Healing," 371; for details, cf. 371-73; *Der Besessene*, 45-47). "At a third stage in the narration, when vv. 18-20 were added, the mission in the Gentile world is even more clearly the focus of attention" ("Healing," 373; for details 373-74; *Der Besessene*, 45-47). Finally, cf. n. 27 with regard to the fourth and last pre-Markan stage reconstructed by Pesch.

[44]   Cf. Gundry, *Mark*, 266: "To follow Pesch . . . in tracing this story through five stages, each having a different point, requires much imagination and runs the danger of too hastily giving up the attempt to find coherence in the story as we presently have it."

correspondence between his results and the observation I made above that the episode with the pigs might be omitted without harming the coherence of the narrative. In the following, we must investigate whether this fact is purely coincidental, or whether it reflects a traditio-historical expansion at an earlier stage of the transmission.

THE EPISODE WITH THE PIGS

A review of the history of research[45] shows that the episode with the pigs has long been considered the most difficult or disturbing part of the story. To the extent that objections against it are rooted in a feeling of distaste for the alleged coarseness and primitiveness, considered to be improper for a person of Jesus' stature to be involved in, they are to be suspected as modern biases, likely produced by alienation to the culture from which the story comes. Related, but admittedly with a closer link to the description of Jesus in the Gospels, is the observation that this incident is the sole example of Jesus' destroying people's livelihood.[46] But to exclude on moral grounds the possibility that Jesus could have been engaged in an incident affecting negatively the living conditions of some people smacks too much of apologetics and, moreover, runs the risk of applying modern sentiments and standards of what is morally acceptable to a society and a culture where things might have been viewed and experienced in a totally different way.

To be taken much more seriously is the consideration that the pigs

---

[45]   Cf. the informative presentation in Annen (*Heil*, 79-101) of the "Forschungsgeschichte," systematically categorised in the subdivisions "1. Ein historischer Bericht" (79-82), "2. Der historische Bericht eines Ereignisses ohne Wunder" (82-86), "3. Eine unhistorische Erzählung" (86-89), "4. Ein historischer Kern erweitert" (90-95), and "5. Keine Stellungnahme zur Historizität" (96-101). In his dissertation (cf. n. 4) Annen gave an even more detailed presentation of the history of research (cf. there pp. 137-88).

[46]   A. D. Martin ("The Loss of the Gadarene Swine," *ExpTim* 25 [1913-14] 380-81) can be mentioned as a representative of those considering "the so-called 'moral difficulty'" as "the one serious objection which remains" (380). Martin's apologetic and hardly convincing solution is to downplay the amount of the loss for the owners of the pigs as much as possible and to describe the effects of the healing of the demoniac as by far compensating the loss of the herd: "Indeed, the final feeling of the owners of the herd may have been one of thankfulness that the hillsides were at last made safe for all live stock. Then, too, the change effected in the man was a personal gain for every one belonging to the locality" (381).

episode might be a secondary proof of Jesus' success in expelling the demon(s). There are clear analogies in contemporary exorcism stories of a demonstration that an exorcism has been successful. Particularly interesting and relevant is the story related by Josephus about the Jewish exorcist Eleazar (*Ant.* 8.2.5 §46-48):[47]

> I have observed a certain Eleazar, of my race, in the presence of Vespasian, his sons, tribunes and a number of other soldiers, release people possessed by demons. Now this was the manner of the cure: Placing to the nostrils of the demon possessed person the ring which had under the seal a root which Solomon had prescribed, he then, as the person smelled it, drew out the demon through the nostrils. When the person fell down, he adjured the demon, speaking Solomon's name and repeating the incantations which he had composed, never to re-enter him. Then, wishing to persuade and to prove to those present that he had this ability, Eleazar would place at a small distance either a cup full of water or a foot basin and command the demon while going out of the human to overturn it and to make known to those watching that he had left him.

To be mentioned is also the story about how Apollonius of Tyana exorcised a demon from a young man in Athens who with a loud and coarse laughter disturbed him while he was speaking. Apollonius realises that it is a demon which makes the young man behave the way he does, and confronts it directly (*Vit. Ap.* 4.20):[48]

> Now when Apollonius gazed on him, the ghost in him began to utter cries of fear and rage, such as one hears from people who are being branded or racked; and the ghost swore that he would leave the young man alone and never take possession of any man again. But Apollonius addressed him with anger, as a master might a shifty, rascally, and shameless slave and so on, and he ordered him to quit the young man and show by a visible sign that he had done so. 'I will throw down yonder statue,' said the devil, and pointed to one of the images which were in the king's portico, for there it was that the scene took place. But when the statue began by moving gently, and then fell down, it would defy anyone to describe the hubbub which arose thereat and the way they clapped their hands with wonder.

Actually, the aspect of a demonstrative additional proof is generally absent form the Gospels' description of Jesus' healing

---

[47] Cited from C. A. Evans, *Jesus and His Contemporaries: Comparative Studies* (AGJU 25; Leiden: Brill, 1995) 237.

[48] The translation is that of F. C. Conybeare in the *LCL* edition. I have cited it from Evans, *Jesus*, 247. Evans adds the comment: "One is reminded of the story of the Gerasene demoniac (Mark 5:1-20)" (248 n. 8). Cf. Twelftree, *Jesus*, 25, as well.

miracles, so if the function of the pigs episode is to deliver such a proof, one can really suspect this to be a later addition. Graham Twelftree, however, argues convincingly that the contrast between the demoniac's earlier state (Mark 5:3-5) and his new condition (v. 15) demonstrates that a successful cure has taken place, and that the fact that "the demons are said to enter into the pigs (εἰσῆλθον εἰς) rather than act upon them as objects," indicates another function for this incident than serving as a proof.[49] The obvious alternative understanding seems to be "that the demons were thought to be displaced from the man into the pigs," an idea with "convincing parallels."[50] Rudolf Pesch describes this widely attested category of *epipompe*, i.e. "the banishment of the demons to a new abode," as an element of exorcistic practice often added to the preceding *apopompe*.[51] The new abode can be either some distant place, objects of different kinds, or animals. There are many references to banishment into the sea, and a Babylonian incantation even witnesses to a pig being offered to demons in place of the human being they have possessed.[52] Thus, "the concept of the *epipompe* in Mk. 5.12 is by no means unusual."[53] Also, the violent effect that the entering demons have on the pigs can easily be explained on the background of ideas related to the phenomenon of *epipompe*.[54] On this background we may safely conclude that it is "more appropriate to view the destruction of the pigs as part of the cure rather than something set up as a deliberate proof of the exorcist's success."[55]

So far we have not found convincing arguments that the episode with the pigs is a secondary addition to our story. It is to be noted, however, that though both the *epipompe* in v. 13 and the preceding plea for lenience in v. 12 have plenty of history-of-religions parallels,[56] the way these two elements are combined in our story is

---

[49]   Twelftree, *Jesus*, 74-75.

[50]   Twelftree, *Jesus*, 75.

[51]   Pesch, "Healing," 365; idem, *Der Besessene*, 36. With regard to the *apopompe*; cf. n. 30 above.

[52]   Pesch, "Healing," 365-67; idem, *Der Besessene*, 36-38. More history of religions parallels are presented by Twelftree, *Jesus*, 75.

[53]   Pesch, "Healing," 367; cf. idem, *Der Besessene*, 38.

[54]   Cf. Pesch, "Healing," 367; idem, *Der Besessene*, 38-39.

[55]   Twelftree, *Jesus*, 75; cf. 155.

[56]   With regard to the plea for lenience, see Pesch, "Healing," 363-65; idem, *Der Besessene*, 34-36; Twelftree, *Jesus*, 23, 51, 154-55.

very unusual. Normally, the activity of the demons is restricted to a non-specified plea for lenience, but here they present a specific request for an *epipompe*.[57] The observation of this combination makes one legitimately ask "whether this distinctive feature points to a dislocation in the tradition."[58] Have we, finally, come across corroborative evidence to our observation that the whole scene with the pigs can be deleted without harming the inner coherence of the story?

If we hypothetically ask what effect a secondary introduction of the episode with the pigs eventually would have on the story, it is not difficult to give a fairly exact answer. Being classified in the Torah as an unclean animal, strictly forbidden for food (Lev 11:7-8; Deut 14:8; cf. Isa 65:4; 66:17), by the time of the first century CE the pig had become the very symbol of paganism to be avoided at any price in the eyes of all Jews. Probably, the violent measures of the Seleucids during the reign of Antiochus IV Epiphanes (175–163 BCE) to force the Jews to sacrifice and eat pigs and the vigorous Jewish resistance against this suppression (cf. 1 Macc 1:47; 2 Macc 6:2, 5; 6:18-7:42) had contributed to making the pig such a prominent token of pagan uncleanness. Besides the story of the Gerasene demoniac, pigs are mentioned in only three other texts in the New Testament (Matt 7:6; Luke 15:15-16 and 2 Pet 2:22 [ὖς]). In all these texts the pig is associated with paganism in a way that corresponds to the current Jewish sentiments. Hence, Franz Annen's conclusion to his extensive *religionsgeschichtliche* investigation about pigs is justified: "Für das zeitgenössische Judentum wie für die frühen Judenchristen, ist das Schwein das Aushängeschild, das Kennzeichen für die Heiden."[59] Consequently, the effect of introducing a herd of

---

57   Usually, *if* there is someone pleading for an *epipompe* that is the suffering possessed human himself. Often there is no plea related to the *epipompe* at all; then it just takes the form of a command on the part of the exorcist. "It is the amalgamation and combination of the two which constitutes the distinctiveness of the Markan narrative" (Pesch, "Healing," 367; cf. idem, *Der Besessene*, 38).

58   Pesch, "Healing," 367. His German original in *Der Besessene*, 38 reads: "Es bleibt zu fragen, ob diese Eigenart nicht . . . eine traditionsgeschichtliche Verwerfung sichtbar werden läßt."

59   Annen, *Heil*, 173. In his investigation of what he labels the "Anschauungshorizont" of the text, i.e. the very "Komplex von Anschauungen . . ., die einen bestimmten Bereich des geistigen, kulturellen, religiösen Lebens der betreffenden Gesellschaft umfassen und von denen aus ein bestimmter Text verfaßt und daher zu

pigs into a story about the exorcism of a non-Jewish person, and assigning to them the role of being the new abode of the exorcised demon(s), would be to focus more strongly and dramatically on the confrontation between the Jewish exorcist—the "son of the most high God" (Mark 5:7)—and the uncleanness related to paganism.

So far I have consistently spoken of "the Gerasene demoniac", respectively—in the conjectured introduction of the pre-Markan version—"a man from Gerasa," seemingly taking for granted that the man Jesus encountered was related to the famous city of Gerasa, situated east of Jordan near the river Jabbok, about 55 km south east of the Sea of Galilee, and belonging to the Decapolis (cf. Mark 5:20).[60] But this localisation is definitely no matter of course because the textual witnesses to the synoptic Gospels in Mark 5:1 and in the parallel references in Matt 8:28 and Luke 8:26 display a variation of alternative readings, among which ἡ χώρα τῶν Γερασηνῶν ("the region of the Gerasenes"), ἡ χώρα τῶν Γαδαρηνῶν ("the region of the Gadarenes") and ἡ χώρα τῶν Γεργεσηνῶν ("the region of the Gergasenes") are the most important. Today there seems to be a clear consensus among textual critics in favour of Γαδαρηνῶν as the original reading in Matt 8:28;[61] thus, the first evangelist relates the incident to the town of Gadara, also belonging to the Decapolis, but situated less than ten km south east of the Sea of Galilee.[62] Perhaps most difficult to decide is the case of Luke 8:26, 37. In the first two editions of the Greek New Testament (1966 and 1968) the variant Γεργεσηνῶν was given preference, but this has been changed in the

---

verstehen ist" (133), he discusses the two themes of "Dämonologie und exorzistische Praktiken" (135-58) and "Die Schweine" (162-73).

60   For the history of Gerasa, see E. Schürer, *The History of the Jewish People in the Age of Jesus Christ (175 B.C.–A.D. 135)* (3 vols., rev. ed.; Edinburgh: T. & T. Clark, 1973-87) 2.149-55; and for the archaeology S. Applebaum and A. Segal, "Gerasa," *The New Encyclopedia of Archaeological Excavations in the Holy Land* (4 vols.; New York: Simon & Schuster, 1993) 2.470-79. For Decapolis, cf. Schürer, *History*, 2.125-27, and S. Thomas Parker, "The Decapolis Revisited," *JBL* 94 (1975) 437-41.

61   Cf. the text and the critical apparatus in Nestle-Aland[26/27], UBSGNT[4], and the argument in B. M. Metzger, *A Textual Commentary on the Greek New Testament* (corrected ed., London and New York: United Bible Societies, 1975) 23-24.

62   See Schürer, *History*, 2.132-36, and, for the archaeology of the site, Y. Hirschfeld, with M. Avi-Yonah, "Ḥammat Gader," *The New Encyclopedia of Archaeological Excavations in the Holy Land*, 2.565-73.

third and fourth editions to Γερασηνῶν.[63] When it comes to the Markan text, for example, Robert H. Gundry has recently advocated the reading Γεργεσηνῶν, i.e. localising the incident in modern Kursi, situated at the eastern side of the Sea of Galilee.[64] However, in spite of some impressive textual witnesses and the obvious advantage of a locale very close to the shore of the Sea of Galilee, the textual evidence in its totality favours Γερασηνῶν.[65] Actually, the acute geographical problem of the reference to "the region of the Gerasenes" in a story presupposing the eastern shore of the Sea of Galilee as its scene strengthens this reading considerably as *lectio difficilior* among the extant variants.[66] The Matthean alternative reading Γαδαρηνῶν is probably due to a conscious editorial change of the text that the evangelist found in his Markan source, and, thus, likely represents a very early witness of the perplexity which the reading Γερασηνῶν caused.[67] On this background, therefore, I join the conclusion of Rudolf Pesch, Franz Annen, and John P. Meier, among others, deciding in favour of "Gerasenes" as the original reading of Mark and his source.[68]

---

[63]   Identical with Nestle-Aland[26/27]; cf. Metzger, *Commentary*, 145.

[64]   Gundry, *Mark*, 255-56. For the archaeology of the site, cf. V. Tzaferis, "Kursi," *The New Encyclopedia of Archaeological Excavations in the Holy Land*, 3.893-96.

[65]   Cf. the text and the critical apparatus in Nestle-Aland[26/27], UBSGNT[4], and Metzger, *Commentary*, 84.

[66]   Gundry (*Mark*, 256) argues, admittedly, cleverly on the basis of internal criteria in favour of "Gergasenes," but in Origen we have an explicit confirmation that in his days and under his influence this reading was introduced to the displacement of "Gerasenes," consciously based on geographical and topographical considerations; cf. T. Baarda, "Gadarenes, Gerasenes, Gergesenes and the 'Diatessaron' Traditions," in E. Earle Ellis and M. Wilcox (eds.), *Neotestamentica et Semitica: Studies in Honour of Matthew Black* (Edinburgh: T. & T. Clark, 1969) 181-97, esp. 183-88; Annen, *Heil*, 204.

[67]   Whereas the region of Gerasa certainly never extended as far as the Sea of Galilee, this might have been the case for the region of Gadara or is, at least, imaginable from the geographical distance. Even though the flight of the herdsmen from the shore of the lake to the town and the arrival of people from there, described in v. 14, still presupposes a very long distance if the town is identified with Gadara, it is not totally incredible as is the case of Gerasa, more than 50 km away. Cf. Annen, *Heil*, 202-203.

[68]   Pesch, "Healing," 352-53; idem, *Der Besessene*, 17-19; Annen, *Heil*, 201-206; Meier, *Marginal Jew*, 2.651.

The demonstration that "Gerasenes" is original in our story reveals a geographical contradiction within it between the inland localisation of Gerasa without any lake in its surrounding region and the presupposed "sea" (θάλασσα) at the site of the event. The role of the sea is, however, restricted to the second scene with the pigs episode (cf. p. 284 above). I have repeatedly claimed that this scene can be dropped without harming the inner coherence of the exorcism story, but so far we had not found any cogent justification for doing so. Now, this has suddenly changed, because we realise that with references both to Gerasa, or the region of the Gerasenes, and to the sea into which the pigs run and are drowned, the text is incoherent. We have already concluded that Γερασηνῶν belongs to the original text, and the question then arises whether the omission of the episode with the pigs might be justified to solve the problem of coherence.

In the search for an answer let me, once more, pick up the thread of the *epipompe*, discussed above. There we noted that the demons' violent effect on the pigs is a feature in complete concordance with general ideas connected to this phenomenon. In line with this Pesch discusses whether the mention of the sea in the narrative has in fact been prompted by the very idea of the *epipompe*, taking due regard to "how widespread the idea of banishment of demons into the sea was."[69] If, as Pesch assumes, the herdsmen and the pigs belonged to the oldest version of the story, functioning as witnesses to Jesus' miracle (cf. pp. 286-87 above), then there would have been a point of connection even in the original version which the dramatic shaping of the *epipompe* banishing the demons in the sea could have used as its point of departure.[70] Of course, it is historically imaginable

---

[69]   Pesch, "Healing," 367: "There is probably still some echo of the idea of an *epipompe* banishing the demons into the sea. This may have prompted the introduction of the sea into the narrative . . .; the *epipompe* banishing demons into the sea is the one which really renders the destructive spirits harmless and banishes them to their own element, the chaos." Cf. idem, *Der Besessene*, 39.

[70]   Pesch ("Healing," 353-54, 370; idem, *Der Besessene*, 19, 43) contemplates whether even the herd had a function in the original version in the sense that "the exit of the demon was originally demonstrated in the narrative by the stampede of the herd of swine" ("Healing," 370), but concludes that this is improbable. If this element had been original, the further dramatizing of the *epipompe* to a destruction in the sea, would have been particularly easy to explain, he correctly notes. But according to Pesch the introduction of the destruction is sufficiently explicable also without this precedent, and he ascribes this innovation to the alleged second stage in

that a herd of pigs might have been grazing in some of the hills adjacent to the city of Gerasa when an exorcism occurred there. But it remains unverifiable and speculative to pose an uninvolved presence of a herd of pigs as the historical and traditio-historical point of departure for the shaping of the episode with the pigs in the later stages of the story. Thus, if we propose to delete this episode in order to regain a coherent story, we must be able to demonstrate that both elements functioning as the new abode of the exorcised demons—the pigs and the sea—plausibly can be conceived of as secondary innovations prompted by the introduction of an *epipompe* with the goal of demonstrating more strongly (than in earlier stages of the story) the complete triumph of Jesus over the demons and the impure pagan setting to which they belong.

As far as I can see, Franz Annen has sufficiently explained how the story could have developed in this way in the course of its transmission (cf. pp. 293-94 above). Already some of the original elements related to the demoniac are for a Jew associated with paganism and uncleanness; we can note particularly the use of the term "unclean spirit(s)" instead of "demon(s)" (vv. 2, 13), the man's dwelling in tombs (vv. 3, 5; cf. Num 19:16, 18) and his nakedness (to be inferred from v. 15).[71] Narrative elements like these and the pagan setting of the exorcism of a gentile demoniac in gentile territory to the east of Jordan gave the story a strong colouring from its inception; and the introduction of the pigs episode was clearly in the line with this tendency. By introducing a new scene in which the pig as the symbol *par excellence* of paganism and the sea as the appropriate *chaos* abode of the demons are the decisive elements, some pre-Markan narrator(s) has/have midrashically expanded and thereby further emphasised the contrast between the distasteful paganism and the liberation from it which Jesus brings in his triumphant exorcism.

My concluding judgement is that we have a sufficient basis for declaring the episode with the pigs in vv. 11-13*—plus the mention

---

the transmission of the story (cf. n. 43 above): "[T]he demons want to enter the swine, the symbol of Gentile uncleanness. The reference to the herd of swine, already provided by the original version, is skilfully exploited by the narrator (v. 11) and expanded into a new scene by the addition of concrete popular magical conceptions" ("Healing," 372; cf. *Der Besessene*, 46).

[71]   See Annen, *Heil*, 159-62, 182-84, for a more elaborate presentation.

of the "seaside" in the conjectured introduction (cf. θάλασσα in v. 1) and of the fleeing herdsmen in v. 14*—a secondary element in the story of Jesus' encounter with a Gerasene demoniac.[72]

THE HISTORICITY OF THE ENCOUNTER

"Without the panicky pigs and their dip in the deep, the environs of Gerasa . . . create no problem for the story."[73] As a matter of fact, exactly this geographical designation is decisive evidence for the historical judgement. If the whole story were a later Christian invention, why is it located in the region of the Gerasenes?[74] To be noted are also other details that surpass standard stereotypic features of exorcism stories and possibly hint at further unique and historically founded elements of the story. I think in particular at the description of the demoniac's state, which suggests that in this instance Jesus was confronted with an especially severe case of demon possession.[75] Neither the indisputable presence of form-

---

[72]   Gundry (*Mark*, 257-58), and Twelftree (*Jesus*, 74-76) consider the pigs episode to be an integral, necessary part of the story and, accordingly, oppose strongly the isolation or omission of it. Twelftree accepts the reading "Gerasenes" (73), but, as far as I can see, he totally ignores the whole problem of the localisation. This is intolerable, all the more so, because he advocates the historicity of the incident. On the contrary, Pesch (cf. above), Annen, *Heil*, 192-93, and Meier, *Marginal Jew*, 2.640-41 (n. 32), 651, 665 (n. 18) view this episode as a secondary addition to the tradition. These authors also cite and refer to other scholars supporting this position; cf. Pesch, *Der Besessene*, 39-40; Meier, *Marginal Jew*, 2.641, and in Annen, *Heil*, particularly his research history survey (cf. n. 45 above) of those who assume behind the story a historical kernel which secondarily has been expanded with new unhistorical material: "Eine gewisse Einigkeit herrscht . . . darüber, . . . daß die Schweine-Episode erst in einem späteren Stadium dazugekommen sei" (95, concluding 90-95).

[73]   Meier, *Marginal Jew*, 2.651.

[74]   Cf. the mention of Decapolis in v. 20, as well, in the New Testament only paralleled in Mark 7:31 and Matt 4:25. Meier (*Marginal Jew*, 2.653) correctly notes: "The sheer oddity of the geographical designation—unparalleled in the Bible and early Christian tradition—may reflect a singular historical event. It could be that the unique connection of one of Jesus' miracles with a particular pagan city in the Decapolis, at a good distance from the Sea of Galilee and Jesus' customary area of activity, may have stuck in the collective memory of Jesus' disciples precisely because of the exorcism's unusual venue."

[75]   I will not, however, exclude possible influence from Scriptural passages, in particular Isaiah 65 and the description of Samson's exceptional strength in Judges

critically typical features (cf. pp. 286-88 above) nor the influence of post-Easter theological convictions[76] can undermine the basic probability that the origin of this tradition is to be found in an authentic exorcism performed by Jesus.

There is a broad consensus among scholars that Jesus actually worked as an exorcist. The total weight of the accumulated evidence of a number of exorcism stories (Mark 1:21-28 par.; 7:24-30 par.; 9:14-29 parr.; Matt 9:32-33; Matt 12:22-23 = Luke 11:14), the brief mention of exorcisms in summary reports (e.g. Mark 1:32-34, 39; 3:7-12[77]), sayings of Jesus referring to or presupposing a ministry of exorcisms (in particular Matt 12:27-28 = Luke 11:19-20; Mark 3:27; Luke 13:32), and affirmations from opponents that Jesus performed exorcisms (Mark 3:22 = Matt 12:24 = Luke 11:15), is very impressive, indeed.[78] In his survey of the research on the miracles of

---

13-16, and from popular notions of frightening effects of demon possession. Cf. the considerations of Annen, *Heil*, 192. Hence, we are well advised in taking note of Meier's warning: "Even if we take the description at face value, all we can be sure of is that Jesus was facing a profoundly disturbed individual. Precise diagnoses over the chasm of 2,000 years (e.g., the demoniac was a paranoid schizophrenic) are speculative at the best" (*Marginal Jew*, 2.666 n. 22).

76 For example, the description of the demoniac falling down in front of Jesus as a *proskynese* in v. 6 is surely a Christian interpretation, but still it does not exclude the possibility that the confrontation with the exorcist had such a disturbing effect on the demoniac that he fell (cf. Twelftree, *Jesus*, 81, 147-48). Whether the formulation of the demon's address to Jesus in v. 7, "son of the most high God," presupposes a Christian Christological confession, or whether it is imaginable as part of the attempt by the demon(iac) to defend itself against and gain control over its adversary by using his name, is disputed. Twelftree (*Jesus*) argues vigorously in favour of the second understanding, see 64-68 (referring to the parallel in Mark 1:24), 81-82, 149-52.

77 Note in particular the reference to Mary Magdalene in Luke 8:2 and the discussion in Meier, *Marginal Jew*, 2.657-59.

78 In spite of a generally unsatisfactory and too superficial treatment of the historical questions related to the single units of evidence, still, Twelftree's monograph on Jesus as an exorcist contributes in its sum to an affirmative evaluation regarding the historical Jesus. See in particular his §16 "Was Jesus an Exorcist?" (*Jesus*, 136-42) and the "Conclusions" (225-28), headed by the justified statement: "The first result we can record from our study is that we are able unhesitatingly to support the view that Jesus was an exorcist" (225). Among the numerous contributions to the discussion of the historicity of Jesus' miracles during recent years concluding in the affirmative with regard to his exorcisms let me mention Evans' chap. 5 "Jesus and Jewish Miracle Stories" in his *Jesus*, 213-43,

Jesus since the rise of form criticism, with special emphasis on the last three decades, Barry L. Blackburn concludes: "[T]hat Jesus acted as an exorcist and healer can easily be described as the consensus of the modern period."[79] When it comes to the individual miracle and exorcism stories, however, scholars are generally very reserved and hesitant to give any positive affirmation of a basic historicity.[80] John P. Meier is one of the few who have undertaken a detailed analysis of individual exorcism stories with the goal of "assessing the possible historical elements in individual cases."[81] His conclusion is that the story of the possessed boy (Mark 9:14-29 parr.) and the brief reference to Mary Magdalene's exorcism (Luke 8:2) are the two strongest individual cases preserved in the gospels that can be traced back to historical events in Jesus' ministry.[82] Next to these two stories, Meier ranks our story of the Gerasene demoniac as third in terms of historical probability, "though in this case the arguments are less probative."[83] Also Franz Annen shows a similar reservation, but concludes that, all in all, the localisation of the story likely reflects its historical origin.[84]

---

and Meier, *Marginal Jew*, 2.404-23, 457-76 (a detailed treatment of Matt 12:28 = Luke 11:20 and Mark 3:24-27 par.), 617-45 (chap. 19, addressing the "global question" of the historicity of Jesus' miracles).

[79]   B. L. Blackburn, "The Miracles of Jesus," in B. Chilton and C. A. Evans (eds.), *Studying the Historical Jesus: Evaluations of the State of Current Research* (NTTS 19; Leiden: Brill, 1994) 353-94, here 362.

[80]   Cf. Blackburn, "Miracles," 363-68, concluding: "That at least a few of the miracle stories rest on reminiscence is commonly held" (368). The story of Jesus' encounter with the Gerasene demoniac is not included among those narratives specified as possibly resting on a degree of reminiscence.

[81]   Meier, *Marginal Jew*, 2.648. In his chap. 20, "Jesus' Exorcisms" (646-77), he discusses seven individual "specimens" of reported exorcisms, namely the five exorcism stories, starting with Mark 1:21-28, mentioned above plus the story of the Gerasene demoniac and the reference to Mary Magdalene (cf. n. 77 above).

[82]   Meier, *Marginal Jew*, 2.660-61. Meier views Mark 7:24-30 and Matt 9:32-33 as Christian redactional creations, but is uncertain with regard to Matt 12:22-23 par. and Mark 1:21-28 par.

[83]   Meier, *Marginal Jew*, 2.661; cf. 653: Meier is inclined to believe "that an exorcism performed by Jesus near Gerasa lies at the basis of the Gospel narrative in Mark 5:1-20. I readily admit, though, that there is no hard proof in the matter. Beyond this, I doubt that much can be said about the historical event; too many layers of literary activity and theological imagination have been superimposed."

[84]   Annen, *Heil*, 197: "Ich bin . . . der Ansicht, daß die Historizität einer Dämonenaustreibung Jesu in Gerasa oder Umgebung bzw. an einem Gerasener

EXORCISM AND PAGANISM

Exorcistic practice played a considerable role in the period of the Early and Old Church.[85] With regard to the reception of the story of the Gerasene demoniac, in which the confrontation with and the liberation from the realm of pagan uncleanness is such a dominating perspective,[86] it is interesting to note that in the Old Church the phenomenon of demon possession was predominantly related to paganism and the idolatry connected with it.[87] As it probably was the miracles, including the exorcisms, that at the most attracted the crowds and made them follow Jesus,[88] the same is true for the ministry of the church during the first centuries: "Excorcism [sic] remained important throughout the Old Church period, partly because excorcisms [sic]—more than healings—were regarded as manifestations of direct and unambiguous confrontations between Christ and Satan, in which Christ's victory could be seen by all."[89] The dramatic story of how Jesus had once triumphed over the multiform demon "Legion" and thereby liberated the poor gentile man who had been suffering so severely under its possession could definitely serve as a motivation and an inspiration for the missionary endeavour of the Old Church when it confronted idolatry and proved victorious in successful exorcisms.

---

zwar keineswegs sicher ist, aber doch recht vieles für sich hat."

[85]   Cf., for example, G. H. Twelftree, *Christ Triumphant: Exorcism Then and Now* (London: Hodder and Stoughton, 1985) 87-134.

[86]   Cf. the discussion of the pigs episode above and for a detailed argument that this perspective is the key to the message of the story; cf. Annen, *Heil.*

[87]   My Norwegian colleague, Prof. Oskar Skarsaune has recently published an interesting article focusing on this aspect, "Besettelse og demonutdrivelse i den oldkirkelige og nytestamentlige litteratur," *Norsk Tidsskrift for Misjon* 51 (1997) 157-71 [English: "Demon Possession and Exorcism in the Literature of the New Testament and the Early Church"]. I quote from the English summary: "In early Christian litterature [sic] the phenomenon of demon possession is not primarily seen as a problem of illness or health in the modern sense, but rather as one possible consequence of idolatry, and therefore interpreted within a framework of religious conflict . . . demon possession is primarily seen as common among Pagans" (170-71).

[88]   Cf. Evans, *Jesus*, 222-23.

[89]   Skarsaune, "Besettelse," 171.

BEDEUTUNG UND RELIGIONSGESCHICHTLICHER HINTERGRUND DER VERWANDLUNG JESU (MARKUS 9:2-8)

Dieter Zeller

APORIEN DER EXEGESE

Die Perikope von der Verwandlung Jesu[1] scheint auf den ersten

---

[1] Eine neuere Bibliographie in Auswahl bietet T. F. Best, "The Transfigura-tion: A Select Bibliography," *JETS* 24 (1981) 157-61. Ich nenne die für mich wichtigsten Veröffentlichungen zur Geschichte als solcher und ihrer markinischen Bearbeitung: E. Lohmeyer, "Die Verklärung Jesu nach dem Markus–Evangelium," *ZNW* 21 (1922) 185-215; C. Masson, "La transfiguration de Jésus (Marc 9,2–13)," *RTP* 97 (1964) 1-14; W. Gerber, "Die Metamorphose Jesu, Mark. 9,2f. par.," *TZ* 23 (1967) 385-95; H. C. Kee, "The Transfiguration in Mark: Epiphany or Apocalyptic Vision?" in J. Reumann (Hg.), *Understanding the Sacred Text* (M. S. Enslin Festschrift; Valley Forge: Judson, 1972) 135-52; U. B. Müller, "Die christologische Absicht des Markusevangeliums und die Verklärungsgeschichte," *ZNW* 64 (1973) 159-93; J. M. Nützel, *Die Verklärungserzählung im Markus-evangelium* (FB 6; Würzburg: Echter, 1973); W. L. Liefeld, "Theological Motifs in the Transfiguration Narrative," in R. N. Longenecker und M. C. Tenney (Hg.), *New Dimensions in New Testament Study* (Grand Rapids: Eerdmans, 1974) 162-79; F. H. Daniel, *The Transfiguration (Mk 9:2–13 and Par.)* (unpublished disser-tation; Nashville: Vanderbilt University, 1976); E. Nardoni, *La Transfiguración de Jesús y el diálogo sobre Elías según el Evangelio de San Marcos* (Teología 2; Buenos Aires: Patria Grande, 1976); B. D. Chilton, "The Transfiguration: Domini-cal Assurance and Apostolic Vision," *NTS* 27 (1981) 115-24; E. Best, "The Markan Redaction of the Transfiguration," in ders., *Disciples and Discipleship: Studies in the Gospel according to Mark* (Edinburgh: T. & T. Clark, 1982) 206-25; J. A. McGuckin, *The Transfiguration of Christ in Scripture and Tradition* (SBEC 9; Lewiston und Queenston: Mellen, 1986); B. Chilton, "Transfiguration," *ABD* 6 (1992) 640-42; A. del Agua, "The Narrative of the Transfiguration as a Derashic Scenification of a Faith Confession (Mark 9.2-8 Par)," *NTS* 39 (1993) 340-54; J. E. Fossum, "Ascensio, Metamorphosis," in ders., *The Image of the Invisible God* (NTOA 30; Fribourg: Universitätsverlag; Göttingen: Vandenhoeck & Ruprecht, 1995) 71-94; M. Öhler, "Die Verklärung (Mk 9:1-8): die Ankunft der Herrschaft Gottes auf der Erde," *NovT* 38 (1996) 197-217; ders., *Elia im Neuen Testament* (BZNW 88; Berlin: de Gruyter, 1997) 118-35; D. Zeller, "La métamorphose de Jésus comme épiphanie (Mc 9, 2-8)," in A. Marchadour (Hg.), *L'évangile exploré* (S. Légasse Festschrift; LD 166; Paris: Cerf, 1996) 167-86. Ich konzentriere mich dort auf das Motiv der Verwandlung.

Blick wenig geeignet, um an ihr das Programm "Authenticating the Activities of Jesus" durchzuführen. Schon formgeschichtlich ist sie nicht leicht einzuordnen. Gewiß haben wir es mit einem Erzähltext zu tun; doch steht darin überhaupt ein Tun Jesu, eine *activity*, im Mittelpunkt? Dies dürfte selbst dann nicht der Fall sein, wenn man mit G. Theißen die Verklärung strukturell unter "Wunder" faßt, dessen Adressat allerdings nicht andere Menschen oder Mächte, sondern der Wundertäter selbst ist.[2] Dann müßte man μετεμορφώθη V. 2c konsequent mit "und er verwandelte sich" übersetzen, was grammatikalisch möglich ist. Angesichts der gezielten Initiative Jesu in V. 2ab liegt diese Wiedergabe sogar nahe.[3] Doch dann treten andere Handlungsträger in den Vordergrund: Mose und Elija, der reagierende Petrus, die Stimme aus der Wolke. In der Proklamation Jesu als geliebter Sohn liegt zweifellos die Pointe der ganzen Szene; hier wird das vorangegangene Geschehen gedeutet. So geht es nicht primär um ein Tun Jesu, sondern darum, daß Jesus in seinem wahren Sein den Jüngern offenbar wird. Deswegen heben manche Formgeschichtler solche "Jesus–Geschichten"—ein anderes Beispiel ist die Taufe Mk 1:9-11—vom übrigen Erzählstoff ab und suchen sie unter der Kategorie des "Mythos" zu begreifen.[4]

Wie steht es dann aber mit der *authenticity?* Die Taufperikope enthält wenigstens ein unbezweifelbares Faktum: daß Jesus von Johannes getauft wurde. Woran kann man sich dagegen bei Mk 9:2-8 halten? Das einzige Konkretum scheinen die "sechs Tage" zu sein, die den Aufstieg Jesu in Beziehung setzen zu einem vorangehenden Ereignis, wohl dem Gespräch mit den Jüngern 8:27–9:1. Deshalb steht die Angabe jedoch von vornherein unter dem Verdacht redaktioneller Bildung, obwohl Markus solche genauen Angaben erst

---

2   G. Theißen, *Urchristliche Wundergeschichten* (SNT 8; Gütersloh: Mohn, 1974) 121-25; 102-105 spricht er von Epiphanie, wenn die Göttlichkeit einer Person nicht nur an ihren Auswirkungen oder Begleiterscheinungen, sondern an ihr selbst erscheint.

3   Gegen die vorschnelle Annahme eines "theologischen Passivs" vgl. Zeller, "La métamorphose," 169. Nur Lk 9:28 weiß, daß Jesus auf den Berg stieg, um zu beten.

4   Vgl. G. Bornkamm, "Formen und Gattungen II im NT," *RGG*[3] 2.999-1005, 1001, im Gefolge von M. Dibelius, *Die Formgeschichte des Evangeliums* (Tübingen: Mohr [Siebeck], [5]1966) Kap. X, bes. 275-76. Theißen (*Wundergeschichten*, 106) präzisiert: eher ein episodaler Ausschnitt aus mythischem Geschehen, der einen menschlichen Standort voraussetzt.

wieder in der Passionsgeschichte macht. Auch können die verschiedenen Versuche, sie als feststehenden Topos zu erweisen und damit für die vormarkinische Überlieferung zu retten,[5] nicht überzeugen. Ältere Autoren hatten hier noch die Spur einer historischen Erinnerung gesehen.[6] Diese beziehe sich auf ein Erlebnis, das man sich oft nach psychologischem Ermessen zurechtschneidert. Harnack etwa hatte die objektiv geschilderte Verwandlung auf eine Vision der Jünger bzw. des Petrus reduziert. Dazu regt freilich der Terminus "es erschienen ihnen" in V. 4 an; aber auch hier denkt der Autor an einen mehreren zugleich sichtbaren Vorgang. Zum mindesten müssen wir seine Darstellung und heutige Versuche einer psychologischen Erklärung unterscheiden. Das jüngste Beispiel eines solchen Reduktionismus bietet J. Murphy-O'Connor. Nach einer abenteuerlichen Literarkritik, wonach in der ersten Hälfte die lukanische Version ursprünglicher als Markus sein soll, in der zweiten aber ein "editor" sekundär Lukas dem Markus angeglichen habe, vermutet er als historischen Kern:

> Jesus decided to withdraw to the top of a mountain to pray about his problem [das Leidenmüssen]. As he prayed, he got the answer—and his face lit up! The glory that Peter and the others saw (Luke 9:32) was the radiant joy that accompanies the resolution of a terrible perplexity.[7]

Mehr als solch ein menschliches Strahlen Jesu darf der Dominikanerexeget die Jünger nicht erfahren lassen; denn er sieht die Schwierigkeit, die ein wörtliches Verständnis der Begebenheit mit

---

5   Zuletzt Fossum, "Ascensio," 79-82. Für Offenbarungsempfang am siebten Tag gibt es zwar einige Beispiele; aber dazu müßte man "nach sechs Tagen" exklusiv verstehen, was wegen Mk 8,31 nicht geht. Die sechs Tage werden bei Mk nicht als Vorbereitungszeit erkennbar. Auch in der rabbinischen Auslegung von Exod 24:16 (*b. Yom.* 4b) erfolgt der Aufstieg des Mose am siebten Tag. *Tg. Ps.-J.* datiert die Ereignisse Exodus 19–24 auf den 6. Tag des Monats, ohne das ausdrücklich zu betonen.

6   A. von Harnack, "Die Verklärungsgeschichte Jesu, der Bericht des Paulus (I. Kor. 15,3ff) und die beiden Christusvisionen des Petrus," *Sitzungsberichte der preußischen Akademie der Wissenschaften* (1922) 62-80, 74ff; J. Blinzler, *Die neutestamentlichen Berichte über die Verklärung Jesu* (NTAbh 17.4; Münster: Aschendorff, 1937); H. Baltensweiler, *Die Verklärung Jesu* (ATANT 33; Zürich: Zwingli, 1959). Ähnlich wie Harnack N. Smith, "The Origin and History of the Transfiguration Story," *USQR* 36 (1980) 39-44.

7   J. Murphy-O'Connor, "What Really Happened at the Transfiguration?" *BibRev* 3 (1987) 8-21.

sich bringt: Wie konnten die Jünger, besonders Petrus, nach einer überwältigenden Schau himmlischer Herrlichkeit an Jesus in der Passion wenig später versagen?[8]

Der Anstoß wäre beseitigt, wenn man mit R. Bultmann in unserer Geschichte eine vorgezogene Osterlegende sehen könnte.[9] Damit wird aber wieder das objektive Geschehen zum Inhalt einer Vision und der eigentliche Iktus verfehlt, daß nämlich schon einmal mitten im Leben Jesu solcher Glanz an ihm sichtbar war (s.u.). Ein neuerer Versuch stellt die Verklärung wenigstens funktional den Erscheinungen des Auferstandenen an die Seite; auch sie habe legitimierende Funktion—nämlich für die drei in V. 2 genannten Jünger.[10] Somit wäre wenigstens ein früher nachösterlicher "Sitz im Leben" gesichert. Allerdings läuft die Geschichte in V. 7 weniger auf eine Legitimation der Jünger als auf eine Legitimation Jesu zu. Außerdem ist die Auswahl der Drei möglicherweise redaktionell (wie 5:37, 40; 14:33), wie auch das κατ' ἰδίαν die Hand des Markus verrät. Sie entspricht auch nicht einer aufweisbaren geschichtlichen Konstellation nach Ostern. Denn daß der Gal 2:9 unter den drei "Säulen" genannte Herrenbruder Jakobus an die Stelle des 42 n. Chr. hingerichteten Zebedaiden Jakobus getreten sei, ist nur eine vage Hypothese.[11] Das einzige Argument dafür, daß die Drei schon

---

8   Vgl. ebd. 9.

9   R. Bultmann, *Geschichte der synoptischen Tradition* (Göttingen: Vandenhoeck & Ruprecht, [6]1964) 278-81 nach Wellhausen, Loisy, Bousset u.a. Weitere Vertreter im Ergänzungsheft [4]1971, 92. Das Für und Wider diskutiert R. H. Stein, "Is the Transfiguration (Mark 9:2–8) a Misplaced Resurrection Account?" *JBL* 95 (1976) 79-96; neu gedruckt in ders., *Gospels and Tradition: Studies on Redaction Criticism of the Synoptic Gospels* (Grand Rapids: Baker, 1991) 97-119. Gegen diese Lösung auch R. H. Gundry, *Mark: A Commentary on His Apology for the Cross* (Grand Rapids: Eerdmans, 1993) 471-74; M. D. Hooker, *The Gospel according to Saint Mark* (BNTC; London: Black, 1991) 213-14, 219.

10   D. Wenham und A. D. A. Moses, "'There are some standing here . . . ': Did They Become the 'Reputed Pillars' of the Jerusalem Church? Some Reflections on Mark 9:1, Galatians 2:9 and the Transfiguration," *NovT* 36 (1994) 146-63, nach einer Anregung von B. Chilton. Unglücklich ist die Beziehung von Mk 9:1 auf die "Säulen." Fairerweise notieren die Autoren auch immer gleich die Schwierigkeiten ihrer "admittedly speculative thesis" (158).

11   Etwa bei H. Kraft, *Die Entstehung des Christentums* (Darmstadt: Wissenschaftliche Buchgesellschaft, 1981) 230, 275. Aber dann sollte man Jakobus in Gal 2:9 nicht an der Spitze, sondern nach Johannes erwarten. Gal 1:19 läßt annehmen, daß der Herrenbruder sich schon vor 42 einer führenden Rolle näherte.

vormarkinisch als Zeugen genannt waren, ist die numerische Entsprechung zu den drei Himmelsgestalten.

ÜBERLIEFERUNGSGESCHICHTLICHE ANHALTSPUNKTE

Eine Analyse, die sich hinter den vorliegenden Text zurücktasten möchte, muß dafür Hinweise im Text selber finden bzw. untersuchen, wie er in einen größeren Zusammenhang eingebaut ist. Möglicherweise helfen auch Parallelversionen, eine ursprünglichere Gestalt herauszuschälen. In Mk 9:6 spricht vor allem die auktoriale Erklärung für die seltsame Rede des Petrus dafür, daß der Evangelist V. 5 schon kannte; dabei kann aber V. 6b durchaus eine topische Jüngerreaktion bewahren. Auch die Tatsache, daß der V. 4 erscheinende Elija in Vv. 12-13 mit dem Täufer identifiziert ist, verrät eine frühere Traditionsstufe des Geschehens auf dem Berg.[12] Sonst fügt es sich aber so bruchlos in den näheren Kontext (das Messiasbekenntnis des Petrus mit der anschließenden Belehrung von Jüngern und Volksmassen 8:27–9:1; das Gespräch beim Abstieg 9:9-13) ein, daß die Annahme eines ursprünglichen Zusammenhangs von Vv. 1 und 11-13[13] als überholt gelten muß. Die Elijafrage knüpft nahtlos an das Stichwort "von den Toten auferstehen," das eine allgemeine Totenerweckung suggeriert, an. Leider tragen auch die Fassungen des Matthäus und Lukas nicht dazu bei, eine Vorform der markinischen Erzählung zu eruieren. Die *minor agreements*,[14] die McGuckin dazu nutzen will,[15] sind gewiß auffällig, aber erklärbar.[16] Noch weniger ist zu vermuten, daß die späte Paraphrase in 2 Petrus 1:16-18, die Daniel heranzieht, Ursprünglicheres enthält.

---

[12]   Vgl. Lohmeyer, "Verklärung," 213.

[13]   Bultmann, *Geschichte*, 279. Die Frage V. 11 entwickelt sich aber aus dem Streit V. 10 ähnlich wie Mk 9:14, 16; 12:8. Eine analoge Jüngersituation schildert Mk 9:43, wo freilich die Frage aus Furcht unterlassen wird.

[14]   Eine extensive Liste bei C. Niemand, *Studien zu den Minor Agreements der synoptischen Verklärungsperikopen* (EHS XXIII 352; Frankfurt am Main: Lang, 1982). Dagegen F. Fendler, *Studien zum Markusevangelium* (GTA 49; Göttingen: Vandenhoeck & Ruprecht, 1991) 180-84.

[15]   McGuckin, *Transfiguration*, 8-14.

[16]   Vgl. F. Neirynck, "Minor Agreements Matthew-Luke in the Transfiguration Story," in Neirynck, *Evangelica I* (BETL 60; Leuven: Peeters und Leuven University Press, 1982) 797-810; ders., "The Minor Agreements and the Two-Source Theory," in ders., *Evangelica II* (BETL 99; Leuven: Peeters und Leuven University Press, 1991) 3-42, bes. 34-40.

Die Untersuchung von Stil und Vokabular[17] kann mehrere
markinische Eigentümlichkeiten aufweisen (vor allem in Vv.
2ab, 5a,
6); sie stößt auch auf einige Hapaxlegomena (bei Markus, in den
Evangelien oder gar im Neuen Testament),[18] aber diese können noch
keine Tradition garantieren, wie die stark markinischer Redaktion
verdächtige Beschreibung V. 3 zeigt. Die Vokabelstatistik allein
genügt nicht; das belegen die recht unterschiedlichen Rekonstruk-
tionsversuche von Nützel und Daniel, die noch andere Kriterien zu
Hilfe nehmen müssen. Aber obwohl Markus das Stück sprachlich und
thematisch vollkommen in sein Evangelium integriert hat, fällt doch
die abwandelnde Wiederholung der Gottesstimme bei der Taufe (Mk
1:11) in V. 7bc auf. Ihre Formulierung dürfte dort ursprünglicher
sein.[19] Denn die Anredeform läßt noch am ehesten Ps 2:7 als
Grundlage erkennen; sollte aber 1:11 eher auf Jes 42:1 zurück-
zuführen sein, wie Lührmann meint, dann hat das Zitat noch sicherer
seinen Sitz in der Taufsituation mit der Geistverleihung. Was Gott
dort Jesus zusprach, wird jetzt den ausgewählten Jüngern verkündet.
An die Stelle des Nachsatzes "An dir habe ich mein Wohlgefallen"
tritt nun die Forderung "Auf ihn sollt ihr hören," die die ganze
autoritative Lehre Jesu im Evangelium im Auge hat. Wegen dieser
beabsichtigten Beziehungen kann die Stimme aus der Wolke kaum
vorredaktionell sein. Man hat deshalb in V. 7bcd eine markinische
Zutat gesehen; die Wolke habe ursprünglich nur die Funktion gehabt,
die himmlischen Gestalten zu verhüllen,[20] während das αὐτοῖς in
seinem jetzigen Bezug unsicher ist.[21] Dagegen spricht zunächst, daß

---

[17]   Außer Nützel, *Verklärungserzählung*, Kap. II, und Daniel, *Transfiguration*,
24-43 vgl. E. J. Pryke, *Redaktional Style in the Marcan Gospel* (SNTSMS 33;
Cambridge: University Press, 1978); und P. Dschulnigg, *Sprache, Redaktion und
Intention des Markus–Evangeliums* (SBB 11; Stuttgart: Katholisches Bibelwerk,
1984).

[18]   ἀναφέρειν, ὑψηλός, μεταμορφοῦσθαι, στίλβειν, γναφεύς, λευκαίνειν,
ὠφθῆναι, συλλαλεῖν, σκηνή, ἔκφοβος γενέσθαι, ἐπισκιάζειν, ἐξάπινα.

[19]   Gegen M. Horstmann, *Studien zur markinischen Christologie* (NTAbh NF
6; Münster: Aschendorff, 1969) 91-92; und D. Lührmann, *Das Markusevangelium*
(HNT 3; Tübingen: Mohr [Siebeck], 1987) 155, nach dem 1:11 aus der Verklärung
vorgezogen ist. Er hat aber inzwischen selbst die Inkonsistenz gegenüber 37-38
bemerkt.

[20]   Nützel, *Verklärungserzählung*, 151-52, nach Masson, Baltensweiler u.a.
Ebenso J. Zmijewski, "Die Sohn-Gottes-Prädikationen im Markusevangelium,"
SNTU 12 (1987) 5-34, 28-31.

[21]   Im jetzigen Zusammenhang schließt es die Jünger mindestens ein, die in

das Erscheinen von Mose und Elija nach Deutung verlangt[22] und das verfehlte Wort des Petrus eine Klarstellung erfordert. Aber genau besehen bleibt die Erscheinung nach wie vor rätselhaft; die Gottesstimme führt über das Vv. 2c-4 Erzählte hinaus. Während dort Jesus nur auf gleicher Ebene mit den alttestamentlichen Gestalten steht, wird er jetzt als der Sohn Gottes über sie hinausgehoben. Die Vermutung ist also erlaubt, daß die jetzige Spitze der Perikope in V. 7 eine vorhergehende Offenbarungsszene verdrängt hat, die vielleicht noch in dem inhaltslosen V. 4b rudimentär zu erkennen ist. Weiter wird man in der Dekomposition aber kaum gehen können;[23] und da wir bezüglich der Vorform des Textes im Dunkeln tappen, muß eine Interpretation nun alle drei Momente zusammenbringen: die Verwandlung Jesu, seine Gleichstellung mit Elija und Mose und die krönende Gottesrede am Schluß.

GEGEN REDAKTIONSGESCHICHTLICHE NIVELLIERUNG

Natürlich muß die Perikope so vom Ganzen des Evangeliums her gelesen und in den näheren Kontext eingebettet werden. Die neueren redaktionsgeschichtlichen Studien (Nützel, Daniel, Nardoni, McGuckin)[24] tun das zur Genüge, manchmal im Übermaß. In erster Linie

---

Vv. 6b und 8 Subjekt sind und denen die Anrede in 7cd gilt.

[22]   Vgl. K. Berger, *Formgeschichte des Neuen Testaments* (Heidelberg: Quelle und Meyer, 1984) 284-85.

[23]   Nützel, *Verklärungserzählung* (mit ihm Zmijewski) meint, mit der auf Deut 18:15 anspielenden Wolkenstimme habe Markus auch Mose in Vv. 4-5 und Bezugnahmen auf die Sinaigeschichte eingefügt. Doch hätte er sie dann doch deutlicher machen müssen. Außerdem wird schwer verständlich, weshalb Mose—im Unterschied zu Elija—im Folgenden keine Rolle mehr spielt. Auch ist die Zweizahl himmlischer Wesen ein verbreiteter Topos: vgl. G. Lohfink, *Die Himmelfahrt Jesu* (SANT 226; München: Kösel, 1971) 198; dazu Ps.-Philon, *LAB* 64:6; K. Berger, *Die Auferstehung des Propheten und die Erscheinung des Menschensohnes* (SUNT 13; Göttingen: Vandenhoeck & Ruprecht, 1976) 269 Anm. 104. Sie fördert hier auch die Symmetrie. Weitere, mehr religionsgeschichtlich argumentierende "Teilungsvorschläge" (Lohmeyer, Hahn, H. P. Müller, Masson) referiert kritisch Horstmann, *Studien*, 74-80. Zuletzt trat Öhler ("Die Verklärung," 199-202) für die "relative Einheitlichkeit der Tradition" ein, die Markus lediglich in einigen Punkten ergänzt habe.

[24]   Außer Horstmann, *Studien*, 80-103, wären noch H.-J. Steichele, *Der leidende Sohn Gottes* (BU 14; Regensburg: Pustet, 1980) 161-92, oder J. Marcus, *The Way of the Lord* (Edinburgh: T. & T. Clark, 1993) 80-93, zur Verwendung der atl. Zitate zu nennen. Weitere Beispiele heutiger Synchronexegese erspare ich

hat sie sicher die Funktion, die Identität des Messias–Menschensohnes Jesus zu bestätigen. Manche Autoren finden in der Verklärung Jesu auch die in der Textumgebung anklingenden Themen Leiden, Auferstehung und Parusie wieder. Weil die Auferweckten in der jüdischen Apokalyptik ihre neue Leiblichkeit durch Verwandlung erreichen,[25] nehme die Metamorphose Jesu diese Auferstehungsherrlichkeit vorweg.[26] Bemerkenswert ist freilich, daß dies hier demonstrativ vor den Augen der Jünger geschieht. Vor allem redet die Wolkenstimme nicht in der Zukunft, sondern von dem, was Jesus jetzt schon ist. Die Auferstehung Jesu ist der terminus a quo für die Verkündigung des auf dem Berg Geschauten (9:9), nicht für seine Wahrheit. Ähnliche Bedenken kommen auf gegen die Deutung des Ereignisses als Antizipation der δόξα des Wiederkommenden,[27] zumal es nicht als Vision von Künftigem erzählt wird. Ganz verfehlt scheint mir die beliebte Auskunft, es stelle die Erfüllung des in 9:1 Geweissagten dar.[28] Der Vers bekräftigt primär den vorangehenden. Weil keine große Gefahr besteht, daß die Jünger binnen sechs Tagen sterben, gilt die Verheißung kaum den Drei von 9:2. Gundry und Öhler müssen zugestehen, daß die "Ankunft der Herrschaft Gottes auf der Erde" in der Verklärung nur vorläufig ist. Solche Ausle-

---

mir, da es in diesem Buch nicht darauf ankommt.

25   Vgl. vor allem *syrBar.* 49, 51; außerdem *äthHen.* 50:1; 108:11-15; Ps.-Philon, *LAB* 28:9; 1 Kor 15:51-52; *hebrHen.* 48C 6-7.

26   Z.B. M. E. Thrall, "Elijah and Moses in Mark's Account of the Transfiguration," *NTS* 16 (1969-70) 305-17; sie nimmt noch eine merkwürdige Polemik gegen die Entrückung (wie bei Elija und Mose) an.

27   Richtig T. A. Burkill, *Mysterious Revelation* (Ithaca: Cornell University Press, 1963) 159-60: "The voice from the cloud does not declare that Jesus *will* be the Son of God at some future date, but simply that he *is* the Son of God . . . Accordingly, St. Mark's account of the transfiguration does not disclose a status which Jesus is to enjoy on a future occasion, whether it be at his resurrection or at his parousia." Textwidrig dagegen Daniel, *Transfiguration* 65: "The revelation of Jesus identity on the mountain is the prediction of a future condition, not a present one." Das schließt nicht aus, daß für den Leser die glorreiche Wiederkunft durch das Berichtete um so gewisser werden soll.

28   So jetzt wieder betont Gundry, *Mark*, 457; Öhler, "Die Verklärung," 216-17 (Der Anm. 1 als Gewährsmann genannte Nardonia heißt allerdings Nardoni). Wenn man Jesus und die Basileia einfach gleichsetzt, was m.E. nicht im Sinn des Redaktors ist, umgeht man elegant das Problem der Mk 9:1 ausgesprochenen Naherwartung. Das hier Gesagte gilt auch gegen Wenham und Moses, "'There are some standing here . . . '," 146-63.

gungen laufen Gefahr, die Tatsache, daß sich die Verwandlung am Irdischen vollzieht und sein ihm bereits eigenes Wesen enthüllt, einzuebnen. Wir müssen also nach zeitgenössischen Modellen Ausschau halten, wo ähnliches zu Lebzeiten bei großen Männern geschieht.

AUF DER SUCHE NACH RELIGIONSGESCHICHTLICHEN ANALOGIEN

Getreu dem Programm des "Authenticating" wird man versuchen, die Begebenheit zunächst aus dem jüdischen Milieu zu erhellen. Sie weist ja auch unübersehbar jüdisches Kolorit auf: das Motiv der weißen Kleider, Mose und Elija, was ihr Erscheinen auch immer bedeutet (s.u.), die Wolke, die die Präsenz Gottes anzeigt; die Gottesstimme, die an die bei Rabbinen ergehende *bat qol* erinnert,[29] die—freilich nicht leicht herauszuhörenden—Anklänge an Ps 2:7 und Deut 18:15 in V. 7cd. Die Parallelen kann man leicht in den Kommentaren zusammengestellt finden.[30] Ich habe jedoch schon darauf aufmerksam gemacht, daß eine übernatürliche Veränderung des Aussehens im Alten Testament und in der zwischentestamentarischen Literatur selten vorkommt.[31] Die LXX kennt dafür nicht den Terminus μεταμορφ–. Aber es gibt immerhin ein vergleichbares Phänomen: den Widerschein der Herrlichkeit Gottes auf dem Antlitz des Mose (Exod 34:29-30), den die jüdische Literatur noch stärker ausmalt (z.B. Philon, *Vita Mosis* 2.70; Ps.-Philon, *LAB* 12:1; *hebrHen.* 15B5).[32] Und Philon gebraucht für den prophetischen ἐνθουσιασμός des Mose auch schon einmal das Verbum μεταβάλλειν,

---

29 So Chilton, "Transfiguration," der ein regelrechtes *genre* "Geschichten mit Himmelsstimmen" behauptet. P. Kuhn (*Offenbarungsstimmen im antiken Judentum* [TSAJ 20; Tübingen: Mohr (Siebeck), 1989]) stellt in seiner Monographie allerdings fest, daß das Motiv in den verschiedensten Gattungen belegt ist.

30 Zuletzt Gundry, *Mark*, speziell 477 zum jüdischen Hintergrund.

31 Vgl. Zeller, "La métamorphose," 167-68. In jüngster Zeit hat U. B. Müller ("'Sohn Gottes'—ein messianischer Hoheitstitel," *ZNW* [1987] 1-39, 22) auch Stellen herangezogen, wo Menschen durch Verzückung "ein anderer werden" (1 Sam 10:6, in Ps.-Philon, *LAB* 20:2 bei der Investitur Josuas verwendet; ähnlich bei Kenas 27:10). Aber hier findet keine äußere Verwandlung statt; bezeichnenderweise geht die Bekleidung mit den Gewändern des Mose (Josua) bzw. mit dem "Geist der Stärke" (Kenas) der Verwandlung voran. Erst beim echten Philon ergreift die prophetische Inspiration auch das Aussehen: vgl. *Vita Mosis* 1.57; 2.272, 280 von Mose, *Virt.* 217 von Abraham.

32 Fossum ("Ascensio, Metamorphosis," 74) führt mehrere samaritanische Texte an, nach denen "his face was clothed with a ray of light."

μεταμορφοῦσθαι.[33] Steht nicht auch das μεταμορφούμεθα 2 Kor 3:18 im Gegenüber zur Verklärung des Mose, wenn es sich jetzt auch auf die Christen bezieht?

Die Mose–Typologie

So hat man in den Exoduskapiteln, die vom Aufstieg und Abstieg des Mose handeln, die narrative Struktur unseres Textes vorgebildet gefunden, der mehrfach auf die Mosegeschichte anspiele, ja geradezu einen Midrasch über Exodus darstelle;[34] die Mose-Typologie liefere nicht nur das Gestaltungsprinzip, sondern auch die Intention: Jesus wird als neuer Mose präsentiert, auf den die Jünger hören sollen (vgl. Deut 18:15 in V. 7d); er ist nicht nur gleichen Ranges, wie V. 4 suggeriert, sondern ihm als "Sohn Gottes" überlegen. Das klingt zunächst plausibel. Doch können die Einzelzüge, auf denen der Indizienschluß aufbaut, für sich genommen meist auch anders erklärt werden. Sie stehen in Exodus in anderem Zusammenhang und in anderer Funktion:

– Exod 24:16 bedeckt eine Wolke sechs Tage lang den Berg bzw. überschattet Mose (*Jub.* 1:2; *äthApkEsr.* 68:12-13), der bereits heraufgestiegen ist. Erst am 7. Tag empfängt er aber die göttlichen Anweisungen. Dagegen ist nach Markus das Widerfahrnis auf dem Berg am 6. Tag zu datieren.[35]

– Schon vorher hatte eine ältere Schicht Mose mit drei Begleitern, aber auch zusammen mit siebzig Ältesten zur Gottesschau hinaufsteigen lassen (Exod 24:9-11); darin kann man ein Vorbild für die Auswahl der drei Jünger finden, die Jesus nach Markus aber auch anderswo trifft.

– Das Strahlen des Antlitzes wird nach Exod 34:29 erst beim Abstieg vom Sinai, wo Mose die steinernen Tafeln beschrieben hatte, sichtbar, "weil er mit dem Herrn geredet hatte," und zwar allen Israeliten. Philo und Ps–Philo verlegen die Verwandlung ins Göttliche aber auch schon in frühere Gottesbegegnungen.[36]

– Daß eine Stimme aus der Wolke ertönt, könnte sich an Exod 24:16

---

33 Vgl. außer den Anm. 31 genannten Stellen noch *Quaest. in Exod.* 2.29, ausführlicher Zeller, "La métamorphose," 176-77. Ich unterstreiche dort, daß solche Verwandlung nicht auf Mose beschränkt ist.

34 In neuerer Zeit del Agua, "Narrative"; Chilton, "Transfiguration," der aber die Bezeichnung "Midrasch" ablehnt und eher eine "explosion of associations" befürwortet.

35 Vgl. die Anm. 5 genannte Schwierigkeit.

36 Vgl. *Quaest. in Exod.* 2.29 zu Exodus 24; Ps.-Philon, *LAB* 11–12 zieht Exodus 19–31 mit Exod 34:29-35 zusammen.

anlehnen, wo aber Mose auf den Gipfel gerufen wird (vgl. noch die Ankündigung 19:9). Das Motiv der Wolke, und auch das der daraus erklingenden Stimme ist jedoch weiter verbreitet.[37]

Vor allem kommt das spezielle Motiv des leuchtenden Angesichtes bei Markus gar nicht vor; erst Matthäus und Lukas ergänzen es, wohl unabhängig voneinander einer Topik folgend,[38] zu den leuchtenden Gewändern, die wiederum in der biblischen Sinaitradition keine Parallele haben (erst in der samaritanischen). D. F. Strauß, der in der evangelischen Geschichte eine Nachbildung der mosaischen erblickte, ging von der Priorität des Matthäus aus.[39] Außerdem wird es nach dem Obigen schwierig, alle Mose-Anspielungen für eine vormarkinische Tradition in Anspruch zu nehmen, da sowohl die 6 Tage wie die Drei, ja vielleicht auch V. 7d auf Markus zurückgehen können. Doch auch Form und Absicht des vorliegenden Textes ist mit einer Mosetypologie nicht ausreichend erklärt.[40] Daß Elija an der Seite des Mose erscheint, bleibt auch so unmotiviert.

Verwandlung in jüdischer Mystik und Apokalyptik

W. Gerber hat darauf hingewiesen, daß die Verklärung Jesu etwas mit dem Gespräch mit himmlischen Gestalten (V. 4) zu tun haben müsse, und Texte der *Hekhalot*-Literatur angeführt, in denen ein ähnlicher Zusammenhang besteht: Bei seinem Aufstieg zur Gottesschau wird der Seher verwandelt.[41] Das Problem ist nur, daß die

---

[37]   Vgl. U. Luz, *Das Evangelium nach Matthäus* (EKKNT 1.2, Zürich und Braunschweig: Benziger; Neukirchen-Vluyn: Neukirchener Verlag, 1990) 507; Öhler, "Die Verklärung," 209-10.

[38]   Vgl. Fossum, "Ascensio," 84-85; seine Beispiele, zu denen man noch *hebrHen.* 48C 6 ergänzen könnte, handeln aber von Henoch und Jesaja. Nur der samaritanische Defter-Hymnus (ebd. 74) verbindet die Bekleidung des Mose mit einem mehr als königlichen Gewand und das Strahlen seines Antlitzes.

[39]   D. F. Strauß, *Das Leben Jesu* (Leipzig: Osiander, 1864) 516-22, vgl. 138-39. Auch in neuerer Zeit gibt A. D. A. Moses (*Matthew's Transfiguration Story and Jewish-Christian Controversy* [JSNTSup 122; Sheffield: Sheffield Academic Press, 1996] 45-49) zu, daß die Sinaitypologie bei Markus—im Unterschied zu Matthäus—"debatable" ist.

[40]   Gegen Aufnahme von Mose-Motiven äußert sich jetzt auch Gundry, *Mark*, 475-76. Öhler ("Die Verklärung," 202-204) stellt sie ebenfalls in Frage.

[41]   Gerber, "Die Metamorphose Jesu" (s. Anm. 1). In "La métamorphose," 172 Anm. 24, habe ich dazu Stellen aus *slavHen.* und *Asc. Jes.* nachgetragen. Vgl. jetzt auch M. Himmelfarb, "Revelation and Rapture: The Transformation of the Visionary in the Ascent Apocalypses," in J. J. Collins und J. H. Charlesworth

Verwandlung Jesu im jetzigen Zusammenhang nicht nur auf die Erscheinung V. 4 ausgerichtet ist. Diese gilt in erster Linie den Jüngern. Die Unterhaltung mit Mose und Elija bringt für Jesus keine eigentliche Offenbarung[42] und entspricht nicht der Schau Gottes. Auch im folgenden ist das Offenbarungsgeschehen auf die Jünger bezogen, die gerade nicht verwandelt werden.

Auch J. E. Fossum sieht die Schwäche des Gerberschen Vorschlages: Während die in den mystischen Texten genannte Umwandlung von menschlicher Natur in himmlisches Feuer eine Voraussetzung dafür ist, daß man Gott oder die Engel sehen kann, ist gerade hier "the parallelism with the Synoptic account . . . not quite in evidence."[43] Dennoch baut er auf diesem Ansatz weiter. Um die Parallele zur Himmelsreise zu verstärken, muß er zunächst einmal den "hohen Berg" als "heavenly locale" wahrscheinlich machen, obwohl er zugesteht, daß er nicht den Ausgangspunkt für den Aufstieg bildet wie in seinen Belegen aus *Apk. Petr.* 17, *Asc. Jes.* 2:8 (Äth); *T. Lev.* 2:5-7.[44] Da Exodus 24 nicht viel Licht auf die Verklärungsperikope werfen kann (76-78), zieht er Weiterbildungen des Sinaiaufenthaltes heran, in denen Mose in den Himmel aufsteigt[45] und dabei eine "glorification" erfährt (83-86). Daß dabei die Kleider verwandelt werden, ist—wie bereits bemerkt—nur einmal von Mose belegt (samaritanischer Defter), dagegen häufiger von anderen Gestalten; ebensowenig ist das strahlende Antlitz spezifisch für Mose. Dennoch versichert Fossum "The Moses pattern continues to hold good," weil Defter und der Tragiker Ezechiel 68ff Mose mit königlichem Gewand bekleidet bzw. auf einem Thron sitzend zeigen.

(Hg.), *Mysteries and Revelations: Apocalyptic Studies since the Uppsala Colloquium* (JSPSup 9; Sheffield: JSOT Press, 1991) 79-90, bes. 84-85; W. F. Smelik, "On Mystical Transformation of the Righteous into Light in Judaism," *JSJ* 226 (1995) 122-44. In beiden Arbeiten müßte deutlicher zwischen einer vorübergehenden und einer finalen Verwandlung (so vor allem die Texte bei Smelik) unterschieden werden.

42 Das will ich für ein früheres Stadium nicht ausschließen. Daß jetzt aber Mose und Elija mit Jesus reden, unterstreicht nur seine Gleichrangigkeit; vgl. *Apk. Soph.* 14:3-4; *Asc. Jes.* 7:6-7.

43 Fossum, "Ascensio, Metamorphosis," 83.

44 Ebd. 72, 79, 82.

45 Überzeugend sind S. 73-74 *Tg.* Ps 69:19; *Sifre Deut.* §357 (zu Deut 34:1-12) und Par.; Ps.-Philon, *LAB* 12:1; 32:9; dazu spätere samaritanische Überlieferungen. Öhler ("Die Verklärung," 205 Anm. 26) möchte nur zwei Stellen aus *TehR* anerkennen.

So werde Jesus nicht nur verwandelt, sondern auch in sein Amt als Gottes Prophet–König installiert mit dem impliziten Auftrag, Gottes Willen zu proklamieren (83). In neuerer Zeit ist aber mit Recht bestritten worden, daß die an die Jünger gerichtete Gottesrede V. 7 als Installation zu verstehen ist.[46] Noch einmal: Es geht um die Offenbarung dessen, was Jesus schon ist. Diese hat freilich die Funktion, die hinter seiner Botschaft stehende Autorität zu verdeutlichen.

Unabhängig von Fossum und vom Mose–Paradigma hat neuerdings M. Öhler versucht, die ganze Motivik (Berg, Verwandlung, Begegnung mit Himmelsbewohnern, Zelte, Präsentation als geliebter Sohn Gottes) in den Kontext von Entrückung bzw. Himmelsreise zu stellen;[47] er bemerkt aber zum Schluß mit Recht, daß von einer Entrückung Jesu in den Himmel gar nicht die Rede ist. Es fehlen die dafür charakteristischen Termini, der Blick in den Himmel, eine Notiz über die Rückkehr. Um dennoch Gewinn aus seinen Funden zu ziehen, behilft sich Öhler mit einem kühnen salto mortale: Das entscheidend Neue unseres Berichtes gegenüber ähnlichen andern bestehe darin, daß die Reise in den Himmel in ein "Kommen des Himmels auf die Erde" transponiert werde: "Gottes Gegenwart wird von den Jüngern auf Erden erlebt und dient zum Aufweis der himmlischen Identität Jesu" (215). Im Ergebnis ist er somit nicht weit entfernt von meinem Vorschlag:

Die Verwandlung als Moment einer Epiphanie

Gerade weil in der vorangehenden Deutung die Verwandlung Jesu nicht befriedigend der Sinnspitze in V. 7 zugeordnet wird, habe ich in meinem Aufsatz[48] auf die eingangs erwähnte Lösung von M. Dibelius zurückgegriffen und versucht, die Verklärung innerhalb der religionsgeschichtlichen Kategorie "Epiphanie eines Gottes in menschlicher Gestalt"[49] zu verstehen, bei der der Gestaltwandel eine

---

46   Vgl. schon Harnack (s.o. Anm. 6) 76 Anm. 3; zuletzt M. Frenschkowski, *Offenbarung und Epiphanie* II (WUNT 2.80; Tübingen: Mohr [Siebeck], 1996) 186; das ist auch gegen die von U. B. Müller ("'Sohn Gottes'," s. Anm. 31) angeführten Parallelen aus Ps.-Philon, *LAB*, zu sagen.

47   Öhler, "Die Verklärung"; er schreibt in Kenntnis des Aufsatzes von Gerber.

48   Zeller, "La métamorphose," 179-81; unabhängig von mir kommt die Mainzer Dissertation von M. Frenschkowski (*Offenbarung und Epiphanie* II, 184-87) zum selben Ergebnis.

49   Zur griechischen Vorstellung vgl. F. Pfister, "Epiphanie," *PRE.S* 4 (1924)

wesentliche Rolle spielt. Wie man dieses Modell bei der heiden-
christlichen Formulierung der Menschwerdung (vor allem in Phil
2,6ff) benutzte,[50] so konnte man sich seiner bedienen, um mitten im
Leben Jesu an ihm göttliche Herrlichkeit aufblitzen zu lassen. Am
Ende einer "verborgenen Epiphanie," bei der Götter sich in menschliche Gestalt hüllen, steht häufig eine Szene, in der sie sich in ihrer
Göttlichkeit zu erkennen geben.[51] Die in unscheinbarer Gestalt
Erschienenen wachsen zu unheimlicher Größe, strahlen vor jugend-
licher Schönheit; ihre Gesichtsfarbe wechselt, ihre Augen leuchten,
ihre prächtigen Gewänder duften. Die Menschen reagieren mit
Erschrecken (vgl. V. 6b). Manchmal suchen sie auch die Erscheinung mit sinnlosen Vorschlägen aufzuhalten wie Petrus in V. 5.[52]
Was in den weißen Gewändern und im Verkehr mit Mose und Elija
zum Ausdruck kommt, spricht dann die Wolkenstimme aus: Jesus ist
ein himmlisches Wesen. "Sohn Gottes" hat hier gewiß von 8:29 her
messianischen Klang. Zugleich verbindet sich damit aber über-
menschliche Schönheit und Lichtglanz wie bei Joseph, der JosAs 6 als
"Sohn Gottes" bekannt wird, wie bei dem Totenrichter, von dem *T.
Abr.* Rez. A 12:5 sagt: "a wondrous man, bright as the sun, like unto
a son of God."[53] Das bedeutet "engelgleich." Natürlich ist dann noch

---

Frenschkowski, *Offenbarung und Epiphanie* II hat den Untertitel *Die
verborgene Epiphanie in Spätantike und frühem Christentum*, zeigt anhand von
Genesis 18, daß die Kategorie nicht auf die griechisch-römische Antike beschränkt
ist und liefert ein reiches Motivrepertoire.

[50]   Vgl. D. Zeller, "Die Menschwerdung des Sohnes Gottes im Neuen
Testament und die antike Religionsgeschichte," in ders. (Hg.), *Menschwerdung
Gottes—Vergöttlichung von Menschen* (NTOA 7; Fribourg: Universitätsverlag,
Göttingen: Vandenhoeck & Ruprecht, 1988) 141-76, 160-63, und U. B. Müller,
Die Menschwerdung des Gottessohnes (SBS 140, Stuttgart: Katholisches Bibel-
werk, 1990); vgl. ders., *Der Brief des Paulus an die Philipper* (THKNT 11.1;
Leipzig: Evangelische Verlagsanstalt, 1993) 93-95.

[51]   Vgl. Frenschkowski, *Offenbarung und Epiphanie* II, 75-76, und das
Scholion zu Homer, *Ilias* 2.791: "Bei den sich verwandelnden Göttern ist es üblich,
beim Weggehen ein Zeichen zur Erkenntnis zu hinterlassen"; ähnlich Ovid, *Met.*
1.220: *signa dedi venisse deum*. Während die Engel Gottes im Alten Testament an
anderen Zeichen nachträglich manifest werden, haben wir in *Herm. Vis.* 5:1-4 und
CH 1.1-5 dem Neuen Testament nahe Texte, in denen die Erkenntnis durch
Metamorphose ausgelöst wird.

[52]   So in atl.-jüdischen Beispielen, wenn körperlosen Engeln Essen oder ein
Lager angeboten wird: vgl. Ri 13:15-16; *T. Abr.* Rez. A 4.

[53]   Übersetzung von E. P. Sanders in J. H. Charlesworth (Hg.), *The Old

einmal ein Schritt von solchen "Söhnen Gottes" zu einem singulären "Sohn Gottes," der aus himmlischem Milieu stammt. Er wurde kaum innerhalb des frühen Judenchristentums getan.[54]

Ein Einwand wird natürlich sofort laut: Solche Selbstenthüllung göttlicher Wesen steht gewöhnlich am Ende ihres verdeckten Wandels auf Erden. Dagegen bedeutet Jesu Verklärung nicht schon seine Rückkehr in die himmlische Welt, sondern währt nur kurz. Das hängt jedoch damit zusammen, daß hier eine ursprünglich für Himmelsbewohner geprägte Vorstellung auf einen irdischen Menschen übertragen worden ist. Dafür lassen sich einige hellenistische—und nur solche—Analogien beibringen. Vor allem habe ich die alte Legende vom goldenen Schenkel des Pythagoras ins Feld geführt, der ihn als den Hyperboreischen Apoll ausweist.[55] Zwar muß man sich ihn wohl als von Geburt an vorhandene Markierung seiner Göttlichkeit vorstellen, aber er wird auch nur für einen Moment entblößt. Besonders interessant für die Abfolge Messiasbekenntnis—Verklärungsepisode ist eine Version der Pythagorasgeschichte, die eine anonyme, vielleicht auf Heraklides Ponticus zurückgehende Quelle (bei Iamblich, *Vit. Pyth.* 91–93) bietet: Abaris, der Diener des Hyperboreischen Apoll, trifft mit Pythagoras zusammen und findet in ihm den Gott, dessen Priester er war. Der Weise "zog, als wäre er wirklich der Gott selbst, den Abaris beiseite und zeigte ihm seinen goldenen Schenkel zum Zeichen dafür, daß er sich nicht getäuscht hatte." Die Szene im Abseits hat ähnlich wie die auf dem Berg die Funktion, ein vorausgehendes Bekenntnis zu bestätigen.

Weiter habe ich auf Beispiele aus Biographien über neuplatonische Philosophen verwiesen;[56] sie liegen mehr auf der Linie von Philons Beschreibung prophetischer Ekstase: Der Geist, die Einheit mit dem

---

Testament Pseudepigrapha, vol. 1 (ABRL; Garden City: Doubleday, 1983) 889.

54 Daß man im jüdischen Denken nicht so leicht eine "Wesensgleichheit des Messias mit den Engeln" behaupten kann, habe ich in "La métamorphose," 173-74, gegen M. Mach, "Christus Mutans," in I. Gruenwald u.a. (Hg.), *Messiah and Christos* (D. Flusser Festschrift; TSAJ 32; Tübingen: Mohr [Siebeck], 1992) 177-98, darzutun versucht.

55 Vgl. die "La métamorphose," 181-83, angegebenen Quellen.

56 Ebd. S. 183-85; vgl. jetzt auch Frenschkowski, *Offenbarung und Epiphanie* II, 185 Anm. 153. Nachzutragen ist die Verwandlung geringeren Grades, die Hippokrates (Brief 17, Littré IX 378, entstanden um die Zeitenwende) an Demokrit nach dessen großer Rede bemerkt: "Er erschien als einer von göttlicher Gestalt; vergessen war sein früheres Aussehen."

Göttlichen, macht sich im Äußeren eines Plotin, Alypios, Proklos, Isidor, bemerkbar, vor allem im Strahlen der Augen und des Gesichtes. Für die Verwandlung der Kleider nach Markus besonders interessant ist ein Gerücht, das sich um Jamblich rankte: Abgesondert von seinen Schülern soll er beim Gebet nicht nur eine erstaunliche Levitation erfahren haben, nein auch sein Leib und das Gewand wandelten sich angeblich zu goldener Schönheit (Eunapios, *Vit. Phil.* 458). Wie das Weiß der Kleider im jüdischen Bereich die Zugehörigkeit zum Göttlichen signalisiert, so das Gold im griechischen. Zugegeben, nur Lukas situiert die Verklärung Jesu beim Gebet; sie zeigt auch etwas an, was Jesus schon ist, nicht was er erst im Kontakt mit dem Göttlichen und bei zunehmender Vergeistigung wird. Insofern kommt das "mythologischere" Beispiel des Pythagoras näher an die neutestamentliche Perikope heran als diese ohnehin erst im 4./5. Jh. niedergeschriebenen Zeugnisse. Die Deutung unserer Jesusgeschichte von hellenistischen Analogien aus wird allerdings erst von einem Gesamtbild markinischer Christologie her plausibel, wie es jetzt Frenschkowski vorlegt.[57] Auf alle Fälle verwendet er für sein Konzept ältere, jüdisch–apokalyptische Elemente, aber er organisiert sie, wie Öhler richtig beobachtet hat, auf unkonventionelle Weise zu einem neuen Sinnzusammenhang. Wir greifen zum Schluß nur ein umstrittenes Moment heraus: das Erscheinen von Elija mit Mose. Kurz soll skizziert werden, welchen Sinn es für ihn gehabt haben könnte und wie es sich mit den vorgetragenen Interpretationen verträgt.

DER SINN VON V. 4 INSBESONDERE

Es ist deutlich, daß das Erscheinen der beiden Prominenten aus der Geschichte Israels indirekt etwas über Jesus aussagen soll, mit dem sie ins Gespräch treten. Aber was?

(a) Weithin aufgegeben ist die früher erwogene Möglichkeit, daß sie das Schriftzeugnis für Jesus, bestehend aus "Gesetz und Propheten," verkörpern. Für die Schriftpropheten wäre Elija ein schlechter Repräsentant. Höchstens Lukas mag die beiden Figuren so aufgefaßt haben, wenn er sie über den "Ausgang Jesu in Jerusalem" reden läßt (9:31; vgl. 24:25-27, 44-45).

(b) Mehr Anhalt im Text (V. 7d) und seiner Umgebung (Vv. 9-13)

---

[57] S. 197-98 meint er, daß Markus eine Präexistenzchristologie *in statu nascendi* impliziere. Das war mir (in "La métamorphose," 174-75) nicht so greifbar.

hat eine andere Sicht: Danach ist Mose der Prototyp des eschato-
logischen Propheten nach Deut 18:15, 18, Elija aber der Vorläufer
des Tages Jahwes nach Mal 3:23-24 oder gar des Messias nach
christlicher Anschauung. Ihr Erscheinen bedeutet dann: Die Endzeit
ist da, und mit ihr der erwartete Prophet wie Mose bzw. der Messias.
Abgesehen davon, daß die Funktionen der beiden etwas ungleich
ausfallen,[58] ist ihr Zusammen in der jüdischen Tradition so nicht
präformiert.[59] Aus der Reaktion des Petrus "Es ist gut, daß wir *hier*
sind" zu schließen, kommt es auch weniger auf die eschatologische
Qualifikation der Zeit, als auf den Ort an: der Himmel senkt sich
gleichsam auf den Berg.

Andere Autoren suchen eine Gemeinsamkeit zwischen Elija und
Mose:

(c) Beide hatten auf einem Berg eine Theophanie.[60] Doch was hat
das mit Jesus zu tun, der selbst keine Gottesschau erfährt? Wird doch
Göttlichkeit an ihm selber anschaulich.

(d) Unter der Voraussetzung, daß Mose und Elija ebenso "in
Herrlichkeit" erscheinen wie Jesus,[61] wird derzeit eine Alternative
favorisiert: Wie das Alte Testament von der Entrückung des Elija
erzählt, so scheint auch ein Teil der jüdischen Tradition Mose ein
ähnliches Ende zugeschrieben zu haben.[62] Er wird in die Gemein-
schaft mit Gott versetzt (Philon), verschwindet plötzlich (Josephus),
steht bei Gott und dient ihm (tannaitische Stimmen). Die Mehrheit
der Rabbinen kann freilich das in der Bibel bezeugte Sterben nicht
umgehen; das erlaubt höchstens eine Aufnahme seiner Seele. Elija
und Mose als notorische menschliche Himmelsbewohner—sie könn-

---

[58]   Liefeld ("Theological Motifs") weist Mose primär eine typologische, Elija
eine eschatologische Rolle zu.

[59]   Es nützt wenig, an die Abfolge von Mal 3:22, 23-24 zu erinnern. Dort steht
zwar die Einschärfung des Gesetzes des Mose neben der Ankündigung des kom-
menden Elija, aber Mose ist nur als Gesetzgeber in der Vergangenheit anvisiert.

[60]   So zuletzt Gundry, *Mark*, 459.

[61]   Das expliziert zwar erst Lk 9:31a; aber auch die Gleichstellung der drei
Gestalten in V. 5 legt einen ähnlichen Zustand nahe. Gegen Gundry, *Mark*, 478.

[62]   Vgl. K. Haacker und P. Schäfer, "Nachbiblische Traditionen vom Tod des
Mose," in O. Betz u.a. (Hg.), *Josephus-Studien* (O. Michel Festschrift; Göttingen:
Vandenhoeck & Ruprecht, 1974) 147-74; B. Ego, "Der Diener im Palast des
himmlischen Königs," in M. Hengel und A. M. Schwemer (Hg.), *Königsherr-
schaft Gottes und himmlischer Kult* (WUNT 55; Tübingen: Mohr [Siebeck], 1991)
361-84, bes. 374-78; J. E. Fossum, *The Name of the God and the Angel of the
Lord* (WUNT 36, Tübingen: Mohr [Siebeck], 1985) 131-36.

ten zu Jesus in den weißen Kleidern passen. Noch besser hätte sich freilich Henoch als Partner des entrückten Elija geeignet. Wenn die Verklärungsgeschichte diese Weiterentwicklung der Mosehaggada als bekannt annimmt, ist sie eher im griechischsprechenden Judenchristentum entstanden als in der aramäischsprechenden Urgemeinde.[63] J. E. Fossum hat diese Deutung in seine Aufstiegshypothese eingebaut; nach ihm bilden die beiden Erscheinenden das Äquivalent zu den zwei himmlischen Wesen, die auch sonst den Aufsteigenden begleiten.[64] Aber da von einem Aufstieg Jesu nach V. 2b nicht mehr die Rede ist, läßt sie sich mindestens ebensogut in meinen Vorschlag integrieren: Mose und Elija erscheinen als Vertreter der himmlischen Welt, in die der Verwandelte einbezogen wird. Die Wolkenstimme stellt dann klar, daß er ihr ursprungsmäßig, als "Sohn Gottes," zugehört.[65]

SCHLUSSFOLGERUNGEN

Der Überblick über die neuere Forschung hat keine Gesamtlösung zutage gefördert, die sich zwingend aufdrängt. Die Mose-Typologie erwies sich gerade am Mk-Text als ungenügend; die Fossumsche These will sie retten, indem sie sie in den weiteren Rahmen des mystischen Aufstiegs von Offenbarungsempfängern stellt; sie stößt aber auf Bedenken, insofern Markus weder einen Aufstieg in den Himmel noch eine ausdrückliche Einsetzung zum Offenbarungsmittler berichtet. Das erstere trifft auch den Versuch von Öhler. Die Verklärung erfolgt zur Aufklärung der Jünger über Jesu verborgenes Wesen. Deshalb bot sich ein Verständnis aus dem Motivkomplex der Epiphanie an. Die Begründung muß allerdings z.T. mit späten Vergleichstexten arbeiten (das gilt im übrigen auch für Fossums samaritanische Parallelen und seine jüdischen Midraschim), die dazu noch aus dem hellenistischen Raum stammen. Diese Schwierigkeit läßt sich entschärfen, wenn man damit rechnet, daß Markus eine vorgefundene Geschichte aus jüdisch-hellenistischem Christentum in seinem Sinne umgestaltet hat. Weiter als zu einer judenchristlich-hellenistischen Erzählung, die zudem in ihren Umrissen und in ihrer Bedeutung unscharf bleibt, kommt man allerdings nicht zurück. So

---

63   Das folgert auch Müller, "Die christologische Absicht" (s. Anm. 1) 183-84.

64   Fossum, "Ascensio, Metamorphosis," 89-90. Er zitiert *Ev. Petr.* 12.39; *Herm. Vis.* 1.4.3; *Mart. Mt.* 30; s. auch die Anm. 23 gegebenen Hinweise.

65   So auch Öhler, "Die Verklärung," 206-207.

zeigen sich an unserem Beispiel auch die Grenzen des *Authenticating the Activities of Jesus.*

JESUS, THE MESSIAH OF ISRAEL
THE DEBATE ABOUT THE "MESSIANIC MISSION" OF JESUS*

Martin Hengel

Χριστός IN PAUL[1]

Paul, the earliest Christian author, gives Jesus the name "Christos" some 270 times. A few texts may retain, at most, a glimmer of its titular use in the sense of Messiah, "The Anointed One," but as a rule the compound name Ἰησοῦς Χριστός has completely absorbed the title ὁ χριστός—there is only one Χριστός, this very Jesus who was crucified. The title has become fully a part of his name.

In Paul's Bible, the LXX, the situation is very different. There the verbal adjective χριστός, translates מָשִׁיחַ, the Anointed One, some 37 times—the Anointed of God, i.e. either the king or the priest.

For Greek, however, χριστός would not have been used with reference to persons. The neutral χριστόν meant "rubbing ointment," and νεόχριστος "newly plastered."[2] The new name Χριστός was so unusual that non-Jews confused it with the common slave name Χρῆστος.[3]

This Χριστός as a personal name for Jesus was already in use long before the letters of Paul, e.g. in Rome, and above all in Antioch, where barely ten years after the death of Jesus the Christians were described as Χριστιανοί.[4] This means that they changed the title "The

---

* I wish to thank Paul A. Cathey for translating my essay, which appeared in an earlier form in German in I. Gruenwald et al. (eds.), *Messiah and Christos* (D. Flusser Festschrift; TSAJ 32; Tübingen: Mohr [Siebeck], 1992) 155-76. It is the summary of a much larger study, The Elisabeth-James Lectures 1991 in Cardiff, published in its fuller form in my collection, *Studies in Early Christology* (Edinburgh: T. & T. Clark, 1995) 1-72. The present, briefer form of this study is a slightly revised and updated version of what appeared in W. R. Farmer (ed.), *Crisis in Christology: Essays in Quest of Resolution* (Livonia: Dove, 1995) 217-40.

[1] See my *Between Jesus and Paul: Studies in the Earliest History of Christianity* (London: SCM Press, 1983) 65-77, 179-88.

[2] LSJ 1170.

[3] Suetonius, *Claudius* 25.4; cf. Tacitus, *Annals* 15.4: *Chrestiani*.

[4] See M. Hengel and A. M. Schwemer, *Paul Between Damascus and Antioch: The Unknown Years* (London: SCM Press; Louisville: Westminster John Knox

Anointed One" into a name within an astonishingly brief period, and thereby usurped it exclusively for their Lord, Jesus of Nazareth.

Accordingly, we find several time in Paul the formula, "Christ died for us."[5] We can still discern in this formula traces of the originally titular meaning, for at the center of the new message was this: it was the sinless *Messiah*, the eschatological emissary and savior—not merely a suffering righteous man or prophet—who sacrificed his life "for the many." Thus Paul speaks of "[the] Christ crucified" as the content of his preaching. The bipartite form of the name, the familiar Ἰησοῦς Χριστός, as well as the Χριστός Ἰησοῦς preferred by Paul, were originally formulaic confessions. Ἰησοῦς Χριστός derives from יֵשׁוּעַ מְשִׁיחָא, Jesus the Messiah, whereas Χριστός Ἰησοῦς originally was probably used analogously to the cry of acclamation κύριος Ἰησοῦς.

That Paul was perfectly acquainted with the Old Testament-Jewish conceptions bound up with the messianic name Ἰησοῦς Χριστός can be seen from any number of texts: thus, the reference to Jesus' descent "from the seed of David" (Rom 1:3-4). Son of David was an epithet for the Messiah. To be numbered here as well is the rehearsal of the salvation-historical privileges of Israel (Rom 9:3-5): " . . . my kinsmen by race . . . are Israelites, and to them belong the sonship, the glory, the covenants . . . the worship, and the promises . . . the patriarchs, *and of their race, according to the flesh, is [the] Christ.*"

The descent of Christ from Israel forms a climax to this series. For Paul Christ is the Messiah promised to Israel—to be sure his salvific work has universal significance. At the end of Romans (15:7-13) he treats this question: Jews and Gentiles in Rome ought to welcome one another "as Christ has welcomed you, for the glory of God. For I tell you that *Christ became a servant to the circumcised* to show God's truthfulness, in order to confirm the promises given to the patriarchs . . . ."

With this "Christ became a servant to the circumcision," Paul refers to the "messianic ministry" of the earthly Jesus to his own people, through which the truth of God's promises to the patriarchs (and later to the prophets) becomes manifest: God has promised nothing in the messianic prophecy of Scripture that he does not keep

---

Press, 1997) 225-30, 4541-56.

[5]   Rom 5:8; cf. 5:6; 14:9, 15; 1 Cor 8:11; 15:3; 2 Cor 5:15; 1 Thess 5:10; Gal 2:21; 1 Pet 3:18.

(cf. Rom 11:28-29). On the other hand, the "Gentiles'" access to salvation in Christ results from his free mercy, and for this reason they ought to give God the glory.

An adoptionist Christology, first valid via the resurrection, was an impossible idea for Paul. This can be seen not only in Paul's pre-existence- and "mission-" Christology,[6] but also in that the earthly Jesus, i.e. the Crucified One, is already Kyrios;[7] it is also apparent in the account of the institution of the Lord's Supper (1 Cor 11:23-25): Jesus dedicates the fruits of his death to his disciples; i.e. already before his death, as Kyrios, he promises them full salvation. Paul holds in common with all the Gospels the certainty that Jesus was the Messiah of Israel promised in Scripture. Even in John Jesus acquires his first disciples because they recognize and confess him to be the Messiah of Israel.

Here the question necessarily arises: "Does this confession of Jesus as Messiah of Israel have anything to do with the real person of Jesus, his ministry and death, or is it confined merely to its "later influence" (*Wirkungsgeschichte*) in the post-Easter communities"?

THE PRE-PAULINE TRADITION AND THE RESURRECTION OF JESUS

The transition of the title "Messiah" into a name, and its fusion with the person of Jesus, happened already early on in the crossover of the gospel from the Aramaic into the Greek language sphere. The description of the Antiochene followers of Jesus as Χριστιανοί (Acts 11:26) presupposes this as long since accomplished. Presumably, the confessional formula "Jesus is the Messiah," by virtue of constant use, gave rise of itself, so to speak, to a permanent name both among Christians, who thereby emphasized that only *one* could bear this name, and their Gentile auditors, who were not particularly conversant with the language of Jewish piety.

This also means, however, that this confession was fundamental to the earliest community in Jerusalem. The persecution of the early

---

6   M. Hengel, *The Son of God* (London: SCM Press; Philadelphia: Fortress, 1976) 48-56, 66-83; idem, Präexistenz bei Paulus?" in C. Landmesser et al. (eds.), *Jesus Christus als die Mitte der Schrift: Studien zur Hermeneutik des Evangeliums* (O. Hofius Festschrift; BZNW 86; Berlin: de Gruyter, 1997) 479-518.

7   1 Cor 7:10; 9:1; cf. 1 Thess 4:5. See Hengel, *Between Damascus and Antioch*, 120-21, 394-95 nn. 632-40, 275-76, 484-85 nn. 1436-41; idem, *The Son of God*, 77-84.

Church in Jerusalem stems from this very confession of Jesus of Nazareth as the crucified Messiah whom God had risen from the death.

The connection is inseparable between the appearances of Jesus, which established the new messianic community of disciples, and the proclamation of the crucified Messiah by the messengers whom he himself authorized, the "apostles of the Messiah, Jesus."[8] However, there is no proof whatever for the current supposition[9] that in the beginning the confession "God raised Jesus from the dead" stood alone—the appearances of Jesus being understood merely as the beginning of the general resurrection—and only after a secondary level of reflection, was the Resurrected One proclaimed as the Messiah. How are we to suppose this to have happened? After waiting vainly for the general resurrection, did someone perhaps suddenly "discover" the messiahship of Jesus' as the solution to the dilemma? Were the beginnings of early Christianity based on a twofold self-deception?

No, the certainty that Jesus' resurrection also meant his exaltation as Messiah-Son of Man to the right hand of God was rather a direct consequence of the appearances; for the commissioning of the disciples as messengers of the Messiah was connected with these.[10] Their task was to proclaim Jesus as the Messiah of Israel, and to offer the people a final opportunity for repentance. The ancient confession, "God raised Jesus from the dead," only became a meaningful part of the proclamation because it originally stood beside the confession "Jesus is the Messiah." The mere revivification of a person or, as the case may be, his translation into the heavenly realm, established neither messianic majesty nor eschatological mission, nor could it, of itself, supply the content of a message of salvation.

Here it is popular to refer to two "adoptionist" statements, Rom 1:3-4 and Acts 2:36.[11] However Rom 1:4 does not say that the Son possessed no messianic claim prior to the resurrection; rather, this is referring to the enthronement of the Son of God in his full

---

8   1 Cor 1:1; cf. 2 Cor 1:1; 11:13; Eph 2:1; Col 1:1.

9   See, e.g., J. Becker, *Auferstehung der Toten im Urchristentum* (SBS 82; Stuttgart: Katholisches Bibelwerk, 1976) 14-15, 28.

10   1 Cor 9:1; 15:1-8; Gal 1:15-16; Acts 1:8; Matt 28:19-20; John 20:21.

11   See Hengel, *The Son of God*, 59-66; cf. also Acts 13:33.

eschatological majesty and power. This is valid for Acts 2:36. This text—formulated by Luke—expresses not an adoptionist Christology, but a radical volte-face of the "powers that be": God made him who had been crucified on the accursed tree to be "Lord and Anointed"; i.e., he installed him in his eschatological office as the Lord and Judge. That an adoptionist Christology in the fullest sense—i.e., in which Jesus is not regarded as the Messiah until his Passion, this first being established through the resurrection—ever existed in early Christianity seems to me more than doubtful.

Jewish *Religionsgeschichte* presents an additional problem To be sure, we have accounts of the translation of certain righteous men, and we hear also of isolated instances of resurrection. But that a righteous man via resurrection from the dead was appointed as Messiah, is absolutely without analogy. Neither resurrection nor translation have anything to do with messiahship. Indeed, the suffering righteous man attains a place of honor in Paradise, but there is never any question of messianic majesty and transfer of eschatological functions in this connection.

If Jesus never possessed a messianic consciousness of divine mission, nor spoke of the coming, or present, "Son of Man," nor was executed as a messianic pretender—as is maintained by radical criticism untroubled by historical arguments—then the emergence of Christology, indeed, the entire early history of primitive Christianity, is incomprehensible. But this is not all—all four gospels, and above all the Passion narrative as their most ancient component, would be a curious product of the imagination very difficult to explain, for the Messiah question is at the center of them all. When all is said and done: if the eleven disciples with Peter at their head, on the basis of the appearances of the resurrected Jesus so difficult for us to comprehend, and completely unprompted, reached the view that Jesus was the Son of Man exalted to God, knowing that in reality he had been merely a proclaimer of the kingdom of God, a rabbi and a prophet, knowing nothing of eschatological offices, did they not then completely falsify the pure (and so unmythologically modern sounding) intention of their master? Is it not the case that not only Judas, but also the disciples, wallowing in messianic mythology against their master's will, were—viewed historically—at bottom betrayers of Jesus, since they misunderstood his cause as thoroughly as it could possibly be misunderstood?

On the other hand, since human beings also had memories then, why do we nowhere find a protest against this "messianic" falsification of Jesus? A pious veneration of a suffering righteous Jesus, who now (as with all the righteous) resided with God, would have given less offense among their own compatriots, and the impending separation from Judaism could have been avoided (removing all the contemporary difficulties of Jewish-Christian dialogue). But such a protest in favor of *the true, unmessianic intention of Jesus is nowhere attested.*

THE PROBLEM IN THE HISTORY OF RESEARCH

The doubts of the messianic certainty of Jesus' self-understanding can be traced to a few nineteenth-century Life of Jesus researchers, such as Volkmar and Scholten; these tended to be outsiders, however. Already in 1873, the anti-Jewish Paul de Lagarde could also emphatically maintain, "that it did not fall to Jesus to present himself as Messiah."[12] On the other hand, no less a Jewish scholar than Samuel Krauss could regard it as questionable, "whether Jesus regarded himself in any sense a Messiah or spiritual ruler";[13] But here and there the direction is clear.

William Wrede first set the unmessianic Jesus in motion with his 1901 study *Das Messiasgeheimnis in den Evangelien [The Messianic Secret in the Gospels]*, with the sub-title *Being a Contribution Toward Understanding the Gospel of Mark.*[14] He regarded the messianic secret in the Gospel of Mark as an apologetic construction of the Evangelist based partly in the community's tradition. He classifies various material under the term "messianic secret": not only Jesus' prohibition of the disciples speaking about his messiahship, but also the commands of silence to those who had been healed, to the demons who knew his true identity, also the unbelief or incomprehension of the disciples in various situations, and finally, the parable theory that Jesus only spoke in parables in order that the

---

[12] H. J. Holtzmann, *Das messianische Bewußtsein Jesu* (Tübingen: Mohr [Siebeck], 1907) 4-6; P. de Lagarde, *Deutsche Schriften* (5th ed., Göttingen: Dieterich, 1920) 58.

[13] S. Krauss, "Jesus," *JE* 4 (1904) 163-64.

[14] W. Wrede, *Das Messiasgeheimnis in den Evangelien: Zugleich ein Beitrag zum Verständnis des Markusevangeliums* (Göttingen: Vandenhoeck & Ruprecht, 1901; 3rd ed., 1963); ET: *The Messianic Secret* (Cambridge and London: James Clarke, 1971).

hearts of the people might be hardened. To be sure, later investigations have shown that this entire complex cannot be traced back to a single motive of masking the unmessianic character of Jesus' ministry, and reading post-Easter Christology into his history. Rather, this is seen as a paradoxical style device intended to allow the hidden "glory" of the Messiah, who goes to the cross, to shine even brighter.

Leading New Testament scholars of the day more or less rejected Wrede's hypothesis. Their criticism focused above all on three points: first, Wrede's denial of the historicity of Peter's confession at Caesarea Philippi, second, his unsatisfactory treatment of the Passion narrative, where in the trial before Pilate the Messiah question stands at the center, and brings Jesus to the cross, and third, his disregard of the religion-historical problem and the question connected with it concerning how, through the Easter visions alone, the disciples suddenly could have made the unmessianic Jesus into the heavenly Son of Man and Messiah. To this list one might add Wrede's failure to recognize the importance of the Galilean-Jewish origin of Jesus and his first hearers and disciples. These queries remain unresolved to this day.[15]

It must be said that these liberal theologians were not particularly interested in Jesus' messiahship. For their enlightened humanistic picture of Jesus it was rather an embarrassment. W. Bousset referred to this problem:

> Inadequate as the conceptions "kingdom of God' and "judgment," were . . . in light of Jesus' preaching, so inadequate . . . also was the title "Messiah" as an expression of his innermost being.[16]

Here one might raise the objection, "Why then did Jesus make use of these messianic hopes at all, so alien to his innermost being—why did he not reject this conception"? Bousset answers:

> Because . . . it was absolutely necessary to him. As the conceptions "kingdom of God" and "judgment" were indispensable for making himself intelligible to his people, so also was the idea "Messiah" indispensable for understanding himself . . . Jesus wanted to be more than one in a series . . . of the Prophets . . . But according to the popular conception, this [could only be] the Messiah . . . He felt himself to be standing in a nearness to God such as no one before him . . . He spoke with confidence the final,

---

[15]   See my *Studies in the Gospel of Mark* (Philadelphia: Fortress, 1985) 31-45.

[16]   W. Bousset, *Jesus* (Religionsgeschichtliche Volksbücher für die deutsche christliche Gegenwart 1. Ser. 2/3; Halle: Gebauer-Schwetschke, 1904) 86.

decisive, word, was convinced that he was the perfecter—after him none other would come.[17]

Although Bousset's language here has been influenced by Carlyle's[18] model of heroic personality veneration, he is no less the expert for Jewish apocalyptic and messianic expectations, and grasped the actual historical basis for the messianic secret in Mark better than his friend Wrede. One the other hand, it must be admitted that the liberal literature at the turn of the century frequently shows a deep aversion against the Jewish messianic hope. It is therefore understandable that the new discovery of the unmessianic Jesus also found an enthusiastic reception. The Heidelberg scholar, Adalbert Merx concluded:

> . . . that Yeshua never claimed to be the Messiah, that his prohibiting his disciples to declare him as the Messiah was not only temporary but absolute, and that consequently Yeshua's true being will remain misunderstood as long as Christians do not resolve to erase this characteristic from his intellectual make-up just as [all other] apocalyptic fanaticism.[19]

Willy Staerck closed a study on Jesus' attitude towards the Jewish Messiah concept with a challenge:

> Now let us also finally be done with speaking of the messiahship of Jesus, pulling him down into *the atmosphere* of ethnic religiosity . . . Jesus [is] not the Messiah, but . . . the Saviour of the world, through the liberation of religion from its bonds of materialism, whether legal, cultic or chauvinistic —*in hoc signo vincemus!*[20]

This false pathos is alien to us today at the close of a century that weighs particularly heavily on us Germans. But the rejection of Jesus' messianic claim has remained, although the reasoning has changed. H. Conzelmann's seminal article, "Jesus Christus," in the third edition of the *RGG*, is one example among many. Conzelmann emphasizes that "the question concerning Jesus' self consciousness" is too quickly attached to the concept "messianic consciousness" and is "not [exhausted]

---

17   Bousset, *Jesus*, 87.

18   For Bousset and Carlyle, see A. F. Verheule, *Wilhelm Bousset: Leben und Werk. Eine theologiegeschichtlicher Versuch* (Amsterdam: Van Bottenburg, 1973) 733-35. See the critique by J. Weiss, *Die Predigt Jesu vom Reiche Gottes* (Göttingen: Vandenhoeck & Ruprecht, 1892; 2nd ed., 1900; 3rd ed. edited by F. Hahn, with introduction by R. Bultmann, 1964) 56; ET: *Jesus' Proclamation of the Kingdom of God* (Philadelphia: Fortress, 1971; repr. Chico: Scholars, 1985) 115.

19   Verheule, *Bousset*, Band II/2, 481.

20   W. Staerck, "Jesu Stellung zum jüdischen Messiasbegriff," *Protestantische Monatshefte* 6 (1902) 309.

in the problem of whether and how J[esus] applied the Jewish christ-ological title to himself.[21] This is certainly correct. However, in the investigation of the titles he concludes that they all derive from "community theology," so "that Jesus' self-understanding is not accessible via the titles.[22] Nor can the words in which Jesus speaks of his sending and coming "be formulated from a retrospect on his completed ministry." However, he admits that, "the conceptions of the prophet and rabbi [typify] only partial aspects(!), yet nothing of the center. Jesus understands himself as *the final herald* ("der letzte Rufer") . . . for after him no one else "comes" but God himself.[23]

Yet by his own interpretation—contra that statements of the primitive Christian texts—grave difficulties must ensue, The *final herald*, after whom "no one else 'comes' but God himself," is not Jesus, but John the Baptist. If Jesus were the "final crier" what then would distinguish him from the Baptist? The synoptic accounts give a clear answer. For example, in Q we find:

> The law and the prophets were until John; since then the good news of the kingdom of God is preached . . . (Luke 16:16). [From that time] the kingdom of heaven has been coming violently and men of violence take it by force (Matt 11:12).

However, where the kingdom of God is breaking through, "*God is already coming*," i.e. in Jesus' activity itself. The treasure in the field, the pearl of great price, will be discovered now or not at all, and appropriated by means of a "violent" decision! Jesus says nothing of a *merely future* "coming" of God. The plea for the coming of the kingdom of God in the Lord's Prayer refers to present *and* future, just as all the other pleas. The future reserves only the revelation of the Son of Man, whatever Jesus may have meant by this, and will make manifest the decision which is consummated now regarding Jesus' message. In contrast to the Baptist, the final and greatest prophet, Jesus brings the eschatological *fulfillment* of the promise:

> Blessed are the eyes which see what you see, and the ears which hear what you hear! For I tell you that many prophets and kings desired to see what you see, and did not see it, and to hear what you hear, and did not hear it (Matt 13:16-17; Luke 10:23).

---

[21]   H. Conzelmann, "Jesus Christus," *RGG* 3 (3rd ed., 1959) cols. 619-53; ET: *Jesus* (Philadelphia: Fortress, 1973).

[22]   Conzelmann, "Jesus Christus," 631.

[23]   Conzelmann, "Jesus Christus," 633 (Conzelmann's emphasis).

Is it not rather the "Fulfiller" who speaks thus, the "Bringer of the Kingdom of God" than the "final crier," and is it not so, given the prophetic promise of the Old Covenant, in which Jesus lives, that (in E. Käsemann's words), "the only category which does justice to this claim . . . is that in which the disciples . . . placed him—namely, that of the Messiah"? If this is so, then is not the construction which has ruled large parts of German Protestant research of the past 90 years, the completely unmessianic Jesus, a fundamental error?

THE RELIGION-HISTORICAL PROBLEM

Earlier research assumed almost as a matter of course the existence of an established, traditional, Jewish "Messiah dogmatic." Under this rubric aspects of Christian teaching from a much later period were read into ancient Judaism. A "firmly established 'Messiah' concept," such as Wrede presupposes[24] and uses to account for an originally unmessianic Jesus, never existed. Instead there were different Messiah pictures with numerous descriptions,[25] often expressing not so much titles as functions. We would do better therefore to speak of a—relatively broad and variable—"Messiah Haggada."

Our knowledge here has been greatly increased by the Qumran texts. But already the material assembled by Billerbeck shows that Judaism had no unified, predominantly *political*, Messiah picture, but rather that the views here were extremely diverse. The messianically interpreted Old Testament texts were already extraordinarily variable. Thus, for example, the contrast between an earthly, political, "Messiah" and a "heavenly, transcendent," Son of Man is questionable, for the "Son of Man" coming from Heaven in Daniel 7 is also victorious against the godless "world powers," and functions there in the Parables of Ethiopic *Enoch* in an even greater capacity as universal judge than the Davidic Messiah in *Psalms of Solomon* 17, whose role seems limited to more immediate nationalistic interests. On the other hand, the Messiah cannot attain his God-given rule without God's help: slaying the army of nations gathered against Jerusalem "with the rod of his mouth and the breath of his lips" (Isa 11:4), is no less a miracle than flying along with the clouds. The earthly and

---

24   Wrede, *Messiasgeheimnis*, 220.
25   For a recent collection of studies in which varieties of Jewish messianism are explored, see J. H. Charlesworth (ed.), *The Messiah: Developments in Earliest Judaism and Christianity* (Minneapolis: Fortress, 1992).

heavenly world formed *one* continuum, were bound together and continually influenced one another.

The timing of the Eschaton is also variable. In the zoomorphic apocalypse of *1 Enoch* the Messiah is not born until after God himself has destroyed the power of the nations and passed judgment. Might not this order sometimes have been reversed? *Psalms of Solomon* 17 already attests that the Messiah will be the Spirit-filled teacher and judge of his people. This refutes the alleged contradiction, emphasized chiefly by Vielhauer, between Messiah and kingdom of God. God sets up his rule through the king from David's house who, taught by God and armed with the gifts of the Spirit mentioned in Isa 11:2-5, will lead and judge his people in righteousness.[26] In *T. Judah* 24 we find a non-warlike Messiah from Judah with an ethical orientation. Alongside this, *T. Levi* 18 speaks of the messianic High Priest as savior. The circumstances of place and time of the Messiah's appearance, his concealment before his public ministry, the forms of his legitimation through God himself, through a prophet like Elijah, or *coram publico*, and his coming in humility or glory, remain astonishingly variable in the later Messiah Haggada. Even the pre-existence Messiah, hidden by God, or the suffering and dying Messiah, are not absent.

The thesis that there is no reference whatever to a pre-Christian suffering Messiah appears questionable in light of the messianic features of the LXX translation of Isaiah 53, and Aramaic text from Cave 4 concerning an atoning revelator.[27] In fact, we have only very few pre-Christian messianic texts, which nonetheless already show an astonishing variety; Qumran has significantly increased these. We now know of the two Anointed figures, the pre-eminent priestly, and the Davidic. To this may be added the eschatological role of Michael

---

[26] *Pss. Sol.* 17:3-4, 21, 36-37, 43. See also the recently published 4Q369, which in 1 ii 5-8 speaks of someone instructed by God: "and you have made clear to him your good judgments [. . .] in eternal light. And you made him a first-bo[rn] son to you [. . .] like him for a prince and ruler in all your earthly land [. . . the] crown of the heavens and the glory of the clouds [you] have set [on him . . .]." The figure described here is probably a Davidic king (if not David himself), but quite possibly a Davidic messianic figure. Note that God has instructed him "in eternal light." See C. A. Evans, "A Note on the 'First-Born Son' of 4Q369," *DSD* 2 (1995) 185-201.

[27] Cf. M. Hengel, *The Atonement: The Origins of the Doctrine in the New Testament* (London: SCM Press; Philadelphia: Fortress, 1981) 58. The text is 4Q541.

as heavenly savior. With such a widely arrayed background, which continues in the rabbinic texts despite the consolidations following AD 70 and 135, it may be presumed that the messianic spectrum was even much broader.[28] A case in point are Josephus' references to radical eschatological groups, and the messianic ambitions of individuals, although he passes over in silence all messianic statements because of their political sensitivity. There can be no question here of a systematic configuration of the Messiah Haggada, to say nothing of a Messiah dogmatic.

The word מְשִׁיחַ refers already in the Old Testament to God's activity. He is the actor in the "anointing" carried out in his name. Thus, מְשִׁיחַ–χριστός is not simply a "title of majesty," which one can adopt, but presupposes God's acting. But the concept need not possess, *a priori*, a greater theocratic-political content, than the metaphor "kingdom of God." Isaiah 61:1-2 is especially fitting as an eschatological text here: "The Spirit of the Lord God is upon me, because the Lord has anointed me to bring good tidings to the afflicted."

I know of no other Old Testament text that better describes the ministry of Jesus in Galilee. Luke, with excellent historical-theological flair, puts this word on Jesus' lips in his sermon at the outset of his public ministry in Nazareth (Luke 4:17-19). The importance of this text for Jesus himself can be seen from his answer to the Baptist's question, and the Beatitudes. The same motif, however, appears in one of the most influential texts of those referring to the "kingly" Messiah, Isa 11:1-5: "And the Spirit of the Lord shall rest upon him . . . ."

The Dead Sea Scrolls have significantly added to our knowledge of Jewish messianism in late antiquity.[29] We know from the Qumran texts that the messianic prophet of Deuteronomy 18 plays a role, not

---

28 This is not to claim that there was no core of common messianic beliefs; cf. J. J. Collins, *The Scepter and the Star: The Messiahs of the Dead Sea Scrolls and Other Ancient Literature* (ABRL 10; New York: Doubleday, 1995); C. A. Evans and P. W. Flint (eds.), *Eschatology, Messianism, and the Dead Sea Scrolls* (Dead Sea Scrolls and Related Literature 1; Grand Rapids: Eerdmans, 1997).

29 See Collins, *The Scepter and the Star*; J. H. Charlesworth (ed.), *The Messiah: Developments in Earliest Judaism and Christianity* (Minneapolis: Fortress, 1992); C. A. Evans and P. W. Flint (eds.), *Eschatology, Messianism, and the Dead Sea Scrolls* (Dead Sea Scrolls and Related Literature 1; Grand Rapids: Eerdmans, 1997); and J. Zimmermann, *Messianische Vorstellungen in den Schriftfunden von Qumran* (dissertation; Tübingen, 1996) [forthcoming in WUNT].

only in the Samaritan eschatology (where there could be no royal Davidic Messiah), and in Christian texts, but also in Jewish texts. Moreover, there the Old Testament prophets are sometimes described as "anointed," for example, we read in 1QM 11:7, "your Anointed ones, seers of the testimonies"; elsewhere we find "Anointed of the Holy Spirit" (CD 2:12, and a further D fragment from 4Q267; cf. 6:1: משיחי רוח הקודש), and "holy Anointed Ones" (CD 6:1). Moses appears once as "God's anointed."[30] In another text the "Shoot of David" is the "Anointed of Righteousness,"[31] while elsewhere we read of one "anointed with the oil of the kingdom" (4Q458 2 ii 6). David was not only the prototype of the kingly Messiah, but, next to Isaiah, the most important prophet as well.[32] What was true for the prophets of Israel was certainly valid for a figure bringing eschatological salvation, as is seen by the appearance of such a one in 11QMelchizedek. There the messenger of good tidings from Isa 52:7, with an allusion to Isa 61:1, is interpreted as the one "Anointed with the Spirit" (משיח הרוח) who "[preaches] good news, proclaims [salvation], of whom it is written, [when it says, 'to comfort [all who mourn in Zion], and to teach them in truth . . . .'"[33] The variability of the משיח manifest in the Qumran texts accords with the possibility of describing the "Son of Man" as Messiah since the *Similitudes of Enoch*.

If, then, a prophetic teacher figure with the authority of God's Spirit appeared with the outrageous claim that with his activity God's eternal reign became reality, if he applied the apocalyptic cipher "(Son of) Man" to himself, and also to the future heavenly Judge, if he also came from a family of the lineage of David, then does it not appear probable, that he was invested with the title "Anointed," and took a position with regard to the title, and under the charge of being the long-awaited "Messiah" and "King of the Jews" was executed on the cross as a political criminal? In other words: the historical sounding of the question, Jesus and "Messiah," must begin with the Passion story.

---

30 4Q377 2 ii 5: "by the mouth of Moses his anointed [מושה משיחו]."
31 4Q252 1 v 3-4: "until the coming of the anointed of righteousness [משיח הצדק], the branch of David [צמח דויד]."
32 J. A. Sanders, *The Psalms Scroll of Qumrân Cave 11* (DJD 4; Oxford: Clarendon, 1965) 96 = 11QPsª 27:9-11.
33 P. J. Kobelski, *Melchizedek and Melchireša^c* (CBQMS 10; Washington: Catholic Biblical Association, 1981) 6 = 11QMelch 2:18-21.

THE CRUCIFIED MESSIAH[34]

H. J. Holtzmann said of Jesus' death on the cross that it was "of all things, the most certain."[35] On this single point, even in research today, there is still a consensus. But here the consensus ends. The workbook by Conzelmann and Lindemann, following R. Bultmann, manages to admit that it must have been "a political accusation that was leveled against Jesus" and "that a trial before the representative of the Roman government actually did take place,"[36] which led to crucifixion; all else is alleged to be redactional, secondarily "spun from" Old Testament material, or simply legend. All that remains of the Markan Passion narrative is what we can otherwise derive from the Pauline statement that Jesus was executed by crucifixion.

On the other hand, it seems that scholarship is widely agreed that, as Bultmann emphasizes, Mark "had already before him a Passion story that was a continuous narrative,"[37] indeed the earliest of all the

---

[34]   On the trial of Jesus, see A. Strobel, *Die Stunde der Wahrheit* (WUNT 21; Tübingen: Mohr [Siebeck], 1980); O. Betz, "Probleme des Prozesses Jesu," *ANRW* II/25.1 (1982) 565-647. See also my studies: *"Mors turpissima crucis*: Die Kreuzignung in der antiken Welt und die 'Torheit' des 'Wortes vom Kreuz'," in J. Friedrich, W. Pöhlmann, and P. Stuhlmacher (eds.), *Rechtfertigung: Festschrift für Ernst Käsemann zum 70. Geburtstag* (Tübingen: Mohr [Siebeck]; Göttingen: Vandenhoeck & Ruprecht, 1976) 125-84; expanded ET: *Crucifixion: In the Ancient World and the Folly of the Message of the Cross* (London: SCM Press; Philadelphia: Fortress, 1977); and *Atonement* (see n. 25 above), which is an expanded English version of my "Der stellvertretende Sühnetod Jesu: Ein Beitrag zur Entstehung des urchristlichen Kerygma," *IKZ* 9 (1980) 1-25, 135-47. The English versions are now published together in one volume: *The Cross of the Son of God* (Philadelphia: Fortress, 1986; repr. London: SCM Press, 1997).

[35]   *GGA* (1901) 959.

[36]   H. Conzelmann and A. Lindemann, *Arbeitsbuch zum Neuen Testament* (9th ed., Tübingen: Mohr [Siebeck], 1988) 331; ET: *Interpreting the New Testament: An Introduction to the Principles and Methods of New Testament Exegesis* (Peabody: Hendricksen, 1988) 333.

[37]   R. Bultmann, *Die Geschichte der synoptischen Tradition* (FRLANT 12; Göttingen: Vandenhoeck & Ruprecht, 1921; 2nd ed., FRLANT 29; 1931); ET: *The History of the Synoptic Tradition* (Oxford: Blackwell, 1972) 275. Close to the ancient kerygma of the "Passion and Death of Jesus, as the analysis has shown, was a short narrative of historical reminiscence about the Arrest, Condemnation and Execution of Jesus." Cf. idem, *Die Erforschung der synoptischen Evangelien* (2nd ed., Giessen: Töpelmann, 1930) 45; ET: "A Study of the Synoptic Gospels," in R. Bultmann and K. Kundsin, *Form Criticism: Two Essays on New Testament Research* (New York: Harper & Row, 1962) 11-76, here 65.

early Church's connected narratives about Jesus. To be sure, there is much disagreement about the date and extent of this pre-Markan "Passion story." Paul provides a hint in 1 Corinthians 11, where he refers to Jesus' last meal. This account may already have existed at the end of the Thirties when Paul was preaching in Syria. Can then the account of Jesus' suffering be very much later? If the oldest narrative account about Jesus, the Passion story, represents a mere conglomerate of "dogmatic" and legendary community formulations, as radical criticism postulates, can anything at all of the Jesus tradition be trustworthy? The disciples must have been much more interested in Jesus' Passion—which formed the basis for the beginning of the Church and the Kerygma—than in individual logia and parables. Wellhausen, the great skeptical historian, comments: "the reminiscences of him are one-sided and sketchy; only the last days of his life remained etched in memory."[38] The early Jerusalem church, under the leadership of Peter and James, the Lord's brother, was for the next three decades the primary church that could gather information about that unique event. If they were not interested in this, but instead, contrary to all memory, freely constructed and historicized, than neither can we expect them to have had any interest in sayings of Jesus. But no one is prepared to accept this consequence. Bultmann wrote a classic study on Jesus, and Conzelmann is able to tell us a good deal about Jesus in his article, "Jesus Christus."

With good reason. For how can the disciples have forgotten the most convulsive day of their lives? If, however, we take the view that the disciples, Peter at their head, held this day in memory, and attempted to supplement their knowledge of their Master's death through additional information from Simon of Cyrene, the women, Joseph of Arimathea, and others, then we cannot ignore that *the Messiah question runs through the Passion story of all the Gospels like a red thread.* This is particularly prominent in the oldest account, Mark's, and is surely true for the pre-Markan story as well.

N. A. Dahl has already pointed out the line of connection between the Pauline message of "Christ crucified," and the statement of the Gospels that Jesus was executed as *King of the Jews.* This was the decisive charge against Jesus, that brought him to the cross; for "the formulation 'King of the Jews' derives neither from a prophetic

---

[38] J. Wellhausen, *Israelitisch-jüdische Geschichte* (8th ed., Berlin: de Gruyter, 1921) 367.

proof nor from the Church's Christology."[39] It is improbable that the early Church, with no reference to historical reality, introduced of itself the politically prejudicial expression, "King of the Jews," since this would have justified the Roman proceedings against Jesus as a rebel. All those who even stretched their hand towards the crown, from the last of the Hasmoneans, Antigonus, to the pseudo-messiah, Bar Cochba, were rebels against Rome and suffered a violent death. Had the earliest Church applied the title, "King of the Jews," to Jesus, it would itself have been responsible for arraying him with the worst of all possible company, defaming both him and itself. But it was unnecessary to invent this charge; it was, in fact, brought by the hierarchs against Jesus before Pilate as the most certain means of bringing this seducer of the people to the cross.

With good reason, Dahl refers her to the *causa poena* on the cross (Mark 15:26): King of the Jews. This informed everyone in Jerusalem of the charge against Jesus. Conzelmann and Lindemann, however, see even in this item, which disadvantaged Christians in the eyes of their opponents, "a christological [motive] without historical back-ground"; for, "there is no evidence for affixing such inscriptions . . . as a Roman custom."[40] But this argument is misleading. For it must be recognized that antiquity has supplied us with very few real descriptions of crucifixion at all.[41] The Gospels are by far the most extensive accounts of execution on the cross. Ancient authors gener-ally considered it far too unsavory a subject. For *this reason* we find hardly any details. The *practice* of publicizing a *causa poena* on a placard for general deterrence at an execution is attested in several texts. These were hung around the delinquent's neck, or carried before him when he was led to the place of execution.[42] With crucifixion however the suffering of the condemned man before his death could last for days; to increase the deterrent effect, the placard will have been affixed to the cross. There is no basis then for

---

[39]   N. A. Dahl, "Der gekreuzigte Messias," in H. Ristow and K. Matthiae (eds.), *Der historische Jesus und der kerygmatische Christus: Beiträge zum Christusverständnis in Forschung und Verkündigung* (Berlin: Evangelische Verlags-anstalt, 1961) 159; ET: "The Crucified Messiah," in Dahl, *The Crucified Messiah and Other Essays* (Minneapolis: Augsburg, 1974) 10-36, here 23-24.

[40]   Conzelmann and Lindemann, *Interpreting the New Testament*, 333.

[41]   See Hengel, *Crucifixion*.

[42]   Suetonius, *Caligula* 32.2; *Domitian* 10.1; Cassius Dio 54.3.7; Eusebius, *Hist. Eccl.* 5.1.44.

dismissing as "dogmatic invention" the reference to the *causa poena*, likely to be understood by ancient readers as a defamation. The *titulus* on the cross is just as historical as the ensuing account that Jesus was crucified between two "robbers," i.e. presumably two political insurrectionists. The same is true of the mocking of Jesus by the anti-Jewish soldier rabble, who deride him in a parody of royal homage as a king wearing a purple mantle and crown of thorns.[43]

Further, I find improbably the view that Pilate's question, "Are you the King of the Jews?," and Jesus' positive answer, was secondarily interpolated into the original unity of 15:1 and 3. For it is incredible that the original account of Jesus' delivery to Pilate should have been no more specific than the banal, "And the chief priests accused him of many things," of 15:3. Is the earliest Church supposed to have believed that Jesus was executed on such unspecified grounds? In fact, v. 3 underscores only the one point of the charge, to which Jesus confesses in v. 2, and in which all four Gospels agree. Jesus' confirming answer to Pilate seals his fate: *confessus pro iudicato est* (*Digestae* 42.2: *de confessis*)

Here, one thing leads to the next. Jesus was delivered to Pilate with the capital charge, "King of the Jews." But how did the hierarchs arrive at *this* charge, graver than any other? Through the previously narrated interrogation at night before the highest Jewish office, the High Priest and the court over which he presided. In favor of the Markan account is the curious note concerning the alleged Temple saying of Jesus. The erection of the new eschatological sanctuary was a messianic task. Thus there was an inner connection between this alleged saying of Jesus and the provocative question of the High Priest concerning Jesus' messianic dignity. Is it not plausible that Jesus answered this question with a word of judgment which, in its turn, provoked the Sanhedrin, confirmed his God-given authority, and at once referred the hierarchs to the coming Son of Man with whom he was inextricably bound? This would explain their indignant reaction, and the abuse he suffered as a false prophet. The precautions taken at Jesus' arrest, and the speed with which he was delivered to Pilate, show that his influence with the people was feared, making it necessary to avoid public proceedings. It was his messianic claim that finally led to their making short work of him.

The Messiah question, according to Mark, was predominant during

---

43   Mark 15:16-20; cf. Philo, *Flacc.* 36-42.

the final, tense days in Jerusalem. He dramatically prepares the way for it with the healing of blind Bartimaeus in Jericho; this healing falls outside the topics of customary miracle stories. The address, "Son of David," marks Jesus as a messianic pretender. Jesus' entry into Jerusalem, riding down from the Mount of Olives into the Holy City—as in Zech 9:9—accompanied by the acclamation of his fellow pilgrims, brings the Messiah question distinctly to the fore. Why should not the crowd of accompanying pilgrims, who knew only too well a prophetic word such as Zech 9:9, have seen in Jesus the messianic Prophet, and have harbored the hope that he would be "one to redeem Israel"? And Jesus himself—why should he not have acted out a messianic symbolism, with the Holy City and its Temple in view?

The Cleansing of the Temple also presupposes a scriptural reference from Zechariah—the last word in the book: "And there shall no longer be a trader in the house of the Lord of hosts on that day" (14:21b).[44] With this second symbolic action, Jesus cleanses the Temple for the kingdom of God in a paradigmatic act in his full authority as Messiah designatus. It is no wonder that the hierarchs question him concerning his authority (11:27-32). A messianic background is evident in other episodes as well. The Parable of the Wicked Vineyard Tenants (Mark 12:1-12), showing a familiarity with Palestinian conditions,[45] threatens the hierarchs with the judgment of God for rejecting his messengers.[46] Other anecdotes demonstrate his authority as a charismatic teacher, "not as the scribes." If Mark has invented all this material—historically appropriate in style to an astonishing degree—then he has done it with ingenious empathy,

---

[44]　On the possible influence of Zechariah on Jesus, see R. M. Grant, "The Coming of the Kingdom," *JBL* 67 (1948) 297-303; F. F. Bruce, "The Book of Zechariah and the Passion Narrative," *BJRL* 43 (1960-61) 336-53; J. D. M. Derrett, "The Zeal of thy House and the Cleansing of the Temple," *Downside Review* 95 (1977) 79-94; and now B. Chilton, *The Temple of Jesus: His Sacrificial Program Within a Cultural History of Sacrifice* (University Park: Penn State Press, 1992) 135-36, as well as the chapter by Evans, "Jesus and Zechariah's Messianic Hope," which appears later in the present volume.

[45]　See M. Hengel, "Das Gleichnis von den Weingärtnern Mc 12:1-12 im Lichte der Zenonpapyri und der rabbinischen Gleichnisse," *ZNW* 59 (1968) 1-39.

[46]　See C. A. Evans, "God's Vineyard and Its Caretakers," in Evans, *Jesus and His Contemporaries: Comparative Studies* (AGJU 25; Leiden: Brill, 1995) 381-406.

intuition, and understanding. But in the opinion of many critics he was a simple anonymous Gentile Christian![47] How is this supposed to have come about?

With these all too brief reflections I have intended no more than to point out that the Passion narrative *can* (and in my opinion must) be viewed very differently than the widespread historical skepticism in contemporary criticism allows. *Absolute proof* for the historicity of the individual episodes in the Markan passion is not the issue here. This can hardly be obtained, given the limited source basis—as is frequently the case in Ancient History. Whoever radically strikes the Messiah question from the Passion story makes the account not only incomprehensible, and a banal torso, but is also unable to explain the Easter events and the origin of post-Easter Christology. This is a high price—much too high a price—to pay for the postulate of an unmessianic Jesus.

THE TITLES "MESSIAH" AND "SON OF MAN"[48]

Might one not object here that in all four Gospels Jesus never applies the appellation "Christ" (anointed) to himself, but, on the contrary, this title is always applied to him by others. However, Jesus never rejects the title—neither in the trial before the High Priest, nor before Peter and the disciples. During the trial before Pilate he might yet have denied this charge, and he explained that he was only a rabbi and prophet declaring the will of God. But even as he refused

---

47   Conzelmann and Lindemann, *Interpreting the New Testament*, 218: "The only thing we can state is that the author of Mk is a Gentile Christian with whom we are not otherwise acquainted." Also: "Mk has quite obviously not been written by a Jew." Such opinions are typical for modern unhistorical "uncritical New Testament criticism." Of course, Mark, the "unjewish author," read neither Strack-Billebeck nor Josephus.

48   See M. Hengel, "Jesus als messianischer Lehrer der Weisheit und die Anfänge der Christologie," in J. Leclant et al. (eds.), *Sagesse et Religion: Colloque de Strasbourg (octobre 1976)* (Paris: Bibliothèque des Centres d'Etudes Supérieures Spécialisés, 1979) 147-88; ET: "Jesus the Messianic Teacher of Wisdom and the Beginnings of Christology," in Hengel, *Studies in Early Christology*, 73-117; as well as the essays by O. Betz, "Die Frage nach dem messianischen Bewußtsein Jesu," "Jesu Evangelium vom Gottesreich," and "Jesus in Nazareth: Bemerkungen zu Markus 6,1-6," in Betz, *Jesus, der Messias Israels: Aufsätze zur biblischen Theologie* (WUNT 42; Tübingen: Mohr [Siebeck], 1987) 140-68, 232-54, and 301-17, respectively.

a hasty flight the night before to avoid arrest, so also he refuses this option. In Mark 8:24-26 he merely forbids Peter and the disciples to betray the secret. The ensuing repudiation of Peter as "Satan" (is this also a product of the earliest Church?) results from Peter's reaction to the revelation that Jesus "must suffer many things." We do not know whether, or how, these accounts originally belonged together.

I would put the question the other way round: Is it not an indication of the relative trustworthiness of the Gospel tradition that the alleged great creativity of the "community" never produced an unambiguous scene in which Jesus announces his claim *coram publico* with a clear "I am the Messiah, the Son of God"? Could this not be the result of the "community" knowing that Jesus never proclaimed himself to be the Messiah in this manner, or even that it was simply impossible thus to proclaim oneself Messiah, for example, because the revelation of God's Anointed in his majesty could only be accomplished by God himself?[49] The messianic secret then would stem *in nuce* from the (eschatological) secret of Jesus himself, and his conduct.

This is known by his use of the disputed cipher, "the man," for himself and the coming Judge. This expression, incomprehensible in Greek and which with one exception (Acts 7:56) occurs only on the lips of Jesus, and always in the four Gospels, is among those imitations of Jesus' speech found in the Gospels such as "the Kingdom of God," "*amen* I say to you," the prayer address, "*Abba*, Father," and "this generation." I am simply unable to believe that the so-called earliest community (i.e. in reality, his closest disciples) made him the resurrected Son of Man after the appearances, and then very quickly suppressed this cipher because it was unsuitable for mission proclamation, while at the same time being extremely careful to insure that in the Gospel tradition only Jesus speaks of the Son of Man, never his disciples, just as the Messiah title was strictly held at a distance from him in the production of the dominical sayings. Radical exegetes seem to be to be too "trusting" here.

Since in the following section I want to treat Jesus' "messianic" conduct and teaching, and no longer the titles, here I address this supremely disputed problem, whose secret we can no longer fully

---

49   Matthew's expansion of Peter's confession reflects this very belief; cf. Matt 16:17: "And Jesus answered him, 'Blessed are you, Simon Bar-Jona! For flesh and blood have not revealed this to you, but my Father who is in heaven.'"

unveil, only briefly. It sometimes seems as it New Testament scholarship has little new to say about this problem. But there is no cause for complete skepticism. It is in any case wrong to construct a thoroughgoing antithesis between the "(Son of) Man," and the "Messiah." Already the (few) Jewish sources referring to the "(Son of) Man" of Dan 7:13 forbid this. Jesus employs "(Son of) Man," an expression characterized both by Dan 7:13, and ordinary, everyday use, because it is a cipher, and not explicitly messianic. It becomes then, paradoxically, the expression for the mystery connected with his mission and passion. Mark appears already to have understood it in this way, and thus for him it is not included in the messianic secret. We meet the expression 81 times in the Gospels. That *all* these texts were secondarily inserted by the Community, I hold to be impossible. In the interest of space, I restrict myself to what seems to me to be the most plausible solution. The earthly and suffering Son of Man are a cipher with which Jesus, in certain situations, expresses both his authority (indeed, we may say as *Messias designatus*), and his humility and tribulation, which ultimately lead him to suffering and death. Regarding the coming Son of Man, who appears as a mysterious heavenly figure, I refer to the seminal study by Carsten Colpe: "The apocalyptic Son of Man is a symbol for Jesus' certainty of perfection."[50] Just as the Son of Man may not be set in opposition to Jesus, neither may he be set over against the Kingdom of God. On the other hand, a precipitous identification in the contemporary ministry of Jesus was impossible. A text such as Luke 12:8-9 emphasizes the inextricable connection between Jesus and the coming Son of Man, but does not remove the dialectical tension between the earthly preacher and the coming judge. Adolf Schlatter, as well, emphasizes that the eschatological dignity of Jesus is indeed one of his "goals," therefore,[51]

> the "Messiah" idea was flexible because it expressed a goal; it did not derive its content from a realized state of affairs. The procession of events had to show how the kingdom of the promised king came into being, and what it accomplished. No promise receives its concrete form until God's government supplies it.[52]

---

[50]   C. Colpe, "ὁ υἱὸς τοῦ ἀνθρώπου," *TDNT* 8 (1972) 400-77.
[51]   A. Schlatter, "Der Zweifel an der Messianität Jesu," *BFCT* 11/7 (1907) 151.
[52]   Schlatter, "Der Zweifel an der Messianität Jesu," 162.

This means, however, that Jesus himself, in obedience to his God-given task of announcing the eschatological fulfillment of the promise, and thereby introducing it, *expounds, through his conduct and his way, just what was really fitting for God's chosen "Anointed."* It was not a given, fixed Jewish "messianology" that determined his service, but rather his service established the standards for what was, in the truest sense, legitimately "messianic." His God-given task, the fulfillment of His will, stood before, and above, the titles. To this messianic ministry to his own people we now turn our attention.

THE MESSIANIC MINISTRY OF JESUS[53]

Despite the widespread aversion to attributing to Jesus a "messianic consciousness," there is broad consensus that Jesus' ministry and conduct can hardly be explained as that of a mere rabbi and prophet: "And they were astonished at his teaching, for he taught them as one who had authority, and *not* as the scribes" (Mark 1:22). For Mark, this is the teaching authority of the perfect Spirit-bearer (1:10, 13), which brings the radically New. This same authority shows itself in Jesus' behavior and conduct. He promises to sinful men and women the forgiveness of their sin, that which is the prerogative of God alone; the scandalous fellowship with tax-collectors and sinners has a similar intention. He justifies it with the saying: "I cam not to call the righteous, but sinners" (Mark 2:17b). The Pauline justification of the sinner derives from Jesus' messianic activity.

His dismissive answer concerning the Pharisees and the Baptist's disciples, "Can the wedding guests fast while the bridegroom is with them?," rests on this mission-consciousness which exceeds the bounds of the prophetic. This saying, even as Jesus' behavior with the tax-collectors and sinners, is only comprehensible if the promise is

---

[53] See M. Hengel, "Jesus und die Tora," *TBei* 9 (1978) 152-72; idem, *Studies in Early Christology*, 1-72; *Nachfolge und Charisma: Eine exegetisch-religions-geschichtliche Studie zu Mt 8,21f und Jesu Ruf in die Nachfolge* (BZNW 34; Berlin: de Gruyter, 1968); ET: *The Charismatic Leader and His Followers* (Edinburgh: T. & T. Clark; New York: Crossroad, 1981); idem, *War Jesus Revolutionär?* (CH 110; Stuttgart: Calwer, 1970); ET: *Was Jesus a Revolutionist?* (FBBS 28; Philadelphia: Fortress, 1971); idem, *Die Zeloten: Untersuchungen zur jüdischen Freiheitsbewegung in der Zeit von Herodes I. bis 70 n. Chr.* (AGJU 1; Leiden: Brill, 1961; 2nd ed., 1976); ET: *The Zealots: Investigations into the Jewish Freedom Movement in the Period from Herod I until 70 A.D.* (Edinburgh: T. & T. Clark, 1989).

already *present* in Jesus' ministry, if the Kingdom of God *comes with him*. Because the promises are now being fulfilled, those who witness with eye and ear are counted blessed; thus the cry of acclamation that the eschatological revelation of the Heavenly Father's salvation for the poor and dis-enfranchised is come (Luke 10:21 = Matt 11:25); thus also healings and exorcisms, the deeds of him in whom the fulfillment of the promises becomes reality. "But if it is by the finger of God that I cast out demons, then the Kingdom of God has come upon you" (Luke 11:20 = Matt 12:28).[54]

The Kingdom of God, overcoming the old aeon and the kingdom of Evil, is not only near, it is present in Jesus' ministry. When Jesus speaks of the earthly Son of Man on the one hand, and the coming Son of Man on the other, the tension between the two corresponds to that between the presence of the kingdom in his ministry—which undergoes testing and trial—and his coming in power. Jesus' answer to the charge of being in league with the Devil tends in this direction: " . . . how can one enter a strong man's house and plunder his goods, unless he first binds the strong man? Then indeed he may plunder his house" (Matt 12:29). Jesus is he who brings "liberty to the captives" (Isa 61:1-2). As the victor in this battle he can also call out to his disciples as they return full of joy from their exorcisms: "I saw Satan fall like lightning from heaven" (Luke 10:18). What follows this is no less astonishing:

> Behold, I have given you authority to tread upon serpents and scorpions, and over all the power of the enemy; and nothing shall hurt you. Nevertheless do not rejoice in this . . . but rejoice that your names are written in heaven (Luke 10:19-20).

Who utters such an outrage is not only certain, in his high-flying, god-inspired enthusiasm, that the power of the "Enemy" is broken here and now, but he also dares to anticipate the judgment of God. Thus also, in three blessings (following Isaiah 61), he can promise the poor, the hungry, and the grieving, unconditional participation in the Kingdom of God. As he already now promises salvation with absolute certainty, so also he can anticipate the word of the last judgment; thus, we find the woes pronounced against Chorazin and Bethsaida, where he had done such "mighty works," and even more

---

[54]   See M. Hengel, "Lk 11,20 = Mt 12,28: Der Finger and die Herrschaft Gottes in Lk 11,20," in R. Kiefer and J. Bergman (eds.), *La Main de Dieu / Die Hand Gottes* (WUNT 94; Tübingen: Mohr [Siebeck], 1997) 87-106.

sharply, against the center of his activity: "And you, Capernaum, will you be exalted to heaven? You shall be brought down to Hades" (Matt 11:20-24 = Luke 10:12-15 [Q]).

We meet the same "messianic" self-consciousness in the answer to the Baptist to his question whether he was "he who is to come." Jesus refers to his healing and salvific ministry in which the promises of Isaiah are fulfilled, as well as his liberating good news to the poor. He emphasizes his eschatological authority and majesty with the concluding, "blesses is he who takes no offense at me" (Luke 7:23 = Matt 11:6 [Q]).

For this very reason, then, one cannot demand a sign of him—as from a prophet. Rather, Gentiles will rise up as witnesses against this generation of Jesus' contemporaries: the Queen of the South, who came to hear the wisdom of Solomon, the wisest of the wise, and the Ninevites, who repented at the preaching of Jonah, the most success- ful of the prophets; for "behold, a greater than Solomon is here," and "behold, a greater than Jonah is here" (Matt 12:42 = Luke 11:32 [Q]). How are we to understand this "behold, a greater than Solomon is here" if not in the sense of the end of the old "salvation history," and the dawning of the Kingdom of God in the work of Jesus himself? Because he is "more than a prophet" he does not begin his authorita- tive words with the Old Testament's "Thus says the Lord," but with the unique "Amen, I say to you."

In my judgment, the real Jesus was more enthusiastic, more ecsta- tic, more passionate, and that means also, more alien to us, than we enlightened Westerners care to admit today. We all tend to shape him theologically "in our image." The enthusiastic, messianic Jesus is further from us than the "rabbi and prophet" who has become dear to us, or even the "herald before the end."

Jesus' "ethical" preaching, as well, stands under his "messianic au- thority," which can anticipate God's judgment: whoever judges, will himself be judged, only he who hears and obeys his word builds upon the rock, whoever is anxious makes mammon his idol. This very say- ing, "Do not be anxious," contradicting all wisdom and experience, presupposes that limitless care of God, which is part of his Kingdom. With the seeking of the Kingdom of God as a present power, anxiety and fear fall by the wayside. This command, "Do not be anxious," is just as much part of his divine "messianic" certainty as the saying about faith that moves mountains, and the certainty of answer to prayer. That he reveals the Kingdom of God in parables shows that he (alone) knows its present *and* future secret.

The trial of Jesus, which ends with his execution as messianic pre–tender, and the unique authority, which determines his preaching, his ministry, and his conduct, illuminate each other. Therefore, it seems to me also probable that he goes to Jerusalem in this very authority, with his death before his eyes as the way that the Father has determined for him. The double saying, "I came to cast fire upon the earth; and would that it were already kindled! I have a baptism with which to be baptized; and how I am constrained until it is accomplished!" (Luke 12:49-50), indicates that he is going to his death for the sake of his mission. This is also true of the question by the sons of Zebedee, the debated ransom saying (Mark 10:45), and above all, the words spoken at the Last Supper. Jesus goes to his death for the sake of his messianic ministry to Israel.

That he intended to address not only the Galilean population, but all Israel, is seen by his call and appointment of the Twelve and his sending them out among the people. He calls them to follow him as God once called the prophets, and commissions them with his message.

Just as the Son of Man and the Messiah cannot be fundamentally separated, neither may one *a priori* completely tear the "prophetic" from the "kingly" Messiah. Each is "Spirit-bearer" in a unique way, and this connects the two. Also, the "kingly," and the "prophetic," Messiah can be teacher and proclaimer of God's will, and even more so, judge. At first, the motif of the political Messiah can recede into the background: the overcoming of the worldly powers at enmity with God, not only the ruling political kingdoms, but above all in Satan as their lord, was accomplished "in power" by God's miracle. One cannot deny all political consequences to Jesus' efficacy, but this was of a very different kind than that of the various "messianic" pretenders of his time.

About Jesus, one may say that he made his appearance in Galilee as "Anointed of the Spirit," in the manner of Isaiah 61, and was executed in Jerusalem as "King of the Jews." That his family was reported to be descended from David, that he addressed the entire "twelve tribes" with the fulfillment of promise and the dawning Kingdom, that he not only entered Jerusalem accompanied by a crowd greeting him as a messianic figure, but entered with eschatological authority, all may have played a role here. With regard to the charges at his trial, he did not renounce the messianic claim.

How he himself viewed the eschatological *accomplishment* of his work, we may only *presume* by examining such texts as Mark 14:25; 10:37; or 14:62. In our lack of knowledge, however, we should not forget that Jesus' disciples knew infinitely more about Jesus than we today, and that this knowledge also flowed into the earliest Christology which began directly with, and after, the Easter appearances. How could this have been otherwise! Easter did not alter the direct *remembrance* of Jesus. This experience burned it into the hearts of the disciples.

With our extant sources, we *today* can sketch only a very fragmentary "picture" of Jesus' ministry. To be sure, this is true of many great figures from antiquity. I am reminded of the debate over the "historical Socrates." Many features remain obscure. However, we ought not therefore to make of necessity a virtue, and, with radical critical skepticism, reject *a limine* information which is plausible. That Jesus neither intended to be a mere "rabbi and prophet," nor *one* "eschatological prophet" among many, ought no longer to be disputed. Just as one-sided is the picture, so popular today, of the supertemporal, benevolent teacher of brotherly love and humane principles, who died in the end as a martyr for his good cause. Here, aspects appealing to the modern mind are emphasized in a one-sided manner. Orthodox-fundamental biblicism has its counterpart in critical biblicism.[55] Both are naïve and in danger of doing violence to historical reality—the one, because of its ahistorical biblical literalism, and the other, because it selects and interprets in accordance with its modern world-view, and theological interests. Against the view, since Wrede, of the unmessianic Jesus, it must be admitted that Jesus conducted himself with "messianic" authority, and was executed as a messianic pretender. Only thus are the development of post-Easter Christology, the accounts of his Passion, and his efficacy, historically comprehensible.

With his messianic claim, Jesus the Jew may appear alien, indeed vexing, since his "mythical" characteristics obscure our ethically determined, demythologized picture of him. But the real Jesus was very different. He lived in the language and imagery of the Old Testament and its Jewish-Galilean environment, and he conducted

---

55   One immediately thinks of the North American Jesus Seminar. For trenchant criticisms of this group's presuppositions, methods, and conclusions, see the chapter in this volume by N. T. Wright.

himself with the—in the truest sense of the word—"apocalyptic" (the word comes from ἀποκαλύπτειν, "to reveal") right to usher in God's reign over Israel (and all nations), and, as the "Anointed of God," to fulfill the promises made to the fathers and the prophets. His death—which he consciously affirmed—placed the seal of confirmation on this right.

That Jesus conducted himself in this manner, I hold to be provable by the methods of historical-critical research. From this flow consequences for theological reflection as well; for, as the messianic bringer of salvation, he is the fundament of our faith, who fulfilled the Old Covenant, and breathed the breath of life into the New. His person and work charge us with the task of a "whole" biblical theology that realizes its Jewish heritage (and the present Israel), a biblical theology that does not eradicate the lines between the Old and the New, but properly defines them, and, remembering a long and checkered history, considers them afresh. I could also express this in the words of Paul with which I began (Rom 15:8): The Jew, Jesus of Nazareth, became the Messiah of Israel in order to fulfill the promises made to the fathers, and he became for us, the Gentiles, "the author of our salvation," because we experience in him what the love of God is, that we might, for the sake of such grace, praise as *our* Father, the God of Israel and Father of Jesus Christ.

ASSESSING THE HISTORICITY
OF JESUS' WALKING ON THE SEA
INSIGHTS FROM CROSS-CULTURAL SOCIAL PSYCHOLOGY

Bruce J. Malina

The task of assessing the authentically historical deeds of Jesus can only be undertaken by means of the imaginary constructs of readers and/or hearers of the Gospel documents. Readers and/or hearers read or hear the documentary sources for a life of Jesus in order to imagine and assess the written descriptions of the deeds in question. Every person seeking to evaluate the historical authenticity of Jesus' deeds thus must necessarily assume and apply some theory of reading, of language and of social meaning, whether they are aware of it or not (see Malina 1996). While a number of scholars do invoke the Romantic, aesthetic category of the Gospels as "literature," nearly all give no thought to the fact that the descriptions in question initially had meaning because of some first-century Mediterranean social system context. And if they have any meaning today at all, it is only because the reader or hearer brings to his or her reading or listening imaginative scenarios of social interaction from a social system context, more often than not that of their own contemporary society. In the quest for evaluating the authentic deeds of Jesus, I suggest that an appreciation of the social system of those who attest to Jesus's deeds as well as that of those who read those deeds today is fundamental.

CURRENT ASSESSMENTS OF THE EPISODE OF
JESUS' WALKING ON THE SEA

This study is about the episode of Jesus walking on the sea (Matt 14:22-33; Mark 6:45-52; John 6:16-21). The most recent overview of previous interpretations of this episode is that of Patrick J. Madden (1997, a dissertation directed by Joseph A. Fitzmyer). Madden describes five types of assessment of this passage:

> The first group withholds any judgment concerning the historicity of the pericope. They engage merely in source and literary analyses, often

stressing the symbolic meaning of the story, but make no judgement whether or not there was a historical event underlying the symbolism. The second group regards the story as a historical account of a miracle that took place during the ministry of Jesus. The third group of interpreters proposes that an originally natural event during the life of Jesus has been given a miraculous interpretation. The fourth group of commentators regards the walking on the sea as a symbolic story with no concrete event as its basis. This group differs from the first group in that for them the story is definitely not historical. The fifth group argues that the story is a displaced resurrection narrative (Madden 1996: 1).

After duly describing the positions of all these groups, Madden himself opts to join the fifth group. He presents his position as follows:

> While absolute certainty is not to be had, it appears more likely that an originally postresurrectional narrative has been transposed to the Galilean ministry rather than vice-versa. There are no real parallels to the sea-walking narrative in the OT or in pre-Gospel pagan literature. So it is likely that this unique narrative is related to Christianity's unique event, the resurrection of Jesus (Madden 1996: 138-39).

From Madden's excellent survey and summary, it is apparent that Jesus' walking on the sea is one of those culturally unfamiliar, problem-filled behaviors in the traditions about Jesus. These include his healings, exorcisms, his hearing voices from the sky, seeing visions of Satan and angels in the wilderness, wonders such as his multiplication of loaves and fishes, or the disciples' visionary experience (transfiguration, appearances of the resurrected Jesus) and the like. Such behaviors are a problem largely because there is no room for them among the patterns of conduct and perception available in contemporary U.S. and northern European social systems. They are anomalies, not replicable in terms of contemporary cultural cues.

The problems posed by such behaviors are variously solved. Conservative, "believing" scholars have recourse to the category, "miracle," and trace the behavior to some supernatural agency. The reason for this, it seems, is that if the behavior in question occurred in the way it is described in the Gospels, then modern witnesses would have to say it was miraculous, obviously supernaturally caused. These scholars seem innocent of the fact that the category "miracle" as they use it is traceable to rather recent times (see Brown 1984; Remus 1983), while the label, "supernatural," invented by Origen in the third century, was of little significance in the world of Jesus and much of the world today (see De Lubac 1948; Saler 1977).

Liberal scholars, on the other hand, judge such behavior as simply impossible, either in the first-century Mediterranean or today. Hence some modern, more enlightened explanations must be used to clarify what our benighted first century Mediterranean authors describe. Such more enlightened explanations include modern psychology and its psychosomatic inventory, psychiatry with its neurosis and psychosis: psychotic interludes, group delusions, or even total shamanistic hoaxes (see Noll 1983). Among these enlightened moderns, there are the literati who would assess these behaviors as literary fiction, fictional accounts developed for some such purpose as supporting weak faith or symbolically expressing some truth or even rooted in misperceptions on the part of first-century witnesses (see Hesse 1965; Keller and Keller 1969).

As a rule, any behavior not readily verifiable in terms of the conceptions available from the contemporary social system into which the interpreter has been enculturated is judged to be a problem. As Jung long ago noted: "all human beings are bad observers of things that are unfamiliar to them" (1976: 307). Since the inquiry into the historical authenticity of Jesus' deeds is largely carried out by liberally enlightened scholars, the general presumption is that none of these extraordinary deeds is historically authentic in the way the Gospel authors describe them. Thus Jesus surely healed, but psychophysical problems were the real issue and Jesus was a master as instilling confidence and allaying anxiety. Hence he could "heal" people. Exorcisms are a case in point. They are instances of psychological projections produced by psychoses. Jesus' techniques were successful in redirecting the projections and bolstering the patient's crippled ego. The multiplication of the loaves and fishes and the subsequent walking on the sea simply highlight Jesus as the new Moses, in a graphic retelling of God's Exodus wonders (water and food) pointing up the role of God's new prophet (see Betz and Grimm 1977; and the range of explanations in Theissen 1983: *passim*).

VIEWING JESUS' WALKING ON THE SEA
FROM ANOTHER PERSPECTIVE

A cross-cultural, anthropological approach to understanding these extraordinary behaviors in the story of Jesus has produced a rather different set of explanations. For such behaviors still exist on the planet in general, and in the Mediterranean as well. The US and its parent northern Europe have grown selectively inattentive to such behaviors. Taking his cue from anthropologists, John Pilch has demonstrated the historical accuracy and plausibility of Jesus' healings in terms of models drawn from a number non-Western societies (see Pilch 1992; 1993a for a list of his previous work). Pilch has also taken the lead in introducing the explanation-rich category of altered (or alternate) states of consciousness (= ASC) into New Testament study (Pilch 1993; 1995; 1996; 1998a; 1998b).

Some twenty-five years ago, Erika Bourguignon has demonstrated that visionary, trance-state experiences and other forms of ASCs exist in institutionalized form among most societies comprising world's population. Pilch offers an overview of her data, as follows:

> ASCs can be induced either directly and intentionally or indirectly and unintentionally. On a continuum, such experiences extend from REM sleep (rapid eye movement) on one end through trance and culminate in possession trance on the other, with many different experiences in between. These insights and further details about them are based on a meticulous analysis of the ethnographic literature from 488 societies in all parts of the world including 44 circum-Mediterranean societies. Ninety percent of these societies reported one or more institutionalized, culturally patterned forms of ASC. Eighty percent of circum-Mediterranean societies shared the same experience. Since ancient Palestine and neighboring societies such as Ancient Egypt and Greece were included in the data bank, the ASC experience is a highly plausible, cultural explanatory model for New Testament reports of circum-Mediterranean people seeing the Risen Jesus (Pilch 1998a).

In recent years a goodly number of researchers have taken serious, experiential, participatory cross-cultural looks into such phenomena, revealing our ignorance of the broad range of possible altered states of consciousness available in human experience (Goodman 1988; 1990; Walsh 1993). There is significant evidence that ASCs represent core experiential features of human living in most societies on the planet, where they are "a matter of major importance, not merely a bit of anthropological esoterica" (Bourguignon 1973: 11). ASCs serve to explain visionary, trance, and ecstatic experience, often combined with extraordinary feats of behavior (e.g. walking on a ladder of sharp knives unscathed, walking over a bed of coals unharmed, walking over an unrolled sheet of paper held off the ground without tearing the paper, self-piercings without bleeding and rather rapid healing, and the like—all now documented on film, available on videocasettes, and sporadically televised on *The Discovery Channel*). Any incident presumably rooted in an ASC may be difficult for Westerners to believe because people in this cultural area have been enculturated to discount such states of awareness except in dreams. Pilch (1994: 233) has noted:

> The physician-anthropologist Arthur Kleinman offers an explanation for the West's deficiency in this matter. "Only the modern, secular West seems to have blocked individual's access to these otherwise pan-human dimensions of the self." What is the Western problem? The advent of modern science in about the seventeenth century disrupted the bio-psycho-spiritual unity of human consciousness that had existed until then. According to Kleinman, we have developed an "acquired consciousness," whereby we dissociate self and look at self "objectively." Western culture socializes individuals to develop a metaself, a critical observer who monitors and comments on experience. The metaself does not allow the total absorption in lived experience which is the very essence of highly focused ASCs (= alternate states of consciousness). The metaself stands in the way of unreflected, unmediated experience which now becomes distanced.

If we recall that "objectivity" is simply socially tutored subjectivity, we might be more empathetic with persons of other cultures who report perceptions that we find incredible, whether miraculous or not, because they are socially dysfunctional for us.

We have come along a bit further than Kant, whose *Critique of Pure Reason* (1781) is devoted to showing how our perceptions, so far from conforming to the objects themselves, can only conform to the conditions imposed by our own minds—which include even such apparently objective external conditions as space and time. For Kant, the "real" world of "things-in-themselves" is both unknown and unknowable. We inhabit a universe of our own personal constructs (see Prickett 1996: 184). The Kantian spin-off known as the "sociology of knowledge" (so often confused in religious studies with the academic discipline of sociology) would go a step further and proclaim that reality is socially constructed. But this Romantic view normally conflicts with U.S. pragmatism that insists that it is not reality that is socially constructed, but rather the social conceptions by which we produce our culturally rooted perceptions. This means that reality is socially interpreted. While I might stub my toe on a hard object in my path and interpret the object as a "a large stone," the object and my immediately felt pain are personally experienced realities that are not socially constructed (see Borhek and Curtis 1975). The reason for insisting on the radical difference between the social construction of reality and the social interpretation of reality is that for the former, ASCs are mere socially contrived mental constructs, while for the latter, ASCs are realities. Yet various cultures deal with these realities differently or not at all, even to the point of denying their existence as anomalies. Anomalies are always full of problems for members of a given social system (see Malina 1993: 154-59).

WALKING ON THE SEA AS AN ASC EXPERIENCE

The Gospel descriptions of Jesus walking on the sea have all the hallmarks of a report of an ASC experience. As a matter of fact, Jesus is regularly described in the Gospels as a "shamanistic holy man," to use an etic designation (see Pilch 1998a; also 1996). The category is well-known and much used by biblical scholars (Theissen 1983: 266). In emic terms, Jesus was said to be a person like John the Baptist, Elijah, Jeremiah or one of the old prophets (Matt 16:14; Mark 8:28; Luke 9:19). In modern descriptions, these persons can "voluntarily enter altered states of consciousness in which they experience themselves or their spirit(s), traveling to other realms at will and interacting with other entities in order to serve their communities" (Walsh 1993: 742). This service consists of solving social problems, providing unavailable information, healings, rescues and the like. Initial experiences that indicate one is able to experience ASC usually befall persons who are effective in personal interaction, superior in energy, concentration, memory, knowledge and leadership. In antiquity such persons had access to the realm of God, and in Hellenism they could be called sons of God, divine men, those with the power of god, divine teachers, wise men, and the like (Gallagher 1982: 72). Pilch was the first to apply ASC anthropological models to the Gospel episodes of the transfiguration and the resurrection appearances of Jesus (Pilch 1995; 1998a; 1998b). Malina applied this perspective in explaining the ecstatic journeys of the author of Revelation (John took his sky readings while "in spirit," 1:10; 4:2; 17:3; 21:10; see Malina 1995, following Pilch 1993b).

Felicitas Goodman, a foremost researcher into ASCs (see Goodman 1988; 1990) has identified four elements almost invariably found in ASC experiences (summarized in Pilch 1993). (1) Those experiencing the vision are initially frightened and (2) do not recognize the figure. (3) The figure in the vision offers calming assurance (e.g. "fear not") and (4) identifies self ("it is I . . ." often giving a name). After this opening gambit, the visionary figure then proceeds to interact with the visionaries in terms of the purpose for the ASC: provide information, healing, rescue and the like. For example, in the Jesus tradition, reports tell of the figure in the vision offering information sought by the one having the vision: a clearer grasp of the identity of the figure in the vision as in the Baptism or Transfiguration accounts, explanation of a difficult problem (Matt 11:25), or the granting of a favor, most often healing (Acts 9:17-18).

Why is it that persons falling into ASCs, where these are institutionalized, invariably encounter expected figures offering quite relevant information, timely rescue or appropriate healing? Goodman offers data indicating that such experiences are always culturally significant for the persons undergoing them because they have been socialized in ASC experiences. Again, she lists four requisite conditions found among the persons she has studied who have experienced ASCs and expect to have them: (1) The person needs to know how to find the crack between the earth, ordinary reality, and the sky on the horizon, the alternate reality. (2) The human body is an intruder in that alternate reality, hence by bodily preparation and posture, the person must tune the physical self to the alternate reality in order to properly perceive it. (3) The person needs the readily learnable proper angle of vision. (4) The event perceived in the experience of the alternate reality is sketched out very hazily; hence the experience must be filled in with elements provided by the general cultural story as well as by any specific story to appreciate a particular experience (Goodman 1990: *passim*, summarized by Pilch 1994). Goodman has, in fact, demonstrated that it is not difficult to teach individuals how to access ASC states; she has done so in public with rather incredulous Western subjects (graduating German medical students). But persons from social systems where ASCs are not institutionalized find their experiences to be vacuous, contentless. It seems the reason for this is that they bring no culturally significant and expected scenarios to the experience (1990: 17). In other words, as Walsh likewise notes, "[ASC] experiences are consistent with the world view and ontocosmology of the tradition. This suggests that there is an intriguing complementarity between a tradition's world view and its technology of transcendence such that an effective technology (set of practices) elicits experiences consistent with and supportive of the world-view" (Walsh 1993: 158, citing Walsh 1991).

Consequently, if descriptions of this experience are so rich in activity and imagery, it is only because participants were culturally prepared to have such experiences and to know what is left unsaid in them. Hence any interpretation of the ASCs in the Gospel requires that the interpreter delve into the available dimensions of persons enculturated in ASC experiences and compare them with features in the Jesus tradition. ASC scenarios might be equally composed from data provided by Israel's traditions that report events that took place in an alternate dimension of reality and that involved people or beings who straddled the two dimensions. For example, the stories of Elijah and Elisha as well as descriptions in the books of Ezekiel, Zechariah, Daniel, Enoch and John's Revelation are excellent examples of available stories.

CULTURAL FEATURES IN THE EPISODE OF
JESUS WALKING ON THE SEA

The account of Jesus' walking on the sea is reported in Matt 14:22-33, Mark 6:45-52 and John 6:16-21 (for a brief literary analysis based on "tradition-historical" criteria, see Bultmann 1968: 216). Interestingly, this incident intervenes between the feeding of the 5000 and events at the other side of the sea in all three sources. The events on the other side are healings at Gennesaret in Matt and Mark, seeking Jesus in John. The sequence presents a scenario that covers "evening," "dark" (explicit in John 6:17, "fourth watch" in Matt and Mark), and "the next day" (explicit in John 6:22, implicit in Matt and Mark). The sequence marks an entire night. Jesus thus comes to his disciples at sea on a stormy night.

The actors in the story include Jesus and his disciples as well as the wind and the sea. The fact alone that the wind and sea are actors is indicative of a society in which one might expect to find persons with ASC abilities. Jesus had already been presented as a person capable of ASC experience. First, there was the sky voice at baptism (Mark 1:11; Luke 3:22; in Matt 3:17 the voice may be directed to the other holy man in the story, John the Prophet; and in another context, the sky voice in John 12:28). Then there was the interlude in the wilderness where Jesus' loyalty to God is tested by Satan/devil (Matt 4:1-11; Mark 1:12-13; Luke 4:1-13), and where God's sky-servants, the angels, minister to Jesus (note in Luke). And the first activity of Jesus described in the tradition is his ability to exorcize (Mark

1:23-28; Luke 4:33-37; not mentioned at this point by Matthew or at all by John). Along with exorcizing and healing, Jesus likewise demonstrates ability as an astral prophet (see Malina 1997). In sum, he is like one of Israel's prophets of old, for whom ASC experiences were quite normal.

Heavy windstorms are a common occurrence on the Sea of Galilee at certain times of the year, and the suddenness with which they can arise is truly astonishing. In antiquity, winds and seasons of the year were personified, or attributed to certain non-visible, person-like cosmic forces or powers.

It is important to note that in all three sources, we are told that "they (the disciples) saw him (Jesus) walking on the sea" (Matt 14:26; Mark 6:49; John 6:19). As Malina and Rohrbaugh note (1998), the sea is an animate being, essentially different entity from water (see Renaud 1997). To walk on the sea is to trample on a being that can engulf people with its waves, swallow them in its deep, and support all sorts of living beings. Given the structure of boats in the period, people who traveled over or worked on the sea literally put their lives in the hands of the spirit(s) or deity that revealed its moods in the varying movements of the sea, from stormy, to rough, to calm, and the like. The Greco-Romans identified the "living" sea with the important deity, Poseidon/Neptune (Semites called this deity: Tiamat or Tehom), a deity noted for violent power. Jesus' ability to walk on the sea is evidence of his place in the hierarchy of cosmic powers.

The point is that in the world of Jesus, the wind and the sea, fevers and unclean spirits, were person-like entities who could be spoken to and who might obey or not. Jesus could command the wind and the sea (Matt 8:26-27; Mark 4:39-41; Luke 8:24-25), just as he commanded unclean spirits (Mark 1:25; Luke 4:35; and again Matt 17:18; Mark 9:25; Luke 9:42) and human beings! Luke (4:39) also reports that fevers could be commanded.

The story reports that the disciples were in a boat in the middle of the sea in the middle of the night. They experienced an ASC of a waking vision (as Matt 14:28 indicates this with: "Lord, if it is you . . ."). That the disciples should have such visions is not surprising. After all they were chosen to deal with unclean spirits, thanks to Jesus' authorization (Matt 10:1; Mark 3:15; 6:7; Luke 9:1). Perhaps it is significant that while Matt 10:1 notes: "he gave them authority over unclean spirits to cast them out, and to heal every disease and every infirmity"; and Luke 9:1-2 states: "[he] gave them power and authority over all demons and to cure diseases, and he sent them out to preach the kingdom of God and to heal," Mark has no mention of Jesus giving his disciples healing power. Mark's only information, repeated twice, is that Jesus "appointed twelve to be with him and have authority to cast out demons" (Mark 3:14-15), and again, Jesus "gave them authority over the unclean spirits" (Mark 6:7). And yet Mark reports that the disciples "cast out many demons, and anointed with oil many that were sick and healed them" (Mark 6:13). The implication is that in the Markan tradition, Jesus chose persons who could heal! Further, the triple tradition reports that the disciples were not always successful even in what they were empowered and authorized to do, that is expel evil spirits/demons (Matt 17:16; Mark 9:18; Luke 9:40). The point is that the disciples were no strangers to the powers that normally were connected to persons capable at ASCs. While the tradition notes the visionary experience of Peter, James and John at the transfiguration (Matt 17:1-9; Mark 9:2-10; Luke 9:28-36), it likewise tells of the visionary experience of all the disciples here on the sea of Galilee and after Jesus' death (Matt 28:16; Luke 23:36-43; repeatedly in John 20:19-23, 24-29; 21:1-14; only in the longer ending to Mark 16:9-20).

The accounts report Jesus' initial intention in the episode. Again, for Matthew and Mark, Jesus was walking across the sea to get to the other side, that is to reach the point toward which the disciples were traveling (Mark 6:48b states that Jesus wished to pass them by!). Hence it was only fortuitously that the disciples had their vision of the sea-traversing Jesus. In the Gospel narratives, Jesus previously demonstrated his mastery over the sea (Matt 8:26-27; Mark 4:39-41), so this episode comes as no total surprise. On the other hand, John has Jesus "walking on the sea and drawing near the boat" (6:19); after prayer Jesus was simply catching up with his disciples. In sum, the whole episode focuses on the disciples and their visionary experience of Jesus on the sea. What sort of cultural sense would this account have for its first-century Mediterranean audience?

WALSH'S MODEL FOR MAPPING ASC EXPERIENCES

Walsh has developed a model that provides for a multidimensional description and phenomenological mapping of features allowing for a comparison of alternate states of consciousness based on ten years of research and personal experience. He uses the model to highlight significant features that characterize the profiles of schizophrenics described in the American Psychiatric Association's *Diagnostic and Statistical Manual of Mental Disorders* (1980). He then sets out these features in comparative array alongside characteristics of shamans in journey trance states, Buddhist Vipassana meditaters and Patanjali yogins (Walsh 1993: 751-52, Table I). The comparison demonstrates that ASCs are not pathological, as ethnocentric Western observers might think. His cross-cultural comparison indicates quite clearly that the three ASC traditions he cites have almost nothing in common with schizophrenia. His model runs as follows:

Key Dimensions for Mapping Altered States

1. Degree of reduction of awareness of the experiential context or environment: ranging from complete to minimal or none

2. Ability to communicate

3. Concentration: important factors here include:
(a) The degree of concentration and
(b) Whether the attention is fixed immovably on a single object (e.g. Buddhist jhanas or yogic samadhi states) or momentary or fluid, where attention is allowed to shift between selected objects e.g. in shamanic journeys)

4. Degree of control.
Here there are two important types of control:
(a) Ability to enter and leave the ASC at will
(b) Ability to control the content of experience while in the ASC

5. Degree of arousal

6. Degree of calm. This refers to more than low arousal, which refers simply to the level of activation, since calm also implies low levels of agitation and distractibility (Nyanoponika Thera).

7. Sensitivity or subtlety of sensory perception. This may be either reduced, as in hypnotic anesthesia, or enhanced, as in Buddhist insight meditation.

8. Nature of the sense of self or identity

9. Affect: especially whether the experience is pleasurable or painful

10. Out of body experience (OBE)
Does the subject experience perceiving from a point that seems outside the body?

11. Content of inner experience:
Here many further differentiations can be made such as: Is the content formless or with form?
(a) Formless, i.e. without differentiation into specific objects or

forms, e.g. an experience of undifferentiated light or clear space, as in the Buddhist jhanas

(b) With form, differentiated, having specific objects, e.g. visual images. If the content is differentiated then it and the state of consciousness can be divided along several subdivisions. Critical subdivisions include:

(1) Degree of organization

(2) Modality of the predominant objects, e.g. auditory,   visual, somatic

(3) Intensity of the objects

(4) Psychological "level" of the objects, e.g. personal or archetypal imagery

12.   The developmental level of the state. In some disciplines different ASCs emerge in a fixed sequence of stages, e.g. the formless samadhi states of yoga emerge after earlier stages in which attention is focused on specific images (Wilber 1980; Wilber et al.). There does not seem to be clear evidence in the literature of a distinct developmental progression of states in shamanism, and so this dimension is not discussed further in this paper (Walsh 1993: 746-47).

PILCH'S ADAPTATION APPLIED TO THE EPISODE
OF JESUS WALKING ON THE SEA

Pilch has adapted and applied Walsh's model in his ground-breaking study of the transfiguration account (Pilch 1995). That essay readily serves as a pattern for studying other ASC described in the New Testament. In the following chart, the features to be mapped are listed in the first column, while the next columns indicate these features in the account of Jesus' walking on the sea:

Dimensions	Matt 14:22-33	Mark 6:45-52	John 6:16-21
1. Reduced Awareness of Environment	Disciples - No Jesus - Yes	Disciples - No Jesus - Yes	Disciples - No Jesus - Yes
2. Ability to Communicate	Disciples - Yes Jesus - Yes	Disciples - Yes Jesus - Yes	Disciples - Yes Jesus - Yes
3. Concentration fixed fluid	Jesus - first fixed, then fluid Disciples - fluid	Jesus - first fixed, then fluid Disciples - fluid	Jesus - first fixed, then fluid Disciples - fixed
4. Control Of ASC: enter and leave at will Of ASC content	Jesus - Yes Disciples - No Peter - No	Jesus - Yes Disciples - No	Jesus - Yes Disciples - No
5. Arousal	Jesus - None Disciples - Yes	Jesus - None Disciples - Yes	Jesus - None Disciples - Yes

6. Calm	Jesus - Yes	Jesus - Yes	Jesus - Yes
	Disciples - No	Disciples - No	Disciples - No
7. Self-sense	Jesus - shift	Jesus - shift	Jesus - shift
	Disciples - no shift	Disciples - no shift	Disciples - no shift
	Peter - unsuccessful		
8. Affect	Jesus - NC	Jesus - NC	Jesus - NC
	Disciples - fear, then	Disciples - fear, then	Disciples - fear, then
	worship of Jesus	worship of Jesus	worship of Jesus
9. Content*	Jesus - mastery of sea	Jesus - mastery of sea	Jesus - mastery of sea
	Disciples - vision	Disciples - vision	Disciples - vision
	Peter - unsuccessful		
	master		

*Content consistent with learned cosmology and traditions that shape culturally patterned waking dreams or trances.

We now consider the dimension of this phenomenological map relative to the episode in question.

1. Degree of reduced awareness of the experiential context or environment

All three accounts variously state that the episode took place on "the sea." That it was the sea of Galilee can only be known from the general narrative context of Matthew and Mark, although John specifies the location in his immediate context, noting the alternate name of the sea, "that is the sea of Tiberias" (John 6:1). It is difficult to assess how long the proposed trip across the sea was to take. However the accounts indicate the disciples left late evening (it was already evening when the feeding of the crowd took place Matt 14:15; cf. Mark 6:35; Luke 9:12). It was already the fourth watch of the night while "they were making headway painfully, for the wind was against them!" (Mark 6:48; Matt 14:24 states they were far from land). Thus the authors indicate the exhausting nature of the trip. Both the exhausted state of the disciples and the nighttime situation are highly favorable to experiencing an ASC.

In the experience itself, the disciples in Matthew and Mark are focused exclusively on their toil in a hostile environment; hence they were quite conscious of their environment, not directly prepared for any visionary experience. As for Jesus, both Matthew and Mark indicate that Jesus spend the night in prayer, entailing his intense focus on God. John simply says Jesus withdrew alone to "the" mountain, presumably also to pray as Matthew and Mark infer. Modern research indicates that in the meditative experience "consciousness of one's physical positioning and environment rapidly fade away" (Forman 1993: 716).

2. Ability to communicate

In all accounts, the wind and sea take the initiative by threatening the disciples with strong waves accompanied by heavy winds. The wind and the sea in this episode function like the cloud in the transfiguration account. In Matthew and Mark, the disciples do not recognize Jesus, but think a sea ghost of sorts approaches them on the sea. Jesus does not communicate with the disciple until he comes toward the boat. In Matthew and Mark, the disciples cry out (Matt 14:26; Mark 6:49). In John's account, the disciples say nothing, but were frightened (John 6:20). But in all three reports, Jesus addresses the frightened disciples with an "it is I" message, features typical of ASC experiences. It is because Jesus speaks to them that they finally recognize him (except, again, for John 6:19 where they knew it was Jesus walking on the sea).

In Matthew, there is a further datum; Peter speaks to the apparition of Jesus (as in the transfiguration account). However here Peter tests the apparition ("if it is you" Matt 14:28); to verify if it in fact is Jesus. He asks to be commanded to come to Jesus "on the waters." It is important to note that Jesus is not walking "on the waters," but "on the sea." Peter interprets the ASC experience wrongly for when the apparition invites him to come, he step out "on the water" successfully, but eventually "sees the wind" (Matt 14:30). The wind with the sea are an integral part of the environment that allow for the ASC. Peter's presence "on the water," along with his "seeing the wind" cause him to fall out of the ASC. He thus sinks "in the waters."

3. Concentration

Two things must be considered: the degree of concentration, and whether it is fixed immovably on a single object or momentary and fluid, with shifting attention. Jesus appears to be intensely concentrated on a single object as he is lost in prayer on "the" mountain, God. In this concentrated state, Mark explicitly (and Matthew implicitly) would have us believe Jesus intended to make his way across the sea where he would catch up with his disciples ("He meant to pass by them" Mark 6:48; Matt 14:25 simply mentions Jesus was walking on the sea toward the boat, without specifying his intention; John 6:19 describes Jesus walking directly to the boat). It is the disciples whose attention is fluid as it moves from their situation on the hostile sea to the coming apparition, with no recognition of Jesus until he speaks. But even then Peter doubts (Matt 14:28).

4. Control

Two elements of the ASC enter into the consideration of control. First, can the subjects enter and leave the ASC at will? Since the tradition of Jesus alone in prayer on "the" mountain is attested to by all three witnesses (John indirectly), then one might conjecture that Jesus was able to enter (and presumably leave) the ASC at will as well as redirect it (from prayer to crossing the sea). The disciples, on the other, seem to slip easily into the ASC in their sleep-deprived, exhausted situation, a common experience documented in cross-cultural research.

Second, can the subjects control the content of the ASC? In Walsh's model, the question seeks to determine whether the one experiencing an ASC is able to employ the experience to his or her own ends: to obtain answers to specific questions, solutions to problems, abilities to heal, to rescue and the like. In Matthew and Mark, the disciples' request of Jesus to help them and the successful outcome of the request points to their control of their ASC experience. Furthermore, in Matthew's account Peter's testing of the apparition and willingness to step out of the boat on the sea could be interpreted as an attempt to manipulate or control the ASC. This interpretation takes on greater likelihood as Peter in fact wakens from his ASC experience when he "sees the wind." It is plausible that the author envisions Peter in some in-between state, not a dream but not fully awake either. In contemporary ASC experience, this is the realm of "waking dreams," guided meditation, healing states, and similar visualization strategies which a trained person can manipulate to suit social needs and personal interest.

At another level, it seems each narrator wishes to explain the nagging concern over Jesus' true identity that "brings on" the ASC. Such indeed is the case with the transfiguration experience, "brought on" by the concern over Jesus' identity raised just prior to the episode ("Who do people say I am?" Matt 16:13; Mark 8:27; Luke 9:18). Such a question would weigh heavily on the collectivist mind-sets of people who live in group-centered rather than individualistic cultures (see Malina 1994). For Mark 6:52 says the problem was that "they did not understand about the loaves, but their hearts were hardened"; Matt 14:33 has all in the boat acknowledge: "Truly you are the Son of God." John, on the other hand, tells of this event in a context in which Jesus is proclaimed a prophet (John 6:14) and a king (John 6:15). A visionary ASC like the transfiguration account would bring enlightenment and relief.

5. Arousal

Here Jesus' heightened arousal is reflected in the fact that he can walk over the sea at will in the ASC, as all accounts agree. That the disciples see this apparition of Jesus on the sea in the middle of a stormy night indicates that something about him must have shone forth. This is not unlike the transfiguration accounts which mention that Jesus experienced heightened arousal reflected in the change of facial appearance (Matt 17:2 and Luke 9:29) and glistening garments (all three: Matt 17:2; Mark 9:3; Luke 9:29). This sounds similar to the contemporary ASC experience of a person's "aura." Some people believe that every person emanates an aura that is visible to those who know how to see it. The aura glistens or changes colors as that person becomes stimulated or aroused. The disciples similarly experience heightened arousal in all three accounts: fear.

6. Calm

Throughout the account, Jesus remains quite calm and in control. The disciples, on the other hand, are rather agitated. Matthew and Mark best describe this condition; John leaves it implicit in his assertion that the disciples were frightened. But with Jesus's assuaging word "have no fear" (Matt 14:27; Mark 6:50; John 6:20), the disciples presumably felt a sense of calm. This feeling is replicated in what happens when Jesus enters the boat. Matthew and Mark note how the storm ceased as Jesus took his feet off the sea and entered the boat (Matt 16:32; Mark 6:51). For John, Jesus no sooner entered the boat than it hit the shore (John 6:21).

7. Sense of self, or identity

In Walsh's model, this feature looks to whether the person undergoing the ASC has a shift in identity, a "disidentification from the conventional egoic body-bound self-sense" (Walsh 1993: 758). In other words does the person in an ASC lose self-identity, take up an "out of the body" posture, or become enveloped in the some All or something similar. Something of the sort does occur in this episode of Jesus walking on the sea, but it has nothing to do with Jesus' identity. Rather his "egoic body-bound self-sense" loses its mooring in the gravity determined, land bound limitations of human being, enabling him to walk on the sea. This change in Jesus' normal bearing leads the disciples to conclude that they do indeed see a vision (explicitly in Matt 14:26; Mark 6:49: "it is a ghost"; implicit in John 6:20). Jesus' distinctive identity is gradually but clearly discerned by the disciples after he speaks to them. While he is initially confused with an apparition of some sea entity, eventually he is perceived quite distinctly. Incidentally, Matthew reports that Peter, too, has an in-vision experience of altered physical bearing. He is initially successful, but his "seeing the wind" snaps him out of it (Matt 14:28-30).

8. Affect

Was the experience pleasurable or painful? The three accounts indicate that the experience was initially totally frightening for the disciples, but eventually quite pleasurable. The reaction of the disciples differs in each account: in Matthew they show reverence to Jesus (Matt 14:33); in Mark they show astonishment (Mark 6:51); while in John they are overjoyed, "glad" (John 6:21). Yet these are normal reactions, typical of ASC cultural patterns (Walsh 785). People often confront frightening experiences, which are followed by pleasant, ecstatic, and blissful experiences.

9. Content of the experience

Is the content formless or with form? The content of the experience of Jesus walking on the sea is surely not formless, although the nature of the sea deities, like that of the sea itself, often is. On the contrary, the content has differentiated form: a person walking up to the boat, perceivable in the storm, hence gleaming in some way, giving words of assurance to the disciples, then entering the boat. The disciples' vision of Jesus walking on the sea as reported in Matthew, Mark and John is well organized. The episode features Jesus' mastery over the sea and what it represents in first-century Mediterranean Hellenism. Peter's inability to demonstrate similar mastery is duly noted by Matthew. The modality of the predominant objects (Jesus, the sea and wind, the disciples, their boat) is mixed: that is, there are somatic, visual, and auditory dimensions to this ASC. The objects appear to have equal intensity (sound, color, appearance), and the imagery of the vision is cultural specific rather than archetypal.

In conclusion, this overall phenomenological mapping of the reports of Jesus' walking on the sea confirms that the etic categories of Walsh's model have sufficient breadth to encompass the emic descriptions presented by the Matthew, Mark and John. What does this analysis contribute to judgments of authenticity? Consider the rather abstract, general principles used to evaluate the authenticity of statements attributed to Jesus: criteria of discontinuity, embarrassment, incongruity, multiple attestation, explanation and coherence (Barr 1995: 467-73; Duling 1994: 520-23). When these are applied to the deeds of Jesus, specifically to the episode of the disciples' vision of Jesus walking on the sea, the following conclusions seem in order. As for discontinuity, reports of Jesus acting as a shamanistic holy man, a saddiq, surely did not feed into the project adopted by later Jesus Messiah groups. They would have Jesus as teacher for their new fictive kinship groups. Similarly, the sentiments and values represented by Jesus as shamanistic holy man more befit a Hellenistic magician than a Messiah or Israelite son of God, a position awkward for Jesus Messiah groups. While there is nothing in this activity in tension with what Jesus is reported to have said to his followers, the incident is found attested to in a number of early sources, including John. Finally the episode of Jesus walking on the sea does contribute to a cogent portrait of a "believable" person (coherence) with a culturally specific social role: the shamanistic holy man, a prophet like John the Baptist and others with whom Jesus was compared "Elijah, Jeremiah or one of the prophets of old" (Matt 16:14; Mark 8:28; Luke 9:19). Jesus' walking on the sea fits in with the other visionary experiences we have noted as well as with his healing and exorcizing and astral prophetic abilities (see Malina 1997).

In sum, the Gospel tradition offers sufficient indication that both Jesus and his disciples were capable of ASCs. Hence the visionary experience in the episode of Jesus' walking on the sea is not totally exceptional. Bultmann, among others, offers a number of parallel incidents (Bultmann 1968: 236-37). Madden presents a sampling of these reports, only to conclude that he could find no precise ancient *literary* parallel for the episode (1997: 49-73). Again, to cite his conclusion: "There are no real parallels to the sea-walking narrative in the OT or in pre-Gospel pagan literature" (1997: 139). But ASC experiences are not literary or narrative forms, they are experiences that take cultural shape and can be reported in a number of ways, in fact in all the ways Madden has found in his sources. As ASC experiences, the episode of Jesus walking on the sea has many parallels! As reported in the Gospels, the incident has all the hallmarks of historical verisimilitude and should be ranked as a historically authentic episode.

The foregoing application of a cross-cultural model of altered states of consciousness experience only reinforces what Pilch has noted in his study of the transfiguration account:

> [T]he social sciences reduce the number of plausible interpretations of texts like the transfiguration, but the choices that remain have a high degree of Mediterranean cultural plausibility and would make perfect sense to illiterate peasants who constituted 90% of population of first century Palestine. The ASC is undoubtedly an epiphany or theophany for Jesus and his select companions, even if these words are not used. For people who have no control over their lives and who believe that God alone is in charge of life, ASCs like ecstatic visions are as essential to well being as aspirin or Tylenol is to modern Westerners. (Pilch 1995: 64)

BIBLIOGRAPHY

Barr, David L. *New Testament Story: An Introduction*. 2nd ed. Belmont: Wordsworth, 1995.

Betz, Otto and Werner Grimm. *Wesen und Wirklichkeit der Wunder Jesu: Heilungen — Rettungen — Zeichen — Aufleuchtungen*. ANTJ 2. Frankfurt am Main/Bern/Las Vegas: Lang, 1977.

Borhek, James T. and Curtis, Richard F. *A Sociology of Belief*. New York: Wiley-Interscience, 1975.

Bourguignon, Erika. *Religion, Altered States of Consciousness, and Social Change*. Columbus: Ohio State University Press, 1973.

—. *Culture and the Varieties of Consciousness*. An Addison-Wesley Module in Anthropology, No. 47. Reading: Addison-Wesley. 1974.

Brown, Colin. *Miracles and the Critical Mind*. Grand Rapids: Eerdmans, 1984.

Bultmann, Rudolf. *History of the Synoptic Tradition*. Rev. ed. Trans. John Marsh. New York: Harper & Row, 1968.

De Lubac, Henri. *Sûrnaturel: Études historiques*. Paris : Aubier, 1946.

Duling, Dennis C. *The New Testament: Proclamation and Parenesis, Myth and History*. 3rd ed. Fort Worth: Harcourt, Brace, 1994.

Gallagher, Eugene V. *Divine Man or Magician? Celsus and Origen on Jesus.* SBLDS 64. Chico: Scholars Press, 1982.

Forman, Robert K. C. "Mystical Knowledge: Knowledge by Identity." *JAAR* 61 (1993) 705-38.

Goodman, Felicitas D. *Ecstasy, Ritual and Alternate Reality: Religion in a Pluralistic World.* Bloomington and Indianapolis: Indiana University Press, 1988.

—. *Where the Spirits Ride the Wind: Trance Journeys and Other Ecstatic Experiences.* Bloomington and Indianapolis: Indiana University Press, 1990.

Hesse, Mary. "Miracles and the Laws of Nature." Pp. 33-42 in C. F. D. Moule, ed. *Miracles: Cambridge Studies in their Philosophy and History.* London: Mowbray, 1965.

Jung, Carl G. *The Symbolic Life: Miscellaneous Writings.* Collected Works 18. Princeton: Princeton University Press, 1976.

Keller, Ernst and Marie-Luise Keller. *Miracles in Dispute: A Continuing Debate.* Philadelphia: Fortress, 1969.

Madden, Patrick J. *Jesus' Walking on the Sea: An Investigation of the Origin of the Narrative Account.* BZNW 81. Berlin and New York: De Gruyter, 1979.

Malina, Bruce J. *New Testament World: Insights from Cultural Anthropology.* Rev. ed. Louisville: Westminster/John Knox, 1993.

—. "'Let Him Deny Himself' (Mark 8:34//): A Social Psychological Model of Self-Denial." *BTB* 24 (1994) 106-19.

—. *On the Genre and Message of Revelation: Star Visions and Sky Journeys.* Peabody: Hendrickson, 1995.

—. "Reading Theory Perspectives." Pp. 3-31. In *The Social World of Jesus and the Gospels.* London and New York: Routledge, 1996.

—. "Jesus as Astral Prophet." *BTB* 27 (1997) 83-98.

Noll, Richard. "Shamanism and Schizophrenia: A State Specific Approach to the 'Schizophrenia Metaphor' of Shamanic States." *American Ethnologist* 10 (1983) 443-59.

Pilch, John J. "BTB Readers Guide: Understanding Healing in the Social World of Early Christianity." *BTB* 22 (1992) 26-33.

—. "Insights and Models for Understanding the Healing Activity of the Historical Jesus." Pp. 154-77 in E. H. Lovering, Jr., ed. *Society of Biblical Literature 1993 Seminar Papers.* SBLSP 32. Atlanta: Scholars, 1993a.

—. "Visions in Revelation and Alternate Consciousness: A Perspective from Cultural Anthropology." *Listening: Journal of Religion and Culture* 28 (1993b) 231-44.

—. "The Transfiguration of Jesus: An Experience of Alternate Reality." Pp. 47-64 in Philip F. Esler, ed. *Modelling Early Christianity: Social Scientific Studies of the New Testament in its Context.* London and New York: Routledge, 1995.

—. "Altered States of Consciousness: A 'Kitbashed' Model." *BTB* 26 (1996) 133-38.

—. "Psychological and Psychoanalytical Approaches to Interpreting the Bible in Social-Scientific Context." *BTB* 27 (1997) 112-16.

—. "Appearances of the Risen Jesus in Cultural Context: Experiences of Alternate Reality," *BTB* 28 (1998a) forthcoming.

—. "A Window into the Biblical World: Walking on the Sea," *The Bible Today* 36 (1998b) 117-23.

Prickett, Stephen, *Origins of Narrative: The Romantic Appropriation of the Bible.* Cambridge: University Press, 1996.

Remus, Harold. *Pagan-Christian Conflict over Miracle in the Second Century.* Patristic Monograph Series, No. 10. Philadelphia: Philadelphia Patristic Foundation, 1983.

Renaud, Bernard. "La 'Grande mer' dans l'Ancien Testament: de la géographie au symbole." Pp. 75-101 in Augusti Borrell, Alfonso de la Fuente, and Armand Puig, eds., *La Bíblia i el Mediterrani — La Biblia y el Mediterráneo — La Bible et la Méditerranée — La Bibbia e il Mediterraneo.* Actes del Congrés de Barcelona 18-22 de setembre de 1995. Vol. 1. Abadia de Montserrat: Associació Bíblica de Catalunya, 1997.

Saler, Benson. "Supernatural as a Western Category." *Ethos* 5 (1977) 31-53.

Theissen, Gerd. *The Miracle Stories of the Early Christian Tradition.* Trans. Francis McDonagh. Philadelphia: Fortress, 1983.

Walsh, Roger. "Phenomenological Mapping and Comparisons of Shamanic, Buddhist, Yogic and Schizophrenic Experiences." *JAAR* 61 (1993) 739-69.

—. "Shamanic Cosmology." *ReVision* 13 (1991) 86-100.

JESUS AND ZECHARIAH'S MESSIANIC HOPE

Craig A. Evans

Jesus' entry into Jerusalem and his activities during the course of the Passion Week are marked by biblical symbolism, at least as they are described by the evangelists: Jesus enters Jerusalem mounted on an animal, evidently enacting the prophetic vision of Zechariah. In anticipation of his approach to the Temple precincts his disciples shout out some of the words of Ps 118:26 ("Blessed be he who enters in the name of the Lord! We bless you from the house of the Lord"). He encounters a fruitless fig tree and curses it, perhaps echoing the prophetic words of Jeremiah who laments that "there are no figs on the fig tree," symbolizing that there are no righteous persons for God to redeem (Jer 8:13). He enters the Temple precincts and drives out merchants, perhaps in the spirit of Zechariah's vision, and then appeals to oracles from Isaiah and Jeremiah: "Is it not written, 'My house shall be called a house of prayer for the all the nations'? But you have made it a 'cave of robbers'" (Mark 11:17; cf. Isa 56:7; Jer 7:11). Reviewing a larger part of Mark 11 Deborah Krause, in a recent study, finds several points of contact with Hos 9:10-17. She believes the Hosean oracle has influenced the Markan evangelist in his selection, arrangement, and editing of material.[1] Finally, mention should also be made of the Passion itself. Jesus refuses the mixed drink (Mark 15:23, 34), perhaps alluding to Ps 69:21. The guards cast lots for Jesus' clothes (Mark 15:24), perhaps alluding to Ps 22:18. Jesus is mocked (Mark 15:29), which probably alludes to Ps 22:7. And in dying (Mark 15:34), Jesus quotes Ps 22:1.

Many of these scriptural allusions are deliberate, originating in the earliest stages in telling the story and supplemented by the evangelists

---

[1] D. Krause, "Narrated Prophecy in Mark 11.12-21: The Divine Authorization of Judgment," in C. A. Evans and W. R. Stegner (eds.), *The Gospels and the Scriptures of Israel* (JSNTSup 104; SSEJC 3; Sheffield: Sheffield Academic Press, 1994) 235-48. In a study in the same volume G. W. Buchanan ("Withering Trees and Progression in Midrash," 249-69) attempts to identify the prophetic passages that lay behind Jesus' (and the evangelists') expectation to find fruit on the fig tree in the spring.

themselves (as comparison of the later evangelists with Mark makes clear). The details from the lament Psalms are especially compelling evidence of the intentional blending of the story of Jesus with images and details of Scripture. After all, some of these details are acted out by Roman soldiers who could hardly be deliberately imitating the patterns of the Jewish scriptures.

Having said that, however, it is unjustified to assume that all actions that reflect biblical themes and images are the product of later tradents who wished to cast the stories of Jesus into a biblical light. As will be shown below, there were many persons in the approximate time of Jesus whose actions were clearly based on the patterns of Scripture. Indeed, these actions were intentional and pedagogical, meant to clarify the agenda of the figure. The embellishment of the Gospel narratives with words, phrases, and details drawn from the biblical text did not originate with the evangelists and the tradents that preceded them; it originated with Jesus himself. Early Christian tradents and the later evangelists embellished, formalized, and made explicit what in the *Sitz im Leben Jesu* was implicit and allusive.

What is necessary, therefore, is a nuanced approach in which the embellishing and apologetic tendencies of tradents and evangelists are recognized, on the one hand, and the implicit, symbolic actions of Jesus are uncovered, on the other. This approach recommends itself, for many features of the Jesus narratives are not readily explicable as productions of the early Church (such as Jesus cursing the fig tree or "triumphantly" entering the Temple precincts, only to be ignored, or later becoming involved in an altercation in the precincts, the consequences of which are later mitigated, or quoting Ps 22:1 while dying on the cross, which hardly painted an impressive portrait of the Church's Messiah and Lord). Many of these features are not easily explained as part of Jewish eschatological or messianic expectation. I invoke here, in general terms, the criterion of dissimilarity, a criterion which has been justly criticized. My appeal to it is heuristic and positive, for it is in its negative application (i.e. because this is not dissimilar to Judaism Jesus could not have said or done it) that the criterion loses its validity.

Whether or not Scripture serves an apologetical use may also distinguish between the *Sitz im Leben Jesu* and the later enrichment of the story of tradents and evangelists. In one way or another Jesus' shameful death on the cross was an embarrassment for Christians, which needed explanation. Whereas the resurrection itself may have been sufficient for Gentiles, Jews would have required convincing arguments from Scripture. Scriptural apologetics are pronounced in Matthew in John, which repeatedly cite texts as "fulfilled" by the events that overtake Jesus. The appearance of allusions to the lament Psalms in the Markan Passion exemplifies this tendency.

Some narrative traditions are complex. The story of Judas' handing over of Jesus is an interesting case in point. That Jesus was betrayed by one of his disciples is highly probable, for it is very difficult to imagine why a tradition of this nature would have been invented by the early Church.[2] The appearance of allusions to Scripture (such as the allusion to Zech 11:12 in Matt 26:15, and Zech 11:12-13 [with influence from Jer 18:2-3; 32:6-15] in Matt 27:3-10) testify both to the authenticity of the story of Judas and to the need to explain it in prophetic terms. But the scriptural traditions themselves did not invent the story. No one reading Zechariah 11 and Jeremiah 18 and 32 would have dreamed up the story of Judas. But one searching the scriptures for clarification of this shocking story could have found in these ancient prophecies helpful details and the sense that the actions of this disciple were foreordained.

Other events required no apologetic and, in the opinion of some, no explanation. The so-called triumphal entry appears to be a case in point. The Markan evangelist narrates the story, without so much as an allusion to Zech 9:9 (in contrast to Matthew and John). For Mark the entry into Jerusalem created no embarrassment. Jesus cut an impressive figure. He does not ride on an ass, but on a colt (cf. Mark 11:2, 5, 7: πῶλος), entering the city amidst cries of acclamation.

With these issues in mind, this study will focus on the apparent allusions to Zechariah clustered in the passion narratives of the Gospels. It is proposed that Jesus consciously patterned his entry into and ministry within the city of Jerusalem in the light of themes and imagery found in this prophetic book. This proposal gains support not only from the observation of the many allusions to Zechariah, but also from the observation that others from the approximate time of Jesus, apparently motivated out of hopes for Israel's restoration, acted out patterns found in Scripture.[3]

---

2   The importance of the tradition of the "Twelve" apostles is so strong that Judas must be replaced, even if there is no story of anything ever accomplished by his replacement (cf. Acts 1:26).

3   My assumptions here run squarely counter to those of the North American

ACTING OUT SCRIPTURE AS PHENOMENON IN JUDAISM

In a recent study Jeffrey Trumbower makes a compelling case that the prophecies of Malachi "had a profound influence on the career of the historical John the Baptist."[4] The Baptist's dire warning of the coming judgment of fire and the threat of an ax striking the root of trees (Matt 3:7-9 = Luke 3:7-9) echoes the language of Mal 3:2-3, 19-20. Of especial importance is Malachi's reference to one who is coming. Trumbower notes that although other prophetic texts, such as Isa 5:24 and 33:10-12, make use of similar imagery, only Malachi speaks of a coming one. Indeed, Malachi's sharp attack on divorce (Mal 2:13-16) coheres with John's criticism of Herod's divorce and remarriage (cf. Mark 6:18; Josephus, *Ant.* 18.5.4 §136).

The geographical setting of the Baptist is also intriguing. His presence at the Jordan River may hint at either the story of the crossing of the Jordan by Joshua or its crossing by Elisha (2 Kgs 2:13-14). John's comparison elsewhere with Elijah, Elisha's predecessor, possibly favors the latter identification. But his reference to "these stones" (Matt 3:9 = Luke 3:8) may allude to the twelve stones of Joshua 4. It is possible that John had erected a memorial of twelve stones, taken from the Jordan, to recall Israel's crossing into the promised land and to remind his contemporaries of the nation's commitment to the Lord (see my comments on pp. 7-9 above).

For support, Trumbower appeals to the examples of men like Theudas whose actions appear to be directly inspired by the stories, as well as prophecies, of Scripture. These men and their provocative claims offer additional features of interest for the present study.[5]

Jesus Seminar, especially as seen in its most recent publication. See R. W. Funk (ed.), *The Acts of Jesus: What Did Jesus Really Do? The Search for the Authentic Deeds of Jesus* (San Francisco: HarperCollins, 1998). Throughout this book the narrated actions of Jesus are deemed inauthentic, if they appear based in any way on Israel's scriptures.

[4]   J. A. Trumbower, "The Role of Malachi in the Career of John the Baptist," in Evans and Stegner (eds.), *The Gospels and the Scriptures of Israel*, 28-41. See also J. D. G. Dunn, "John the Baptist's Use of Scripture," in Evans and Stegner (eds.), *The Gospels and the Scriptures of Israel*, 42-54.

[5]   In another study J. A. Trumbower ("The Historical Jesus and the Speech of Gamaliel (Acts 5.35-9)," *NTS* 39 [1993] 500-517) recommends comparing Jesus with Theudas and the Egyptian Jew. See also C. A. Evans, "Aspects of Exile and Restoration in the Proclamation of Jesus and the Gospels," in J. M. Scott (ed.), *Exile: Old Testament, Jewish, and Christian Conceptions* (JSJSup 56; Leiden:

According to Josephus, two Jewish men in the first century promised fellow Israelites signs of salvation; one by parting the Jordan
River, the other by bringing down the walls of Jerusalem. We begin
with Theudas (cf. Josephus, *Ant.* 20.5.1 §97-98):

> 97 During the period when Fadus was procurator of Judaea, a certain
> impostor name Theudas persuaded the majority of the masses to take up
> their possessions and to follow him to the Jordan River. He stated that he
> was a prophet and that at his command the river would be parted and would
> provide them an easy passage. 98 With this talk he deceived many. Fadus,
> however, did not permit them to reap the fruit of their folly, but sent against
> them a squadron of cavalry. These fell upon them unexpectedly, slew many
> of them and took many prisoners. Theudas himself was captured, where-
> upon they cut off his head and brought it to Jerusalem.[6]

Next we may consider the episode of the Jew from Egypt (cf.
Josephus, *J.W.* 2.13.4–5 §258-263; *Ant.* 20.8.6 §167-172):

> 258 Besides these there arose another body of villains, with purer hands but
> more impious intentions, who no less than the assassins ruined the peace of
> the city. 259 Deceivers and impostors, under the pretence of divine inspira-
> tion fostering revolutionary changes, they persuaded the multitude to act like
> madmen, and led them out into the desert under the belief that God would
> there give them signs of freedom. 260 Against them Felix, regarding this as
> but the preliminary to insurrection, sent a body of cavalry and heavy-armed
> infantry, and put a large number to the sword.
>
> 261 A still worse blow was dealt at the Jews by the Egyptian false pro-
> phet. A charlatan, who had gained for himself the reputation of a prophet,
> this man appeared in the country, collected a following of about thirty
> thousand dupes, 262 and led them by a circuitous route from the desert to
> the mount called the Mount of Olives. From there he proposed to force an
> entrance into Jerusalem and, after overpowering the Roman garrison, to set
> himself up as tyrant of the people, employing those who poured in with him
> as his bodyguard. 263 His attack was anticipated by Felix, who went to
> meet him with the Roman heavy infantry, the whole population joining him
> in the defence. The outcome of the ensuing engagement was that the
> Egyptian escaped with a few of his followers; most of his force were killed

---

Brill, 1997) 299-328, esp. 300-305, 324-25. Also see R. A. Horsley, "Popular
Messianic Movements around the Time of Jesus," *CBQ* 46 (1984) 471-95; idem,
"Popular Prophetic Movements at the Time of Jesus: Their Principal Features and
Social Origins," *JSNT* 26 (1986) 3-27; idem, "Les groupes juifs palestiniens et
leurs messies à la fin de l'époque du second Temple," *Concilium* 245 (1993) 29-46.

[6]   Translation, with some modifications, from L. H. Feldman, *Josephus IX*
(LCL 433; London: Heinemann; Cambridge: Harvard University Press, 1965) 441,
443.

or taken prisoners; the remainder dispersed and stealthily escaped to their several homes.[7]

167 With such pollution did the deeds of the brigands infect the city. Moreover, impostors and deceivers called upon the mob to follow them into the desert. 168 For they said that they would show them unmistakable signs that would be wrought in harmony with God's design. Many were, in fact, persuaded and paid the penalty of their folly; for they were brought before Felix and he punished them. 169 At this time there came to Jerusalem from Egypt a man who declared that he was a prophet and advised the masses of the common people to go out with him to the mountain called the Mount of Olives, which lies opposite the city at a distance of five furlongs. 170 For he asserted that he wished to demonstrate from there that at his command Jerusalem's walls would fall down, through which he promised to provide them an entrance into the city. 171 When Felix heard of this he ordered his soldiers to take up their arms. Setting out from Jerusalem with a large force of cavalry and infantry, he fell upon the Egyptian and his followers, slaying four hundred of them and taking two hundred prisoners. 172 The Egyptian himself escaped from the battle and disappeared. And now the brigands once more incited the populace to war with Rome, telling them not to obey them. They also fired and pillaged the villages of those who refused to comply.[8]

Theudas and the Egyptian Jew were offering their contemporaries confirming signs, in keeping with the traditions of the exodus.[9] It is probable that they were laying claim to the Deuteronomistic promise that someday God would "raise up a prophet like Moses" (Deut 18:15, 18). Such a prophet would have to be confirmed by the fulfillment of a prediction or sign.

The actions of Theudas are reminiscent of Joshua, the successor to Moses. According to Josephus, this man "persuaded the majority of the masses to take up their possessions and to follow him to the Jordan River." Theudas claimed to be a "prophet" (προφήτης) at

---

7 Translation, with some modifications, from H. St. J. Thackeray, *Josephus II* (LCL 203; London: Heinemann; Cambridge: Harvard University Press, 1927) 423, 425.

8 Translation, with some modifications, from Feldman, *Josephus IX*, 479, 481.

9 The word "signs" (σημεῖα) is very common in the exodus story (some three dozen occurrences). The combination τέρατα καὶ σημεῖα ("wonders and signs"; cf. *Ant.* 20.8.6 §168) is common in the exodus story, especially as retold in Deuteronomy (Exod 7:3, 9; 11:9, 10; Deut 4:34; 6:22; 7:19; 11:3; 13:3 [in reference to false "signs and wonders"]; 26:8; 28:46; 29:2; 34:11), while reference to "signs" taking place "in the wilderness" is also attested in the exodus tradition (Num 14:22).

whose "command the river would be parted" allowing for "an easy passage" (*Ant.* 20.5.1 §97). Calling himself a prophet coheres with the Mosaic promise of Deuteronomy 18. Persuading people to gather at the Jordan River, whose waters will be divided and which will then be crossed with ease, is surely patterned after the example of the generation of Israelites who crossed the Jordan, following Joshua (Joshua 1–4). Taking up possessions heightens the parallel, for the ancient Israelites carried their possessions across the Jordan to the promised land.

In the case of the Egyptian Jew the details are somewhat different, but the Joshua-successor-to-Moses pattern is just as obvious. Josephus speaks of people being led out into the desert (*J.W.* 2.13.4 §259). As already mentioned, this theme is common to the exodus story, but it also is a feature in the story of the great Joshua, conqueror of the promised land (Josh 1:4; 5:6; 24:7). Very revealing is Josephus' reference to the "circuitous route" (περιάγω = "led around"). This word occurs in an important passage in LXX Amos 2:10 ("and I led you up from the land of Egypt and led you around [περιάγω] in the desert [ἐν τῇ ἐρήμῳ] forty years . . ."). As the usage of the word in Amos shows, what Josephus seems to be describing is a reenactment of the exodus. Finally, in the later account in *Antiquities*, Josephus says that this man "wished to demonstrate from there that at his command Jerusalem's walls would fall down, through which he promised to provide them an entrance into the city" (*Ant.* 20.8.6 §170). Here we have an unmistakable reference to Joshua's first major conquest in the promised land—the collapse of the walls surrounding the city of Jericho. Indeed, even the closing comment, "the brigands . . . also fired [ἐμπιπράναι] and pillaged the villages of those who refused to comply" (*Ant.* 20.8.6 §172), may very well recall Israel's burning (cf. LXX Josh 6:24: "And the city was burned [ἐμπιπράναι] with fire . . . "; cf. 8:19; 11:11) and plundering (11:14) of several cities in Canaan. That the "brigands" did this to those who "disobeyed" (ἀπειθεῖν) also coheres with the presentation of Joshua (cf. 1:18; 5:6).

Although Josephus did not discuss the biblical precedents and goals of men like Theudas and the Egyptian Jew, we are able, nevertheless, to catch glimpses of their true purposes. It is very probable that both of these men promised a new conquest of the land, perhaps reflecting hopes of an eschatological jubilee, in which the dispossessed could reclaim their lost patrimony, and, in keeping with the requirement of

Deuteronomy 18, offered confirming signs.[10] Their popularity and the resultant violent responses from the authorities testify to the broad appeal of their message, as well as to its intelligibility. The populace understood and identified with the promised biblical deliverance. The authorities understood it also and took steps to eradicate it.

JESUS AND ZECHARIAH

The scholarly literature that has investigated the extent, if any, of Zechariah's influence on Jesus is modest.[11] Much of the discussion has focused on the formal usage of Zechariah, perhaps with the result of diverting attention away from the parallels between Jesus' behavior and themes in this prophetic book. Quotations and allusions to Zechariah in the Gospels have been tabulated in the standard Greek New Testament editions as follows:

UBSGNT:

Zech 1:1	Matt 23:35
Zech 2:6, 10	Mark 13:27
Zech 2:6	Matt 24:31
Zech 8:6 (LXX)	Mark 10:27 = Matt 19:26
Zech 9:2-4	Matt 11:21-22 = Luke 10:13-14
Zech 9:9	Matt 21:5; John 12:15
Zech 9:11	Mark 14:24 = Matt 26:28 = Luke 22:20
Zech 10:2	Mark 6:34 = Matt 9:36
Zech 11:12-13	Matt 27:9-10
Zech 11:12	Matt 26:15

---

10   Josephus' description of the Egyptian Jew as a "false prophet" (ψευδο-προφήτης) is consistent with and may even consciously reflect Deut 18:22, which identifies the wicked prophet as one whose prophecies do not come to pass. In the case of Theudas also the tradition of the test of the true prophet probably applied; after all, the promised parting of the Jordan did not take place.

11   F. F. Bruce, "The Book of Zechariah and the Passion Narrative," *BJRL* 43 (1960-61) 336-53; idem, *New Testament Development of Old Testament Themes* (Grand Rapids: Eerdmans, 1969) 100-114; C. F. Evans, "'I Will Go before You into Galilee'," *JTS* 5 (1954) 3-18, esp. 5-8; R. T. France, *Jesus and the Old Testament* (London: Tyndale, 1971) 103-10; R. M. Grant, "The Coming of the Kingdom," *JBL* 67 (1948) 297-303; S. Kim, "Jesus—The Son of God, the Stone, the Son of Man, and the Servant: The Role of Zechariah in the Self-Identification of Jesus," in G. F. Hawthorne and O. Betz (eds.), *Tradition and Interpretation in the New Testament: Essays in Honor of E. Earle Ellis for His 60th Birthday* (Tübingen: Mohr [Siebeck]; Grand Rapids: Eerdmans, 1987) 134-48.

Zech 12:3 (LXX)	Luke 21:24
Zech 12:10	Matt 24:30; John 19:37
Zech 12:14	Matt 24:30
Zech 13:4	Mark 1:6
Zech 13:7	Mark 14:27, 50 = Matt 26:31, 56; John 16:32
Zech 14:5	Matt 25:31

NA[27]:

Zech 1:1	Matt 23:35 = Luke 11:51
Zech 1:5	John 8:52
Zech 2:6	Mark 13:27
Zech 2:10	Matt 24:31
Zech 3:8	Luke 1:78
Zech 6:12	Luke 1:78
Zech 7:9	Matt 23:23
Zech 8:6 (LXX)	Mark 10:27 = Matt 19:26
Zech 8:17	Matt 5:33; 9:4
Zech 9:9	Mark 11:2; Matt 21:5; John 12:15
Zech 9:11	Mark 14:24 = Matt 26:28 = Luke 22:20
Zech 11:12	Matt 26:15
Zech 11:13	Matt 27:9
Zech 12:3	Luke 21:24
Zech 12:10, 12, 14	Matt 24:30; Luke 23:27
Zech 12:10	John 19:37
Zech 13:3	Mark 3:21
Zech 13:4	Mark 1:6
Zech 13:7	Mark 14:27 = Matt 26:31; John 16:32
Zech 14:4	Mark 11:1 = Matt 21:1
Zech 14:5	Matt 25:31
Zech 14:7	Mark 13:32 = Matt 24:36
Zech 14:8	John 4:10; 7:38
Zech 14:21	Matt 21:12; John 2:16

To these one should probably add:

Zech 14:5	Mark 13:8; Matt 27:51[12]

---

[12]   In an imaginative retelling of 2 Chr 26:16-21 Josephus says that after king Uzziah's angry outburst in the Temple, "a great tremor shook the earth, and, as the Sanctuary [ὁ ναός] was divided [διΐστημι], a brilliant shaft of sunlight gleamed through it and fell upon the king's face so that leprosy at once struck him, while ... half of the western hill was broken off and rolled four stadia until it stopped at the eastern hill ..." (*Ant.* 9.10.4 §225). Josephus' paraphrase doubtlessly draws upon Zech 14:5 ("And you shall flee by the valley of the Lord's mountain, for the valley between the mountains shall reach to Azal; and you shall flee as you fled from the earthquake in the days of King Uzziah of Judah"). See R. Marcus, *Josephus VI* (LCL 326; London: Heinemann; Cambridge: Harvard University Press, 1937) 118

Zech 1:1   Matt 23:35[13]

Besides specific quotations and allusions, at many points themes of Zechariah cohere with actions and emphases in the ministry and teaching of Jesus. We are particularly interested in (1) the manner of Jesus' entry into Jerusalem the week of his passion, (2) his subsequent activity in the Temple precincts, and (3) his appeal to Zech 13:7 to explain his anticipated fate and the scattering of his followers. Most interpreters appear to be willing to accept the first item as historical and authentic, but many dispute the historicity of the second and third items. In my opinion when all factors are considered, the balance tips in favor of the second item but is undecided with respect to the third. However, a nuanced interpretation of the first two items may tip the balance in favor of the third as well.[14] Let us consider in order these possible points of contact with Zechariah.

1. *Mounted on a colt.* Jesus' entrance into Jerusalem marks the beginning of passion week. The entrance itself, in which Jesus mounts a colt, appears to be deliberately modeled after Zech 9:9: "Tell the daughter of Zion, Behold, your king is coming to you, humble, and mounted on an ass, and on a colt, the foal of an ass." Mark's account (Mark 11:1-11) does not quote the passage from Zechariah, but the Matthean and Johannine accounts do (Matt 21:4-5; John 12:14-15). Mark's failure to exploit an important proof text argues both for his Gospel's priority and for the essential historicity of the account. The explicit and formal quotation of Zech 9:9 in Matthew and John is consistent with their scriptural apologetic, an apologetic it seems that is primarily fashioned with the synagogue in mind.

The shouts of the crowd, which allude to Ps 118:26 ("Blessed is he who comes in the name of the Lord"), is consistent with the imagery of Jesus mounted on the royal mule, much as Solomon did shortly

---

n. e and marginal note on p. 119. Marcus notes that Zech 14:5 was associated with 2 Chr 16:19 in the Rabbis as well. The association of an earthquake in the Temple precincts, with eschatological overtones (see Zechariah 14 in the Targum), may in some way be reflected in the Markan eschatological discourse, as well as in the rending of the Sanctuary veil. This interpretive tradition may account for Matthew's addition of the Easter story about the earthquake and the splitting of the rocks.

13   Matthew's "Zechariah the son of Barachiah" may have in mind the prophet, rather than "Zechariah the son of Jehoida the priest" (2 Chr 24:20).

14   Grant ("The Coming of the Kingdom," 298) rightly comments that the "evangelist has not constructed this scene [i.e. Mark 11], for he is apparently unaware" of its relationship to Zechariah.

before the death of his father David (1 Kgs 1:32-40). The crowd interpretively adds to Psalm 118 the words: "Blessed is the kingdom of our father David that is coming!" (Mark 11:10). In the Aramaic, Psalm 118 is understood to be speaking of David "who is worthy to be ruler and king." The coherence of Aramaic Psalm 118 with Jesus' Zechariah-inspired action of mounting the colt argues for antiquity of the tradition, probably its authenticity. The explicit quotation of Zech 9:9 in Matthew points to later elaboration and apologetic. The rephrasing of the shout of the crowd in Matt 21:9 draws the parallel closer to the text of Ps 118:26, chiefly through simplification of Mark's clumsy version, and explicitly identifies Jesus as the "son of David."[15]

2. *Interference with Temple trade.* In the Temple incident, which Christians have traditionally (and somewhat misleadingly) called the "cleansing of the Temple" (Mark 11:15-19), Jesus is said to have tried to "prevent any one from carrying anything through the Temple" (Mark 11:16). Bruce Chilton and others have rightly suggested that Jesus may very well have been acting out Zechariah's vision that "on that day" everything in the Temple precincts would be regarded as holy and that no merchant would be allowed in the house of the Lord (Zech 14:20-21).[16] Chilton argues that Jesus' actions are consistent with his concerns for purity; and he offers several important examples from Josephus and early rabbinic tradition that document similar actions on the part of religious teachers.[17]

E. P. Sanders's dismissal of the historicity of Mark 11:16 and its apparent allusion to Zechariah 14 amounts to little more than special pleading.[18] Failure on our part to understand the significance of Jesus' action does not provide warrant for a negative judgment.

---

[15] Mark 11:10 reads "Blessed is the kingdom of our father David that is coming," while Matt 21:9 reads "Hosanna to the son of David! Blessed is he who comes . . ."

[16] J. Jeremias, *Jesus' Promise to the Nations* (SBT 24; London: SCM Press, 1958) 65-70; C. Roth, "The Cleansing of the Temple and Zechariah xiv 21," *NovT* 4 (1960) 174-81; B. Chilton, *The Temple of Jesus: His Sacrificial Program Within a Cultural History of Sacrifice* (University Park: Penn State Press, 1992) 135-36; cf. Grant, "The Coming of the Kingdom," 300; J. D. M. Derrett, "The Zeal of thy House and the Cleansing of the Temple," *Downside Review* 95 (1977) 79-94.

[17] Chilton, *The Temple of Jesus*, 100-110.

[18] E. P. Sanders, *Jesus and Judaism* (Philadelphia: Fortress, 1985) 67, with 364 n. 1.

Jesus' action not only reflects Zechariah's prophetic hope, it is also consistent with Josephus' comment that "no vessel whatever might be carried into the Temple" (*Apion* 2.8 §106).

With Zechariah forming a scriptural backdrop to Jesus' activities in the Temple precinct we may have at hand a clue to the strange saying, and its context, in Mark 11:23: "Truly I tell you, if you say to this mountain, 'Be taken up and thrown into the sea,' and if you do not doubt in your heart, but believe that what you say will come to pass, it will be done for you." Robert Gundry has suggested that Jesus is speaking of the Mount of Olives being cast into the Dead Sea (which is visible from the Mount).[19] He could be correct, but Zechariah's prediction in 14:4 suggests a different direction: "On that day his feet shall stand on the Mount of Olives, which lies before Jerusalem on the east; and the Mount of Olives shall be split in two from east to west by a very wide valley . . ." The Hebrew's "from east to west" can also read literally "from east to the sea" (i.e. the Mediterranean!).[20] In other words, Jesus' saying is eschatological, and not simply a lesson on faith, and again reflects the language and imagery of Zechariah. If his followers have faith, they will participate in, perhaps even precipitate the fulfillment of Zechariah's prophecy.[21]

3. The stricken shepherd. Finally, following several verbal altercations with the ruling priests and their allies (see Mark 11:27–12:41), Jesus demoralizes his disciples by speaking of his death and of their betrayal of him (Mark 14:7-8, 17-21, 26-31). Jesus is said to have applied to himself the words of Zech 13:7: "I will strike the shepherd, and the sheep will be scattered" (Mark 14:27). Again the Matthean and Johannine evangelists exploit the association with Zechariah. Matthew alludes to Zech 11:12-13, which speaks of the thirty pieces of silver cast into the house of God as part of his description of Judas' betrayal of Jesus (Matt 27:3-10). John alludes to Zech 12:10, which prophesies that "They shall look on him whom they have pierced" (John 19:37).

---

[19]   R. H. Gundry, *Mark: A Commentary on His Apology for the Cross* (Grand Rapids: Eerdmans, 1993) 649, 654.

[20]   מִזְרָחָה וְיָמָּה. See Grant, "The Coming of the Kingdom," 300.

[21]   W. Manson, *Jesus the Messiah* (London: Hodder & Stoughton, 1943) 29-40; Bruce, "The Book of Zechariah," 347-48. Bruce comments: "The logion is then a picturesque way of saying, 'If only you have sufficient faith in God, the promised Day of the Lord will come swiftly.'"

Support of the authenticity of this tradition is found in the presence of the Zechariah pattern. That is, if Jesus entered Jerusalem to effect the prophecy of Zechariah, if his actions in the Temple precincts were in part inspired by Zechariah's eschatological vision, then he may have applied the image of the stricken shepherd to himself as well. Further support for the authenticity of this saying is seen in the improbability of the early Church applying this text to Jesus. In context the stricken shepherd of Zechariah is the target of God's wrath: "Awake, O sword, against my shepherd . . . Strike the shepherd, that the sheep may be scattered . . ." Again, the Aramaic paraphrase makes explicit the royal element implicit in Zechariah's oracle: "O sword, be revealed against the king and against the prince . . . slay the king and the princes . . ."

But there are other indications that Jesus understood himself as Israel's eschatological shepherd. A saying from Q, in which Jesus likens his followers to sheep, may imply that he saw himself in the role of Israel's shepherd: "See, I am sending you out like sheep into the midst of wolves; so be wise as serpents and innocent as doves" (Matt 10:16 = Luke 10:3). In defending his policy of seeking out the lost, Jesus illustrates it with the Parable of the Lost Sheep, again implying that he is the shepherd: "What do you think? If a shepherd has a hundred sheep, and one of them has gone astray, does he not leave the ninety-nine on the mountains and go in search of the one that went astray?" (Matt 18:12 = Luke 15:4-6). In what may be Matthean not Jesuanic utterances, the instructions to "Go nowhere among the Gentiles, and enter no town of the Samaritans, but go rather to the lost sheep of the house of Israel" (Matt 10:6), the explanation "I was sent only to the lost sheep of the house of Israel" (Matt 15:24), and the halakic argument about healing someone on the Sabbath by comparison to rescuing a sheep that has fallen into a pit (Matt 12:11) probably do represent Jesus' disposition.[22] Likewise we should regard the evangelists' editorial comment, "he had compassion for them, because they were like sheep without a shepherd" (Mark 6:34 = Matt 9:36), as a reminiscence of the kind of language Jesus used to describe his mission to Israel, language that suggestively

---

[22]   See Bruce, "The Book of Zechariah," 342-46; N. T. Wright, *Jesus and the Victory of God* (Christian Origins and the Question of God 2; London: SPCK; Minneapolis: Fortress, 1996) 533-34. Luke's "Fear not, little flock" (Luke 12:32) may also be genuine dominical tradition.

alluded to Old Testament imagery and themes (cf. Num 27:17; Zech 10:2; 1 Kgs 22:17).[23] Finally, according to *Pss. Sol.* 17:40 the scion of David was expected to "shepherd faithfully and righteously the Lord's flock." This expectation is once again consistent with the eschatology of Zechariah: "On that day the LORD their God will save them, for they are the flock of his people . . . " (9:16a).

Jesus' words in Mark 14:24, "This is my blood of the covenant," echo those in Exod 24:8, where Moses says, "See the blood of the covenant that the LORD has made with you in accordance with all these words," and those in Zech 9:11: "As for you also, because of the blood of my covenant with you, I will set your prisoners free from the waterless pit." The eschatological perspective of Zechariah, especially its anticipation of the gathering of Israel's exiles, again suits well Jesus' program.[24] However, Jesus has interpreted the blood of God's covenant in the light of the words that speak of striking the shepherd. Jesus' blood will restore Israel's covenant relationship with God and will make possible the nation's renewal.[25]

CONCLUSION

The three principal points of contact with Zechariah that have just been reviewed lead us to consider the possibility that the theology of the prophet Zechariah may have informed Jesus' understanding of his mission to Jerusalem. In acting out the entrance of the humble messianic king by riding on the donkey—right up to the Temple precincts—Jesus may very well have been guided by Zechariah's vision of diarchic restoration, of the anointed royal figure serving alongside the faithful anointed priest.[26] The shouts of Hosanna, which are drawn from Psalm 118, are consistent with this expectation. For according to the Aramaic version of this Psalm, the priests (or builders) are to welcome the approaching David, who as a boy had

---

23   T. W. Manson, *The Servant Messiah* (Cambridge: Cambridge University Press, 1953) 70; Bruce, "The Book of Zechariah," 344.

24   Evans ("'I will Go before You into Galilee'," 6) suspects that Jesus' saying has in mind the words of Zechariah, more than those of Exodus.

25   Grant, "The Coming of the Kingdom," 301. Zechariah's "blood of my covenant" alludes to the great Sinai covenant. Because of this covenant Israel may expect redemption in the day when "the LORD will appear over them" (Zech 9:14).

26   Zechariah's "two sons of oil" (Zech 4:14) were expected to administer justice over a restored Israel.

been earlier rejected.[27] But Jesus receives no such greeting from the High Priest or from any of the ruling priests. He enters the precincts but is ignored. Such a scenario makes sense of the awkward conclusion of the triumphal entry, at least as it is depicted in Mark's Gospel: "And he entered Jerusalem, and went into the Temple; and when he had looked around at everything, as it was already late, he went out to Bethany with the twelve" (Mark 11:11). The abrupt conclusion of the entry contrasts sharply with the careful preparations that earlier had been made (Mark 11:1-6).

The anticlimactic conclusion of this triumphal parade is almost painful. Was the whole point simply to enter the Temple precincts and "look around"? It is more likely that a priestly reception was anticipated. But none occurred. From this point on tension between Jesus and the ruling priests escalated. The High Priest's refusal to acknowledge and cooperate with Jesus' eschatological agenda triggers denunciations, which escalate in a series of challenges and threats, culminating in Jesus' execution. Jesus is crucified by Rome as "king of the Jews" (Mark 15:26), a charge that makes no sense apart from the presence of royal messianic sayings or actions.

Given the correlation with ideas in Zechariah, it is possible that Jesus' entry into the Temple precincts and his expressions of authority were intended to forge the messianic diarchy envisioned by Zechariah (see esp. Zech 4:14), and evidently presupposed by the authors of some of the texts from Qumran, whereby the anointed of David and the anointed of Aaron serve the Lord side-by-side and

---

27   The Targum of Ps 118:21-26 reads: "21 I will give thanks before You, for You have received my prayer and You have become for me a Savior. 22 The boy which the builders abandoned was among the sons of Jesse and he is worthy to be appointed king and ruler. 23 'From before the Lord this came about,' said the builders. 'It is marvelous before us,' said the sons of Jesse. 24 'This is the day the Lord has made,' said the builders. 'Let us rejoice and be glad in it,' said the sons of Jesse. 25 'If it please You, O Lord, <save us> now,' said the builders. 'If it please You, O Lord, prosper (us) now,' said Jesse and his wife. 26 'Blessed is one who comes in the name of word of the Lord,' said the builders. 'They will bless you from the house of the sanctuary of the Lord,' said David." For further details of the exegetical and liturgical features of Psalm 118 and how they may relate to the function of Psalm 118 in the entrance narrative, see J. A. Sanders, "A New Testament Hermeneutic Fabric: Psalm 118 in the Entrance Narrative," in C. A. Evans and W. F. Stinespring (eds.), *Early Jewish and Christian Exegesis: Studies in Memory of William Hugh Brownlee* (Homage 10; Atlanta: Scholars Press, 1987) 177-98, esp. 179-85.

inaugurate the anticipated era of restoration. Jesus' allusion to Isaiah 56, which envisions the day when all nations will worship at Jerusalem's Temple, is consistent with this proposal.[28]

Finally, given the observation that other Jewish figures in the late second Temple period acted out scriptural patterns and oracles, we should resist the "critical" impulse to assign scriptural correlations in the Gospel narratives to the theological and literary creativity of the evangelists (or tradents before them). In my judgment it is probable that Jesus' behavior while in Jerusalem was guided by elements and themes in Zechariah, only one of which the Markan evangelist clearly exhibits—and only then because it was part of a dominical utterance. The other Zecharian elements in Mark appear without special notice and give no indication of resulting from Christian theology or apologetic. Thus, we may have attested here and there in the Markan Gospel important clues to Jesus' self-understanding and mission.

---

28   C. A. Evans, "From 'House of Prayer' to 'Cave of Robbers': Jesus' Prophetic Criticism of the Temple Establishment," in C. A. Evans and S. Talmon (eds.), *The Quest for Context and Meaning: Studies in Biblical Intertextuality in Honor of James A. Sanders* (BIS 28; Leiden: Brill, 1997) 417-442. Just as the oracle of Isaiah 56 expected all peoples to come to Jerusalem to worship the Lord, so also Zechariah speaks of an ecumenical gathering: "Then all who survive of the nations that have come against Jerusalem shall go up year after year to worship the King, the LORD of hosts, and to keep the festival of booths" (14:16).

THE AUTHENTICITY OF JUDAS' PARTICIPATION IN THE ARREST OF JESUS

William Klassen

THE STATE OF THE QUESTION

The role of Judas in the arrest of Jesus is a matter of some considerable disagreement among scholars. There is probably no clearer case of the confusion New Testament scholars spread among the people than our answer to the question: What act did Judas commit? What role did he play in the death of Jesus? Few scholars share James Charlesworth's confidence that anything can be said with certainty about Judas. He describes the betrayal of Jesus by Judas as "bedrock historical fact."[1] Others have affirmed that no one in the early church would invent such a "slime ball," as Professor Ruth Tucker recently called him.[2] John Dominic Crossan accepts "Judas as a historical follower of Jesus who betrayed him . . . Judas' existence and betrayal are historical because Christians would never have made up such a character . . . He is too bad to be false."[3]

Others, perplexed by the problems created by the narrative,[4]

---

[1] J. H. Charlesworth, *Jesus within Judaism* (ABRL; New York: Doubleday, 1988) 14. Later he avers that Jesus suffered through the betrayal of Judas, which, along with the denial of Peter, appears among a list of items which are "relatively trustworthy" (p. 169). No clue is given on how we know that Jesus suffered on account of the betrayal or what indeed the word "betray" means in the case of a disciple doing what the Master said he would do. So also M. J. Borg, *Jesus: A New Vision* (San Francisco: Harper & Row, 1987) 177: "He had been betrayed by one of his own."

[2] On the Arts and Entertainment network special in the series, "Mysteries of the Bible" on Judas aired in early December, 1997. She concluded that he was quite plausible.

[3] J. D. Crossan, *Who Killed Jesus? Exposing the Roots of Anti-Semitism in the Gospel Story of the Death of Jesus* (San Francisco: HarperCollins, 1995) 75, 71.

[4] For example, how can a person predict one's own betrayal and even point out the individual who will betray? Why did the arresting party need someone to help them find a person who daily taught in broad daylight in the Temple and who was surely known by face to many people?

assume that the character of Judas was a construct of the imagination, invented in order to feed the Jewish Christian controversy. Bishop Spong, a good Anglican from the circle of the Jesus Seminar, urges us to read the Bible "through Jewish eyes" and as we realize that the Passion narratives of the Gospels were written "with their Hebrew Bible open before them" we will recognize that "everything about the Judas narrative screams that this was a late-developing legend created out of the midrashic method to serve the apologetic needs of the Christians in the last half of the first century in order to transfer the guilt and blame for Jesus' death from the Romans to the Jews."[5]

Spong, like many of his contemporaries, knows that the word used in the New Testament to describe the action of Judas does not mean "betray" but literally means "hand over" but that does not in the least inhibit him from using the word "betray" to describe his action.[6]

---

[5]   J. S. Spong, *Liberating the Gospels: Reading the Bible With Jewish Eyes.* (San Francisco:Harper Collins, 1996). He deals with Judas on pp. 257-276. See also his article, "Did Christians invent Judas?" *The Fourth R* (March\April 1994) 3-11, 16. Here we learn that certain stories from the Hebrew scriptures "suggest that most of the details about the life of Judas may not be literal at all" (p. 8). Presumably one cannot have similar stories in Hebrew scriptures and the New Testament without one of them becoming inauthentic. More judiciously Raymond Brown (*The Death of the Messiah: From Gethsemane to the Grave. A Commentary on the Passion Narratives in the Four Gospels* [2 vols., ABRL 7; New York: Doubleday, 1994] 1.61) allows for the possibility that in Matthew's account of the death of Judas, "the OT background may have actually generated the stories." He rejects the notion that a person like Judas was created at a later level. Attention to "all the evidence supports the thesis that one of the Twelve named Judas gave Jesus over to the authorities." In the tradition, Brown believes "little more than that may have been known about Judas, except that he died a sudden, violent death and that his name was associated in the Jerusalem area with 'the Field/Acreage of Blood'" (*Death*, 2.1396-97).

[6]   Indeed it would seem that "reading the Bible with Jewish eyes" leads him to conclude that we "recognize that the Jewish word for betrayal" means to hand over. Not a clue is given to which "Jewish" word [Hebrew? Aramaic?] he has in mind (Spong, *Liberating the Gospels*, 267). Unfortunately he cites not one instance in which a Jew of the first century hands over a fellow Jew to the High Priest, nor does he draw a distinction between handing someone over to the High Priest, according to Jewish belief, God's installed servant, and Pilate a pagan ruler appointed by Rome. Perhaps most insulting is his assumption that the "midrashic" method is well-known and understood but that we need an Anglican bishop to help us read "the Bible with Jewish eyes." Ironical also is the fact that the leaders of the Jesus Seminar who pride themselves in their independence from all ecclesiastical

Spong is right in trying to connect with the "Jewishness" of Judas and of Jesus. Unfortunately he failed to do his homework. There is no doubt that Judas has been of special interest as a historical problem to many Jews. Symptomatic, perhaps, is that Hyam Maccoby cannot decide whether Judas was a historical figure or a mythical figure.[7] The tradition about Judas went its own way in Judaism and is invariably connected with the treatment of the trial of Jesus.[8] Jewish interpreters tended to treat Judas or the act of betrayal as either unhistorical or with a certain predilection for this disciple.[9] In any case, although some Jewish sources are aware that all the disciples had left Jesus in the lurch during his last days, as far as one can tell, they "betray no knowledge of an actual betrayal by an individual disciple."[10] This is a significant historical observation and bears on our reading of the New Testament sources as well.

The evidence that I have offered elsewhere on this point need not be repeated here.[11] I simply reaffirm that every book written about the death of Jesus and certainly Judas' role in it will be different if you take the translation of that one word seriously. One reviewer has suggested that I have not paid sufficient attention to three occurrences of the word παραδίδωμι in Mark 13:9, 11, 12, where it is argued the translation "betray" fits the situation.[12]

But look at each of them briefly: In the first the disciples are warned to look out for those eager to hand them over to the "courts

---

authority are delighted to have a bishop in their midst. Spong seems to have said farewell to any concern about scholarly integrity, shows no awareness of the methods of research used to deal with an issue like the historicity of Judas (Vogler, Klauck, and Dieckmann do not appear on his horizon). Nor is any attention paid to manners in how one treats Jews as partners in dialogue. All in all a sad spectacle.

7   W. Klassen, *Judas: Betrayer or Friend of Jesus?* (Minneapolis: Fortress Press, 1996) 197-98. Maccoby's terms are, "the story of Judas is almost entirely fictitious" (cf. "Who was Judas Iscariot?" *Jewish Quarterly* [1991] 8); "Judas Iscariot, the Betrayer of Jesus never existed" (cf. *Judas Iscariot and the Myth of Jewish Evil* [New York: Free Press, 1992] 153). Yet he affirms that "to some extent the historical Judas can be recovered" (*Judas Iscariot,* 137).

8   E. Bammel, "Judas in der jüdischen Überlieferung," in Bammel, *Judaica et Paulina: Kleine Schriften II* (WUNT 91; Tübingen: Mohr [Siebeck], 1997) 24-33.

9   Bammel, "Judas in der jüdischen Überlieferung," 33 n. 73.

10   Bammel, "Judas in der jüdischen Überlieferung," 24.

11   See n. 7 above.

12   W. Braun in *The Mennonite Reporter* (Fall 1996).

and they will be flogged in the synagogues." Surely the meaning of "handed over" or arrested makes good sense here, better sense than "betray." It may involve betrayal. I suggest it need not if the provisions of the Jewish practice of rebuke are followed.

Likewise in Mark 13:11 "being arrested and taken away" makes an adequate translation. In v. 12 this action moves to the inner family circle and while it is possible that betrayal is involved, a warning would most likely precede such a "handing over." In any case Mark uses the same verb for all three instances. Had he wanted to say "betray" as the NEB does only in the last instance he surely could have used the Greek word προδίδωμι. Obviously, the question of authenticity of the act of Judas hinges to some extent on the translation of παραδίδωμι.

This essay seeks to arrive at some historical conclusions on the matter of Judas' role in the arrest of Jesus. I consider as authentic the tradition that Judas was a disciple of Jesus, indeed one of the Twelve, a group which I also consider as authentic,[13] facts which are recorded by all the four Gospels after the event of Jesus' arrest. I also consider it likely that Judas served as treasurer of the group (John 12:6) which traveled with Jesus.[14] Since there is only one witness who describes him as a "thief" (John 12:6) we will allow that to stand as a rumor and not necessarily a fact; indeed we take it as a rumor from the pen of one who seeks wherever possible to discredit Judas. We are, moreover, convinced that the category of rumor might serve us well in analyzing the progressive blackening of Judas' character.

Perhaps also since we have two accounts of Judas' death we have at least two alternatives. Either Luke sought to soften the rumors about Judas' demise by providing his version in which Judas does not commit suicide (Acts 1:15-22). Indeed it is singularly striking that Luke puts into Peter's mouth a speech in which Peter describes what Judas did as a "ministry" (διακονία, Acts 1:17), the implications of which are too seldom noted.[15]

---

13   As demonstrated by R. P. Meye, *Jesus and the Twelve* (Grand Rapids: Eerdmans, 1968). See my *Judas*, 34-37; and also J. P. Meier, "The Circle of the Twelve: Did it Exist During Jesus' Public Ministry?"*JBL* 116 (1997) 635-72.

14   D. Schirmer, *Rechtsgeschichtliche Untersuchungen zum Johannes-Evangelium* [Berlin: Ernst Reuter Gesellschaft, 1964] 191-93) notes that John does not report that money is a factor in Judas's task. According to Schirmer the purse carrier was responsible for paying toll and taxes for the group which travelled.

15   Note, however, Hanse's comment: "The two words together [κλῆρος and

Or Matthew sought to depict Judas' demise in a negative manner. At the same time in telling us this story, it is quite explicitly stated that Judas was the one disciple who stood before the High Priest and made a remarkable confession about Jesus: "I handed over an innocent man" (Matt 27:4). To be sure, this affirmation was made after Caiaphas had already consigned Jesus to Pilate; nevertheless it stands as part of the recorded tradition. In either case we must assume that suicide was considered blameworthy, a risky assumption.[16] There is simply too much that we do not know to make a firm judgment.

But modern study of rumor should help us to be wary of treating as accurate Gospel narratives that put anyone in a bad light. That would apply, it would seem to stories about Peter, Thomas, James and John, or Judas. At the same time we must take the criterion of embarrassment seriously. I have, for example, no doubt that at one time or another the relatives of Jesus came to take him away because they thought he was daft (Mark 3:21).[17] I cannot imagine Mark or anyone else in the early church inventing such a story when every effort was bent upon presenting Jesus in a good light. So too my historical sense leads me to believe that Paul did curse the High Priest, as Luke reports, because it does not put Paul in a good light and Luke's contemporaries, especially the Stoics and Cynics, would have little respect for Paul's heated reaction or for his strange dodge that he did not recognize the High Priest (Acts 23:1-5).

διακονία] express the fact that Judas, like the others, had not grasped the office for himself, but that it has been allotted to him by God through Christ" (*TDNT* 4 [1967] 2). Even more strongly Foerster says: "Judas ἔλαχεν τὸν κλῆρον τῆς διακονίας ταύτης (Ac. 1:17); this ministry is something which was assigned. κλῆρος and λαγχάνειν both emphasise the freedom of the divine will" (*TDNT* 3 [1965] 763); "κλῆρος denotes the heavenly gift which God has allotted to each called believer in fellowship with all the saints, not so much as a "lot," but as a present benefit which God apportions to each, thus giving him a share, his individual share, in that which is prepared for the community" (p. 764). On the overall meaning of διακονεῖν and cognates, see Beyer, *TDNT* 2 (1964) 81-93.

16   It is not likely that Matthew viewed suicide simply as a "noble death," nor indeed did the deed carry the heavy connotation of sin often associated with it today. One can only conclude that one who commits suicide is profoundly depressed and leave to God all final judgments. It may be fruitful however, to view the reaction of the church to Judas's death as the response of suicide survivors. For further discussion, see Klassen, *Judas*, 160-76.

17   This issue as well as several others is very ably dealt with by J. W. Miller, *Jesus at Thirty* (Minneapolis: Fortress, 1997).

One instance in respect to rumor and Judas must suffice. In the various accounts of the anointing of Jesus by the woman (Mark 14:3-9; Matt 26:6-13; John 12:1-8) the oldest account (Mark 14:4) states simply that "certain" people (τινες) who were standing around were angry and expressed their anger among themselves.[18] Jesus rebuked them in a spirited way. A later account, Matthew's, tells us simply that "his disciples were angered by it."[19] By the time John tells the story he has thickened the narrative down to a much simpler stage in which it is Judas *and he alone* who questions this prodigious waste of money. Moreover, according to John and he alone, the complaint has nothing to do with Judas' concern for the poor but rather arises from his own greed and desire for money. It is most likely that John's source did not specify who did the complaining and that the latest redactor of John's Gospel wanted someone named and also had a grudge against Judas.

Which story has carried the day since then? John's of course. For one thing it is more dramatic and can be used to frighten children into goodness more effectively for the good woman and the bad man are sharply contrasted. In addition the stories of Jesus were always conflated, still are, before the Gospels were viewed as separate and individual documents. But, in this case, tragically, we face if not a perverted view of Judas, certainly one based on only one person's account and therefore must be treated as rumor. When, however, an account is so firmly embedded in folklore, legendary accretions and homilies it is more difficult to decide: Which one is authentic?

My historical instincts would lead me to give the nod to Mark. So if people ask, Did Judas complain at the anointing, the answer, from my perspective, has to be, "Perhaps, along with other disciples standing around" (Mark 14:4).

Once we take the evidence seriously that Judas handed Jesus over and did so with Jesus' full knowledge, perhaps even at his direction[20]

---

18   It is a difficult construction; see BAGD.

19   Both Mark and Matthew use the strong term ἀνανακτεῖν. By contrast, in John Judas merely asks the question: "Why was this ointment not sold and the money given to the poor?" (John 12:5). There can be no blame in raising the question, nor does Jesus rebuke Judas for raising it.

20   So G. Schwarz (*Jesus und Judas: Aramaistische Untersuchungen zur Jesus-Judas-Überlieferung der Evangelien und der Apostelgeschichte* [BWANT 123; Stuttgart: Kohlhammer, 1988] 12-31) interprets John 13:27: Jesus says to Judas, "What you do, do quickly." Brown (*Death*, 2.1403) rejects that position as

the issue of Jesus's own participation in the act of handing over has to be addressed. Simply put, Jesus increasingly saw himself as the suffering servant who had to lay down his life for his people. The agony this created for him is vividly portrayed in the wrestling with the will of God in Gethsemane, the utter loneliness he experienced in those hours and the total desertion he felt on the Cross as revealed in the cry of dereliction. Even God whom he sought to obey deserted him and left him in the lurch.[21]

Is it too much to assume that he preferred to be handed over by one he loved, whose feet he had washed and with whom he had experienced many meals, including his last one? At first the Gospels indicate that God would be handing him over.[22] In the Pauline theology of this act this is first enunciated for it is God who handed Jesus over (Rom 8:32), or Jesus who handed himself over (Gal 2:20). Paul certainly did not hesitate to use the handing over terminology[23] and he can even use the expression, "on the night when Jesus was handed over" (1 Cor 11:23), to describe the whole passion of the Lord. Paul sees no need to name Judas, and from his perspective Judas may have been simply God's chosen instrument.[24]

This essay builds on a book published on Judas several years ago. On the whole it has had an encouraging response.[25] Chapter three of

---

"idiosyncratic." He had himself described it as a "command," and as a "permission" (*The Gospel according to John* (2 vols., AB 29 and 29A; Garden City: Doubleday, 1966-70) 2.575, 579. "Indeed, having recognized the irrevocability of Judas' malice, Jesus hastens him on" (p. 578). Brown also warns us of too much skepticism with regard to John's additions, when trying to sort out his "better storytelling sense" and "historical memory" (*Death*, 1.244-45).

21   The theme of the "remoteness of God," in one's hour of greatest need, is found in many stories of the Hebrews. On its importance for the arrest narrative, see Klassen, *Judas*, 86-88; and above all R. Feldmeier, *Der Krisis des Gottessohnes: Die Gethsemaneerzählung als Schlüssel der Markuspassion* (WUNT 2.21; Tübingen: Mohr [Siebeck], 1987).

22   See Klassen, *Judas*, 52-53.

23   Note that it is the same term which is always translated "betray" when used in connection with the act of Judas.

24   According to Bammel ("Judas in der jüdischen Überlieferung," 30), in the Aramaic *Toledoth Yeshu* Judas is portrayed as the one who acts for God and he is designated as the one sent by the Most High God.

25   See n. 7. The most discerning reviews have been by W. Braun, *Mennonite Reporter* (October 1996); J. Murphy-O'Connor, in *RB* 105 (1998) 151-52; D. M. Scholer, in *Christian Century* (August 1997); M. Desjardins, in *Conrad Grebel*

that book seeks to establish a linguistic basis for our understanding of the act of Judas. It has received the most widespread approval; to my knowledge no author-scholar has tried to refute it or indeed offered new evidence to show that mine is flawed. In that chapter evidence demonstrated that the word to describe Judas's act could not by any stretching or distortion be taken to mean "betray." It is gratifying, not only that scholars have accepted that point but also that others unaware of my work reached similar conclusions alongside of and prior to my work.[26]

Martin Dibelius, maintains that Judas "'betrayed' nothing except the meeting place; rather, he 'handed over.'"[27] He explicitly states that "the actual meaning of the word which we usually translate 'betray' is to 'surrender or extradite.'"[28]

Wolfgang Reinbold in his study of the death of Jesus concluded that the "word παραδίδωμι means 'hand over' (ausliefern) not the commonly used term 'betray' (verraten) . . . The word available for 'betray' (προδίδωμι) never appears in the New Testament (except the variant reading Mark 14:10 D and the designation, προδότης for Judas in Luke 6:16)." Precisely because of this it has never been possible to determine "what" Judas actually betrayed. As an example

---

Review; L. Houlden, in the Times Literary Supplement (October 1996) and in the Theological Book Review (February 1997); G. Wigoder, in the Jerusalem Post Magazine (December 1997); P. Cockburn, in The Independent (March 1997); F. Kermode, in the London Review of Books; K. Armstrong, in the Guardian; P. Perkins, in Bible Review (December 1997); Professor Cane, in Reviews in Religion and Theology (August 1997); and W. McCready in Studies in Religion. I am grateful also to Raymond Brown (JBL) who took the book's thesis seriously, even though he could not agree with my conclusions. His rejoinder to my criticism of some of his positions is deeply appreciated. I find it quite impossible to accept the notion that Jesus cursed Judas (Brown, Death, 2.1399), or to accept the view that Matthew attributes guilt to Judas for the death of Jesus. Nevertheless, I share his confidence that the traditions about Judas existed early and that he had a critical role in the arrest of Jesus.

26   W. Reinbold, Der älteste Bericht über den Tod Jesu: Literarische Analyse und historische Kritik der Passionsdarstellungen der Evangelien (BZNW 69; Berlin and New York: de Gruyter, 1994).

27   M. Dibelius, "Judas und der Judaskuss," in Dibelius, Botschaft und Geschichte: Gesammelte Aufsätze I (Tübingen: Mohr [Siebeck], 1953) 277. Many others have followed Dibelius in this specification of the meeting place without heeding his caveat about the meaning of the word παραδίδωμι.

28   Dibelius, "Judas und der Judaskuss," 273.

he cites Gnilka who, to be sure, correctly translates "hand over" but still concludes: "What Judas betrayed, remains uncertain."[29]

Reinbold continues: "Once more it should be specifically pointed out that *paradidonai* cannot be translated betray."[30] He is aware that Bauer has misled us here and writes: "That Bauer (*ibid.* 1243) nevertheless speaks of the 'betrayal,' of Judas, is in my opinion only explainable from habit [*ist meines Erachtens 'nur wirkungsgeschichtlich' erklärbar*]."[31] He adds that the translation "'betray' is in spite of its widespread usage a straightforward mistranslation [*eine glatte Fehlübersetzung*]."[32] Matti Myllykoski also concludes: "Historically speaking it is [*sachgemäss*] more appropriate to speak of a handing over by Judas rather than a betrayal."[33]

Wiard Popkes who has made a thorough study of the term, likewise concluded: Judas is always joined to his deed. The tradition of the handing over of Judas originated in the Gospels, mainly in the pre-Markan and pre-Johannine materials and is generally stereotypical. "Certainly the dimension of faithlessness, falsehood, enters from the general context [*Sachzusammenhang*] perhaps also from the nickname (Iscariot) given him."[34] Moreover he suggested that "Both the stereotypical designation, "the one who handed him over" as well as that "he was one of the Twelve point in the direction of an apocalyptic horizon. Perhaps one can even say with Lightfoot that 'Judas represents the anti-Christ—shall we say?—of the first advent'; but the analogy should not be pressed."[35] With respect to the authenticity of the act of Judas he cautions that "We cannot deduce that there is an original or early connection between the deed of Judas and the 'handing over of the Son of Man.'"[36]

---

[29] Reinbold, *Der älteste Bericht*, 137 n. 137, citing J. Gnilka, *Das Evangelium nach Markus* (2 vols., EKKNT 2.1-2; Zürich: Benziger; Neukirchen-Vluyn: Neukirchener Verlag, 1978) 2.230.

[30] Reinbold, *Der älteste Bericht*, 235 n. 28.

[31] Reinbold, *Der älteste Bericht*, 235 n. 28.

[32] Reinbold, *Der älteste Bericht*, 137, 235.

[33] M. Myllykoski, *Die letzten Tage Jesu: Markus und Johannes, ihre Traditionen und die historische Frage*, vol. 1 (Annales Academiae Scientiarum Fennicae B/256; Helsinki: Suomalainen Tiedeakatemia, 1994) 172 n. 7.

[34] W. Popkes, *Christus Traditus: Eine Untersuchung zum Begriff der Dahingabe im NT* (ATANT 49; Zürich: Zwingli, 1967) 174-89, here 178.

[35] Popkes, *Christus Traditus*, 179 n. 492; cf. p. 181.

[36] Popkes, *Christus Traditus*, 181.

Two monographs on Judas, by scholars of first rank of recent times, both arrive at similar conclusions. So for example, Hans-Josef Klauck states: "The connotation, "betrayal" associated in the Christian tradition with this vocabulary with Judas has to be considered very much on the fringes of the semantic field."[37] For Klauck the texts see the action of Judas as a "delivering up" or a "surrendering." "The expression 'betray' is more easily designed to distort its content." The term that becomes strongest for Klauck is deserter (*Überläufer*).[38]

He perceives as the historical kernel of the legendary Judas tradition of the New Testament the following:

> Judas turned away from Jesus, externally as well as internally, and during the events of the arrest of Jesus in some manner played an unpraiseworthy role . . . Independent of all that he may have been or become he was above all this: a disciple of the Lord, like the rest a loyal and true fellow traveler of Jesus. The least speculative reason still would seem to be to base his defection on a deep disappointment with his presumed messianic expectations.[39]

Finally Werner Vogler in the first study based on modern source analysis, concludes:

> A totally different understanding of the word (from the prediction of suffering and 1 Cor) comes in connection with Judas. A formal difference is noticeable: the verb is always active and never passive. The subject, Judas, is always expressly named. Never is Judas named without reference to this deed. Before all the other disciples did, Judas separated himself from Jesus. He transferred his loyalties to the other side and it was on the side of Jesus' enemies that he was found when Jesus was arrested. That, and only that could have been the historical deed of Judas.[40]

Two scholars of Jewish faith, may be cited: Hyam Maccoby states that "παραδίδωμι need not mean betray. It can simply mean 'handed over' without any connotation of betrayal."[41] David Flusser likewise concludes: "To hand over never means betray but always to deliver, ausliefern. If Jesus has commanded Judas to do so, there is no blame

---

37   H.-J. Klauck, *Judas* (Freiburg: Herder, 1987) 45-48, 53-54, here 45.

38   Klauck, *Judas*, 46, 48-49.

39   Klauck, *Judas*, 55.

40   W. Vogler, *Judas Iskarioth: Untersuchungen zu Tradition und Redaktion von Texten des Neuen Testaments und außerkanonischer Schriften* (2nd ed., Theologische Arbeiten 42; Berlin: Evangelische Verlagsanstalt, 1985): "The Deed of Judas," 30-36, here 35.

41   Maccoby, *Judas Iscariot*, 36.

in it. Naturally if one 'ausliefert' *to the colonial power* or to the enemy then it is a crime for which there is no pardon."[42]

One of the more ingenious treatments of Judas appears in the work of Hugh Schonfield. He argues that Jesus himself was "in fact the comprehensive engineer of the Passover Plot," that he set up his own scenario for the passion, and that he was in complete control of the events leading to his crucifixion. Whatever temptation Judas had, "it came in the guise of his Master."[43] Furthermore he suggests that revealing the traitor must have been one of the most painful tasks Jesus had to perform. Although on one level he sees the betrayal of Judas as preceded by Jesus' betrayal of Judas it is the strength of Schonfield's position that he views Jesus' action in the light of Jewish apocalypticism of his day and that Jesus acted fully in the belief that the prophecies of the Messiah, including the Passion, were being fulfilled in his actions. He concludes:

> It was a singular, fantastic and heroic enterprise, though in the strange apocalypticism of the time perfectly comprehensible. It called for intense messianic faith, acute perceptiveness, an iron will, and a very high order of intelligence.

He depicts vividly the high state of tension during the last days in Jerusalem and suggests that Judas may well have been the "most sensitive and high strung of the disciples" and near the breaking point. While we may question terms like "conspiracy" or "plot" what Schonfield affirms is that Jesus is in control of his own destiny. All, including the traitor, respond to the orchestrations of Jesus, based on his understanding of the scriptures.

What is missing in this as well as in virtually all presentations of Judas is the lexicographical dimension. What are we told about the act of Judas? In order to answer that question we must pay attention not only to the history of research but above all to that lowly discipline of examining words and their meaning in the various contexts in which they appear. It is the thesis of this paper that apart from one text in Luke there is no assertion that Judas betrayed Jesus. What he did is still open to debate. But for now we must simply retire the

---

[42]   See Klassen, *Judas*, 74. Citing a letter from David Flusser and his article, "Ein Sendschreiben aus Qumran (4Q MMT) und der Ketzersegen," *Bulletin der Schweizerischen Gesellschaft für Judaistische Forschung (Beiheft für Judaica)* 3 (1995) 6-57.

[43]   H. J. Schonfield, *The Passover Plot* (New York: Bantam, 1965) 125.

notion that Judas betrayed Jesus.

Nearly a hundred years ago, B. F. Westcott, one of the leading scholars to study critically the New Testament in Greek, noted that "the rendering, 'betray' adds something to the force of the original (Greek) word." Thus at the very beginning of the critical study of the New Testament in the original Greek language, it has been recognized that the rendering "betray" is incorrect. "The exact word 'traitor' (προδότης) is applied to Judas only in Luke vi.6. Elsewhere the word used of him is some part of the verb 'to deliver up' (παραδιδόναι), and not of the word 'to betray' (προδιδόναι)."[44]

To be sure, some, like Raymond Brown, concede the linguistic point, but do not yield on the historical question: Did Judas betray Jesus? That is still answered in the affirmative on the basis of the overall picture derived from reading the Gospels. That is a point which can be discussed. We then explore other evidence and evaluate it before we reach a conclusion. That conclusion however must not be contaminated by evidence which no longer exists, such as the meaning of the word used always to describe the act of Judas. But we lose a vital methodological point—and I am not willing to concede it —if we do not take the meaning of words seriously, indeed, where possible, literally.

THE MEANING OF BETRAYAL

I remain adamant that "betray" must have its ordinary meaning involving the following:

Betrayal can only take place in the context of a relationship of trust, even friendship. In the case of Judas and Jesus there is simply no evidence that either mistrusted the other so we can assume that there was trust and warmth between them. Moreover the betrayal to be such must have harmful results or a harmful effect upon the one who is betrayed. These conditions having been met the act of betrayal involves the following three elements:

1. The Betrayer does something harmful, damaging or hurtful directed against the betrayed and against the will of the Betrayed. There is a breach of a spoken or unspoken bond or trust between them.

2. The Betrayer does something that comes as a hurtful surprise to the

---

44 B. F. Westcott, *The Gospel according to St. John: The Authorized Version with Introduction and Notes* (2nd ed., London: Murray, 1881; repr. Grand Rapids: Eerdmans, 1973) 192. See my book, *Judas*, 41-61.

Betrayed or is not expected by the Betrayed.
3. The Betrayer does something that benefits the self and harms the Betrayed.

On the face of it, none of these conditions are met in the Passion narratives. It is therefore consistent with sound translation techniques and the reproduction of historical records that Raymond Brown does not once use the term "betray" or "traitor" when he provides us with a new translation of the Passion narrative in his magisterial book on the death of the Messiah.[45]

It is especially appropriate to speak of the Judas act as an authentic deed of Jesus. It is only to be remembered that this is not so much something Jesus did as something he elicited in order to be done on his behalf. Canon Vanstone in his book, *The Stature of Waiting*, has reminded us that Jesus was a thoroughly passive person after the wrestling in Gethsemane.[46] He hardly lifted a finger on his own behalf and during his interrogations before both Caiaphas and Pilate did not try to vindicate himself. Modern religious protesters, e.g. Daniel and Philip Berrigan and many others have refused to dignify the system by participating in it when they were in court. So it is highly likely that both Judas and the disciple who hacked off the High Priest's servant's ear were taken aback when Jesus reacted in the thoroughly non-violent way he did. Before Gethsemane Jesus commanded them to acquire swords (Luke 22:36). After Gethsemane, he refused to allow them to use them, even to defend him (Luke 22:51). The existence of Jesus after Gethsemane was defined by what

---

[45]   Brown, *Death*, 2.1583-1608. His section on Judas, "Overall View of Judas Iscariot," is a very valuable contribution, marred only by a sharp edge of judgment against Judas, who "failed definitively" (1.49), while "the others succeeded" (1.141), some excessive name calling, "a mysterious villainous figure" (1.242), "idle, otiose, iniquitous," who acted against Jesus (1.241). His critique of my book that I have not made a sharp enough distinction between the various layers of tradition is correct. But I wonder whether he has not allowed himself to be too deeply influenced by a profound theological aversion to the character of Judas so deeply ingrained in virtually all layers of Christian history.

[46]   Since my *Judas* was published W. H. Vanstone's *The Stature of Waiting* (London: Dartman and Long, 1982, often reprinted) was kindly given to me by Heather McKay. Vanstone's intriguing study of the term παραδίδωμι focuses on the change from active to passive mode in Jesus' life after Gethsemane. The net effect is to minimise the role of Judas, although in Vanstone's theory he retains his position as "traitor."

happened to him and not by what he did. How could the disciples still think of him as king or Messiah? If Jesus was handed over by Caiaphas to Pilate, what was there left for Judas to live for?

I have never argued that it was impossible for Judas, as one of the Twelve, to betray Jesus and even for a paltry sum of money. The point at issue is first whether the linguistic evidence of the Gospels allows us to conclude that Judas was a traitor. We argue that it does not; or at least only in one text, Luke 6:16 where the word for "traitor" προδότης stands in contrast to παραδίδωμι. Why Luke uses this term only here and never elsewhere in the Gospel or in Acts to describe the action of Judas, if he had access only to traditions that portrayed Judas as a classic traitor, is hard to understand.

I rest my case with three observations:

> 1. This single occurrence of the word meaning to betray can surely not override all the other occurrences in which Luke says not that Judas betrayed him but that he "handed him over" (Luke 9:44; 18:32; 20:20; 22:4, 6, 21, 22, 48; 24:7, 20). At the very least we must recognize this discrepancy.
>
> 2. The fact that Luke alone uses the word "traitor" is significant for both Matthew and Mark could have done the same. Are we not forced to invoke once more the legal principle: It takes more than one witness to provide a plausible case. Here we have only one.
>
> 3. In 2 Maccabees there are a number of actions clearly described as betrayals and in none of the cases is the word used which is always attached to the act of Judas. Simon the traitor (ἐνδείκτης) slandered the High Priest, Onias (2 Macc 4:1). Jason was hated by all, betrayed (προδότης) both the laws and his country, and was an apostate showing the way to Antiochus who plundered the temple (2 Macc 5:15). A Jewish soldier Rhodocus by name betrayed secrets to the enemy (2 Macc 13:21). In none of these cases is the word, παραδίδωμι used. In the Martyrdom of Polycarp, about 155 CE reference is made to Polycarp's being handed over παραδίδωμι (1:2), and that Polycarp patiently waited for that to happen even as our Lord had done. He does not commend "those who give themselves up, since the Gospel does not give this teaching" (4:1). Those who betrayed πρόδιδωμι Polycarp "were of his own house" (6:2), and those who betrayed (προδόντες) him "should undergo the same punishment as Judas" (6:2). One has the impression that the author knows a difference although it is not wholly consistent.

While the conclusion that the linguistic evidence of the New Testament cannot sustain the freight of the traitor theory has been found convincing by many scholars now, it has been more difficult to come up with an alternative explanation for the action of Judas.

The action which I attribute to Judas is that he "handed Jesus over to Jewish authorities" and that such a handing over was standard practice in Judaism of the time. To be sure we have very few sources that illuminate it and we have apparently few cases in which the one being handed over has consented to it. That is the critical point.

Shortly after my book was published a German colleague, Luise Schottroff, provided me with a copy of the doctoral thesis prepared for Ethelbert Stauffer and Leonard Rost by Dietrich Schirmer on the legal aspects of the arrest of Jesus as portrayed in John.[47] With respect to the Old Testament, Schirmer observed that in the many concrete cases of betrayal where money is not explicitly mentioned it is surely to be explained that it is not needed since it is simply taken for granted.[48]

This is the most thorough study of Jewish practices of "handing over," betrayal, and informing available to me. Schirmer concludes that the fourth Gospel contains sections in which Jewish legal relationships appear which can be found in later rabbinic sources. The juristic character of these texts and their martyrological narrative elements distinguish them as a specific literary genre.[49] Schirmer notes that John 11:53 introduces a formal process which seeks to bring Jesus to his death. Moreover he notes that the encounters of Jesus with the Jewish authorities in all of the Gospels make visible a provocative, aggressive and uncompromising element. "We must therefore ascribe basic historical integrity to those passages which describe Jesus as fleeing from the authorities again and again, especially in the fourth Gospel."[50]

The study of the Jewish organs of policing is especially important. His chapter on the interpretation of Judas in the Fourth Gospel and indeed his total treatment of Judas is very important even though it lies almost entirely in traditional categories. For example he suggests that in all lists, Judas' name appears last and that he is always described as the "one who handed him over" signifies that Judas "seen from the perspective of his deed stands on the outer edges of the apostolic circle.[51] Schirmer concludes that not once is the word מסר,

---

[47]   Schirmer, *Rechtsgeschichtliche Untersuchungen*, esp. 179-97.
[48]   Schirmer, *Rechtsgeschichtliche Untersuchungen*, 61.
[49]   Schirmer, *Rechtsgeschichtliche Untersuchungen*, 164.
[50]   Schirmer, *Rechtsgeschichtliche Untersuchungen*, 175.
[51]   Schirmer, *Rechtsgeschichtliche Untersuchungen*, 180.

which corresponds to it most closely, translated in the LXX as παραδίδωμι. This was a theological expression for a military act, summarized in 2 Ezra 9:7: "They will be handed over to the violence of the kings of the lands, to the sword, to prison, to plundering and to deprivation."[52] He gives the examples of Judg 16:23 and 1 Kgs 23:12-14 and concludes: "These two cases illustrate that the handing over of one person by others at times is understood as a process which seen theologically is actually carried out by God." That needs to be considered for a theological understanding of the deed of Judas described as παραδίδωμι.[53]

In 1 Sam 22:9; 23:19-23 "to hand over" means to reveal where the wanted person is. That is also the case in 2 Macc 14:31-33. "When the LXX translates this process with παραδίδωμι it is to be observed in trying to clarify the meaning of παραδίδωμι in connection with Judas."[54] It has to be treated as of highest certainty that the "informer" is paid money (p. 187) mostly to the Romans in any case.

What παραδίδωμι signifies is that Judas brought Jesus under the power of his enemies (p. 190). It designates a two-sided act: Judas revealed some information which made it possible for the Jewish authorities to arrest Jesus and that Judas actively participated in that arrest. All four Gospels support this understanding of παραδίδωμι.[55]

Dietrich Schirmer's book studies the record of John's Gospel—the only one who tells us that the Jews were looking for an informer to help them arrest Jesus. This publication makes it clear that in Judaism of the Second Temple period the institution of "informing" was well established and that John may well have been aware of certain procedures which later Jewish sources fully document. In any case both Luke and John report that the authorities were looking for an informer (John 11:57; Luke 19:47-48; 20:19-21; 22:2; 1 Cor 10:28).

The evidence from Josephus has been treated by Ceslas Spicq in a detailed study of the word, which carefully classified many usages of the word. With the fourth category however he concludes that the predominant sense of παραδίδωμι in the Old Testament is pejorative. When God does the handing over the outcome is generally bad. He further concludes that the New Testament "inherits this theology."

52   Schirmer, *Rechtsgeschichtliche Untersuchungen*, 184.
53   Schirmer, *Rechtsgeschichtliche Untersuchungen*, 184.
54   Schirmer, *Rechtsgeschichtliche Untersuchungen*, 185.
55   Schirmer, *Rechtsgeschichtliche Untersuchungen*, 190.

Spicq notes that the term becomes a technical term in the passion of Jesus. "The term is to be taken first in its legal and judicial sense, but it conveys moreover a moral or psychological nuance and a theological value. *Paradosis* was also used for treason (*prodosia*). Judas Iscariot is always called *ho paradidous,* 'the traitor,' the one who betrayed or betrays Jesus."[56] Spicq states that the verb "rather often connotes this nuance of criminality . . . betrayal of someone's trust"; and in a footnote to Josephus he claims to support that.

When Spicq then affirms that the early Christians saw Christ's death as less of pain and torture and more as "a result of perfidy" and that the whole "handing over" means that he was betrayed, he has departed far from his evidence. He insists that the shame of the cross was betrayal rather than torture and again his conclusions are not verifiable. They surely cannot be built on the evidence he cites. He has strayed very far indeed from lexicography.

No reference is made to the absence of this meaning in the papyri[57] and all the usages he cites from Josephus prove exactly the opposite. Apparently he hopelessly confuses the two words, προδίδω-μι, meaning "betrayal" and παραδίδωμι meaning "hand over." One can only say that theology here then determines lexicography not the other way around.

In the case of Raymond Brown the matter is more complicated. He writes: "I insisted that the verb παραδίδοναι, applied to Judas, means 'to give over,' not 'to betray.'"[58] He noted that there is a Greek word for "betray" and that it appears only once in the New Testament with reference to Judas. The tendency to translate παραδίδωμι with "betray" "blurs the parallelism to the agency of others expressed by this verb."[59] He therefore prefers the verb to "give over" or hand

---

[56]   C. Spicq, "παραδίδωμι," in Spicq, *Theological Lexicon of the New Testament* (3 vols., Peabody: Hendrickson, 1994) 3.13-23, here 21.

[57]   See J. H. Moulton and G. Milligan, *The Vocabulary of the Greek New Testament Illustrated from the Papyri and Other Non-Literary Sources* (London: Hodder & Stoughton, 1930; repr. Grand Rapids: Eerdmans, 1974); F. Preisigke, *Wörterbuch der griechischen Papyrusurkunden*, vol. 2 (Berlin: G. Preisgke, 1927); H.-A. Rupprecht and A. Jördens, *Wörterbuch der griechischen Papyrusurkunden* (Wiesbaden: Harrassowitz, 1991), who provide not one instance where it might mean "betray." See also G. H. R. Horsley, (ed.), *New Documents Illustrating Early Christianity*, vol. 4 (North Ryde: Macquarie University, 1987) 165 (§73).

[58]   Brown, *Death* , 2.1399.

[59]   Brown, *Death*, 1.211.

over and if I mistake not never uses the word "betray" or "traitor" in his careful translation of the passion narrative at the end of his two volume work. Indeed Brown deals with the theories of betrayal and designates as their "fatal objection" the fact that Judas did not appear as a witness at the trial of Jesus. At the same time Brown states that "because Jesus was given over (nay[60], betrayed) to his judges by his trusted friend and because Jesus was innocent, there is a stigma of guilt in the human chain of those who gave Jesus over: Judas gave him over to the chief priests, the chief priests gave him over to Pilate . . . Pilate gave him over to the soldiers to be crucified. In trying to assess whom John 19:11 designates as the primary perpetrator, Brown leaves the question open although considers it possible that the Satanic Prince of the world, the agent behind the scene, may well be meant as well as Caiaphas.[61]

He concludes: "Peter was not responsible for Jesus' death and Judas was . . . Judas had done something so heinous that no ordinary repentance affects it."[62] "God's punishment for that guilt was evidenced in Judas' suicide."[63]

A most important book in this area is by Bernhard Dieckmann.[64] Dieckmann's mastery of literature and art in this area is extremely illuminating even though the history of Judas in the church is only one part of his larger treatment.

In the history of Christian art a more positive aspect of the relationship between Judas and Jesus comes out in the scene of Judas getting his feet washed. Only one portrayal is known to exist in which Judas has his feet washed by Jesus. Dieckmann presents a woodcut depicting that act, from just before 1485.[65] In contrast many portrayals of the Last Supper from the Middle Ages have only eleven disciples present.

Quite different is the case of the earliest (fourth century) depiction of Jesus on the Cross with Judas by his side, also hanging from a tree. Only the tree of Judas has life in it and in the leaves above Judas a bird is feeding its young. This ivory carving which is in the British

---

60   Meaning, "not this, but also."

61   Brown, *Death*, 1.211.

62   Brown, *Death*, 1.641.

63   Brown, *Death*, 1.836.

64   B. Dieckmann, *Judas als Sündenbock: Eine verhängnisvolle Geschichte von Angst und Vergeltung* (Munich: Kösel, 1991).

65   Dieckmann, *Judas als Sündenbock*, 105.

Museum could well come from those circles of the Christian church which praised the role of Judas in the death of Christ. We will never know. But it could, being the earliest depiction of Jesus on the cross, and probably the earliest depiction of Judas, remind us that Judas died with Jesus and that their solidarity in death should not necessarily drive us to conclude that Judas was evil and Jesus was good. Perhaps the "handing over of Jesus," the ministry to which Judas was called and which he faithfully performed can be seen as an authentic act; an act which to be sure was deeply misunderstood and continues to baffle us.

The evidence allows us to conclude that Judas acted in obedience to Christ's will and that in his act of handing over could have been obedient to God's will for there is no doubt that eventually Jesus came to believe and then the early Christians all believed that the handing over of Jesus was God's will if not God's act. Perhaps the greatest New Testament interpreter of the twentieth century concluded: "The one who 'handed him over' and condemned him to death is none other than God."[66] In that statement the profoundest reading of Judaism and Christianity come together. What God achieves on this earth is eventually brought about by the people of God who live in covenant faithfulness.

Klauck concludes his book by dealing with the problematic interpretations of the Judas act:

> Already in the New Testament the traditions have taken different ways. The oldest attempts to explain we can see in the explanation of the word, παραδίδωμι, understood as handing over, or turning in the prophetic warning and woe statement of Mark 14:21. Both weld into a unity of understanding [*Gesamtdeutung*] which remains strongly theologically oriented and therefore not least for this reason provides us most easily with acceptable aspects or dimensions. This prediction of judgment rests on adapting an apocalyptic speech pattern and in content stands under an eschatological reservation. This presumption [*Vorbegriff*] of the final judgment must be eventually honored by God and it remains for him whether he will do it and how.

> The term *ausliefern* sets a theological paradox which in the figure of Judas is driven to its high point. The debate centers in the not resolvable dialectical tension between human action and the Divine Will. What God wishes to accomplish, the giving up of his son on the cross to save the world, one

---

[66] A. Schlatter, *Das Evangelium Lukas* (2nd ed., Stuttgart: Calwer, 1960) 445-46.

person freely decides to transform into an act.

Here we are in the presence of problems very difficult to solve. Likewise the secret which surrounds and protects Judas is formulated theologically and therefore is protected both from the black-white painting of the ecclesiastical orthodoxy as well as from a flat rationalism. Nothing is more precarious or risky here than the presumed simple solution. The character portrait of Judas is muddied in the synoptics increasingly by psychological insertions. From the handing over they make a long planned despicable betrayal. As driving motive they diagnose greed for money. Satan whispers in Judas' ear in Luke. The Jewish authorities in Luke and the Jewish people in Matthew come ever closer to Judas and his actions then devolve on their shoulders.

The logical conclusion to all this is found in John. Early on Judas is a devil. All overtures of love towards him from Jesus make no impression. The only reason he remains a follower is to take more money out of the treasury. He belongs to the opposition, the Jews, to the world, to the personification of the evil one, That ties him to his Jewish people which, as is well known, belongs to the devil since he is their father (8:44).

The narratives' high point [*Glanzstueck*] of the Judas traditions is the death accounts offered by both Matthew and Luke. His death is portrayed after an Old Testament pattern as a horrible and revolting death. It had undoubtedly nothing to do with the place mentioned in Jerusalem. Thus it is apparent that we cannot take the accounts of Judas found in the New Testament naively and leave them untested without doing a grave injustice to the historical Judas whatever he may have done. Rehabilitation does not necessarily mean a declaration of freedom from all guilt or responsibility. It is quite adequate to push back his deed to an intelligent and historically plausible degree. We must deal with the sources critically in which the question is more important than the answer. The New Testament itself gives contradictory portraits of Judas.

In the mean-time hate against Judas has to be curbed. A drastic course correction has to be undertaken. For the hatred of Judas leads too quickly to a hatred towards the Jews and the nourishment for that hatred must be cut.

Therefore one may be allowed to make one suggestion that we guard ourselves against calling Judas a traitor or at least to put those words into footnotes which explain that we are dealing here not with a historical reality but a questionable interpretation to which early Christian writers were captive. Judas was neither the hero that the *Toledoth Jeschu* and the Gospel according to Judas thought he was, nor the villain some church fathers considered him. Better to confess to know too little than too much. No answer is better than a false one. Just remove the extremes and then let the rest stand in mystery.

We do not need psychodynamics to understand Judas. But we need it to understand ourselves, especially when it comes to the scape goating technique against someone who fell from faith or became hardened against it. Daub and Hengstenberg's verdict over Judas has been taken over by most the systematic theologians. We need to remember that no humans can draw the limits of God's mercy and forgiveness . . . . We should accept and respect Judas as he encounters us in the critical analysis of the texts, as a disciple of the Lord, snarled up in a deep contradiction, which can at any time become ours as well.[67]

We have made considerable progress when we read in Dieckmann that it is not permissible to demonize Judas and that it is not helpful to treat our portrait of Judas as identical to the antijudaism of the Christians. Hard as they may be to separate from each other it is necessary to differentiate between them. Even our interest in opposing antijudaism is not adequate access to the form and problems of Judas. Dieckmann reminds us that in our study of Judas we are dealing in the first instance with a brother who was a disciple of Jesus who went his own way. It is already a sign of hardening if he is treated as an outsider, a foreigner.[68]

CONCLUSION

Our study leads us to the conclusion that Judas was a disciple of Jesus, he was one of the Twelve. We consider his defining deed the act of handing over Jesus to the Jewish authorities. He served as a go between and brought about a meeting between the Temple authorities and Jesus. Since this act was fully anticipated by Jesus and Judas was pointed out at the Supper Table and since Jesus warmly greeted Judas[69] in the garden during the arrest, we have no reason to believe that Jesus considered the act of Judas sinful or wrong. I consider it probable that Jesus did express a woe, a commiseration towards the

---

[67]   The above materials are taken from Klauck, *Judas*, 144-47.

[68]   Dieckmann, *Judas als Sündenbock*, 262.

[69]   Jerome Murphy-O'Connor (in his review) questions my use of the term "embrace" (Klassen, *Judas*, 111) for that encounter. I should have spelled out the way in which a fervent kiss was executed then. Again Raymond Brown (*Death*, 1.1531, 1584) in his translation of this text has it right when he translates: "he kissed him warmly." Both Matthew and Mark use the term κατεφιλεῖν (Mark 14:45; cf. v. 44; Matt 26:49; cf. v. 48), signalling a warm or affectionate kiss (compare Luke 7:38; 22:47; 15:20; Acts 20:37). The usual word is φιλεῖν. On this point, see W. Klassen, "The Sacred Kiss in the New Testament: An Example of Social Boundary Lines," *NTS* 39 (1993) 122-35. The kiss is an expression of ἀγάπη and of peace.

one who had been selected to do this task. The authenticity of this act would be further enhanced if more examples of similar acts could be adduced. There remains then the task of trying to understand that act and to examine its historical roots before we begin any theologizing about it. Since our understanding of that event impinges upon our understanding of the death of Jesus and the role so often imputed to Judas has had such disastrous effects on Jewish Christian relations we can be grateful that the lexicographical base for a classical "betrayal" does not exist. Altogether a stronger incentive for further study and further questioning about the role of Judas cannot be imagined.

DID JESUS WASH HIS DISCIPLES' FEET?

Richard Bauckham

Few narratives in the Fourth Gospel have made as strong an impression on its readers over the centuries as that of Jesus washing his disciples' feet (John 13:2-11). Does its symbolic power stem from Jesus' own prophetic daring, as most readers have assumed, or from the evangelist's creative imagination? The legacy of the nineteenth-century liberals' distinction between historically reliable, early sources (Mark and Q) and late, theological fiction (John) endures, even if only subliminally, in the minds of many New Testament scholars and students. Uniquely Johannine narratives are still often attributed to narrative creativity in the service of theology, at some stage in the Fourth Gospel's history of development. At least, the burden of proof tends to be thrust onto any who would maintain otherwise in any specific instance. That John is indebted to Gospel traditions independent of the Synoptic Gospels (whether or not he is also dependent on one or more of these) is now very widely accepted, but still rarely ensures a level playing field between John and the Synoptics when it comes to evaluating the historical value of their narrative traditions.[1] The issue has to be tackled both in general and in particular. In the case of the footwashing, the historical question is rarely discussed in more than a few sentences.[2] For many Johannine scholars the question is, in any case, of little interest. Others perhaps assume that, in the nature of this case, there is little to be said on either side of the issue. Must it not hang largely on a general judgment of the historical value of Johannine narratives in general? In fact, there is a good deal more to be said.

---

[1]   Johannine creativity in attributing words to Jesus calls for quite distinct treatment from Johannine creation of narratives about Jesus. For a recent summary of Johannine scholarship, treating many of the issues raised here, see R. Kysar, "John, the Gospel of," *ABD* 3.912-31.

[2]   Substantial arguments for the historicity of the footwashing are provided by C. H. Dodd, *Historical Tradition in the Fourth Gospel* (Cambridge: Cambridge University Press, 1963) 59-63; J. A. T. Robinson, *Twelve More New Testament Studies* (London: SCM Press, 1984) 77-80.

FOOTWASHING IN ANTIQUITY

In the first place, it is important to be clear about the nature and social significance of footwashing.[3] For the ancients footwashing was as necessary and regular a chore as brushing teeth is for most modern people. Feet were protected by no more than open sandals, and so, after walking in the heat and in the dust and dirt of country roads or town streets, washing feet was necessary both for comfort and for cleanliness, especially before sitting down to a meal. Footwashing appears in the literature most often as preparation for a meal, and also as a duty of hospitality, either to expected guests or to passing strangers, who needed both to be refreshed after their journey and to be properly prepared for sharing a meal with the host. But it was certainly not a host's duty to wash his guests' feet himself. Either a slave or a servant would do it, or the host would provide a basin of water and a towel for the guests to wash their own feet. Washing someone else's feet was an unpleasant task which no one except a servant or slave could be expected to do. So menial a task was it that in a household with a hierarchy of slaves and servants, it would be the duty of the slaves, not of the servants who performed less demeaning tasks such as waiting at table.[4] It was, in fact, the quintessentially servile task, the one thing that no one else would do. In a household without servants, everyone washed their own feet.

Exceptions in ancient literature are all recorded precisely as exceptional cases. In most, if not all, such cases it is clear that the person washing another's feet is deliberately playing the role of a servant or slave. This is explicitly the case with Abigail (1 Sam 25:41), Aseneth (*Jos. Asen.* 13:15; 20:1-5), and Favonius (Plutarch, *Pomp.* 73.6-7). In some other exceptional cases, the footwashing is clearly an exceptional act of devotion or flattery (Aristophanes, *Vespae* 605-611; Meleager in *Anthol. Pal.* 12.68;[5] Plutarch *Mor.*

---

[3]   For the evidence on which this section is based, see especially J. C. Thomas, *Footwashing in John 13 and the Johannine Community* (JSNTSup 61; Sheffield: JSOT Press, 1991) chap. 3. Thomas himself is much indebted to B. Kötting, "Fusswaschung," *RAC* 8.743-59.

[4]   Cf. P. K. Nelson, *Leadership and Discipleship: A Study of Luke 22:24-30* (SBLDS 38; Atlanta: Scholars Press, 1994) 164.

[5]   The point in this case, not brought out by Thomas, is that poet renounces any claim on the boy he loves because he sees him as cupbearer to Zeus on

12.249d).[6] Even when the person washing the feet is not actually a servant or slave, the social significance of the act remains the same. In a society highly conscious of relative status, it would be unthinkable for this uniquely servile act to be performed for an inferior by a superior in the social scale. Exceptionally an inferior who is not actually a servant or slave may perform the act as a kind of extravagant expression of their willingness to be subject to the superior, but for a superior to perform the act for an inferior would be an incomprehensible contradiction of their social relationship.

Abraham was famous for his hospitality to strangers, on the basis of Gen 18:1-8. Even though he treats his visitors as his social superiors (18:3), he has water brought for them to wash their own feet (18:4), or, in the Septuagint, for his servants to do so. No doubt, the translators, knowing from the text itself that Abraham has servants, thought it, in those circumstances, more hospitable for the guests not to be left to wash their own feet (cf. the similar difference between Hebrew and LXX texts in Gen 43:24). But according to the *Testament of Abraham*, it was Abraham himself who washed the three guests' feet (A6:6; cf. B3:9), and who performs the same act when one of the three, the archangel Michael, visits him again (A3:6-9). Of course, these angelic visitors really are Abraham's social superiors, and it is only the B recension (3:6-9) that implies it was Abraham's regular practice himself to wash the feet of visiting strangers. This might be a Christian touch (since, as we shall see below in "History of a Practice," early Christian hosts did wash their guests' feet themselves),[7] though in general it is the A recension that shows most signs of the Christian transmission of the text.[8] But in any case the social significance of footwashing is not lost. Abraham, exceptional in his hospitality to strangers (A1:5; 4:6; B2:10), is the

---

Olympus, thus too superior for anything other than the poet's metaphorical washing of his feet to be appropriate. The image is the extravagant opposite of a homosexual act, whose social significance would be the inferiority of the boy.

[6]   All these texts are quoted and discussed in Thomas, *Footwashing*, 37-40, 52-55.

[7]   Note that Origen, *Hom. in Gen.* 4.2, treats Abraham's example of washing his guests' feet as one which Christians should follow.

[8]   E. P. Sanders ("Testament of Abraham," in J. H. Charlesworth [ed.], *The Old Testament Pseudepigrapha* [2 vols., ABRL 13-14; New York: Doubleday, 1983-85] 1.879-80) does not include B3:6-9 among passages he suspects Christians may have reworked.

exceptionally humble host who treats all his guests as his social superiors.

THE JOHANNINE INTERPRETATION OF THE FOOTWASHING

The meaning of the footwashing in John 13 has been much debated.[9] Lacking the space to rehearse the debate, I can here argue only briefly for my own view, as a preliminary to considering the issue of historicity. The passage (13:1-20) provides the initial statement of the theme of Jesus' lordship in self-humiliation and service, which is the major overarching theme of John's passion narrative. That narrative culminates with Jesus' dying the death of slaves and criminals, while designated king of the Jews for all the world to see (19:19-21) and subsequently buried with the honour due to a king (19:39-41). It begins with the stark paradox of 13:3-5: Jesus, knowing that the Father had given him the uniquely divine lordship over all creation, undertook the role of a slave, performing for his disciples the act most expressive of servile status. The one who can claim the highest status in all reality, sovereign over all creation, humbles himself to the lowest human status, expressing his lordship in self-humiliating service for his social inferiors. A radical overturning of common cultural values with respect to status is implied.

There can be no doubt that John understands the footwashing in relation to the cross, where the Jesus who in chapter 13 undertakes the role of a slave finally dies the death of a slave. The footwashing both provides an interpretation of the meaning of the cross, as Jesus' voluntary self-humiliation and service for others, and also gains its own fullest meaning when seen in the light of the cross it prefigures. In this respect it parallels the Synoptic accounts of "the institution of the Lord's Supper," accounts whose function in these Gospels is not

---

9   See the survey of interpretations in Thomas, *Footwashing*, chap. 1; and the assessment of the main types of interpretation in R. B. Edwards, "The Christological Basis of the Johannine Footwashing," in J. B. Green and M. Turner (eds.), *Jesus of Nazareth: Lord and Christ* (I. H. Marshall Festschrift; Grand Rapids: Eerdmans; Carlisle: Paternoster, 1994) 367-83. See now also the cultural anthropological interpretation in J. H. Neyrey, "The Footwashing in John 13:6-11: Transformation Ritual or Ceremony?," in L. M. White and O. L. Yarbrough (eds.), *The Social World of the First Christians* (W. A. Meeks Festschrift; Minneapolis: Augsburg Fortress, 1995) 197-213.

to record the institution as such (only the disputed verse Luke 22:19b indicates that the rite is to be repeated by the disciples), but rather to provide an interpretation of Jesus' coming death. John's omission of such an account must be due, not only to the fact that he has already spoken of Jesus' death in eucharistic language in chap. 6, but also to the fact that he gives Jesus' death a sacrificial interpretation in his narration of the death itself (19:34, 36). This leaves him free to narrate a different symbolic action at the Supper, supplying a different perspective on the meaning of Jesus' coming death.

As has frequently been argued, John 13 provides two interpretations of the act of footwashing, one in Jesus' dialogue with Peter (vv. 6-11), the other in Jesus' speech to the disciples after resuming his seat (vv. 12-20).[10] The two interpretations are related, but distinct. Both are christological, taking their meaning from the fact that it is Jesus the Lord who serves as a slave, but the first is christological and soteriological, the second christological and exemplary. The first is a meaning which the disciples will not be able to understand until after the resurrection (13:7; cf. 2:22; 12:16), a clear indication that it is a meaning connected with Jesus' death. This meaning is conveyed by Jesus' words only in a way that to the disciples within the narrative hides it (vv. 8-10), including the characteristically Johannine double entendre of v. 8b: "Unless I wash you, you have no share in me [μέρος μετ' ἐμοῦ]." At the literal level, this can mean that unless Peter's feet are washed he cannot share the meal with Jesus. At the level of true significance, it means that without the cleansing to be effected by Jesus' death, Peter cannot participate in the eternal life to be had in union with Jesus' life. Whereas this first, soteriological interpretation of the meaning of the footwashing cannot be understood by the disciples within the narrative, as Peter demonstrates, there is nothing about the second interpretation which could not be clear to them. It portrays Jesus' act as an example the disciples are to follow. If he, their Lord and Master, serves them as a slave, so should they serve each other. What is not beneath his dignity can certainly no longer be considered beneath theirs. Here the socially revolutionary nature of Jesus' act is evident in the

---

[10] D. A. Carson (*The Gospel according to John* [Leicester: Inter-Varsity Press; Grand Rapids: Eerdmans, 1991] 465) sees a distinct, third interpretation in vv. 10-11, but if his exegesis is correct, it would be more appropriate to see these verses as providing a second development of the first interpretation.

abolition of relationships based on status which is its consequence among the disciples. If footwashing is not beneath anyone's dignity, then nothing is. A social group in which each washes the feet of the others can have no social hierarchy, at least of the type symbolized by the limitation of such menial tasks to those of lowest status.[11]

The question arises whether the command in vv. 14-15 is meant to be followed literally or whether footwashing here functions as a symbol of humble service. In the light of the practice and significance of footwashing in the ancient world, this is surely a false dilemma. There is no indication that the command is not meant literally, but literal footwashing is a concrete instance of the practice of humble service in ordinary life. The reference is to the regular washing of feet which the disciples, like everyone else, must practise. This ordinary, daily chore is what they should do for each other. Since it is the most menial task, which noone but a servant or slave would ordinarily think of doing, it is the extreme case which carries with it every less humiliating kind of service for each other that might arise. If this is not beneath them, nothing is.

Those exegetes who see in vv. 14-15 the institution of a special religious rite of footwashing[12] miss the ordinariness of footwashing as one of the most frequent of life's chores. To confine mutual footwashing to a ritual context while continuing to treat ordinary footwashing as the task only of slaves would create a scarcely tolerable contradiction in the social significance of the act. This

---

[11]   J. Massyngbaerde Ford (*Redeemer – Friend and Mother: Salvation in Antiquity and in the Gospel of John* [Minneapolis: Augsburg Fortress, 1997] chap. 8) understands the footwashing as an act of ritualized friendship. Friendship is probably the best ancient model for the kind of radically non-hierarchical relationships which mutual footwashing would symbolize and enact. In 13:13 Jesus says that the disciples rightly call him Teacher and Lord, for so he is (cf. also 16), but in 15:15 he says that he no longer calls them servants but friends.

[12]   Thomas (*Footwashing*) offers the fullest recent argument for such a view. He lists earlier views of this kind on pp. 14-16; for more recent advocates, see Edwards, "The Christological Basis," 378-79; M. F. Connell, "*Nisi Pedes*, Except for the Feet: Footwashing in the Community of John's Gospel," *Worship* 7 (1996) 517-31. Many of the arguments for a rite of footwashing depend rather heavily on the hypothesis that the Fourth Gospel reflects and addresses a "Johannine community" with distinctive practices not necessarily found in other churches. Against this general hypothesis, see R. Bauckham (ed.), *The Gospels for All Christians: Rethinking the Gospel Audiences* (Edinburgh: T. & T. Clark; Grand Rapids: Eerdmans, 1997).

ritual (or "sacramental") understanding of the footwashing—for example, as a rite of remission of post-baptismal sin—is often connected with a blurring of the distinction between the two interpretations of Jesus' act provided in John 13.[13] Something of the soteriological significance of Jesus' act of washing his disciples feet is carried over into the practice of footwashing as the disciples are to continue it, as was the case in the repetition of the eucharistic acts in the Lord's Supper. But here the analogy of the Lord's Supper has proved misleading. The eucharistic acts would have no particular meaning without their close connexion to the soteriological signifi-cance of Jesus' death, but mutual footwashing has a clear meaning as the key to a rejection of social hierarchy and a new form of social relationships based on Jesus' example. There is no need to carry over the soteriological focus of the first interpretation in order to make sense of vv. 13-20, which themselves contain no soteriological allusion and are fully intelligible in their own terms.

The kind of exegesis which blurs or abolishes the distinction between the two interpretations, usually by thinking of footwashing in the church as a rite with salvific significance, is partly motivated by a dissatisfaction with the idea of two different interpretations merely placed side by side, especially as this idea has often been connected with theories of sources and redaction[14] which see the evangelist or the final redactor as in less than full control of his material. However, rejecting the ritual meaning of mutual footwash-ing does not mean that the two interpretations are unconnected. Both are developed from the fundamental meaning of Jesus' act: his expression of his lordship in self-humiliating service. Moreover, both can be seen in relation to Jesus' death, which for the first interpretation is the act of salvific service for others to which the footwashing points, while for the second interpretation it would be the culminating act of Jesus' self-humiliating service as an example for the disciples to follow. Those who follow Jesus in acting like a slave for others may also, like Jesus, incur a slave's death for others. The difference between the two interpretations is that one is

---

[13]   Thus Thomas (*Footwashing*, chap. 4) argues forcibly against the view that there are two different interpretations.

[14]   One of the most recent discussions of this type is M. C. de Boer, *Johannine Perspectives on the Death of Jesus* (Contributions to Biblical Exegesis and Theology 17; Kampen: Pharos, 1996) 283-92.

concerned with the unique soteriological significance of Jesus' self-humiliation and service, while the second presents these as an example his disciples should follow.

This juxtaposition of the uniqueness and the exemplariness of Jesus' self-giving service is not at all incongruous. It is found elsewhere in the New Testament, notably in Mark 10:43-45 (a passage thematically close to John 13: see "John and the Synoptics" below) and in 1 Pet 2:21-24.[15] The well-known christological passage in Phil 2:5-11, which strikingly resembles John 13 in its fundamental themes, also combines these two aspects. In the passage often identified as a hymn (vv. 6-11), Jesus' self-humiliation in service and servile death are envisioned as unique, at least insofar as they lead to his unique exaltation to the position of divine sovereignty over all things (cf. John 13:5), but the function of this passage in its wider context (vv. 3-5) is to exemplify the kind of self-denying humility towards each other that the Philippian Christians are encouraged to practise. That the fourth evangelist should highlight both aspects in relation to the footwashing is not at all surprising, and needs no theories of sources and redaction to explain it. This also means that no confidence can be placed in attempts to argue that one of the two interpretations is older and the other added. While this may be the case,[16] we have no way of knowing it. Our consideration of the historicity of the footwashing must manage without such speculations about Johannine tradition history.

ORIGINAL CREATION OR INTERPRETATION OF TRADITION?

In considering the historicity of the footwashing, we shall follow three lines of inquiry: the first considering evidence within the Fourth Gospel, the second the evidence of the relationship between John 13:1-20 and sayings of Jesus in the Synoptics, the third the evidence of the Christian practice of footwashing outside the Gospels.

As far as the internal evidence of the Fourth Gospel itself is concerned, much depends on our general views about the Johannine narratives of which this is one. A remarkable fact, though it is rarely

---

[15] See also 1 John 4:10-12 and 3:16, as pointed out by de Boer, *Johannine Perspectives*, 291-92.

[16] But the parallel with Mark 10:43-45 (see "John and the Synoptics" below) tends to suggest otherwise.

remarked on, perhaps because it is considered too obvious to merit comment, is the relatively small number of events in Jesus' ministry which the Fourth Gospel recounts. Compared with the Synoptic Gospels, John's narratives are characteristically much longer, inviting the reader or hearer into a more reflective participation in a narrative whose form often provides significant indications of the meaning of the event recounted, while many narratives also incorporate or precede passages in which Jesus himself draws out the meaning of the events. In selecting rather few events to include in his Gospel, John has left himself the space to expound their significance at length. Whatever might be the relationships between John and the Synoptic Gospels, it is scarcely credible that John did not have far more stories about Jesus available to him than he includes in the Gospel (cf. 20:30). This being so, his selection is no doubt determined by the potential of the stories for the kind of interpretation they receive within the Gospel. But given the scope for selectivity which he must have had and given that some of the stories most important to him (such as the cleansing of the temple or the feeding of the five thousand) were, as we can tell from their parallels in the Synoptics, certainly traditional, an easy resort to free creation of narratives, which has often been attributed to him, would seem unnecessary. John's genius as a narrator and interpreter of the story of Jesus seems to lie in telling the traditional stories in such a way as to indicate and incorporate profound and extensive reflection on their meaning. Since he undoubtedly does this in some cases, the onus of proof would seem to lie with those who attribute to him in other cases a kind of theological fiction, consciously inventing stories as carriers of the theological meaning he wishes to propound.

Of course, an argument that all John's narratives have a basis in tradition cannot show that all such traditions are historically reliable, but it can dispel the residue of suspicion about specifically Johannine narratives that the scholarly tradition of emphasizing John's theological creativity has left. That suspicion derives from the older view of the fourth evangelist as dependent on all three Synoptic Gospels and having no other Gospel traditions available to him. This view is held by few today. Without it there is no good reason to attribute to John's theological creativity the free creation of narratives *ex nihilo,* as distinct from and in addition to the interpretation of existing stories.

A further consideration is more specific to the footwashing. Jesus' statement that Peter cannot understand what he is doing but will do so "later" (μετὰ ταῦτα: 13:7; cf. 13:36), i.e. after the resurrection, is paralleled earlier in the Gospel by two statements of the evangelist to the effect that the disciples did not understand at the time, but did so after Jesus' resurrection (2:22) or after his glorification (12:16). In one case the reference is to a saying of Jesus which was already known in the tradition (2:19; cf. Matt 26:61; Mark 14:58), in the other case to an event, Jesus' entry into Jerusalem on a donkey, which was already known in the tradition (12:14-15). The probability is that in chap. 13, as in the other two cases, John sees, with post-resurrection hindsight, a deeper significance in a feature of the traditions of Jesus' words and deeds, rather than creating an event to which he attributes such significance.

JOHN AND THE SYNOPTICS

There is a saying of Jesus well-attested in the Synoptic traditions to the effect that the greatest among the disciples must be their servant. It is found in a variety of contexts, of which those closest to John 13 are Luke 22:24-27 and Mark 10:41-45 = Matt 20:24-28. Whereas Matthew[17] has followed Mark's version of this pericope closely, Luke's version differs considerably and probably derives from another source.[18] The two versions of our saying (the Greatest as Servant: Luke 22:26-27a; Mark 10:43-44) show little verbal correspondence but close resemblance in sense. The same is true of the sayings of Jesus which are placed before and after it and to which in both cases it is very closely linked. The sequence must represent an early tradition which we have in two pre-Lukan forms:

Luke 22:24-27	*Mark 10:41-45 = Matt 20:24-28*
The disciples dispute which is the greatest	The disciples indignant at the request of James and John to sit beside Jesus
(A) Kings of the Gentiles	(A) Rulers of the Gentiles
(B) Greatest as Servant	(B) Greatest as Servant and Slave
(C) Jesus as Servant	(C) Jesus as Servant
	(D) Ransom

---

[17]   The following discussion assumes Markan priority.

[18]   So, e.g., I. H. Marshall, *The Gospel of Luke* (NIGTC; Exeter: Paternoster, 1978) 811; J. Nolland, *Luke 18:35-24:53* (WBC 35C; Dallas: Word, 1993) 1062-63.

In both versions of this sequence, the fact that saying (B) is related to saying (C)—so that explicitly or implicitly it is because of Jesus' example of service that greatness among the disciples is defined in terms of service—brings this sequence much closer to John 13:12-20 than other occurrences of saying (B). Moreover, in both versions Jesus' service is probably to be understood as culminating in his death. This is explicit in the Markan version in the close link between (C) and the ransom saying (D). In Luke the placing of the sequence, at the Last Supper following the institution of the eucharist and the prediction of the betrayal, suggests that saying (C) should be connected with Jesus' closely approaching death, just as John's placing of the footwashing at the Last Supper suggests the same connexion. However, in neither the Markan nor the Lukan version is it clear in what Jesus' service prior to his death consists.[19] The general image of servant or slave in Mark's version becomes the more specific image of the servant who waits at table in the two questions which are unique to Luke's version of (B) (v. 27a). This coheres with a striking occurrence of the same image elsewhere in Luke (12:37) and with the Lukan setting at the Last Supper. But whether Luke's version is meant to imply that Jesus' serving is his actual waiting at table at the Last Supper is unclear, especially as in 22:14-21 Jesus is reclining at table, not waiting at table, and indeed presiding at the meal, not serving. In both versions it is probably best to think of Jesus' whole ministry as one of self-giving service, culminating in his death as the giving of his life for others.

It is Luke's version of this sequence that has usually been seen as especially close to John 13:1-20.[20] Luke's version is part of Jesus' "farewell discourse"[21] at the Last Supper, as John 13:12-20 is the beginning of the much longer "farewell discourse" in John (whereas Matthew and Mark have no such discourse). But it is doubtful how much significance can be attached to this. Luke or his tradition has highlighted the relationship of this material to Jesus' death by placing it on the last occasion on which Jesus teaches his disciples prior to his death, just as John has done with the footwashing and its interpretation. But Mark's placing is functionally similar, since he locates it after the third of the three passion predictions (Mark 10:32-34) and

---

[19] For Luke, see the full discussion by Nelson, *Leadership*, 160-71.

[20] For various views of the relationship, see Nelson, *Leadership*, 161-65.

[21] Nelson, *Leadership*, 97-119.

closely preceding Jesus' entry into Jerusalem. Moreover, whereas the table setting is explicit within Luke's version of saying (B) itself (22:27a), the correspondence with John is not as close as might at first appear. Luke refers to waiting at table as the servant's role. This is a different role from washing feet, and a less menial one, which, in a household with a number of slaves and servants, would be performed by the servants, whereas footwashing would be left to the slaves. The image of waiting at table, while it evokes a humble, serving role, is rather less shockingly demeaning than that of footwashing. While it is tempting to classify Luke 22:24-27 and John 13:1-20 among the rather numerous instances of shared tradition exclusive to Luke and John, it is doubtful whether the contact between John and Luke at this point is in fact significantly greater than that between John and Mark 10:41-45.

Saying (B), the Greatest as Servant, also occurs in another context represented in all three Synoptics:

Matt 18:1-5	*Mark 9:33-37*	*Luke 9:46-48*
Disciples dispute who is the greatest	Disciples dispute who is the greatest	Disciples dispute who is the greatest
	(B) First as Servant	
Jesus takes a child	Jesus takes a child	Jesus takes a child
(E) Entering Kingdom like a Child		
(B) Greatest like a Child		
(F) Receiving Child is Receiving Me	(F) Receiving Child is Receiving Me	(F) Receiving Child is Receiving Me
		(B) Greatest as Least

The core of this tradition consists of the narrative material and saying (F). It may well be Mark himself who has added saying (B), in a form which looks like an abbreviated form of the version in Mark 10:43-44 (which lacks πάντων ἔσχατος but has all the other vocabulary of the version in Mark 9:35). It is unlikely to be an independent version of the saying. Matthew's and Luke's changes stem from the recognition that, whereas the saying is appropriate to the context in that it speaks of the reversal (or abolition) of social status among the disciples, it is inappropriate to the extent that a child, though lacking social status, is not a servant. Both therefore transfer the saying into Jesus' words subsequent to his taking the child and adapt it to the example of the child by removing the "servant" terminology. The Matthean and Lukan versions of saying (B) are not independent versions, but sufficiently explained as adaptations of Mark 9:35 to the context. Finally, Matthew has also transferred saying (E) to this context from its Markan context in the other Synoptic pericope featuring children, where Mark and Luke have it but Matthew omits it (Matt 19:13-15; Mark 10:13-16; Luke 18:15-17). It forms an appropriate companion to Matthew's version of saying (B) which follows it in Matt 18:3-4. The conclusion must be that it is unlikely that any of the three Synoptic versions of saying (B) in this tradition are independent versions, but all stem originally from the form in Mark 10:43-44.

Finally, one more Synoptic version of saying (B), the Greatest as Servant, occurs in Matthew 23:11 in a quite different sequence of sayings. Whether this is Matthew's abbreviation of the version in Mark 10:43-44 = Matt 20:26-27 or an independent version from Matthew's special tradition, it is impossible to be sure. It is likely enough that such a saying should circulate widely and appear in more than one collected sequence of sayings, as is the case with the saying that follows it here (Matt 23:12; cf. Luke 14:11; 18:14).

Thus we have two independent versions of sayings (B) and (C) connected within a sequence of sayings that contrasts kingship among the Gentiles with service among the disciples of Jesus and roots this contrast in Jesus' own example:

> The kings of the Gentiles lord it over them;
> and those in authority over them are called benefactors.
> But not so with you:
> rather the greatest among you must become like the youngest,
> and the leader like one who serves.
> For who is greater, the one who is at table or the one who serves?
> Is it not the one at table?
> But I am among you as one who serves (Luke 22:25-27).

> You know that those who are considered rulers over the Gentiles lord it over them,
> and their great ones tyrannize over them.
> But it is not so among you;
> but whoever wishes to become great among you must be your servant,
> and whoever wishes to be first among you must be slave of all.
> For the Son of Man came not to be served but to serve,
> and to give his life a ransom for many (Mark 10:42-45).

There is also another plausibly independent version of saying (B):

The greatest among you will be your servant (Matt 23:11).

It should be noted that in John 13:1-20 there are no verbal parallels at all with these Synoptic sayings, except that δοῦλος occurs both in John 13:16 and in Mark 10:44 (= Matt 20:27). But John 13:16 is a saying paralleled in Matt 10:24, where δοῦλος occurs.

Though verbally unrelated, John 13:1-20 has strong thematic similarities with Luke 22:25-27 and Mark 10:42-45. How are these to be understood? The question arises whether John is dependent on nothing more in the tradition than a version of these Synoptic sayings, and has created the narrative of the footwashing as a vivid illustration of the point made in these traditional sayings of Jesus. It has not seldom been suggested that the footwashing is an imaginative construction on the basis of Luke 22:27.[22] Such a process seems to lack parallels. While Gospels scholars sometimes suggest that the evangelists or their traditions have created narrative settings for traditional sayings, the creation of a narrative to *replace* a traditional saying has been suggested with any plausibility at all only in the case of parables,[23] where the traditional saying could not have been retained in the context of the narrative. There is no convincing example in John.[24] In the case of the footwashing, there is no reason why John should not have included a version of the sayings in Luke 22:25-27 and Mark 10:42-45 as Jesus' interpretation of his action, had these sayings been the source from which he created the narrative. That he has created, not a setting for the sayings, but a

---

[22]   E.g. C. K. Barrett, *The Gospel according to St John* (2nd edition; London: SPCK, 1978) 436; for earlier supporters of this view, see J. A. Bailey, *The Traditions Common to the Gospels of Luke and John* (NovTSup 7; Leiden: Brill, 1963) 36 n. 7.

[23]   Notably, the suggestion that the parable in Luke 13:6-9 is the origin of the story of the barren fig tree (Mark 11:12-14, 20-21): see W. R. Telford, *The Barren Temple and the Withered Tree* (JSNTSup 1; Sheffield: JSOT Press, 1980) 13-14.

[24]   The suggestion (e.g. by M. Davies, *Rhetoric and Reference in the Fourth Gospel* [JSNTSup 69; Sheffield: JSOT Press, 1992] 256) that John's narrative of the raising of Lazarus (11) is based on the parable of the rich man and Lazarus (Luke 16:10-31) is entirely unconvincing. Lazarus (Eleazar) was one of the most common Jewish names of the period, so that the coincidence of the name is of no significance. John's Lazarus is not raised so that he may warn unrepentant Jews of the punishment that awaits them in the next life, as it is suggested Luke's Lazarus should be (though the request is refused). It is impossible to see how Luke's parable could have generated John's narrative.

narrative replacement of the sayings is implausible. Moreover, it should be observed that in Jesus' interpretation of the footwashing John does in fact cite two traditional sayings of Jesus, highlighted by the "Amen, amen, I say to you" formula which John often uses to mark out traditional logia. These have parallels in the Synoptics (John 13:16; cf. Matt 10:24-25; Luke 6:40; John 13:20; cf. Matt 10:40; Luke 10:16),[25] but in different contexts, unrelated to the Greatest as Servant sayings.

If the Synoptic sayings are not a source of John's footwashing narrative, then they can be invoked in support of the historical value of John's narrative by the criterion of coherence. The two independent versions Luke 22:25-27 and Mark 10:42-45 provide this series of sayings with good attestation in the tradition, indicating that Jesus both spoke of leadership among his disciples as the role of the slave or the servant of all,[26] and also spoke of his own example to them in the same terms. The embodiment of these ideas in a striking, even extreme instance of what he meant—washing the disciples' feet —is coherent with the Synoptic sayings, with Jesus' practice of enacting symbolic and demonstrative illustrations of his teaching, widely evidenced in the Gospel traditions, and with the hyperbolic style characteristic of Jesus' teaching.

HISTORY OF A PRACTICE

Outside John 13 there is only one New Testament reference to a Christian practice of washing the feet of fellow-Christians. In 1 Tim 5:10, the good works expected of a widow include that she has "shown hospitality, washed the saints' feet, helped the afflicted." The association with hospitality is not unexpected in the light of the general evidence about footwashing from the ancient world, and tends to preclude the possibility that the footwashing here is a religious rite. Rather, among the good works expected of widows, is

---

[25] Cf. also Matt 18:5 = Mark 9:37 = Luke 9:46, where a version of this saying makes reference to the child Jesus takes as an example of the lack of status required of disciples. In Luke 9:46 this brings it into combination with a version of the Greatest as Servant saying. But this is the version of the latter furthest from resembling John 13 (since it makes no reference to servant or serving), while John 13:20 is similarly closer to Matt 10:40 than to Mark 9:37 or Luke 9:46.

[26] The subversion of social status in the community of the disciples is a theme also more widely attested in the tradition of the sayings of Jesus: e.g. Mark 10:31 and parallels; Matt 23:12 and parallels.

that they should perform for their house guests the footwashing which, had they not been Christians, they would have expected a slave or the guests themselves to perform. Besides hospitality in their own homes, another possible context for the widows' footwashing, suggested by a passage of Tertullian we shall cite below, is the agape meal, at which the feet of all who arrived for the meal would have to be washed in some way. That footwashing is here mentioned among the good works of widows in no way implies that only widows practised it in the context addressed by 1 Timothy.

This passage joins the scattered evidence from the following centuries for Christian practice of footwashing. Except in connexion with this other evidence, it might not be especially significant, while the later evidence alone could not be presumed to refer to a practice going back to the New Testament period were it not for 1 Tim 5:10. Together the evidence is sufficient to indicate a widespread practice, highly distinctive to early Christianity, which originated at an early date. The fact that 1 Tim 5:10 itself clearly presumes an established practice should be noted, and makes it very unlikely that it itself reflects the influence of the Fourth Gospel.

J. C. Thomas has collected and discussed the relevant patristic evidence,[27] but his discussion is marred by his view that, like his interpretation of John 13, this material evidences a widespread religious rite of footwashing in early Christianity. On the contrary, most of the evidence is best understood as referring to the practice of washing the feet of fellow-Christians (or others) on occasions when footwashing would take place in any case. There need be no special significance in the footwashing itself, only in the fact that Christians are performing the act.

Tertullian writes of the way a non-Christian husband might be expected to regard his Christian wife, especially the good works and religious meetings for which she would leave his home:

> For who would suffer his wife, for the sake of visiting the brethren, to go round from street to street to other men's, and indeed all the poorer, cottages? Who will willingly bear her being taken from his side by nocturnal convocations, if need so be? Who, finally, will without anxiety endure her absence all the night long at the paschal solemnities? Who will, without some suspicion of his own, dismiss her to attend the Lord's Supper which

---

[27]   Thomas, *Footwashing*, chap. 5. His treatment of the patristic evidence is also criticized by R. B. Edwards in a review in *EvQ* 66 (1994) 278-80.

they defame? Who will suffer her to creep into prison to kiss a martyr's bonds? Nay, truly, to meet any one of the brethren to exchange the kiss? to offer water for the saints' feet? to snatch (somewhat for them) from her food, from her cup? to yearn (after them)? to have (them) in her mind? If a pilgrim brother arrive, what hospitality for him in an alien home? (*Ad Uxorem* 2.4)[28]

The husband's concern is probably envisaged as primarily for the dishonour such activities by his wife would bring on his own reputation. Some of the activities are of dubious propriety or worse, especially in view of the persistent pagan rumours about what happened in secret Christian meetings during the hours of darkness. But there is also evidently a concern about activities that demean the wife (and thereby her husband), such as entering the homes of the poor and honouring convicted criminals (the martyrs in prison). Washing the feet of the saints (perhaps a deliberate echo of 1 Tim 5:10) would be seen as a socially degrading act. We cannot here think of hospitality in the woman's home as the context, since the last sentence of the quotation excludes what in any case would not be conceivable in the case of the wife of an unbeliever. Probably, therefore, the most plausible context is the agape meal, at which, Tertullian elsewhere notes, 'a peculiar respect is shown to the lowly' (*Apol.* 39), though the later evidence associating footwashing with visiting the sick (*Apost. Const.* 3.19) suggests, alternatively, that this could be in view. Elsewhere Tertullian seems to imply that Christians were known for practising footwashing in a religious context (*De Corona* 8); reference to footwashing preceding the agape meal would be very plausible here too.

From the late fourth century come two references to washing the feet of those unable to do this for themselves. The Canons of Athanasius instruct bishops to serve at meals with their priests, and to wash the feet of those too weak to do this for themselves. The *Apostolic Constitutions* instruct deacons, as part of their ministry of visiting the sick, to wash the feet of "such of the brethren as are weak and inform" (3.19).[29] While these references may seem to minimize the practice in envisaging it only as a service to those unable to wash their own feet, they also make clear that it is no religious rite. It is

---

28 Quoted by Thomas, *Footwashing*, 140, in the translation by Roberts and Donaldson (*Ante-Nicene Fathers*).

29 The two passages are quoted by Thomas, *Footwashing*, 130-32.

the regular footwashing for comfort and hygiene, such as before a meal. Bishops and deacons are not to think it beneath their dignity to perform this ordinary but servile act for those who needed it done for them.

Other references to the practice, by Origen, Chrysostom, Pachomius, Caesarius of Arles, Sulpicius Severus, Sozomen and Benedict of Nursia clearly envisage hospitality to strangers as the context, whether in private homes or in monastic communities,[30] while Caesarius also, like the *Apostolic Constitutions*, associates it with visiting the sick.[31]

Some of the evidence Thomas cites for footwashing as a rite signifying forgiveness of sins is not really such. Some passages mean that the meritorious act of washing the feet of others procures forgiveness of sins for the one who washes (Ambrose, *De Spiritu Sancto* 1.15) or procures prayers for his forgiveness by those whose feet he has washed (Cassian, *Inst.* 4.19; Caesarius, *Serm.* 202), while Augustine understands Christ to be daily cleansing our feet (metaphorically) from sin by interceding for us, with no apparent reference to an actual ritual practice (*In Joan. Ev.* 56.5; 58.5).[32] However, there is good evidence that, from at least *c.* 300 onwards, in certain parts of the western church, there was a common practice of washing the feet of the newly baptized.[33] Ambrose, reflecting on the fact that this custom was observed in Milan but not in Rome, cites the view of some that footwashing was to be observed as a practice of hospitality only, not as a ritual element in the sacrament of baptism. His response is that the former "belongs to humility," the latter "to sanctification" (*De Myst.* 3.5).[34] This makes a clear distinction between the special soteriological significance attached to the footwashing that in some churches accompanied baptism, and the significance of the common Christian practice of footwashing as part

---

[30]The relevant passages are quoted by Thomas, *Footwashing*, 132-34, 141, 143-45.

[31]   *Serm.* 60.4, quoted by Thomas, *Footwashing*, 145.

[32]   All these passages are quoted by Thomas, *Footwashing*, 158-61.

[33]   The evidence, from the Synod of Elvira, Ambrose, Augustine and Caesarius of Arles, is quoted by Thomas, *Footwashing*, 142-43, 145, 178.

[34]   Quoted by Thomas, *Footwashing*, 178. Caesarius (*Serm.* 104.3, quoted by Thomas, *Footwashing*, 145) says of the baptized: "Let them receive strangers and, in accord with what was done for themselves in baptism, wash the feet of their guests."

of the hospitality offered to strangers and guests. The latter is not a religious rite, but a feature of everyday life which Christians expressed their humility—their disregard of social status—in undertaking. As late as the sixth century it is clear that the practice was a stumbling-block for some high status Christians, who felt it to be degrading.[35] The socially radical significance of Christian footwashing persisted throughout the patristic period.

The practice of footwashing following baptism may well have been based on John 13:5-10, from which its soteriological significance and its connexion with baptism could have been derived. The everyday practice of footwashing—in hospitality and visiting the sick—is also associated in the texts with John 13, as obedience to Jesus' command that his example be followed (vv. 14-15). These texts make it clear that the command was understood to apply to ordinary occasions when footwashing would be natural and necessary, requiring that Christians should not on these occasions hesitate to perform the act which would otherwise be the duty of slaves. Though for the period from the first century to the third the only clear evidence is that provided by 1 Timothy, Tertullian and Origen,[36] the incidental character of these references is indicative of a practice taken for granted and well-known, despite its counter-cultural nature. The nature of our evidence for early Christianity in the first three centuries makes it unsurprising that references are not more plentiful. The evidence we have is sufficient to suggest a practice established already in the first century independently of the influence of the Fourth Gospel.

Footwashing was one of the most counter-cultural practices of early Christianity, symbolizing most radically the status-rejecting ideals of the early Christian communities. Its origin calls for explanation. It might be a practice initiated within earliest Christianity, under the inspiration of those sayings of Jesus which require his disciples to relate to each other by humble service rather than by self-aggrandizing lordship. John's story of the footwashing might then be an aetiological myth, projecting the origin of this distinctive practice back into Jesus' ministry. But such a speculation is less plausible than the obvious alternative: that, just as Jesus dined with outcasts and blessed children, so also he washed his disciples' feet.

---

35   Caesarius, *Serm.* 202, quoted by Thomas, *Footwashing*, 133.
36   Cf. also, less clearly, Cyprian, quoted by Thomas, *Footwashing*, 141.

"WHERE NO ONE HAD YET BEEN LAID"
THE SHAME OF JESUS' BURIAL

Byron R. McCane

Recent studies have posed provocative questions about Jesus' burial, as a steady stream of books and articles has increasingly raised the possibility that the body of Jesus might have been disposed of in shame and dishonor.[1] While some scholars still hold that Jesus was buried with dignity, it is now quite common to read assertions to the contrary. Raymond E. Brown, for example, has argued that Jesus was buried in a tomb reserved for criminals, and John Dominic Crossan has concluded that no one really knew what became of the body—it may have been thrown out to be eaten by dogs.[2] The problems surrounding Jesus' burial are extremely difficult, for reasons which are all too familiar to scholars of the historical Jesus: the event took place long ago, the sources are scarce, and most of the textual evidence is heavily shaded in Christian ideologies. All the same, in my judgment it is possible to reach a very high degree of historical confidence about the burial of Jesus. He was, after all, a Palestinian Jew crucified by Romans, and quite a lot is known about Jewish and Roman practices regarding the dead. In addition, anthropologists and sociologists have thoroughly analyzed the ways in which societies and cultures treat the remains of the dead. Accordingly, this chapter will draw upon evidence from archaeology

---

[1]   J. Blinzler, "Die Grablegung Jesu in historischer Sicht," in E. Dhanis (ed.), *Resurrexit* (Vatican City: Editrice Vaticana, 1974) 56-107; F. M. Braun, "La sépulture de Jesus," *RB* 45 (1936) 34-52, 184-200, 346-63; A. Buchler, "L'enterrement des criminels d'après le Talmud et le Midrasch," *REJ* 46 (1903) 74-88; H. Cousin, "Sépulture criminelle et sépulture prophétique," *RB* 81 (1974) 375-93; D. Daube, *The New Testament and Rabbinic Judaism.* (London: Athlone, 1956), 310-11; E. Dhanis, "L'ensevelissement de Jésus et la visite au tombeau dans l'évangile de saint Marc (xv,40–xvi,8)," *Greg* 39 (1958) 367-410.

[2]   R. E. Brown, "The Burial of Jesus (Mark 15:42-47)," *CBQ* 50 (1988) 233-45; idem, *The Death of the Messiah* (New York: Doubleday, 1994) 1201-1317; J. D. Crossan, *The Historical Jesus* (San Francisco: Harper, 1991) 391-94; idem, *Who Killed Jesus?* (San Francisco: HarperCollins, 1995) 160-88.

and literature, along with theory from anthropology and sociology, to argue that Jesus was indeed buried in disgrace in a criminals' tomb. Based on what we know of Roman practice and Jewish custom, one or more members of the Sanhedrin must have obtained the body of Jesus from Pilate and arranged for a dishonorable interment. From an early date the Christian tradition tried to conceal this unpleasant fact, but the best evidence clearly shows that Jesus was buried in shame.

I

Jesus was crucified by Romans, and at the time of his death his body was in the hands of Romans, so any historical investigation of his burial must begin with the Romans. What would Pilate and the soldiers guarding the cross, who were in charge of the body of Jesus, have been most likely to do with it? There is a distinct possibility that they might have done nothing at all with the body, but simply left it hanging on the cross. As Martin Hengel has observed, the Romans used crucifixion not only as a punishment but also as a deterrent, and while the punitive effect of crucifixion may have ended when the victim died, the deterrent effect did not have to.[3] The impact of crucifixion could go on for days at a time, as the body of one who had crossed the purposes of Rome was left hanging in public view, rotting in the sun, with birds pecking away at it.

Several Roman writers mention that condemned criminals could be denied a decent burial, and that victims of crucifixion in particular could be left on their crosses for days at a time. Suetonius, for example, writes that when Augustus avenged the murder of Julius Caesar, he not only took the lives of Brutus and his supporters but also denied them customary rites of burial. One victim who pleaded for a decent burial was told, "The carrion-birds will soon take care of that" (Suetonius, *Augustus* 13.1-2). Later, in 31 CE, when Tiberius moved against Sejanus and his supporters, some of them committed suicide rather than be executed, "because people sentenced to death forfeited their property and were forbidden burial" (Tacitus, *Annals* 6.29). Also from the first century is Petronius' amusing (to Romans, at least) story about a soldier who was assigned to guard some crosses "in order to prevent anyone from taking a body down for burial" (Petronius, *Satyricon* 111). The unfortunate soldier loses one

---

3   M. Hengel, *Crucifixion in the Ancient World and the Folly of the Message of the Cross* (Philadelphia: Fortress, 1977) 86-88.

of the bodies, however, when he diverts his attention from the crosses in order to pursue an amorous interlude with a widow. While he is thus distracted, parents of one of the victims take the body down and bury it. The story is full of bawdy themes—it is from the *Satyricon*, after all—but two incidental details suggest the seriousness with which Romans could take the matter of guarding crucifixion victims: the soldier guards the crosses for three nights, and he fears for his life when the theft is discovered. Finally, Horace mentions that a slave who is innocent of murder need not fear "hanging on a cross to feed crows" (Horace, *Epistles* 1.16.48).

In each of these cases the central issue appears to be an assertion of power, and specifically *Roman* power. In typical Roman fashion, opponents and enemies are not merely subdued but utterly vanquished and even made an example of. Certainly the limp, putrefying body of a crucifixion victim would have displayed the might of Rome in viscerally graphic fashion. Something else was also at work in these practices, however, something which had to do with the Roman social order. Ordinarily, death is an event which disrupts the functioning of a social order, for the death of any particular individual tears away a member of a social network and forces the network to reconstitute itself. Death rituals—i.e., burial customs and rites of mourning—are social processes which heal the wounds which death inflicts on the social group.[4] By burying the dead and mourning their absence, members of a society affirm that someone significant has been lost. When the Romans did not permit the burial of crucifixion victims, then, they were doing more than merely showing off the power of Rome: they were also declaring that the deaths of these victims were not a loss to Roman society. Far from it, the deaths of condemned criminals actually served to strengthen and preserve Rome, protecting and defending the social order of the Empire.

Certainly there were times when Roman officials in Judea behaved like their counterparts in the rest of the Empire. When Varus, for example, the Roman legate of Syria, moved into Judea in 4 BCE to quell civil unrest after the death of Herod the Great, he reportedly crucified two thousand of those who participated in the uprising in and around Jerusalem (*Ant.* 17.10.10 §295). Later, as the First Jewish War was breaking out in 66 CE, the Roman procurator Gessius Florus is said to have ordered indiscriminate crucifixions,

---

4   R. Hertz, *Death and the Right Hand* (New York: Free Press, 1960).

including among his victims even some citizens of equestrian rank (*J.W.* 2.14.9 §306-307). And in 70 CE the Roman general Titus is reported to have crucified hundreds of Jewish captives around the walls of Jerusalem, in the hope "that the spectacle might perhaps induce the Jews to surrender" (*J.W.* 5.11.1 §450). Josephus does not specifically state that bodies were left hanging on crosses in these cases, but that would be entirely consistent with the general purpose of these crucifixions. It is likely, then, that on at least three occasions Roman authorities in Judea left victims of crucifixion hanging on crosses in just the way described by Petronius and Horace.

These actions, however, are certainly not typical of the way Romans usually behaved in Judea. These mass crucifixions, it turns out, all come from times of acute crisis, when Roman military officers were being called in to stabilize situations which had gotten out of control. Varus and Titus, for example, were putting down armed rebellions, and even before Florus' action in 66, the legate of Syria (Cestius Gallus at the time) had already become involved with the escalating troubles in Judea (*J.W.* 2.14.3 §280-283). Throughout most of the first century, by contrast, and especially at the time of Jesus' death, Judea was not in open revolt against Rome and was not under the control of Roman generals commanding legions of soldiers.[5] It was instead administered by a prefect who had only a small contingent of troops at his disposal. Certainly the prefect could mobilize those forces to suppress potential rebellion, as Theudas and "the Egyptian" discovered (*J.W.* 2.13.4–5 §258-263; *Ant.* 20.5.1 §97-99; 20.8.6 §167-172; Acts 5:36), but such events were brief, intermittent, and did not involve mass crucifixions. Most of the time, in other words, the city walls of Jerusalem were not ringed by hundreds of crosses. At the time of Jesus, in fact, the situation was peaceful enough that events in and around Jerusalem were not always under the direct control of the Roman prefect. Pilate did not reside in Jerusalem, but at Caesarea on the coast in a palace built by Herod the Great, and he came to Jerusalem only on special occasions, such as Passover. A small Roman force was stationed in the city in the fortress Antonia, but the routine day-to-day government of Jerusalem was largely in Jewish hands, specifically the High Priest and the

---

[5]   E. P. Sanders, *The Historical Figure of Jesus* (New York: Penguin, 1993) 15-32; F. Millar, *The Roman Near East 31 BC – AD 337* (Cambridge: Harvard University Press, 1993) 43-56.

council, who were accountable to Pilate for the maintenance of public order. Pilate himself was accountable to the legate of Syria, and it was in the interest of all concerned to avoid disruption of the status quo. It would be a mistake, then, to conclude that episodes like those involving Varus, Florus, and Titus are typical of the situation surrounding Jesus' burial. They were military commanders putting their foot down—*hard*—on open rebellion against Rome. Pilate was a bureaucrat trying to keep the wheels of government running smoothly.

Roman prefects like Pilate, in fact, often allowed crucifixion victims to be buried. Cicero, for example, mentions a governor in Sicily who released bodies to family members in return for a fee (*In Verrem* 2.5.45), and Philo writes that on the eve of Roman holidays in Egypt, crucified bodies were taken down and given to their families, "because it was thought well to give them burial and allow them ordinary rites" (*In Flaccum* 10.83-84). In addition, as Crossan has pointed out, the famous case of Yehoḥanan, the crucified man whose skeletal remains were found in a family tomb at Givʿat ha-Mivtar, proves that a Roman governor in Jerusalem had released the body of a crucifixion victim for burial.[6] Finally, the Gospels'

---

[6] Crossan, *Who Killed Jesus?*, 167-68. For the archaeology, cf. V. Tzaferis, "Jewish Tombs at and near Givʿat ha-Mivtar, Jerusalem," *IEJ* 20 (1970) 18-32. For two differing analyses of the skeletal remains—and two different reconstructions of the Roman method of crucifixion—cf. N. Haas, "Anthropological Observations on the Skeletal Remains from Givʿat ha-Mivtar," *IEJ* 20 (1970) 38-59; and J. Zias and E. Sekeles, "The Crucified Man from Givʿat ha-Mivtar: A Reappraisal," *IEJ* 35 (1985) 22-27. Crossan, however, completely misunderstands the significance of this find when he writes, "With all those thousands of people crucified around Jerusalem in the first century alone, we have so far found only a single crucified skeleton . . . Was burial, then, the exception rather than the rule?" (168). The archaeological report plainly states that it was only an accident which caused Yehoḥanan's remains to be preserved in such a way as to identify him as a crucifixion victim. Only the nail through his ankle provided evidence of crucifixion. And why was the nail still in Yehoḥanan's ankle? Because the soldiers who had crucified him could not extract it from the cross. When the nail had been driven in, it had struck a knot in the wood, bending back the point of the nail. As any carpenter (or fisherman) knows, it is almost impossible to extract a nail with a point that has been bent back like the barb of a hook. Thus if there had not been a knot strategically located in the wood of Yehoḥanan's cross, the soldiers would have easily pulled the nail out of the cross. It never would have been buried with Yehoḥanan, and we would never have known that he had been crucified. It is not

assertion that Pilate "used to release for them one prisoner for whom they asked" (Mark 15:6 par.) is also relevant here, for it shows that during the first century CE one could plausibly tell stories of Roman judicial clemency, especially around religious holidays. Thus the fate of Jesus' body in Roman hands should not be regarded as automatic. The occasion of Jesus' death was a Jewish holiday, and Pilate was not in the process of suppressing a revolt, but rather simply trying to protect public order.

On balance, then, the Romans involved with the death of Jesus naturally would have expected that the body would remain on the cross, unless Pilate ordered otherwise. It was something of a commonplace in the Empire that victims of crucifixion would become food for carrion-birds, unless the clemency of a governor intervened. Certainly Rome had its reasons for leaving its victims on public display. This fact can help to explain an interesting detail in Mark's account of the burial of Jesus: Mark 15:43 says that Joseph of Arimathea "dared" (τολμήσας) to approach Pilate and request the body of Jesus. Why "dared?" Because such a request would indeed have been daring in light of the fact that victims often remained hanging on crosses as symbols of Roman will.[7] On the other hand, a request by a Jewish leader for the body of Jesus would not have been out of place, either, since Roman prefects—including at least one that we know of in first-century Jerusalem—did allow the burial of crucifixion victims. In the case of Jesus, such an allowance was likely, since Jesus was not caught up in a mass crucifixion, and his death did not come at a time of revolt against Rome. The Jewish leaders of Jesus' day generally cooperated with Pilate in preserving public order in Jerusalem, and the occasion of Jesus' death was a Jewish religious holiday. It may have taken a little nerve, then, but someone like Joseph of Arimathea could have reasonably expected that Pilate would grant his request for the body of Jesus.

II

But would a member of the council have approached Pilate about the body of Jesus? Or would the Jewish leaders of first-century

---

surprising, in other words, that we have found the remains of only one crucifixion victim: it is surprising that we have identified even one. Crossan's inference on p. 168 is quite misguided.

7   Brown, *The Death of the Messiah*, 1216-17.

Jerusalem have been content to let Pilate do whatever he wanted with the body? The evidence indicates that they would *not* have wanted the body of Jesus to be left hanging on the cross. Based on what we know of Jewish culture, they would have preferred for Jesus to be buried, and promptly. Jewish burial practices in the days of Jesus are well-known: hundreds of tombs have been excavated, and many texts—from Josephus, the Mishnah, and the tractate *Semaḥot*[8]— explicitly discuss the care of the dead. Indeed, the archaeological and literary evidence presents a remarkably complete picture, and the following portrait of a typical Jewish funeral is based on the combined witness of texts and tombs.[9]

---

[8]   The tractate *Semaḥot* (lit. "rejoicings," certainly a euphemistic title) dates from the third century CE and is an earlier form of the Talmudic tractate ʿEbel *Rabbati*. For this date and a discussion of the evidence, see D. Zlotnick, trans., *The Tractate "Mourning" (Semaḥot)* (New York: Yale University Press, 1966).

[9] Comment is called for here on current scholarly suspicions regarding the value (or lack thereof) of the Mishnah as a historical source for the world of Jesus. Of course one cannot naively assume that this third-century text preserves reliable information about first-century Jewish life. In many cases it demonstrably does not. *On the specific topic of burial practices, however*, there is strong evidence in favor of using the Mishnah. First, at points where it can be checked against the archaeological evidence the Mishnah has already been shown to be accurate. *m. B. Bat.* 6:8, for example, records a rabbinic discussion about the ideal dimensions for burial niches, and the dimensions given in the Mishnaic text correspond closely to the actual dimensions of so-called "loculus" niches typically found in first-century Jewish tombs in Palestine. *m. B. Bat.* 2:9 stipulates that tombs should be located at least fifty cubits outside of a town or city, and archaeology confirms that this practice was typically followed both in first-century Jerusalem and at Qumran. Second, it is an anthropological commonplace that burial practices change very slowly (see below). Theological ideas about death and the afterlife are typically vague and fluid, but burial practices and customs have a weight and mass all their own. From this point of view, there would be nothing particularly remarkable about a third-century text which accurately preserved information about burial customs from two centuries earlier. For these reasons I do not hesitate to make critical use of the Mishnah—along with the tractate *Semaḥot*—in conjunction with other sources of evidence *on this specific topic*. Cf. B. R. McCane, *Jews, Christians, and Burial in Roman Palestine* (Ph.D. diss., Duke University, 1992); P. Figueras, *Decorated Jewish Ossuaries* (Leiden: Brill, 1985); D. Goldenberg, *Halakhah in Josephus and in Tannaitic Literature: A Comparative Study* (Ph.D. diss., Dropsie University, 1978); R. Hachlili, *Ancient Jewish Art and Archaeology in the Land of Israel* (Leiden: Brill, 1988); S. Klein, *Tod und Begräbnis in Palästina zur Zeit der Tannaiten* (Berlin: Itzowski, 1908); E. M. Meyers, *Jewish Ossuaries: Reburial and Rebirth* (Rome: Pontifical Biblical Institute, 1971); L. Y. Rahmani, "Ancient

The Jews of Early Roman Palestine had a long tradition of prompt burial of the dead. Most funerals took place as soon as possible after death, and almost always on the same day.[10] As soon as death occurred, preparations began: the eyes of the deceased were closed, the corpse was washed with perfumes and ointments, its bodily orifices were stopped, and strips of cloth were wrapped tightly around the body—binding the jaw closed, holding the hand to the sides, and tying the feet together.[11] Thus prepared, the corpse was placed on a bier or in a coffin and carried out of town in a procession to the family tomb, usually a small rock-cut cave entered through a narrow opening that could be covered with a stone.[12] Upon arriving at the tomb, eulogies were spoken and the corpse was placed inside, either in a niche or on a shelf, along with items of jewelry or other personal effects of the deceased.[13] Expressions of condolence continued as the procession returned to the family home,

---

Jerusalem's Funerary Customs and Tombs, Part Three," *BA* 44 (1981) 43-45; S. Safrai, "Home and Family," in S. Safrai and M. Stern (eds.), *The Jewish People in the First Century* (2 vols., CRINT 1.1-2; Assen: Van Gorcum; Philadelphia: Fortress, 1976) 2.773-87.

[10] *m. Sanh.* 6:5; *Sem.* 1.5. Cf. also Mark 5:38 par., where funerary preparations have already begun after Jairus' daugher has died earlier that day.

[11] *m. Sanh.* 23.5; *Sem.* 1.2-5; 12.10. One prominent rabbi, Rabban Gamaliel, is said to have disapproved of overly ostentatious preparations for burial, and to have ordered his body to be wrapped in flax rather than linen (*b. Ketub.* 86a; *b. Mo'ed Qat.* 27b). Brown appears to misunderstand the point of this gesture when he writes that "a change in burial style is reported to have been introduced" by Gamaliel (*The Death of the Messiah*, 1243). Gamaliel did not, however, introduce any change in Jewish burial practices: his body was wrapped in cloth like any other Jewish corpse. What Gamaliel changed was the degree of ostentation, by insisting on plain simple flax rather than fine linen. Such sentiments are rather common in the anthropology of death ritual. In the ancient world, Solon, Plato, and Cicero are all said to have urged limitations on funerary display (Plutarch, *Sol.* 21.5; Cicero, *de Leg.* 2.23.59; 2.24.60).

[12] *m. B. Bat.* 2:9; cf. also A. Kloner, *The Necropolis of Jerusalem* (Ph.D. diss., Hebrew University, 1980) [Hebrew].

[13] *Sem.* 8.2-7. Two kinds of burial niches typically characterize Jewish tombs in Roman Palestine: (1) the *kokh* or loculus, a deep narrow slot in the wall of the tomb, and (2) the arcosolium, a broad arch-shaped recess along the wall of the tomb. A typical loculus cave can have 5-8 niches (cf. L. Y. Rahmani, "A Jewish Tomb on Shahin Hill, Jerusalem," *IEJ* 8 [1958] 101-105), while a typical arcosolium cave has only three (cf. idem, "The Mahanayim Tomb," *'Atiqot* 3 [1961] 91-120).

and friends and relatives dispersed. The funeral was thus conducted without delay, and in most cases the body had been interred by sunset on the day of death. Once in a while a Jewish funeral might even be a little too hasty: the rabbis told stories of people who had been mistakenly buried before they were actually dead.[14]

This preference for promptness was only heightened in the case of crucifixion victims, for the Torah specifically commanded that those who had been "hung on a tree" should be buried at sunset. Deuteronomy 21:22-23 reads: "if a man has committed a crime punishable by death and he is put to death, and you hang him on a tree, his body shall not remain all night upon the tree, but you shall bury him the same day." Victims of execution could be left hanging in public view, then, but only for a short period of time. In the book of Joshua, the king of Ai is killed, hanged, and then buried at sunset (Josh 8:29), as are the five kings who oppose the Israelites (Josh 10:27). The apocryphal book of Tobit tells of a hero who risked life and limb to bury execution victims at sunset of the day of death (Tob 1:16; 2:4), and Jewish writings from first-century Palestine confirm the ongoing vitality of this ancient cultural norm. The Temple Scroll from Qumran, for example, quotes Deut 21:22-23, and Josephus says that the Jews in Jerusalem were "so careful about funeral rites that even malefactors who have been sentenced to crucifixion were taken down and buried before sunset" (*J.W.* 4.5.2 §317). These norms continued to have currency long after the time of Jesus: *m. Sanh.* 6:4 quotes Deut 21:22-23 verbatim and notes that Jews did not customarily leave bodies of executed criminals hanging past sunset on the day of death. Jews in Palestine, in other words, had long regarded prompt burial as the normal and decent way to treat the dead. The Jewish leaders in first-century Jerusalem would have thought of it as only natural and right to take Jesus' body down from the cross at sunset.

They would not have thought it natural and right, however, to bury Jesus like most other Jews. For there was also a long-standing

---

[14] *Sem.* 8.1: "One may go out to the cemetery for three days to inspect the dead for a sign of life, without fear that this smacks of heathen practice. For it happened that a man was inspected after three days, and he went on to live twenty-five years; still another went on to have five children and died later." Such anecdotal accounts are more likely than rabbinic prescriptions to reflect the realities of everyday life—and death.

Jewish tradition that some bodies ought to be buried differently from others. Some Jews were buried in shame and dishonor, because they were guilty of crimes which made them undeserving of a decent burial. The evidence for the practice of dishonorable burial begins in the Hebrew Bible. In 1 Kgs 13:21-22, for example, a prophet who disobeys the command of the LORD is denounced and told, "Your body shall not go into the tomb of your fathers." Later, in Jer 22:18-19 it is the king himself (in this case, Jehoiakim, son of Josiah) who is so threatened: "They shall not lament for him . . . With the burial of an ass shall he be buried, dragged and cast forth beyond the gates of Jerusalem." Granted, these texts evince only the beginnings of an outline of dishonorable burial by suggesting that there might be offenders who would not be buried in their family tombs, and that there might be deaths for which Israel would not mourn; but this early evidence is reinforced in later periods. Josephus, for example, records a version of the biblical story of Achan (Joshua 7) and his account ends with the statement that Achan was "straightway put to death and at nightfall was given the ignominious (ἄτιμος) burial proper to the condemned" (*Ant.* 5.1.14 §44). Josephus does not specify what "ignominious burial" was—apparently he can safely assume that his readers will know and understand. The Mishnah is much more specific. *m. Sanh.* 6:6 says that criminals condemned by a Jewish court were not interred "in the burial place of their fathers," but in separate places kept by the court specifically for that purpose. Rites of mourning were not observed for these criminals, either. Family members were supposed to keep their grieving to themselves:

> The kinsmen came and greeted the judges and the witnesses as if to say, "We have nothing against you in our hearts, for you have judged the judgment of truth." And they used not to make open lamentation, but they went mourning, for mourning has its place in the heart (*m. Sanh.* 6:6).

Talmudic texts likewise argue that mourning should not be observed for those condemned by a Jewish court (*Šem.* 2.6). Even though these sources do not always spell out in full the exact details of dishonorable burial, certain elements do recur, and enough for us to reach at least one conclusion. From the Hebrew Bible through the rabbinic literature, dishonorable Jewish burial meant two things: burial away from the family tomb, and burial without rites of mourning.

Before proceeding any further, there is a point to be noted here about burial practices—not just Jewish burial practices, but burial practices in general. The point is this: they change very slowly. For centuries on end Israelites and Jews had been burying their dead promptly, and burying their dishonored dead in shame, and these customs did not change much over time. Burial practices are in fact among the most traditional and conservative aspects of human cultures, and they are especially so in unsecularized societies. When a society is still embedded in religion—i.e. when religious beliefs still serve as the foundation for social institutions and customs—burial practices function as ritual vehicles for social and cultural cohesion in the face of death. As such, they change very slowly. It is important to note the significance of this fact for the burial of Jesus.[15] Traditions of prompt burial, and of dishonorable burial, would have exerted a powerful influence on the Jewish leaders of first-century Jerusalem. These customs had been handed down for generations and were invested with the aura of sacred authority. The Jewish leaders were devoutly religious. To imagine that they could have disregarded these traditions, out of indifference or inconvenience, is to misunderstand burial customs in a fundamental way. Worse yet, it is to project post-modern secularized ways of thinking back into an era where they do not belong.

The element of shame in Jewish dishonorable burial is most vividly evident in the specific differences between burial in shame and burial with honor. Honorable burial emphasized precisely what shameful burial left out: the family tomb, and mourning. Burial by family groups in subterranean chambers was the consistent pattern, not just among Israelites and Jews but throughout the ancient near east. The practice of secondary burial (i.e. the reburial of bones after the flesh of the body has decayed) was especially prevalent, going back as far as the Middle Bronze Age (c. 2000-1500 BCE), when circular underground chambers were used and the bones of family members were typically gathered into a pile on one side of the tomb.[16] Similar practices persisted through the Late Bronze Age (c.

---

[15] For the sociology and anthropology of death ritual, see P. Metcalf and R. Huntington, *Celebrations of Death: The Anthropology of Mortuary Ritual* (2nd ed., Cambridge: Cambridge University Press, 1991); M. Bloch and J. Parry (eds.), *Death and the Regeneration of Life* (New York: Cambridge University Press, 1982); R. Chapman, I. Kinnes, and K. Randsborg (eds.), *The Archaeology of Death* (Cambridge: Cambridge University Press, 1981).

[16] S. Campbell and A. Green (eds.), *The Archaeology of Death in the Ancient*

1500-1200 BCE).[17] Later, during Iron Age II (esp. c. 800-700 BCE), benches were carved around the walls of the burial chamber, about waist-high.[18] Bodies were laid on these benches, and when decomposition of the flesh was complete, the bones were moved into repositories beneath the benches. Over time, these repositories came to hold the bones of family members long dead, so that the bones of the deceased rested with those of their forebears. The recurrent biblical idiom, "to be gathered to one's people/fathers" (Gen. 25:8 etc.), vividly depicts this ancient Israelite burial practice. It also gives voice to the Israelite preference for burial in a family tomb.

Secondary burial in family tombs was still being practiced at the time of Jesus. True, the "bench" tomb had been replaced by the "loculus" tomb, in which bodies were placed not on benches but in loculus niches (i.e. deep narrow slots carved into the wall of the tomb). Repositories had also been replaced by "ossuaries" (i.e. limestone boxes), but the basic ancient pattern still held true: bones of family members were reburied together in underground tombs. Archaeological evidence demonstrates that secondary burial in loculus tombs was by far the dominant burial practice among first-century Jews in and around Jerusalem, and inscriptions show that most of these tombs were used by family groups. In the "Goliath" tomb from Jericho, inscriptions enabled the excavators to reconstruct three generations of the family tree.[19] The famous "Caiaphas" tomb demonstrates that the family of the High Priest followed these customs: in that loculus tomb there were 16 ossuaries, one of which was inscribed with the name "Joseph Caiaphas."[20] Secondary burial is discussed at length in the Mishnah and Talmudim, and the tractate *Semahot* is almost entirely devoted to the topic. Here too there is a strong emphasis on ties of kinship and family: *Semaḥot* 12.9, for example, holds a son responsible for the reburial of his father's

---

Near East (New York: Oxford University Press, 1994).

17   R. Gonen, *Burial Patterns and Cultural Diversity in Late Bronze Age Canaan* (ASOR Dissertation Series 7; Winona Lake: Eisenbrauns, 1992).

18   E. Bloch-Smith, *Judahite Burial Practices and Beliefs about the Dead* (JSOTSup 123; Sheffield: JSOT Press, 1992).

19   R. Hachlili, "The Goliath Family in Jericho: Funerary Inscriptions from a First Century AD Jewish Monumental Tomb," *BASOR* 235 (1979) 31-65; idem and P. Smith, "The Geneology of the Goliath Family," *BASOR* 235 (1979) 67-70.

20   Z. Greenhut, "The Caiaphas Tomb in North Talpiyot, Jerusalem," *ʿAtiqot* 21 (1992) 63-71.

bones. Archaeological corroboration of the rabbinic sources is found in the second and third-century catacombs at Beth She'arim, where secondary burial is frequent and where inscriptions show that individual burial chambers were purchased and used by family groups.[21]

The element of mourning which was included in honorable burial also emphasized ties of kinship and family, and here too the traditions reach far back into Israelite history. Jacob was said to have rent his garments and put on sackcloth after being told that Joseph has died (Gen 37:34), and Bathsheba first "made lamentation for her husband" before becoming David's wife (2 Sam 11:26-27). Sometimes a specific length of time is mentioned: the people of Israel mourn the death of Aaron for thirty days (Num. 20:29), and Job sits with his comforters for seven days and seven nights (Job 2:12-13). References to the length of time spent in mourning also appear in Jewish literature from the first century, as for example when Josephus writes that Archelaus "kept seven days of mourning for his father" (J.W. 2.1.1 §1), and Mary and Martha are said to have been mourning their brother Lazarus for four days before Jesus arrives (John 11:17-19). The rabbinic literature supplies details of a more highly developed ritual. Here the period of mourning unfolds in two stages: first a seven-day period of intense grieving (called שבעה), when family members "stay away from work, sitting at home upon low couches, heads covered, receiving the condolences of relatives and friends,"[22] and then a thirty-day period of less severe mourning (called שלשים), during which family members still did not leave town, cut their hair, or attend social gatherings. The rabbinic literature strongly emphasizes family ties: the longest period of mourning—an entire year—is said to occur when a son mourns for his parents (Sem. 9.15).

These customs of honorable burial expose an important feature of the Jewish culture of Roman Palestine. When they tended to their dead in this way, Jews were doing more than simply disposing of a body and dealing with their grief; they were also making a symbolic statement about their most basic cultural norms and values.

---

[21]   M. Schwabe and B. Lifshitz, *Beth She'arim, Vol. II: The Greek Inscriptions* (New Brunswick: Rutgers University Press, 1974) 223.

[22]   L. Y. Rahmani, "Ancient Jerusalem's Funerary Customs and Tombs, Part One," *BA* 44 (1981) 175.

Anthropologists have found that death rituals typically feature symbolic representations of the most cherished values in a culture, because "the issue of death throws into relief the most important cultural values by which people live their lives and evaluate their experiences."[23] For Jews, one of those values was the importance of belonging to an extended family group. The foundational narrative for Jewish culture was a story about a man whose descendants were to be more numerous than the stars in the sky, and respect for the family was enshrined in the moral charter of Judaism: "honor your father and mother." Jews in Jesus' day typically lived in extended family groups, and routinely identified themselves in legal documents, inscriptions, and literature as "X, son (or daughter) of Y." At life's end, they thought it best to be buried with their nearest kin. To be buried away from the family tomb—by design, not by fate—was to be cast adrift from these cultural patterns, and dislodged from a place in the family. To be unmourned by one's nearest relatives was to be effaced from the cultural landscape. It was worse than unfortunate; it was a shame.

How does all of this affect the burial of Jesus? To begin, it is certain that the Jewish leaders did not want the body of Jesus left hanging on the cross. Instead they wanted it to be taken down and buried before sunset on the day of his death. They would not have placed the body in a family tomb, nor would they have felt any obligation to mourn, but failure to bury Jesus would have been an offense against everything decent and good. At the season of Passover such sensibilities would only have been heightened. Thus it is to be expected that someone from the council approached Pilate about the body of Jesus. It is not necessary to assume that most, or even many, of the council members were involved in the events which led to Jesus' death. Nor is it necessary to suppose that any of the council members had any secret allegiance to Jesus. It is only necessary to recognize that at least a few of them were involved in the proceedings against Jesus, and that they were devout Jews. In that situation, Jewish religious and cultural norms would have prompted them to see that Jesus was buried in shame at sunset on the day of his death. And to do that, someone had to approach Pilate about the body of Jesus.

Jewish burial customs, in fact, can explain a detail in the Gospels

---

23   Metcalf and Huntington, *Celebrations of Death*, 25.

which has puzzled some interpreters: why does Joseph of Arimathea bury *only* the body of Jesus? Why doesn't he also bury the others crucified with Jesus?[24] Jewish traditions of dishonorable burial can make sense of this turn of events in the story, because burial in shame was relevant only to those criminals who had been condemned by the action of some Jewish (or Israelite) authority. Dishonorable burial was reserved for those who had been condemned by *the people of Israel. Semahot* 2.9, in fact, specifically exempts those who die at the hands of other authorities. Mark's narrative conforms to this tradition. Since at least a few of the Jewish leaders had been involved in the condemnation of Jesus, they had an obligation to bury him in shame. But they were not necessarily responsible for Pilate's other victims.

III

In describing the burial of Jesus, John 19:39 says, "Nicodemus, who had at first come to Jesus by night, also came, bringing a mixture of myrrh and aloes, weighing about a hundred pounds." This brief sentence showcases the kind of problems which bedevil the Christian accounts of Jesus' burial. In a word, the Christian stories are shot through with theology. Nicodemus, for example, is not mentioned in any other Christian story about the burial, but he figures prominently in the Gospel of John, both in the burial story and in his late-night conversation with Jesus in chapter 3. His appearance in the burial narrative has been linked to a specific theological agenda in the Fourth Gospel: he represents those who believe but do not openly declare their faith in Jesus.[25] In addition, the reference to "a hundred pounds" of spices is also problematic. That much myrrh and aloes would "fill a considerable space in the tomb and smother the corpse under a mound."[26] This exorbitant quantity of spices, however, can also be linked to a theological interest, since ancient texts often depict extravagant preparations for the burials of important people. In both of these cases, John has added details which advance a theological purpose, and that in a nutshell is the basic historical problem with the burial narratives.

---

24   Crossan, *Who Killed Jesus?*, 173.

25   R. A. Culpepper, *Anatomy of the Fourth Gospel* (Philadelphia: Fortress, 1983) 136.

26   Brown, *The Death of the Messiah*, 1260.

These texts stand at the intersection between the death of Jesus and his resurrection, and as such they are thickly woven with expressions of early Christian theology.

It is tempting to try to solve this problem in one of two ways. First, it is possible to try to identify a pre-Gospel tradition which underlies and precedes the written Gospels, and which can then be used to bypass the difficulties of the written Gospel narratives. Brown offers just such a reconstruction in his magisterial work, *The Death of the Messiah*. The results are often persuasive, as for example when Brown argues that the pre-Gospel tradition probably included the designation that Jesus was buried on "the day of preparation."[27] Yet reservations about such conclusions will always persist, since any effort to recover a pre-Gospel tradition is inevitably beset by intractable theoretical problems. We simply do not know enough about oral tradition in general, or about the pre-Gospel burial tradition in particular, to speak with confidence in this area. In the absence of any external confirmation it is practically impossible for us to know what preceded the burial narrative in the Gospel of Mark.

It is also tempting to go to the opposite extreme and conclude that the Christian accounts of Jesus' burial contain no historically useful information at all. John Dominic Crossan argues for this view in *Who Killed Jesus?* Setting the burial texts against the background of early Jewish and Christian polemics, Crossan asserts that the Gospels tell us absolutely nothing reliable about the fate of Jesus' body: "The burial stories are hope and hyperbole expanded into apologetics and polemics."[28] Certainly there are elements in the burial texts which express Christian hope—Nicodemus, for one—and there are elements which obviously derive from Christian apologetics—the guard at the tomb, for another. Be that as it may, *Who Killed Jesus?* still reads like an exercise in throwing the baby out with the bath water. Even if everything in all the burial narratives has been constructed entirely from Christian theology and apologetics, these texts could still be instructive. It is precisely by looking closely at the ways in which Christian theology has shaped these stories—what has been changed, what has been emphasized, and (most especially) what has been presupposed and even tacitly admitted—that we can turn up

---

27   Brown, *The Death of the Messiah*, 1238-41.
28   Crossan, *Who Killed Jesus?*, 188.

a revealing clue about the historical circumstances of Jesus' burial.

I refer, of course, to the well-known fact that the Gospels embellish and glamorize the burial of Jesus. Many scholars have already commented on this tendency in the Gospels.[29] Because he held such a prominent place in the worship of early Christians, their stories naturally seek to refine, polish and beautify the circumstances of his interment. A few bottles of ointment might suffice for washing an ordinary corpse, but for Jesus, no less than one hundred pounds will do. Examples of this sort can be repeated several times over. It is not necessary to rehearse in detail the studies which have already covered this material thoroughly and well; it will suffice merely to summarize their conclusions. Virtually all studies agree that as the tradition develops, every detail in the story is enhanced and improved upon. Mark begins the written tradition by saying that on Friday evening, Joseph of Arimathea, a respected member of the Council, requested the body of Jesus from Pilate, wrapped it in linen and sealed it in a rock-cut tomb. Never again would the story be told so simply. Joseph of Arimathea becomes a "good and righteous man" who did not consent to the action against Jesus (Luke 23:51), and then evolves into a secret disciple of Jesus (Matt 27:57; John 19:38). The "rock-cut" tomb in Mark becomes a "new" tomb (Matt 27:60), "where no one had yet been laid" (Luke 23:53). John not only combines those descriptions—the tomb is both "new" and "where no one had yet been laid" (John 19:41)—but also adds that the tomb was located in a garden. In Mark Joseph wraps the body in linen—nothing more—but subsequent Gospels describe the linen as "clean" (Matt 27:59) and claim that the body was bathed in vast quantities of perfume (John 19:39). By the time of the *Gospel of Peter*, during the mid-second century CE, Christians were going so far as to assert that Jesus had been sumptuously buried in the family tomb of one of Jerusalem's most powerful and wealthy families. The tendency of this tradition is unmistakable, and Crossan is right to describe it as

---

29   See, inter alia, Blinzler, "Die Grablegung Jesu," 74; Brown, "The Burial of Jesus," 242-43; Crossan, *The Historical Jesus*, 393-94; Daube, *The New Testament and Rabbinic Judaism*, 311; R. Pesch, *Das Markusevangelium* (HTKNT 2.1-2; 2 vols., Freiburg: Herder, 1977) 2.516; J. A. Fitzmyer, *The Gospel according to Luke* (AB 28 and 28A; Garden City: Doubleday, 1981) 2.1523-25. R. Schnackenburg, *Das Johannesevangelium* (HTKNT 4.1-3; 3 vols., Freiburg: Herder, 1965-75) 2.346.

"damage control."[30]

In view of this clear tendency, one characteristic of the burial narratives stands out as strikingly significant: *the canonical Gospels depict Jesus' burial as shameful.* Even though they take obvious steps to dignify the burial of Jesus, these documents still depict a burial which a Jew in Roman Palestine would have recognized as dishonorable. For in every Gospel up to the *Gospel of Peter*, Jesus is not buried in a family tomb, and he is not mourned. This fact is both surprising and revealing. It is surprising because it shows that even with all their embellishments and improvements, there was a limit beyond which the early stages of the tradition would not go. Brown, for example, has demonstrated that the burial described in the Gospel of Mark is a dishonorable burial at the hands of a Torah-observant council member.[31] In keeping with Jewish custom, Joseph of Arimathea buries the body at sunset, probably in a tomb reserved for criminals. What has been shown for Mark holds true for the other canonical burial narratives as well. The story is steadily improved upon, but the two defining marks of shame continue and persist: no family tomb, and no mourning. A detail added by Matthew, Luke, and John is particularly revealing in this regard. The tomb of Jesus, they all say, is new, "where not one had yet been laid" (Matt 27:60; Luke 23:3; John 19:43). Many scholars have noted that this description lends dignity to Jesus' burial, because it clearly differentiates his resting place from a criminals' burial place like the ones mentioned in the Mishnah. But as both David Daube and Josef Blinzler have pointed out, a new tomb would still be a shameful place of interment.[32] In fact a new tomb, never before used by sinner or saint, would be the only culturally acceptable alternative to a criminals' burial place, for it would be the only other way to preserve the boundary of shame which separated Jesus from his people. By putting him alone in a new tomb, Matthew, Luke, and John do not deny the shame of Jesus' burial; they merely spare him the disgrace of being placed in a criminals' tomb. A residue of shame still clings to him as an executed convict.

Rites of mourning are absent from these narratives as well. When

---

30   Crossan, *The Historical Jesus*, 394.
31   Brown, "The Burial of Jesus."
32   Blinzler, "Die Grablegung Jesu," 101-102; Daube, *The New Testament and Rabbinic Judaism*, 311.

Jesus dies, no one sits שבעה: a few women merely note the location of the tomb, and later visit it after the Sabbath. They go there, however, not to mourn, but merely to anoint the body or "to see the tomb." The omission of mourning from the canonical Gospels is significant because in other contexts all four of these Gospels have clear depictions of the initial stages of mourning for the dead. Resuscitation stories like the raising of Jairus' daughter (Mark 5:21-43 par.), for example, or the Lazarus narrative (John 11:1-44) include explicit depictions of typical Jewish rituals of mourning. Indeed, in each of these stories the portrayal of mourning actually serves to heighten the narrative impact of the miracle by establishing that the unfortunate victim is truly dead, beyond all human help. Clearly these writers knew how to depict mourning for the dead and were willing to do so when it would advance the point of their story. What a shame that they did not put any such depictions in their stories of Jesus' burial.

Contradictions against Jewish practices of dishonorable burial first appear in the *Gospel of Peter*, which both places Jesus in a family tomb and depicts specific acts of mourning. According to *GPet.* 6.22, for example, Joseph of Arimathea washes the body of Jesus, wraps it linen and places in "his own tomb"—nothing about newness here—which was called "Joseph's Garden." Later, women come to the tomb with the stated intention of performing the customary rites of mourning for the dead (ἃ εἰώθεσαν ποιεῖν; *GPet.* 12.52) True, the Jews are said to have prevented such mourning on the day of Jesus' crucifixion, but the women resolutely intend to do so after the Sabbath (καὶ νῦν ἐπὶ τοῦ μνήματος αὐτοῦ ποιήσωμεν ταῦτα; *GPet.* 12.53). They determine not to confine their grieving to the privacy of their own hearts: they will do "what ought to be done" (τὰ ὀφειλόμενα; *GPet.* 12.54). With these depictions the tradition of Jesus' burial has turned a corner, crossing the boundaries of Jewish custom and making the burial of Jesus honorable.

In the early stages of the written tradition, then, culturally appropriate efforts were made to dignify the burial of Jesus. To that end, the canonical Gospels tell stories about a member of the Sanhedrin named Joseph of Arimathea, a new tomb, clean linen, and large amounts of perfume. Specific mention of either a criminals' burial place or rites of mourning is, however, discreetly avoided. Not until the *Gospel of Peter* are these stories embellished to the point that they denied what an earlier generation of Christians had tacitly admitted: Jesus had been buried in shame.

This analysis is consistent with a fact which can all too easily get lost in the confusing shuffle of the burial narratives: the people who first told this story were Jews from first-century Palestine. The earliest layers of the Gospel tradition originated in first-century Palestine—certainly Matthew and possibly also Mark and John were written there—and as such these early stories of Jesus' burial were necessarily shaped by the burial practices of that place and time, customs which belonged to the contemporary social system and the prevailing cultural landscape. The earliest Christians lived and died by these customs, most of the time rather unreflectively, and their narratives inevitably presupposed them. From a distance of twenty centuries we can now imagine all kinds of reasons why their stories might have taken the shape they did. There are, for example, possible answers in literary criticism: perhaps the shameful burial completes the ongoing conflict between Jesus and the Jewish leaders in Matthew, or maybe it is Mark's final statement on the cost of discipleship. On the other hand, an ideological explanation will be more plausible to some: perhaps women *did* mourn the death of Jesus, but male Gospel writers, suspicious of what might happen if women began meeting in groups, expunged them from the written record. Frankly, all sorts of possibilities suggest themselves, none of which played any role at all in first-century Palestine. In that place and time, the answer was not so complicated. A story about the honorable burial of a criminal condemned by Jewish authorities was simply not plausible. Everyone knew it did not work that way.

Certainly the early Christians in Palestine who first told the story of Jesus' burial knew it, for when it came to matters of death and burial, they appear to have been ordinary and typical Jews. Their narratives clearly display a thorough familiarity with most of the Jewish burial practices of first-century Palestine. They knew, for example, that bodies were customarily buried promptly on the day of death, after being washed with ointment and wrapped in linen. They knew that the dead were customarily buried in underground tombs, and that they were mourned by their nearest relatives. And by the subtle ways in which they dignified the burial of Jesus without crossing the boundaries of Jewish custom, the texts show that the earliest Christians also knew that condemned criminals were not buried with their families and were not mourned. It is reasonable to conclude, in other words, that the early Christians in Palestine buried their dead no differently from other Jews in that place and time.[33]

IV

E. P. Sanders, in attempting to reconstruct the course of events at Jesus' trial, has pointed out that probably no single individual was in a position to know fully the exact course of events that night.[34] The point is well taken and should serve as a reminder that a degree of uncertainty will always inhere in any effort to reconstruct what happened at the death and burial of Jesus. It was, after all, almost two thousand years ago. John Dominic Crossan, of course, takes scepticism a good deal further and argues that "*nobody knew what had happened to Jesus' body* . . . With regard to the body of Jesus, by Easter Sunday morning, those who cared did not know, and those who knew did not care."[35] There are reasons to agree with this sobering assessment, at least in part. Certainly few—if any—of Jesus' followers directly witnessed his death and burial, and the glamorized Christian stories of his interment cannot be trusted to describe *wie es eigentlich war*. Yet there are good reasons to stop short of complete scepticism about the fate of Jesus' body. Indeed, the evidence from Roman, Jewish, and Christian sources all coheres around a single conclusion: Jesus was buried in shame. Someone from the Council approached Pilate about the body and put it in an underground tomb reserved for Jewish criminals.

The evidence has shown that even though Roman authorities like Pilate might sometimes have left crucifixion victims hanging, they often allowed bodies to be buried. Such allowances, in fact, were all the more likely during a religious holiday, or when the crucifixion was not part of a mass operation to suppress an open and armed revolt, or when the request for the body came from a person who was cooperative with Rome. The evidence has further shown that the Jewish leaders who participated in the proceedings against Jesus had strong religious and cultural motives for seeking to bury him in shame. Such motives came not from any secret allegiance to Jesus, but from observance of traditional law and custom. Finally, the

---

[33]The absence of distinctively Christian funerary archaeology in Roman Palestine further reinforces this conclusion. For the details of the archaeological and literary evidence, cf. McCane, "Jews, Christians, and Burial in Roman Palestine."

[34]   E. P. Sanders, *Jesus and Judaism* (Philadelphia: Fortress, 1985) 300.

[35]   Crossan, *The Historical Jesus*, 394 (his emphasis).

evidence has also shown that the early followers of Jesus described his burial in terms which were dishonorable. They dignified it as much as possible but did not deny its shame.

On the basis of the evidence, then, the following scenario emerges as a likely course of events for the deposition of Jesus' body: late on the day of his death, one or more of the Jewish leaders in Jerusalem —later personified by Christian tradition as Joseph of Arimathea— requested custody of the body for purposes of dishonorable burial. These leaders, having collaborated with the Romans in the condemnation of Jesus, had both the means and the motive to bury him in shame: means, in their access to Pilate, and motive, in Jewish law and custom. Pilate did not hesitate to grant dishonorable burial to one of their condemned criminals. Only the most rudimentary burial preparations were administered—the body was wrapped and taken directly to the tomb, without a funeral procession, eulogies, or the deposition of any personal effects. By sunset on the day of his death, the body of Jesus lay within a burial cave reserved for criminals condemned by Jewish courts. No one mourned.

The shame of Jesus' burial is not only consistent with the best evidence, but can also help to account for an historical fact which has long been puzzling to historians of early Christianity: why did the primitive church not venerate the tomb of Jesus? Joachim Jeremias, for one, thought it inconceivable (*undenkbar*) that the primitive community would have let the grave of Jesus sink into oblivion.[36] Yet the earliest hints of Christian veneration of Jesus' tomb do not surface until the early fourth century CE.[37] It is a striking fact—and not at all unthinkable—that the tomb of Jesus was not venerated until it was no longer remembered as a place of shame.[38]

---

[36]   J. Jeremias, *Heilegengräber in Jesu Umwelt* (Göttingen: Vandenhoeck & Ruprecht, 1958) 145.

[37]   Eusebius, *Vita Constantini* 3.25-32.

[38]   I am grateful to my colleague at the Sepphoris Regional Project, Jonathan L. Reed, and to my colleagues at Converse College, Robert J. Hauck and Melissa Walker, all of whom read an earlier version of this article and offered constructive criticisms.